Patient Advocacy for Health Care Quality

Strategies for Achieving Patient-Centered Care

Jo Anne L. Earp, ScD
Professor and Chair, Health Behavior and Health Education
University of North Carolina at Chapel Hill

Elizabeth A. French, MA
Lecturer, Health Behavior and Health Education
University of North Carolina at Chapel Hill

Melissa B. Gilkey, MPH
John Hopkins Bloomberg School of Public Health
Baltimore, Maryland

JONES AND BARTLETT PUBLISHERS
Sudbury, Massachusetts
BOSTON   TORONTO   LONDON   SINGAPORE

World Headquarters

Jones and Bartlett Publishers
40 Tall Pine Drive
Sudbury, MA 01776
978-443-5000
info@jbpub.com
www.jbpub.com

Jones and Bartlett Publishers
Canada
6339 Ormindale Way
Mississauga, Ontario L5V 1J2
Canada

Jones and Bartlett Publishers
International
Barb House, Barb Mews
London W6 7PA
United Kingdom

Jones and Bartlett's books and products are available through most bookstores and online booksellers. To contact Jones and Bartlett Publishers directly, call 800-832-0034, fax 978-443-8000, or visit our website www.jbpub.com.

Substantial discounts on bulk quantities of Jones and Bartlett's publications are available to corporations, professional associations, and other qualified organizations. For details and specific discount information, contact the special sales department at Jones and Bartlett via the above contact information or send an email to specialsales@jbpub.com.

This publication is designed to provide accurate and authoritative information in regard to the Subject Matter covered. It is sold with the understanding that the publisher is not engaged in rendering legal, accounting, or other professional service. If legal advice or other expert assistance is required, the service of a competent professional person should be sought.

6048

Production Credits
Publisher: Michael Brown
Production Director: Amy Rose
Associate Editor: Katey Birtcher
Associate Production Editor: Rachel Rossi
Associate Production Editor: Jamie Chase
Marketing Manager: Sophie Fleck
Manufacturing Buyer: Therese Connell
Composition: Paw Print Media
Cover Design: Kristin E. Ohlin
Cover Image Top Left: © Creatas/Jupiterimages
Cover Image Top Right: © Courtesy of Will Owens
Cover Image Bottom Left: © Courtesy of Will Owens
Cover Image Bottom Right: © Courtesy of Dreyfus and Associates Photography
Printing and Binding: Malloy, Inc.
Cover Printing: Malloy, Inc.

Library of Congress Cataloging-in-Publication Data
Patient advocacy for health care quality : strategies for achieving patient-centered care / [edited by] Joanne L. Earp, Elizabeth French, and Melissa B. Gilkey.
    p. ; cm.
    Includes bibliographical references and index.
    ISBN-13: 978-0-7637-4961-3
    ISBN-10: 0-7637-4961-3
    1. Patient advocacy—United States. 2. Medical care—United States—Quality control. I. Earp, Joanne L. II. French, Elizabeth (Elizabeth A.) III. Gilkey, Melissa B.
    [DNLM: 1. Patient Advocacy. 2. Health Services Accessibility. 3. Insurance, Health. 4. Patient-Centered Care. 5. Quality of Health Care. W 85 P29725 2007]
    R727.45.P43 2007
    362.1068—dc22

                 2007001642

Printed in the United States of America
11 10 09 08 07 10 9 8 7 6 5 4 3 2 1

We cannot seek or attain health, wealth, learning, justice or kindness in general. Action is always specific, concrete, individualized, unique.

—John Dewey

To Scott Pearson, whose untimely death inspired this work, and to Tom Ferguson, whose optimism and energy propelled us forward.

Contents

Foreward   ix

Preface   xv

Acknowledgments   xxi

About the Editors   xxiii

Contributors   xxv

INTRODUCTION   **1**

Chapter 1—What Is Patient Advocacy?   3
Melissa B. Gilkey, Jo Anne L. Earp, and Elizabeth A. French

Chapter 2—The U.S. Healthcare System and the Need for
Patient Advocacy   29
Pam Silberman, Thomas C. Ricketts, III, and Donna Cohen Ross

**STRATEGY ONE: UNDERSTANDING WHAT PATIENTS
ARE DOING NOW AND WHAT PROVIDERS CAN DO
TO SUPPORT THEM**   **59**

Chapter 3—Family-Centered Care: Why It Is Important,
How to Provide It, and What Parents and Children Are
Doing to Make It Happen   61
Beth Seyda, Terri Shelton, and Nancy DiVenere

Chapter 4—E-Patients: How They Can Help Us Heal Healthcare   93
Tom Ferguson

Chapter 5—The Long Reach to Basic Healthcare Services:
Partnering With Lay Health Advisors to Improve Health Equity   121
Alexis Moore and Jo Anne L. Earp

**STRATEGY TWO: IMPROVING PROVIDERS' ABILITY
TO COMMUNICATE AND CREATE RELATIONSHIPS**   **151**

Chapter 6—The Clinician's Experience: Incorporating Advocacy
Into the 20-Minute Medical Encounter   153
Beth A. Lown and Adina Kalet

Chapter 7—Accessing the Patient's World: Patient-Physician
Communication About Psychosocial Issues   185
Carol E. Golin, Carolyn Thorpe, and M. Robin DiMatteo

Chapter 8—Advocacy and Patient Literacy: What Healthcare
Professionals Can Do To Help Patients Overcome Patient Literacy
Barriers   215
Darren A. DeWalt and Mike P. Pignone

Chapter 9—Improving the Quality of Care Through Research:
Measuring Patient Activation   241
Judith H. Hibbard

**STRATEGY THREE: TRANSFORMING HOSPITAL
AND MEDICAL SCHOOL CULTURE TO SUPPORT
PATIENT- AND FAMILY-CENTERED CARE**   **261**

Chapter 10—The Contributions of Patient Advocacy in
Patient Safety   263
James Conway

Chapter 11—Planetree, a Hospital Model for
Patient-Centered Care   289
Susan B. Frampton and Laura Gilpin

Chapter 12—Confronting the Hidden Curriculum in Medical
Education: The Challenge Faced by Patients, Families,
Educators, and Administrators in Changing Medical School
and Hospital Culture   313
Kathy Zoppi, Patricia Sodomka, and Julie Moretz

Chapter 13—Advocacy for Improving End-of-Life Care:
A 30-Year Healthcare Cultural Revolution   333
Gary S. Winzelberg and Laura C. Hanson

**STRATEGY FOUR: MAKING CONSUMERS' VOICE
HEARD IN POLICY AND LAW**   **359**

Chapter 14—Did Patient/Consumers Cause the Healthcare Crisis?
Historical Talking Points for the 21st Century Patient Advocate   361
Nancy Tomes

Chapter 15—Advocacy for Residents in Long Term Care:
Lessons and Challenges   387
Elma L. Holder and Barbara Frank

Chapter 16—Access to Healthcare: Using Data From
a Nonprofit Advocacy Practice to Drive Policy Change   419
Nancy Davenport-Ennis

Chapter 17—Research Advocacy in Traditional Research Settings:
Questions of Influence and Legitimacy   445
Margo Michaels and Deborah Collyar

**STRATEGY FIVE: ADVANCING EDUCATION AND
PROFESSIONAL ROLES IN ADVOCACY**   **479**

Chapter 18—Educating for Health Advocacy in Settings of
Higher Learning   481
*Marsha Hurst, Martha E. Gaines, Rachel N. Grob, Laura Weil,
and Sarah Davis*

Chapter 19—Clinical Advocacy—Clinicians Advocating for
Patients and Families Facing Complex, Life-Threatening Illness   507
Mark Renneker, Gwendolyn Stritter, and Paul Jentes

Chapter 20—Using the Law to Strengthen the Patient's Voice   533
Virginia L. Morrison and Nicola B. Truppin

CONCLUSION   **567**

Chapter 21—Patient Advocacy: A Bridge to Improving
Healthcare Quality   569
Jo Anne L. Earp, Katie Emmet, and Elizabeth A. French

Index   603

FOREWORD

Much of my career has been spent considering what makes a good and safe healthcare environment, from my days as a local public health officer to my role today leading a top academic healthcare system.

In 1986, when I served as administrator of the Health Care Financing Administration, we published the first mortality information on Medicare beneficiaries at the nation's hospitals. The importance and role of quality in health and healthcare outcomes were relatively new ideas at the time. Despite the sophisticated statistical approaches we used and the efforts we made to include a range of experts in the process, the report's release was controversial. As I look back on that project, the mortality rates themselves were the least important aspect of that effort, although they were the focus of the most discussion. At the time, we did not have common agreement on what quality in healthcare meant, and the idea of measuring and changing was a pretty radical notion. Nonetheless, the concept of measuring, changing, and expecting quality was compelling, and in 1988, we launched the Health Care Financing Administration Effectiveness Initiative, premised on the idea that quality of care should be a unifying concept in all of healthcare.

Over the next 10 years, a number of distinguished scientists, policy makers, and healthcare advocates worked through panels, individual research, and well-known reports to add greatly to our understanding of healthcare quality. Ultimately, the Institute of Medicine defined it as "the degree to which health services for individuals and populations increases the likelihood of desired health outcomes and are consistent with current professional knowledge." Later, the Institute of Medicine added the ideas that high-quality care should be patient-centered, timely, efficient, effective, safe, and equitable. It should also be coordinated, compassionate, and innovative.

Overlaying each of these elements of quality care is the basic premise that they are achieved through systemic change and commitment to care. Quality improvement, whether focused on decreasing medication errors or increasing sensitivity to patients' cultural needs, only happens when systems are in place to support the good efforts of individuals within the system. In the landmark Institute of Medicine report *To Err Is Human*, a strong case was made that the best way to reduce medical errors was to focus on systemic failures, not individual human ones. Indeed, I contend that failure on *any* of the quality of care constructs is generally attributable to system-wide weaknesses. That fact substantially increases the potential impact of advocacy on healthcare and health outcomes—applying pressure on the healthcare system can affect the behaviors of many individual caregivers simultaneously by changing the systems that support their work.

This important book focuses on the key question—where does patient advocacy fit? What role does it play in changing the healthcare quality landscape? In 2003, more than 60 leaders from a number of disciplines met at a critical patient advocacy summit in Chapel Hill, North Carolina. At that time, Dr. Carolyn Clancy, director of the Agency for Healthcare Research and Quality, asked what I thought was the right question: "Do we need an 'army' of good advocates, or do we need a better system in which advocates are not necessary?" The answer was and is simply "yes"- we need both. Changing the quality of our healthcare and ensuring that it is appropriate and safe will demand that individuals advocate for themselves and others on the basis of each of the elements of quality listed previously here. But as the system changes, each new healthcare iteration also means that advocates will need to adapt their approach if they are to continue playing a significant role in quality improvement in the foreseeable future.

The authors of the IOM's *Crossing the Quality Chasm* described an approach to change based on the idea of evidence-based, patient-centered, and systems-minded care. Advocacy can and should have an important role in each element of this approach—in gathering and interpreting data and ensuring that care is based on good science, in ensuring that the patient and the patient's needs and wishes are at the center of every healthcare decision, and in insisting that the care delivered be cooperative and coordinated across disciplines and organizations. Authors of the *Quality Chasm* went further to endorse 10 simple rules as a framework for high quality care, each of which describes a touch point for advocates and the advocacy process. These rules are not easy to implement, but they are straightforward and compelling in this simplicity.

For example, although the old model of care was focused on healthcare visits, the new model embraces the idea of a continuous healing relationship. Yet to attain this ideal, we need the constant advocacy of patients, their families, and the clinicians who care for them. In turn, a system based on continuous healing relationships will be one in which patients' needs are more easily and naturally communicated so that the system itself advocates for patient-centered care.

In another of the 10 simple rules, providers whose decision making was primarily based on training and experience should now also base their decisions on evidence. Evidence-based care is or should be consistent across individual clinicians. The scientific basis for many healthcare approaches is increasingly available to patients and their advocates, for example, at *www.ahrq.gov*, and can be a powerful tool in the advocacy process.

As a final example, in the old system of care, secrecy (e.g., about error rates) is necessary, but if the 10 simple rules are followed, transparency is essential. Transparency means that patients and their families can easily obtain the information they need to make good healthcare decisions and to advocate for the care they need from providers and health systems. The trend toward transparent care began with the publication of Medicare mortality information in the mid 1980s and continues, for example, with data on hospital care published by the Department of Health and Human Services at *www.hospitalcompare.hhs.gov*. Organizations such as the Institute for Healthcare Improvement, as well as patients and their families, have made advocating for greater transparency with patients when and if errors do take place a priority.

Unfortunately, the backdrop for this trend is one in which the gap between the best possible care and the care routinely given remains large, and studies bear out that the consumer's widespread demand for quality healthcare is not yet a reality. Six years ago, in *To Err Is Human*, the Institute of Medicine reported that tens of thousands of deaths each year are directly attributable to medical errors that occur in hospitals alone. Recently, the Institute's *Preventing Medication Errors* report stated, among other significant findings, that medication errors harm at least 1.5 million people and cost $3.5 billion in additional costs in the inpatient setting annually. The report finds that adverse drug events are common, costly, and preventable. Eliminating them requires a change in the patient–provider relationship, a greater reliance on information technologies and electronic prescribing, proper training to make sure that new technologies are well-integrated into the system and are not just an add-on, and improved labeling and packaging of medications.

I believe that a critical role for advocates today and in the near future will be in supporting the use of electronic resources in medical decision making. Physicians, patients, and their families should have access to every bit of information they need to make good healthcare decisions. They should understand the costs involved, their options, and their risks. Doctors and nurses should have at their fingertips information on best practices and standards of care and feel confident that the system in which they operate fully supports them. Through the adoption of clinical information systems, outcomes data collection, and the use of electronic medical records, we are taking incremental steps to ensure that healthcare quality measurement, reporting, and decision-making will yield more valid and reliable results. Standardization is important in driving safety and reducing errors, whereas more efficient seamless systems will dramatically encourage adoption of electronic medical records and other cost-saving technologies.

Developing a system of care based on state-of-the-art electronic resources requires that forward-thinking individuals advocate for it, that individuals and groups use the system to advocate for better care, and that the system itself be continuously improved through the efforts of individuals advocating for even better science.

Patient advocacy, in essence, is a central driver of all aspects of quality improvement. As this timely and comprehensive book demonstrates, patient advocacy—in its many forms—is a powerful source of pressure to initiate and follow through on the needed changes in our healthcare system. As we see in this volume, patient advocacy may occur with individuals advocating on behalf of individual patients, or it may take a broader organizational form. Regardless, an essential tenet is the encouragement—even the insistence—of the partnership in which patients participate with the healthcare system to affect their outcomes.

We may very well see patient advocacy taking root as an academic discipline as its importance becomes better understood. I have strongly supported the idea of a university-based center for consumer health advocacy that could be a powerful mechanism for gathering information, conducting research, evaluating advocacy approaches, and disseminating key findings. Whatever the direction patient advocacy takes, this important book will set the stage, providing a starting point, a taxonomy, and a common language for understanding, studying, encouraging, and developing advocacy in healthcare.

Our healthcare system is in need of change. Advocacy will be an important lever to affect key touch points in the system that will in turn support patient care that adheres to the quality tenets we all value. As the system supports advocacy, advocates will support an improving system. Advocating for better healthcare is not an optimal choice—I believe it is our imperative.

William L. Roper, MD, MPH
Dean, School of Medicine
CEO, UNC Health Care System
Vice Chancellor for Medical Affairs
The University of North Carolina at Chapel Hill

PREFACE

The Public Health and Medical Continuum

The common denominator shared by public health, with its focus on prevention, and medical care, with its focus on cure, is the end user—the individual viewed as patient, client, customer, or consumer. Public health and medical care have been linked sporadically, but they are more often regarded as distinct and separate fields—prevention versus cure—rather than as equal and complementary partners in the health care system of the United States. The citizen is supported by the many public health facilities and services offered at local, state, and federal levels. When that citizen becomes ill, the medical care system—private physician, public clinic, or hospital—takes over. Yet rather than looking at these modalities as separate entities, this book examines major points of intersection between public health and medical systems. In analyzing what happens to patients, from entry into the healthcare system until their ultimate outcome, this book focuses on public health tools that can help ameliorate the problems many citizens face when they become ill.

What mechanisms are available to ensure citizens that the links in the chain of public health and medical care—the two most important system components—are not broken? Patient advocacy is the navigator, both in its aim to help and guide patients to make well-informed decisions about their health for the best outcomes, and in its quest to create more effective systems and policies.

The Role of Personal Experience

As in many health and social movements in the United States, the authors of this preface became increasingly aware of the need for patient advocates through personal experiences. After helping two close family members through life-threatening illnesses, Clarence realized that there was great need, but not formal and consistent recourse, for effecting positive change in the lives of patients everywhere. His first wife, June, died in 1967, when their son was a toddler. Then, in 2001, his son Scott died of malignant melanoma at age 38.

During Scott's battle with cancer, Clarence and Laurie Norris, Scott's stepmother, witnessed Scott's frustration with a treatment regimen orchestrated by multiple providers, with little acknowledgment of Scott or his family as decision-makers or partners in care; neither Scott nor his family were given options for participation as full and informed partners in healthcare decision-making. They saw a system in disarray, with doctors not communicating, hospital records not being shared among various institutions providing Scott's care, and patients often treated with little respect or dignity.

Critically ill patients often must serve as their own advocates. They often must react to multiple healthcare providers, research their own illnesses, and negotiate with insurance providers even as they face financial strain, negotiate for reduced work time, and cope with the stress of illness. Scott Pearson's case was hardly an exception. During the course of his care, Scott was moved seven times among five institutions. His hospital bills, representing seven months of care in the five institutions, listed 49 physicians as healthcare providers. Although Clarence visited his son every day throughout that time, he met only five physicians. From the day Scott was referred by his family physician to a hospital, neither Scott nor his father heard from this physician again.

The night the hospital called to tell his family that Scott had died, Laurie and Clarence discussed with Dr. Alison Norris (Laurie's sister) about what action the family could take as a memorial to Scott and his struggle. Dr. Norris, an intensivist, nephrologist, and long-term patient advocate in her own practice, served as Scott's patient advocate, helping the family understand in plain terms what was happening and what kind of information his providers should have shared with them to facilitate patient and family decision-making. Yet much of this communication with Scott's providers was characterized by a struggle to elicit information. More often than not, Dr. Norris experienced a lack of cooperation or resistance as she tried to advocate for Scott with her peers. The family recognized that theirs was not an isolated case. If Scott had experienced so many barriers to excellent care, even with the advocacy of an attentive family and a highly trained physician, others must be suffering even more. After the family discussed various options, Alison suggested a fund to support what would have made a difference for Scott's care; patient advocacy practiced effectively in an environment supporting such actions and with full participation of all the actors in a patient's case.

Clarence Pearson and Laurie Norris whole-heartedly agreed and, soon thereafter, established a fund in memory of their relatives to advance the aims of patient advocacy at the University of North Carolina School of Public Health at Chapel Hill. The Scott and June Pearson Fund for Patient Advocacy has allowed the school to research patient advocacy, develop this textbook and curriculum, disseminate findings to all stakeholders, and develop research-driven, theory-based strategies that can improve conditions for patients and their families.

In our vision, patient advocacy empowers patients and their families as partners in their own healthcare by fostering interactive communication with the patient's team of healthcare providers and by offering resources for well-informed decision-making. The patient advocate helps ease a patient's "administrative" burdens by taking such steps as: making sure providers talk to each other, getting the go-ahead for procedures, finding out what insurance policies cover, or extending a hospital stay. Moreover, as explored in this book, the roles advocates play can extend beyond one-on-one efforts and across professional disciplines so that they develop materials, websites, and organizations for patients, restructure systems to make them safer, and lobby for policies that ensure people's access to care. Many people can serve as patient advocates—family members, doctors, nurses, and insurance providers as well as patients themselves.

There are still many things to learn about the basic problems patient advocates attempt to solve. For example, how do cultural, gender, and literacy differences change the way patients and providers share and understand information? How do these differences affect what questions get asked, how questions are framed, and the kind of answers given? By posing such questions, and by delineating what we already know, this book marks an important goal in the search for viable answers.

Public Health Education: The Roots of Patient Advocacy

The term "patient advocacy" is of recent use but has its roots in the much broader field of public health education that became a social force beginning in the early 1900s. Clarence Pearson, as a public health educator, was well acquainted with the early history of advocacy for health, having worked at MetLife, a leading insurance company, for much of his career. Early in the nineteenth century, the private sector—principally the insurance industry—established the first organized, private-sector, public health education program. Metropolitan Life took the lead in this area by establishing a very early example of an advocacy program directed to a specific audience—

"industrial policyholders." The working class policyholders of the time—the year was 1909—represented many nationalities, reflecting the large influx of immigrants into the U.S. in that era. In many cases, these immigrant populations were poor, had minimal access to health care, and had little exposure to modern educational movements for what MetLife called "the preservation of health and the conservation of life."

MetLife clearly had a stake in making sure their policyholders remained healthy and had increased longevity. At the same time, however, MetLife felt that in dealing with these members of the industrial classes, it had an obligation beyond that contained in the policy contract. They put this commitment into action by designing an innovative, extensive, and socially useful program.

Visiting the homes of industrial policyholders weekly to collect small premium payments—as little as 10 cents per payment—MetLife's agents were as familiar as the milkman and the mailman. Agents distributed company publications on health, hygiene, and safety. They became pioneers and early advocates for patient health, sharing with their clients *The Metropolitan*, a quarterly magazine published by MetLife written in popular style on subjects dealing with the health of the family, and particularly with the health of children. Each edition was printed in eight languages. One of the many pamphlets published by MetLife in 1913, "All About Milk," was authored by Professor Milton J. Rosenau, Professor of Preventive Medicine at Harvard University and later the first Dean of the School of Public Health at the University of North Carolina at Chapel Hill.

As an advocate for good health, MetLife realized early on that literature in itself was insufficient for the complete development of its campaign of advocacy for education and prevention. Recognizing the effective role of nurses, both in assuring some continuity of care and in serving as key advocates for the patient, in June 1909 MetLife organized the Visiting Nurse Service. Through this program, nurses visited the homes of sick industrial policyholders to provide onsite services. The visiting nurses, as advocates of the patient through their work, provided the personal contact that connected the policyholder, the insurance company, and the healthcare system.

To "get the word out" about this innovative program, MetLife agents distributed circulars explaining details of the service, emphasizing that it was without cost to policyholders and that visiting nurses would work under the guidance of the physician in charge. Agents provided each policyholder with a mailing card addressed to MetLife's local office. The card was filled out and mailed by the policyholder in case of need, and the visiting nurse called at the earliest possible time. But insurance agents, continuing in their advocacy role, reported a large number of cases directly over the telephone when they encountered ill clients during their weekly rounds.

Visits were primarily requested for acute diseases and conditions where there was a strong possibility of recovery. In those days, illnesses under this heading included pneumonia, influenza, bronchitis, and various children's ailments. MetLife also provided maternity service after the mother had been insured for one year.

Under the rules of the service, a nurse was not permitted to make more than one visit without a physician in attendance. Where patients were too poor to engage a physician, the nurse frequently took on the duty of securing the voluntary service of some physician he or she knew or requesting the attendance of the city or county physician. The nurse helped the patient through the healthcare system of that time—an early example of patient advocacy. The service of visiting nurses introduced by MetLife also influenced the establishment of Visiting Nurse Services, Inc., a national nonprofit organization.

The MetLife visiting nurse service ended in the 1950s; its health and safety education division activities continued into the 1990s. Myriad letters of appreciation sent to MetLife from patients, nurses, and physicians testified to the invaluable work of the visiting nurse; without this home care, many patients would not have been restored to health or even have survived. MetLife's service supported the concept attributed to many great business organizations, "Doing Good While Doing Well." The MetLife Foundation carried on health and safety education activities after the Health and Safety Education Division of MetLife was dissolved.

Patient Education and Advocacy in Medical Care Settings

In the early 1960s, only a handful of the existing 7,500 hospitals in the U.S. had organized patient education programs—another important component of patient advocacy. Yet as hospitals and clinics began to evince a growing interest in capitalizing on "teachable moments" to educate both inpatients and outpatients, MetLife's Health and Safety Education Division responded by providing a grant to the American Hospital Association. These funds allowed experts in the field to convene to establish guidelines for hospital-based patient and community health education programs sponsored and implemented by hospitals.

Patient Advocacy and Medical Care Delivery in Changing Times: Some Thoughts for Moving Ahead

The "family physician" was once a cornerstone of person-centered care over the course of a patient's life. The physician delivered babies, treated sickness, visited or called the patient daily during an illness, admitted the patient to a hospital and followed the patient during hospital treatment through recovery at home, helped the patient find a nursing home or after-care facility if needed, and would most likely be in attendance at the patient's eventual funeral service. Yet this "personal touch" between patient and provider—the continuity of care so important to the generation of the 1930s, 1940s, and 1950s—has been overshadowed in the last 50 years by the reliance on new technologies and specialists, the need to contain rising healthcare costs, and the emergence of more complex health systems. These dramatic changes in the healthcare environment have meant that few physicians are able to carry out the multiple roles they once embraced. Unfortunately, as the authors of this preface have themselves experienced, the gap created by this change in physician roles has yet to be filled.

What measures must we take to make the healthcare industry accountable to the patient—as both customer and client? One answer is patient advocacy, which has the patient's interests as a priority. The father of American management, Peter Drucker, suggested the first action of leadership. An industry, in this case health care, should ask itself, "What is our mission? Who is our customer? What does the customer value? What are our results? What is our plan?" Peter Drucker also offered this guidance, "You determine your primary customer—the person whose life is changed because of your work."

This book represents leadership and innovative thinking in the field of patient advocacy. The values, practices, and points of view represented here can further the dialogue on healthcare reform. These chapters contain stimuli for all participants in the system—ranging from patients to providers to policymakers—to take action for progressive change.

Alison Norris, MD
Laurie Norris, MA
Clarence Pearson, MPH

ACKNOWLEDGMENTS

In the four years since we began planning the first patient advocacy conference at the University of North Carolina at Chapel Hill through to the editing and publication of this volume, we have been repeatedly—and forcibly—reminded of the urgent need for patient advocacy and patient-centered responses to the healthcare crisis we face today. The efforts of more than one hundred patient advocacy conference participants in 2003 and 2005, the many patient advocacy education and research programs around the country, as well as the insights of sixteen Carolina students and twenty guest speakers in our first patient advocacy course all attest to the vigor of this emerging field and demonstrate its significance to the quality of people's lives.

As editors we were supported in important ways, large and small, by many individuals and groups who helped make this book possible. First and foremost, we wish to thank Katie Emmet. Katie provided expert review, insightful commentary, and invaluable editorial assistance in helping us write, cut, and generally shape virtually every chapter in this book. In many ways she served as a fourth editor, at the same time that she completed her MPH program with high honors. Similarly, Susan Keesee applied her magic as a medical librarian and former journal editor to hundreds and hundreds of citations. She worked rapidly, tirelessly, and unerringly to review, correct, and complete the many references cited in this volume.

To our authors, we are deeply grateful not only for writing such stimulating, critically nuanced chapters, every one of them illuminated by narratives or case studies, but also for putting up with our numerous requests for "just one more rewrite." You were a delight to work with; we could not have asked for a better group of colleagues.

We wish to thank, too, a number of thought leaders in patient advocacy whose ideas found their way into one or more chapters, including: George Annas, Don Berwick, Erica Breslau, Scott Brown, Fran Castellow, Carolyn Clancy, Elizabeth Clark, Allan Ettinger, Connie Ginsberg, Roxeanne Goeltz, Joe and Terri Graedon, Alice Hedt, Maggie Hoffman, Charlie Inlander, Bev Johnson, Art Levin, Liz Lyons, Andrea Meier, Elda Railey, Barbara Rimer, Deborah Simmons, Julie Sweedler, Charlene Voyce, and Christine Williams.

We note with sadness the untimely death of Tom Ferguson, a nationally recognized physician and Web presence who advocated as "DocTom.com" and in other venues for patients until the very last days of his life. Tom's contributions to patient advocacy are exemplified, though extend far beyond, his chapter in this volume.

Another significant set of people worked diligently behind the scenes in one capacity or another reviewing or helping to revise early drafts. Among them were Peggy Cohn, Joe and Terri Graedon, Ashley Hammarth, Stephen Kosnar, Art Levin, and Wayne Weston. Melissa McPheeters played a major role in assisting Bill Roper shape his foreward for the book. We are especially grateful to several early supporters of our patient advocacy summits, the place where our ideas for this volume first took shape. Among those supporters were Julie Sweedler, Sue Havala Hobbs, and Alexis Moore. Their brainstorming with us was instrumental in the formation of our early ideas.

Completion of the manuscript would not have been possible without the dedicated staff assistance of Laura Pearson, office assistant for the UNC Chapel Hill Department of Health Behavior and Health Education; Cat Vorick and Robin Perkins, as well as graduate students Hillary Anderson, Emily Waters, and Jennifer Wieland, who also provided technical support. Without the crucial advice of Kate Torrey, editor of *The University of North Carolina Press*, at a pivotal time in this book's journey to print, we might not yet have published it. Similarly, to our editor, Mike Brown, who believed in us from the very first moment we "met," we give our most heartfelt thanks.

We are most indebted to one couple for making our foray into patient advocacy happen. Without the support, financial and emotional, of Clarence Pearson and his wife Laurie Norris, and particularly the Scott and June Pearson Fund for Patient Advocacy and its many contributors, including Metropolitan Life, the Agency for Health Care Quality, GlaxoSmithKline, the UNC Health Care System, and the Robert Wood Johnson Foundation, this book would not exist. Clarence and Laurie provided backing for this project, support for our decisions, and belief in our abilities every step of the way. To them we express our enormous gratitude.

Finally, to our colleagues, friends, and especially our partners, Shelley Earp, Barry Feiler, and Martin Johnson, we owe unconditional thanks for their encouragement, tolerance, and sense of humor when we most needed these qualities.

Jo Anne L. Earp
Elizabeth A. French
Melissa B. Gilkey

ABOUT THE EDITORS

Jo Anne L. Earp, ScD, professor and chair, Department of Health Behavior and Health Education, University of North Carolina at Chapel Hill, is a medical sociologist whose research interests focus on the role of social and attitudinal factors in explaining variation in health behaviors. Her current research projects concern the barriers preventing older minority women from getting mammograms and pap smears, community and physician strategies for overcoming these barriers, and an examination of the factors responsible for high-risk behaviors among persons with or at risk for sexually transmitted diseases and AIDS, as well as strategies for altering these behaviors. Earp has published widely in peer-reviewed journals (over 100 articles and chapters) and has extensive experience in curriculum development. Notable works include "Increasing Use of Mammography Among Older, Rural African American Women: Results from a Community Trial," published in the *American Journal of Public Health* in 2002, as well as "Conceptual Models for Health Education Research and Practice," published in *Health Education Research* in 1991. She earned her ScD from the Johns Hopkins School of Public Health.

Elizabeth A. French, MA, is a writer, editor, and lecturer in the Department of Health Behavior and Health Education at University of North Carolina at Chapel Hill. With 7 years in the Department and over 10 years in the profession, she has extensive experience in both scientific and literary writing. She teaches courses in patient advocacy and scientific writing, as well as a required doctoral seminar, "Historical and Conceptual Bases of Public Health." She received her MA in English from the University of North Carolina at Chapel Hill and is currently pursuing an MPH in public health.

Melissa B. Gilkey, MPH, is presently pursuing a doctoral degree at the Johns Hopkins Bloomberg School of Public Health in the Department of Health, Behavior & Society. She previously was a research associate in the Department of Health Behavior and Health Education at the University of North Carolina. Her interests are service learning, health communications, and interdisciplinary training in the health sciences. Formerly a health educator in the San Francisco Unified School District, she has experience in classroom teaching and curriculum development. She received her MPH from the University of North Carolina at Chapel Hill.

CONTRIBUTING AUTHORS

Deborah Collyar, BS
Patient Advocates in Research

James Conway, MS
Institute for Healthcare Improvement

Nancy Davenport-Ennis, BA
CEO and Founder, National Patient Advocate Foundation

Sarah Davis, JD
Center for Patient Partnerships
University of Wisconsin-Madison Law School

Darren A. DeWalt, MD, MPH
Division of General Internal Medicine and Clinical Epidemiology
University of North Carolina School of Medicine

Nancy DiVenere, BA
Board of Directors
Institute for Family Centered Care

M. Robin DiMatteo, PhD
Professor of Psychology
University of California-Riverside

Jo Anne L. Earp, ScD
Professor and Chair, Health Behavior and Health Education
University of North Carolina at Chapel Hill

Katie Emmet, MPH
Evaluation Consultant
North Carolina Prevention Partners

Tom Ferguson, MD (Deceased)
Senior Research Fellow for Online Health at the Pew Internet and
    American Life Project

Susan B. Frampton, PhD
President, Planetree

Barbara Frank, MPA
National Citizens' Coalition for Nursing Home Reform
B & F Consulting

Elizabeth A. French, MA
Lecturer, Health Behavior and Health Education
University of North Carolina at Chapel Hill

Martha E. Gaines, LLM, JD
Center for Patient Partnerships
University of Wisconsin-Madison Law School

Melissa B. Gilkey, MPH
John Hopkins Bloomberg School of Public Health
Baltimore, Maryland

Laura Gilpin, MA
Planetree

Carol E. Golin, MD
Assistant Professor
Departments of Medicine and Health Behavior and Health Education
University of North Carolina at Chapel Hill

Rachel N. Grob, PhD
Associate Dean of Graduate Studies
Sarah Lawrence College

Laura C. Hanson, MD, MPH
Associate Professor
Division of Geriatric Medicine
University of North Carolina School of Medicine

Judith H. Hibbard, DrPH
Professor of Planning, Public Policy, and Management
University of Oregon

Elma L. Holder, MSPH
Founder, National Citizens' Coalition for Nursing Home Reform

Marsha Hurst, PhD
Director, Health Advocacy Program
Sarah Lawrence College

Paul Jentes, MPH
Ohio State University

Adina Kalet, MD, MPH
Associate Professor, New York University School of Medicine

Beth A. Lown, MD
Assistant Professor, Department of Medicine, Harvard University

Margo Michaels, MPH
Education Network to Advance Cancer Clinical Trials

Alexis Moore, MPH
Lineberger Comprehensive Cancer Center
University of North Carolina at Chapel Hill

Julie Moretz, BA
Director of Special Projects
The Institute for Family-Centered Care

Virginia L. Morrison, JD
Healthcare Mediations

Michael P. Pignone, MD, MPH
Division of General Internal Medicine and Clinical Epidemiology
University of North Carolina School of Medicine

Mark Renneker, MD, MPH
Associate Clinicial Professor,
Department of Family and Community Medicine
University of California at San Francisco

Thomas C. Ricketts, III, PhD
Deputy Director, Cecil G. Sheps Center for Health Services Research
Professor, Health Policy and Administration
University of North Carolina at Chapel Hill School of Public Health

Donna Cohen Ross
Outreach Director, Center on Budget and Policy Priorities

Pam Silberman, JD, DrPH
Clinical Associate Professor, Health Policy and Administration,
University of North Carolina at Chapel Hill School of Public Health
President and CEO, North Carolina Institute of Medicine

Beth Seyda, BA
Co-Director, Compassionate Passages, Inc.

Terri Shelton, PhD
Professor, Department of Psychology
Director, Center for Youth, Family, and Community Partnerships
University of North Carolina at Greensboro

Gwendolyn Stritter, MD
Stritter Consulting

Patricia Sodomka, FACHE, MHA
Director, Center for Patient and Family Centered Care
Medical College of Georgia

Carolyn Thorpe, PhD
VA Medical Center

Nancy Tomes, PhD
Professor of History
Stony Brook University

Nicola B. Truppin, JD
Health Navigator Partners, LLC

Laura Weil, MA
Health Advocacy Program
Sarah Lawrence College

Gary S. Winzelberg, MD, MPH
Assistant Professor, Division of Geriatric Medicine
University of North Carolina School of Medicine

Kathy Zoppi, PhD, MPH
Indiana University and Community Hospital Family Practice

Introduction

CHAPTER 1

What Is Patient Advocacy?

Melissa B. Gilkey, Jo Anne L. Earp, and Elizabeth A. French

OBJECTIVES

- To introduce traditions of advocacy, including those related to nursing, palliative care, and breast cancer activism
- To show the importance of the patient safety and quality of care movement in establishing a vocabulary and a greater urgency for patient advocacy efforts
- To discuss the primary goals of patient advocacy: patient-centered care, patient safety systems, and patient involvement and leadership in healthcare design, delivery, and access
- To describe the different levels of the advocacy continuum using an ecological framework

Patient advocacy is often borne of personal necessity. A woman with ovarian cancer researches experimental treatment options, finding one that puts her cancer into remission. The mother of a child with autism learns to navigate the complex healthcare system, coordinating the many specialists involved in her child's care. A physician double-checks the tests ordered by a colleague for his aunt and, in doing so, identifies a misdiagnosis. These examples are only a few of the ways patients and their family members advocate for their own healthcare quality in the face of a system that is often frustrating, fragmented, and even dangerous.

Not surprisingly, many of these patient advocates envision a better system, one in which patients have access to high-quality information when they need it, services are better coordinated, and medical errors are avoided through careful surveillance. In some cases, the desire to prevent others from reliving their own frightening experience is so powerful that patients and their loved ones are inspired to work for broader change. For example, they may establish online support groups to inform and assist other patients, develop medical curricula to improve patient–provider communication, or found nonprofit organizations devoted to organizing patient groups and promoting their interests in public policy. The shift from personal, or "case," advocacy to class advocacy on behalf of a larger group is the basis for many of the quality improvement efforts undertaken in recent years and is a primary concern of this book.

Patients, however, are not alone in seeking to change the status quo in healthcare. Numerous professionals have also recognized the need to make the healthcare system more responsive to patients' needs. Physicians, frustrated by the recalcitrance of chronic disease, create educational materials for low-literacy patients to increase their involvement in managing their diabetes. Researchers develop tools to aid providers in eliciting their patients' care preferences. Hospital administrators institute patient representative programs to help patients successfully navigate the hospital system. Attorneys explore the use of mediation, rather than litigation, as a tool for asserting patients' rights. In such ways, professionals can also become patient advocates. Often swimming upstream against their own professional and organizational norms, these advocates help provide safer and more satisfying care, while at the same time changing the systems-level problems that generate the need for advocacy in the first place.

Subsequent chapters explore each of these examples of patient advocacy in greater depth; they are presented here to illustrate the breadth of the subject. Patient advocates share an interest in improving patient safety and patient experience, but they hail from a wide range of personal and professional backgrounds. In fact, this diversity has been a barrier to organization and collaboration. Patient advocates often report their greatest frustration to be the feeling that they are working in isolation. As challengers to the status quo, they do not always feel comfortable in their given roles as patients or healthcare professionals, but neither do they have easy access to other reform-minded people who could share lessons learned and provide much needed information and support.

The purpose of this chapter is to identify some of the primary forms of patient advocacy and to show how, despite their differences, many advocates are now working to realize the goals of patient-centered care, patient safety, and patient involvement. We discuss traditions of patient advocacy related to specific health topics such as palliative care and breast cancer as well as those that have arisen in particular professions such as nursing. We also examine the contributions of the patient safety movement. With *To Err Is Human,* the Institute of Medicine (IOM) succeeded in creating a sense of urgency about systemic problems underlying the need for patient advocacy (2000). A subsequent report, *Crossing the Quality Chasm*, furthered this discussion by describing a gold standard of healthcare, one characterized by principles such as patient centeredness, equity, and timeliness (2001). With these reports, the issue of healthcare quality gained national prominence and gave patient advocacy a new focus and imperative. In this environment, the time is ripe to discuss ways in which patient advocacy shows important signs of coalescing to become a focus of action and research.

In addition to discussing the origins of patient advocacy, this chapter sets forth a framework that can be used to understand better who the advocates are and how their work is interconnected. Beginning at the level of the individual patient, we show how advocates provide patients with the information and support they need to navigate the healthcare system and to make informed decisions about their health. At the interpersonal level, we examine how advocates work to improve patient–provider communication and to maximize opportunities for peer support. We then broaden our focus to examine the organizational and policy levels where advocates are changing hospitals, medical schools, and nonprofit agencies so that they are more accountable to the patients they serve. Using an ecological framework such as this one offers a more holistic view of advocacy that, in turn, enables patient advocates to identify potential supporters and collaborators more easily.

TRADITIONS IN PATIENT ADVOCACY

To speak of traditions of patient advocacy may sound premature in the context of an emerging area of inquiry; nevertheless, it has a history, and it is possible to identify the "roots" of patient advocacy in several contexts. The "helping professions" of nursing and social work, for example, have a long history of advocacy, connected as they are with the day-to-day work of caring for patients (Mallik, 1997). Other forms of patient advocacy are associated with particular kinds of care, such as mental health or palliative care, in which patients' autonomy may be in jeopardy (Casarett, Karlawish, & Byock, 2002). A third and closely related type of advocacy is that of activists, often disease survivors, who work to improve healthcare for people marginalized by socially stigmatizing diseases

(Davenport-Ennis, Cover, Ades, & Stovall, 2002). Whether in regard to HIV/AIDS or breast cancer, patient advocacy in this context is often tied to broader social movements such as the gay rights, women's, or consumer health movements. Examples of each type of advocacy help illustrate patient advocacy's meanings and complexity.

Professional Roles: Nursing

All health professions are founded on the desire to care for patients, but the practice of nursing is particularly salient to the concept of patient advocacy. As intermediaries between the world of patients and medical institutions, nurses have been among the first in healthcare to define their professional role in terms of advocacy, and as a result, the nursing literature is rich in its discussion of the concept of patient advocacy, its moral underpinnings, and its practice. The literature suggests that nurses in the United States increasingly embrace patient advocacy as a professional role (Mallik, 1997). Although definitions of nursing-related advocacy vary, they tend to center on the nurse's role in protecting patients' autonomy (Kubsch, Sternard, Hovarter, & Matzke, 2004; Mallik, 1997). For example, a concept analysis by Moyra Baldwin (2003) identifies three "essential attributes" of patient advocacy in nursing: (1) *valuing* patients' right to self-determination, (2) *apprising* patients though a combination of education and advising so that they may take part in decision making, and (3) *interceding* for patients with others, including family members and physicians, to ensure that patients' wishes are honored. Challenges to patient advocacy in nursing include the lack of formal training for advocacy and the risk of alienating other members of the healthcare team, particularly physicians (Grace, 2001; Mallik, 1997). Despite these concerns, many leaders in nursing consider patient advocacy to be a central goal of their profession, and the conceptual work accomplished by nurses is a valuable resource for others as they work to understand and develop advocacy roles within their own professions (Mallik, 1997).

Types of Healthcare: End of Life and Palliative Care

In addition to its professional origins, patient advocacy has roots in particular areas of healthcare, such as end of life care. As in the nursing profession, advocates in end of life and palliative care are often concerned with protecting and extending patients' comfort and autonomy. Leaders in the field emphasize (1) open communication between patients and providers about care preferences, (2) the importance of cultural and spiritual dimensions of care, and (3) the need for adequate pain management (IOM, 1997).

Palliative care adds to our understanding of patient advocacy in that these concerns have led to the development of new care models. In the 1970s, advocates in end of life care established hospice programs designed to offer comprehensive services for patients very close to death (Byock, 2000). In this model, physicians and nurses joined families, religious and spiritual practitioners, volunteers, and others in a coordinated effort to minimize patients' suffering as they progressed through a natural stage of life (Byock, 2000). Today, palliative care advocates continue to face challenges in integrating models such as hospice into the healthcare system (Byock, 2000), but their success in designing and disseminating the hospice model illustrates advocates' abilities to redesign the healthcare system at an organizational level to provide more holistic, satisfying care.

Activism: Breast Cancer

Activism represents a third tradition in advocacy. As several chapters in this book illustrate, breast cancer activism is one of several powerful examples of the potential for patient advocacy (Davenport-Ennis et al., 2002). Breast cancer patients and survivors have helped change how clinicians approach this once-stigmatizing disease; advocacy efforts have resulted in greater transparency in patient–provider communication as well as changes in treatment guidelines with less invasive lumpectomies replacing radical mastectomies (Ganz, 1995). Through awareness campaigns, fundraising, lobbying, and coalition building, advocates have also pursued broader goals; following the lead of AIDS activists before them, they have increased access to screening and treatment services (Earp et al., 2002), secured funding for research, and introduced patients as experts in the process of designing and conducting breast cancer research (Lerner, 2002). Efforts such as these lend a new meaning to the idea of patient autonomy, involving patients as both the recipients and the source of advocacy.

Breast cancer activism is also important because it shows how patient advocacy is related to broader social movements. In the case of breast cancer, the women's health movement and the consumer movement helped create the conditions in which survivors could unite to confront the medical establishment (Lerner, 2002). The challenges of patient advocacy in this context are similar to those of other social movements and include sustaining public interest and support, building coalitions and other collaborative relationships, and securing funding (Davenport-Ennis et al., 2002).

Nursing, palliative care, and breast cancer activism are only three of many overlapping advocacy traditions, but each illustrates themes that continue to be important in patient advocacy today. First, advocates believe patients' rights to autonomy are paramount; echoing well-established ethical codes such as the Belmont Report, advocates argue from a rights-based perspective that every effort should be made to keep patients informed of their options and involved in their care. Second, change is often needed at the organizational level to ensure that medical and research institutions meet the needs of traditionally vulnerable groups such as children, the mentally ill, those with disabilities, and those at the end of life, as well as underserved groups such as ethnic minorities. Third, patients themselves are an important source of this change, and their approach may be confrontational, as in the case of early breast cancer or AIDS activism, or collaborative, as with more recent breast cancer advocacy efforts in which patients have been integrated to varying extents into research review boards (see Chapter 17). These themes, of course, are broad, but they gain greater clarity in light of a fourth source of patient advocacy, the patient safety movement.

THE MOVEMENT FOR PATIENT SAFETY AND HEALTHCARE QUALITY

Medical researchers have studied medical error and iatrogenic injuries for decades, but only recently did the subject of patient safety gain widespread attention. In 2000, the IOM published an alarming report on medical error, *To Err Is Human: Building a Safer Health System*. In that report, the Committee on the Quality of Health Care in America extrapolated the findings of two prominent Harvard studies to illustrate the scope of preventable "adverse events," otherwise known as medical errors. These included mistakes in prescribing or administering prescription drugs, poor surgical technique, or failure to identify diagnosable illnesses

(IOM, 2000). The report captured the attention of the scientific community as well as the popular media by estimating that between 44,000 and 98,000 people die each year in the United States because of preventable medical errors (IOM, 2000).

In addition to stating the problem, the IOM committee set an ambitious goal of cutting medical error deaths in half in a 5-year period. In making recommendations toward this goal, the committee emphasized that "the problem is not bad people; the problem is that the system needs to be made safer" (IOM, 2000, p. 49). For example, a pharmacist who reads hand-written prescriptions will almost inevitably misinterpret a physician's handwriting every once in a while, resulting in potentially fatal prescription drug errors. From the point of view of the IOM committee, the fault in this scenario lies not so much with the pharmacist, as with the procedure of handwriting prescriptions. Such errors could be avoided by changing the system to one in which prescriptions are keyed in to a patient's electronic medical record and then printed out. In accordance with this systems-level, nonpunitive, nonreductionist perspective, the committee's recommendations focused on both mandatory and voluntary reporting of medical errors and increased systems analysis, not on greater scrutiny of individual providers.

The IOM's famous "body count," although hotly contested by some, was convincing enough to inspire action by many (Levin, 2005, p. 91). The federal government, for example, called on the Agency for Health Care Research and Quality (AHRQ) to step up patient safety efforts at the national level (Levin, 2005). New organizations such as the Leapfrog Group and the American Medical Association's National Patient Safety Foundation were also established (Levin, 2005). At the same time, medical organizations across the country investigated technologic solutions such as the adoption of electronic medical records to the systems-level problems identified by the IOM committee (Leape & Berwick, 2005). The IOM committee's goal has not yet been met. Indeed, as recently as 2006, the IOM's newest report in the patient safety area, *Preventing Medication Errors*, indicated that anywhere from 380,000 to 450,000 preventable adverse drug events take place in hospitals each year, with another estimated 800,000 adverse drug events occurring in long-term care facilities. Nevertheless, *To Err Is Human* clearly conferred a new legitimacy on efforts to improve the healthcare system, giving would-be reformers the quantitative evidence they needed to demand change (Stelfox, Palmisani, Scurlock, Orav, & Bates, 2006).

Perhaps even more important, however, to galvanizing the patient safety movement was a second IOM report, *Crossing the Quality Chasm: A New Health System for the 21st Century,* published in 2001. In that document, the committee addressed the broader topic of healthcare quality, including not only issues of patient safety but also those of patient experience, cost, and access to services. Establishing six "aims" for the healthcare system, the committee identified the characteristics most important to healthcare quality. They envisioned a system described as (1) *safe,* protecting patients from medical error; (2) *effective* so as to avoid both under-use and over-use of services; (3) *patient centered,* meaning that care is anchored in patients' values; (4) *timely,* providing services when they are needed so as to prevent more serious problems later on; (5) *efficient* in the use of material and human resources; and (6) *equitable,* so as to provide quality care to all people regardless of their gender, ethnicity, or socioeconomic status (IOM, 2001, pp. 5–6). Based on these six patient-centered aims, the committee made recommendations for federal agencies, healthcare organizations, and healthcare purchasers (IOM, 2001).

One of the most striking aspects of *Crossing the Quality Chasm* is the report's emphasis on patient experience and patient authority. The concept of patient-centered care as one of the committee's six aims is the most obvious example; this concept is defined in the report as "care that is respectful of and responsive to individual patient preferences, needs, and values and ensure[s] that patient values guide all clinical decisions" (IOM, 2001, p. 6). The ensuing chapters in this volume offer extensive examples of what it means to respect and respond to such preferences, needs, and values. In addition to overarching aims, the committee also set forth 10 "rules" for reforming the healthcare system. Patients also feature prominently in this context. Rules include "customization [of care] based on patient needs and values," "the patient as the source of control" in decision making, "shared knowledge and the free flow of information" between patient and providers, and "the need for transparency" (IOM, 2001, p. 8). Finally, the committee asserted a role for patients in enacting these aims and rules, naming patients, along with healthcare organizations, purchasers, and providers, as one of the stakeholders responsible for change. If *To Err Is Human* emphasized the importance of systems analysis in healthcare, *Crossing the Quality Chasm* established the patient at the center of those systems.

The IOM reports have a number of important implications for patient advocacy. First, they have provided advocates with the data needed to prove that widespread structural problems *do* exist in the healthcare system and that these problems are serious, resulting in the loss of thousands of lives each year. Second, the reports have illustrated the need to think beyond the culpability of individual providers to consider systems-level factors that determine healthcare quality. Third, the IOM has established, or at least popularized, a vocabulary and an approach that have helped patient advocates articulate their goals. *Patient-centered care* is now an often-used term among patient advocates, even in the midst of debate about how exactly to conceptualize and implement it. Finally, the IOM reports may be credited more generally with bringing awareness to issues important to patient advocates, thereby drawing more people and funding to their efforts. That the healthcare system is frustrating and dangerous has, in effect, been transformed from experiential or anecdotal knowledge to an empirically testable, scientific knowledge that is accepted by those both inside and outside of the medical establishment.

OVERARCHING GOALS OF PATIENT ADVOCACY

The various "traditions" of patient advocacy reveal commonalities that are not surprising in light of the widespread systems-level problems identified by the IOM. The stories of individuals who become advocates out of personal necessity are replicated across a number of professions and disease foci. Despite their different origins, patient advocacy efforts are primarily inspired by three main goals: patient-centered care, safer medical systems, and greater patient involvement in healthcare delivery and design.

Patient-Centered Care

Perhaps no other term evokes the aims of patient advocacy as fully as *patient-centered care*, a concept that has drawn considerable attention from patients and professionals alike. Though definitions vary, many begin with the IOM's aforementioned emphasis on patient preferences and values. The Picker Institute has furthered this definition with research that identifies seven dimensions of the concept: (1) "respect for patients' values, preferences, and expressed needs," (2) "coordination and integration of care" among providers and healthcare institutions, (3) "information, communication, and education" tailored to patients' needs, (4) "physical comfort," especially freedom from pain, (5) "emotional support" to reduce the fear and worry associated with illness and treatment, (6) "involvement of family and friends" in caregiving and decision making, and (7) planning for "transition and continuity" to ensure patients continue to heal after they leave the hospital (Gerteis, Edgman-Levitan, Daley, & Delbanco, 1993, pp. 5–10). These dimensions illustrate the assumption underlying patient-centered healthcare as both a personal and social process aimed not solely at treating disease, but also at promoting a more holistic well-being through supportive interpersonal, cultural, and organizational interactions.

At the same time, the term "patient-centered care" is not without controversy. Although most advocates would agree with the dimensions outlined by the Picker Institute, some take issue with the name itself, preferring instead "person-centered," "family-centered," or "relationship-centered" care. Others feel that "patient-centered care" is a concept that has been co-opted to some degree by those with a business interest in healthcare and may be too easily confused with terms such as "consumer-centered" or "consumer-driven" healthcare. This area of discussion reflects a broader debate about the terminology of patient advocacy that must be considered carefully by patients and professionals as they define their own work (Textbox 1.1).

Safer Systems

A second goal of patient advocacy is to establish systems that will ensure patient safety. As defined by Longo, Hewett, and Schubert, these systems are the "various policies, procedures, technologies, services, and numerous interactions among them necessary for the proper functioning of hospital care" (2005, p. 2859). Patient safety systems, in other words, are diverse, and they may extend to any healthcare setting from hospitals to pharmacies to long-term care facilities. Patient safety systems include (1) *technological innovations* such as electronic medical records and prescription tracking systems that improve the accuracy and availability of medical information, (2) *procedures* such as the marking of surgical sites that introduce reminders and reduce chances for miscommunication, and (3) *policies* that ensure medical errors, or even "near misses," are reported, analyzed, and addressed (Longo et al., 2005). Even though many systems

Textbox 1.1   Advocacy Terminology: What Is in a Name?

As social reformers, patient advocates are often interested in updating both popular and professional language to better convey the values they aim to support. The very language that we use frames how we think about a set of problems, defining and limiting categories of knowledge. Since at least the 1970s, healthcare reformers have argued about the appropriate words to use for people who receive care. For many, the term *patient* evokes the image of a powerless layperson submitting passively to medical authority (Neuberger, 1999). Others point out that the term is poorly suited for describing people who are essentially healthy, but require health-related services, such as people living in long-term care facilities, pregnant women, and others (Herxheimer & Goodare, 1999). Some feel that these connotations of passivity and illness are serious enough to warrant abandoning the term *patient* altogether (Neuberger, 1999).

Alternatives to *patient* include *partner, consumer, client*, and *user*, each of which carries its own connotations and limitations. *Partner* is effective in communicating shared power, but is not health specific and requires additional modifiers to distinguish between the person receiving services and the professional providing them. On the other hand, *consumer, client*, and *user* have commercial connotations, conceptualizing healthcare as a commodity best regulated through market forces rather than as a personal need or right (Herxheimer & Goodare, 1999). In the end, context and tradition often decide word choice. For example, *client* is the preferred term of certain professions such as psychology and social work, whereas *consumer* is often used to refer to patients collectively, especially at the level of policy advocacy efforts. Interestingly, after weighing the merits of these various terms for years, advocacy educators at Sarah Lawrence College opted finally for "person." Depending on context, this book uses many forms of the term: patient, partner, consumer, client, and person.

Semantic debate extends to other advocacy terms, including *patient-centered care*. Advocates who work in residential settings, for example, may favor *person-centered care*, possibly a more appropriate term for healthy people. Pediatric advocates, on the other hand, use *family-centered care* to emphasize the social dimension of care they feel is so often lacking in traditional medical practice.

These distinctions are of no small consequence to a text devoted to *patient advocacy*, a conflicted term that gives rise to debate. One particular interest is how the term is distinct from other, closely related concepts. For the purposes of this text, patient advocacy has been defined very broadly to include interventions targeting individual empowerment, interpersonal interactions, organizational and cultural change, and policy development related

(continued)

Textbox 1.1   Advocacy Terminology: What Is in a Name? (continued)

to healthcare delivery and design. An even broader term, however, is *health advocacy*. It encompasses these dimensions as well as efforts to impact determinants of health outside the healthcare system. *Health advocacy* implies community and environmental efforts directed at, for example, lead paint abatement in low-income communities. Distinguishing patient advocacy from similar concepts, although frustrating at times, can help scholars and practitioners reach a more precise understanding of *patient advocacy*, even as we recognize the limitations of the vocabulary we use.

Given the nature of language and meaning—that is, the ways in which a word has the power to categorize and limit—variants in terminology will undoubtedly persist. With this recognition, this volume aims to recognize the significance of terminology, to demonstrate an understanding and respect for the tradeoffs made in choosing one term over another, and to introduce readers to different advocacy dialects.

---

solutions are technical and organizational in nature, suggesting a throwback to technocratic rather than social solutions to healthcare problems, they are based on a "culture of patient safety" in which healthcare administrators, providers, and patients value and promote safety (Clancy, 2005, p. 277). Like patient centeredness, patient safety implies an attitudinal shift toward healthcare governed by a set of values focused on human beings within their social milieus.

Patient Involvement in Healthcare

A third goal of patient advocacy, implicit in both patient centeredness and patient safety, is the desire to give patients a greater voice in healthcare. Patient advocates recognize that the biomedical orientation of the U.S. healthcare system often champions the scientific knowledge of healthcare professionals while undervaluing the lay knowledge of patients. At the level of the individual medical encounter, patients are not encouraged often enough to be partners in their own care, resulting in the loss of valuable information as well as motivation on the part of the patient to contribute to and follow treatment plans. Advocates wish to improve patient–provider communication by "activating" patients, educating providers, and creating models of patient-centered communication

(Chapters 7, 8, and 9). The rise in chronic diseases such as diabetes is creating an ever greater need for such patient engagement as more and more healthcare becomes self-care, which must be managed by the patient outside of the healthcare system.

The neglect of "patient voice" has broader consequences as well. Patients have a valuable perspective to offer those in medical education and medical research. When given the opportunity, patients can, for example, develop and teach medical school curricula in patient–provider communication, compose and pretest health education materials and consent forms to improve their readability and relevance to lay people, and serve alongside scientists on research review boards. True patient participation is rarely invited in these ways, but patient advocates hope to correct this imbalance by changing institutional cultures so that patients' contributions become more valued by and accessible to health professionals.

Patient or consumer voice is often similarly underrepresented in health policy and administration, leading to healthcare organizations and public policies that do not serve public interests as effectively as they might (Davis, Schoenbaum, & Audet, 2005). This danger is particularly acute for minority groups and low-income communities whose access to even the most basic of healthcare services is often at stake. Improving healthcare access involves many factors central to patient advocacy, including making healthcare more affordable (e.g., by enacting state or federal policies that extend health insurance to the over 45 million uninsured); reducing barriers to the use of medical institutions (e.g., by increasing hours of operation and providing translation services); and reaching out, through lay health advisor and patient navigator programs, to populations who have been alienated by the healthcare system. Patient advocates believe that patient input is crucial to tackling issues such as these, and they seek to mobilize patients through public awareness campaigns and grassroots organizing so that patients' voices are heard.

The three goals of patient advocacy outlined here (i.e., patient-centered care, patient safety, and patient involvement) are broad and have the potential to overlap. For example, increasing patient involvement in healthcare is often identified as an essential part of both patient-centered care as well as the improvement of patient safety systems. Although the distinction among the three goals is in some ways artificial, conceptualizing patient advocacy as the intersection of patient-centered care, patient safety, and patient involvement helps us more easily map the intellectual streams we perceive as contributing to these related sets of endeavors

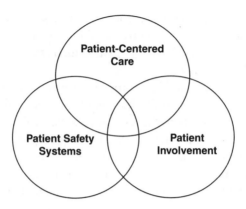

Figure 1.1   Patient Advocacy Goals

(Figure 1.1). In the case of each goal, patient advocacy occurs along a continuum from individual medical encounters to organizational and systems efforts to policy and grassroots initiatives. Like the problems they are meant to address, patient advocacy efforts are designed to be widespread and systemic in nature.

MAPPING THE ADVOCACY CONTINUUM: AN ECOLOGICAL FRAMEWORK

Given the breadth of patient advocacy's goals, it is not surprising that advocacy's roles and methods, not to mention its actors, are diverse and resist being categorized under one umbrella. Nevertheless, developing a "taxonomy" of patient advocacy is an important first step toward fostering understanding and collaboration among various stakeholders. The social ecological framework is a useful heuristic often employed in public health and may serve as a helpful conceptual framework for mapping the advocacy continuum (McLeroy, Bibeau, Steckler, & Glanz, 1988). The social ecological framework divides interventions by their level of influence and is well suited for addressing the multiple modalities of patient advocacy. By considering advocacy at the individual, interpersonal, organizational, and policy levels, as delineated by the social ecological framework, we can map the patient advocacy continuum in a way that increases our understanding of who advocates are and how their work is interrelated (see Figure 1.2).

The Individual Level: Informing Patients

The social ecological framework begins at the level of the individual and considers interventions that target the personal beliefs, attitudes, and knowledge needed to achieve health. Many efforts examined in this volume begin with these "individual level" determinants, both patients' own efforts to educate and orient themselves, and with other efforts that seek to bolster patients' knowledge and confidence so that they may more fully participate in their own care. Sometimes falling under the rubric of "self-help," patient advocates may develop patient education materials that address a particular disease or that more generally help patients navigate the healthcare system more safely and effectively. Patients' literacy and access to information are related concerns for both practitioners and researchers, especially as chronic diseases force patients to take an ever greater role in the treatment process (Chapter 8).

In the realm of "individual-level" advocacy, e-health is a dynamic new area of interest to patient advocates, with recent studies showing that as

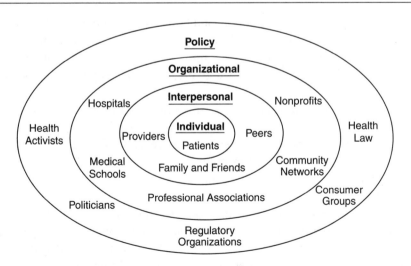

Figure 1.2   Patient Advocacy from a Social Ecological Perspective

many as 80% of Internet users seek health information online (Fox, 2005). Sites devoted to informing patients include those sponsored by nonprofit and government agencies (e.g., AARP and Agency for Health Care Research and Quality (AHRQ)), well-known professionals (e.g., Tom Ferguson's DocTom.Com and Alan Greene's DocGreene.Com), and patients themselves (e.g., Karen Parles's lungcanceronline.org). The content of these sites is as diverse as their sponsors and includes information and advice related to (1) choosing a health plan, medical center, or healthcare provider; (2) learning about diseases and treatment options; (3) preventing medical error and increasing participation in treatment decisions; and (4) understanding the lived experience of patients as they face specific illnesses. Although only a small sampling, these resources demonstrate the wide range of advocacy efforts devoted to giving patients the knowledge that they need to become actively involved in their own care (Chapter 4). Of course, e-health interventions are not limited to the "individual level" alone. In addition to providing information, some e-health efforts focus on helping patients cultivate interpersonal relationships with other patients and providers through, for example, e-mail or online support groups.

The Interpersonal Level: Supporting and Empowering Patients

In addition to their own beliefs and knowledge, people are often influenced by others in their social network. The second "level" of the social ecological framework therefore focuses on the interpersonal interactions that support health, such as advice giving, emotional support, and the provision of resources and other help. In the case of patient advocacy, the most relevant interpersonal relationships may be those between patients and their family members and friends, their healthcare providers, and other patients in similar circumstances. Advocacy efforts at the interpersonal level are devoted to connecting patients to people who can be most helpful to them and to improving the quality of communication and support given.

Patient–provider communication is probably the most well-studied example of patient advocacy efforts at the interpersonal level. In particular, advocates are interested in advancing patient-centered models of communication in which providers take not only a biomedical interest in patients' physical symptoms, but also consider psychosocial aspects of care, including the social, cultural, and financial factors that impact patients' health (Mead & Bower, 2000). Both medical researchers and patients themselves have worked to develop models of patient-centered communications, such as motivational interviewing, and then have trained providers in using these methods (Chapters 3, 6, 7, and 9). At the same time, advocates are pushing for the adoption for new technologies in electronic medical records that would better capture this patient information, allowing for greater continuity of care between visits and among providers.

Patient advocates also recognize the importance of nonmedical relationships. Family members and friends, for example, provide patients with much needed emotional and instrumental support. They also have an important role to play in asserting patients' rights, preventing adverse drug events or other medical errors, and helping patients understand and follow treatment regimens. Patient advocates help patients benefit from the involvement of friends and family members by encouraging these people to become involved in the care process and by addressing barriers, such as limited visiting hours or attitudes of healthcare employees, that make it difficult for loved ones to act as advocates. Patient advocates also work to connect patients with other lay people, such as disease survivors, who can help orient and support patients; these interventions may take the form of online or in-person support groups, hospital-based peer navigation programs, or community outreach efforts (Chapters 3, 4, and 5). In these ways, patient advocates support and expand patients' social networks to provide care that is socially specific and culturally appropriate.

The Organizational and Community Levels: Transforming Culture

Social networks are organized more broadly by community and organizational structures, and the third level of the social ecological framework addresses interventions aimed at these macro-level environments. In patient advocacy, organizations that determine the patient centeredness and safety of healthcare include hospitals, professional associations, medical and other health science schools, and advocacy-related community organizations. These organizations play a major role in governing how and where healthcare is practiced as well as who may participate in the process of giving and receiving care. More generally, these organizations are responsible for establishing a tone or culture that can either support or discourage patient centeredness, patient safety, and patient involvement.

Not surprisingly, hospitals are the center of many patient advocacy efforts, and patient advocacy in this setting includes efforts to establish new models and systems. Hospital administrators and health services researchers, for example, develop and implement hospital models of patient-centered care that engage patients by increasing the accessibility of medical information, improving the navigability and appearance of hospital buildings, and offering greater access to complementary and alternative therapies (Chapters 11 and 13). At the same time, others work to make hospital settings more conducive to patient safety by instituting systems that prevent error as well as those that monitor and analyze errors that do occur. Patient advocates are among those responsible for developing these systems and for helping to get them adopted (i.e., building support among patient and hospital administrators, aligning financials and prestige-related incentives, training hospital providers and staff, and organizing patient and consumer support) (Chapter 10). In these ways, patient advocates attempt to change the entire organizational culture of medical institutions from hospitals to medical schools to professional associations so as to bring them into better alignment with the goals of patient advocacy (Chapter 12).

One long-standing example of patient advocacy at the organizational level is the patient representative program. In these hospital-based efforts, representatives are assigned to patients who need assistance in navigating the hospital system, especially with regard to voicing and addressing complaints related to their care (Ravich & Schmolka, 1993). Patient representatives are meant to be problem solvers who help personalize care and assert patient rights. They may range from professional representatives who are employed by the hospital to trained volunteers who serve on a part-time basis. Although critics have argued that such hospital-sponsored efforts present a serious conflict of interest, patient representative programs have become a common feature of hospitals across the country and are a well-known quality improvement tool (Ravich & Schmolka, 1993).

The Policy Level: Translating Consumer Voice into Policy and Law

In addition to organizational rules and procedures, the social ecological framework recognizes the importance of broader policies and laws. In patient advocacy, important policies are those that (1) control access to care; (2) regulate healthcare organizations, especially with regard to patient safety surveillance; and (3) protect healthcare consumers. Patient advocates work to influence policy making through activism, ombuds programs, and political lobbying so that lay people have a voice in a healthcare system otherwise dominated by the beliefs and practices of health professionals and business interests.

Grassroots organizing is one important example of patient advocacy at the policy level. Advocates representing vulnerable communities such as children, older adults, and the uninsured are responsible for gauging the interests and needs of their constituencies, communicating and promoting these priorities to policy makers, and enforcing the regulation of policies once they have been established (Chapters 15, 16, and 17). Additionally, advocates work to protect consumers' access to information and promote a higher level of truth in advertising (Chapter 14). In these ways, patient advocates address the macro-level forces that govern organizations, interpersonal interactions, and individual health behaviors.

The different levels of the social ecological framework are useful for categorizing advocacy efforts, allowing for an understanding of patient advocacy that moves beyond the activities of individuals helping patients move through complex health systems. The framework also suggests how levels are related. The social ecological framework is based on the premise that health promotion efforts can be significantly strengthened by intervening at multiple levels simultaneously (McLeroy et al., 1988). For example, patients who have been "activated" through interventions at the individual level are better able to take part in patient-centered communication fostered by interventions at the interpersonal level. At the same time, improved interpersonal communication results in more activated patients. These interactions can only happen to the extent that organizations and policies encourage patients to access the healthcare system in the first place, but activated patients and physicians are more likely than others to participate in the organizational and political processes that determine access to care. In other words, gains at one level of advocacy carry over to other levels, and this idea of reciprocal determinism has important implications for patient advocacy (McLeroy et al., 1988). The social ecological framework suggests the ways in which the multiplicity of patient advocacy efforts are a strength, rather than a liability, and that better communication and coordination among advocates working at different levels may have a synergistic effect that benefits everyone involved (see Table 1.1).

PATIENT ADVOCACY, AN EMERGING FIELD?

This text is based on a social ecological conceptualization of patient advocacy that includes individual, interpersonal, organizational, and policy-level components. Subsequent chapters explore these levels of advocacy in greater depth, showing that from patients to healthcare providers to nonprofit leaders to researchers, every stakeholder in the healthcare system has the potential to contribute to efforts to promote patient-centered care, patient safety, and patient involvement. This view is supported by patient advocacy leaders, as this book defines them, from every level of the healthcare system, as evidenced by advocacy-related literature as well as recent survey research (see Textbox 1.2) (Casarett et al., 2002; Davenport-Ennis et al., 2002; Ganz, 1995).

Although not all stakeholders perceive patient advocacy as a movement, much less a field, this volume makes a case that this collection of efforts points to the emergence of a distinct professional area. As the chapters that follow show, advocates increasingly recognize the need to collaborate around their shared goals and challenges (Chapter 2). As a result, individual advocates are beginning to coalesce into broader networks and organizations. At the same time, roles for advocacy are becoming more numerous, both for professional patient advocates such as patient representatives and those in other professions such as medicine and law who wish to specialize in advocacy (Chapters 19 and 20). A corresponding increase in interest in advocacy education is also evident, as shown by the growing number of graduate-level courses devoted to the topic (Chapter 18). From a social ecological perspective, these efforts to unify and coordinate patient advocacy efforts may provide the external and internal pressure needed to significantly improve healthcare quality.

Table 1.1 Patient Advocacy Intervention Matrix: Examples by Level of Influence

	LEVEL OF INFLUENCE			
Patient Advocacy Goals	*Individual*	*Interpersonal*	*Organizational and Community*	*Policy and Consumer Health*
Patient-Centered Care	• Provide patients with information about illness and treatment options • Help patients assess and choose medical care facilities, providers • Increase patients' access to information through written, video, or electronic resources • Increase readability and cultural relevance of patient education materials	• Engage family members and friends in care • Connect patients to peers through support groups, peer navigator programs • Develop models and tools of patient-centered communication • Train providers in patient-centered communication	• Design organizational models that support patient-centered care • Change hospital rules and physical environments to better support family involvement • Reward providers for practicing patient-centered care • Coordinate patient representative and lay health advisor programs that help both existing patients and those facing barriers to accessing care	• Support efforts to ensure access to care • Conduct assessments of medical centers, health-care plans for consumer reports

(continued)

Table 1.1   Patient Advocacy Intervention Matrix: Examples by Level of Influence

	LEVEL OF INFLUENCE			
Patient Advocacy Goals	*Individual*	*Interpersonal*	*Organizational and Community*	*Policy and Consumer Health*
Patient Safety	• Engage patients in patient safety practices (e.g., verifying medication doses) • Inform patients and providers about risk of medical error • Engage patients in care process	• Engage families in patient safety practices • Institute electronic medical records and other technological supports for communication and information sharing	• Develop systems for capturing and addressing medical errors • Change medical school and hospital culture to encourage more collaborative relationships among providers	• Prioritize safety-related organizations for financial and political support • Raise awareness among consumers about the pervasiveness of medical error
Patient Involvement	• Include patients in development and pretesting of patient education materials	• Integrate patients in design and implementation of communication curricula for providers • Recruit patients and survivors to act as peer educators	• Coordinate and train patients to contribute to medical research design and funding	• Organize health activism and grassroots advocacy • Include patients and survivors in developing and funding research studies

Textbox 1.2   The University of North Carolina (UNC) Patient Advocacy Survey: What Is Patient Advocacy?

A national survey by the UNC School of Public Health explored the topic of patient advocacy. In 2005, a purposive sample of advocacy leaders from all levels of healthcare were invited to complete an online questionnaire. Respondents were asked to define patient advocacy and to identify important roles, aims, and methods related to the concept. A total of 112 respondents completed the survey, representing a response rate of 55%.

Survey respondents perceived patient advocacy efforts as involving a broad spectrum of actors from patients to providers to heads of non-profits and others.

- When asked which of seven groups "often" or "sometimes" take on the role of patient advocate, about three quarters of respondents indicated patients themselves (72%), family members or friends (81%), nurses (76%), social workers (81%), and hospital patient representatives (72%). Almost half (47%) indicated that physicians do so as well.
- The majority of respondents wished these groups were more active in advocacy efforts, with over three quarters indicating that they would like to see patients themselves (78%) and physicians (79%) take even more of a role in patient advocacy.
- The majority of respondents also felt that a "big role" or "somewhat of a role" is played by leaders of nonprofit organizations (79%), educators of patient advocates (86%), and activists and grassroots organizers (89%).
- About three quarters of respondents (71%) wished to see hospital administrators take more of a role in patient advocacy.
- Respondents indicated a number of reasons for getting involved in health-related advocacy, with one quarter (25%) citing the experience of a friend or family member as their main motivation.

Respondents rated the importance of advocacy-related goals, methods, and competencies.

- The vast majority of respondents indicated that "very important" goals in patient advocacy include quality improvement and patient safety (84%), more patient-centered care (86%), improved patient-provider communication (88%), and increased access to care (79%).
- Over half of our respondents (57%) reported that patient/consumer education is a method "often" used by patient advocates. In terms of methods that should be used more often than they currently are, about two thirds mentioned organizational change in hospitals (69%) and provider education/curriculum reform (65%).
- In terms of "next steps" for patient advocacy, over half the respondents assigned a "high priority" rating to coordinating advocacy efforts more

(continued)

Textbox 1.2   The University of North Carolina (UNC) Patient Advocacy Survey: What Is Patient Advocacy? (continued)

effectively (61%), raising public awareness about advocacy issues (59%), and training more advocates/training advocates more effectively (51%).

- In regard to advocacy competencies, respondents most often assigned a "very important" rating to communication skills (86%) and an understanding of the patient's perspective (83%).

Respondents defined patient advocacy via four themes: (1) taking a multilevel approach that includes both individual- and systems-level advocacy, (2) increasing patient power by facilitating patients' education, involvement in decision making and ability to navigate the healthcare system, (3) changing hospital and provider culture to be more patient centered, and (4) improving healthcare quality, particularly in regard to patient safety and access to care. A few illustrative responses included the following:

- *Patient advocacy is supporting and empowering patients to make informed decisions, navigate the system to get the healthcare they need, build strong partnerships with providers while working toward system improvement to support patient-centered care. Patient advocates are dedicated first and foremost to the well being of the patients they serve.*
- *Assisting people (either as case advocacy on behalf of individuals or class advocacy on behalf of a group) with the process of receiving healthcare, maximizing their health, and ensuring that all people have access to safe and comprehensive healthcare.*
- *Standing with patients to assist them in meeting their needs by intervening at various levels of the health and social care system.*
- *Efforts to ensure that patients have the information and the self-determination they need so that patient needs are forefront in decisions about patient care.*
- *Patient advocacy is the bilateral appreciation that the focus of medical intervention should be "patient centered." This includes the sharing of decision making, risks, cost effectiveness, treatment regimens, goals, and expectations. This must be implemented with an appreciation of the individual patient and physician in the global context of healthcare.*

Although this cross-sectional study of a relatively small, purposive sample of people already involved in patient advocacy work cannot be seen as the defining standard in what we are positing as the emerging field that is patient advocacy, it was useful in both confirming what policy makers and researchers have been writing about for almost a decade and suggesting directions for future research and programmatic efforts.

Source: Gilkey, MD & Earp, JA. University of North Carolina Patient Advocacy Survey. Unpublished. Completed in 2005.

REFERENCES

Baldwin, M. A. (2003). Patient advocacy: A concept analysis. *Nursing Standard, 17*(21), 33–39.

Byock, I. (2000). Completing the continuum of cancer care: Integrating life-prolongation and palliation. *CA: A Cancer Journal for Clinicians, 50*(2), 123–132.

Casarett, D. J., Karlawish, J. H., & Byock, I. (2002). Advocacy and activism: Missing pieces in the quest to improve end-of-life care. *Journal of Palliative Medicine, 5*(1), 3–12.

Clancy, C. M. (2005). Training health care professionals for patient safety. *American Journal of Medical Quality, 20*(5), 277–279.

Davenport-Ennis, N., Cover, M., Ades, T. B., & Stovall, E. (2002). An analysis of advocacy: A collaborative essay. *Seminars in Oncology Nursing, 18*(4), 290–296.

Davis, K., Schoenbaum, S. C., & Audet, A. M. (2005). A 2020 vision of patient-centered primary care. *Journal of General Internal Medicine, 20*(10), 953–957.

Earp, J. A., Eng, E., O'Malley, M. S., Altpeter, M., Rauscher, G., & Mayne, L., et al. (2002). Increasing use of mammography among older rural, African American women: Results from a community trial. *American Journal of Public Health, 92*(4), 646–654.

Fox, S. (2005). *Health information online: Eight in ten users have looked for health information online, with increased interest in diet, fitness, drugs, health insurance, experimental treatments, and particular doctors and hospitals. Pew Internet & American Life Project.* Retrieved June 1, 2006, from http://www.pewinternet.org/pdfs/pip_healthtopics_may05.pdf.

Ganz, P. A. (1995). Advocating for the woman with breast cancer. *CA: A Cancer Journal for Clinicians, 42*(2), 114–126.

Gerteis M., Edgman-Levitan S., Daley J., & Delbanco T. L. (Eds.). (1993). *Through the patient's eyes: Understanding and promoting patient-centered care.* San Francisco: Jossey-Bass.

Grace, P. J. (2001). Professional advocacy: Widening the scope of accountability. *Nursing Philosophy, 2*(2), 151–162.

Herxheimer, A., & Goodare, H. (1999). Who are you, and who are we? Looking through some key words. *Health Expectations, 2*(1), 3–6.

Institute of Medicine. (2000). In L. T. Kohn, J. M. Corrigan, & M. S. Donaldson (Eds.), *To err is human: Building a safer health system.* Washington, DC: National Academy Press.

Institute of Medicine. (2001). *Crossing the quality chasm: A new health system for the 21st century.* Washington, DC: National Academy Press.

Institute of Medicine, Committee on Care at the End of Life. (1997). In M. J. Field, C. K. Cassel (Eds.), *Approaching death: Improving care at the end of life.* Washington, DC: National Academy Press.

Kubsch, S. M., Sternard, M. J., Hovarter, R., & Matzke, V. (2004). A holistic model of advocacy: Factors that influence its use. *Complementary Therapies in Nursing & Midwifery, 10*(1), 37–45.

Leape, L. L., & Berwick, D. M. (2005). Five years after to err is human: What have we learned? *Journal of the American Medical Association, 293*(19), 2384–2390.

Lerner, B. H. (2002). Breast cancer activism: Past lessons, future directions. *Nature Reviews Cancer, 2*(3), 225–230.

Levin, A. A. (2005). Patient safety: Rejecting the status quo. *North Carolina Medical Journal, 66*(2), 91–95.

Longo, D. R., Hewett, J. E., Ge, B., & Schubert, S. (2005). The long road to patient safety: A status report on patient safety systems. *Journal of the American Medical Association, 294*(22), 2858–2865.

Mallik, M. (1997). Advocacy in nursing: A review of the literature. *Journal of Advanced Nursing, 25*(1), 130–138.

McLeroy, K. R., Bibeau, D., Steckler, A., & Glanz, K. (1988). An ecological perspective on health promotion programs. *Health Education Quarterly, 15*(4), 351–377.

Mead, N., & Bower, P. (2000). Patient-centeredness: A conceptual framework and review of the empirical literature. *Social Science and Medicine, 51*(7), 1087–1110.

Neuberger, J. (1999). Do we need a new word for patients? Let's do away with "patients." *British Medical Journal, 318*(7200), 1756–1758.

Ravich, R., & Schmolka, L. (1993). Patient representation as a quality improvement tool. *Mount Sinai Journal of Medicine, 60*(5), 374–378.

Stelfox, H. T., Palmisani, S., Scurlock, C., Orav, E. J., & Bates, D. W. (2006). The "To Err is Human" report and the patient safety literature. *Quality & Safety in Health Care, 15*(3), 174–178.

CHAPTER 2

The U.S. Healthcare System and the Need for Patient Advocacy

Pam Silberman, Thomas C. Ricketts, III, and Donna Cohen Ross

OBJECTIVES

- To describe several different types of private and public insurance coverage offered in the United States and the ways in which this "nonsystem" contributes to problems with healthcare access and quality
- To identify factors that contribute to increased healthcare spending and escalating insurance premiums
- To explain who the uninsured are, why they are uninsured, what safety net options exist, and why these provisions are insufficient to meet the need
- To illustrate how advocacy groups have been active in preserving and expanding access to healthcare for children in two different states

Mary Smith has two children: Ben, age 3, and Sarah, age 7. For years, she worked at a local manufacturing company through which she received health insurance for herself and her family. The company paid 90% of her costs and 50% of the costs of dependent coverage. About a year ago, Mary lost her manufacturing job. The only job she could find in the service industry does not offer health insurance coverage. Her son, Ben, is enrolled in a Medicaid-managed care organization and is required to see his primary care provider for preventive, primary care, and specialty referrals. Sarah receives health insurance through the State Children's Health Insurance Program.

29

She has a different set of providers. Mary has diabetes, but has no insurance coverage. She pays for her health visits out of pocket. Some of her providers accept payments on a sliding scale basis; however, she has not been able to pay for all her doctor's visits and cannot always pay for her medicine or testing strips.

This story illustrates some of the complexities of accessing healthcare in the United States. This country does not have a single healthcare "system" with a unified financing or delivery method to meet the basic health needs of the entire population. Instead, healthcare services are financed through both public and private payers, including the federal, state, and local governments, employers, and families. Healthcare institutions can be government owned and operated or may be run by private nonprofit or for-profit organizations. Most people have some form of health insurance, but insurance benefit designs, cost sharing, scope of services covered, and provider networks vary widely.

This chapter provides an overview of our healthcare "nonsystem," with the aim of showing how access to healthcare in the United States requires expert navigation skills. To paraphrase a former U.S. District Court judge, "The U.S. health system is almost unintelligible to the uninitiated" (Judge Friendly, 1976). This chapter starts with a brief history of U.S. financing mechanisms to illuminate how this "nonsystem" emerged and then provides overviews of how healthcare services are financed and sources of insurance coverage. The last section focuses on the uninsured and the safety net system set up to address their needs. Throughout, this chapter illustrates the need for advocacy in helping people know where to obtain services, how to jump through procedural hoops, and how to stand up for their own rights. Aside from one-on-one patient advocacy, the chapter also shows how broader policy advocacy is needed to promote adoption of laws and policies to improve healthcare access and quality and to oppose changes that will impede certain groups' access to needed services.

HISTORY OF THE U.S. HEALTH SYSTEM

At the time of the founding of the republic, public health was not a recognized responsibility of government, and medicine was a craft that was neither very effective nor very costly. The structure of our current healthcare and public health system developed haphazardly, arising out a blend of competing interests at the local, state, and federal levels.

Public health measures and responsibilities originally arose from local demands for protection from disease. City health departments emerged first, well before organized state structures coalesced. In turn, the states drew on traditions of "police power" to create necessary public health laws and regulations as well as to establish health departments and public health officers. The police power comes from the 10th Amendment to the Constitution, which gives states the powers not given to the federal government, including the authority to protect the health, welfare, and safety of the public.

Initially, federal level public health responses focused narrowly on securing borders and enforcing quarantine laws. The first foray into directly providing healthcare services came in 1798 with the creation of marine hospitals to care for sick and injured merchant seamen. The Marine Hospital Service later took over responsibility of caring for people quarantined with certain infectious diseases and of providing medical inspections for arriving immigrants. By 1912, this system of care had evolved into the Public Health Service. The federal government has also historically provided health services to active military personnel, authorizing the first healthcare facility for veterans in 1811. Care for veterans expanded rapidly after the Civil War, and in 1930, Congress created the Veteran's Administration to oversee these efforts.

Aside from providing care for veterans, the federal government was reluctant to support direct healthcare services for the broader population. This sentiment began to change in the 1960s, when the government began supporting neighborhood health centers as part of its War on Poverty. Later, funding was designated to support clinics providing services for certain groups of people experiencing financial, social, or geographic barriers to healthcare, including farm workers and the homeless; nevertheless, the government has remained reluctant to fund healthcare services for the population as a whole.

The plurality of our healthcare system evolved from many different sources. Hospitals and curative healthcare systems emerged from local nonprofit civic and religious groups as well as local governmental entities. These different types of caregiving institutions sprang from different traditions of governance. For example, in a single community, a secular community board might control one hospital, whereas a church-affiliated body would run another and an elected commission yet another. Each of these governing bodies felt an obligation to slightly different constituencies. Private, for-profit hospitals and clinics, although rare, did exist and grow in some communities. The medical profession began to dominate delivery of health services in the late 19th and 20th centuries after protracted battles with other types of healthcare providers (e.g., osteopaths, midwives) (Starr, 1982). State licensure laws began to regulate entry into practice. Organized medicine also resisted national health reform efforts that could undercut the entrepreneurial tradition of private financing and delivery of health services.

By mid-century, money began flowing into the health sector as the science of healthcare evolved, and the public began demanding more, and better, healthcare services. Health insurance became more prevalent during World War II when Roosevelt established wage ceilings to control inflation and employers responded by offering health insurance as an alternative means of attracting scarce employees. The early success of Blue Cross health insurance plans before World War II, and the later spread of tax-advantaged insurance for employees, tightly linked the financing of healthcare to employment and gave business a stake in supporting a healthcare system.

In the 1960s, after recognizing that the older population and the poor had no access to employer-based insurance, Congress created Medicare (initially limited to older adults) and Medicaid (limited to certain groups of low-income people). These reforms resulted in a huge transfer of tax funds into healthcare. Medicare, initially structured along the lines of existing Blue Cross and Blue Shield insurance systems, paid providers their usual and customary fees. Profits from this early payment structure allowed institutions to invest in technology and upgrade buildings. Additionally, the government helped underwrite physicians' training costs through the Medicare graduate medical education program, even as the National Institutes of Health helped support the development of new technology, medical care, and pharmaceutical research.

During the 1970s, expansion of third-party payments, more sophisticated technology, and medical advances led to rapid increases in healthcare expenditures. In an effort to control these cost increases, Congress attempted to limit unnecessary duplication of services by regulating placement of health services and facilities based on geographic, demographic, and economic considerations. Many of these planning efforts were later abandoned, however, as profit and expansion pressures overwhelmed efforts for constraint.

When attempts at healthcare planning failed, government and other third-party payers tried to restrain the growth in healthcare spending by restricting provider payments. In the 1980s and 1990s, Medicare, private insurers, and other third-party payers implemented prospective payment systems and standardized fee schedules and initiated utilization review and other care management systems (see glossary). Managed care—in particular health maintenance organizations—became popular as a means of improving care and reducing unnecessary services; however, a consumer backlash in the late 1990s led to the abandonment of most of the more tightly controlled care management systems. Quality is now the watchword for 21st century healthcare as the institutions and individuals who pay for services begin to focus on what they are getting for their money.

The United States continues to be deeply conflicted about who has ultimate responsibility for financing and providing healthcare services. This ambivalence has led to a patchwork system in which government, employers, and individuals all help cover these expenses. Over time, government has assumed responsibility for providing health insurance to certain "deserving" populations (e.g., children, older persons, the disabled, and some poor people), but has generally avoided financing care for working adults. Instead, many working adults either obtain insurance through their employer or by purchasing coverage on their own, or they go without. Furthermore, no single unifying "system" of services exists. Health services are provided directly by governmental organizations (such as the Veterans Administration or public health), organizations supported by federal or state funding, and private providers. Healthcare services are offered by both for-profit and not-for-profit organizations. In addition, many physicians provide care through solo or small practices, whereas others practice as employees of larger group practices or as part of a hospital system or medical school. Because the United States lacks a cohesive universal healthcare system, many people fall through the cracks, failing to get the medical care they need. In addition to impeding consumers' access to care, the patchwork system also results in poor healthcare quality (Institute of Medicine, 2001).

FINANCING HEALTHCARE

In 2004, the United States spent approximately $1.9 trillion on healthcare, or 16% of the Gross Domestic Product (GDP) (Smith, Cowan,

Heffler, Catlin, & National Health Accounts Team, 2006), an amount that exceeded the healthcare spending, both per capita and as a percentage of the GDP, of any other major industrialized country (Anderson, Reinhardt, Hussey, & Petrosyan, 2003). Despite these enormous expenditures, key indicators show that the United States lags behind other countries in terms of health outcomes. In 2003, for example, U.S. life expectancies for the total population at birth (77.2 years) tied for 22nd place out of 30 countries (Organisation for Economic Cooperation and Development [OECD], 2005a).[a,b] Similarly, in 2003, the United States had the 25th highest infant mortality rate (OECD, 2005b). In short, even as the United States spends more on healthcare than any other country worldwide, by many indicators, we have poorer health outcomes.

More than half (55%) of all healthcare spending in 2004 came from private sources, including private insurance (35%) and out-of-pocket payments (13%) (Smith et al., 2006); the rest came from governmental sources (45%), with the federal government accounting for 32% of the spending, and state and local governments accounting for 13%. Most federal spending is allocated to Medicare (16%), Medicaid, and the State Children's Health Insurance Program (SCHIP) (9%). State and local spending is about equally split between Medicaid and SCHIP (6.4%) and other state and local health spending (6.8%).

The share of healthcare spending from private and public sources has remained relatively constant over the last 10 years. In 1993, private sources covered 56% of healthcare costs, compared to 55% in 2004 (Heffler et al., 2005); however, the difference between private and public spending is expected to narrow in 2006 because of the introduction of Medicare prescription drug coverage (Medicare Part D; discussed later here). Federal spending on Medicare is predicted to increase from 16% in 2003 to more than 20% of all health-related spending in 2006. As a result, governmental spending in 2006 may account for as much as 49% of healthcare expenditures, whereas private spending may drop to 51% (Heffler et al., 2005).

Most of the $1.9 trillion spent in healthcare in 2004 (83%) was spent on personal healthcare services, including hospital care, professional services, nursing home and home health, prescription drugs, and medical products (Heffler et al., 2005). Another 7% of healthcare spending pays for healthcare administration (both governmental and private insurance administrative costs). Only 3% of the $1.9 trillion supports government public health initiatives, and the remaining funding (7%) is used for research and construction.

INSURANCE COVERAGE

Most Americans have some form of health insurance coverage, but the source of coverage varies greatly depending on whether the person is younger or older than 65. Of people younger than 65, most (63%) have employer-sponsored insurance. Seven percent have private direct-purchase coverage (U.S. Census, n.d. a), and 18% have governmental insurance (either Medicaid or the SCHIP: 13%; Medicare for disabled individuals: 2.5%; or military coverage: 3%). Another 18% of the younger population is uninsured.[c] In contrast, almost all older persons (95%) have health insurance coverage through Medicare (U.S. Census, n.d. b). These different types of insurance coverage are described here in five subsections: employer-sponsored insurance, private nongroup coverage, Medicaid, the SCHIP, and Medicare.

Employer-Sponsored Insurance Coverage

Most people receive health insurance coverage through their job or through a working family member. More than two thirds of those younger than 65 (U.S. Census, n.d. c) and one third of those 65 and older have employer-sponsored insurance coverage (U.S. Census, n.d. b);[d] nevertheless, the percentage of people under 65 with employer-sponsored coverage has been declining steadily over the last 5 years, from 68% in 2000 to 63% in 2005 (U.S. Census, n.d. a). To obtain employer-sponsored insurance, an individual (or his or her spouse or parent) must work for a company that offers coverage. Although more than 90% of employers with 100 or more employees do so, only 36% of the smallest employers (those with fewer than 10 employees) offer coverage to their employees (Medical Expenditure Panel Survey). Moreover, the percentage of small firms offering health insurance coverage declined from 57% in 2000 to 47% in 2005 (Gabel et al., 2005). Rising healthcare premiums account for much of this decline (Gilmer & Kronick, 2005). Between 2000 and 2005, the cost of premiums increased by 73%, far more than the increase in overall inflation (14%) or workers' earnings (15%) (Kaiser Family Foundation and Health Research and Education Trust (2005; OECD, n.d. b). The average total premium cost for an employee in 2005 was $4,024 per year, whereas premiums for family coverage averaged $10,880 (Kaiser Family Foundation and Health Research and Education Trust, 2005, Chart 11; OECD, n.d. b).

These increases in health insurance premiums are primarily because of the underlying costs of healthcare. Simply conceptualized, healthcare spending is a product of the number of services used and the cost per service, both of which have increased in recent years. In some cases, technological advancements have driven the increased cost per service; in others, labor costs may have risen. Increased use is driven by changes in disease prevalence,[e] increased population, and consumer demand for health services (Sturm, 2002; Thorpe, Florence, & Joski, 2004). Providers also contribute to increased utilization, as changes in treatment protocols or technology can lead to an increased use of certain services or procedures.

Employers have passed on rising costs of health insurance premiums to their workers through increased out-of-pocket costs, including higher premiums, deductibles, and co-payments. Between 2000 and 2005, the average premium paid by a worker rose from $28 to $51 per month, or from $135 to $226 per month for family coverage. The average deductible for a Preferred Provider Organization plan (the dominant form of health insurance coverage) increased from $175 to $323 per individual (see glossary sidebar). Additionally, employees are now more likely to be enrolled in a plan with a tiered drug benefit, meaning that they pay more for certain brand name or specialty drugs compared with generics. Currently, the most widely used forms of employer-sponsored insurance include

- Preferred provider organizations (61% of market share), a network of healthcare providers willing to offer services at lower rates to large groups of insured consumers (see Textbox 2.2 for a more complete description of different types of insurance models)
- Health maintenance organizations (HMOs) (21% of market share), which offer lower premiums and out of pocket costs while limiting people's choice of providers to those within the HMO network. Restrictions on choice of providers led to a "managed-care" backlash, resulting in HMO enrollment declines from 29% of market share in 2000 to 21% in 2005.

- Point-of-service plans (15% of market share). Similar to HMOs, but these plans give people the option to seek care outside provider networks for higher out-of-pocket costs.
- Indemnity coverage (3% of market share). Enrollees can see any provider with little insurance oversight to examine appropriateness of services provided.

To address rising healthcare premiums, one fifth of employers have started offering high-deductible plans. These plans offer lower monthly premiums, but have a minimum deductible of at least $1,000 for individual or $2,000 for family coverage. Four percent of employers offer high-deductible plans coupled with a health reimbursement account (HRA) or a health savings account (HSA), a pre-tax account that helps pay some of the medical expenses an enrollee incurs before meeting the deductible. High-deductible health plans, health reimbursement accounts, and health savings accounts are all predicated on the belief that patients will be less voracious consumers of healthcare if they are required to pay more for them. Past studies confirm that consumers use fewer services when faced with higher out-of-pocket costs (Newhouse, 2004); nevertheless, consumers are just as likely to forgo necessary care as unnecessary care. Health outcomes for some subpopulations—the poor and the sick—suffer as a result. Moreover, these plans do little to control the high costs incurred by the small subsection of the population that accounts for the majority of healthcare spending. In 1996, 10% of the population used more than two thirds of all healthcare expenditures, or approximately $11,000 per capita in 1996 (Berk & Monheit, 2001). Individuals with these high medical costs are likely to incur expenses that exceed the high-deductible amount, thereby negating somewhat any cost savings among these high-cost individuals.

Private Direct Purchase Coverage

Approximately 7% of people under 65 are covered through private, "direct-purchase" health insurance coverage. Policies purchased by individuals for themselves and/or other family members are often referred to as "nongroup" policies because they are not purchased as part of a larger employer-based association or other group plan.

Individually purchased health insurance coverage has some advantages over employer provided insurance. First, individuals are not tied to an employer, allowing them to choose the coverage they need and to continue the same coverage even if they switch jobs; however, the availability and affordability of individually purchased insurance are limited. Administrative expenses are higher in the nongroup market, and these costs are passed onto consumers through higher premiums (Pauly & Nichols, 2002). Because people are not required to have insurance coverage, some wait until they are sick before seeking coverage, meaning that the nongroup market is more vulnerable to "adverse selection." In these groups, there are fewer healthy individuals over whom to spread the costs of a high-risk population, and costs are higher (Buntin, Marquis, & Yegian, 2004). Insurers try to prevent adverse selection through underwriting rules that prevent those with pre-existing conditions from purchasing coverage or excluding coverage for certain conditions. For example, one study tested the willingness of insurers to provide nongroup health coverage to people with different health conditions. Eight percent of insurers denied coverage to a hypothetical 26-year-old client with seasonal hay fever, whereas 100% denied coverage to a hypothetical HIV-positive patient (Pollitz & Sorian, 2002). This study suggests that some populations without group coverage simply cannot purchase health insurance. Insurers that do provide coverage for these individuals often charge higher rates to help cover the higher than average anticipated claims costs.

As a response to the "adverse selection" problem, 32 states have created high-risk pools to provide more affordable coverage to those with pre-existing health problems. States that operate high-risk pools set caps on their premiums, typically between 125% and 200% of the amount charged to individuals without pre-existing health problems. State and federal subsidies help cover losses incurred in the pool (Abbe, 2004). Despite caps on the premiums charged, these plans typically have very low enrollment, suggesting that they may still be unaffordable to many individuals with pre-existing conditions.

Medicaid

Medicaid, a government-financed health insurance program, covered 52 million low-income individuals in 2003 (Kaiser Commission on Medicaid and the Uninsured, 2005). Program costs are split between the federal and state governments, with the federal government paying a larger share of program costs for states with lower per capita income. The federal government establishes certain requirements that states must follow in order to receive federal funding; however, states have considerable flexibility in program administration and eligibility rules (Community Catalyst, 2006).

Contrary to popular belief, being in the low-income bracket is not sufficient for an individual to qualify for Medicaid. Certain categorical eligibility requirements apply as well. These categories include pregnant women, children under the age of 21 years, families with dependent children, people with disabilities, and older adults (age 65 years or older). Relatively recent Congressional amendments added women diagnosed with breast or cervical cancer and certain disabled individuals (who would not otherwise qualify) to the list of individuals who might qualify for Medicaid. These Medicaid expansions at both the federal and state levels have often been enacted as the result of consumer advocacy (see Textbox 2.2). Nonetheless, in most states, a childless adult who is not disabled or older will not qualify for Medicaid, regardless of how poor he or she is.

In addition to being the right "type" of individual, a person must also meet income and sometimes resource restrictions to be eligible. The federal Medicaid law establishes certain minimum income eligibility standards, but states are generally free to increase the income limits for most groups. Typically, Medicaid income limits vary depending on the program category and, for children, by the age of the child[f] (see Figure 2.1). States also establish resource limits for certain program categories. These limits are intended to ensure that publicly financed insurance covers only those who are most in need. Individuals with other resources—such as savings accounts or real property other than a primary residence—are expected to use those resources before enrolling.

Medicaid covers hospitalizations, doctors and other health professional services, prescription drugs, and long-term care (as well as many other services); however, Medicaid often reimburses these entities at lower rates than commercial insurance plans do, leading many private providers to be less willing to treat Medicaid patients than commercially insured individuals (Zuckerman, McFeeters, Cunningham, & Nichols, 2004). Thus, consumer groups advocating for low-income populations often team up with provider organizations to push for increases in reimbursement rates to increase Medicaid patients' access to providers.

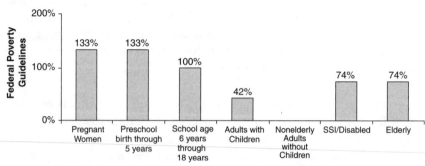

Figure 2.1   Federal Medicaid Eligibility Minimum

Source: Kaiser Commission on Medicaid and the Uninsured. Who Needs Medicaid? April 2006. Figure 1. Available online at http://www.kff.org/medicaid/upload/7496.pdf (Accessed September 11, 2006).

Medicaid enrollment grows during downturns in the economy, when people lose their jobs or have reduced earnings. During these periods, more people qualify because their incomes are lower. This increased enrollment, coupled with increases in healthcare costs, causes Medicaid costs to escalate rapidly at a time when state revenues are declining (Figure 2.2).

In 2004, Medicaid constituted 16.5% of states' general fund spending, or nearly 22% of total state expenditures when federal Medicaid funds are included (National Governors Association and National Association of State Budget Offices, 2004). Moreover, between 2004 and 2005, Medicaid expenditures increased by 12%, far faster than general state revenues. Because Medicaid is an entitlement program, the state and federal government must pay for covered services for all individuals meeting the state's eligibility rules. To address these rising costs over the last 4 years, many states have either cut or frozen provider payments, cut eligibility or service coverage, reduced pharmacy benefits, added recipient cost-sharing, and/or changed the program structure (Smith, Ramesh, Gifford, Ellis, & Wachino, 2003). Low-income families led by advocacy groups are often involved in policy advocacy at the state and federal levels to fight Medicaid cuts or to support Medicaid expansions to cover more of the uninsured (see Textbox 2.1 on Washington state).

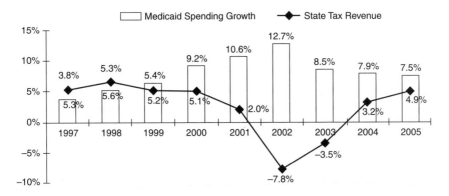

Figure 2.2 Medicaid Spending Growth and State Tax Revenue (1997–2005)

Source: Smith V, Gifford K, Ellis E, Wile A, Rudowitz R, & O'Malley M. Medicaid Budgets, Spending and Policy Initiatives in State Fiscal Years 2005 and 2006. Results from a 50-State Survey. Kaiser Commission on Medicaid and the Uninsured. October 2005. Available online at http://www.kff.org/medicaid/upload/Medicaid-Budgets-Spending-and-Policy-Initiatives-in-State-Fiscal-Years-2005-and-2006-report.pdf (Accessed August 26, 2006).

SCHIP

SCHIP is a government-funded program that provides health insurance coverage to low-income, uninsured children with family incomes too high to qualify for Medicaid but too low to pay for private health insurance coverage. The program provided health insurance coverage to 3.9 million children in 2004 (Kaiser Family Foundation, statehealthfacts.org, 2004). States are given discretion in determining some of the eligibility criteria, resulting in great variability in coverage. Some states have limited eligibility to children with incomes no greater than 140% of the federal poverty guidelines ($28,000 per year for a family of four in 2006), whereas other states use their SCHIP funds to cover children with incomes up to 350% of the federal poverty guidelines ($70,000 per year for a family of four) (Kaiser Family Foundation, statehealthfacts.org, 2005; U.S. Department of Health and Human Services, 2005).

States can use their SCHIP program to expand Medicaid coverage to children or can create a separate program distinct from Medicaid. Some states have "combination" programs, with some children covered through

Medicaid and others covered through a stand-alone SCHIP program. The federal government pays a higher portion of SCHIP's program costs than it does for Medicaid, even as it limits the amount it will contribute toward each state's SCHIP costs. Unlike Medicaid, which is an entitlement program, SCHIP is funded through block grants to the states, based on both the number of children covered under the program and the number of uninsured children with incomes below 200% of the federal poverty guidelines. Because of these federal funding limits, some states have run out of monies in specific years for the program.[g] For example, North Carolina was the first state in the country to close enrollment to new enrollees in 2001; subsequently, seven states have had to close their SCHIP enrollment for a period of time (Silberman, Walsh, Slifkin, & Poley, 2003).

Medicare

Medicare is a national health insurance program that provides coverage for Americans 65 years old and older as well as some younger people with disabilities. Approximately 95% of older adults have Medicare coverage (U.S. Census, n.d. b). Medicare coverage has several parts, including hospital insurance (Part A), coverage for physicians and other providers (Part B), and prescription drug coverage (Part D). In addition, Medicare Advantage (Part C) allows beneficiaries to obtain their Medicare coverage through private HMOs, preferred provider organizations (PPOs), or private fee-for-service insurers. Medicare Part A and Part B constitute the traditional Medicare coverage. Only in 2006 did Medicare begin offering prescription drug coverage.

Traditional Medicare coverage includes significant cost sharing, with separate deductibles for hospitals and physician services, coinsurance, and premiums (for Part B and Part D). Some services are not covered, including routine physicals, hearing aids, dental care, and long-term care services (until 2006, prescription drugs). As a result, Medicare has historically paid for only about 45% of a person's healthcare costs (Cubanski, Voris, Kitchman, Neuman, & Potetz, 2005). Most beneficiaries supplement their traditional Medicare coverage with an additional policy that helps pay costs not covered by Medicare.[h] Those with Medicare as their sole source of coverage are far more likely to report access barriers in obtaining needed healthcare services (Kaiser Commission on Medicaid and the Uninsured, 2001).

Textbox 2.1   Examples of Consumer Advocacy

Publicly financed health insurance programs—notably Medicaid and the State Children's Health Insurance Program (SCHIP)—provide basic health-care and life-saving medical treatments for those unable to afford coverage. As healthcare costs rise and the number of people enrolled increases, expenses to the state and federal governments that jointly finance the programs also increase. Pressure on states can be particularly fierce when poor economic conditions result in diminished revenues and high unemployment, precisely the time when more people need assistance obtaining health coverage. These situations lead to considerable tension about whether to expand coverage to more people in need or to retract coverage to curtail state spending. Many interest groups, including low-income families, advocates for low-income consumers, healthcare providers, and others, have a stake in the outcome of such decisions. Examples from two states, Washington and Illinois, demonstrate how effective advocacy efforts can influence whether health coverage is available and affordable for uninsured people.

Washington: Advocates Persuade State to Abandon Medicaid Premiums for Children

Washington State has a long history of providing generous Medicaid coverage to children in families with incomes up to twice the federal poverty line. During the robust economic years that followed the enactment of SCHIP, Washington further expanded eligibility, greatly simplified enrollment procedures, and invested in aggressive outreach activities to cover more eligible children. As the economic tide turned, advocates found themselves struggling to fend off program cuts. In 2003, the state legislature took steps to limit Medicaid spending by making it more difficult for eligible children to obtain and maintain coverage. Children's enrollment plummeted, with the program ultimately sustaining a decline of over 39,000 children.

At the same time, the state legislature was preparing to impose new financial barriers, jeopardizing access to health coverage for children on Medicaid, a group traditionally protected from having to pay premiums. The state obtained a federal waiver which allowed it to charge families $15 to $20 per child, including children with incomes just above the federal poverty line, then $15,670 for a family of three. The state also planned to raise premiums for children in SCHIP. In an attempt to prevent this blow to children's health, the Children's Alliance, a children's advocacy group, mobilized the state's Health Coalition for Children and Youth to resist the imposition of a premium. This network of children's advocates, healthcare providers, hospitals, clinics and the Washington State PTA focused full attention on eliminating the proposed premiums. The following strategies were central to their campaign:

(continued)

Textbox 2.1   Examples of Consumer Advocacy (continued)

The coalition used respected research to make the case. The coalition shared with policy makers and the media research from Maryland and Oregon that found significant drops in enrollment when premiums were imposed on low-income beneficiaries. In addition, advocates asked the Center on Budget and Policy Priorities (CBPP), a national organization that conducts research and policy analysis, to investigate the likely effects of the state's plan. Using an econometric model of the relationship between premiums and participation, CBPP estimated that 24,000 low-income children would lose coverage, increasing the number of uninsured children in the state by 57%.

The coalition offered an alternative financing plan. Advocates showed that new federal legislation, enabling Washington to redirect about $25 to $26 million in SCHIP funds to Medicaid, could ease pressure on the Medicaid budget. In addition, they argued that the temporary increase in federal Medicaid payments, passed to help states in the tight economy, could also be used to avoid implementing the premiums.

Coalition members applied political pressure. Arguing that imposing a premium would result in substantial hardship for very low-income families, advocates lobbied the legislature to repeal them and succeeded in getting the charges rescinded for the lowest income children. Next, they pushed the exiting governor to delay implementation of the remaining premiums, pitching this move as vital to his legacy. They succeeded one month before the new charges were set to take effect. In 2004, advocates persuaded Christine Gregoire, a candidate for governor, to focus on children's health coverage. After taking office, her first policy action was to further delay the premiums, but the threat still loomed large. Then, in 2005, the legislature declared its intent to cover all children by 2010, but remained silent on the premium issue. Persuaded that premiums would thwart the success of this vision, the governor requested a bill to prohibit premiums on children in families with incomes less than twice the federal poverty line. The bill passed and became law in February 2006.

After a hard-fought, determined campaign, advocates succeeded in getting the state legislature and the governor to establish an important principle: that premium-free coverage for low-income children is essential to the viability of a plan to provide coverage for all children.

Illinois: Steady Steps Forward Set the Stage for a Bold Jump on Children's Health Coverage

Beginning in 2001, Illinois faced the same bleak economic conditions confronting most of the nation, yet the state managed to expand health coverage to low-income children and their parents during the 5 years that followed. A sequence of modest steps helped build the momentum that led to

(continued)

Textbox 2.1   Examples of Consumer Advocacy (continued)

the governor's announcement in 2006 of a bold plan to cover all children. Advocacy efforts by nongovernmental stakeholders were central to this progress, creating a political environment in which Republicans and Democrats alike supported increased coverage as a vital, and attainable, priority. Several advocacy strategies cultivated the ground for the incremental expansions:

Building a broad coalition helped enlist groups with a mix of skills, such as research, lobbying, and grassroots organizing, all of which are needed for an effective campaign. Participants included consumer health organizations, providers (such as hospitals, clinics, and pharmacies), antipoverty groups, advocates for children and people with disabilities, labor unions, community organizations, and religious groups. Participation of unusual allies strengthened the public perception that cutbacks were unacceptable and that expanding health coverage served broad societal interests. Groups dedicated to improving K-12 education and public safety emphasized how a strong health coverage system helps achieve these other public priorities. Coalition leaders leveraged the support of business organizations and employers by incorporating an optional premium assistance component into the expansion plan, allowing individuals to use Medicaid or SCHIP funds to help subsidize the costs of dependent coverage for workers with access to employer-sponsored insurance. Businesses regarded this option as essential to retaining lower income employees.

Organizing around commonly held principles was key. The coalition fostered cohesion by promoting the message that the budget should not be balanced by cutting programs for vulnerable people and that augmenting total revenue would help everyone. Coalition leaders vigorously advanced alternatives to harmful cuts to counteract the assertion that the state had "no choice" but to cut. Ultimately, the legislature adopted an increase in the cigarette tax and other revenue measures. Strategies maximizing the influx of federal dollars also helped improve the fiscal picture; for example, the state obtained a waiver of federal SCHIP laws to cover pregnant women not eligible for Medicaid. This enabled the state to get federal matching funds for services previously covered through state funds only. This measure freed up state funds to use for the expansion.

The coalition pursued concrete, measurable goals emphasizing that "success" was within reach. The process of incremental expansion, begun in a prior administration before the economic crisis, had gained public recognition, making it harder for state politicians to roll-back reforms. Thus, between 2003 and 2004, when a number of states reacted to tight fiscal pressures by paring back health coverage expansions, Illinois extended its publicly subsidized program to thousands more parents and increased the number of children covered under "KidCare," its Medicaid and SCHIP programs. The state

(continued)

Textbox 2.1   Examples of Consumer Advocacy (continued)

also continued to simplify enrollment procedures and invest in community-based outreach so that eligible individuals could easily enroll in the new coverage programs.

Against this backdrop, in 2005 the governor championed his proposal to "Cover All Kids," a most ambitious plan in the face of continuing fiscal constraints. The bill, co-sponsored in the legislature by the Speaker of the House and the Senate president, provided healthcare for 253,000 children, including immigrant children not eligible for existing federal programs. It amassed strong bipartisan support in both houses and easily passed. As the nation stays focused on this bold program, other states, including Hawaii, Pennsylvania, and Wisconsin, have proposed "Cover All Kids" plans of their own. These developments underscore the power of consistent, well-conceived advocacy efforts.

Source: The major source for the above discussion was data from: Bouman, John, *The Path to Universal Health Coverage for Children in Illinois*, Clearinghouse Review Journal of Poverty Law and Policy, March–April 2006. For additional background: Cohen Ross, Donna and Laura Cox, *Beneath the Surface: Barriers Threaten to Slow Progress on Expanding Health Coverage of Children and Families*, Kaiser Commission on Medicaid and the Uninsured, October 2004.

In 2005, 88% of Medicare beneficiaries were enrolled in traditional Medicare (Kaiser Family Foundation, 2005). Beneficiaries can also enroll in a private Medicare health insurance plan called Medicare Advantage, or Medicare Part C. Medicare Advantage includes health maintenance organizations, point of service plans, preferred provider organizations, and private fee-for-service plans (see Textbox 2.2 for a description of these types of health plans). About 12% of Medicare beneficiaries were enrolled in Medicare Advantage plans in 2005.

In January 2006, Medicare began covering prescription drugs through Medicare Part D. Medicare beneficiaries who want prescription drug coverage can voluntarily enroll, but they must obtain coverage through a Medicare Advantage plan (listed previously) or through a separate Prescription Drug Plan. Thus, Medicare beneficiaries may now have three sources of health insurance coverage: traditional Medicare (Parts A and B) for most Medicare-covered services, a prescription drug plan that covers only prescription drugs, and a Medicare supplement policy to pay for some of the cost sharing and other uncovered Medicare services. In addition, some individuals choose to purchase separate long-term care policies,

Textbox 2.2   Key Healthcare Terms

Block grant program: A program funded through a set amount of money. Block grants are generally distributed by the federal government to state and/or local governments. Block grant recipients have some discretion in how they spend funds, within broad federal parameters. Unlike entitlements, no further federal funds are available once the block grant is spent, even if additional people meet the program's eligibility rules. The State Children's Health Insurance Program (SCHIP) is an example of a block grant program.

Entitlement program: A program that guarantees coverage to individuals who meet eligibility rules, regardless of how much it costs the federal or state government. Social Security, Medicare, and Medicaid are examples of entitlement programs.

Health maintenance organizations (HMOs): A type of healthcare organization that manages and finances healthcare services provided to its enrollees. Enrollees must obtain care from the HMO's network of providers. Some HMOs require enrollees to obtain all nonemergency care or referrals from their primary care provider; others have open access plans that allow patients to choose from any primary care provider or specialist in the network without a referral.

Conventional indemnity plans (also called private fee-for-service in Medicare Advantage): Under an indemnity plan, individuals can go to whatever provider they choose. Insurers do not typically create "networks" of providers, as they do within PPOs, POS, or HMOs. The provider is paid each time a covered service is provided.

Cost-sharing: A generic term used to describe the payment insured individuals must make for certain covered services. Different cost-sharing methods may include deductibles (an amount the individual has to pay out-of-pocket before the insurance begins paying), co-insurance (a percentage of the bill that the insured individual must pay), and co-payments (a fixed amount per covered service).

Federal poverty guidelines (FPG): The U.S. Department of Health and Human Services sets the federal poverty guidelines annually to determine eligibility for certain federal programs. They are based on a federal poverty threshold developed by the U.S. Census. The federal poverty guidelines vary by size of the family and attempt to determine the amount of money families need to meet basic subsistence needs.

Health Reimbursement Accounts (HRAs): These are high-deductible policies combined with pretax spending accounts. Only employers may contribute to the savings account. Employees can use HRA funds to pay for healthcare services; withdrawals are not subject to taxes or penalties if used for healthcare services.

(continued)

Textbox 2.2   Key Healthcare Terms (continued)

Health savings accounts (HSAs): Like HRAs, HSAs are high-deductible policies combined with pretax spending accounts; however, unlike HRAs, both employer and employee can contribute to an HSA savings account with pretax dollars. Furthermore, the savings account is portable and can follow the employee if he or she leaves employment.

Managed care organization (MCO): A general term applied to managed-care companies such as health maintenance organizations (HMOs), preferred provider organizations (PPOs), and point of service (POS) plans.

Medicare: A national health insurance program that covers most older adults (age 65 years or older) and people with disabilities who receive Social Security, Railroad Retirement, or Disability payments. Medicare Part A covers hospitals, nursing facilities, hospice, and some home health. Part B covers physicians and other outpatient providers. Part D provides prescription drug coverage. In addition, Part C (Medicare Advantage) allows Medicare beneficiaries to purchase their Medicare coverage through private HMOs, PPOs, or private fee-for-service insurers.

Medicaid: A health insurance system jointly financed between the state and federal governments to provide health insurance to some—but not all—low-income individuals.

Point of Service (POS): POS plans are types of managed care arrangements typically offered by HMOs. HMOs generally will not pay for care obtained from a provider outside their network. In POS plans, individuals can obtain care from non-network providers, but will have to pay more of the costs themselves. The insurer or HMO will pay for some of the costs as long as the individual meets all other requirements (e.g., the insurer/HMO may require that the insured individual first obtain approval from his or her primary care provider before authorizing the out-of-network care).

Preferred provider organizations (PPOs): PPOs are insurance arrangements that try to manage costs by creating a network of providers willing to accept lower reimbursement rates. Insured individuals may choose any healthcare provider, but they have to pay additional money if they choose a provider who is not part of the PPO network.

Prescription drug plans (PDP): Medicare Part D insurance plans cover prescription drugs only. PDPs do not cover other health services, such as hospitalizations and/or physicians' services. PDPs differ from Medicare Advantage plans, which although they may provide prescription drug coverage, also cover other Medicare services as well.

Prospective payment systems: A reimbursement system that establishes payment amounts before services are provided, usually based on patients' underlying health condition. Hospitals are often paid under a prospective

(continued)

Textbox 2.2   Key Healthcare Terms (continued)

payment system, which encourages efficiency because hospitals do not get paid more for longer hospital stays.

State children's health insurance (SCHIP): A health insurance system jointly financed between the state and federal government, SCHIP provides health insurance to uninsured children with incomes too high to qualify for Medicaid, but lower than a state-specified threshold (often 200% of the federal poverty guidelines).

Utilization review: A process used by many insurers/MCOs to monitor the use, or evaluate the appropriateness, of healthcare services, procedures, providers, or facilities. For example, some insurers or managed care organizations require patients to get prior approval from their primary care provider or from the insurer/MCO before a high-cost procedure ("prior authorization"). Insurers/MCOs may also review a person's length of stay in a hospital to determine if he or she still needs to be hospitalized ("concurrent review"). Some insurers and MCOs also offer case management services to help manage care provided to members with complex or costly medical conditions. Typically, utilization review procedures are intended to reduce unnecessary healthcare costs by ensuring that patients receive appropriate care in the least costly setting.

---

which help pay for nursing home care or home and community-based services for individuals who need assistance with activities of daily living.

THE UNINSURED

The number and percentage of uninsured has been growing steadily over the last 5 years, from 39.8 million people, or 14.2% of the population, in 2000 to 46.6 million (15.9%) in 2005 (U.S. Census, n.d. d). Two thirds of the uninsured have incomes below 200% of the federal poverty guidelines, or $40,000 for a family of four in 2006 (Kaiser Commission on Medicaid and the Uninsured, 2004a). Racial and ethnic minorities are also more likely to be uninsured (11% of non-Hispanic whites, 20% of African Americans, and 33% of Latinos) (U.S. Census, n.d. e), as are noncitizens (44%).[i] Younger adults between the ages of 18 and 34 years are also more likely to be uninsured than children or older adults.

More than two thirds of the uninsured are full-time workers or are in a family with at least one full-time worker (Kaiser Commission on Medicaid and the Uninsured, 2004b) Nevertheless, full-time workers have uneven access to employer-sponsored insurance, which varies by the size of employer and industry type. Smaller companies and certain industries such as construction, agriculture, and hospitality are less likely to offer coverage. Moreover, lower income individuals are both less likely to be offered coverage and less likely to enroll in a plan if coverage is offered (Garrett, 2004).

The most significant reason many people do not have health insurance coverage is due to cost. Seventy percent of the uninsured point to the high cost of premiums as the most important reason that they lacked coverage in 2005 (USA Today/KFF/HSPH Healthcare Costs Survey, 2005). Employers cite the same problem to explain why they do not offer coverage (Claxton et al., 2005). For every 10% increase in health insurance premiums, the number of firms offering health insurance coverage to their employees drops by approximately 2.5% (Gruber & Lettau, 2004). In addition, some low-income uninsured individuals could qualify for publicly subsidized insurance such as Medicaid or SCHIP, but do not enroll, either because they do not know they are eligible, because the application is too complicated, or because they fear the stigma attached to enrolling in a public program (Stuber, Maloy, Rosenbaum, & Jones, 2000).

People without health insurance have more problems accessing needed health services than those with insurance (Hadley, 2002; Institute of Medicine, Committee on the Consequences of Uninsurance, 2002). They are less likely to have a regular doctor, get preventive screenings, or care for chronic health problems. They are also *more* likely to report delaying needed care because of costs. As a result, they are more likely to be diagnosed with severe health problems such as late-stage cancer. The uninsured are also more likely to be hospitalized for preventable conditions such as diabetes, asthma, or pneumonia. In addition, some studies suggest that the uninsured are 10% to 15% more likely to die prematurely than those with insurance (Institute of Medicine, Committee on the Consequences of Uninsurance, 2002).

SAFETY NET PROVIDERS

A variety of healthcare safety net providers have a mission or a legal obligation (because of state or federal laws) to provide care to the uninsured (Institute of Medicine, 2000), offering services on a sliding scale for those with lower incomes. These organizations include community and migrant health centers, homeless or public housing clinics, health departments, free clinics staffed by volunteer physicians, hospital outpatient clinics, and other nonprofit organizations. Unfortunately, safety net organizations do not exist in every community, and research indicates that only about half of the uninsured are even aware such organizations exist, even when the organization is within 5 miles of the person's home (May, Cunningham, & Hadley, 2004). Instead, the uninsured receive much of their healthcare through private physicians' offices where services are not always provided on a sliding scale or discounted basis. In an environment where the number of physicians providing free or reduced-cost care to the uninsured is dropping (from 76.3% in 1997 to 68.2% in 2005) (Cunningham, 2006), the uninsured often end up with high bills they cannot pay (Reed, Cunningham, & Stoddard, 2001). In addition, many uninsured people access hospital emergency departments for care because of hospitals' legal obligation to screen and stabilize anyone requesting treatment at an emergency room, regardless of ability to pay (EMTALA, 42 USC §1395dd); however, receiving care in hospital emergency departments is both more costly than care provided in physicians' offices and is often less than optimal. In an emergency room setting, patients are less likely to establish an ongoing relationship with a specific provider who knows the patient's health history and can help manage his or her care over time.

A robust system of safety net organizations familiar to the community helps improve access to health services for the uninsured; nevertheless, even communities that ensure adequate patient access to safety net primary care services can rarely meet the other healthcare needs of the uninsured, including specialty referrals, access to mental health and substance abuse services, dental care, or prescription drugs (Felland, Felt-Lisk, & McHugh, 2004). In this context, expanding insurance coverage helps ensure better access to health services than expanding the safety net (Cunningham & Hadley, 2004).

Nationally, the public generally agrees on the need to curtail the costs of, and improve access to, healthcare. As revealed in one national survey, 23% of people cited improved access to care and insurance as the most important healthcare problem for the government to address in 2005; 39% cited the need to reduce healthcare costs. These two problems are interrelated. When healthcare costs rise, so does the number of uninsured; healthcare organizations then shift the costs of providing care to the uninsured to those with insurance coverage, whose premiums then go up (Families USA, 2005). One national study suggested that insured people pay an extra $341 for individual coverage, or $922 for family coverage, per year to help cover the costs of providing care to the uninsured.

Despite this untenable situation, policy makers have achieved no consensus on how best to expand coverage to the uninsured. Generally, advocates take one of three approaches: (1) expanding coverage through employers (Sheils & Haught, 2003), (2) divorcing coverage from employment while requiring or encouraging individuals and their families to purchase health insurance (with tax subsidies or vouchers for lower income individuals), or (3) initiating a government-sponsored health insurance program (e.g., single payer approach) by expanding Medicaid, Medicare, or the Federal Employees Health Insurance program to everyone. These options are not mutually exclusive; a government-sponsored program for low-income individuals could be combined with an employer-based model or individual mandate for individuals with higher incomes (Davis & Schoen, 2006). In general, consumer advocacy groups are much more likely to support a government-based approach, whereas insurers, providers, and employers generally support tax-based subsidies or individual mandates and/or employment-based approaches. The public is also divided about its preference for healthcare coverage expansion, with roughly equal numbers supporting instituting a single payer system, requiring employers to offer coverage to all, offering tax credits for people purchasing health insurance coverage in the private market, or expanding public programs for low-income populations (Blendon, Benson, & DesRoches, 2003). Regardless of the approach taken, consumer involvement is critical to health insurance expansion. The recent initiative in Illinois to cover all children is a prime example, where consumer advocates worked in broad coalitions with providers and employer groups to support expanded coverage for all children.

Table 2.1   Selected Web Resources

Academy for Health Services Research and Policy:
  http://www.academyhealth.org

Agency for Healthcare Research and Quality (AHRQ): http://www.ahrq.gov

Alliance for Healthcare Reform: http://www.allhealth.org

American Association for Retired Persons (AARP): http://www.aarp.org

American Health Insurance Plans: http://www.ahip.org

American Hospital Association (AHA): http://www.hospitalconnect.com

Blue Cross and Blue Shield Association: http://www.bcbshealthissues.com

The Brookings Institution: http://www.brook.edu

Center on Budget and Policy Priorities (CBPP): http://www.cbpp.org

Center for Healthcare Strategies, Inc. (CHCS): http://www.chcs.org

Center for Studying Health System Change (HSC): http://www.hschange.org

Centers for Medicare and Medicaid Services (CMS): http://cms.hhs.gov

Children's Defense Fund (CDF): http://www.childrensdefense.org

The Commonwealth Fund: http://www.cmwf.org

Department of Health and Human Services (DHHS): http://www.dhhs.gov

Economic and Social Research Institute (ESRI): http://www.esresearch.org

Employee Benefit Research Institute (EBRI): http://www.ebri.org

FamiliesUSA: http://www.familiesusa.org

General Accounting Office (GAO): http://www.gao.gov/index.html

Henry J. Kaiser Family Foundation: http://www.kff.org

The Heritage Foundation: http://www.heritage.org

Institute of Medicine (IOM): http://www.iom.edu

National Academy for State Health Policy (NASHP): http://www.nashp.org

National Center for Health Statistics (NCHS): http://www.cdc.gov/nchs/index.htm

State Health Facts: http://statehealthfacts.kff.org/cgi-bin/healthfacts.cgi?

Congressional legislation: http://thomas.loc.gov

The Urban Institute: http://www.urban.org

ENDNOTES

a. Countries studied include Australia, Austria, Belgium, Canada, Czech Republic, Denmark, Finland, France, Germany, Greece, Hungary, Iceland, Ireland, Italy, Japan, Korea, Luxembourg, Mexico, Netherlands, New Zealand, Norway, Poland, Portugal, Slovak Republic, Spain, Sweden, Switzerland, Turkey, United Kingdom, and United States.

b. Some economists suggest that the reason the United States spends so much is that we pay more for the healthcare services we receive. Spending measured either as a percentage of the Gross Domestic Produce or per-capita spending was higher in the United States than in any other OECD country. In contrast, the United States used fewer services (e.g., physician visits or hospital days per capita).

c. Individuals with insurance coverage can have multiple sources of coverage, and thus, the percentages add up to more than 100%.

d. Almost two thirds of children (61%) and nonolder adults (63%) have employer-sponsored insurance, as do more than one third (36%) of the older population.

e. Between 1987 and 2000, five health conditions (heart disease, mental disorders, pulmonary disorders, cancer, and trauma) accounted for 30% of the increase in health spending. Fifteen health conditions accounted for approximately half of the increase in healthcare spending. Certain lifestyle-related illnesses contribute to rising healthcare costs. Smoking, heavy drinking, and obesity contribute to the incidence of certain chronic diseases. For example, people who are obese have a higher risk of developing diabetes, hypertension, and heart disease. Smokers are more likely to develop certain types of cancer and heart disease. These chronic illnesses translate into higher healthcare costs. One study showed that obesity increased inpatient and ambulatory healthcare costs by $395 per year, current or past smoking by $230 per year, and problem drinking by $150 per year. The aging of the population also affects healthcare spending, as older adults generally use more services than younger people. Although aging may have a longer-term impact on healthcare spending, the average age of the population does not vary significantly from year to year, and thus, the aging population does not explain the increase in healthcare spending on a yearly basis.

f. In most states, categorically eligible individuals with higher incomes may qualify for Medicaid under a separate program category called the medically needy program. These individuals must incur medical bills equaling the difference between their countable income and the medically needy income limits. This is similar in some respects to a health insurance deductible; however, the amount of the "deductible" varies depending on the person's income. After the Medicaid recipient incurs medical bills equaling the Medicaid deductible, then Medicaid will pay the remaining bills.

g. States that use their SCHIP funds to expand Medicaid will still receive federal Medicaid funding to cover children even after the state uses all its federal SCHIP allotment (albeit at a lower federal match rate); however, states that operate stand-alone SCHIP programs must either use 100% of state funds to continue to operate the program or can create a waiting list to close enrollment to new eligibles after they spend their federal allotment.

h. In 2002, about one third of the older population (35%) had employer-based retiree benefits. Twenty-one percent had private Medicare supplement policies. Fifteen percent had Medicare managed-care plans, and 17% had Medicaid coverage. Only 12% of Medicare beneficiaries lacked any form of supplemental coverage.

i. The term noncitizen is not synonymous with being undocumented. Many noncitizens live in the United States with many different types of immigration classifications, such as work or student visas. Federal immigration laws, passed in 1996, make it more difficult for recent immigrants residing legally in the United States under a visa to qualify for federally funded programs. Even if otherwise eligible for a public program (e.g., by meeting categorical, income, and resource requirements), immigrants cannot qualify for Medicaid or SCHIP unless they are citizens or qualified immigrants who have resided in the United States for at least 5 years. Certain immigrants such as Latinos are more likely to work in industries such as construction, agriculture, or hospitality, which are less likely to offer coverage.

REFERENCES

Abbe, B. (2004). *Comprehensive health insurance for high risk individuals: A state-by-state analysis: 2004/2005* (18th ed.). Fergus Falls, MN: Communicating for Agriculture for the Self-Employed.

Anderson, G. F., Reinhardt, U. E., Hussey, P. S., & Petrosyan, V. (2003). It's the prices, stupid: Why the United States is so different from other countries. *Health Affairs, 22*(3), 89–105.

Berk, M. L., & Monheit, A. C. (2001). The concentration of healthcare expenditures, revisited. *Health Affairs, 20*(2), 9–18.

Blendon, R. J., Benson, J. M., & DesRoches, C. M. (2003). Americans' views of the uninsured: An era for hybrid proposals. *Health Affairs, Web Exclusive* (W3-405-414). Retrieved September 26, 2006, from http://content.healthaffairs.org/cgi/reprint/hlthaff.w3.405v1.

Buntin, M. B., Marquis, M. S., & Yegian, J. M. (2004). The role of the individual health insurance market and prospects for change. *Health Affairs, 23*(6), 79–90.

Claxton, G., Gile, I., Finder, B., Gabel, J., Pickreign, J., Whitmore, H., et al. (2005). *Employer health benefits: 2005 annual survey.* Retrieved August 26, 2006, from http://www.kff.org/insurance/7315/upload/7315.pdf.

Community Catalyst. (2006). *Consumer health advocacy: A view from 16 states: October 2006.* Retrieved October 7, 2006, from http://www.communitycatalyst.org/resource.php?base_id=1075.

Cubanski, J., Voris, M., Kitchman, M, Neuman, T., & Potetz, L. (2005). *Medicare chartbook: Publication #7284* (3rd ed.). Henry J. Kaiser Family Foundation. Retrieved October 6, 2006, from http://www.kff.org.libproxy.lib.unc.edu/medicare/upload/Medicare-Chart-Book-3rd-Edition-Summer-2005-Report.pdf.

Cunningham, P., & Hadley, J. (2004). Expanding care versus expanding coverage: How to improve access to care. *Health Affairs, 23*(4), 234–244.

Cunningham, P. J. (2006). *A growing hole in the safety net: Physician charity care declines again.* Retrieved August 26, 2006, from http://www.hschange.org/CONTENT/826/826.pdf.

Davis, K., & Schoen, C. (2003). Creating consensus on coverage choices. *Health Affairs, Web Exclusive* (W3-199-211), February 15, 2006, from http://content.healthaffairs.org/cgi/reprint/hlthaff.w3.199v1.

EMTALA, the Emergency Medical Treatment and Active Labor Act, 42 USC §1395dd.

Families USA. (2005, June). *Paying a premium: The added cost of care for the uninsured.* Retrieved February 16, 2006, from http://www.familiesusa.org/assets/pdfs/Paying_a_Premium_rev_July_13731e.pdf.

Felland, L. E., Felt-Lisk, S., & McHugh, M. (2004, June). *Healthcare access for low-income people: Significant safety net gaps remain: Issue brief. No. 84.* Retrieved February 15, 2006, from http://www.hschange.org/CONTENT/682/.

Gabel, J., Claxton, G., Gil, I., Pickreign, J., Whitmore, H., & Finder, B., et al. (2005). Health benefits in 2005: Premium increases slow down, coverage continues to erode. *Health Affairs, 24*(5), 1273–1280.

Garrett, B. (2004). *Employer-sponsored health insurance coverage: Sponsorship, eligibility and participation patterns in 2001.* Kaiser Commission on Medicaid and the Uninsured.

Gilmer, T., & Kronick, R. (2005). It's the premiums, stupid: Projections of the uninsured through 2013. *Health Affairs, Web Exclusive,* W5-143–W5-151.

Gruber, J., & Lettau, M. (2004). How elastic is the firm's demand for health insurance? *Journal of Public Economics, 88,* 1273–1293.

Hadley, J. (2002). *Sicker and poorer: The consequences of being uninsured.* Kaiser Commission on Medicaid and the Uninsured. Retrieved January 17, 2007, from http://www.kff.org/uninsured/20020510-index.cfm.

Heffler, S., Smith, S., Keehan, S., Borger, C., Clemens, M. K., & Truffer, C. (2005). U.S. health spending projections for 2004–2014. *Health Affairs, Supplement, Web Exclusives,* W5-74–W5-85.

Institute of Medicine. (2000). *America's healthcare safety-net: Intact but endangered.* Washington, DC: National Academy Press.

Institute of Medicine. (2001). *Crossing the quality chasm: A new health system for the 21st century.* Washington, DC: National Academy Press.

Institute of Medicine, Committee on the Consequences of Uninsurance. (2002). *Care without coverage: Too little, too late.* Washington, DC: National Academy Press.

Judge Friendly. Friedman v. Berger, 547 F.2d 724, 272 n. 7 (2nd Circuit 1976).

Kaiser Commission on Medicaid and the Uninsured. (2001). *Medicare and medicaid for the elderly and disabled poor.* Retrieved January 17, 2007, from http://www.kff.org/medicaid/2132-poor.cfm.

Kaiser Commission on Medicaid and the Uninsured. (2004a, November). *The uninsured: A primer: Table 1.* Retrieved January 17, 2007, from http://www.kff.org/uninsured/7451.cfm.

Kaiser Commission on Medicaid and the Uninsured. (2004b, November). *The uninsured: A primer.* Retrieved January 17, 2007, from http://www.kff.org/uninsured/7451.cfm.

Kaiser Commission on Medicaid and the Uninsured. (2005). *The Medicaid program at a glance.* Retrieved January 17, 2007, from http://www.kff.org/medicaid/upload/The-Medicaid-Program-at-a-Glance-Fact-Sheet.pdf.

Kaiser Family Foundation. (2005). *Medicare fact sheet: Medicare advantage.* Retrieved August 26, 2006, from http://www.kff.org/medicare/upload/Medicare-Advantage-April-2005-Fact-Sheet.pdf.

Kaiser Family Foundation and Health Research and Education Trust. (2005a). *Employer health benefits: Summary of findings 2005.* Retrieved November 30, 2005, from http://www.kff.org/insurance/7315/sections/upload/7316.pdf.

Kaiser Family Foundation and Health Research and Education Trust. (2005b). *Employer health benefits, 2005 annual survey: Chart #11.* Retrieved October 11, 2005, from http://www.kff.org/insurance/7315/sections/upload/7375.pdf.

Kaiser Family Foundation, statehealthfacts.org. (2004). *Current monthly SCHIP enrollment, Dec. 2004.* Retrieved January 31, 2006, from www.statehealthfacts.org; accessed October 6, 2006, from http://tinyurl.com/jr9hn.

Kaiser Family Foundation, statehealthfacts.org. (2005). *Income eligibility levels for children's separate SCHIP programs by annual incomes and as a percent of federal poverty level, 2005.* Retrieved January 31, 2006, from www.statehealthfacts.org.

May, J. H., Cunningham, P. J., & Hadley, J. (2004, November). *Most uninsured people unaware of healthcare safety net providers: Center for Studying Health System Change: Issue Brief No. 90.* Retrieved February 15, 2005, from http://www.hschange.org/CONTENT/718.

Medical Expenditure Panel Survey. (2003). *Table IA2: Percent of private-sector establishments that offer insurance by firm size, 2003.* Retrieved September 20, 2006, from http://www.meps.ahrq.gov/mepsweb/data_stats/summ_tables/insr/national/series_1/2003/tia2.htm.

National Association of State Budget Offices. (2004, December). *The Fiscal Survey of State: April 2004.* Washington, DC: National Governors Association.

Newhouse, J. P. (2004). Consumer-directed health plans and the RAND health insurance experiment. *Health Affairs, 23*(6), 107–113.

Organisation for Economic Cooperation and Development (2005a). *Charts 1.1 and 1.2: OECD health data 2005: Health status: Life expectancy at birth.* Retrieved August 28, 2006, from http://ocde.p4.siteinternet.com/publications/doifiles/812005171G001.xls.

Organisation for Economic Cooperation and Development (2005b). *Chart 1.20: OECD health data 2005: Health status: Infant mortality.* Retrieved August 28, 2006, from http://ocde.p4.siteinternet.com/publications/doifiles/812005171G007.xls.

Pauly, M. V., & Nichols, L. (2002). The nongroup insurance market: Short on facts, long on opinions and policy disputes. *Health Affairs, Supplement, Web Exclusives,* W325–W344.

Pollitz, K., & Sorian, R. (2002). Ensuring health security: Is the individual market ready for prime time? *Health Affairs, Web Exclusive,* W372–W376.

Reed, M. R., Cunningham, P. J., & Stoddard, J. (2001). *Physicians pulling back from charity care: Issue Brief No. 42: Center for Studying Health System Change.* Retrieved February 15, 2006, from http://www.hschange.org/CONTENT/356/.

Sheils, J., & Haught, R. (2003, October). *Cost and coverage analysis of ten proposals to expand health insurance coverage: Covering America: Executive summary.* Retrieved February 16, 2006, from http://www.esresearch.org/publications/SheilsLewinall/Sheils%20Report%20Final.pdf.

Silberman, P., Walsh, J., Slifkin, R., & Poley, S. (2003, January). *The North Carolina Health Choice Enrollment Freeze of 2001.* Kaiser Commission on Medicaid and the Uninsured. Retrieved January 31, 2006, from http://www.kff.org/medicaid/upload/The-North-Carolina-Health-Choice-Enrollment-Freeze-of-2001-Findings-in-Brief-Report-2.pdf.

Smith C., Cowan C., Heffler S., Catlin A., & National Health Accounts Team. (2006). National health spending in 2004: Recent slowdown led by prescription drug spending. *Health Affairs, 25*(1), 186–196.

Smith, V., Ramesh, R., Gifford, K., Ellis, E., & Wachino, V. (2003). *States respond to fiscal pressure: State Medicaid spending growth and cost containment in fiscal years 2003 and 2004.* Kaiser Commission on Medicaid and the Uninsured. Retrieved January 17, 2007, from http://www.kff.org/medicaid/loader.cfm?url=/commonspot/security/getfile.cfm&PageID=22126.

Starr, P. (1982). *The social transformation of American medicine.* New York: Basic Books.

Stuber, J. P., Maloy, K. A., Rosenbaum, S., & Jones, K. C. (2000, July). Beyond stigma: What barriers actually affect the decisions of low-income families to enroll in Medicaid? *Issue Brief.* Retrieved August 26, 2006, from http://www.gwumc.edu/sphhs/healthpolicy//chsrp/downloads/beyond_stigma_no3.pdf.

Sturm, R. (2002). The effects of obesity, smoking and drinking on medical problems and costs. *Health Affairs, 21*(2), 245–253.

Thorpe, K. E., Florence, C. S., & Joski, P. (2004). Which medical conditions account for the rise in health spending? *Health Affairs, Web Exclusive,* W4-437–W4-445.

U.S. Census. (n.d. a). *Health insurance coverage status and type of coverage by state: People under 65: 1987 to 2005.* Retrieved August 29, 2006, from http://www.census.gov/hhes/www/hlthins/historic/hihistt6.html.

U.S. Census. (n.d. b). *Table HI-2. health insurance coverage status and type of coverage: All people by age and sex: 1987 to 2004.* Retrieved November 29, 2005, from http://www.census.gov/hhes/www/hlthins/historic/hihistt2.html.

U.S. Census. (n.d. c). *Table HI-3: Health insurance coverage status and type of coverage: Children under 18 by age: 1987 to 2004.* Retrieved November 29, 2005, from http://www.census.gov/hhes/www/hlthins/historic/hihistt3.html.

U.S. Census. (n.d. d). *Health historical insurance tables: Table HI-6: Health insurance coverage status and type of coverage by state: All people: 1987–2005.* Retrieved August 29, 2006, from http://www.census.gov/hhes/www/hlthins/historic/hihistt4.html.

U.S. Census. (n.d. e). *People with or without health insurance coverage by selected characteristics: 2004 and 2005.* Retrieved August 29, 2006, from http://www.census.gov/hhes/www/hlthins/hlthin05/hi05t8.pdf.

U.S. Department of Health and Human Services. (2005). *The 2005 HHS federal poverty guidelines.* Retrieved February 1, 2006, from http://aspe.hhs.gov/poverty/05poverty.shtml.

USA Today/KFF/HSPH Healthcare Costs Survey. (2005). *The uninsured: Reasons for not having health insurance.* Retrieved February 16, 2006, from http://www.kff.org/spotlight/healthcosts/16.cfm.

Zuckerman, S., McFeeters, J., Cunningham, P., & Nichols, L. (2004). Changes in medicaid physician fees, 1998-2003: Implications for physician participation. *Health Affairs, Web Exclusive,* 24-374-384.

Strategy One: Understanding What Patients Are Doing Now and What Providers Can Do to Support Them

Patient advocacy is based on the premise that patients and their families can and should have a direct impact on the way healthcare is practiced. At the individual and systems level, patient involvement is often predicated on knowledge of health and the healthcare system that many people lack. For this reason, many resources have been developed to help patients and their families learn about the risk factors and illnesses they are facing, how to marshal resources in a fragmented system, how to go about navigating the day-to-day hurdles encountered when coping with an illness, and more generally how to negotiate an often frustrating healthcare system. Supporting patients' learning processes and increasing their feelings of competency in these areas are important capacity-building steps in "activating" patients as partners in their own care.

In addition to health-related knowledge and confidence, peer relationships and social networks are important to patient activation, and a second patient advocacy thread involves connecting patients with others who can help. Whether family members, disease survivors, or outreach workers, many kinds of lay people can work alongside healthcare professionals to increase patients' knowledge, comfort, and self-efficacy in negotiating the healthcare system. Identifying who is best positioned to act in this supportive capacity and how such aid is most effectively delivered is another key concern of patient advocacy.

As this unit will demonstrate, patients have already done a great deal to increase the availability of knowledge and support; a fundamental strategy of patient advocacy is to learn about, encourage, and pass along these efforts. In Chapter 3, Seyda, Shelton, and DiVenere discuss ways in which patient communities are working to create care geared toward the needs of families, not only toward the support of individuals. After describing the core principles of family-centered care, the authors discuss ways of fostering such care, including examples of parent-to-parent networking, medical education by patients, and patient involvement in hospital administration and research.

In Chapter 4, Ferguson explores the adoption of information technologies by patients and patient groups. The author details the ways in which the Internet has provided unprecedented access to information as well as how modes of electronic communication have allowed patients to overcome the geographic boundaries that once prevented them from sharing information with each other or staying in close contact with health professionals. This chapter outlines the ways that patients use e-health as well as areas, such as the availability of patient–provider e-mail, that they believe are still lacking.

In Chapter 5, Moore and Earp discuss the lay health advisor outreach model as one method for overcoming persistent health disparities between minority and majority groups in the United States. By engaging "natural helpers" in marginalized communities to act as intermediaries, community health outreach programs empower community members to overcome cultural, logistical, and financial barriers to accessing and navigating a fractured healthcare system. Using the North Carolina Breast Cancer Screening Program as an example, the authors show how this community-based approach to breast cancer screening can translate the power and influence of lay people into health-enhancing behaviors.

CHAPTER 3

Family-Centered Care: Why It Is Important, How to Provide It, and What Parents and Children Are Doing to Make It Happen

Beth Seyda, Terri Shelton, and Nancy DiVenere

OBJECTIVES

- To define family-centered care and its central tenets
- To understand the importance of family-centered care for patients, families, and providers and its relevance for patient advocacy
- To explore the benefits of practicing family-centered care, including improved health outcomes, reduced medical errors, greater family and professional satisfaction, increased patient/family self-efficacy/ advocacy, and improved medical/health education
- To learn about ways in which programs across the country have incorporated the principles of family-centered care in practice, research, and education

I think it's really important that a doctor listens to you as a human being instead of just treating you like an object that they're trying to cure or trying to help. To really listen to you, not necessarily to be able to solve everything but to listen and to understand how the patient's feeling. . . . My doctor always asked if I wanted to have certain things done. She would say, "Do you feel okay about this?" She made me feel like I was really part of my health, I was part of the team trying to get me better.

Child/patient (Center for Attitudinal Healing, 1991)

I am Charlie's mother, and the doctors always respected that. I felt in charge and was confident in the fact that those who had my trust advised me. It was a comfortable arrangement. I knew my child best.

Parent of ill child (Hilden, Tobin, & Lindsey, 2003)

Most important of all, we are committed to making ourselves available to patients and their families. To this end, I wanted to make the environment as informal and accessible as possible. Our doors stay open whenever we're not seeing patients. Patients and families often deal with us on a first-name basis. We don't talk over their head in medical jargon. We don't wear white coats. I give out my home number to patients and their families because I know how important a doctor's accessibility is to peace of mind.

Physician (Epstein & Horwitz, 2003)

At its most basic, advocacy means expressing support for and/or taking action on a specific "cause." As it relates to healthcare, advocacy can range from individuals exercising their right to make their own healthcare decisions to ensuring that they receive accurate and up-to-date information about procedures and outcomes to raising awareness or influencing policy decisions. It can and should occur whether the patient is a child or an adult, and it has benefits for both patients and staff. Whatever the form, the "cause" is the same: better health outcomes. So, why have a chapter on family-centered care in a book about patient advocacy? Briefly, family-centered care is the context for patient and family advocacy; the principles of family-centered care provide the roadmap for patients advocating for quality healthcare. Although patient advocacy can be expressed in many ways, it is likely to be most effective when couched within the tenets of family-centered care. Without this philosophical grounding, patient advocacy can easily become just one more thing that the healthcare system does "to" or "for" and not "with" a patient. The individuals quoted at the beginning of this chapter are advocates . . . advocates for themselves and advocates for one another; they epitomize the links between family-centered care (e.g., respectful partnerships, open communication, honesty, and trust) and patient advocacy. This chapter further defines family-centered care as it applies to all patients, particularly with children, and provides concrete examples of how family-centered care has been translated into practice.

WHAT IS FAMILY-CENTERED CARE?

As noted by Conway et al. (2006):

> Efforts to enhance patient and family partnerships in health care redesign must be based on a shared understanding of key terms that often come up in the health care literature and in discussions of quality improvement. Of these terms, none may be as critical as patient- and family-centered care. (p. 5)

The historical roots of patient- and family-centered care date back the middle of the 20th century. Several movements and initiatives helped define this concept, including family-centered maternity care movements in Canada in the late 1950s, the consumer movements of the 1960s and 1970s (see Chapter 14), and federal programs and legislation such as Head Start. The term "patient-centered medicine," first introduced by Balint, Ball, and Hare (1969), was later adopted by the Picker Commonwealth Program for Patient-Centered Care (subsequently the Picker Institute) as they began to research what patients defined as quality care.

However, Surgeon General C. Everett Koop most effectively brought family-centered care to the forefront in the late 1980s by responding to the advocacy efforts of parents caring for children with chronic healthcare needs and disabilities. Specifically, he called for a national agenda in which families would work together with professionals to improve the care of children with special health needs. In 1989, Congress amended the Social Security Act requiring Maternal and Child Health Title V programs that focused on children with special healthcare needs to "provide and promote family-centered, community-based, coordinated care (including care coordination services) and to facilitate the development of community-based systems of services for such children and their families." The Maternal and Child Health Bureau extended this mandate to all of its program grantees. It was through these initiatives and legislation that the concept of family-centered care was further defined (Shelton & Stepanek, 1994).

Since the time of Surgeon General Koop's initiatives, family support groups, hospitals, agencies, and provider groups have further refined, adopted, and advanced the principles of family-centered care. Indeed, the Institute of Medicine (IOM, 2001) placed family-centered care at the center of its major report, *Crossing the Quality Chasm*, when it emphasized the need for providers to involve patients in their own healthcare decisions, better inform families of treatment options, and improve patients' and families' timely access to information. The American Academy of Pediatrics (AAP, 2003) also led the way in incorporating family-centered care principles into a number of its policy statements, including its 2003 report *Family-Centered Care and the Pediatrician's Role*. Both the IOM's 2001 report and the AAP's 2003 policy statement also emphasize family-centered care principles, including partnering with consumers in healthcare decision making, providing improved access to information, and using peer support, including parent-to-parent networking. The AAP has incorporated family-centered care principles in many of its initiatives, including the concept of the medical home, in which a pediatrician or primary care physician coordinates care so that all of the patient's medical and nonmedical needs are met, including access and coordination of specialty care, educational services, and out-of-home care (AAP, 2006). Finally, family-centered philosophy has been incorporated into major pieces of legislation, including the Omnibus Budget Reconciliation Act (1989) and the Developmental Disabilities Assistance and Bill of Rights Act (1990).

Family-centered care is a partnership approach to the planning, delivery, and evaluation of healthcare and is grounded in a belief that each participant in a clinical encounter brings valuable experience to the table. Numerous benefits result when patients and family members have the opportunity to share their expertise with providers, both for those individuals directly involved and for the healthcare system as a whole. Family-centered care applies to people of all ages and to any healthcare setting but is most often referred to when the patient is a child (Institute for Family-Centered Care; U.S. Department of Health and Human Services, Maternal and Child Health Bureau).

Definitions of family-centered care vary (see Chapter 1), yet most contain four principles highlighted by the Institute for Family-Centered Care (see resource list), founded in 1992. The four definitions are listed in Textbox 3.1.

The concept of "family" has been defined in a variety of ways; however, for the purposes of this chapter, the family is whomever the patient or con-

---

Textbox 3.1   Core Principles of Family-Centered Care

- *Dignity and Respect.* Healthcare practitioners listen to and honor patient and family perspectives and choices. Patient and family knowledge, values, beliefs, and cultural backgrounds are incorporated into the planning and delivery of care.
- *Information Sharing.* Healthcare practitioners communicate and share complete and unbiased information with patients and families in ways that are affirming and useful. Patients and families receive timely, complete, and accurate information in order to effectively participate in care and decision making.
- *Participation.* Patients and families are encouraged and supported in participating in care and decision making at the level they choose.
- *Collaboration.* Patients and families are also included on an institution-wide basis. Healthcare leaders collaborate with patients and families in policy and program development, implementation, and evaluation; healthcare facility design; and professional education, as well as the delivery of care.

---

sumer defines as family. They may be related by blood, marriage, adoption, friendship, or some other kinship tie, as illustrated by the following quote (New Mexico Coalition for Youth and Families, 2006):

> We all come from families. Families are big, small, extended, nuclear, multi-generational, with one parent, two parents, and grandparents. We live under one roof or many. A family can be as temporary as a few weeks, as permanent as forever. We become part of a family by birth, adoption, marriage, or from a desire for mutual support. . . . A family is a culture unto itself with different values and unique ways of realizing its dreams. Together, our families become the source of our rich cultural heritage and spiritual diversity. Our families create neighborhoods, communities, states, and nations.

WHAT ARE THE BENEFITS OF ADOPTING FAMILY-CENTERED CARE?

With its tenets of respectful partnership, open communication, shared decision-making, and strength-based approaches, the philosophy behind family-centered care may seem like common sense, yet these tenets often run counter to the traditional ways in which healthcare is taught and practiced, despite the accumulating body of research demonstrating that family-centered care benefits everyone involved—patients, families, healthcare providers, as well as healthcare insurers. Family-centered care is increasingly linked to improved health outcomes, lower healthcare costs, more effective allocation of resources, reduced medical errors and litigation, greater patient, family, and professional satisfaction, increased patient/family self-efficacy/advocacy, and improved medical/health education. Finally, family-centered care, with its reliance on having providers and care systems work respectfully with families, can help build trust with traditionally marginalized populations, making it a promising approach for helping to reduce health disparities between minority and majority populations (see Chapter 5).

Better Health Outcomes Lead to Decreased Healthcare Costs

Perhaps the most relevant outcome of family-centered care is improved health, both immediate and long term (see AAP, 2003, for a review of family-centered care outcomes). For example, almost 40 years ago, research demonstrated that having a mother present when her child received anesthesia resulted in the child feeling more prepared for and less anxious about surgery (Schulman, Foley, Vernon, & Allan, 1967). Subsequent studies have continued to highlight the benefits of parental presence for children's health outcomes. Even simple collaboration between families and the healthcare team, such as having a parent present when blood is taken, has immediate benefits, such as less distress for the child (Hannallah & Rosales, 1983; Hannallah, Abramowitz, Oh, & Ruttimann, 1984; LaRosa-Nash & Murphy, 1997; Smerling, Lieberman, & Rothstein, 1988; Vessey, Caserza, & Bogetz, 1990; Wolfram & Turner, 1996). Researchers have shown that having parents play a more active role in their children's care improves other outcomes as well. A scan of the literature shows the following:

- Children whose mothers are involved in their post-tonsillectomy care recover faster and are discharged earlier than those whose mothers did not participate in their care.

- Parents more successfully transition the management of their baby's care from hospital to home when participating in a collaborative discharge process where parents are ongoing full participants with medical staff. An example of this outcome is found at Rainbow Babies and Children's Hospital in Cleveland, Ohio. With specific input from parents, the stepdown unit of the hospital's neonatal intensive care unit was redesigned to provide a quieter, more homelike environment with private living/sleeping units so that families could reside with and learn to care for their infants on a daily basis. In addition, the unit began offering structured educational sessions on evenings and weekends when both parents could be present. Home care equipment was brought in for parents to learn to use, and daily interdisciplinary infant care rounds were conducted at the bedside with parents giving and receiving information and participating in care decisions. After this transitional care center was designed, the hospital experienced a 30% to 50% decrease in infants' length of stay in the hospital, fewer readmissions, and a decreased use of the pediatric emergency department (Forsythe, 1998).

These examples demonstrate how family-centered care improved health outcomes for patients and families; however, earlier discharges and fewer rehospitalizations also produce a significant ancillary benefit for the healthcare system as a whole by decreasing costs for families, providers, and insurers.

Increased Satisfaction for Patients, Families, and Providers

Research consistently demonstrates a link between family-centered practices and consumer satisfaction. The Care-by-Family Units program in the Child Health Center of the University of Texas Medical Branch in Galveston is an example where family members are trained to take a more formalized active role in providing both routine care taking as well as performing more complicated medical procedures. Compared with traditional units where families are not encouraged to provide direct dare, care-by-family units have been associated with increased parent satisfaction (Caldwell & Lockhart, 1981), positive ratings from 3rd-year medical students (Lerner, Haley, Hall, & McVarish, 1972), and cost savings of 13.5% to 33% (Evans & Robinson, 1983). The immediate outcomes of this program include increased trust,

---

Textbox 3.1   Focus on Family Advocacy

For more than 20 years I have given a voice to consumers—what they like or dislike about services and what new services they seek—via qualitative and quantitative research. Compassionate Passages, Inc. was created by combining my professional expertise in consumer research with the personal experience from the illness and death of my son. I was 16-weeks pregnant with Dylan when I learned from an ultrasound that he had a serious birth defect that would prevent his lungs from growing and developing properly. We were told Dylan had a 50% chance to survive and would require intensive medical treatment and surgery when he was born. At that point, I knew I had to advocate for myself and Dylan—I would do everything I could to help him live. For the most part, we had a wonderful healthcare team that practiced family-centered care—we were treated with respect, were well-informed, participated in decisions, and took care of Dylan. Unfortunately, we also experienced what it was like when the principles of family-centered care are absent. After Dylan died, I wrote to the healthcare team about the ups and downs of our experience—they needed to understand the patient/family point of view—and I also gave them recommendations for improvement. The team appreciated my feedback but, more importantly, made changes to policy/procedures and incorporated my suggestions into the design of the new children's hospital. I learned a huge lesson—that sharing the family perspective could improve care for future families.

Compassionate Passages, Inc. (www.compassionatepassages.org) is a nonprofit organization that advocates, educates, and conducts research to assist families, healthcare professionals/students, and the community in being supportive during and after the death of a child. Its vision is to be the leading "family voice" for pediatric end-of-life care—to ensure that families receive family-centered care at the end of their child's life. They do this by advocating on behalf of dying children and by empowering families to self-advocate, educating healthcare professionals and students about the patient/family perspective, and conducting research that will change policy/procedures and create resources that support dying children and their families.

—*Beth Seyda, Co-founder and Executive Director, Compassionate Passages, Inc., Chapel Hill, NC*

---

respect, and open dialogue. In turn, these elements of family-centered care are thought to improve patients' overall satisfaction.

Effective, sensitive communication seems to be particularly important among vulnerable and minority populations. For example, Ngui and Flores

(2006) found that in a recent study of nearly 40,000 children with special healthcare needs, black and Hispanic parents were significantly more likely than white parents to be dissatisfied with care (13% and 16% versus 7%, respectively) and to report greater problems with accessing services (35% and 34% versus 23%). A lack of family-centered practices was associated significantly with these groups' dissatisfaction and access problems. Indeed, when family-centered care practices were controlled, the statistical differences among different ethnic groups were reduced or eliminated.

In another example, through the Families as Faculty program at the University of Vermont College of Medicine (Johnson, Yoder, & Richardson-Nassif, 2006), medical students visited the family of a child with disabilities in their home and then wrote a reflection paper about the experience. Analysis of these papers indicated that the students learned first hand from families about how focusing on family strengths, supporting family relationships and normalcy, physician–family collaboration, and clear communication can improve satisfaction with care and health outcomes.

Finally, providing family-centered care can make a significant improvement in patients' and families' end-of-life experiences (see Chapter 13). The AAP affirms that "parents and guardians should be offered the opportunity to be present with their child during medical procedures and offered support before, during, and after the procedure" (AAP, 2003, p. 694). In some cases, family members may even be present during the administration of CPR. Indeed, family choice and family presence during CPR has been linked to greater family satisfaction and more positive grieving, even if the child dies (Knapp, Mulligan-Smith, & AAP Committee on Pediatric Emergency Medicine, 2005). The IOM Committee on Palliative and End of Life Care for Children and Their Families recommends that more research be done on palliative, end-of-life, and bereavement care for children and their families (IOM, 2003).

As telling as these studies are, the evidence base for family-centered care still largely relies on case studies and anecdotal data. The challenge to document the active ingredients that lead to improvements, as well as the cost effectiveness of this philosophy, remains. Although increasing the number of patients and families satisfied with their children's hospital experience is a positive step, knowing what elements of care contributed to that satisfaction is the key to quality improvement. To that end, six hospitals under Evanston Northwestern Healthcare in Evanston, Illinois, developed models of factors that predicted satisfaction (Dowling, Vender, Guilianelli, & Wang, 2005). Nothing was found to be as effective in promoting well-being among families and staff as consistent communication, a key principle of family-centered care. Helping patients/families understand tests and treatments and being sensitive and responsive to their needs were key aspects of staff communication that influenced satisfaction.

Fewer Medical Errors and Less Litigation

Family-centered care also addresses many of the patient safety concerns that have recently captured public attention. Since publication of the IOM report on medical errors, *To Err Is Human*, hospital administrators, researchers, and the lay public alike have trained a spotlight on how to reduce medical errors (IOM, 2000). Open communication about patient safety and transparency about system failure seem to be the most promising pathways to achieve these goals, as demonstrated by several hospitals' recent efforts. For example, Boston's Dana-Farber Cancer Institute has significantly reduced medical errors through its family–faculty program. Specifically, hospital leaders helped improve communication by involving patients and family members at all levels of institutional planning through patient and family advisory councils in their adult and pediatric programs. These councils work side by side with doctors, nurses, and other healthcare providers to ensure that patients receive the highest possible levels of care. "Most of our active committees have patients and family members sitting on them. We don't have to wait three or six months or a year for surveys to tell us what's up," says former Dana-Farber Cancer Institute chief operating officer, James B. Conway. "We've built up, through our relationships with patients and families, a system in which if there's something that's not working, we know that right away" (Shaw, 2000).

Indeed, risk-management literature indicates that in situations in which the practitioner has established open and effective communication and trusting relationships with patients and families, those patients and families are significantly *less* likely to initiate lawsuits, even when mistakes are made (Duclos et al., 2005; Hobgood, Tamayo-Sarver, Elms, & Weiner, 2005; Levinson, 1997; Maggioni, 2003; Mendelson, 2003; Udey, 2005) (see Chapter 20). More specifically, Levinson, Roter, Mullooly, Dull, and Frankel (1997) found that, relative to physicians experiencing malpractice claims, primary care physicians with no malpractice claims against them spent more time with patients and their families during routine visits, provided more anticipatory guidance, engaged patients more in collaborative discussions, and used humor more often.

The converse is also true—a lack of communication can lead to litigation. Patients and families are more likely to sue when they feel their provider has failed to understand their perspectives, delivered information poorly, devalued their point of view, or been unavailable to them (Beckman, Markakis, Suchman, & Franken, 1994) (see Chapter 10).

CASE STUDY: CINCINNATI CHILDREN'S HOSPITAL MEDICAL CENTER

> I feel very grateful to be a part of this program, to be able to offer my unique perspective as a parent, to have a physician look into my eyes and really listen to what it's like from my side. . . . Fears and concerns are laid out on the table. . . . We are working together to move things forward.
>
> *Tracey Blackwelder, Cystic Fibrosis Improvement Team Member*

The following case study illustrates how the comprehensive adoption of family-centered care principles can improve patients' health outcomes and medical care. In 1996, the Cincinnati Children's Hospital Medical Center crafted a vision statement asserting its intention to be the nation's leader in improving children's health. To support this vision, leaders wrote a comprehensive strategic plan, sent a group of senior management and staff to attend the Institute for Family-Centered Care's "Hospitals Moving Forward" Seminar, and began implementing family-centered care principles throughout their institution. They also committed themselves to measuring the impact of their changes. As a result, this hospital was the only pediatric and academic medical center selected to participate in the Institute for Healthcare Improvement's Pursuing Perfection program in 2001 (Institute for Healthcare Improvement, 2006).

Quality Improvement Teams

At this writing, patients and families are involved with 18 of the hospital's strategic quality improvement teams. These teams aim to improve the entire care continuum for their patients, including access to care, flow, patient safety, clinical excellence, and team well-being. More broadly, the teams help the hospital work towards fulfilling their larger goal of creating a safe, effective, timely, and equitable patient and family-centered care delivery system.

Family Support Programs

In addition to initiating the 18 quality improvement teams, Cincinnati Children's Hospital also aims to support and partner with patients and families through two other programs. The first program, the Family Resource Center, helps parents find information about a child's health condition, offers access to Internet and e-mail, helps families build a CarePage (a personal website for families to keep relatives/friends updated about their child's condition), and helps facilitate parent-to-parent networking and resources for the Hispanic/Latino community. A second program, the Chronic Condition Clinical Portals (Cincinnati Children's Hospital Medical Center, 2006a), provides parents with the information they need to be active and informed members of their child's healthcare team. Via a secure website, the portals offer up-to-date medical record information, such as laboratory results, medications, and procedures, and include a Q&A section for nonurgent questions to the healthcare team from patients/families.

Communication and Discharge Planning

"Family First Rounds" and "Discharge When" have increased patient/family satisfaction as well as improved quality and timeliness of care. The objective of Family First Rounds is to increase communication and coordination of care through a team approach to physician rounds. The unique aspect of these rounds is that the team includes the patient and family, which ensures that everyone hears the same information at the same time. The team, including parents, develops specific discharge criteria for "Discharge When" so that it is clear that when patients meet these goals, they go home. Progress toward meeting discharge goals is discussed during Family First Rounds. Before "Discharge When," approximately 50% of patients on the general pediatric unit at Cincinnati Children's Hospital went home within four hours after meeting goals, compared with 80% after "Discharge When" was introduced. Families are more satisfied with their hospital experience, feel better informed, and are discharged with less delay since the implementation of both these approaches. Another trickle-down effect from "Discharge When" is improved timeliness in admitting new patients, as hospitalized patients are often discharged earlier in the day.

Major Cultural and Procedural Changes

Three major cultural and procedural initiatives arose as a result of adopting family-centered care methods at Cincinnati Children's Hospital Medical Center, including (1) developing clinical guidelines for common illnesses, (2) addressing health disparities, and (3) improving transparency.

Developing Clinical Guidelines for Common Illnesses

To prevent needless emergency and inpatient care, Cincinnati Children's developed family-centered, evidence-based clinical guidelines for common childhood conditions such as asthma and bronchitis. Created with parent input, these guidelines help clinicians and families make healthcare decisions based on the best available evidence. From 1996 to 2005, the hospital documented shorter lengths of stay and decreased hospital admissions for children with diseases targeted by their improvement initiatives.

Reducing Disparities

In their continuous effort to both measure improvement and respond to problems identified through evaluation, Cincinnati Children's has identified some inequities in their system (Cincinnati Children's Hospital Medical Center, 2006b). Specifically, their juvenile rheumatoid arthritis care team found disparities in outcomes between children who were privately insured and those on Medicaid. The team, which includes parents, examined its practices and found they were providing the same quality of care, the same medications, and the same frequency of visits to both groups, but with different outcomes. As a result, they developed new processes that provided more intensive case management for at-risk patients, including preplanned occupational therapy and physical therapy visits, closer ties to a nurse and social worker, and an emphasis on self-management and goal setting. The percentage of juvenile rheumatoid arthritis patients achieving optimal functional status increased dramatically among government-insured (Medicaid) patients so that the gap between publicly and privately insured patients decreased significantly, from more than 40% to less than 20%. The team is also applying these family-centered case management approaches to privately insured patients to improve outcomes for everyone.

Increasing Transparency

The Cystic Fibrosis Center at Cincinnati Children's sought to achieve better health outcomes by increasing transparency and collaboration among patients, families, and the healthcare team. Specifically, the team began sharing with families how the center was performing. This decision was based upon the recommendations of two IOM reports published in 2000 and 2001, which assert that disclosing patient outcomes data to the public (i.e., transparency) is an essential aspect of patient-centered care. Families were given access to data comparing the health of their children with that of other children with the disease at the 116 other cystic fibrosis centers across the country. Cincinnati Children's was "in the middle of the pack" on important predictors of life expectancy, including lung function and nutritional status. "The fact that they were not hiding these numbers, and were asking us to join them in moving forward, that was a pretty big step," recalled Tracey Blackwelder, a mother of four children who received care at the Cystic Fibrosis Center. Despite the less than stellar data shown to parents, Blackwelder reported an excitement in the room. "We all left feeling enthusiastic about the prospect of working together to improve things."

> Transparency brings its own benefits and complications, but you can't create a meaningful partnership without it. Beneath it all must be a willingness to accept the data and believe in it, to admit that you are not doing as well as you would like, and to commit to doing it better. That's the motivation for partnering: accepting reality and the need to change it.
>
> *Jim Acton, MD, Director, Cincinnati Children's Hospital Medical Center*
> *Cystic Fibrosis Center (Institute for Healthcare Improvement, 2006)*

Many strategies were implemented as part of the new thrust, including clinicians taking more frequent respiratory cultures from patients, tracking lung function and nutritional status more carefully, initiating an aggressive flu vaccine program, refining protocols for airway clearance techniques, and creating a formal parent-to-parent network. The impact of this initiative is reflected in tangible health improvements: the percentage of cystic fibrosis patients under the 10th percentile for weight dropped from more than 40% to less than 25%. The percentage of patients receiving flu vaccines increased to 95% in one season as compared with an estimated 40% before the new program, and the percentage of patients having a respiratory culture increased to 85% as compared with less than 50% three years previously. Simultaneously, patients and parents reported feeling more supported, involved, and valued as members of the health-care team.

HOW IS FAMILY-CENTERED CARE TRANSLATED INTO PRACTICE?

In examining where family-centered care has been implemented successfully, one common thread is that these principles are integral to organizational policy, woven into the fabric of the program; they are not merely an "add on" or special project. This comprehensive approach to implementation is probably best illustrated in the Johnson, Jeppson, and Redburn 1992 publication, *Caring for Children and Families: Guidelines for Hospitals.* Its chapters outline a number of areas in which family-centered practice can be integrated, along with examples of ways in which to do this. These include administrative and governance issues, facility design and space allocation, personnel policies, programs and practices, training and education, supporting families and supporting the child's development through programming, education, and information, care coordination, as well as specific applications within transitions, critical care, and ambulatory care.

In the following sections, more detail is provided on four ways in which family-centered care is integrated in policy and practice through parent-to-parent networking, medical education and training, direct service, and research.

Parent-to-Parent Networking

The AAP Policy Statement on Family-Centered Care and the Pediatrician's Role emphasizes the importance of using parent to parent support as a family-centered practice to improve health outcomes in children. The experience of parenting a child with a serious and/or chronic illness can be extremely demanding. Stress can compromise a parent's ability to be available for her sick child and for the rest of her family. As one parent said, "When I'm overwhelmed, I'm not eating, sleeping, or utilizing my support systems. Then I become cranky, tired, and short-tempered, shout, cry, throw, ignore" (Orloff & Huff, 2003). A parent of a child with special needs specifically addressed caring for siblings when she said, "Guilt about being away from your other child can be hard to handle. Often caregivers overindulge the siblings due to guilt. Don't be afraid to ask for support" (Fields, n.d.).

State and local peer support networks such as Parent to Parent continue to be one of the most effective and often one of the most underused resources by professionals in helping families adjust to having a child with special health needs or a disability. Barriers to peer networking include a lack of understanding on the part of professionals as to the critical and unique role this support plays; policies such as confidentiality may be invoked to explain why referrals are not made. In addition, logistic barriers such as the need for transportation and child care make it difficult for parents to get to support groups. There is solid research evidence for the efficacy of parent-to-parent support (e.g., Ireys, Chernoff, Stein, DeVet, & Silver, 2001; Singer et al., 1999) and the growth of family support groups and Parent to Parent support indicates that the other barriers can be overcome. Parent to Parent USA (www.P2PUSA.org) was established in 2005 as a national nonprofit organization dedicated to ensuring access to research-based emotional and informational peer support for all families with children or youth who have special health needs or a disability. Through Parent to Parent USA, families can access a Parent to Parent program in their state and be matched in a one-to-one relationship with an experienced support parent. Parents are carefully matched in one-on-one relationships with parents in their geographic area. Many parents experience tremendous relief in being able to share their experiences and challenges with others who understand (Valdez-Honeyman, 1992):

No matter whether we're a step parent, a foster parent, single parent, the birth parent, adoptive parent, grandparent—we need each other, and we can help each other by supporting, mentoring, role modeling, whatever it is that links us together—we need each other.

The support parent is able to provide a unique form of support that only another parent who has "been there" can.

Medical Education and Training

Graduate medical education (i.e., medical school) teaches many of the same fundamentals of healthcare provision that were taught 40 years ago; however, medical education is beginning to evolve to meet the changing needs of a rapidly changing society and is recognizing the benefits of partnering with patients and families in healthcare education and training. This recognition has led bodies such as the American College of Graduate Medical Education (Accreditation Council for Graduate Medical Education, 2003) to include patient care interpersonal skills and communication professionalism as key competencies. More specifically, pediatric residency programs require graduates to demonstrate competence in six areas, including (1) patient care that is compassionate, appropriate, and effective for the treatment of health problems and the promotion of health, and (2) interpersonal and communication skills that result in the effective exchange of information and collaboration with patients, their families, and other health professionals.

It is essential for both families and professionals to learn to actively listen to each other, and to use open and honest communication—not just in what is said, but also in how something is said.

Jeni Stepanek (1994), mother of son, Mattie, who had a rare form of muscular dystrophy

One way to develop these key communication skills is to learn directly from patients and families. A growing number of innovative and successful approaches to healthcare education not only emphasize the principles of family-centered care in their content (e.g., effective communication), but also model family-centered care in how that content is taught. According to Jordan Cohen, MD, former president of the Association of American Medical Colleges, "In the modern medical school, a teacher doesn't always wear a white coat or carry the title 'M.D.' Quite often the best 'teaching' comes from the patient" (Cohen, 2000). According to the Association of American Medical Colleges (2006), 80 of the 142 U.S./Canadian medical schools report using patients and families as teachers in the educational training of medical students graduating in 2007. Two particular programs that use family as faculty for medical school and residency teaching are Families in Resident/Student Teaching (FIRST) and Project DOCC (Delivery of Chronic Care).

In 1997, Parent to Parent of Vermont and the University of Vermont College of Medicine began the FIRST program to ensure that pediatric residents had the knowledge and skills necessary to provide family-centered, community-based care for children with special health needs and their families. Hospital-based pediatric residents are matched with a teaching family and share and observe their experiences through a series of home visits over their three-year training. The FIRST program epitomizes family-centered care in that families are the teachers, and their homes and communities become the classroom. Residents are also given the opportunity to question and reflect on what they are learning from families and to develop strategies for applying this knowledge to their clinical experiences. According to Shilpa Patel, MD, a third-year resident who participated in FIRST, "The program has helped me understand on a concrete level what some families go through with the multiple stressors of life when having a child with a disability. . . . It amazes me that they are willing to take the time to train me."

Another example is Project DOCC. Founded in 1994 by parents of children with disabilities, Project DOCC improves the quality of care for children with severe chronic illness by educating pediatricians-in-training about children's special needs from a parent's perspective (www.uhfnyc.org). The curriculum is taught by parents and has three components: grand rounds, home visits, and parent interviews (Associated Press, 2005).

Ongoing learning from patients and families can also be accomplished via in-service training (e.g., continuing education for hospital staff held in-house), grand rounds, and patient/family advisory councils. For example, The Family Faculty program at the Children's Hospital of Philadelphia trains parents of children with special healthcare needs to present classes on family-centered care to physicians, nurses, and other hospital staff (Heller & McKlindon, 1996). The classes weave family-centered care philosophy with stories that relate individual families' experiences of illness as well as their care needs; the classes also model effective communication and enhanced collaboration between hospital staff and families. During its first year of existence, this program educated over 900 employees, 25% of its entire workforce.

Direct Service

Patients and families can serve as advisors in healthcare in education and training as well as in direct service. According to Maureen Connor, director of Quality and Risk Management at Dana-Farber Cancer Institute, "Patients and family members provide a unique perspective that we would not have otherwise. Experience is a great teacher and they clearly have a wealth of experience to share." As outlined in guidance materials available from the Institute for Family-Centered Care (see http://www.familycenteredcare.org/advance/IFFCC_checklist.pdf and http://www.familycenteredcare.org/advance/supporting-pafam.html), patients and families can collaborate with professionals in numerous ways: as members of committees such as task forces, facility design committees, or quality improvement initiatives; as advisory board members and members of boards of trustees; in hiring new staff; evaluating programs and reviewing policies; as grant reviewers or focus group participants; or as paid program staff consulting with or mentoring families, providing family-to-family support or training health advocates.

A good example of such collaboration is the Patient and Family Advisory Councils at Cincinnati's Children's Hospital (www.cincinnatichildrens.org). The Patient Advisory Council is made up of patients ages 10 to 18 who help staff understand what it is like to be a young patient and how to be supportive of patients. They also help identify quality-improvement strategies.

One of the most comprehensive examples of how to apply family-centered care principles is the concept of the Medical Home (www.medical homeimprovement.org). Arising from concerns about fragmentation of medical care for children with special healthcare needs, the AAP and other groups recommended the concept of the medical home as a way to centralize and coordinate care as standard practice (Cooley & McAllister, 2004; Knapp et al., 2005; Williams, 2006). A medical home is not a building, house, or hospital, but rather an approach to providing comprehensive primary care. A medical home is defined as primary care that is centrally facilitated by a pediatrician or primary care physician from her office. It is accessible, continuous, comprehensive, family centered, coordinated, compassionate, and culturally effective. In a medical home, a clinician partners with the family/patient to ensure that *all* of the patient's medical and nonmedical needs are met, including access and coordination of specialty care, educational services, out-of-home care, family support, and other public and private community services important to the overall health of the child/youth and family (see the National Center for Medical Home Initiatives, http://www.medical-homeinfo.org/). With its emphasis on collaboration among all healthcare team members, including the patient's family (Kitchen, 2005), the medical home provides a clear example of how family-centered care can be operationalized (see recommendations in Table 3.2).

CONDUCTING RESEARCH ON FAMILY-CENTERED CARE IN A FAMILY-CENTERED WAY

> Research must be more inclusive and participatory, involving not only consumers but also other stakeholders in understanding and interpreting research, in disseminating and applying research findings, and in planning, conducting, and evaluating research.

U.S. Department of Education (1998)

Early on in the development of family-centered care, the "evidence" base for its effectiveness consisted of case studies, anecdotes, project descriptions, and recommended guidelines. Although important, these "stories" often lacked the empirical data needed in assessing its efficacy; over the last decade, however, a significant increase in both qualitative and quantitative studies has documented that family-centered care yields better outcomes. This research also demonstrates that the experience of care, not just the outcome, is important. Practitioner communication with patients and families and active patient and family participation in clinical care and program development have been linked to health outcomes. The Institute for Family-Centered Care has compiled an annotated bibliography (http://www.family-centeredcare.org/advance/supporting.html) summarizing this

Table 3.2   Desirable Characteristics of a Medical Home

- Mutual responsibility and trust exists between the patient and family and the medical home physician.
- The family is recognized as the principal caregiver and center of strength and support for the child.
- Clear, unbiased, and complete information and options are shared on an ongoing basis with the family.
- Families and youth are supported so they can play a central role in care coordination.
- Families, youth, and physicians share responsibility in decision making.
- The family is recognized as the expert in their child's care, and youth are recognized as the experts in their own care.
- A plan of care is developed by the physician, child or youth, and family and is shared with other providers, agencies, and organizations involved with the care of the patient.
- The medical home physician shares information among the child or youth, family, and consultant and provides specific reasons for referral to appropriate pediatric medical subspecialists, surgical specialists, and mental health/developmental professionals.
- Families are linked to family support groups, parent-to-parent groups, and other family resources.
- Concern for the well-being of the child or youth and family is expressed and demonstrated in verbal and nonverbal interactions.
- Efforts are made to understand and empathize with the feelings and perspectives of the family as well as the child or youth.
- The child or youth and family's cultural background, including beliefs, rituals, and customs, are recognized, valued, respected, and incorporated into the care plan.
- All efforts are made to ensure that the child or youth and family understand the results of the medical encounter and the care plan, including the provision of (para)professional translators or interpreters, as needed.
- Written materials are provided in the family's primary language.

From the American Academy of Pediatrics, 2002

research across a number of dimensions, including adult healthcare, facility design, maternity care, newborn intensive care, patients and families as advisors, parent-to-parent support, pediatrics professional education, and risk management.

Conducting research in a way consistent with the philosophical tenets of family-centered care reflects good research practice, including being open to what the data imply; yet, putting these tenets into practice is not as easy as it may appear (see Table 3.2). The difficulties involved with putting these principles into practice are underscored in two research articles, published many years ago, examining the impact on the family of having a child with disability. In an initial article, Wikler, Wasow, and Hatfield (1981) identified what they called the "chronic sorrow" experienced by parents of children with mental retardation. Yet while most parents did report experiencing feelings of sadness, they also indicated that they had become much stronger individuals because of their experiences. The authors chose not to report these more positive findings because the results so contradicted their prior assumptions. They attributed these unanticipated findings to methodologic problems; however, in an unprecedented move, the authors published another article two years later in which they re-analyzed the data. They reported that they "considered this initial dismissal to be another example of a pervasive stance adopted among professionals, in which problems instead of strength and instances of coping are concentrated on" (Wikler, Wasow, & Hatfield, 1983). Both articles illustrate the major role researchers' assumptions can play, how important it is for researchers to listen to the full spectrum of what families are saying, and the benefits of collaborating with families in the interpretation of research findings.

What can researchers do to guard against these potential biases? They can use family-centered care principles as a roadmap. First, whenever possible, research concerning patient, family, and child outcomes is greatly improved by using community-based participatory research strategies (IOM, 2003). Community-based participatory research is a method in which researchers collaborate in all aspects of research, including the design and interpretation of the data, with the very people who may eventually benefit from that research (Leung, Yen, & Minkler, 2004). Had Wikler, Wasow, and Hatfield employed this strategy, they might have avoided misrepresenting their data. Because of their unique experience, family members can contribute an invaluable perspective to a research study. They can add richness to the hypotheses generated, help ensure that strength-based measures are used, and provide significant insight into the interpretation of the results.

The family-centered care principle of emphasizing and reinforcing strengths can also be used to select measures for a study. Based on the growing body of research on developmental assets (Prilleltensky, 2005; Scales, Leffert, & Vraa, 2003; Search Institute, 2005a, 2005b), family-centered research tools now include ways to measure strengths directly and not simply as the absence of deficits. Dunst and colleagues have been instrumental in creating many of these measures, including the Inventory of Social Support (Dunst & Trivette, 1998; Dunst, Trivette, & Deal, 1988; Trivette, Dunst, & Hamby, 1996). Others have created scales specifically to examine family-centered practices (e.g., A Measure of Processes of Care [King, Rasenbaum, & King, 1995]; and Enabling Practices Scale [Dempsey, 1995]). These and other instruments can be extremely helpful in documenting the degree to which programs are family centered.

Another approach is to partner with families and youth in data collection. Particularly with sensitive data or when families are receiving services from the same providers who are conducting the research, families may feel more comfortable giving open responses when questions are asked by other families. This approach is particularly important when evaluating programs or services. If the purpose is to obtain honest and reliable information about the service, consulting the perspectives of patients, families, and youth can be critical in determining whether the measures will, in fact, yield the information desired. In addition, with respect to issues of informed consent and participation, working with patients and their families as researchers is one of the most effective ways to ensure that families and youth are truly comfortable in choosing whether to participate in a study. Family members can also review recruitment procedures, research protocols, and written communication for excessive length and potentially offensive language, thereby helping to ensure that research is conducted in a culturally appropriate and family-centered way. Patients, families, and youth also benefit from partnering in research. Their participation gives them the opportunity to understand the research findings, the theories that support them, and how the data are obtained and to increase their comfort and skills in advocacy. These advocacy benefits are well illustrated by several ongoing initiatives through the Federation of Families for Children's Mental Health (2006). As they noted, partnering in research can yield powerful advocacy tools for families and youth. Finally, it is important to include the family once the research has been completed. Are there mechanisms for youth and families to provide feedback about the research experience? Is this information incorporated into the next steps of the research? Too often, research participants never receive any information about the

Table 3.3   Checklist for Conducting Family-Centered Research

- What are the ways in which families and youth collaborate with professionals in the design of the research?
- How does the research design and data analysis allow for a balanced approach, focusing on family and child strengths as well as needs?
- What steps are taken to ensure that families feel that they will not jeopardize the quality of services they receive if they do not wish to participate?
- What are the mechanisms for ensuring that consent forms are easy to understand and are validly translated into other languages or media as needed?
- If a number of research studies are being conducted in one agency or clinic, what are the mechanisms for ensuring that families are not overwhelmed with multiple requests?
- What are the mechanisms for ensuring that the results of the research are communicated and explained to the families and youth who participated?
- How do families provide feedback to the researchers on their perceptions as participants?

Source: Adapted from Shelton & Stepanek, 1994.

findings. Sharing the results of the research with the families and patients who participated in it in the first place demonstrates a respect for their partnership and helps to build good will for their continued participation. The checklist, shown in Table 3.3, can help researchers if they wish to put family-centered care principles into practice.

SUMMARY

Historically, patient advocacy was often restricted to professional staff assisting patients with complaints or concerns, often after a negative medical outcome. Families caring for children with special health needs advocating on behalf of their children helped transform this notion of advocacy into a self-advocacy movement, giving voice to the philosophy framed in the principles of family-centered care. As the examples in this chapter illustrate, healthcare is improved when professionals, patients, and their families work in partnership.

Textbox 3.2   Resource List

Institute for Family-Centered Care (www.family-centeredcare.org)

   The Institute for Family-Centered Care, a nonprofit organization founded in 1992, promotes the understanding and practice of patient- and family-centered care. The Institute's initiatives support the implementation of patient- and family-centered care in all systems providing care and support to individuals and families, including health, education, mental health, and social services. Through consultation, training, and technical assistance, materials development and information dissemination, and research and public policy initiatives, the Institute serves as a central resource for policy makers, administrators, program planners, direct service providers, educators, design professionals, and patient and family leaders. By promoting collaborative, empowering relationships among patients, families, and healthcare professionals, the Institute facilitates patient- and family-centered change in all settings where individuals and families receive care and support.

Parent to Parent USA (www.P2PUSA.org)

   Parent to Parent USA, established in 2005, is a national nonprofit organization dedicated to ensuring access to research-based parent-to-parent support for all families with children or youth who have a special health need or a disability. Parent-to-parent programs provide emotional and informational support to parents of children who have special needs. To provide this support, trained and experienced support parents are carefully matched in one-on-one relationships with parents who are newly referred to the program. Because the support parent has shared the experience of disability or special health need in the family, he or she is able to provide a unique form of support that only another parent who has "been there" can. Research conducted on this model of peer support has proven it to be effective and has identified evidence-based practices endorsed, promoted, and supported by P2PUSA (Chernoff, Ireys, DeVet, & Kim, 2002).

   More specifically, the benefits of advocacy on behalf of family-centered care are visible when healthcare practitioners listen to and honor patient and family perspectives and choices and incorporate patient and family knowledge, values, beliefs, and cultural backgrounds into the planning and delivery of care. Patients and families need timely, complete, and accurate information in order to participate in their care and decision making effectively. When healthcare professionals share complete and unbiased information in supportive and useful ways, they are building a partnership with patients and families and are promoting self-knowledge and self-advocacy to ensure better health outcomes. Reframing patient advocacy from this perspective broadens the approach from what can often be a reactive and sometimes adversarial activity to one that seeks a partnership to improve healthcare in a proactive way.

As a review of the history of family-centered care can attest, developing policies and implementing practices that are exemplary of family-centered care philosophy is a process that takes time. As Ireys (1987) noted, this philosophy rests on a mutual respect and a shared commitment to working together in an imperfect world. As such, barriers and impediments to family-centered care still exist. One is a lack of awareness of the benefits of this approach. Although the research base is growing, additional research incorporating both solid qualitative and quantitative methodologic designs is needed. In addition, more consumers need to be involved in all aspects of this research and not just as participants. Likewise, the benefits of family-centered care for professionals need to be better articulated.

Second, we need better information about what aspects of family-centered care are the "active ingredients" in these improved outcomes. If we want professionals to practice family-centered care, we need to continue to articulate clearly what those competencies are and what outcomes we expect to achieve. One area that appears to be promising is the link between family-centered care and patient, youth, and family efficacy or empowerment. In several studies from the mental health, early intervention, and developmental disabilities fields (e.g., Dunst, Boyd, Trivette, & Hamby, 2002; Graves & Shelton, in press), practices consistent with family-centered care lead to better child outcomes; however, these outcomes seem to be linked or mediated by improvements in family efficacy, that is, in families' belief in and ability to advocate for their child. This type of more detailed research can help to ensure the adoption of family-centered care throughout the healthcare system.

Third, we need to disseminate information about how family-centered care looks when implemented in practice. Principles such as dignity, trust, honesty, and collaboration can be quite abstract. Information such as the examples contained in this chapter and through organizations such as the Institute for Family-Centered Care can help to increase the adoption of such care into educational training, healthcare programs, family support, and policies. As family-centered practices permeate all aspects of healthcare design and delivery, patients, families, and providers will become more and more convinced that this is the most effective way to practice medicine; furthermore, it is the right thing to do.

REFERENCES

Accreditation Council for Graduate Medical Education. (2003, November). A crosswalk between the ACGME and IOM competencies. *ACGME Bulletin, 7.*

American Academy of Pediatrics. (2002). The medical home. *Pediatrics, 110*(1), 184–186.

American Academy of Pediatrics. (2003). Family-centered care and the pediatrician's role, policy statement. *Pediatrics, 112*(3), 691–696.

American Academy of Pediatrics. (2006). *Family-centered care publications.* Retrieved October 8, 2006, from http://www.medicalhomeinfo.org/publications/family.html.

Association of American Medical Colleges. (2006, June). *AAMC Curriculum Management and Information Tool (Curr MIT).* Washington, DC.

Associated Press. (2005, February). Moms teach doctors to care for children: Program trains pediatricians to better treat disabled kids. MSNBC, October 9, 2006, from http://www.msnbc.msn.com/id/6913185/.

Balint, M., Ball, D. H., & Hare, M. L. (1969). Training medical students in patient-centered medicine. *Comprehensive Psychiatry, 10*(4), 249–258.

Beckman, H. B., Markakis, K. M., Suchman, A. L., & Franken, R. M. (1994). The doctor–patient relationship and malpractice: Lessons from plaintiff depositions. *Archives of Internal Medicine, 154*(12), 1365–1370.

Caldwell, B. S., & Lockhart, L. H. (1981). A care-by-parent unit: Its planning, implementation and patient satisfaction. *Children's Health Care, 10*(1), 4–7.

Center for Attitudinal Healing. (1991). *Advice to doctors & other big people from kids.* Berkeley, CA: Celestial Arts.

Chernoff, R. G., Ireys, H. T., DeVet, K. A., & Kim, Y. J. (2002). A randomized, controlled trial of community-based support program for families of children with chronic illness: Pediatric outcomes. *Archive Pediatrics and Adolescent Medicine, 156*(6), 533–539.

Cincinnati Children's Hospital Medical Center. (2006a). *Find a service by topic: Chronic condition clinical portals.* Retrieved October 11, 2006, from http://www.cincinnatichildrens.org/svc/topics/universal-portal.htm.

Cincinnati Children's Hospital Medical Center. (2006b). *Transformation: The Quality Initiative at Cincinnati Children's.* Cincinnati, Ohio. Retrieved January 23, 2007, from http://www.cincinnatichildrens.org/about/measures/perfect.htm.

Cohen, J. (2000, September 22). *Medical education's quiet revolution to meet America's health care needs.* Retrieved January 23, 2007, from http://www.aamc.org: Association of American Medical Colleges.

Conway, J, Johnson, B., Edgman-Levitan, S., Schlucter, J., Ford, D., Sodomka, P., et al. (2006). *Partnering with patients and families to design a patient- and family-centered health care system: A roadmap for the future.* Retrieved October 9, 2006, from http://www.ihi.org/IHI/Topics/PatientCenteredCare/PatientCenteredCareGeneral/Literature/PartneringwithPatientsandFamilies.htm.

Cooley, W. C., & McAllister, J. W. (2004). Building medical homes: Improvement strategies in primary care for children with special health care needs. *Pediatrics, 113*(5 Suppl), 1499–1506.

Dempsey, I. (1995). The enabling practices scale: The development of an assessment instrument for disability services. *Journal of Intellectual & Developmental Disability, 20*(1), 67–73.

Developmental Disabilities Assistance and Bill of Rights Act of 1990, Public Law 101-496. (1990).

Dowling, J., Vender, J., Guilianelli, S., & Wang, B. (2005). A model of family-centered care and satisfaction predictors: The critical care family assistance program. *Chest, 128*(3 Suppl), 81S–92S.

Duclos, C. W., Eichler, M., Taylor, L., Quintela, J., Main, D. S., Pace, W., et al. (2005). Patient perspectives of patient-provider communication after adverse events. *International Journal for Quality in Health Care, 17*(6), 479–486.

Dunst, C. J., Boyd, K., Trivette, C. M., & Hamby, D. W. (2002). Family-oriented program models and professional help giving practices. *Family Relations: Interdisciplinary Journal of Applied Family Studies, 51*(3), 221–229.

Dunst, C. J., & Trivette, C. M. (1998). *Current and prospective use of family-centered principles and practices in early elementary grades.* Asheville, NC: Orelina Hawks Puckett Institute.

Dunst, C. J., Trivette, C. M., & Deal, A. G. (1988). *Enabling and empowering families: Principles and guidelines for practice.* Cambridge, MA: Brookline Books.

Epstein, F., & Horwitz, J. (2003). *If I get to five: What children can teach us about courage and character.* New York: Henry Holt.

Evans, R. G., & Robinson, G. C. (1983). An economic study of cost savings on a care-by-parent ward. *Medical Care, 21*(8), 768–782.

Federation of Families for Children's Mental Health. (2006). *Family leadership through evaluation.* Retrieved October 9, 2006, from http://www.ffcmh.org/evaluation.htm.

Fields, S. (n.d.). *Personal communication: Mother of a Child with Special Needs and Area Coordinator for Family Connection of South Carolina.*

Forsythe, P. (1998). New practices in the transitional care center improve outcomes for babies and their families. *Journal of Perinatology, 18*(6 Pt 2 Su), S13–S17.

Graves, K., & Shelton, T. L. (in press). Family empowerment as a mediator between family-centered systems of care and changes in child functioning: Identifying an important mechanism of change. 18th Annual Research Conference for the Research and Training Center for Children's Mental Health. University of South Florida. March 8, 2005.

Hannallah, R. S., Abramowitz, M. D., Oh, T. H., & Ruttimann, U. E. (1984). Residents' attitudes toward parents' presence during anesthesia induction in children: Does experience make a difference? *Anesthesiology, 60*(6), 598–601.

Hannallah, R. S., & Rosales, J. K. (1983). Experience with parents' presence during anaesthesia induction in children. *Canadian Anaesthetist's Society Journal, 30*(3 Pt 1), 286–289.

Heller, R., & McKlindon, D. (1996). Families as "faculty": Parents educating caregivers about family-centered care. *Pediatric Nursing, 22*(5), 428–431.

Hilden, J. M., Tobin, D. R., & Lindsey, K. (2003). *Shelter from the storm: Caring for a child with a life-threatening illness.* Cambridge, MA: Perseus.

Hobgood, C., Tamayo-Sarver, J. H., Elms, A., & Weiner, B. (2005). Parental preferences for error disclosure, reporting, and legal action after medical error in the care of their children. *Pediatrics, 116*(6), 1276–1286.

Institute for Family-Centered Care. Retrieved October 8, 2006, from http://www.familycenteredcare.org.

Institute for Healthcare Improvement. (2006). *Pursing perfection: Report from Cincinnati Children's on improving family-centered care for cystic fibrosis patients.* Retrieved September 30, 2006, from http://www.ihi.org/IHI/Topics/ChronicConditions/AllConditions/ImprovementStories/PursuingPerfectionReportfromCincinnatiChildren sImprovingFamilyCenteredCare.htm.

Institute of Medicine. (2000). In L. T. Kohn, J. M. Corrigan, & M. S. Donaldson (Eds.), *To err is human: Building a safer health system.* Washington, DC: National Academy Press.

Institute of Medicine. (2001). *Crossing the quality chasm: A new health system for the 21st century.* Washington, DC: National Academy Press.

Institute of Medicine. (2003). In M. J. Field & R. E. Behrman (Eds.), *When children die: Improving palliative and end-of-life care for children and their families.* Washington, DC: National Academy Press.

Ireys, H. (1987, January). *Family-centered care management: Issues for the professional.* Panel presentation at the Conference on Case Management Services for Disabled Children. Washington, DC.

Ireys, H. T., Chernoff, R., Stein, R. E. K., DeVet, K. A., & Silver, E. J. (2001). Outcomes of community-based family-to-family support: Lessons learned from a decade of randomized trials. *Children's Services: Social Policy, Research, and Practice, 4*(4), 203–216.

Johnson, B. H., Jeppson, E. S., & Redburn, L. (1992). *Caring for children and families: Guidelines for hospitals.* Bethesda, MD: Association for the Care of Children's Health.

Johnson, A. M., Yoder, J., & Richardson-Nassif, K. (2006). Using families as faculty in teaching medical students family-centered care: What are students learning? *Teaching and Learning in Medicine, 18*(3), 222–225.

King, S., Rasenbaum, P. L., & King, G. (1995). *The measure of processes of care (MPOC): A means to assess family-centered behaviors of health care providers.* O. N. Hamilton (Ed.), McMaster University: Neurodevelopmental Clinical Research Unit.

Kitchen, B. E. (2005). Family-centered care: A case study. *Journal for Specialists in Pediatric Nursing, 10*(2), 93–97.

Knapp, J., Mulligan-Smith, D., & American Academy of Pediatrics Committee on Pediatric Emergency Medicine. (2005). Death of a child in the emergency department. *Pediatrics, 115*(5), 1432–1437.

LaRosa-Nash, P. A., & Murphy, J. M. (1997). An approach to pediatric perioperative care: Parent-present induction. *Nursing Clinics of North America, 32*(1), 183–199.

Lerner, M. J., Haley, J. V., Hall, D. S., & McVarish, D. (1972). Hospital care-by-parent: An evaluative look. *Medical Care, 10*(5), 430–436.

Leung, M. W., Yen, I. H., & Minkler, M. (2004). Community based participatory research: A promising approach for increasing epidemiology's relevance in the 21st century. *International Journal of Epidemiology, 33*(3), 499–506.

Levinson, W. (1997). Doctor-patient communication and medical malpractice: Implications for pediatricians. *Pediatric Annals, 26*(3), 186–193.

Levinson, W., Roter, D. L., Mullooly, J. P., Dull, V. T., & Frankel, R. M. (1997). Physician-patient communication. the relationship with malpractice claims among primary care physicians and surgeons. *Journal of the American Medical Association, 277*(7), 553–559.

Maggioni, A. (2003). Communication helps reduce risks for hospitalists, PCPs. *AAP News, 23*(2), 60.

Mendelson, R. A. (2003). Reduce risk of malpractice suits by forging patient relationships. *AAP News, 22*(6), 260.

New Mexico Coalition for Youth and Families. (2006). *Adapted from a statement prepared by the New Mexico for youth and families, and the New Mexico young children's continuum.* Retrieved October 11, 2006, from http://www.familyvoices.org/info/about.php or http://www.familyvoices.org/states.php?state=NM2.

Ngui, E. M., & Flores, G. (2006). Satisfaction with care and ease of using health care services among parents of children with special health care needs: The roles of race/ethnicity, insurance, language, and adequacy of family-centered care. *Pediatrics, 117*(4), 1184–1196.

Omnibus Budget Reconciliation Act of 1989, Public Law 101-239. House Resolution 3299U.S.C.

Orloff, S., & Huff, S. M. (2003). *Home care for seriously ill children: A manual for parents.* Alexandria, VA: Children's Hospice International.

Prilleltensky, I. (2005, October). Promoting well-being: Time for a paradigm shift in health and human services. *Scandinavian Journal of Public Health, Supplement, 66*, 53–60.

Scales, P. C., Leffert, N., & Vraa, R. (2003). The relation of community developmental attentiveness to adolescent health. *American Journal of Health Behavior, 27*(Suppl 1), S22–S34.

Schulman, J. L., Foley, J. M., Vernon, D. T., & Allan, D. (1967). A study of the effect of the mother's presence during anesthesia induction. *Pediatrics, 39*(1), 111–114.

Search Institute. (2005a). *Introduction to assets: What are developmental assets?* Retrieved October 10, 2006, from http://www.search-institute.org/assets.

Search Institute. (2005b). *Positive human development.* Retrieved October 10, 2006, from http://www.search-institute.org/research/HDindex.html.

Shaw, G. (2000). Teaching hospitals, medical schools combat error. *AAMC Reporter, 9*(4), October 9, 2006, from http://www.aamc.org/newsroom/reporter/feb2000/teaching.htm.

Shelton, T. L., & Stepanek, J. S. (1994). *Family-centered care for children needing specialized health and developmental services.* Bethesda, MD: Association for the Care of Children's Health.

Singer, G. H. S., Marquis, J., Powers, L. K., Blanchard, L., DiVenere, N., & Santelli, B. (1999). A multi-site evaluation of parent to parent programs for parents of children with disabilities. *Journal of Early Intervention, 22*(3), 217–229.

Smerling, A. J., Lieberman, I., & Rothstein, P. (1988). Parents' presence during induction of anesthesia in children: Parents' viewpoint. *Anesthesiology, 69*, A743.

Stepanek, J. S. (1994). The end—but just the beginning. *ACCH's Family-Centered Care Network, 11*(2), 1–2.

Trivette, C. M., Dunst, C. J., & Hamby, D. W. (1996). Factors associated with perceived control appraisals in a family-centered intervention program. *Journal of Early Intervention, 20*(2), 165–178.

U.S. Department of Education. (1998, October 26). Part III: National institute on disability and rehabilitation research; notice of proposed long-range plan for fiscal years 1999–2004 (new focus of research inquiries). *Federal Register, 63*(206) 57194. Retrieved October 8, 2006.

U.S. Department of Health and Human Services, Maternal and Child Health Bureau. *Achieving and measuring success: A national agenda for children with special health care needs.* Retrieved October 10, 2006, from http://mchb.hrsa.gov/programs/specialneeds/measuresuccess.htm.

Udey, D. (2005). Listen, show compassion when dealing with angry patients. *AAP News, 26*(2), 17.

Valdez-Honeyman, E. (1992). Parents speak out for America's children: Report of the surgeon general's conference: Healthy children ready to learn: The critical role of parents. Retrieved October 8, 2006, from http://profiles.nlm.nih.gov/NN/B/C/T/M/.

Vessey, J. A., Caserza, C. L., & Bogetz, M. S. (1990). Another Pandora's Box? Parental participation in anesthetic induction. *Children's Health Care, 19*(2), 116–118.

Wikler, L., Wasow, M., & Hatfield, E. (1981). Chronic sorrow revisited: Parent vs. professional depiction of the adjustment of parents of mentally retarded children. *American Journal of Orthopsychiatry, 51*(1), 63–70.

Wikler, L., Wasow, M., & Hatfield, E. (1983). Seeking strengths in families of developmentally disabled children. *Social Work, 28*(4), 313–315.

Williams, W. G. (2006). Family-centered care: Advanced practice nurses in a medical home. *Journal for Specialists in Pediatric Nursing, 11*(3), 203–206.

Wolfram, R. W., & Turner, E. D. (1996). Effects of parental presence during children's venipuncture. *Academic Emergency Medicine, 3*(1), 58–64.

CHAPTER 4

E-Patients: How They Can Help Us Heal Healthcare

Tom Ferguson

OBJECTIVES

- To learn about who looks for and uses online health information, according to the health status of the individual (healthy, acutely ill, chronically ill)
- To see how online health information is changing e-patients' decision-making processes and communication patterns with clinicians
- To understand ways in which online support groups provide emotional, informational, and instrumental support to e-patients
- To learn about what expert e-patients are doing to disseminate cutting-edge information and provide support to newly diagnosed patients worldwide

Back in 2003 when Jo Anne Earp and I were planning a national conference on patient advocacy, we were aware that Tom Ferguson was one of the leading voices in the emerging field of e-health. We did not know him personally then, but to our delight, he said "yes" to our invitation and then set the room abuzz at our conference with forays into topics ranging from advocacy education for children to where he saw e-health going in the near future.

Two years and one patient advocacy conference later, in November 2005, Tom agreed to author a chapter for this book. My co-editors and I were both thrilled and humbled—thrilled that such a major thinker in this area would commit to the project and humbled that, despite his protracted and ongoing battle with cancer (he had been undergoing treatment for multiple myeloma on and off for almost 15 years), Tom would shoehorn this assignment into a schedule already filled with projects. At the time of our conversation,

Tom alerted our editorial team that he might need an extended dead-line to get his materials in to us. More treatments were on the horizon, and he would need some time afterward to regain energy.

What struck me during our conversations in winter 2005 was the way Tom spoke about his illness and treatments. Noted philosopher and art critic Susan Sontag (1990) discusses, and finally rejects, many of the narrative typologies (i.e., categories or genres) that we use to speak about illness and its effects. In a similar resistance to these categories, Tom spoke about illness and treatments as if they were so much background noise, a giant hassle that had the most irritating way of interrupting a life filled with interesting people and fascinating, vital work – as if even *this* lens for talking about illness were confining to him. I surmised at the time that, to the extent Tom's illness propelled his work, it did so by fueling his curiosity, leading him to observe closely how others responded to and took charge of their health, to ask the kinds of researchable questions explored in this chapter, and to develop thoughtful frameworks for understanding how our new information technologies affect our culture, specifically how we view and respond to health issues.

Several months after our November 2005 conversation, Tom sent me an e-mail with four chapters from the book he was writing on e-patients. He knew our own book deadline was fast approaching, so he asked me to "wave my magic pencil" over his materials to weave them into a chapter. When he made this request, I had anticipated that we would collaborate on this endeavor and that we would decide together what to cut and how to shape the chapter. To my great sadness, that turned out not to be the case. Tom died in April 2006 following a final round of cancer treatments.

Absent Tom's direction, what follows are my efforts to carve a single chapter out of an absorbing, provocative set of essays he had been incubating for some time (essays that may eventually be published elsewhere in their more complete form). These essays emerged from Tom's experience as a pioneer in consumer health informatics, from his work with the Pew Internet and American Life Project (he was their senior research fellow for Online Health), and from his interactions with an e-Patient Scholars Working Group he put together several years ago. These experiences supply part of the context for this chapter. Yet Tom's work also draws on the "thousands of free text responses to e-patient surveys" that he and his Pew Internet and American Life Project colleagues conducted, together with "e-patient insights passed on via the e-Patients Scholars working group," from e-patient weblogs, home pages, support groups, mailing lists, chat rooms, and web forums (Ferguson, 2006). "So," as Tom concludes, "in addition to summarizing the opinions of some of the most knowledgeable professionals and researchers, I have tried, whenever possible, to let the reader hear the contemporary e-patient's voice" (Ferguson, 2006).

In going over the work Tom shared with me, I have tried to edit with a light hand, retaining his voice, his first-person perspective in the introduction, and his collegial use of the word "we," by which he meant himself and the e-Patients Scholars Working Group. Particularly difficult for me in paring down Tom's materials has been the need to cut some of the extensive observations e-patients have made about how the Internet has changed the ways they care for themselves and their families. Similar to Tom, I have retained as many e-patient observations as I could in the knowledge that details of people's experience, in their own words, breathe life into statistical summaries. My hope is that, even in this condensed form, Tom's arguments will reach their mark, leading readers to consider the ways in which the time is ripe for "a major conceptual shift . . . from viewing lay people as consumers of health care to seeing them as they really are: its primary providers" (Levin & Idler, 1981, p.5)[a]

Elizabeth French

INTRODUCTION

I collect old toy robots. My Atomic Robot Man (Japan, 1948) (Figure 4.1) is a personal favorite. For many years I did not understand the powerful hold these dented little metal men maintained on my imagination. One day I finally got it; they show us how the culture of the 1940s and 1950s imagined the future. Cast-metal humanoid automatons would do the work previously supplied by human labor.

That was not how things turned out, of course. By making more productive forms of work possible, our changing technologies made older forms of work unnecessary. So instead of millions of humanoid robots laboring in factories, we have millions of information workers sitting at

Figure 4.1   Atomic Robot Man, 5″ high, Japan, 1948

computers. We did not just automate our earlier forms of work; the under-lying nature of work itself changed.[b]

Similarly, we have been projecting the assumptions of our familiar 20th-century medical model onto our unknown healthcare future, assuming that the healthcare of 2030, 2040, and 2050 will be much the same as that of 1960, 1970, and 1980. Yet bringing healthcare into the new century will not merely be a matter of automating or upgrading existing clinical processes. The underlying nature of healthcare itself must change.

This is not some techno-romantic vision of an impossibly idealist future. It is already happening. Physician and patient roles are already changing; and millions of knowledge workers are emerging as unexpected healthcare heroes. As this chapter seeks to demonstrate, when they or a loved one become ill, they turn into e-patients—citizens who use the Internet as a health resource, studying up on their own diseases (and those of friends and family members), finding better treatment centers, insisting on better care, providing others with medical assistance and support, and collaborating with their clinicians. In doing so, they are creating commu-nities of care through online support groups and friendship networks; they are pooling their knowledge and sharing it with each other and with their providers in easy-to-grasp language and a supportive milieu. Ultimately, as this chapter emphasizes, indicators suggest that these e-patients are improving their own and other people's access to and quality of care as measured by several yardsticks. In *Escape Fire*, Donald Berwick (2002) calls for healthcare that is accessible 24 hours a day, 7 days a week, 365 days a year. In looking at what is happening online, even now, we get a glimpse of what that kind of healthcare might look like.

This phenomenon may be a harbinger of a major paradigm shift within healthcare. In 1964, Thomas Kuhn identified two contrasting types of scientific work relevant to paradigm change. The first, *normal science*, involves the gradual accumulation of knowledge within a still timely and effective professional paradigm. The discovery of the structure of DNA is one example of normal science: Investigators knew what they were looking for, knew the methods that they needed to use, had faith in their underlying paradigm, and immediately knew it when they found the answer (Kuhn, 1964, 2000, pp. 165–177).

A healthy professional paradigm helps members of a profession work together; but there can be a dark side to professional paradigms as well. Because observations, approaches, and strategies contrary to accepted tenets of a dominant paradigm are typically ignored, denied, or explained away, an outdated paradigm can insulate a professional community from new developments, and the understandable impulse to protect a valued paradigm can stifle needed change. In times of rapid technological and/or cultural evolution, when the dominant professional paradigm in its traditional form may no longer serve the needs of the greater community, a second type of scientific work becomes necessary.

Disruptive science seeks to identify and understand the underlying limitations of an older paradigm and to facilitate development of a more sustainable scientific worldview. Galileo's identification of the sun, rather than the earth, as the center of the solar system is one familiar example of disruptive science that precipitated a major paradigm shift. For our purposes, the medical paradigm can be defined as a commonly held understanding of how the medical profession functions, that is, how the profession defines appropriate roles of the professional and those they care for, the type of work done, types of problems studied, and appropriate methods used. As this chapter suggests, e-patients may have a major impact on each of these dimensions of the medical paradigm, e-patients may indeed be the engines of the new paradigm—the source of disruption—dramatically changing how people care for themselves and make medical decisions. Yet the paucity of research in this area suggests that this promising new world view has, to date, somehow remained off the radar screens of most health policy makers, medical professionals, federal and state health officials, and other healthcare stakeholders. In this context, simply paying attention may be the most important step we can take toward the goal of developing a more sustainable healthcare system that draws on the knowledge and skill of activated e-patients.

But as the battered little robot beside my computer constantly reminds me, we are in the early stages of this process. Our current and future new technologies may change the nature of healthcare in ways we can, as yet, only vaguely imagine. As Massachusetts Institute of Technology's Sherry Turkle has suggested, instead of asking how these new technologies can help us make the familiar processes of medical care more efficient and effective, we should ask ourselves how they are "changing the ways we deal with one another, raise our children, and think about ourselves" (Open Door, 2003).

HUNTERS AND GATHERERS OF MEDICAL INFORMATION: E-PATIENT INFORMATION SEEKING TRENDS

Background

One morning in 1994, the same year Netscape released the first commercial web browser, the Englewood Hospital library in Englewood, New Jersey, received an unusual call. Identifying himself as Dr. Harold Blakely, a local family practitioner, the caller gave the librarian a citation for an article in a medical journal and asked her to make him a copy and leave it on the table outside the library door.[c] This request was not atypical. Hospital librarians frequently left copies of journal articles for doctors to pick up after the library had closed.

Later that afternoon, the caller phoned again, checking to be sure his article was ready. This time, however, the call was taken by the library's director, Kathy Lindner. Although she knew Dr. Blakely, she did not recognize the caller's voice. After a brief discussion with a colleague, she phoned Dr. Blakely's office. When a bewildered Dr. Blakely came to the phone, he assured Ms. Lindner that neither he nor anyone in his office had called the hospital library that day.

Half an hour after the library closed, a nervous, well-dressed man entered the hospital through a side entrance. Walking with a cane, he passed the elevator, climbed the stairs with some difficulty, and continued down the second floor hallway toward the medical library. As he picked up the envelope with Dr. Blakely's name on it, a hospital security guard stepped out of the doorway and asked him to identify himself.

After being questioned by the hospital's security service, the man admitted that he was Edwin Murphy, a 58-year-old insurance agent with a chronic hip problem. Dr. Blakely, his physician, had been urging him to undergo a promising new surgical procedure. Mr. Murphy, intrigued but not convinced, wanted to know more about the procedure's potential risks and benefits. He had repeatedly asked Dr. Blakely to help him obtain a copy of the definitive review article that had recently appeared in a major medical journal, but Dr. Blakely had not done so. Finally, in desperation, Mr. Murphy decided that there was only one way to obtain this vital information. He would have to impersonate his physician (K. Linder, personal communication, Englewood Hospital Library, March 14, 2002).

Dr. Blakely's reluctance to provide Mr. Murphy with such medical information may strike contemporary readers as strange. Yet in 1994, it was not at all unusual. Indeed, Dr. Blakely's response was the rule, not the exception. "For most of the twentieth century, patients were routinely and systematically denied access to the best available in-depth medical information about their conditions and the medical treatments currently available," said Alan Greene, a clinical professor of pediatrics at Stanford and an attending pediatrician at Stanford Children's Hospital. "I was trained never to share the deeper levels of my thinking with patients" (A. Greene, personal communication, November 7 and 9, 2003).

Five years later, in a completely different context, Marian Sandmaier's 16-year-old daughter, Darrah, had been experiencing severe headaches and a "sloshing" noise inside her head (Sandmaier, 2003). Her family physician took her vital signs, peered into her eyes, checked her balance and reflexes, and pronounced Darrah more or less healthy. "It may just be sinuses," she observed.

"But what about the pain in her neck and that odd sound she's been hearing?" the elder Ms. Sandmaier wanted to know.

The doctor paused at the exam room door. "Hard to say," she said vaguely. "Call back in 2 weeks if she's still having problems."

Unlike Mr. Murphy, however, Marian Sandmaier, a medical journalist, was a skilled Internet user. Remembering that Darrah had been taking a new antibiotic for a tenacious skin problem, she used Google to find hits for "minocycline" and "side effects." There she read about a rare side effect called *pseudotumor cerebri*, an accumulation of fluid around the brain that can produce severe headaches, neck pain, and vision problems. One symptom of this rare condition is a sloshing or roaring sound heard inside the head. Reading further, Sandmaier discovered that *pseudotumor cerebri* can damage the optic nerve, producing severe vision difficulties and, in some cases, blindness. She asked her daughter to stop taking the antibiotic and returned to the dermatologist who had prescribed the suspect medication. The doctor dismissed Sandmaier's diagnosis but switched Darrah to a new antibiotic nonetheless. Sandmaier checked its side effects on Google. The list included *pseudotumor cerebri*.

> Two doctors had now shrugged their shoulders at my daughter's symptoms. . . . Yet who was I to diagnose a rare disorder—on the Internet, no less? . . . Then another voice within me rose up, urgent, unbowed. If my child has it, I don't care how rare it is.
>
> I called Darrah's dermatologist and pediatrician and told them that I had rejected their diagnoses. . . . When I said the words *pseudotumor cerebri*, they both became very quiet. (Sandmaier, personal communication, May 17, 2004)

Sandmaier took Darrah to a top neuro-ophthalmologist at the University of Pennsylvania, saying nothing about her suspicions. After a lengthy battery of neurological tests, the specialist announced her verdict. "Your daughter is experiencing a rare side effect called *pseudotumor cerebri*." She indicated that the buildup in cerebral fluid sometimes reverses itself-if the patient stops taking the toxic drug in time. In the weeks that followed, Darrah's symptoms slowly subsided and finally disappeared. Her mother's quick action may have saved her sight (Sandmaier, 2003).

From Passive Patients to Active Healthcare Participants: How E-Patients Are Using the Internet to Find Information and Make Decisions

The year 2004 marked the end of the first decade in which the Internet came into wide public use. Over those 10 years, it changed the way we care for ourselves and others. It has changed the way we educate ourselves. It has also transformed the list of things we are now capable of. Fully 77% of Americans now go online, with 70% having Internet access from their homes (HarrisInteractive, 2006). For e-patients like Marian Sandmaier, online health resources now supplement the information and guidance their clinicians are able to offer within the time limits of medical encounters. They use the Internet to prepare and follow up on doctor visits. They go online to explore treatment options their clinicians did not mention, to double check diagnoses, to learn about alternative and complementary treatments, and to compare the treatments their doctors suggest with those used by other patients in other locales.

Five major surveys of e-patients conducted as part of the Pew Internet & American Life Project since 2000 provide a good deal of underlying data to support the observations, ideas, trends, and conclusions offered here (Fox, 2005; Fox & Rainie, 2000, 2002; Fox & Fallows, 2003; Madden & Fox, 2006). The free online newsletter *Health Care News*, published by HarrisInteractive since 2001, has been another valuable resource. Recent studies in the *Journal of Medical Internet Research*, the *Journal of the American Informatics Association*, the *International Journal of Medical Informatics*, and *Health Expectations* have provided additional insights. Here is a brief summary of what we know about e-patients so far:

- Eighty percent of U.S. adult Internet users have searched online for at least one of 16 major health topics, including a specific disease (63%), a certain treatment (47%), diet and nutrition (44%), fitness (36%), and prescription or over-the-counter drugs (34%) (Fox & Rainie, 2002).
- Women are more likely to search for specific diseases and other medical problems, reflecting their traditional role as family health-care givers. Men are more likely to search for information relating to sexual health, drugs, alcohol, and smoking (Fox, 2005).
- Although young people use online health resources more frequently than their older counterparts (HarrisInteractive Health Care News, 2002), Internet use is increasing rapidly among older citizens (Horrigan & Rainie, 2002).

E-Patients According to Health Status

Recent survey data suggest that segmenting e-patients according to how they use online health resources can shine a clearer light on their potential to shape healthcare in the future. Cain, Sarasohn-Kahn, and Wayne (2000) recently identified three types of e-patients whose online behavior differs according to their state of health and wellness. These categories include the well, the newly diagnosed, and the chronically ill and their caregivers. The e-Patient Scholars Working Group and I have tweaked this identification of patient types as follows: (1) the well and their caregivers, (2) acutely ill patients and their caregivers, and (3) chronically ill patients and their caregivers.

The Well and Their Caregivers

About 60% to 65% of e-patients are well. Although some may "keep an eye out" for particular health-related concerns (e.g., exercise, stress, and nutrition), most browse for general health and wellness information in much the same way as they might look for news or feature stories. They are the lightest users of online health resources (Cain et al., 2000). At the same time, however, well e-patients, especially women, often serve as managers for other family members' health concerns (Fox & Rainie, 2000).

Acutely Ill Patients and Their Caregivers

About 5% to 10% of e-patients are facing a new medical challenge. Some have just received a new diagnosis for a serious condition such as HIV/AIDS, cancer, or diabetes. Others are dealing with a challenging new development for a previously diagnosed condition; for example, their treatment is no longer working, they are experiencing troublesome side effects, or they must make a choice about a new therapy. These e-patients search online resources intensively, casting a wide net for information, communicating with other patients with the same condition, participating in online support communities, and enlisting the help of online medical experts. They are the heaviest users of online health resources (Cain et al., 2000), often using the Internet every day (Fox & Rainie, 2000).

Because their numbers are so small, surveys of the general e-patient population can easily miss acutely ill patients. Yet they play a much more important role in generating total online health traffic (web searching plus participation in online communities and health-related e-mail) than their low numbers suggest. Personal accounts by acutely ill e-patients often describe exhaustive searches extending over hundreds of hours and many days or weeks (Fox & Rainie, 2002). For example, when a 35-year-old e-patient named Jack learned he had tested positive for HIV/AIDS, he devoted himself to an intense series of "wildly generic searches" to learn everything he could about the condition (Reeves, 2001). In one early session, he found several newsgroups where patients discussed his condition:

> I went through and pulled a list of everything that had to do with HIV.
> . . . I went through each newsgroup and I literally . . . sat there for
> three days and read every single post. There were 2,476 of them. I
> read them all.

Chronically Ill Patients and Their Caregivers

About 30% to 35% of e-patients have stable chronic illnesses and are not currently dealing with a medical challenge. They use online health resources regularly to manage their illnesses and to keep up to date on their conditions. They look up pertinent information before and after a doctor's visit, communicate with other patients and caretakers, and use e-mail to keep in touch with their own network of family and friends. They are moderately frequent users of online health resources, using them several times a month (Cain et al., 2000).

In addition to managing their own medical conditions, many chronically ill patients spend a great deal of time caring for others. Often the most active participants in online support communities, they frequently serve as hosts, "community elders," and "big brothers/big sisters" to the newly diagnosed. Chronic patients are typically the most likely to develop web sites for their condition, post content designed to help others, and respond to the questions of others.

E-patients and Their Activation Levels: The Accepting, the Informed, the Involved, and the "In Control"

A second useful typology for understanding how e-patients are changing the healthcare environment has been proposed by Von Knoop, Lovich, Silverstein, and Tutty (2003). They relate patients' empowerment levels to two independent factors: the severity of their condition and their attitude toward their physician. In this schema, the more severe and long-lasting a condition, the more likely a patient is to seek out sophisticated information and then use that information to make decisions.

"The Accepting," Doctor Dependent and Uninformed

These patients consider their doctors the ultimate medical authorities, relying entirely or almost entirely on them for medical guidance. They feel it is their doctors' prerogative to provide any medical information they need and to make all their medical decisions for them. They rarely or never go online to seek health information or guidance.

"The Informed," Doctor Dependent but Active Information Seekers

These patients also consider physicians the unquestioned leaders of the healthcare team, relying on them to make many of their medical decisions, but they go online to learn more about their condition and its treatments, often doing so just before or after a doctor's visit. They are occasional users of e-health resources and appreciate the fact that they can find medical information without "wasting the doctor's time with their questions."

"The Involved," Junior Medical Partners

"The involved" regard themselves as respectful junior partners to their physicians. When possible, they would prefer making medical decisions in collaboration with their providers. They use the Internet extensively, seeking in-depth information on their conditions. They may attempt to discuss the material they find with their doctors, but often they are not particularly assertive, will typically allow the doctor to control the interaction, and will usually defer to doctors' preferences in cases of disagreement.

"In Control," Autonomous Patients

These patients believe in making their own medical choices, even when they disagree with their physicians. These are the power users of the e-patient world and could be considered "expert patients." Although they usually try to confirm their conclusions with a clinician, they use online resources, tentatively diagnosing their own conditions. They may make decisions about their treatment preferences independently of their providers and then attempt to persuade their clinicians to treat them accordingly. They are the most active of all e-patients in offering guidance, support, and resources to help others with the same condition. Von Knoop et al. (2003) found that dealing with a continuing or increasingly severe illness tends to drive e-patients from a medically passive to a more medically autonomous role.

Studies by Ziebland et al. (2004) confirm these typologies, describing how patients with cancer use the Internet "to gain, maintain, and display familiarity with a remarkable body of medical and experiential knowledge about their illness" (p. 566). In doing so, they increase their sense of competence, develop effective coping skills in the face of serious illness, and present themselves as technically proficient and discriminating users of medical information and professional services.

What E-Patients Like Best and What They Say Is Lacking

Given a context in which acutely and chronically ill patients use Internet resources extensively, understanding what kinds of information and services they look for, how they use the information they find, and what they would like to see more of can further shape our conceptualizations of what 24–7–365 healthcare might look like. E-patients are generally satisfied with most aspects of using online health resources (Fox & Fallows, 2003).

- Eighty percent find the information they look for online most or all of the time.
- Sixty-eight percent say that their last online search affected their decisions about how to treat an illness, whether to visit a doctor, whether to ask new questions, and whether to get a second opinion.
- Sixty-one percent of e-patients say that getting health and medical information from the Internet has improved the way they take care of their health either "a lot" or "some" (Fox & Rainie, 2002).

Nevertheless, a significant percentage of e-patients said that they would have liked more availability of certain online services or features (Fox & Fallows, 2003; Sciamanna, Clark, Houston, & Diaz, 2002), including

- Doctor–patient e-mail
- How to determine whether a doctor is ordering the correct tests and treatments
- More information about the quality of care both doctor and local hospitals provide
- The ability to schedule doctor's appointments online
- Direct Internet access to online doctors
- Free access to fee-only online medical journals
- More information about drug interactions
- More information and support for caregivers
- Better ways to connect with local resources

- Online diagnostic tools or "symptom finders"
- Access to medical records and test results
- A private place to store records of illnesses, tests, and treatments

How Is the Internet Changing E-Patient/Clinician Interactions?

Since 2000, all practicing U.S. clinicians have been seeing patients and caregivers who have searched the Internet for medical information, but most have been unaware of it. Only 38% of patients ever discuss their use of online medical resources with any clinician (Fox & Fallows, 2003, pp. 15–19); however, even though many doctors still overlook its importance, the Internet has already become an important factor in patient care. One e-patient in seven has made an appointment to see a doctor because of information or advice received online (Taylor & Leitman, 2002). Patients who have searched for medical information online are more likely to consult doctors than are non-e-patients (Fox & Fallows, 2003, p. 15), and because their ability to use the Internet makes them feel less dependent, less fearful of the unknown, more capable of asking well-informed questions, and more capable of evaluating the care medical professionals provide (Fox & Fallows, 2003, p. 16), e-patients likely come to clinic better prepared than those who have not used online health resources.

The range of clinicians' responses to e-patients' online research efforts was nicely summarized by one participant in a Pew survey who wrote that he had encountered two distinctly different attitudes among his clinicians. One group encouraged his online efforts, supported his desire to become more medically competent, and thought of him as a "partner in my care." A second group of clinicians seemed uncomfortable with or offended by his attempts to learn more about his condition via online resources. Internet-hostile clinicians sometimes try to discourage their patients from going online. But when they do, one of two things usually happen: (1) the patient finds a new physician or (2) she "goes underground," continuing her Internet research but no longer sharing it with her physicians (Fox, 2004).

Regardless of their clinicians' response, nearly all e-patients feel that Internet health resources are a very good thing, indeed. Most e-patients report that their use of the Internet makes them feel more autonomous and capable, not only in dealing with the health challenges they face, but also in dealing with their clinicians and provider institutions. As one e-patient explained, "Knowledge is power. [What I find online] helps me feel prepared to talk with doctors and nurses. I know the terminology and the options." E-patients who have "studied up" on their diseases online say they have less fear of the unknown and more confidence in their ability to deal with whatever the future may bring because of what they have learned during their online health research (Fox & Fallows, 2003, p. 16).

PATIENT-CENTERED NETWORKS: CONNECTED COMMUNITIES OF CARE

Social Network Theory and the Internet

Searching the Internet for medical information represents only one aspect of the e-patient experience. For many, online interactions with their own personal networks may be equally or more important, providing several new dimensions of social, informational, and logistical support for those facing health concerns.

An individual's social network, that is, the web of social relationships that surrounds an individual and the characteristics of those ties, has long been recognized as an important factor in maintaining health and managing disease more effectively (Granovetter, 1972; Heaney & Israel, 2002). Not surprisingly, these social networks have expanded with our use of the Internet. According to a classification system proposed by Haythornthwaite (2003), those with whom we communicate weekly or more often are defined as our closest ties; our weekly to monthly contacts are our significant ties; and those with whom we communicate monthly or less frequently are our extended ties. In addition, we may sometimes correspond on a one-time or short-term basis with friends or others we have "met" online (a weak tie link).

Network Members Serve as Internet Surrogates

Interestingly, more e-patients (81%) have gone online for a friend or family member diagnosed with a new illness than to find information for themselves, and moreover, almost half of e-patients say that their last health search was done on behalf of someone else (Fox & Rainie, 2002). These Internet surrogates (i.e., people who turn to the Internet to help others) are typically ordinary people who have stepped in to help friends or family members facing a medical challenge. As one woman in an online focus group explained, "I am just a mom with absolutely no special training or education in healthcare, but because I have been able to access resources for information online, I have been able to truly play a part in our care" (Pew Internet & American Life Project, 2001).

Internet surrogates also serve as key decision makers for the sickest and most vulnerable patients. Many not only search for static medical content on their friend or family member's behalf, they also exchange e-mail or other electronic communications with expert patients they find online. The online efforts of these friends and family members have direct effects on medical care. Nearly half (46%) said that their last online search affected their decisions about how to treat an illness. Thirty-nine percent said that the information they found online led them to ask their loved one's doctor new questions, and 34% said that online health resources had changed their overall approach to medical care (Fox & Rainie, 2002).

Helping Patients and Families Deal With a New Diagnosis

When a new illness is diagnosed within a wired family, a patient's original network may expand as different friends and family members activate their own networks. "If I e-mail my friend Tricia to tell her I've just been diagnosed with hypothyroidism, she may begin by doing a Google search for me," explains e-Patient Scholars' Working Group member Allan Greene, a Stanford pediatrician (personal communication, September 14, 2005).

> [Tricia] may e-mail her friend Suzie who has become something of an expert on this topic after receiving a similar diagnosis last year. Tricia may then report back to me with the advice and resources Suzie recommends. Or she may put me directly in touch with Suzie herself (a new weak tie link). Suzie may then refer me to a good online support group for this condition. . . . Because we're mutual friends of Tricia's, and because we are now disease-mates as well, there's frequently a surprisingly high level of altruism in these relationships (A. Greene, personal communication, September 14, 2005).

Patient-Centered Support Networks in Serious Illness

Just as people's online networks evolve with a new diagnosis, they also evolve during long-term serious illnesses, where e-mail and other online resources help friends and family become more intimately involved in their loved one's medical experiences. One example involving a Seattle psychotherapist, Lenny, and his wife, Judy, helps illustrate this dynamic. An initial e-mail sent to about a dozen close friends and family members in 2001 informed Lenny's friends that Judy had been diagnosed with Calciphylaxis, a rare, poorly understood condition found only in people with kidney disease. Lenny explained to his social network the symptoms, likely trajectory of the disease, and that she had decided on a highly experimental course of treatment. "We are e-mailing this information," he wrote, "because we thought you would like to know—and because it is stressful and upsetting for us to have to explain this frightening disease over and over again to all our caring family members and friends."[d]

Over the following 16 months, Lenny sent out a total of 128 "Judy Updates" to a list that grew to include more than 80 names—other family members and friends, new friends, health workers who had become friends, and many others. Its members, in short, became Lenny and Judy's *patient-centered support network*. In explaining what his regular "Judy Updates" and the community that grew up around these e-mails—meant to him, Lenny shared a number of insights.

> It was wonderful to be able to share our struggles and triumphs with a loving, supportive group of friends who were eager to hear from us. And since our friends knew exactly what we were going through, we knew that we were not alone. We did not have to spend hours and hours on the phone, bringing everyone up to date. And since some of our medical experiences had been so unpleasant, it would have been unpleasant to relive them over and over.

Wired caregiver Charlene Voyce amplifies on this perspective:

> Immediately after my daughter had surgery for her brain tumor at age 6, lots of people stepped in to help. But my support network dwindled fast when I couldn't return calls or simply felt too exhausted to encounter one more person's grief over my daughter's difficulties. But once I began posting regular Emma updates online, that support network got reactivated, and eventually expanded to include lots of very supportive people. (Personal communication, UNC at Chapel Hill, October 12, 2006)

Professional medicine is often at its worst in providing continuing comfort and care for patients facing serious illnesses beyond the hope of cure.

In this context, Internet support groups and social networks may help fill this gap in meaningful ways; yet research in this area is in its infancy. For example, no studies have been done and no statistics kept to suggest how many of the more than 12,000 different online discussion groups for "individual families" (*Yahoo Family Groups*, 2006) are currently being used to manage a loved one's illness. The e-Patient Scholars Working Group wrote to a dozen groups that appeared, from the public group description, to include family caretaking among their functions, but no one from these groups was willing to share their online caregiving processes.

ONLINE PATIENT HELPERS

Spotlight on an Online Patient Helper

Karen Parles was a research librarian at a major New York art museum until January 1998, when she learned she had advanced lung cancer.

> My doctors told me my cancer was incurable, that even with chemotherapy I had only a year or so to live. I'd never smoked, I have two great kids, and I was only 38. So the whole thing came as quite a shock. I was pretty overwhelmed at first. But, as soon as I could, I went onto the Internet, looking for information. (K. Parles, personal communication, 1999–2002)
>
> I'm pretty good at finding things online. But even so, I had a hard time locating all the information and people I needed. . . . There was no comprehensive site that provided links to all the best online information for this disease.

She did find an excellent support group, the Lung-Onc mailing list, whose members gave her invaluable support and information (http://listserv.acor.org/archives/lung-onc.html). When a surgical team recommended an experimental treatment that involved removing a lung, she shared her fears about going ahead with the procedure with her Lung-Onc friends:

> I heard right back from eight or ten others who'd had a pneumonectomy. They assured me that I could do it and encouraged me to give it a shot. . . . I can't overemphasize the importance of their help in those early weeks and months. My membership in the group provided

instant access to the wisdom and experience of hundreds of other lung cancer patients. (K. Parles, personal communication, 1999–2002).

Reflecting on her experience, Parles recalls that she had "found my life-saving treatment by a combination of Net-smarts, luck, and personal contacts." Yet the idea that others might not be so lucky led her to create an online resource just for lung cancer, "a single, centralized site where patients could find links to everything they needed to help them get the best possible medical care, a place where they could learn to manage their disease in the best possible way" (K Parles, personal communication, 1999–2002).

Parles launched her site, Lung Cancer Online (www.luncanceronline.org), in 1999. It lists and describes all the best sites containing information about lung cancer. Visitors will find guidelines and databases to help them find the top-rated lung cancer specialists and the best medical centers for each type of lung cancer. They will also discover practical advice and survivors' stories, up-to-date information on the latest clinical trials, a list of online support groups, guides to the best bibliographic databases, medical libraries, conference proceedings, and medical journal articles; the site even offers access to Parles herself. "Because I'm an experienced lung cancer survivor, I've found that many patients and family members want to interact with me personally, by phone or e-mail or in person," she explains.

Why does Parles devote 30 or more unpaid hours a week to maintaining her site and helping other patients? "They keep me pretty busy sometimes," she admits. "But then I have to ask myself, 'Do I really have something to do that's more important than helping and comforting a terrified fellow patient who's just learned they have the same deadly disease that I do?'"

E-Patient Support Groups Change the Experience of a Serious Illness by Supplementing, but Not Replacing, Doctors

For millions of patients across the country and around the world, access to support groups and online patient helpers has changed the experience of having a serious chronic disease. A Pew Internet study of online communities found that 28% of U.S. adult Internet users had connected with an online support group for a medical condition or a personal problem (Horrigan, Rainie, & Fox, 2001). The Internet now offers online groups for almost every imaginable medical challenge—from AIDS and breast cancer to depression and stress.

Although research in this area is scant, initial findings from an early study of 191 members of an online support community (most of them seriously ill patients with conditions like breast cancer, prostate cancer, ovarian cancer, fibromyalgia, and hepatitis C) help explain why online support groups are such a valuable resource. Respondents were asked to identify which of three resources—specialist physicians, primary care physicians, or online support groups—they would rate most highly in a number of categories (Ferguson, 1999). Table 4.1 illustrates the findings.

The value of online groups as perceived by e-patients was substantially greater than most health professionals had realized. In terms of cost-effectiveness, in-depth information, emotional support, convenience, and several other factors, online support groups were the clear winners. Yet it appeared that online groups had relatively little to offer in some areas, as for example, the process of diagnosis. Doctors' abilities to advise patients on an ongoing treatment plan were also highly valued, as were their technical knowledge and capacity for support and empathy. In fact, the findings suggested that the combination of a good doctor and a good support group might offer e-patients the best of all possible worlds.

Online Support Groups Help Those with Rare Diseases or Limited Access to Healthcare

Not only are online support groups helpful to e-patients seeking information and support, they can offer special benefits for those with rare conditions. Gilles Frydman, founder and executive director of the Association of Cancer Online Resources, explains why.

> Patients with rare cancers are often the first example of this disease their local oncologist has ever seen. So, most doctors aren't up-to-date on the latest treatments. E-patients can learn about the treatments currently in use at the leading treatment centers from their online communities. And they can then pass this information on to their physicians. (G. Frydman, personal communication, November 16, 2003)

Table 4.1   Most Useful Resources for 12 Dimensions of Medical Care [Rated by the Members of an Online Support Community (*N* = 191), by Percent]

	Online Groups	Specialist MD	Primary Care MD
Most cost-effective	82.7	8.4	8.9
Best in-depth information on my condition	76.9	20.9	2.2
Best help with emotional issues	74.7	9.9	15.4
Most convenient	72.7	14.2	13.1
Best for helping me find other medical resources	68.7	14.3	17.0
Best practical knowledge of my condition	68.5	23.4	8.2
Best help with issues of death and dying	57.5	15.0	17.5
Most compassion and empathy	52.5	17.5	30.1
Most likely to be there for me in the long run	49.4	21	29.6
Best technical knowledge of my condition	47.5	44.8	7.7
Best help to diagnose my problem correctly	11.4	73.5	15.1
Best help and advice on management after diagnosis	34.6	42.7	22.7

Adapted from Ferguson, 1999.

Expert caregiver Charlene Voyce agrees. For six years, this parent has been helping her daughter (now age 12) negotiate multiple complications that attended the removal of a brain tumor in 2000. "Doctors sometimes don't even *know* they're not up to date," said Voyce.

So bringing these materials in to specialists can be an eye-opening experience for them and can have a significant impact on the care they give. What's more, all boats rise with the rising tide. I'm not just able to advocate for more up-to-date treatments for my own daughter.

> By sharing this information with providers, I'm helping to dissemi-
> nate cutting edge information, meaning that other children may ben-
> efit too. (C. Voyce, personal communication, UNC at Chapel Hill,
> October 12, 2006)

Finally, online support groups are an important resource for those with
limited access to professional care. As a member of the Brain Talk
Communities (www.braintalk.org) recently observed

> When I talk to my doctor, I hear myself asking questions that my
> online "family" needs to know. It's as if all these other people—the
> members of my group—are asking questions through me. And what-
> ever answers I hear from my doctor, I know I'll share with them
> online. (Ferguson, 2002)

Gilles Frydman of the Association of Cancer Online Resources concurs:

> Some uninsured and offshore members of our lists have told me that
> their online support group is their only source of medical guidance.
> Many English members of the breast cancer groups learned about
> Herceptin years before the anti-cancer agent was approved in the U.K.
> And a number of foreign patients suffering from gastrointestinal
> stromal tumor recently learned about an early-stage European clinical
> trial long before it was listed in the NCI's PDQ database. (G.
> Frydman, personal communication, November 16, 2003)

CONCLUSIONS ABOUT THE IMPACT AND FUTURE OF THE E-PATIENT

This chapter opened with the claim that, with the advent of e-health, we
are witnessing an instance of disruptive science, a paradigm shift in which
e-patients are as much providers of care as they are consumers. In this paradigm, patients seek and share highly sophisticated information found on
the Internet, make well-informed decisions based on this information,
gain confidence in managing their conditions, reach out to others to help
them manage their illnesses, and much more.

Drawbacks of the Internet?

Despite these benefits, many researchers and clinicians have expressed concern about the Internet's possible downsides, including the impact of misinformation on e-patients, the possibility that some e-patients will push physicians to prescribe inappropriate medications, and the impact of the digital divide between white and black populations as well as those with more and less education (Ferguson & Frydman, 2004). These are legitimate concerns. Low literacy, for example, affects 90 million American adults (Kutner, Greenberg, & Baer, 2005), making Internet searches and e-mail correspondence a major challenge for many (see Chapter 8). Indeed, those who have not completed high school are much less likely to go online (32%) than those with college degrees (88%) (Pew Internet & American Life Project, 2006).

Yet as Eysenbach (2003) noted, medical researchers have become so "distracted by focusing on the negative aspects of the Internet that they have overlooked the benefits it provides." Specifically, fears of patient suffering based on consequences of online advice are countered by frequent reports that they obtain better care, avoid medical mistakes, or even save their own lives due to online health sites (Fox & Fallows, 2003; Spadaro, 2003). Many e-patients even say that the "medical information and guidance they can find online is more complete and useful than what they receive from their clinicians" (Fox & Rainie, 2002; Spadaro, 2003). Similarly, although patients may now ask their doctors to prescribe a specific medication learned about online (Taylor & Leitman, 2002), one study suggested that health information on the Internet has not yet resulted in many requests for inappropriate care (Murray et al., 2003a, 2003b). Finally, the digital divide does persist across race and education lines. Yet a merging of technologies such as television, Internet, and cell phones, combined with more visual content and greater ease of use across all of these media, may help ameliorate these inequities.

Final Thoughts

Based on our findings thus far, the e-Patient Scholars Working Group has formulated several tentative conclusions regarding the emerging world of the e-patient that together sum up the impact of patients' health information-seeking behaviors in recent years and what needs to happen in the near future to harness the power of these changes (Ferguson & Frydman, 2004). Over the last several years, we have seen the following:

1. Medical online support groups have become an important healthcare resource, providing emotional support, guidance, health information, and referrals for most medical conditions, around the clock, for free.

2. Doctors willing to discuss health information from the Internet with patients may enhance the doctor–patient relationship by being open to new information and revealing confidence in their own abilities as doctors. On the other hand, doctors who respond negatively may damage the doctor–patient relationship, as patients may perceive their doctors as threatened by a challenge to their authority (Murray et al., 2003a, 2003b).

3. E-patients often become extremely well informed, often experts, on their own conditions. When this expertise is acknowledged, it can elevate the quality of medical care.

Returning to the metaphor of the atomic robot at my desk, it is likely that no one in the 20th century had quite envisioned the ability of patients to develop such a powerful forum for healthcare information. As a result, the medical world still lags behind in legitimizing the new technology and its uses. E-patients and the information they create and share with one another need to be recognized as a valuable new type of renewable resource—managing much of their own care, providing care for others, helping professionals improve the quality of their services, and participating in collaborations between patients and professionals. Only when we have recognized the enormous ramifications of the e-patient's shift in roles can we begin responding as creatively to this e-revolution as patients have themselves.

ENDNOTES

a. Particular thanks go to Tom's friends and colleagues, Joe and Terry Graedon, who reviewed this chapter before it went to press; thanks also to members of the e-patient scholars' working group (Susannah Fox, Gilles Frydman, Terry and Joe Graedon, Alan Greene, Cheryl Greene, Dan Hoch, John Lester, Charlie Smith and Connie Smith), who generously allowed me to quiz them during a meeting held in Durham in summer 2006.

b. For an overview of the rise of the "knowledge worker" in western society, see Peter F. Drucker, "Knowledge Work and Knowledge Society: The Social Transformations of this Century," the 1994 Edwin L. Godkin Lecture, presented May 4, 1994, John F. Kennedy School of Government, Harvard University.

c. Names and identifying characteristics have been changed to protect the privacy of those involved.

d. Names have been changed to protect patient and caregiver identities.

REFERENCES

Berwick, D. M. (2002). *Escape fire: Lessons for the future of health care.* New York: The Commonwealth Fund.

Cain, M. M., Sarasohn-Kahn, J., & Wayne, J. C. (2000). *Health e-people: The online consumer experience: Five-year forecast.* Institute for the future. California HealthCare foundation. Retrieved September 20, 2006, from http://www.chcf.org/documents/ihealth/HealthEPeople.pdf.

Eysenbach, G. (2003). The impact of the Internet on cancer outcomes. *CA: A Cancer Journal for Clinicians, 53*(6), 356–371.

Ferguson, T. (1999). *Original research: E-patients prefer eGroups to doctors for 10 of 12 aspects of health care. The Ferguson Report,* Number 1, March 1999. Retrieved September 22, 2006, from http://www.fergusonreport.com/articles/fr039905.htm.

Ferguson, T. (2002). *"Expert driver" interview: Medical knowledge as a social process: An interview with John Lester. The Ferguson Report,* Number 9, September 2002. Retrieved October 29, 2006, from http://www.fergusonreport.com/articles/fr039905.htm.

Ferguson, T. (2006). *Preface.* Unpublished manuscript.

Ferguson, T., & Frydman, G. (2004). The first generation of e-patients. *British Medical Journal, 328,* 1148–1149.

Fox, S. (2004). *Today's E-patients: Hunters and gatherers of health information online.* Information therapy conference, Park City, Utah, September 27, 2004. Retrieved October 29, 2006, from http://www.pewinternet.org/ppt/Fox_Ix_Speech_Sept04.pdf#search='hunters%20and%20gatherers%20of%20health%20information%20online.

Fox, S. (2005). *Health information online: Eight in ten users have looked for health information online, with increased interest in diet, fitness, drugs, health insurance, experimental treatments, and particular doctors and hospitals.* Pew Internet & American Life Project. Retrieved September 20, 2006, from http://www.pewinternet.org/pdfs/PIP_Healthtopics_May05.pdf.

Fox, S., & Fallows, D. (2003). *Internet health resources: Health searches and email have become more commonplace, but there is room for improvement in searches and overall Internet access.* Pew Internet & American Life Project. Retrieved September 20, 2006, from http://www.pewinternet.org/pdfs/PIP_Health_Report_July_2003.pdf.

Fox, S., & Rainie, L. (2000). *The online health care revolution: How the web helps Americans take better care of themselves.* Pew Internet & American Life Project. Retrieved September 20, 2006, from http://www.pewinternet.org/pdfs/PIP_Health_Report.pdf.

Fox, S., & Rainie, L. (2002). *Vital decisions: How Internet users decide what information to trust when they or their loved ones are sick.* Pew Internet & American Life Project. Retrieved September 20, 2006, from http://www.pewinternet.org/pdfs/PIP_Vital_Decisions_May2002.pdf.

Granovetter, M. (1972). The strength of weak ties. *American Journal of Sociology, 78,* 1360–1380.

HarrisInteractive. (2006). *Over three-quarters of all U.S. adults—an estimated 172 million—now go online. The Harris Poll. #41.* Retrieved October 23, 2006, from http://www.harrisinteractive.com/harris_poll/index.asp?PID=668.

HarrisInteractive Health Care News. (2002). *Cyberchondriacs continue to grow in America.* 2(9). Retrieved October 23, 2006, from http://www.harrisinteractive.com/news/newsletters/healthnews/HI_HealthCareNews2002Vol2_Iss09.pdf.

Haythornthwaite, C. (2003). *A social network theory of tie strength and media use: A framework for evaluating multi-level impacts of new media (technical report).* Champaign: University of Illinois, Graduate School of Library and Information Science. Retrieved September 20, 2006, from http://classweb.lis.uiuc.edu/~haythorn/Publications/Reports/Hay_TechReport_sna_theory.html.

Heaney, C. A., & Israel, B. A. (2002). Social networks and support. In K. Glanz, B. Rimer, & F. M. Lewis (Eds.), *Health behavior and health education* (3rd ed., pp. 185–209). San Francisco: Jossey Bass.

Horrigan, J. B., & Rainie, L. (2002). *Getting serious online: As Americans gain experience, they use the web more at work, write emails with more significant content, perform more online transactions, and pursue more activities online.* Retrieved September 20, 2006, from http://www.pewinternet.org/pdfs/PIP_Getting_Serious_Online3ng.pdf.

Horrigan, J. B., Rainie, L., & Fox, S. (2001). *Online communities: Networks that nurture long-distance relationships and local ties.* Pew Internet & American Life Project. Retrieved October 29, 2006, from http://www.pewinternet.org/pdfs/PIP_Communities_Report.pdf.

Kuhn, T. S. (1964). *The structure of scientific revolutions.* Chicago: University of Chicago Press.

Kuhn, T. S. (2000). *The road since structure.* Chicago: University of Chicago Press.

Kutner, M., Greenberg, E., & Baer, J. (2005). *A first look at the literacy of America's adults in the 21st century.* U.S. Department of Education. NCES 2006-470. Retrieved October 29, 2006, from http://nces.ed.gov/pubsearch/pubsinfo.asp?pubid=2006470.

Levin, L. S., & Idler, E. L. (1981). *The hidden health care system: Mediating structures and medicine.* Cambridge, MA: Ballinger.

Madden, M., & Fox, S. (2006). *Finding answers online in sickness and in health.* Pew Internet & American Life Project. Retrieved September 20, 2006, from http://www.pewinternet.org/pdfs/PIP_Health_Decisions_2006.pdf.

Murray, E., Lo, B, Pollack, L, Donelan, K, Catania, J, White, M, et al. (2003a). The impact of health information on the Internet on health care and the physician–patient relationship: National U.S. survey among 1,050 U.S. physicians. *Journal of Medical Internet Research, 5(3), e17.* Retrieved March 20, 2004, from http://www.jmir.org/2003/3/e17/.

Murray, E., Lo, B., Pollack, L., Donelan, K., Catania, J., & White, M., et al. (2003b). The impact of health information on the Internet on the physician-patient relationship: Patient perceptions. *Archives of Internal Medicine, 163*(14), 1727–1731.

Open Door: Ideas and Voices from MIT. (2003). *Interview with Professor Sherry Turkle.* Retrieved October 23, 2006, from http://alumweb.mit.edu/opendoor/200307/turkle.shtml.

Pew Internet & American Life Project. (2001). *Healthcare callback survey.* Unpublished data.

Pew Internet & American Life Project. (2006). *Demographics of Internet users.* Retrieved October 13, 2006, from http://www.pewinternet.org/trends/User_Demo_4.26.06.htm.

Reeves, P. A. (2001). How individuals coping with HIV/AIDS use the Internet. *Health Education Research, 16*(6), 709–719.

Sandmaier, M. (2003, June 3). Listening to zebras. *Washington Post.*

Sciamanna, C. N., Clark, M. A., Houston, T. K., & Diaz, J. A. (2002). *Unmet needs of primary care patients in using the Internet for health-related activities. Journal of Medical Internet Research, 4(3), E19.* Retrieved November 7, 2004, from http://www.jmir.org/2002/3/e19/.

Sontag, S. (1990). *Illness as a metaphor and AIDS and its metaphors.* New York: Doubleday.

Spadaro, R. (2003). *European union citizens and sources of information about health. Eurobarometer 58.0.* The European opinion research group, European Union, Brussels Belgium. Retrieved October 23, 2006, from http://ec.europa.eu/health/ph_information/documents/eb_58_en.pdf.

Taylor, H., & Leitman, R. (2002). *Four-country study finds most cyberchondriacs believe online information is trustworthy, easy to find and understand. HarrisInteractive health care news, 2(12).* Retrieved October 29, 2006, from http://www.harrisinteractive.com/news/newsletters/healthnews/HI_HealthCareNews2002Vol2_Iss12.pdf.

Von Knoop, C., Lovich, D., Silverstein, M. B., & Tutty, M. (2003). *Vital signs: E-health in the United States.* The Boston Consulting Group. Retrieved September 20, 2006, from http://www.bcg.com/publications/files/Vital_Signs_Rpt_Jan03.pdf.

Yahoo Family Groups. (2006). Retrieved January 24, 2006, from http://dir.groups.yahoo.com/dir/Family___Home/Families/Individual_Families.

Ziebland, S., Chapple, A., Dumelow, C., Evans, J., Prinjha, S., & Rozmovits, L. (2004). How the Internet affects patients' experience of cancer: A qualitative study. *British Medical Journal, 328,* 564–569.

CHAPTER 5

The Long Reach to Basic Healthcare Services: Partnering With Lay Health Advisors to Improve Health Equity

Alexis Moore and Jo Anne L. Earp

OBJECTIVES

- To review national trend data to demonstrate that receipt of timely, high-quality healthcare varies across population groups, resulting in poorer health outcomes for racial and ethnic minorities, those without insurance, and people with disabilities
- To understand how sociocultural and economic factors influence healthcare access and healthcare quality at the individual and population levels
- To learn how one strategy, lay health advising, can increase and improve healthcare delivery in population groups with high rates of morbidity and disease mortality
- To describe social science theories and research evidence that substantiate lay health advising as an effective strategy for increasing individual access to patient-centered care and healthcare equity across population groups
- To compare and contrast lay health advising to other clinical and allied health roles
- To describe some of the key elements of effective community-based and clinic-based lay health advisor programs

No matter how full the river, it still wants to grow.

Congolese proverb

Data from national samples and recent reports on quality of care and access to care suggest that the health of average Americans, although not the best in the world, is good by most measures (Mathers, Sadana, Salomon, Murray, & Lopez, 2001). Life spans continue to lengthen. Survival rates for those living with cancer are increasing (Edwards et al., 2005). Recovery rates from acute cardiovascular events such as stroke are higher than in other countries (Gray et al., 2006), and childhood immunization rates are at record high levels (Barker, Santoli, & McCauley, 2004). Concealed within national trend data, however, is evidence of inequities in health and healthcare that are hard to tolerate.

The National Healthcare Disparities Report, launched in 2003 and published annually by the Agency for Healthcare Research and Quality (AHRQ), drives home the urgency of the inequities issue by highlighting the most serious gaps in healthcare access and quality. The aim of the AHRQ report is to instigate policy and practice improvements where the needs are most acute. The report's measures of healthcare access include insurance status, utilization of preventive and primary care and emergency departments, "potentially avoidable" hospital admission rates, and patient perceptions of accessibility. Healthcare quality is assessed along dimensions of effectiveness, patient safety, timeliness, and patient centeredness. According to the report, for almost every measure of healthcare access and healthcare quality, disparities persist along racial, ethnic, and socioeconomic lines. Although progress has been made in closing many of the gaps, some types of disparities, particularly those affecting Hispanics, are expanding (AHRQ, 2005) (see Table 5.1).

The extent of these disparities between whites and other racial and ethnic groups—across virtually all diseases and conditions—exposes America's failure to deliver basic health services humanely and fairly. Because income and wealth are among the most important predictors of health, it is not surprising that in the United States, where race and poverty are intertwined, the health of minorities relative to whites is generally worse; however, even when researchers take into account and adjust for socioeconomic factors, health disparities between whites and other population groups do not altogether disappear (Institute of Medicine, 2002). This fact suggests that, in addition to socioeconomic status, other factors

Table 5.1   Health Inequities Across Several Divides:
A Few Cases in Point

- Overall, the healthcare utilization gap between Hispanics and whites is widening, not narrowing (AHRQ, 2005).

- For blacks, virtually all health indices are worse than for whites. Life expectancy for blacks is lower at birth and at every age (Hoyert, Heron, Murphy, & Kung, 2006).

- Mexican American women are more than twice as likely as non-Hispanic white women to delay prenatal care until the third trimester or to forgo it completely (Office of Minority Health, 2006).

- For black women, breast cancer death rates are higher than they are for whites, although death rates for both groups are dropping (Smigal et al., 2006).

- The rate of cervical cancer, a largely preventable disease, is five times more common in Vietnamese American women compared with non-Hispanic white women (National Cancer Institute, 1996).

- American Indians experience a high prevalence of type II diabetes compared with other U.S. populations. Among Pima Indians of Arizona aged 30 to 64 years, diabetes prevalence is 50% compared with 7% in the general population (Office of Minority Health, 2005).

- Although health statistics derived from Asian American samples generally deliver positive news, in fact, the incidence rate for liver cancer is 41.8/100,000 for Vietnamese men compared with only 3.3/100,000 for non-Hispanic white males. The high prevalence of liver cancer in Vietnamese and other Asian American communities is due mostly to low rates of vaccination for Hepatitis B (Chen, 2005).

- Colorectal cancer incidence increased 11% for blacks between 1975 and 2000 while decreasing 2% for whites. Blacks are also more likely to die from colorectal cancer (Ries et al., 2006).

- Oral health is essential to general health. Almost 20% of surveyed adults with disabilities reported not having had a dental visit in the past 5 years compared with 9.4% of adults without disabilities (Havercamp, Roth, Scandlin, Herrick, & Gizlice, 2004).

associated with race, ethnicity, and culture also interact with behaviors related to health outcomes.

Ethnic minority groups represented 25% of Americans in 2004 and will comprise nearly half the U.S. population by 2050 (U.S. Census Bureau, 2004). In an increasingly multicultural society in which so many are underinsured and uninsured (see Chapter 2), examining health trends within and across population groups allows for more effective planning and placement of patient advocacy efforts. Patient advocates generally believe that, regardless of individual financial resources or cultural background, each of us is equally entitled to receive respect, trust, compassion, and clear communication from our healthcare providers. Yet patient advocacy efforts that remain tightly focused on providing services and support primarily to individual patients as they enter the healthcare system for treatment of acute disease are exclusionary by design. To achieve greater equity, the public health establishment and patient advocate groups must also expand the scope of their efforts to reach and include individuals from communities estranged from medical systems (see Chapter 18). Otherwise, patient advocacy efforts risk contributing to the problem of health disparities even as they work to improve quality of care for individual patients whose attendance at hospital clinics and physicians' offices may signal that they already confront fewer obstacles to initiating healthcare visits and adhering to beneficial treatment plans.

To ensure the timely delivery of healthcare responsive to diverse patient preferences and needs, today's patient advocates have critical roles to play in two spheres. The first is improving outreach to people who cannot find their way into health services because these "systems" are inaccessible— culturally, financially, and/or physically. The second is elevating the importance of ensuring patient-centered, culturally sensitive healthcare for those most in need: ethnic and cultural minorities, people with disabilities, and the underinsured and uninsured.

HISTORIES OF EXCLUSION BASED ON RACE, RURALITY, DISABILITY, INCOME, AND CULTURE

For much of the 20th century, blacks in the United States were routinely denied access to medical facilities. The federal government ended racial segregation on the floors of its Veterans' Administration hospitals starting in 1948, setting a precedent for equal access to government-provided healthcare. Unfortunately, few other types of medical institutions followed the VA's lead. The passage of the 1964 Civil Rights Act, which prohibited payment of federal funds (including Medicare payments) to institutions that maintained segregated facilities and staff, finally expanded healthcare access for blacks. Threatened with losing potential revenue, most segregated hospitals quickly moved to comply with the mandate to provide equal access to healthcare regardless of race. The unanticipated fallout from hospital desegregation toward the end of the sixties, however, was that many historically black hospitals closed, resulting in interrupted healthcare services for some blacks (Institute of Medicine, 2002). The extent to which healthcare facilities, especially those providing primary care, still remain racially divided on the basis of *de facto* residential segregation continues to be a problem (Smith, 2005).

Health disparities are often attributed to the problem of uneven access to medical facilities and providers. In rural communities, for example, shortages of primary care providers (Eberhardt, Ingram, & Makuc, 2001), greater distances from medical facilities, and a lack of public transportation are frequently noted geographic barriers to the receipt of healthcare (Arcury, Preisser, Gesler, & Powers, 2005; Chan, Hart, & Goodman, 2006; Schroen, Brenin, Kelly, Knaus, & Slingluff, 2005). Physically inaccessible facilities and services also limit healthcare use for people with disabilities in rural and urban settings alike. Nearly 20% of all Americans report a disability, and the rate is higher yet, 25%, among blacks and Native Americans. As the U.S. population ages, disability rates are expected to continue climbing (U.S. Census Bureau, 2000a). The Americans with Disabilities Act passed in 1990 has been fundamental in bringing about more equitable access to healthcare for people with physical, sensory, or cognitive disabilities. Title III of the act ensures access to all types of public facilities and businesses, including healthcare institutions. As a result, many health facilities have modified their policies and building design, for example, by allowing guide animals to accompany the visually impaired or constructing wheelchair ramps at their entryways. Nevertheless, because compliance with Title III is not systematically monitored or enforced, people with disabilities are still less likely to receive primary care than the U.S. population as a whole (Iezzoni, McCarthy, Davis, & Siebens, 2000; Krahn, Hammond, & Turner, 2006; Mele, Archer, & Pusch, 2005). Architectural design accounts only partly for the inaccessibility of healthcare for people with disabilities. Prevailing barriers to primary and preventive care also stem from lack of knowledge on the part of providers about how to modify procedures for patients with specific disabilities and perceived lack of time to accommodate their special needs (Grabois, Nosek, & Rossi, 1999). In an era when most of us believe that overt discrimination in the delivery of goods and services has become rare or virtually nonexistent, people with disabilities continue to report being denied access to care and encountering healthcare providers who are reluctant to serve them (Smeltzer, 2006).

More than physical or geographic barriers, today, the leading determinants of who receives quality healthcare in the United States are personal wealth and health insurance status. For a country that spends a larger percentage of its gross national product on healthcare than any other, the United States has the ironic distinction among developed nations of having a large percentage of uninsured citizens—about 16% of Americans younger than 65 years old, totaling approximately 46 million people overall (Reinhardt, Hussey, & Anderson, 2004). In fact, the lack of health insurance is the leading barrier to healthcare access in the United States for all ethnic groups except Asians and whites (AHRQ, 2005). For underinsured and uninsured people, a disproportionate number of them minorities, the pursuit of healthcare is often cut short when the medical practice receptionist or hospital intake nurse requests an insurance card (see Textbox 5.1).

Textbox 5.1   Poverty Causes Treatment Delays

I was talking with a friend of mine on the phone, and she said, "I can never catch you at home." So I started telling her, I was taking this class, the *Save our Sisters* (breast cancer screening) program. She did not say anything. Thus, I said, "Have you had a mammogram recently?" She said, "No. You know, I have no funds. I have no insurance or anything." I said, "Well, you just hold on. Let me call you right back." I went and called the coordinator for my lay health group and told her the problem. This friend of mine *did* have a problem! She was told she had a lump in her breast but never followed up because she couldn't afford it."

My coordinator told me to help this lady get in touch with the nurse at our rural health center. She needed more information than I could give her. It was too late to save her breast—she had to have a mastectomy. I've been in constant contact with her. We talk just about every day. She's so happy that she went and got that mammogram. I don't know where the funds are coming from, but they gave her the mastectomy.

If I hadn't asked her about mammograms, there is no telling how this would have turned out because she did not want anyone to know that she did not have insurance or to even go back to check.

I feel like I really saved her. She said the lump in her breast turned out to be about the size of a quarter.

— *Lay Health Advisor for the NC Breast Cancer Screening Program*

A growing body of evidence suggests that cultural differences also contribute directly and independently to health disparities. In studies confined to people who have access to healthcare, quality of care received appears to differ by ethnicity and culture (Institute of Medicine, 2002). The Institute of Medicine's surpassingly comprehensive report, *Unequal Treatment*, explores the extent and causes of racial and ethnic healthcare inequalities that are not associated with access or insurance status. The overarching conclusion of the IOM's literature review spanning hundreds of studies is that

> Racial and ethnic disparities in healthcare exist. These disparities are consistent and extensive across a range of medical conditions and healthcare services, are associated with worse health outcomes, and occur independently of insurance status, income, and education, among other factors that influence access to health care. These disparities are unacceptable. (Institute of Medicine, 2002)

WHEN HEALTHCARE AND CULTURE CONVERGE

Limited English Proficiency

Research shows that after controlling for health insurance and relevant economic factors, Hispanic patients who are not fluent in English have had fewer physician visits, receive less preventive care, and are more dissatisfied with their care compared with their bilingual peers (Fiscella, Franks, Doescher, & Saver, 2002). Compared with Latinos, who comprise a growing population sector, some other immigrant groups are likely to be even more linguistically isolated. For example, 96%, of the approximately 170,000 Hmong refugees resettled in the United States do not use English at home, and 64% report they are unable to communicate in English (Reeves & Bennett, 2004). Nationwide, 18% of Americans spoke a language other than English at home at the time of the 2000 census, and half of those reported that they did not speak English well (U.S. Census Bureau, 2000b). Trust and understanding between a patient and her doctor can only emerge through communication. President Clinton's signature in 2002 on Executive Order 13166, Improving Access to Services for Persons with Limited English Proficiency, sought to ensure better access

> "I think that what's really gonna happen to you is gonna happen no matter what you do. I just don't feel that you can stop it, and so if it is intended for you, if you are fat, small, skinny, or what you eat, I really do not think that has a lot to do with it. I think God has total control over all of that."
> —Eastern NC Focus Group Participant

to high-quality healthcare across linguistically diverse U.S. communities by expanding translation services where possible. Efforts to repeal the order at the grassroots levels and in the Senate, however, indicate wavering national commitment to improving services for people with limited English proficiency.

Values, Beliefs, and Practices

Language is only one of many cultural factors that can influence doctor–patient interactions and whether a person receives optimal healthcare. We are all members of multiple, overlapping, and interrelated cultural groups characterized by shared values, beliefs, and practices. Cultural identity is not static; it changes depending on our attachment to various groups defined by nationality, race or ethnicity, regional identity, hometown, education level, urban or rural residential history, household income, religious affiliations, political beliefs, club memberships and affiliations, disability (physical, sensory, and cognitive), gender identity, age, child-rearing experiences, sexual preferences, military service, career pathways, use of tobacco, alcohol or drugs, hobbies, comfort with computer technology, and the list goes on.

The complexity and variability of culture make its influence on health difficult to measure or predict. Operating through a complex web of causation, cultural factors can either inhibit or promote interpersonal understanding and collaboration. Cultural commonalities between a patient and provider can help facilitate trust and agreement about primary and secondary prevention and treatment efficacy, but too often these cultural compatibilities are missing in medical encounters. When patients and providers are more culturally disconnected from each other, medical misunderstandings are particularly likely to arise if time and communication skills are also lacking. During a brief clinic visit, a rushed healthcare provider relying too much on cultural stereotypes might unconsciously use an authoritative tone to engage a patient rather than the participatory communication style she usually employs. This communication technique might then influence whether the patient shares additional information about his case or whether he trusts the doctor's advice and recommendations. The consequences of culturally based misunderstanding can manifest subtly as a patient's mild resistance or gradual decline in willingness to seek preventive care or even life-saving treatment or, more overtly, a patient's unqualified rejection of a recommended treatment plan (Ashton et al., 2003). Research evidence indicates that cultural factors can and do influence our health behavior and the quality of our interactions with the healthcare system and, ultimately, contribute to health disparities.

HEALTHCARE DISPARITIES: A ROLE FOR PATIENT ADVOCATES?

Inequalities in healthcare access and utilization have important implications for patient advocacy. The right to receive patient-centered healthcare should not be accorded on the basis of an individual's cultural or socioeconomic characteristics. Opportunities to deliver meaningful patient-centered healthcare already have been lost when social conditions compel some Americans to delay healthcare, possibly foregoing essential treatment. Using the example of breast cancer, this chapter explores gaps in disease incidence, severity, and mortality that could be dramatically reduced or possibly even eliminated if more patient advocates were aware of and able to concentrate on the problem of barriers to healthcare access, including cultural bias. What follows are four key questions that help illuminate the impact of cultural bias on health seeking behavior.

1. **How often do poor patient–provider communication and a lack of cross-cultural awareness prevent patients from making**

"I don't like people feeling over me. That made me jumpy when I took my mammogram, and (the mammographer) was laughing because I was jumpy. I couldn't stand it."

—Eastern NC Focus Group Participant

informed choices about preventive care? Screening mammography, which has been associated with decreased mortality and earlier stages of breast cancer diagnosis, is recommended every 1 to 2 years for women 40 years old and older (National Cancer Institute, 2002). Although the value of routine screening for breast cancer is widely acknowledged to improve chances of earlier detection and is increasingly viewed as expanding a woman's opportunities to receive more effective and less invasive treatments, cultural misunderstandings may still cause some patients to feel confused or even alarmed by a doctor's recommendation for routine mammography. Some Vietnamese and Latina women, for example, may associate mammography screening with disreputable personality traits such as a lack of modesty or a tendency to "go looking for trouble" when no problems are suspected (Bird, Otero-Sabogal, Ha, & McPhee, 1996).

2. **Are patients sometimes deterred from returning for follow-up visits, counseling, or treatment because of a healthcare provider's lack of personal or cultural sensitivity?** Repeat screening mammograms every 1 to 2 years, not one-time use, is necessary for earlier disease detection. Despite a significant national increase in mammography use, long-term adherence to screening is still low across certain population groups and, in particular, for African American women (Rauscher, Hawley, & Earp, 2005; Smith-Bindman et al., 2006; Song & Fletcher, 1998). In general, patients who have had a negative experience with a healthcare provider are more likely to avoid follow-up and future treatments (Moore et al., 2004). Although prejudicial treatment is likely to be unconscious rather than intentional, African American focus group participants reported a preference for black doctors specifically because of prior negative experiences with providers who were not black (Malat & van Ryn, 2005). In the case of mammography, women who are extremely anxious about the procedure are half as likely as those with little or no anxiety to participate in repeat mammography screening (Lerman et al., 1993). Mammographers who show interest in their patients, provide them with emotional support and guidance, and encourage them to ask questions during the procedure are less likely to generate complaints of pain than those who fail to develop rapport with their patients (Keefe, Hauck, Egert, Rimer, & Kornguth, 1994). Technologists who administer mammograms can play an important role in shaping women's attitudes about future mammography (Moyer, Lennartz, Moore, & Earp, 2001).

3. **How often do healthcare services disregard or turn away from the needs of individuals or population groups outside the mainstream?** Primary care practices and mammography centers should be equipped to serve all patients including, according to the Americans with Disabilities Act, those with mobility, cognitive, or sensory impairments. Of 62 primary care practitioners who volunteered to complete a national survey on accessibility, 18% said they had turned away at least one patient in the previous 12 months because their facility was not fully compliant with the Americans with Disabilities Act. A lack of suitable equipment or adequate personnel made it necessary for 19% of providers to examine patients in their wheelchairs, resulting in less comprehensive care than is typically offered to non-disabled patients (Grabois et al., 1999).

   A lack of preparation to deliver healthcare to people with disabilities extends to other populations and other types of patient support services. Black breast cancer survivors in eastern North Carolina found that posttreatment support services were lacking (Lopez, Eng, Randall-David, & Robinson, 2005). Resourceful survivors, as described later in this chapter, sometimes develop new programs and services, but these programs and services are often supported and housed outside the existing healthcare system or national support group networks such as those offered by the American Cancer Society.

4. **From prenatal care to end-of-life, are support and allied health programs compatible with the cultural and physical needs and preferences of all populations?** Despite their lower incidence of breast cancer, black women are more likely than white women to die from the disease (Smigal et al., 2006). At the end of life, blacks, compared with whites, are less likely to enroll in hospice services or receive palliative care (Anderson et al., 2002; Kapo, MacMoran, & Casarett, 2005) (see Chapter 17). Individual patient preferences or cultural norms, not culturally biased treatment or access barriers, may partly explain disproportionate use of pain management, palliative care, and hospice across ethnic groups and between men and women (Duffy, Jackson, Schim, Ronis, & Fowler, 2006). On the other hand, the Balm of Gilead program, designed to serve terminally ill black patients in Birmingham, Alabama, suggests that end-of-life care can be restructured so it is more culturally appropriate and financially and structurally accessible.

"I came up with the idea of self help groups for African American women because I had no support for my cancer. I felt so alone."

To find out about models for her self-help program, this community leader attended a local program jointly sponsored by the American Cancer Society and a regional hospital that aimed to give women undergoing cancer treatment free makeovers, styling tips for wigs and scarves, and free make-up kits.

In a county where 43% (U.S. Census Bureau, 1996 statistics) of the population is black, she found that support group programs did not have wigs or accessories suitable for African American women on hand. "What if I had been reaching out? I would have felt even more isolated . . . I would have been in a room with a beautician who had no supplies to meet my needs!"

—Testimonial from Eastern NC Cancer Survivor
and Community Activist, Bernice M.

Traditionally, hospice has been available only to those with a stable place of residence and an able-bodied caregiver in the home. In contrast, Balm of Gilead designed a program that took into account high levels of homelessness, poverty, and lack of insurance in its service area, as well as the strong social and community service networks of the surrounding black community. A 10-bed palliative care unit was established in the local hospital. Boarding houses were recruited to rent rooms to hospice patients who lacked family nearby or a permanent residence, and eventually an inpatient hospice program was established. Black churches supplied volunteers to give care and support. In contrast to commonly held perceptions that hospice and end-of-life planning are inconsistent with black cultural norms, the majority of patients were black, and the program operated with a waiting list (Kvale, Williams, Bolden, Padgett, & Bailey, 2004).

EXTENDING OUR REACH: DO WE HAVE THE TOOLS TO DO IT?

Culturally sensitive care, like patient-centered care, will require changes on multiple fronts and at various levels of our healthcare system (Betancourt, Green, Carrillo, & Ananeh-Firempong, 2003). Through a review of cultural competency healthcare disparity literature, Brach and Fraser (2000) identified nine theoretically and programmatically sound strategies already in use in some healthcare organizations to improve delivery of clinical services to ethnic and cultural minority groups (see Table 5.2). Many of the techniques are based on the premise that patient-centered care for ethnically diverse populations requires advocacy and intervention prior to hospitalization. These nine mutually reinforcing techniques target clinical training, administration, and service delivery. Used in combination, several or all of these strategies can help achieve more patient-centered care in cross-cultural medical encounters. They are entirely consistent with patient advocacy recommendations.

The rest of this chapter explores one recommended cultural competency technique, cited by Brach and Fraser, the use of community health workers. It draws primarily on the example of the North Carolina Breast Cancer Screening Program (NC-BCSP), an intervention study in effect from 1992–2002, which was aimed at increasing access to mammography screening among older black women in eastern North Carolina. Although black women are less likely than white women to be diagnosed with breast

Table 5.2   Cultural Competency Techniques to Improve Patient Care

1. Interpreter services for patients who need them
2. Recruitment and retention of minority staff that share cultural beliefs and language with prospective patient communities
3. Cultural competency trainings for administrative as well as clinical staff
4. Coordinating with traditional healers to ensure that patients receive compatible therapies from their allopathic and alternative providers
5. Use of community health workers to reach communities that have been socially, culturally, and economically isolated from receiving appropriate healthcare services
6. Emphasizing health promotion as much or more often as acute or emergency treatment
7. Including family and community members in as many aspects of care in accordance with their wishes
8. Creating opportunities for healthcare professionals and personnel to become immersed in another culture with the aim of increasing cultural sensitivity and acquisition of culturally compatible practices
9. Administrative and organizational changes, such as changing hours and reminder systems, that make care provision more user friendly

Brach and Fraser, 2000.

cancer, they face a greater likelihood of dying from the disease. Poorer survival rates among black women are partly attributed to lower rates of routine mammography use and a subsequently higher prevalence of later stage diagnoses (Smigal et al., 2006; Smith-Bindman et al., 2006). To close the breast cancer mortality gap between blacks and whites, NC-BCSP relied on trained lay health advisors (LHAs) to promote mammography screening among black women ages 50 years and older in five rural eastern North Carolina counties. The intervention underwent rigorous evaluation from 1994 to 2000 and proved to be effective for increasing mammography use among black women (Earp et al., 2002).

COMMUNITY HEALTH WORKERS AND LHAS, IMPROVING HEALTHCARE QUALITY

Community health workers are part of a public health movement to recruit and train groups of lay individuals, usually women, to provide one-on-one information and support about pressing health needs of disadvantaged populations (Rosenthal, Wiggins, Brownstein, & Johnson, 1998). Mostly in communities of color and in low-income neighborhoods, groups of volunteer community health workers, often called LHAs as in the case of NC-BCSP, are organized to take on the problems of persistent inequalities in access to healthcare and to stimulate greater awareness and activism about health issues at the neighborhood level (Swider, 2002) (see Chapter 14). An increasing number of health centers, managed-care organizations, and specialty clinics have also begun to train community members to assist in outreach and case management. These outreach efforts indicate an openness on the part of healthcare professionals to affirm that, with training and support, "ordinary people" can relay accurate health information and strengthen ties between health agencies and medically underserved neighborhoods and communities.

Despite increasingly widespread use of LHAs in the United States since the 1950s, a universally recognized label has not yet been coined for these individuals. Brach and Fraser selected the term *community health worker* while noting that sundry terms are being used to capture the range of serv-. ices and functions provided by lay leaders who have received brief training to enhance their ability to deliver health information and mobilize people in their communities to access healthcare services appropriately (Brach &

Fraser, 2000). NC-BCSP, one of hundreds of such programs that have been documented in the United States, used the term LHA. We will employ it throughout the rest of this chapter unless a specific program being described uses a different title.

Just as LHA titles vary from one organization to the next, so do LHA roles and responsibilities. This variation is probably the necessary consequence of developing health promotion efforts in collaboration with community stakeholders. A growing body of community-based participatory action research indicates that involving the intended beneficiaries of a proposed intervention program as collaborators increases its cultural acceptability (Viswanathan et al., 2004). In contrast to one-size-fits-all approaches, these community-tailored methods help to create locally relevant services likely to be used and sustained.

Nationally, the abundance of LHA programs underscores how well this type of intervention is accepted by communities often viewed as "hard to reach." LHAs have been successfully recruited, trained, and organized to promote health among American Indian women (Burhansstipanov, Dignan, Wound, Tenney, & Vigil, 2000; Dignan et al., 1996), blacks (Earp et al., 2002; Gary et al., 2004; Sung et al., 1997; Tatum, Wilson, Dignan, Paskett, & Velez, 1997), Vietnamese immigrants (Bird et al., 1998), and Hispanic and Latino populations (Alcalay, Alvarado, Balcazar, Newman, & Huerta, 1999; Brown, Garcia, Kouzekanani, & Hanis, 2002; Corkery et al., 1997; Kim, Koniak-Griffin, Flaskerud, & Guarnero, 2004; McQuiston, Choi-Hevel, & Clawson, 2001; Meister, Warrick, de Zapien, & Wood, 1992; Navarro et al., 1998; Taylor, Serrano, Anderson, & Kendall, 2000; Watkins et al., 1994).

LHA outreach programs have maintained a particularly strong record in promoting women's health, including improving access to and utilization of prenatal care and children's health services (Bradley & Martin, 1994; Butz et al., 1994; Downing et al., 1999; Hutcheson et al., 1997; St. James, Shapiro, & Waisbren, 1999; Taylor et al., 2000; Watkins et al., 1994; Zuvekas, Nolan, Tumaylle, & Griffin, 1999). LHAs also have an extensive history in promoting cancer screening, especially for breast and cervical cancer sites (Bird et al., 1998; Brownstein, Cheal, Ackermann, Bassford, & Campos-Outcalt, 1992; Burhansstipanov et al., 2000; Campbell, MacDonald, & McKiernan, 1996; Dignan et al., 1996; Earp et al., 2002; Margolis, Lurie, McGovern, Tyrrell, & Slater, 1998; Navarro et al., 1998; Sung et al., 1997; Tatum et al., 1997). More recently, LHA programs have expanded to focus on changing lifestyle behaviors for the prevention of cancer onset or recurrence. These LHA programs include a focus on dietary changes, increasing physical activity, and promoting adoption of disease self-management skills (Swider, 2002).

In rural (Earp et al., 2002; Meister et al., 1992) as well as in urban populations (Butz et al., 1994; Gary et al., 2004; Hutcheson et al., 1997; Kim et al., 2004; Krieger, Collier, Song, & Martin, 1999; Parker, Schulz, Israel, & Hollis, 1998; Sung et al., 1997), LHAs have proven their effectiveness in promoting health and building bridges between communities and healthcare systems. Efforts to reach into every corner and neglected outpost of a region have led many LHAs, including NC-BCSPs, to rely on local religious institutions, especially churches, for disseminating health information and mobilizing individual and community action.

PROGRAM IMPLEMENTATION: THE NC-BCSP EXAMPLE

The NC-BCSP LHA network ultimately recruited and trained nearly 200 women living and volunteering in five contiguous counties. As needed, the entire network occasionally came together to gain strength and insights from the common purpose they served. Usually, however, the LHAs planned and carried out their activities in small groups that served their own close-by communities. Local nuances had a marked impact on how the programs evolved in these communities: the presence of a particular church as a popular venue for health fairs in one town; a strong program endorsement and access to office supplies and equipment from a black clinic director in another region; and, just as importantly, each LHA group's interests and wishes for its own community. These and other factors produced variations in how the program was implemented across NC-BCSP's five counties spanning 2700 square miles.

LHA and Staff Recruitment

The basis for any LHA program is the complex web of interpersonal relationships that already exist naturally in a community. These relationships link together family units, neighborhoods, churches, workplaces, schools, and clubs in a large social support network. We have all relied on our personal network of friends and family at one time or another to lead us to resources or support, especially during important life events such as the birth of a child or coping with disease or injury. Where health is concerned, research shows that people are often more likely to seek advice from family members or friends than from professionals (Ayers, 1989; Jackson & Parks, 1997). Thus, LHA networks are natural extensions of a community's existing informal infrastructure for disseminating, in a culturally sensitive manner, information, support, and advocacy services to people who may not be receiving adequate care.

The potential of these social networks can be understood in light of relevant social science theories. Social learning theory and the theory of reasoned action describe psychosocial dynamics that shape health decisions and behavior (Bandura, 1986). These theories take into account factors in a person's external environment that can influence behavior. Using mammography as an example, these factors might include receiving a recommendation from a doctor, living near a mammography facility or perhaps knowing a friend who approves of and supports screening. LHAs can use their presence in the community to help create a supportive environment for timely breast cancer screening.

The effectiveness of a LHA program for promoting health depends greatly on the personal qualities of its members. To identify and recruit the NC-BCSP LHA network, program planners relied on personal recommendations from at least one, but usually several, community members who were likely to know which of their peers had reputations for being particularly helpful. Interviews with local community leaders, healthcare providers, and other key influential people helped identify local residents to serve on advisory groups in each county. These advisory groups, in turn, selected women as LHAs who had reputations for being discrete, knowledgeable, nonjudgmental, empathetic, and particularly helpful.

Training

LHAs rely heavily on interpersonal communication, especially giving one-on-one information and support that link people to resources and alleviate fear or anxiety about pursuing a particular course of treatment or care. LHAs are trained to deliver appropriate types of social support, including emotional (trust, concern, empathy), instrumental (tangible help such as transportation services and access to cost reductions), informational (advice, instruction, suggestion), and appraisal (affirmation, feedback) support (Earp & Flax, 1999). By offering empathy and hands-on technical support as well as information, LHAs encourage women to take action to protect their health.

NC-BCSP LHAs were required to complete 10 to 12 hours of training focused on providing all four types of social support to older black women specifically with the goal of increasing breast cancer screening rates in this group. Training requirements for LHAs can be less or more extensive (up to 120 hours), depending on the complexity of the health messages being disseminated and the level of outreach, leadership, and administrative responsibility (Rosenthal et al., 1998). NC-BCSP scheduled training according to the needs and preferences of the participating LHAs.

Completion of LHA training, whether 10 hours or 120 hours, calls for a graduation ceremony to publicly acknowledge participants' readiness to assume the new role of linking their personal communities and informal social groups to formal institutions and organizations delivering health and social services to within their communities. NC-BCSP invited friends and families of LHAs and agency leaders to attend a celebration with each graduating class. Announcements and graduation photos of the LHAs were published in local newspapers. The ceremony acknowledged the prestige associated with this new role, extending beyond the respect the women had already earned within their communities.

Compensation

NC-BCSP LHAs comprised a volunteer network. They did not receive pay for their services. NC-BCSP program planners deliberately designed a program that made the most of LHAs' day-to-day routines and habits and did not require a large time commitment from them. Essentially, LHAs were asked to share information and give support, one on one, at all the places they usually frequented—church, the grocery store line, the hair salon, and family reunions. They were asked to introduce the topic of breast cancer and mammography screening into discussions whenever and wherever it felt comfortable and likely to be of benefit to someone they knew. Some LHAs expanded their role greatly by driving women to appointments, providing food for LHA meetings, and engaging in community organizing. Whether paid or volunteer, it is important to develop systems that ensure LHAs are reimbursed promptly and appropriately for any expenses they incur as a result of carrying out activities to help the intervention reach its goals (Schulz, Israel, Becker, & Hollis, 1997). NC-BCSP created a petty cash account to facilitate prompt reimbursement by cash or check.

Coordination and Community Involvement

One aim of LHA programs is to increase bidirectional communication between community members and health system administrators and providers. Ideally, the LHA network can become a zone where the formal healthcare organizational structure and the community merge. In the case of NC-BCSP, a salaried community outreach specialist based in a health department or community health center coordinated LHAs in each county. In addition to supporting the LHAs, the outreach specialists built collaboration among diverse individuals and groups, bridging the institutional and community spheres. They needed culturally appropriate skills and knowledge to move easily from clinical and office settings to all types of community venues. They were responsible for ensuring that accurate health information was relayed from service providers and researchers to community members. Just as importantly, they served as a direct communication line for LHAs into the health system.

Being situated within the organizational structure of a healthcare system can ensure financial stability, access to equipment, and administrative support. It comes, however, with the risk that corporate culture will undermine the egalitarian peer networks that make community-based LHA programs effective. The National Community Health Advisor Study noted that health advisors sometimes have difficulty being accepted as colleagues within the agencies where they work because of their more casual dress, flexible schedules, familiarity with clients, and focus on community-based health promotion rather than clinical care (Rosenthal et al., 1998). NC-BCSP outreach specialists based in some agencies reported similar experiences.

Involving LHAs and program coordinators in key decision-making and executive teams within the health organization increases the likelihood of producing measurable improvements in healthcare accessibility and user friendliness. LHA programs cannot succeed in agencies that strongly emphasize the divide between professionals and "clients." The goal is to involve community members more in the design and implementation of medical and social services, thereby ensuring that better health for everyone is actually achieved.

Roles of LHAs

The National Community Health Advisor Study defined seven major roles currently and routinely provided by lay or community health advisors (Rosenthal et al., 1998). Each of the roles identified by the national study is listed in Textbox 5.2 and annotated with examples from the North Carolina Breast Cancer Screening Program.

NC-BCSP LHAs became competent in these seven roles through a combination of personal characteristics and training.

Textbox 5.2   Lay Health Advisor Roles

Cultural mediation between communities and health and human services systems. LHAs sometimes provide bilingual translation, but more often they are needed to render biomedical information into lay or colloquial terms. Timely follow-up of an abnormal mammogram can depend on how well a woman understands the meaning of terms such as diagnostic mammogram, 3-month follow-up, digital screening, or biopsy.

Culturally appropriate health education. To raise awareness about the effectiveness of mammography relative to other screening options, NC-BCSP LHAs wore specially designed beaded necklaces. Each polished wooden bead on the necklace indicated the size of a lump detectable during a self-breast exam, clinical breast exam, or mammogram. The smallest bead represented a lump that could only be found with annual mammography screening. Women said being able to touch the different beads made it easier for them to appreciate the importance of mammography (see Figure 5.1).

Providing direct services to individuals. NC-BCSP lay health advisors' one-on-one advising did not end with giving information and emotional support. They also helped women schedule mammography appointments, arranged transportation, and accompanied them to their radiology appointments.

Providing informal counseling and support. Although many NC-BCSP LHAs made formal group presentations about the value of mammography

(continued)

Textbox 5.2   Lay Health Advisor Roles

screening, most of their volunteer hours were dedicated to providing individual, confidential counseling and support to women they knew. Their conversations focused on who should get a mammogram, where to get a mammogram, and how to pay for it. They also responded to women's fears about having a mammogram.

Advocating for individual and community needs. When NC-BCSP LHAs became aware of a woman's confusion about her doctor's advice, they encouraged her to go back for more information and to ask as many questions as needed to understand her health status and options. They also negotiated with local agencies to obtain transportation vouchers to assist other women in obtaining treatment for diagnosed breast cancer.

Providing clinical services and basic needs. For women with meager incomes, mammography screening was a low priority compared with keeping the lights on in their homes. NC-BCSP LHAs often helped women obtain food, transportation assistance, and emergency funds. Two NC-BCSP paid staff also spent several hours weekly in local health clinics conducting eligibility screenings for women to help them get free or low-cost mammograms.

Building individual and community capacity. After visiting various cancer survivor support groups, one LHA, a breast cancer survivor in the NC-BCSP network, proposed funding efforts to improve support services for rural African American survivors. With NC-BCSP backing, she convened breast cancer survivors and local agency representatives for a brainstorming session. Their plans resulted in Make Today Count (MTC), a self-help group program that met monthly for nearly 6 years and served more than 200 African American breast cancer survivors. MTC advocated for local prosthetic fitters to stock supplies designed for African Americans and collaborated with the American Cancer Society to train black cosmetologists for its "Look Good . . . Feel Better" program designed to help patients adapt to hair loss and other dermatological changes resulting from treatment. Several members of Make Today Count later used photography and journals to document and study their own survivorship experiences, an effort that culminated in the publication of a peer-reviewed article.

Rosenthal et al., 1998.

DISTINGUISHING LHAS FROM OTHER TYPES OF HEALTHCARE PROFESSIONALS

Looking at LHA programs as they have manifested nationally, LHAs generally have been employed to provide outreach, education, and social

Figure 5.1   NC-BCSP LHA Breast Cancer Education Necklace

Source: Photo courtesy of NC Breast Cancer Screening Program, Lineberger Comprehensive Cancer Center, University of North Carolina at Chapel Hill.

support to promote healthy habits in community settings. In U.S. programs, LHAs are more intensely involved in primary prevention, helping people initiate and maintain healthy habits and access health services, and usually less involved in activities related to diagnosis and treatment (see Figure 5.2). In some clinic-based programs, paid or volunteer LHAs have also been recruited to directly assist patients after treatment by delivering health information and peer support for managing chronic conditions such as asthma (Butz et al., 1994; Parker et al., 1998), diabetes (Brown et al., 2002; Corkery et al., 1997; Gary et al., 2004; Wilson & Pratt, 1987), or high blood pressure (Bone et al., 1989; Kim et al., 2004; Krieger et al., 1999; Levine et al., 2003). Considering healthcare as a sequence of services and interactions that begins with primary prevention and, when there is acute illness, extends to diagnosis, treatment, disease management, and secondary prevention, LHAs have traditionally been engaged to give support at each end of the spectrum rather than in the center.

Medical facilities, however, recognizing the potential contributions of LHAs, also sometimes rely on them to help reduce cultural barriers within clinical settings or as members of the medical team (Love et al., 2004). One program evaluated the effectiveness of matching recently discharged cardiac patients with a trained peer further along in recovery from the same or a similar treatment (Riegel & Carlson, 2004). Another clinic-based program assigned lay home visitors to families of children diagnosed with failure to thrive to provide support on parenting and child

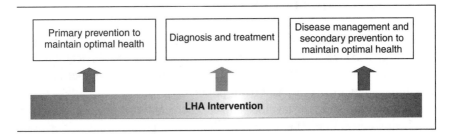

Figure 5.2   Intensity of LHA Activity Across the Healthcare Continuum

development issues and ensure that parents were receiving services they qualified for (Hutcheson et al., 1997).

Some have questioned whether a clinical role is consistent with the LHA tradition. Working or volunteering in clinical settings requires reaching out to people outside one's own social networks. In this regard, and especially if the hospital or the community is large, clinic-based LHAs are a variant of the naturally occurring community network advisors described previously in this chapter. Clinic-based LHAs differ from other medical and allied health providers, however, in that they deliver peer, rather than professional, support. Eng describes the various types of LHA programs and individual LHA styles as residing "along a continuum of informal to formal helping" (Eng, Parker, & Harlan, 1997). At one end of the continuum are paid outreach workers sponsored by a specific agency for the purpose of improving delivery of particular services. Anchoring the other end of the continuum are unpaid "natural helpers" who provide informal advice to those in their own social networks; however, LHAs often engage in a combination of natural helping and formal advising.

One type of community health advising is not necessarily better than another; the needs and objectives of an agency or program and the community it serves must necessarily determine the program design. In virtually every case, however, the role of LHAs is to inform people about healthcare opportunities and to lead and support them in developing safe, trusting relationships with local medical providers. Local needs and interests will determine the most suitable program components for making healthcare services more accessible and user friendly at every stage of wellness or of diagnosing, treating, and managing disease.

LOOKING TO THE FUTURE

The scope and magnitude of health disparities in the United States have raised urgent concern from the Institute of Medicine, the AHRQ, and all who are concerned about medical outcomes, both as they impact individuals and as they affect the American population.

If patient advocates develop and implement strategies mainly for healthcare consumers (i.e., those with buying power), disparities will grow. Patient advocacy risks becoming a service predominantly reserved for the insured and more affluent (see Chapter 19) insofar as advances in healthcare practices and technology can often exacerbate inequities. They are likely to be too expensive for potential consumers, or they are not designed and used in ways that take into account cultural differences (Starfield, 2004). As health system administrators and policy makers have come to recognize, the delivery of patient-centered care requires greater focus on creating programs that bring down financial, cultural, and structural barriers to healthcare access and delivery.

In considering potential criteria for identifying and selecting such programs, it is helpful to return to the four questions presented earlier in the chapter about perceived barriers to care. Is it a program that holds promise to do the following?

- Improve cross-cultural awareness so that more patients, including recent immigrants, can make more informed choices about preventive care and treatment?
- Increase patients' access to clinical and service providers who are culturally sensitive, thereby increasing their willingness to return for follow-up visits and additional support?
- Expand or enhance the cultural suitability of healthcare and patient support services for a wider base of American consumers?
- Provide an essential patient service that is currently not available to some populations?

In response to these questions, lay health advising is an example of one strategy that can enable patient advocates to play a larger role in promoting health equity while simultaneously continuing to improve healthcare quality for individual patients.

Over many years, patient advocates, a diverse community of lay and professionally trained experts on the needs of patients, have created a dynamic collage of recommendations, techniques, technologies, and opportunities. Yet there is no overarching plan or perfect model that addresses all the complexities of patient care or inequities in how patients are served. A key strength of an expansive, amorphous patient advocacy network is that its boundaries and mission can be expanded when necessary to incorporate innovations such as lay health advising. By helping health and advocacy organizations build stronger alliances with individuals and communities that are currently disenfranchised from the healthcare system, LHAs can help communities play a larger role in patient advocacy, and patients play a larger role in their own treatment.

REFERENCES

Agency for Healthcare Research and Quality. (2005). *National healthcare disparities report.* No. 06-0017. Rockville, MD.

Alcalay, R., Alvarado, M., Balcazar, H., Newman, E., & Huerta, E. (1999). Salud para su corazon: A community-based Latino cardiovascular disease prevention and outreach model. *Journal of Community Health, 24*(5), 359–379.

Anderson, K. O., Richman, S. P., Hurley, J., Palos, G., Valero, V., & Mendoza, T. R., et al. (2002). Cancer pain management among underserved minority outpatients: Perceived needs and barriers to optimal control. *Cancer, 94*(8), 2295–2304.

Arcury, T. A., Preisser, J. S., Gesler, W. M., & Powers, J. M. (2005). Access to transportation and health care utilization in a rural region. *Journal of Rural Health, 21*(1), 31–38.

Ashton, C. M., Haidet, P., Paterniti, D. A., Collins, T. C., Gordon, H. S., & O'Malley, K., et al. (2003). Racial and ethnic disparities in the use of health services: Bias, preferences, or poor communication? *Journal of General Internal Medicine, 18*(2), 146–152.

Ayers, T. D. (1989). Dimensions and characteristics of lay helping. *American Journal of Orthopsychiatry, 59*(2), 215–225.

Bandura, A. (1986). *Social foundations of thought and action.* Englewood Cliffs, NJ: Prentice Hall.

Barker, L., Santoli, J., & McCauley, M. (2004). National, state, and urban area vaccination coverage levels among children aged 19–35 months: United States, 2003. *MMWR Morbidity and Mortality Weekly Report, 53*(29), 658–661.

Betancourt, J. R., Green, A. R., Carrillo, J. E., & Ananeh-Firempong, O. (2003). Defining cultural competence: A practical framework for addressing racial/ethnic disparities in health and health care. *Public Health Reports, 118*(4), 293–302.

Bird, J., Otero-Sabogal, R., Ha, N., & McPhee, S. (1996). Tailoring lay health worker interventions for diverse cultures: Lessons learned from Vietnamese and Latina communities. *Health Education Quarterly, 23*(Suppl), S105–S122.

Bird, J. A., McPhee, S. J., Ha, N. T., Le, B., Davis, T., & Jenkins, C. N. (1998). Opening pathways to cancer screening for Vietnamese-American women: Lay health workers hold a key. *Preventive Medicine, 27*(6), 821–829.

Bone, L. R., Mamon, J., Levine, D. M., Walrath, J. M., Nanda, J., & Gurley, H. T., et al. (1989). Emergency department detection and follow-up of high blood pressure: Use and effectiveness of community health workers. *American Journal of Emergency Medicine, 7*(1), 16–20.

Brach, C., & Fraser, I. (2000). Can cultural competency reduce racial and ethnic health disparities? A review and conceptual model. *Medical Care Research & Review, 57*(Suppl 1), 181–217.

Bradley, P. J., & Martin, J. (1994). The impact of home visits on enrollment patterns in pregnancy-related services among low-income women. *Public Health Nursing, 11*(6), 392–398.

Brown, S. A., Garcia, A. A., Kouzekanani, K., & Hanis, C. L. (2002). Culturally competent diabetes self-management education for Mexican Americans: The Starr County border health initiative. *Diabetes Care, 25*(2), 259–268.

Brownstein, J. N., Cheal, N., Ackermann, S. P., Bassford, T. L., & Campos-Outcalt, D. (1992). Breast and cervical cancer screening in minority populations: A model for using lay health educators. *Journal of Cancer Education, 7*(4), 321–326.

Burhansstipanov, L., Dignan, M. B., Wound, D. B., Tenney, M., & Vigil, G. (2000). Native American recruitment into breast cancer screening: The NAWWA project. *Journal of Cancer Education, 15*(1), 28–32.

Butz, A. M., Malveaux, F. J., Eggleston, P., Thompson, L., Schneider, S., & Weeks, K., et al. (1994). Use of community health workers with inner-city children who have asthma. *Clinical Pediatrics, 33*(3), 135–141.

Campbell, H., MacDonald, S., & McKiernan, M. (1996). Promotion of cervical screening uptake by health visitor follow-up of women who repeatedly failed to attend. *Journal of Public Health Medicine, 18*(1), 94–97.

Chan, L., Hart, L. G., & Goodman, D. C. (2006). Geographic access to health care for rural Medicare beneficiaries. *Journal of Rural Health, 22*(2), 140–146.

Chen, M. S., Jr. (2005). Cancer health disparities among Asian Americans: What we do and what we need to do. *Cancer, 104*(12 Suppl), 2895–2902.

Corkery, E., Palmer, C., Foley, M. E., Schechter, C. B., Frisher, L., & Roman, S. H. (1997). Effect of a bicultural community health worker on completion of diabetes education in a Hispanic population. *Diabetes Care, 20*(3), 254–257.

Dignan, M., Michielutte, R., Blinson, K., Wells, H. B., Case, L. D., & Sharp, P., et al. (1996). Effectiveness of health education to increase screening for cervical cancer among eastern-band Cherokee Indian women in North Carolina. *Journal of the National Cancer Institute, 88*(22), 1670–1676.

Downing, M., Knight, K. R., Vernon, K. A., Seigel, S., Ajaniku, I., & Acosta, P. S., et al. (1999). This is my story: A descriptive analysis of a peer education HIV/STD risk reduction program for women living in housing developments. *AIDS Education & Prevention, 11*(3), 243–261.

Duffy, S. A., Jackson, F. C., Schim, S. M., Ronis, D. L., & Fowler, K. E. (2006). Racial/ethnic preferences, sex preferences, and perceived discrimination related to end-of-life care. *Journal of the American Geriatrics Society, 54*(1), 150–157.

Earp, J. A., Eng, E., O'Malley, M. S., Altpeter, M., Rauscher, G., & Mayne, L., et al. (2002). Increasing use of mammography among older rural, African American women: Results from a community trial. *American Journal of Public Health, 92*(4), 646–654.

Earp, J. A., & Flax, V. L. (1999). What lay health advisors do: An evaluation of advisors' activities. *Cancer Practice, 7*(1), 16–21.

Eberhardt, M. S., Ingram, D. D., & Makuc, D. M. (2001). *Urban and rural health chartbook: United States, 2001.* Hyattsville, MD: National Center for Health Statistics.

Edwards, B. K., Brown, M. L., Wingo, P. A., Howe, H. L., Ward, E., & Ries, L. A., et al. (2005). Annual report to the nation on the status of cancer, 1975–2002, featuring population-based trends in cancer treatment. *Journal of the National Cancer Institute, 97*(19), 1407–1427.

Eng, E., Parker, E., & Harlan, C. (1997). Lay health advisor intervention strategies: A continuum from natural helping to paraprofessional helping. *Health Education and Behavior, 24*(4), 413–417.

Fiscella, K., Franks, P., Doescher, M. P., & Saver, B. G. (2002). Disparities in health care by race, ethnicity, and language among the insured: Findings from a national sample. *Medical Care, 40*(1), 52–59.

Gary, T. L., Batts-Turner, M., Bone, L. R., Yeh, H. C., Wang, N. Y., & Hill-Briggs, F., et al. (2004). A randomized controlled trial of the effects of nurse case manager and community health worker team interventions in urban African-Americans with type 2 diabetes. *Controlled Clinical Trials, 25*(1), 53–66.

Grabois, E. W., Nosek, M. A., & Rossi, C. D. (1999). Accessibility of primary care physicians' offices for people with disabilities: An analysis of compliance with the Americans with Disabilities Act. *Archives of Family Medicine, 8*(1), 44–51.

Gray, L. J., Sprigg, N., Bath, P. M., Sorensen, P., Lindenstrom, E., & Boysen, G., et al. (2006). Significant variation in mortality and functional outcome after acute ischaemic stroke between western countries: Data from the tinzaparin in acute ischaemic stroke trial (TAIST). *Journal of Neurology, Neurosurgery, and Psychiatry, 77*(3), 327–333.

Havercamp, S., Roth, M. S., Scandlin, D., Herrick, H., & Gizlice, Z. (2004). *Health and disability in North Carolina.* Chapel Hill, NC: North Carolina Office on Disability and Health, The State Center for Health Statistics.

Hoyert, D. L., Heron, M. P., Murphy, S. L., & Kung, H. C. (2006). Deaths: Final data for 2003. *National Vital Statistics Reports: From the Centers for Disease Control and Prevention, National Center for Health Statistics, National Vital Statistics System, 54*(13), 1–120.

Hutcheson, J. J., Black, M. M., Talley, M., Dubowitz, H., Howard, J. B., & Starr, R. H., Jr., et al. (1997). Risk status and home intervention among children with failure-to-thrive: Follow-up at age 4. *Journal of Pediatric Psychology, 22*(5), 651–668.

Iezzoni, L. I., McCarthy, E. P., Davis, R. B., & Siebens, H. (2000). Mobility impairments and use of screening and preventive services. *American Journal of Public Health, 90*(6), 955–961.

Institute of Medicine. (2002). In B. D. Smedley, A. Y. Stith, & A. R. Nelson (Eds.), *Unequal treatment: Confronting racial and ethnic disparities in health care.* Washington, DC: National Academy Press.

Jackson, E. J., & Parks, C. P. (1997). Recruitment and training issues from selected lay health advisor programs among African Americans: A 20-year perspective. *Health Education and Behavior, 24*(4), 418–431.

Kapo, J., MacMoran, H., & Casarett, D. (2005). "Lost to follow-up": Ethnic disparities in continuity of hospice care at the end of life. *Journal of Palliative Medicine, 8*(3), 603–608.

Keefe, F. J., Hauck, E. R., Egert, J., Rimer, B., & Kornguth, P. (1994). Mammography pain and discomfort: A cognitive-behavioral perspective. *Pain, 56*(3), 247–260.

Kim, S., Koniak-Griffin, D., Flaskerud, J. H., & Guarnero, P. A. (2004). The impact of lay health advisors on cardiovascular health promotion: Using a community-based partici- patory approach. *Journal of Cardiovascular Nursing, 19*(3), 192–199.

Krahn, G. L., Hammond, L., & Turner, A. (2006). A cascade of disparities: Health and health care access for people with intellectual disabilities. *Mental Retardation and Developmental Disabilities Research Reviews, 12*(1), 70–82.

Krieger, J., Collier, C., Song, L., & Martin, D. (1999). Linking community-based blood pres- sure measurement to clinical care: A randomized controlled trial of outreach and tracking by community health workers. *American Journal of Public Health, 89*(6), 856–861.

Kvale, E. A., Williams, B. R., Bolden, J. L., Padgett, C. G., & Bailey, F. A. (2004). The Balm of Gilead Project: A demonstration project on end-of-life care for safety-net pop- ulations. *Journal of Palliative Medicine, 7*(3), 486–493.

Lerman, C., Daly, M., Sands, C., Balshem, A., Lustbader, E., & Heggan, T., et al. (1993). Mammography adherence and psychological distress among women at risk for breast cancer. *Journal of the National Cancer Institute, 85*(13), 1074–1080.

Levine, D. M., Bone, L. R., Hill, M. N., Stallings, R., Gelber, A. C., & Barker, A., et al. (2003). Community health workers help to reduce high blood pressure. *Ethnicity & Disease, 13*(3), 403.

Lopez, E. D., Eng, E., Randall-David, E., & Robinson, N. (2005). Quality-of-life concerns of African American breast cancer survivors within rural North Carolina: Blending the tech- niques of photovoice and grounded theory. *Qualitative Health Research, 15*(1), 99–115.

Love, M. B., Legion, V., Shim, J. K., Tsai, C., Quijano, V., & Davis, C. (2004). CHWs get credit: A 10-year history of the first college-credit certificate for community health workers in the United States. *Health Promotion Practice, 5*(4), 418–428.

Malat, J., & van Ryn, M. (2005). African-American preference for same-race healthcare providers: The role of healthcare discrimination. *Ethnicity & Disease, 15*(4), 740–747.

Margolis, K. L., Lurie, N., McGovern, P. G., Tyrrell, M., & Slater, J. S. (1998). Increasing breast and cervical cancer screening in low-income women. *Journal of General Internal Medicine, 13*(8), 515–521.

Mathers, C. D., Sadana, R., Salomon, J. A., Murray, C. J., & Lopez, A. D. (2001). Healthy life expectancy in 191 countries, 1999. *Lancet, 357*(9269), 1685–1691.

McQuiston, C., Choi-Hevel, S., & Clawson, M. (2001). Protegiendo nuestra comunidad: Empowerment participatory education for HIV prevention. *Journal of Transcultural Nursing, 12*(4), 275–283.

Meister, J. S., Warrick, L. H., de Zapien, J. G., & Wood, A. H. (1992). Using lay health workers: Case study of a community-based prenatal intervention. *Journal of Community Health, 17*(1), 37–51.

Mele, N., Archer, J., & Pusch, B. D. (2005). Access to breast cancer screening services for women with disabilities. *Journal of Obstetric, Gynecologic, and Neonatal Nursing, 34*(4), 453–464.

Miller B. A., Kolonel L. N., Bernstein L., Young, J. L., Jr. Swanson G. M., West D., Key C. R., Liff J. M., Glover C. S., Alexander G. A., et al. (eds). *Racial/Ethnic Patterns of Cancer in the United States 1988-1992*, National Cancer Institute. NIH Pub. No. 96-4104. Bethesda, MD, 1996.

Moore, P. J., Sickel, A. E., Malat, J., Williams, D., Jackson, J., & Adler, N. E. (2004). Psychosocial factors in medical and psychological treatment avoidance: The role of the doctor-patient relationship. *Journal of Health Psychology, 9*(3), 421–433.

Moyer, C. A., Lennartz, H., Moore, A. A., & Earp, J. A. (2001). Expanding the role of mammographers: A training strategy to enhance mammographer-patient interaction. *Breast Disease, 13*, 13–19.

National Cancer Institute. (2002, February 21). *NCI statement on mammography screening.* Retrieved January 23, 2007, from http://www.cancer.gov/newscenter/ mammstatement31jan02.

Navarro, A. M., Senn, K. L., McNicholas, L. J., Kaplan, R. M., Roppe, B., & Campo, M. C. (1998). Por la vida model intervention enhances use of cancer screening tests among Latinas. *American Journal of Preventive Medicine, 15*(1), 32–41.

Office of Minority Health. (2005). *Health status of American Indian and Alaska native women.* Retrieved October 19, 2006, from http://www.omhrc.gov/templates/content.aspx?ID=3724.

Office of Minority Health. (2006). *Infant Mortality/SIDS and Hispanic Americans.* Retrieved October 19, 2006, from http://www.omhrc.gov/templates/content.aspx?ID=3329.

Parker, E. A., Schulz, A. J., Israel, B. A., & Hollis, R. (1998). Detroit's East Side Village Health Worker Partnership: Community-based lay health advisor intervention in an urban area. *Health Education and Behavior, 25*(1), 24–45.

Rauscher, G. H., Hawley, S. T., & Earp, J. A. (2005). Baseline predictors of initiation vs. maintenance of regular mammography use among rural women. *Preventive Medicine, 40*(6), 822–830.

Reeves, T. J., & Bennett, C. E. (2004). *We the People: Asians in the United States. Census 2000 special reports* (No. CENSR-17). U.S. Census Bureau, U.S. Department of Commerce, Washington, D.C.

Reinhardt, U. E., Hussey, P. S., & Anderson, G. F. (2004). U.S. health care spending in an international context. *Health Affairs, 23*(3), 10–25.

Riegel, B., & Carlson, B. (2004). Is individual peer support a promising intervention for persons with heart failure? *Journal of Cardiovascular Nursing, 19*(3), 174–183.

Ries, L. A. G., Harkins, D., Krapcho, M., Mariotto, A., Miller, B. A., & Feuer, E. J., et al. (2006). *SEER cancer statistics review, 1975–2003.* Bethesda, MD: National Cancer Institute.

Rosenthal, E., Wiggins, N., Brownstein, N., & Johnson, S. (1998). *A summary of the National Community Health Advisor Study: Weaving the future.* Baltimore, MD: Anne E. Casey Foundation.

Schroen, A. T., Brenin, D. R., Kelly, M. D., Knaus, W. A., & Slingluff, C. L., Jr. (2005). Impact of patient distance to radiation therapy on mastectomy use in early-stage breast cancer patients. *Journal of Clinical Oncology, 23*(28), 7074–7080.

Schulz, A. J., Israel, B. A., Becker, A. B., & Hollis, R. M. (1997). "It's a 24-hour thing . . . a living-for-each-other concept": Identity, networks, and community in an urban village health worker project. *Health Education and Behavior, 24*(4), 465–480.

Smeltzer, S. C. (2006). Preventive health screening for breast and cervical cancer and osteoporosis in women with physical disabilities. *Family & Community Health, 29*(1 Suppl), 35S–43S.

150   CHAPTER 5   THE LONG REACH TO BASIC HEALTHCARE SERVICES

Smigal, C., Jemal, A., Ward, E., Cokkinides, V., Smith, R., & Howe, H. L., et al. (2006). Trends in breast cancer by race and ethnicity: Update 2006. *CA: A Cancer Journal for Clinicians, 56*(3), 168–183.

Smith, D. B. (2005). Racial and ethnic health disparities and the unfinished civil rights agenda. *Health Affairs, 24*(2), 317–324.

Smith-Bindman, R., Miglioretti, D. L., Lurie, N., Abraham, L., Barbash, R. B., & Strzelczyk, J., et al. (2006). Does utilization of screening mammography explain racial and ethnic differences in breast cancer? *Annals of Internal Medicine, 144*(8), 541–553.

Song, L., & Fletcher, R. (1998). Breast cancer rescreening in low-income women. *American Journal of Preventive Medicine, 15*(2), 128–133.

St. James, P. S., Shapiro, E., & Waisbren, S. E. (1999). The Resource Mothers Program for maternal phenylketonuria. *American Journal of Public Health, 89*(5), 762–764.

Starfield, B. (2004). Promoting equity in health through research and understanding. *Developing World Bioethics, 4*(1), 76–95.

Sung, J. F., Blumenthal, D. S., Coates, R. J., Williams, J. E., Alema-Mensah, E., & Liff, J. M. (1997). Effect of a cancer screening intervention conducted by lay health workers among inner-city women. *American Journal of Preventive Medicine, 13*(1), 51–57.

Swider, S. M. (2002). Outcome effectiveness of community health workers: An integrative literature review. *Public Health Nursing, 19*(1), 11–20.

Tatum, C., Wilson, A., Dignan, M., Paskett, E. D., & Velez, R. (1997). Development and implementation of outreach strategies for breast and cervical cancer prevention among African American women. FoCaS project. Forsyth County cancer screening. *Journal of Cancer Education, 12*(1), 43–50.

Taylor, T., Serrano, E., Anderson, J., & Kendall, P. (2000). Knowledge, skills, and behavior improvements on peer educators and low-income Hispanic participants after a stage of change-based bilingual nutrition education program. *Journal of Community Health, 25*(3), 241–262.

U.S. Census Bureau. (2000a). *Census 2000. Summary file 3.* Retrieved July 17, 2006, from http://factfinder.census.gov/servlet/DatasetMainPageServlet.

U.S. Census Bureau. (2000b). *Profile of general demographic characteristics: 2000. Geographic area: United States.* Retrieved July 17, 2006, from http://www.census.gov/Press-Release/www/2002/demoprofiles.html.

U.S. Census Bureau. (2004). *U.S. interim projections by age, sex, race, and Hispanic origin.* Retrieved January 23, 2007, from http://www.census.gov/ipc/www/usinterimproj.

Viswanathan, M., Ammerman, A., Eng, E., Garlehner, G., Lohr, K. N., & Griffith, D., et al. (2004). Community-based participatory research: Assessing the evidence. *Evidence Report/Technology Assessment (Summary), (99)*, 1–8.

Watkins, E. L., Harlan, C., Eng, E., Gansky, S. A., Gehan, D., & Larsan, K. (1994). Assessing the effectiveness of lay health advisors with migrant farm workers. *Family & Community Health, 16*(4), 72–87.

Wilson, W., & Pratt, C. (1987). The impact of diabetes education and peer support upon weight and glycemic control of elderly persons with noninsulin dependent diabetes mellitus (NIDDM). *American Journal of Public Health, 77*(5), 634–635.

Zuvekas, A., Nolan, L., Tumaylle, C., & Griffin, L. (1999). Impact of community health workers on access, use of services, and patient knowledge and behavior. *Journal of Ambulatory Care Management, 22*(4), 33–44.

Strategy Two: Improving Providers' Abilities to Communicate and Create Relationships

The second section of this text considers patient advocacy from the perspective of healthcare professionals as they strive to provide patient-centered care. Whether clinicians, administrators, or researchers, many healthcare "insiders" support patients' assertions that good care is based on good communication. In particular, patient-centered care requires providers to elicit their patients' points of view, bringing to light the personal values, care preferences, and psychosocial factors that impact health. The following chapters explore the provider's role in fostering patient-centered care, the tools needed to support this practice, as well as the limitations to provider advocacy. Throughout these chapters, the theme of patient empowerment continues to emerge as authors think about how to help patients achieve as much autonomy as possible without placing undue burden on them.

In Chapter 6, Lown and Kalet share a "day in the life" of a primary care physician and illustrate how clinicians can practice patient-centered care despite struggling against many of the same systemic problems that challenge patients. Through case studies, the authors provide examples of best practices for physicians and describe the attitudinal commitments and practice competencies needed to achieve patient-centered care. By cultivating an understanding of the healthcare system and helping patients navigate that system, physicians can do a great deal to advocate for patients. At the same time, physicians' professional roles dictate certain ethical and practical limitations to advocacy that must be acknowledged.

In Chapter 7, Golin, Thorpe, and DiMatteo introduce patient–provider communication, a central concern of patient advocacy, and devote particular attention to the psychological and social factors that contribute to patients' illnesses. Conditions such as depression or poverty have a serious impact on patients' health and, until uncovered, limit providers' abilities to establish rapport, help patients make fully informed health decisions, and manage chronic illnesses. Sharing techniques for creating an open dialogue with patients, the authors give an overview of motivational interviewing, a proven method for uncovering patients' concerns and goals. By allowing patients to articulate their own motivations, supports, and barriers to behavior change, clinicians may make more informed and effective decisions about how to counsel their patients.

Chapter 8 expands on the topic of health communication by discussing patient literacy and its effects on patient care and health outcomes. DeWalt and Pignone describe the prevalence of low literacy, which affects over 90 million adults in the United States, and outline the ways in which insufficient literacy skills prevent patients from navigating a healthcare system that relies heavily on written communication. Not only does low literacy prevent people from actively partnering with their providers, it renders them unable to follow crucial instructions related to their treatment, billing, and matters of informed consent. The authors discuss providers' roles in both lessening the literacy demands placed on patients and helping patients meet those demands that cannot be avoided.

In Chapter 9, Hibbard provides a social science researcher's perspective on improving patient–provider communication through the development of clinical measures. "Patient activation" is one promising example of research that will give clinicians tools to assess psychological factors such as engagement and readiness in the same way they would measure physical factors such as blood pressure or cholesterol. The information provided by patient activation questionnaires allows clinicians to tailor patients' healthcare experiences, encourage self-management, and track progress from visit to visit. Chronicling how the patient activation measure has been developed and tested, the author outlines the ways in which research has contributed to clinical encounters and to patient advocacy as a whole.

CHAPTER 6

The Clinician's Experience: Incorporating Advocacy Into the 20-Minute Medical Encounter

Beth A. Lown* and Adina Kalet

OBJECTIVES

- To show the ways in which physicians advocate for individual patients on a daily basis
- To discuss the five attitudinal commitments a physician must make to be an effective advocate
- To present 11 competencies physicians need to master in order to fulfill these commitments
- To discuss ethical and practical limitations to physician advocacy
- To show current initiatives, changes in medical education, and resources to help physicians advocate more effectively

Effective physician–advocates embrace five core commitments based on a relationship-centered approach to healthcare and advocacy (Tresolini & The Pew-Fetzer Task Force, 1994). Relationship-centered caregivers view the patient as a whole person within the context of his or her unique psychological and social context and integrate the patient's needs with the best medical practices. Relationship-centered advocacy requires the mastery of certain key competencies, which may help clinicians overcome the constraints of the medical system, the boundaries of their own profession, and the limits of their professional education. Medical schools and residency

*Beth A. Lown is a board member of both the American Academy on Communication in Healthcare and the Kenneth B. Schwartz Center.

training programs are expanding their efforts to teach some of the competencies that enable clinicians to be effective advocates. Nevertheless, the biotechnical culture of medicine, the slow pace of curricular reform, and the complex systemic and economic pressures experienced by physicians comprise formidable barriers to effective patient advocacy.

The dual goals of this chapter are first to explore the meaning of patient advocacy in the context of the patient–physician relationship from the perspective of two primary care physicians. Second, we seek to explore avenues for curricular reform to train physicians to be effective advocates. Our focus on the patient–physician relationship represents but one lens through which to view some of the current challenges facing those primary care physicians attempting to practice humanistic, relationship-centered care with their patients on a daily basis. We welcome the multiple perspectives represented in this book and recognize that only through our coordinated efforts will patient and family advocacy be realized.

CORE COMMITMENTS

Above and beyond the primary commitment to maintain an up-to-date knowledge base and technical skills, physicians must make five core commitments in order to advocate effectively on behalf of their patients.

If one defines health advocacy as the act of providing patients with "access to the best care that integrates the patient's and clinician's values, needs and preferences, safety from mistakes and compassion for suffering" (Earp, French, & Gilkey, 2003), each patient–physician encounter contains numerous opportunities for advocacy. On a typical day, a primary care physician may see an older patient who needs a hearing aid that is not paid for by Medicare, a child with asthma who is not getting the help that she needs to use her medications properly, a woman with small children who suddenly finds herself homeless and without health insurance after leaving her abusive husband, or a patient unable to afford a procedure or medication that may save his life. This physician may be called on to intervene on behalf of a hospitalized patient who needs an expensive treatment not authorized by his insurance company or to repair the fractured communication among healthcare professionals who may not communicate adequately with each other or the patient. She hears from her patients that a valuable community resource such as "Meals-on-Wheels" or a hospital-based free pharmacy is about to lose its funding or add unaffordable co-pays. The challenges are daunting and plentiful, even on a "slow" day. Physicians battle the ailing healthcare system on a daily basis in order to provide quality care to their patients.

Patient advocacy requires a relationship-centered approach to health-care (Tresolini & The Pew-Fetzer Task Force, 1994). The philosophical premise of this approach is that the relationships among practitioners, patients, and their communities are the primary drivers of health. In contrast, in a physician-centered, paternalistic model of the patient–physician relationship, the physician elicits information for diagnosis, shares information that he or she thinks is important, and makes and implements decisions on behalf of the patient. The patient and his or her autonomy in this model are marginalized as the physician holds power, control, and responsibility in the relationship. Physicians who supply information and technical services without the caring and guidance based on their knowledge of the patient abandon their professional responsibility (Quill & Cassel, 1995). In the more recent informed-consumer relationship model, the patient brings information to the physician, seeks additional information and expert opinion, and makes decisions independently (Charles, Gafni, & Whelan, 1997). Neither of these models will enable us to fulfill the goals stated previously here.

In the relationship-centered model, patient advocacy is situated within relationships mutually constructed by the patient and physician on behalf of the patient's health and well-being. In such relationships, the physician cares about as well as for the patient (Peabody, 1927) and strives to understand the patient's perspective. The physician integrates case-specific medical knowledge and best medical practice into her approach to healing. She reaches agreement with patients about how to integrate their needs and preferences with medically appropriate care. This mutually constructed understanding then informs decision making and patient-appropriate advocacy. Because the care of each patient is so complex, the physician is often called on to fulfill multiple commitments in any given situation. The following case histories are typical, fictional examples of a few patients among many who might be seen during brief appointments in a busy primary care practitioner's office. These cases are intended to contextualize the commitments necessary to advocate for specific patients and describe the competencies necessary to operationalize them in a clinician's daily practice (see Table 6.1 and Table 6.2).

Table 6.1   Commitments, Competencies, and Curricular Domains

Commitments	Competencies	Institute of Medicine Curricular Domains
Commitment to understand the patient as a person within his or her unique psychosocial context	Acquire and maintain knowledge about the links and consequences of biological, psychological, social, and emotional issues in health. Demonstrate the ability to elicit patient-specific biopsychosocial information.	Mind-body interactions in health and disease Patient behavior Social and cultural aspects of health
Commitment to understand and help patients navigate the healthcare system	Acquire and maintain knowledge of community resources, and how healthcare systems work nationally, locally, and within one's own institution. Demonstrate the ability to apply this knowledge to meet patients' and families' needs.	Health policy and economics
Commitment to the importance of using effective interpersonal and communication skills	Acquire and maintain knowledge about links between communication and patient outcomes. Demonstrate essential and advanced communication skills with patients, families, and members of the healthcare team.	Physician-patient interactions
Commitment to self-awareness	Acquire and maintain knowledge about barriers to, and positive outcomes of, self-awareness. Act with awareness of one's personal assumptions, biases, and emotional "hot buttons." Demonstrate nonjudgmental respect.	Physician role and behavior

(continued)

Table 6.1   Commitments, Competencies, and Curricular Domains
(continued)

Commitments	Competencies	Institute of Medicine *Curricular Domains*
Commitment to integrate current biomedical knowledge and expertise with the human and relational dimensions of care	Acquire and maintain the knowledge base necessary for excellent clinical care. Integrate this knowledge with expertise in clinical diagnosis and reasoning, interactional skills, knowledge of the patient, his/her family and community, and knowledge of the healthcare system.	

Table 6.2   Dr. Advocate's Appointment Schedule

8:00-8:20	Mr. Ames. Age: 80. Insurance: Medicare, Veterans' Administration service connected. Reason for visit: hypertension, diabetes follow-up.
8:20-8:40	Mrs. Smith. Age: 26. Insurance: managed care, no mental health benefits. Reason for visit: Gynecological check-up.
8:40-9:00	Mrs. Jones. Age: 56. Insurance: Social Security Insurance/Social Security Disabled, Medicaid. Reason for visit: chest pain.
9:00-9:20	Urgent care slot.
9:20- . . .	

All patient names are fictitious. No reference to actual patients or their histories is intended.

PATIENT CASE HISTORY: MR. AMES

Mr. Ames: "Hi Doc. I went to see that hearing doctor you sent me to and he told me to get a hearing aid. Damn thing costs $1,000 and they tell me Medicare won't pay for it. What am I supposed to do, rob a bank?"

Joe Ames is an 80-year-old retired plumber with high blood pressure and diabetes for which he takes medications, as well as macular degeneration with deteriorating vision and hearing loss. He has been widowed for 10 years and lives alone in a private senior citizen's building in the city. He has sufficient assets to make him ineligible for Medicaid but does have Medicare for insurance. He has a son and daughter who live out of state and see him once or twice yearly. He prepares his own breakfast and depends on "Meals-on-Wheels" for his main meal of the day, which is delivered to his apartment. He treasures his independence and is concerned about his diminishing vision and hearing. He sees Dr. A. every four months for scheduled follow-up visits.

CASE-SPECIFIC MEDICAL KNOWLEDGE

Dr. A is concerned about Mr. Ames's progressive sensory losses, as they constitute the most immediate threats to his continued independence, safety, and well-being. She has referred Mr. Ames for ophthalmologic treatment and is aware that patients with moderate macular degeneration liken their quality of life to those suffering from severe heart disease, moderate strokes, and chronic renal dialysis (Brown et al., 2005). She is aware of research suggesting that the adverse effects on quality of life associated with hearing loss can be reversed with hearing aids (Gates & Mills, 2005; Mulrow et al., 1990; Yueh, Shapiro, MacLean, & Shekelle, 2003), and visual loss can be ameliorated by available treatments (Complications of Age-Related Macular Degeneration Prevention Trial Study Group, 2004; Wormald, Evans, Smeeth, & Henshaw, 2005). She wonders if a multidisciplinary rehabilitation program is available to address the medical and psychosocial consequences of this patient's dual sensory losses in an integrated fashion (Heine & Browning, 2002).

Dr. A. checks Mr. Ames's blood pressure and recent laboratory work, discusses these with him, refills his prescriptions, tells him that she will find out what needs to be done to get his hearing aid paid for, and will call him later.

Phone call 1, 9:41 a.m. (3 minutes): Dr. A. calls the social work department at her hospital for advice; after spending several minutes on hold, the secretary tells Dr. A. that she will try to have someone call her back.

Phone call 2, 1 p.m. (2 minutes): Dr. A. calls the office of the otolaryngologist who examined Mr. A and sent him to an audiologist for a hearing test. The secretary leaves a message asking the audiologist to return Dr. A.'s call.

Phone call 3, 4 p.m. (2 minutes): Dr. A. calls a colleague in geriatrics for advice. The colleague informs Dr. A. that if the patient is Veterans' Administration (VA) service connected, he can get a hearing aid paid for through the VA system. Dr. A. files this information in her personal information files for later reference.

Phone call 4, 5:30 p.m. (3 minutes): Dr. A. calls Mr. Ames to tell him the VA will pay for his hearing aid, but he may have to be re-evaluated within that system. He grumbles about having to start all over again but accepts the phone number.

She decides that she will have to research interdisciplinary programs for the evaluation and treatment of multiple sensory losses later because she has to finish her phone calls, dictate her notes, review the day's laboratory results, and see patients in the hospital before she can leave for the evening. She is uncertain whether Mr. Ames will be willing to go through a re-evaluation for his hearing loss and makes a mental note to call him back to discuss this further.

COMMITMENT TO UNDERSTAND AND HELP PATIENTS NAVIGATE THE HEALTHCARE SYSTEM

Dr. A. could have left these phone calls to the patient or his family; however, her knowledge of the patient's circumstances informed her concern that this older patient would be unable to obtain the help needed from his family or navigate the phone calls to obtain necessary information and recommendations, especially with his sensory deficits. Her caring about the patient stimulated her to go ahead and make the calls on his behalf.

No one tells physicians or patients how to access this sort of practical information, which is neither readily available nor easily acquired. Dr. A. had to acquire rapidly a knowledge base about how and where to access the resources needed by this patient and then used two frequently employed avenues to do so: colleagues and the Internet. It is left to the individual physician to compile, update, apply, and share such information with his or her patients.

PATIENT CASE HISTORY: MRS. SMITH

Commitment to Understand the Patient as a Person Within His or Her Unique Psychosocial Context

Barbara Smith is a 26-year-old mother of two children, ages 2 and 4, returning to see Dr. A. for a gynecologic evaluation. In response to Dr. A.'s query, "What's happened since I last saw you?" Mrs. Smith replies that she has left her husband who had been physically abusive to her and is now living in a homeless shelter with her children. Dr. A. listens carefully until Mrs. Smith has finished speaking. She leans forward, expresses her concern, looks intently at Mrs. Smith, and says, "That is an enormously courageous act. You do not deserve to be beaten." She ascertains that the spouse has not been abusing the children and discusses with Mrs. Smith what they should prioritize during this visit today. Mrs. Smith wants to be checked for sexually transmitted diseases, including HIV, and directed to someone who can help her find resources for housing and health insurance. Dr. A. brings Mrs. Smith into the examining room to change and gives her a consent form for HIV testing to read while she is waiting to be examined.

When Dr. A. returns to the examining room, she asks Mrs. Smith, "Will this exam be upsetting for you?" Mrs. Smith reassures Dr. A. that she will be fine, and Dr. A. speaks to her throughout the examination, telling her what she is going to do in advance of every step. When she is finished, Dr. A. notices that Mrs. Smith has not signed the HIV consent form and asks whether she has any questions. Mrs. Smith looks down at the floor. "What's the matter?" Mrs. Smith's eyes fill with tears as she shamefully confesses that she cannot read the form. Dr. A. gently touches her arm and says, "You needn't feel ashamed. Many of my patients have trouble reading. We'll help you." Dr. A. reads the consent form to her and answers her questions. Dr. A. requests and receives Mrs. Smith's permission to call a social worker to inquire about services available to her. While Mrs. Smith is getting dressed, Dr. A., following through on Mrs. Smith's wishes, begins to make inquiries for her patient.

COMMITMENT TO UNDERSTAND AND GUIDE PATIENTS THROUGH THE HEALTHCARE SYSTEM

Phone call 1 (15 minutes): Hospital Social Work Department: Dr. A. calls the department of social work to make an appointment for Mrs. Smith. She speaks to a social worker colleague whom she trusts will help her advocate for her patient. Her colleague tells her that they could help Mrs. Smith apply for subsidized housing, WIC (Women, Infants, and Children) assistance for her youngest child, and food stamps, Transitional Aid to Families with Dependent Children, Medicaid, and free care at the hospital until Medicaid kicks in, a process that usually takes 1 to 2 months. Dr. A. makes an appointment for Mrs. Smith to see her colleague in the social work department later that week. Dr. A. also asks the patient to make another appointment to see her over the next few weeks so that she can review her laboratory tests with her and check on how she is doing. "You know how to reach me if you need me in the meantime!" Mrs. Smith thanked her, smiled briefly, and left.

Dr. A. paused for a moment, thinking, "How could I have missed the fact that Mrs. Smith was not only being abused, but was unable to read?" She set this thought aside for the time being in order to finish seeing the rest of her patients. Perhaps after the dust settles and the family's basic needs are attended to, Mrs. Smith would be interested in literacy programs in the city.

Internet Search 2 (10 minutes): Adult Literacy Services: That evening, Dr. A. searches the Internet to find out about adult literacy services in her area. She is happy to find an adult literacy hotline and a listing of adult basic education programs on her state's Department of Education website. She saves it for future reference to place in her collection of general resources for her patients.

CASE-SPECIFIC MEDICAL KNOWLEDGE

Dr. A. knows that the life-time prevalence of intimate partner violence against women ranges from 25% to 30% (Tjaden & Thoennes, 2000), and that approximately 11 million U.S. adults are nonliterate in English (National Center for Education Statistics). She also knows that both conditions impose a significant burden of emotional, psychological, and economic suffering as well as poor health (DeWalt, Berkman, Sheridan, Lohr,

Textbox 6.1   An Example of Patient Advocacy Training in Action: New York University School of Medicine/Bellevue Hospital Center, Primary Care Internal Medicine

The NYU School of Medicine/Bellevue Hospital Center residency program in Primary Care Internal Medicine believes the issues of patient advocacy and greater social consciousness are crucial to high-quality, patient-centered medical practice. Each aspect of the curriculum from the first year of training to graduation is developed with the goal of educating residents who are skilled at defining the medical, psychological, and socioeconomic needs of the patient and then developing a therapeutic plan of care aligned with these needs. By the end of training, it is not uncommon to hear a third-year resident describe a case where the final plan is to call the local Department of Aging.

Through an intensive course in psychosocial medicine focusing on the finer aspects of cultural competency, doctor-patient relationships, medical ethics, substance use and abuse, and the medical interview, our residents gain the tools needed to perform a needs assessment of their patients' biopsychosocial needs. They are then taught to use that information to develop patient-centered therapeutic plans. They also participate in a clinical epidemiology course that includes skills building in patient-centered risk communication and medical decision making. Finally, they participate in a health policy course that focuses on the field of healthcare economics and policy and the techniques of political lobbying and advocacy for vulnerable populations.

An In-Depth Look at the Health Policy Curriculum

For 8 weeks, third-year (senior) residents participate in the annual health policy block that includes three 3-hour seminars a week, an advocacy project, and lobbying field trips to Albany, New York, and Washington, DC. The goals of the block are to (1) provide residents in training with a working understanding of health policy, health economics, and the structure of the U.S. and international healthcare markets, (2) help residents develop an appreciation of the impact of health systems on patients and physicians, and (3) ensure that trainees recognize the role of patient advocacy in improving health outcomes.

There are two main components of this block: the seminar-based curriculum in health economics and health policy and the hands-on political lobbying and patient advocacy project. The seminar-based curriculum is coordinated by the program director and chief resident and are led by prominent area legislators, healthcare administrators, health policy researchers, and lobbyists. The focus of these sessions is a discussion of the topic and a brief synopsis of the invited seminar leader's career. The

(continued)

Textbox 6.1   An Example of Patient Advocacy Training in Action: New York University School of Medicine/Bellevue Hospital Center, Primary Care Internal Medicine (continued)

hands-on component of the course is a lobbying field trip and is directed by the medical center lobbyist who also serves as the director of government affairs for the medical school. Under her leadership, the residents' lobbying projects are conceived and refined. Although the focus of the projects is determined by the residents, they virtually all select topics relevant to their experiences as physicians serving the patients of Bellevue Hospital.

In summary, through this block, NYU residents are introduced to basic topics in health policy and economics such as who are the people and institutions that make health policy, how these people and institutions are influenced, how health policy impacts health outcomes, and the basics of macroeconomics and health insurance. By the end of the block, residents have been taught the basics of lobbying and advocacy and have gained first-hand experience in advocating for vulnerable populations through a lobbying trip to state and federal legislatures.

& Pignone, 2004; Tjaden & Thoennes, 2000). Despite this knowledge base, Dr. A. had not asked screening questions that might have uncovered these conditions. Even if she had, Mrs. Smith may have chosen not to share this information with her for a variety of reasons, including fear and shame (Parikh, Parker, Nurss, Baker, & Williams, 1996; Petersen, Moracco, Goldstein, & Clark, 2004; Rodriguez, Bauer, McLoughlin, & Grumbach, 1999).

COMMITMENT TO USING EFFECTIVE INTERPERSONAL AND COMMUNICATION SKILLS WITH PATIENTS

Dr. A. tries to use a patient-centered communication style. Patient-centered communication involves inquiring about and responding to patients' perspectives, concerns, and emotions, and their unique psychosocial context and helping patients' understand and participate in discussions, decisions, and care (Stewart et al., 1995). Physicians vary in their beliefs about the importance of psychosocial issues in healthcare. Physicians with positive attitudes toward psychosocial aspects of care invite dialogue, and their patients participate more actively in their care (Levinson & Roter,

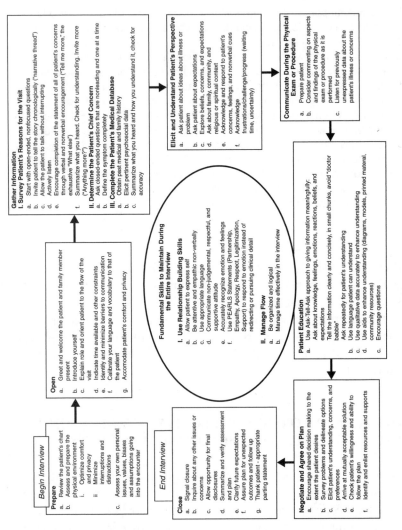

Figure 6.1   The Macy Model of Physician–Patient Communication

1995). Patient participation and patient-centered communication have, in turn, been correlated with patient satisfaction and trust (Cooper-Patrick et al., 1999; Fiscella et al., 2004), efficiency of diagnosis (Epstein et al., 2005; Stewart et al., 2000), enhanced health outcomes, and perceived quality of care (Flocke, Miller, & Crabtree, 2002; Stewart, 1995; Stewart et al., 1999). Many believe that communication is an intuitive art that one either does or does not possess. Yet research suggests that communication skills can be taught and are learned, particularly when, similar to other clinical skills, they are practiced and cultivated with feedback from faculty and/or patients (Aspegren, 1999).

During this brief but complex visit, Dr. A. uses several essential elements of patient- or relationship-centered communication elucidated in consensus statements (Makoul, 2001; Simpson et al., 1991) and educational communication models (Kalet et al., 2004). For example, she uses words and nonverbal signals to convey care and concern and to build the relationship. She reaches agreement with the patient about priorities for the visit. She respects her patient's feelings, inquires whether the examination will be difficult, and sensitively guides and orients her throughout the process. She validates her patient's courage and responds to her emotions. She tries to understand the patient's perspective and gathers information not only about her medical symptoms but also about her social situation. She shares information the patient needs to understand, including the pros and cons of HIV testing and how to access the resources she needs. They reach agreement on the appointment with the social worker and finally close the visit by agreeing on a follow-up and contact plan.

Dr. A. also acts as a liaison between other members of the healthcare profession, systems of care and financing, and her patient. She seeks a trusted colleague to assist her in helping her patient. To do this, she must communicate effectively with colleagues and other members of the healthcare service system.

PATIENT CASE HISTORY: MRS. JONES

Carla Jones is a 56-year-old African American poet with a history of poorly controlled insulin-dependent diabetes and bipolar (manic-depressive) disorder, who has always insisted on managing her illnesses in her own way. Dr. A. has known her for several years and has at times found

Table 6.3   Essential Elements of Communication in Medical Encounters: The Kalamazoo Consensus Statement

Open the Discussion
- Allow the patient to complete his or her opening statement
- Elicit the patient's full set of concerns
- Establish/maintain a personal connection

Gather Information
- Use open-ended and closed-ended questions appropriately
- Structure, clarify, and summarize information
- Actively listen using nonverbal (e.g., eye contact) and verbal (e.g., words of encouragement) techniques

Understand the Patient's Perspective
- Explore contextual factors (e.g., family, culture, gender, age, socioeconomic status, spirituality)
- Explore beliefs, concerns, and expectations about health and illness
- Acknowledge and respond to the patient's ideas, feelings, and values

Share Information
- Use language the patient can understand
- Check for understanding
- Encourage questions

Reach Agreement on Problems and Plans
- Encourage the patient to participate in decisions to the extent he or she desires
- Check the patient's willingness and ability to follow the plan
- Identify and enlist resources and supports

Provide Closure
- Ask whether the patient has other issues or concerns
- Summarize and affirm agreement with the plan of action
- Discuss follow-up (e.g., next visit, plan for unexpected outcomes)

Makoul, 2001

her to be a challenging patient. Her bipolar disease has been problematic because of her reluctance to take medications that might suppress her manic symptoms and therefore her desire and ability to write. Despite her difficulty working with Mrs. Jones, Dr. A. had come to respect her ability to cope with her illnesses and the socioeconomic hardship she continued to endure and to admire her flair and zest for life.

On this particular day, Mrs. Jones greeted Dr. A. with the new onset of chest pressure radiating to her left arm and associated with recent EKG changes. Dr. A. was puzzled because Mrs. Jones had recently had a normal cardiac exercise test. Concerned nevertheless about the likelihood of unstable coronary artery disease in this high-risk patient, Dr. A. sent her immediately to the emergency department with a transfer note asking the admitting intern or resident to call her. She assumed that her patient would be admitted by the hospitalist service, seen in consultation by the cardiology service, and undergo cardiac catheterization during her hospital admission.

When Dr. A. checked back in, the doctors in the hospital were irritated with Mrs. Jones. She insisted on managing her own insulin, refused the doses prescribed by the intern or resident, and insisted on taking only brand-name medications, not the generic medications available in this public hospital. The nurses were also aggravated with her, saying she behaved in a supercilious, condescending manner to them and was unreasonably demanding of their attention. The doctors were eager to discharge her, suggesting that her report of symptoms was unreliable because of her psychiatric history and recent negative exercise test. Dr. A. assured them that she knew this patient quite well and reasoned that the constellation of her new symptoms, risk factors, and EKG changes made it highly likely that she was having an evolving heart attack. It became apparent to Dr. A. that she was getting nowhere and that she would need to speak with the hospital staff in person despite the fact that she generally turned her patients over to a hospitalist when they required admission.

After multiple, lengthy conversations by Dr. A. with the cardiologist, nurses, interns, and residents, Mrs. Jones finally underwent cardiac catheterization. The catheterization showed triple vessel coronary disease, and the patient underwent coronary bypass surgery shortly thereafter. When Dr. A. came by to see her patient before her discharge and to arrange her outpatient follow-up, Mrs. Jones complained about the inattentive physicians and poor nursing care in the hospital. She made no mention of the role Dr. A. had played in facilitating her care and demanded to know when she would call her prescriptions into the pharmacy.

CASE-SPECIFIC MEDICAL KNOWLEDGE

Dr. A. has read the medical literature documenting disparities in healthcare in the United States (Institute of Medicine, 2003). These studies have shown that African American patients receive fewer cardiac catheterizations, coronary angioplasties, and bypass surgeries, even when the researchers controlled for variables, including clinical indications, sociodemographic factors, type of healthcare system, and availability of the procedures (Kressin & Petersen, 2001). Lower bypass surgery rates for African American patients have resulted in lower adjusted 5-year survival rates, indicating that these discrepancies are clinically meaningful. Such disparities in healthcare have been found in other areas as well, ranging from cancer care to renal transplantation (Simpson et al., 1991).

COMMITMENT TO SELF-AWARENESS

Dr. A. had to consider carefully her own thoughts and feelings in order to manage her frustration and resentment with the patient for her controlling style and seeming lack of appreciation. Dr. A. was able to draw on her longstanding relationship with this patient, her memories of the episodes of illness and recovery they had sojourned together, and her understanding of Mrs. Jones' past psychosocial history and current context. She also had to manage her feelings toward the team for their resistance to her recommendations and their assumptions about the patient. Dr. A's self-awareness protected her from the judgment-clouding reactions displayed by other members of the healthcare team.

In Dr. A's view, Mrs. Jones' presentation was classical, and her medical management plan should have been straightforward. Why did the admitting team behave as it did? Mrs. Jones' personality style made interactions with her difficult, but Dr. A. was also concerned that the healthcare team in her own hospital may have been reacting to her patient at least in part based on unconscious stereotypes, including racism and the stigma associated with mental illness. In retrospect, the biomedical decisions were straightforward, but in stressful, time-limited interactions people may react on the basis of subconscious or unconscious beliefs and feelings. Clinicians are not immune to this phenomenon (Gilbert & Hixon, 1991).

A commitment to self-awareness begins with a willingness to reflect on one's thoughts, feelings, and actions in the moment and in retrospect in order to learn and grow. It includes an examination of one's own patterns of identification, projection, and defenses, and how these affect the care of our patients. This commitment includes a willingness to embrace diversity and to examine, recognize, and address one's personal assumptions and biases with their resultant potential for perpetuating disparities in care. Finally, this commitment begins and ends with compassion for ourselves as well as for others.

COMMITMENT TO THE IMPORTANCE OF USING EFFECTIVE INTERPERSONAL AND COMMUNICATION SKILLS WITH OTHER MEMBERS OF THE HEALTHCARE TEAM

The practice of medicine has become increasingly specialized over the past several decades. Subspecialists care for disorders of a single-organ system or surgical problem. Gynecologists no longer necessarily deliver babies, and psychopharmacologists oversee the medications of other therapists' patients. With the recent advent of the hospitalist movement, primary care physicians may not follow their patients when they require hospitalization. The trend toward subspecialist and hospitalist care has contributed to the increasing discontinuity and fragmentation of care (Moore & Showstack, 2003). This requires increased efforts by the physician–advocate to communicate effectively with other members of the healthcare team, especially at times of transition of care among providers, teams, and institutions. When these efforts fail to occur, the tasks of communication and coordination of care falls on the shoulders of the patient and family with all of the resultant stress, anxiety, and dissatisfaction this shift incurs. This communication during transitions in care is extremely challenging for individual providers, let alone patients and their families, especially in the absence of supportive infrastructure and information systems. Dr. A. accepts the responsibility of communicating with the hospital team and for making sure she picks up the follow-up care during the patient's transition back home. Her commitment to this responsibility may have affected her patient's clinical outcome.

COMMITMENT TO INTEGRATE CURRENT BIOMEDICAL KNOWLEDGE AND EXPERTISE WITH THE HUMAN DIMENSIONS OF CARE

Dr. A. conceives of her professional and personal identity within partnered relationships, seeks case- and patient-specific knowledge, uses effective communication skills with other members of the healthcare system as well as with her patients, and integrates these beliefs, skills, and knowledge to implement jointly agreed-on plans. This is relationship-centered care and advocacy.

ETHICAL AND PRACTICAL LIMITATIONS TO PATIENT ADVOCACY

The previous case studies illustrate the important role that primary care physicians can play in helping their patients navigate the healthcare system, but it is important to acknowledge that many barriers to such advocacy exist. Physicians may confront ethical dilemmas in managing competing demands and needs. They must and should adhere to quality and evidence-based guidelines to improve patient care (Joint Commission on Accreditation of Healthcare, 2006) and, in some institutions, will be paid for performance that demonstrates such adherence (Centers for Medicare and Medicaid Services, 2005). They must also integrate the application of these guidelines with their knowledge of each individual patient's values and wishes and to know when and how to adapt the guidelines to meet the needs of the patient as much as possible while still upholding their own professional standards. Physicians must think about costs spent on panels and populations of patients in addition to the needs of each individual. Furthermore, many managed-care organizations create financial incentives for physicians to limit costs of testing, treatments, and referrals. These incentives may result in actual or perceived conflicts of interest (Gorawara-Bhat, Gallagher, & Levinson, 2003).

Advocacy efforts take time. Physicians are expected to maximize clinical productivity and complete an increasing number of clinical and administrative tasks in a limited amount of time, leaving less time to engage in advocacy on behalf of individual patients, to teach, or to do research (Schindler et al., 2006). Cognitive and patient-centered skills are reimbursed at lower rates than technical procedures, and a large majority of advocacy efforts described previously here are not reimbursed activities.

Advocacy efforts also take emotional energy. Physicians, like other professionals, struggle to balance professional commitment with personal and family needs. Studies of medical students (Dyrbye, Thomas, & Shanafelt, 2006) and academic physician faculty (Gundersen, 2001) suggest that the prevalence of depression, anxiety, and overall psychological distress in these groups is significantly higher than in the general population. Psychologically distressed physicians have fewer emotional reserves to engage in advocacy and provide high-quality care (Gundersen, 2001).

MEDICAL EDUCATION AND TRAINING BARRIERS TO EFFECTIVE ADVOCACY

Medical schools and residency training programs have made progress in implementing curricula and programs to reinforce humanistic values and the skills needed to teach physicians how to advocate effectively for patients and their families and to practice relationship-centered care. Significant barriers persist, however.

Undergraduate Medical Education

Most medical students enter medical school filled with compassion, humanism, and commitment to health and healing. Although many educators have introduced curricula in communication skills (Haq, Steele, Marchand, Seibert, & Brody, 2004; Kalet et al., 2004; Rider, Lown, & Hinrichs, 2004; Smith et al., 1991), physician training still overwhelmingly emphasizes biomedical aspects of disease and technologic approaches to care and undervalues psychosocial and relational issues in care. Students' humanistic values are challenged by the objectification of the person that occurs during the course of clinical training; the suffering witnessed and incurred by both patients and students (Pories, Jain, & Harper, 2006); the "hidden curriculum" (Hafferty, 1998) of unspoken values, practices, and language that promote "clinical productivity" over relationships and patient advocacy; and the ever-burgeoning amount of information and skills to be mastered.

Some of the knowledge, skills, and attitudes necessary to implement the core commitments of patient advocacy may be present in existing courses that address the role of physicians in society, medical ethics, communication skills, primary care, and prevention (Association of American Medical Colleges, 2006); however, curricula focused on relationship-centered patient care and advocacy are sparse, dispersed across various courses, clerkships, and electives, concentrated within the first two years of medical school, and not consistently reinforced thereafter. Few medical schools integrate and develop understanding and performance in these domains throughout the four years of undergraduate medical education (Institute of Medicine, 2004).

In addition to the challenges of supporting and sustaining students' humanism and interest in patient advocacy as well as the need for curricular reform, the venues in which clinical training occurs present additional challenges. The majority of medical student and postgraduate medical training takes place in hospital settings. This tradition is partly due to historical precedent but is also significantly related to service needs and hospital reimbursement for residency training programs. Shortened hospital lengths of stay truncate opportunities for students and trainees to meet and get to know patients, practice fledgling communication and other advocacy skills, and learn about community resources. Hospital-based training may not adequately prepare graduates in the skills needed for patients who require advocacy for long-term health promotion or chronic illness management.

Fewer medical school graduates are entering primary care practice. Primary care physicians (general internal medicine, family physicians, pediatricians, and sometimes obstetricians and gynecologists) are ideally situated to advocate for their patients because of their longitudinal relationships with patients and families. There has been a well-documented and dramatic decrease in the number of medical school graduates planning to pursue careers in primary care medicine, with 33% to 35% fewer graduates entering family practice and internal medicine training programs over the past five years (Garibaldi, Popkave, & Bylsma, 2005). This decline is likely due to a variety of factors, including increasing subspecialization and technologic approaches to patient care; increasing administrative requirements, guidelines, and complexity of clinical encounters; the desire for more personal and family time; decreased professional satisfaction; and widening income gaps between generalists and specialists because of reimbursement policies that favor the latter (Schroeder, 2002). The tendency for physicians to enter more highly reimbursed specialties has been amplified by the fact that 85% of medical school graduates carry a significant educational debt by the time they graduate. The average educational debt of medical school graduates in 2005 was $115,000 (American Medical Association, 2006).

Graduate Medical Education

After four years of medical school, most graduates go on to complete an additional four to seven years in graduate residency training programs. Although essential for educational and professional growth, residency training has traditionally been physically and psychologically grueling and even more so as the pace of hospital-based healthcare delivery has quickened. In July 2003, the Accreditation Council for Graduate Medical Education (ACGME) mandated that all graduate medical education training programs limit resident work hours to no more than 80 hours per week (ACGME, 2003–2004). This mandate was initiated primarily to protect the safety of the public from harm caused by medical errors committed by fatigued or sleep-deprived physicians. Some educators note with concern, however, that these duty hour restrictions are diminishing professional altruism and commitment among young physicians and replacing them with a "shift mentality." They wonder whether these changes are impairing the quality of care delivered by resident physicians because of lack of patient care continuity (Charap, 2004; Goitein, Shanafelt, Wipf, Slatore, & Back, 2005).

CURRENT MANDATES FOR CHANGE

Medical regulatory, licensing, and accreditation organizations now require the teaching and evaluation of competency in a number of domains, including many of those necessary for effective patient advocacy (Liaison Committee on Medical Education, 1998). The Institute of Medicine, recognizing the paucity of curricula in the behavioral and social sciences as a contributor to poor quality of care, recently challenged medical schools in the United States to provide integrated curricula in these domains. The domains proposed include those essential to effective advocacy such as interpersonal and communication skills, understanding of social and cultural issues in healthcare, health policy, and economics (Smith et al., 1991).

The United States Medical Licensing Examination (USMLE) is a rigorous three-step examination required for licensure in the United States. Step 1 is usually taken at the end of the 2nd year of medical school, step 2 in the 4th year, and step 3 during the first or 2nd year of postgraduate training. A clinical skills examination was added to step 2 in 2004, including subcomponents to evaluate an integrated clinical encounter and candidates' interpersonal and communication skills. These skills are evaluated by "standardized patients," people highly trained to consistently portray specific medical scenarios and to reliably evaluate candidates' skills (USMLE.) This is the first time competency in interpersonal and communication skills evaluated by standardized patients has been a requirement for licensure in this country.

The ACGME is responsible for accrediting postgraduate residency training programs in all disciplines. The ACGME has recently defined a set of six core competencies, including medical knowledge, patient care, interpersonal and communication skills, professionalism, practice-based learning and improvement, and systems-based practice. Residency programs in the United States must now evaluate resident competency within each of these six domains (ACGME, 2006).

Many of the previously mentioned domains in which students and trainees must demonstrate competency to receive licensure and to graduate from residency training programs are grounded in the principles, values, and skills that provide the foundation for patient advocacy. Professionalism, for example, is based on the principles of the primacy of patient welfare, patient autonomy, and social justice (ABIM Foundation, 2002). Effective, relationship-centered interpersonal and communication skills are essential for patient advocacy. Medical schools and residency programs must meet the challenge to provide effective training to enhance these values and skills to meet the current mandates. This may in turn enhance their prominence and relative value not only in training, but in medical practice.

FUTURE DIRECTIONS

As medical historian Kenneth Ludmerer pointed out, the current climate of academic medical centers, reflecting the systemic woes of the

United States healthcare system, has made it exceedingly difficult to maintain a nurturing learning environment where teachers have enough time to teach, learners have enough time to learn, and institutional leaders are able to honor their professional commitments to high-quality, safe, and effective patient care, medical education, and research (Ludmerer, 1999). The healthcare system that is frustrating the public with increasingly costly, fragmented, and unsatisfying care is also frustrating physicians.

First and foremost, physicians, and indeed all health advocates, must advocate on behalf of all people who desire health and need care. The first responsibility of those who wish to advocate for patients and families is to advocate for their ability to access the healthcare system.

Second, healthcare systems and medical education must prioritize the primacy of the patient–clinician relationship. Relationships are the vehicle for advocacy, health, and healing. Leaders of healthcare policy, medical education, and the public must advocate for innovative systems of care that facilitate continuity of relationships between patients and clinicians. Given a trade-off between access and convenient appointments versus continuity, the vast majority of adults in the United States prefer continuity (Safran, 2003). Continuity, although important, is not sufficient to ensure positive, effective relationships, however.

We must also pay attention to the well-being of healthcare practitioners. Physicians who feel besieged, disillusioned, and burned out do not have sufficient emotional reserve to care about understanding their patients as whole persons. Equitable reimbursement for effective advocacy as well as technical care, and alternative financing of medical education may help stem the tide of declining enrollment in primary care training programs, but not if quality-of-life issues remain unresolved.

How can we sustain continuity of relationships given the current healthcare terrain of subspecialization, office-based practitioners, hospitalists, and work-hour restrictions? We hypothesize that strategies to build collaboration and strengthen relationships may enhance *perceived* continuity even though patients' care may be shared and contact with a continuous provider dispersed over time. This hypothesis must be tested further by research. To create such strategies, the leadership of medical institutions and medical education across the continuum from medical school to postgraduate training to continuing medical education must cultivate a culture of partnership, caring, communication, collaboration, and teamwork among all members of the healthcare community as well as the public they serve. Creating this culture will require a paradigm shift to focus on the practice, teaching, and assessment of collaborative, relationship-centered care between physicians and their patients.

CURRICULUM DEVELOPMENT FOR PATIENT ADVOCACY

Academic medical centers should implement the Institute of Medicine's recommendations to integrate developmentally appropriate curricula in behavioral and social sciences. The recommended curricular domains overlap and intersect with the commitments and competencies we describe (refer back to Table 6.1).

Commitment to Understand the Patient as a Person Within His or Her Unique Psychosocial Context

Physicians would benefit from curricula to help them understand the patient as a person within his or her unique psychosocial context. Curricula in social and cultural issues, human behavior, and mind–body interactions might include discussions about health risk behaviors, the role of cultural and personal belief systems, and the impact of psychosocial stressors on health and illness. Some medical schools are beginning to offer curricula in cultural competency (Betancourt, 2003; Rapp, 2006). Some also offer courses in the arts, literature, and the humanities to enhance empathy and a holistic understanding of the experience of illness (DasGupta, Meyer, Calero-Breckheimer, Costley, & Guillen, 2006; Jones & Carson, 2003; Krackov et al., 2003; Sirridge & Welch, 2003).

Commitment to Understand and Help Patients Navigate the Healthcare System

Curricula in health policy and economics would help learners understand how healthcare and reimbursement systems work on both the national and local level. Medical schools could collaborate with schools of public health to offer courses in health policy and economics. Community-based education and training offer learners local immersion experiences and enrich their understanding of the interactions among community context, resources, and the health of its inhabitants. These students learn about advocacy for vulnerable populations. A few medical schools offer courses in legislative advocacy, lobbying skills, and research-based advocacy (Quraishi, Orkin, Weitekamp, Khalid, & Sassani, 2005).

Commitment to the Importance of Using Effective Interpersonal and Communication Skills

We must improve our teaching and evaluation of both basic and advanced interpersonal and communication skills, particularly in the latter years of medical school and during postgraduate medical training where reinforcement, expansion, and deepening of skills teaching is sparse.

Perceived continuity may be enhanced if clinicians are able to function and communicate within highly integrated, coordinated teams in which their roles and responsibilities are explicitly clear to each other, colleagues, and patients. This will require increased emphasis on interdisciplinary communication and education. Team training, based on the principles of aviation crew resource management, is being implemented to improve team communication among hospital surgery and emergency department staff (Awad et al., 2005). These educational methods may also benefit students and trainees. Training in communication skills and strategies at transitions in care between clinicians and healthcare venues, and from these venues to home are especially important in light of evidence suggesting a correlation between discontinuity of care and medical error (Petersen, Brennan, O'Neil, Cook, & Lee, 1994).

Commitment to Self-Awareness

Self-reflection and personal awareness are essential aspects of personal learning and growth. Students, residents, and faculty rarely have opportunities for the self-reflection necessary to renew one's spirit and sustain meaning in today's fast-paced, high-stakes healthcare environment. Yet without time and venues for reflection and renewal, empathy and humanism may diminish. Various innovative curricula and courses have been developed to enhance reflective practice, empathy, and humanism

(American Academy on Communication in Healthcare; Novack et al., 1997; Novack, Epstein, & Paulsen, 1999). Proponents of "narrative medicine" propose that writing stories and "close reading" enhances reflection and helps practitioners become more attentive to their own stories as well as those of their patients (Charon, 2006). Balint groups, facilitated longitudinal reflective discussion groups first initiated by the British psychoanalyst Michael Balint, have long been a staple in family medicine training programs (Balint, 1964). Programs such as "The Healer's Art," developed in 1992 and now offered nationally, enable participants to explore such topics as grief, loss, awe, and mystery in the practice of medicine (Remen & Rabow, 2005). Many healthcare sites have initiated "Schwartz Center Rounds," multidisciplinary forums where healthcare providers discuss difficult emotional and social issues that arise during the care of patients (Kenneth B. Schwartz Center). At this time, most of these programs are elective and are not integrated within ongoing required curricula.

Commitment to Integrate Biomedical Knowledge with Human Dimensions of Care

We must also teach communication strategies to help clinicians, patients, and families integrate medical recommendations with patients' values and preferences. This approach requires knowledge of the patient as well as best medical practice. We must help clinicians learn how to access the medical and practical information they need for both themselves and their patients together with communication methods for explaining information in culturally competent and literacy-appropriate ways. We need better training in evidence-based medicine and how to translate it into simple language for patients. We should continue to develop electronic information systems that maintain confidentiality while facilitating communication and the sharing of information and resources among clinicians and patients.

Thoughtfully designed curricula to address these commitments should be integrated with existing courses and clinical training. The curricula should be reinforced and expanded to include increasingly complex content and skills consonant with developmental and training stages. This educational approach would enable physicians to understand and implement the actions necessary for patient advocacy at the level of the patient, family, community, and society.

THE DRIVERS OF CHANGE

Medical education and training is at an important crossroad. Licensure and accreditation organizations are requiring the demonstration of competency in the domains and commitments necessary to advocate for patients and families. The leadership in medical schools, postgraduate training programs, and even continuing medical education for practicing clinicians should use these mandates to leverage curriculum implementation in the commitments and competencies necessary for patient advocacy.

It is often said that assessment drives the system. Competency standards in interpersonal and communication skills are already being implemented by the United States Medical Licensure Examination. We propose required assessment of the competencies needed to advocate for patients and families at the developmentally appropriate levels of clinical training and practice. The debate surrounding the implementation of the new accreditation requirements from the USMLE and ACGME are instructive.

Faculty development in all of these commitments and competencies is critical if we are to begin to change the current culture of healthcare, academic medical centers, and their associated training sites. The clinicians who practice and teach in medical schools and training programs must value and model the desired attitudes and demonstrate the skills that provide the foundation for relationship-centered care and patient advocacy if we are to secure this heritage for new generations of practitioners and patients.

People throughout the U.S. want information about their health, their care, and the economic and educational systems in place to ensure that they get the care they need. If we are serious about healthcare as a collaboratively constructed enterprise, medical educators should invite the participation of patients, families, and health advocates into the development of curricula, assessment, and medical education research design. If we do not do so, it will be impossible to incorporate their voices into the processes and evaluation of medical education. Such efforts are beginning around the world, and networks of health professional educators interested in this approach have formed in the United States, Canada, and the United Kingdom (University of British Columbia, 2005).

CONCLUSIONS

We believe that the vast majority of students come to medical training embracing the ideal that they are and should be advocates for the patients they will serve. The mission of medical education must include the need to ensure that physicians maintain these commitments and develop the competencies needed to be effective patient advocates throughout their careers. Medical education reform efforts are needed to implement this mission. Medical schools and training programs are striving to meet this need. Although much has been accomplished, we do not yet provide a comprehensive, integrated approach to teaching and evaluating the competencies necessary for relationship-centered care and advocacy across the continuum of medical education. We can leverage current licensure and accreditation assessment mandates to address this challenge. We believe that important gains can be made if we address the need for curricular reform, institute assessment in the salient commitments and competencies, conduct faculty development activities, and invite patients and families to help shape and implement medical education.

REFERENCES

ABIM Foundation, American Board of Internal Medicine, ACP-ASIM Foundation, American College of Physicians-American Society of Internal Medicine, & European Federation of Internal Medicine. (2002). Medical professionalism in the new millennium: A physician charter. *Annals of Internal Medicine, 136,* 243–246.

Accreditation Council for Graduate Medical Education. (2003–2004). *The ACGME's approach to limit resident duty hours 12 months after implementation: A summary of achievements.* Retrieved March 27, 2006, from http://www.acgme.org/DutyHours/dutyhoursummary2003-04.pdf.

Accreditation Council for Graduate Medical Education. (2006). *Home page.* Retrieved March 28, 2006, from http://www.acgme.org.

American Academy on Communication in Healthcare. *Home page.* Retrieved July 14, 2006, from http://www.aachonline.org/.

American Medical Association. (2006). *Medical student debt.* Retrieved March 27, 2006, from http://www.ama-assn.org/ama/pub/category/5349.html.

Aspegren, K. (1999). BEME guide no. 2: Teaching and learning communication skills in medicine: A review with quality grading of articles. *Medical Teacher, 21,* 563–570.

Association of American Medical Colleges. (2006). *CurrMIT: Curriculum management & information tool.* Retrieved March 28, 2006, from http://www.aamc.org/meded/curric/start.htm.

Awad, S. S., Fagan, S. P., Bellows, C., Albo, D., Green-Rashad, B., De la Garza, M., et al. (2005). Bridging the communication gap in the operating room with medical team training. *American Journal of Surgery, 190,* 770–774.

Balint, M. (1964). *The doctor, his patient, and the illness* (2nd ed.). London: Pitman Medical Publishing.

Betancourt, J. R. (2003). Cross-cultural medical education: Conceptual approaches and frameworks for evaluation. *Academic Medicine, 78,* 560–569.

Brown, M. M., Brown, D. C., Stein, J. D., Roth, Z., Campanella, J., & Beauchamp, G. R. (2005). Age-related macular degeneration: Economic burden and value-based medicine analysis. *Canadian Journal of Ophthalmology, 40,* 277–287.

Centers for Medicare and Medicaid Services. (2005). *Fact sheet: Medicare pay for performance (P4P) initiatives.* Retrieved July 10, 2006, from http://www.cms.hhs.gov/apps/media/press/release.asp?Counter=1343.

Charap, M. (2004). Reducing resident work hours: Unproven assumptions and unforeseen outcomes. *Annals of Internal Medicine, 140,* 814–815.

Charles, C., Gafni, A., & Whelan, T. (1997). Shared decision-making in the medical encounter: What does it mean (or it takes at least two to tango)? *Social Science & Medicine, 44,* 681–692.

Charon, R. (2006). *Attention, representation, affiliation. narrative medicine: Honoring the stories of illness* (pp. 131–153). New York: Oxford University Press.

Complications of Age-Related Macular Degeneration Prevention Trial Study Group. (2004). The complications of age-related macular degeneration prevention trial (CAPT): Rationale, design and methodology. *Clinical Trials, 1,* 91–107.

Cooper-Patrick, L., Gallo, J. J., Gonzales, J. J., Vu, H. T., Powe, N. R., Nelson, C., et al. (1999). Race, gender, and partnership in the patient-physician relationship. *JAMA: Journal of the American Medical Association, 282,* 583–589.

DasGupta, S., Meyer, D., Calero-Breckheimer, A., Costley, A. W., & Guillen, S. (2006). Teaching cultural competency through narrative medicine: Intersections of classroom and community. *Teaching and Learning in Medicine, 18,* 14–17.

Dewalt, D. A., Berkman, N. D., Sheridan, S., Lohr, K. N., & Pignone, M. P. (2004). Literacy and health outcomes: A systematic review of the literature. *Journal of General Internal Medicine, 19,* 1228–1239.

Dyrbye, L. N., Thomas, M. R., & Shanafelt, T. D. (2006). Systematic review of depression, anxiety, and other indicators of psychological distress among U.S. and Canadian medical students. *Academic Medicine, 81,* 354–373.

Earp, J. L., French, E., & Gilkey, M. (2003). *Action items: Where do we go from here? Proceedings from the patient advocacy summit. Patients, families and health care providers: Partners in decision making, advocates in health care,* November 13–14, 2003. (p. 20). Department of Health Behavior and Health Education, School of Public Health, University of North Carolina at Chapel Hill. Chapel Hill, NC.

Epstein, R. M., Franks, P., Shields, C. G., Meldrum, S. C., Miller, K. N., Campbell, T. L., et al. (2005). Patient-centered communication and diagnostic testing. *Annals of Family Medicine, 3,* 415–421.

Fiscella, K., Meldrum, S., Franks, P., Shields, C. G., Duberstein, P., McDaniel, S. H., et al. (2004). Patient trust: Is it related to patient-centered behavior of primary care physicians? *Medical Care, 42,* 1049–1955.

Flocke, S. A., Miller, W. L., & Crabtree, B. F. (2002). Relationships between physician practice style, patient satisfaction, and attributes of primary care. *Journal of Family Practice, 51,* 835–840.

Garibaldi, R. A., Popkave, C., & Bylsma, W. (2005). Career plans for trainees in internal medicine residency programs. *Academic Medicine, 80,* 507–512.

Gates, G. A., & Mills, J. H. (2005). Presbycusis. *Lancet, 366,* 1111–1120.

Gilbert, D. T., & Hixon, J. G. (1991). The trouble of thinking: Activation and application of stereotypic beliefs. *Journal of Personality and Social Psychology, 60,* 509–517.

Goitein, L., Shanafelt, T. D., Wipf, J. E., Slatore, C. G., & Back, A. L. (2005). The effects of work-hour limitations on resident well-being, patient care, and education in an internal medicine residency program. *Archives of Internal Medicine, 165,* 2601–2606.

Gorawara-Bhat, R., Gallagher, T. H., & Levinson, W. (2003). Patient-provider discussions about conflicts of interest in managed care: Physicians' perceptions. *American Journal of Managed Care, 9,* 564–571.

Gundersen, L. (2001). Physician burnout. *Annals of Internal Medicine, 135,* 145–148.

Hafferty, F. W. (1998). Beyond curriculum reform: Confronting medicine's hidden curriculum. *Academic Medicine, 73,* 403–407.

Haq, C., Steele, D. J., Marchand, L., Seibert, C., & Brody, D. (2004). Integrating the art and science of medical practice: Innovations in teaching medical communication skills. *Family Medicine, 36*(Suppl), S43–S50.

Heine, C., & Browning, C. H. (2002). Communication and psychosocial consequences of sensory loss in older adults: Overview and rehabilitation directions. *Disability and Rehabilitation, 24,* 763–773.

Institute of Medicine. (2003). In B. D. Smedley, A. Y. Stith, & A. R. Nelson (Eds.), *Unequal treatment: Confronting racial and ethnic disparities in health care.* Washington, DC: National Academy Press.

Institute of Medicine, Committee on Behavioral and Social Sciences in Medical School Curricula. (2004). In P. A. Cuff & N. A. Vanselow (Eds.), *Improving medical education: Enhancing the behavioral and social science content of medical school curricula.* Washington, DC: National Academies Press.

Joint Commission on Accreditation of Healthcare. (2006). *Performance measurement initiatives.* Retrieved July 10, 2006, from http://www.jointcommission.org/performance-measurement/performancemeasurement.

Jones, A. H., & Carson, R. A. (2003). Medical humanities at the University of Texas Medical Branch at Galveston. *Academic Medicine, 78,* 1006–1009.

Kalet, A., Pugnaire, M. P., Cole-Kelly, K., Janicik, R., Ferrara, E., Schwartz, M. D., et al. (2004). Teaching communication in clinical clerkships: Models from the Macy initiative in health communications. *Academic Medicine, 79,* 511–520.

Kenneth B. Schwartz Center. *Home page.* Retrieved July 14, 2006, from http://www.theschwartzcenter.org/.

Krackov, S. K., Levin, R. I., Catanese, V., Rey, M., Aull, F., Blagev, D., et al. (2003). Medical humanities at New York University School of Medicine: An array of rich programs in diverse settings. *Academic Medicine, 78,* 977–982.

Kressin, N. R., & Petersen, L. A. (2001). Racial differences in the use of invasive cardiovascular procedures: Review of the literature and prescription for future research. *Annals of Internal Medicine, 135,* 352–366.

Levinson, W., & Roter, D. (1995). Physicians' psychosocial beliefs correlate with their patient communication skills. *Journal of General Internal Medicine, 10,* 375–379.

Liaison Committee on Medical Education. (1998). *Functions and structure of a medical school.* Washington, DC: Liaison Committee on Medical Education.

Ludmerer, K. M. (1999). *Time to heal: American medical education from the turn of the century to the era of managed care.* Oxford, UK: Oxford University Press.

Makoul, G. (2001). Essential elements of communication in medical encounters: The Kalamazoo consensus statement. *Academic Medicine, 76,* 390–393.

Moore, G., & Showstack, J. (2003). Primary care medicine in crisis: Toward reconstruction and renewal. *Annals of Internal Medicine, 138,* 244–247.

Mulrow, C. D., Aguilar, C., Endicott, J. E., Tuley, M. R., Velez, R., Charlip, W. S., et al. (1990). Quality-of-life changes and hearing impairment. *Annals of Internal Medicine, 113,* 188–194.

National Center for Education Statistics. *2003 National Assessment of Adult Literacy (NAAL).* Retrieved March 25, 2006, from http://nces.ed.gov/NAAL/index.asp?file=AboutNAAL/WhatIsNAAL.asp&PageId=2.

Novack, D. H., Epstein, R. M., & Paulsen, R. H. (1999). Toward creating physician-healers: Fostering medical students' self-awareness, personal growth, and well-being. *Academic Medicine, 74,* 516–520.

Novack, D. H., Suchman, A. L., Clark, W., Epstein, R. M., Najberg, E., & Kaplan, C. (1997). Calibrating the physician: Personal awareness and effective patient care: Working group on promoting physician personal awareness, American Academy on Physician and Patient. *JAMA: Journal of the American Medical Association, 278,* 502–509.

Parikh, N. S., Parker, R. M., Nurss, J. R., Baker, D. W., & Williams, M. V. (1996). Shame and health literacy: The unspoken connection. *Patient Education and Counseling, 27,* 33–39.

Peabody, F. W. (1927). The care of the patient. *JAMA: Journal of the American Medical Association, 88,* 877–882.

Petersen, L. A., Brennan, T. A., O'Neil, A. C., Cook, E. F., & Lee, T. H. (1994). Does house staff discontinuity of care increase the risk for preventable adverse events? *Annals of Internal Medicine, 121,* 866–872.

Petersen, R., Moracco, K. E., Goldstein, K. M., & Clark, K. A. (2004). Moving beyond disclosure: Women's perspectives on barriers and motivators to seeking assistance for intimate partner violence. *Women & Health, 40,* 63–76.

Pories, S., Jain, S. H., & Harper, G. (2006). *The soul of a doctor: Harvard medical students face life and death.* Chapel Hill, NC: Algonquin Books.

Quill, T. E., & Cassel, C. K. (1995). Nonabandonment: A central obligation for physicians. *Annals of Internal Medicine, 122,* 368–374.

Quraishi, S. A., Orkin, F. K., Weitekamp, M. R., Khalid, A. N., & Sassani, J. W. (2005). The health policy and legislative awareness initiative at the Pennsylvania State University College of Medicine: Theory meets practice. *Academic Medicine, 80,* 443–447.

Rapp, D. E. (2006). Integrating cultural competency into the undergraduate medical curriculum. *Medical Education, 40,* 704–710.

Remen, R. N., & Rabow, M. W. (2005). The healer's art: Professionalism, service and mission. *Medical Education, 39,* 1167–1168.

Rider, E. A., Lown, B. A., & Hinrichs, M. M. (2004). Teaching communication skills. *Medical Education, 38,* 558–559.

Rodriguez, M. A., Bauer, H. M., McLoughlin, E., & Grumbach, K. (1999). Screening and intervention for intimate partner abuse: Practices and attitudes of primary care physicians. *JAMA: Journal of the American Medical Association, 282,* 468–474.

Safran, D. G. (2003). Defining the future of primary care: What can we learn from patients? *Annals of Internal Medicine, 138,* 248–255.

Schindler, B. A., Novack, D. H., Cohen, D. G., Yager, J., Wang, D., Shaheen, N. J., et al. (2006). The impact of the changing health care environment on the health and well-being of faculty at four medical schools. *Academic Medicine, 81,* 27–34.

Schroeder, S. A. (2002). Primary care at a crossroads. *Academic Medicine, 77,* 767–773.

Simpson, M., Buckman, R., Stewart, M., Maguire, P., Lipkin, M., & Novack, D., et al. (1991). Doctor-patient communication: The Toronto consensus statement. *British Medical Journal, 303,* 1385–1387.

Sirridge, M., & Welch, K. (2003). The program in medical humanities at the University of Missouri-Kansas City School of Medicine. *Academic Medicine, 78,* 973–976.

Smith, R. C., Osborn, G., Hoppe, R. B., Lyles, J. S., Van Egeren, L., Henry, R., et al. (1991). Efficacy of a one-month training block in psychosocial medicine for residents: A controlled study. *Journal of General Internal Medicine, 6,* 535–543.

Stewart, M., Brown, J. B., Weston, W. W., McWhinney, I. R., McWilliam, C. L., & Freeman, T. R. (1995). *Patient-centered medicine: Transforming the clinical method.* Thousand Oaks, CA: Sage Publications.

Stewart, M., Brown, J. B., Boon, H., Galajda, J., Meredith, L., & Sangster, M. (1999). Evidence on patient-doctor communication. *Cancer Prevention & Control, 3,* 25–30.

Stewart, M., Brown, J. B., Donner, A., McWhinney, I. R., Oates, J., Weston, W. W., et al. (2000). The impact of patient-centered care on outcomes. *Journal of Family Practice, 49,* 796–804.

Stewart, M. A. (1995). Effective physician-patient communication and health outcomes: A review. *CMAJ: Canadian Medical Association Journal, 152,* 1423–1433.

Tjaden, P., & Thoennes, N. (2000). *Full report of the prevalence, incidence, and consequences of violence against women: Findings from the National Violence Against Women Survey (Research Report NCJ 183781, November 2000).* Retrieved March 25, 2006, from http://www.ncjrs.gov/pdffiles1/nij/183781.pdf.

Tresolini C. P., & The Pew-Fetzer Task Force. (1994). *Health professions education and relationship-centered care.* San Francisco: Pew Health Professions Commission.

United States Medical Licensing Examination. Retrieved July 13, 2006, from http://www.usmle.org.

University of British Columbia. (2005). *2005 conference: "Where's the patient voice in health professional education?"* (log in as a guest). Retrieved July 7, 2006, from http://www.health-disciplines.ubc.ca.libproxy.lib.unc.edu/DHCC.

Wormald, R., Evans, J., Smeeth, L., & Henshaw, K. (2005). Photodynamic therapy for neovascular age-related macular degeneration. *Cochrane Database of Systematic Reviews (Online), 4,* CD002030.

Yueh, B., Shapiro, N., MacLean, C. H., & Shekelle, P. G. (2003). Screening and management of adult hearing loss in primary care: Scientific review. *JAMA: Journal of the American Medical Association, 289,* 1976–1985.

CHAPTER 7

Accessing the Patient's World: Patient–Physician Communication About Psychosocial Issues

Carol E. Golin, Carolyn Thorpe, and M. Robin DiMatteo

OBJECTIVES

- To become familiar with central elements of patient–physician communication
- To understand how these communication styles and behaviors contribute to the delivery of high-quality, patient-centered medical care
- To understand how various types of communication can influence patients' satisfaction, health behaviors, and health outcomes
- To learn about specific communication strategies, including nonverbal communication, shared decision making, and motivational interviewing, that enhance communication about psychosocial issues
- To understand the research evidence linking these communication strategies to better outcomes
- To recognize barriers to using patient-centered communication strategies in the current medical system and possible avenues for overcoming these barriers

Healthcare advocates have been aware for many years that good communication is the basis of an effective relationship between patients and their physicians. Patients consistently articulate their desire for a physician who they trust and who has their best interests in mind and who understands and takes into consideration their social context. Yet among most medical institutions and providers, healthcare communication has not been emphasized as much as the biomedical aspects of care. This perspective is changing, largely because of an increasing body of research evidence over the past 30 years that has shown patient–provider communication to be an essential element of the delivery of high-quality, patient-centered care. In fact, The Institute of Medicine's 2001 proposal to improve the quality of healthcare for the 21st century is built on the premise that optimal healthcare can best be achieved in the context of a long-term, healing relationship between provider and patient (Institute of Medicine, 2001).

Although many definitions have been developed to describe the model of "patient-centered care," a common set of dimensions remains central to this concept (Mead & Bower, 2000). First, this model assumes that a strictly biomedical approach to addressing medical problems—that is, an approach limited to identifying physical signs and symptoms of disease, making a diagnosis, and treating the disease with appropriate therapy—is inadequate for delivering patient-centered care. The more comprehensive biopsychosocial approach is required as well (Mead & Bower, 2000). A *biopsychosocial approach* (Engel, 1977) recognizes that illness involves and is influenced by social and psychological factors in addition to biological factors. A patient's experience living with diabetes, for example, may include having uncontrolled blood glucose but also involves how that patient is affected by the disease: whether she has a supportive network of family and friends, whether she is depressed or anxious, and the extent to which she has access to care and medication. Thus, physicians who take a biopsychosocial approach recognize the need to attend to the "nonmedical" aspects of their patients' problems in order to diagnose and care for them effectively.

Second, patient-centered care requires both the patient and the provider to share responsibility for decision making about the patient's illness and its treatment (DiMatteo, Reiter, & Gambone, 1994; Mead & Bower, 2000). Patient-centered care emphasizes the development of a therapeutic alliance in which both parties have input. As a result, patient preferences are sought out and validated. Patients and physicians form a personal bond, and patients view their physicians as not only clinically competent but also as supportive and engaged (DiMatteo, 1998; Mead & Bower, 2000).

Finally, patient-centered care serves to put a human face on the practice of medicine. Providers approach the "patient-as-person" (rather than patient-as-disease or organ), taking into account the meaning of the illness to the patient in his or her broader life context (Mead & Bower, 2000). To achieve patient-centered care, physicians must strive to understand patients' emotions, beliefs, and attitudes about illness and its impact on their lives. Patient-centered care also recognizes the physician-as-person. In other words, physicians are not interchangeable; their emotional reactions and behavior exert an influence on patient behavior and vice versa (Balint, Courtenay, Elder, Hull, & Julian, 1993; Mead & Bower, 2000). In this model, physicians and patients engage in a relationship that is reciprocal.

Based on this description, communication between physicians and patients is the process through which patient-centered medical care is achieved (Bensing, Verhaak, van Dulmen, & Visser, 2000). In the following sections, we describe specific aspects of patient-centered communication in more detail. We present evidence linking patient-centered communication to self-care behavior, patient satisfaction, health outcomes, and malpractice claims. We discuss ways in which creating more balance between biomedical and psychosocial communication can lead to improved outcomes. In the latter part of the chapter, we describe specific communication strategies that providers use to achieve greater balance between psychosocial and biomedical aspects of care and to facilitate more patient-centered interactions with patients. We end by discussing barriers that physicians face when attempting to adopt these communication strategies and ways in which these barriers can be overcome.

IMPORTANT COMPONENTS OF THE PATIENT–PROVIDER RELATIONSHIP

History of the Patient–Provider Relationship

Over the centuries, the patient–physician relationship has been recognized as a central aspect of medical care (Plato, 1961; Roter, 2000; Szasz & Hollender, 1956). With the rise of modern medical science, however, emphasis on communication between patients and providers greatly diminished (Shorter, 1985). For 30 years after the end of World War II, the purely biomedical perspective reigned supreme in the U.S. medical system (Mead & Bower, 2000), creating what anthropologist Edward T. Hall refers to as a "low-communication context," in which communication is verbally explicit but lacks attention to nuanced aspects of emotive communication (Roter, Frankel, Hall, & Sluyter, 2006). Furthermore, the biomedical model is characterized by paternalism, in the sense that the balance of power and control over decision making leans heavily in favor of the physician (Roter & Hall, 1992). In its most classic expression, as practiced in mid-century, physicians set the agenda for medical encounters, decided what course of action was in the patient's best interest, and determined what information and services to provide. Patients were expected to passively cooperate (Roter & Hall, 1992). In essence, the paternalistic model assumed the physician understood the patient's values and could act as her guardian (Roter, 2000). For example, under the paternalistic model, a physician recognizing symptoms of an anxiety disorder in a patient may decide unilaterally that anxiety is best treated with anti-anxiety medication and prescribe this medication, without any exploration of the context of the anxiety symptoms or the patient's preferences for other treatment options, such as psychotherapy.

Beginning in the 1960s with the rise of the consumer social movement and a growing emphasis on preventive health services, a consumer-based model for the patient–physician relationship began to gain ground (Reeder, 1972). When viewed through a *consumerist* framework, the medical care system is conceived as a marketplace where physician services are based on patient supply and demand. Patients direct the agenda for the medical visit as well as what information and services the physician provides (Roter, 2000; Roter & Hall, 1992). In this model, the physician acts primarily as technical consultant, and the patient's values remain unexamined (Roter, 2000). For example, under the consumerist model, a patient may inform her physician that she has been experiencing symptoms of anxiety and request a prescription for anti-anxiety medication. The physician, in turn, may comply with this request, again without exploring the context of the patients' symptoms or reasons for preferring treatment with medication versus psychotherapy.

Lying between the extremes of paternalism and consumerism is *mutuality*, in which control and decision-making responsibility are shared by patients and physicians. In mutuality, patients and physicians arrive at decisions about care together through informed, collaborative choice in the context of the patient's value system. Mutuality is currently advocated by healthcare communication researchers and experts because it is most congruent with the concept of patient-centered care (Roter, 2000). In fact, some experts in patient–provider relationship research have proposed substituting the term "relationship-centered care" for patient-centered care because mutuality and negotiation lie at the heart of the concept (Beach & Inui, 2006; Roter, 2000). Under this model, the anxious patient and her physician may explore possible reasons for the patient's increase in anxiety symptoms, discuss all available treatment options, consider the patient's preferences for treatment, and arrive together at a decision about the best treatment plan given these circumstances.

Features of Patient-Centered Communication

Patient-centered communication is characterized by high levels of physician *informativeness*, *interpersonal sensitivity*, and *partnership building* (Wissow et al., 1998). Informativeness consists of providing information, both biomedical and psychosocial in nature, to patients spontaneously and in response to their concerns. Interpersonal sensitivity involves eliciting information from patients about social and emotional topics and then responding appropriately. Finally, in partnership building, the physician seeks out the patient's perspective and verifies that he or she understands the patient's thoughts and opinions accurately (e.g., using strategies such as reflective listening and shared decision making, discussed in more detail later). Although these physician behaviors are key aspects in determining the patient centeredness of healthcare communication, patients also play a role. Accordingly, Roter (2000) defined patient-centered communication as that which:

1. Fulfills medical management functions or facilitates the accomplishment of basic medical tasks such as the physical examination, diagnosis, and treatment.
2. Facilitates the elicitation of the patient's agenda for the visit and concerns he or she wishes to address, including psychosocial and quality-of-life issues.
3. Is responsive to the patient's emotional state and concerns.
4. Provides information and behavioral recommendations in an understandable, useful, and motivating way.
5. Encourages patients to participate in decision making.

Table 7.1 provides an additional description of these five components (Roter, 2000), along with specific examples of language that reflects these elements.

Table 7.1   Examples of Patient-Centered Communication Behaviors

Elements of Patient-Centered Communication	Examples

Supports fulfillment of basic medical tasks
    Orients patient to flow of visit
    Gives instructions
    Makes transitional statements
	Well, let's take a look, and
	then we'll talk more about it.
	Breathe normally while I listen to your heart.
	Let's get started with the exam.

Facilitative
    Asks about patients goals and
        concerns they wish to address
    Elicits discussion about psychosocial
        issues
	What concerns would you like to discuss
	today?
	How has your mood been since we last talked?

Responsive
    Looks for clues and probes about
        feelings and emotions
    Expresses support and empathy
	You made a face when I suggested that. How
	are you feeling about this?
	I bet this has been hard for you.

Informative
    Gives biomedical information
 	
    Gives psychosocial information
	The medication might cause your appetite to
	increase. Some people find that having a lot
	of healthy, low-calorie snacks around helps
	them deal with this side effect without gaining
	a lot of weight.
	Let me give you some information about a
	local support group for people with your ill-
	ness. It can really help to talk with others
	who are dealing with the same issues.

Participatory
    Asks about patients' expectations,
        understanding, and concerns
    Asks about impact of the problem on
        functioning and quality of life
    Encourages patient question asking
 	
    Provides opportunities for patients to
        share in decision making
	How do you think this medication plan will
	work for you? What are your concerns about it?
	How has this affected your relationship with
	your family?
	Do you have any questions about the
	medication?
	Which option do you think might work better
	for you?

Links Between Patient-Centered Care and Important Outcomes

Research has consistently shown that patient-centered communication is associated with a variety of improved outcomes. First, patients are more satisfied with their medical care when they experience higher levels of psychosocial talk, encouragement, displays of empathy, biomedical question asking, discussion of treatment effects, and when physicians relinquish control in the latter part of the medical visit (Beck, Daughtridge, & Sloane, 2002). On the other hand, patients tend to be less satisfied when their physicians verbally dominate medical encounters (Bertakis, Roter, & Putnam, 1991). In a recent conference focused on patient advocacy, one participant, a divorced mother of two children, one of whom had suffered from a brain tumor followed by neurologic disorders, articulated how important communication within the doctor–patient relationship is to patients: "Communication isn't just a nice 'extra.' If my doctor is 'nice' or 'polite' to me, that's an extra. What's really important, though, is that he or she takes seriously my knowledge of having lived with the disease, both in terms of symptoms, and in terms of my day-to-day life. Knowing whether or not I have a car, for example, makes a difference in how care is given."

Second, two recent reviews (Roter, 2000; Stewart, 1995) reported that physician informativeness, partnership building, and responsiveness to patients' emotions are consistently linked to better psychological and physiologic outcomes. Specifically, when physicians were more informative, their patients had reduced levels of psychological distress, higher rates of symptom resolution, and improved blood pressure when compared with patients of physicians who were less informative. Also, physicians' attempts to build partnerships and elicit patient participation were associated with improved symptom resolution, lower levels of anxiety and depression, and reduced role and physical limitations among patients. Perhaps most compelling in this line of research was one study using random assignment, which found that patients trained to participate more in medical decision making had improved health outcomes (i.e., improved blood glucose control and functioning) compared with controls (Greenfield, Kaplan, & Ware, 1985; Greenfield, Kaplan, Ware, Yano, & Frank, 1988). Furthermore, these reviews also revealed that physicians' responsiveness to patients' emotional states was related to reduced levels of patient distress and improved symptom resolution, and patients who were encouraged to express psychosocial concerns had improved physical and social functioning, health status, and blood pressure.

Third, several specific patient-centered communication practices have also been linked to improved health behaviors in patients. When physicians explain, provide feedback, share medical data, and demonstrate solidarity with the patient, patients tend to have higher levels of treatment adherence (Beck et al., 2002), defined as the extent to which patients carry out behavioral recommendations they have agreed on with physicians (World Health Organization, 2003).

Finally, patients whose doctors use a patient-centered approach may also be less likely to bring malpractice claims. In one study, physicians who showed higher levels of facilitative behavior (i.e., asking patients to express their opinions, checking their understanding and generally encouraging them to talk more) and who used humor more often were less likely to experience a malpractice claim (Levinson, Roter, Mullooly, Dull, & Frankel, 1997). In summary, this body of research strongly suggests that patient-centered communication leads to a wide range of positive outcomes for both patients and physicians.

The Importance of Psychosocial Communication

One aspect of patient-centered communication that may have a particularly strong influence on patients' satisfaction with their care is the extent to which psychosocial communication occurs during primary care visits. Psychosocial communication elicits information about the social and psychological issues that patients face and provides the physician with an opportunity to offer information and counsel about these issues. For example, an older widow with diabetes may have no way to get to the store to purchase her supplies for glucose testing. Communication about her transportation needs will be a vital component in ensuring that she is able to follow her doctor's recommendations.

Several studies have demonstrated that the balance struck by physicians between psychosocial and biomedical communication in office visits, a distinguishing characteristic of the three models of the patient–physician relationship introduced previously, may influence patients' satisfaction with their medical care. Roter et al. (1997) analyzed primary care visits with adults with ongoing medical problems and identified five distinct patterns of communication: (1) *narrowly biomedical*, characterized by very little talk about psychosocial topics, a large amount of physician information giving about biomedical topics, and extensive question asking by the physician; (2) *expanded biomedical*, characterized by high levels of physician question asking but slightly less imbalance between psychosocial and biomedical issues; (3) *biopsychosocial*, characterized by a greater balance between biomedical and psychosocial exchange, a lower level of question asking by the physician, and a higher level of social talk; (4) *psychosocial*, characterized by an equal balance between psychosocial and biomedical talk by the physician and a higher level of patient psychosocial than biomedical talk, as well as low levels of physician question asking; and (5) *consumerist*, characterized by high levels of patient question asking, low levels of physician question asking, high levels of physician information giving, and low levels of psychosocial and social exchange. The first two styles were the most commonly used, accounting for 32% and 33% of visits, respectively, whereas the biopsychosocial, psychosocial, and consumerist patterns occurred less frequently (20%, 7%, and 8% of visits, respectively). Patient satisfaction was highest in the psychosocial pattern, followed by the biopsychosocial and consumerist patterns, and lowest in the narrowly biomedical and expanded biomedical patterns, suggesting that patients are most satisfied when given ample opportunity to talk about psychosocial issues in addition to biomedical issues.

Mechanisms by Which Psychosocial Communication Affects Patient Outcomes

Why might psychosocial communication have such a significant influence on patient satisfaction, as well as on their psychological, behavioral, and physiologic outcomes? Several possible reasons exist, including enhanced physician understanding of barriers and facilitators to illness management, shared decision making, and perceptions of physician support, trust, and rapport.

Improved Understanding of Barriers and Facilitators to Illness Management

Across a variety of conditions, only about half of all patients adhere to behavioral recommendations made by their healthcare providers (World Health Organization, 2003). Such low rates of adherence can lead directly to poor clinical outcomes (World Health Organization, 2003), particularly when illnesses are chronic (DiMatteo, Giordani, Lepper, & Croghan,

2002). A vast body of research has demonstrated that a variety of psychosocial factors influence the degree to which patients follow medical recommendations. These issues include patients' beliefs about their illness, motivation, intentions, confidence, social relationships, financial resources, literacy levels, culture, emotions, and mental health status (Bosworth & Voils, 2006; World Health Organization, 2003). It follows that physicians willing to devote time to identifying and addressing these types of issues will improve the psychological, behavioral, and even physiologic outcomes of their patients.

Research suggests that through psychosocial communication, physicians become aware of issues affecting their patients' abilities to cope with their health problems. For example, one recent study (Wissow et al., 2002) suggested that when physicians avoided patients' disclosure of social and emotional issues, patients reduced their subsequent disclosures to their physicians, both later in the visit and in subsequent visits (Wissow et al., 2002). In contrast, when physicians asked open-ended questions and demonstrated higher levels of patient-centered communication overall, patients disclosed social and emotional issues more frequently.

Shared Decision Making

Discussion of psychosocial issues also facilitates shared decision making about health problems, another method for enhancing patient-centered care. Although shared decision making is a relatively new concept (Kaplan, 2004), evidence indicates that it improves patient satisfaction (Frosch & Kaplan, 1999; Gattellari, Butow, & Tattersall, 2001). One important feature of shared decision making is discussing patients' values and concerns regarding specific biomedical options, many of which may be psychosocial in nature (O'Connor et al., 1999a). For example, a woman diagnosed with early-stage breast cancer may be an appropriate candidate, from a biomedical perspective, for either mastectomy or breast-conserving therapy with chemotherapy and radiation. Discussion of psychosocial issues, such as her concerns about body image versus fears about breast cancer recurrence, are necessary in order to develop a treatment plan that takes into account her values and preferences.

Enhanced Perceptions of Physician Support, Trust, and Rapport

Psychosocial communication in medical office visits may improve patient outcomes by enhancing patients' trust in their physicians. A patient–provider relationship in which patients perceive high levels of trust, rapport, and physician support is known as a therapeutic alliance and has been linked to improved patient satisfaction (Leach, 2005) and treatment adherence (Kyngas & Rissanen, 2001; Leach, 2005; Stanton, 1987; World Health Organization, 2003). Encouraging discussion about psychosocial topics in office visits may communicate to the patient that the physician is committed to understanding him or her as a person, not just a medical case, thus improving patient trust and rapport. Indeed, research has demonstrated a link between more discussion about psychosocial issues in office visits and higher patient perceptions of emotional support from physicians (Bertakis et al., 1991).

Use of Patient-Centered Communication in Office Visits

Despite what is known about the benefits of patient-centered communication, including psychosocial communication, research suggests that they are underused in patient–physician encounters. Several reports have found that between 35% and 65% of primary care office visits consist of communication that is primarily biomedical in nature (Bensing, Roter, & Hulsman, 2003; Flocke, Miller, & Crabtree, 2002; Roter et al., 1997). A recent study (Levinson, Gorawara-Bhat, & Lamb, 2000) also found that primary care physicians and surgeons often failed to appropriately respond to patients' clues about social and emotional issues they wished to discuss with their doctors. Only 38% of such clues presented to surgeons and 21% of clues presented to primary care physicians elicited a positive response from physicians (i.e., acknowledgment, encouragement, praise, reassurance, or a show of support). The remainder elicited inadequate acknowledgment, inappropriate use of humor, denial of the patient's concerns, or termination of talk about the issue.

In the next sections, we present several specific strategies that physicians can use to facilitate patient-centered communication with their patients. We also examine a number of barriers to engaging in patient-centered and psychosocial communication in office visits and a variety of promising strategies for overcoming these barriers.

COMMUNICATION STRATEGIES FOR BUILDING BETTER RELATIONSHIPS WITH PATIENTS

Nonverbal Strategies

Nonverbal communication skills include nonverbal sensitivity and nonverbal behavior (Roter et al., 2006). Nonverbal sensitivity involves the ability to both encode (convey emotional messages accurately) and decode (read emotions of others accurately) based on nonverbal cues. In cross-sectional studies, physicians with greater nonverbal skill (i.e., those who were better able to decode body movements and more skilled at emotional encoding) received higher patient satisfaction ratings than those without these abilities (DiMatteo, Hays, & Prince, 1986; DiMatteo, Taranta, Friedman, & Prince, 1980; Friedman, DiMatteo, & Taranta, 1980; Harrigan & Rosenthal, 1986). These skills have been associated with improved treatment adherence as well (DiMatteo et al., 1986).

Nonverbal behavior involves a range of communication activities that do not have linguistic content, including eye contact, facial expressions, head movements (such as nodding), hand gestures, and postural positions (Roter et al., 2006). Paralinguistic behaviors are also nonverbal, such as the rate, volume, and pitch of speech, pauses, and interruptions (Harrigan & Rosenthal, 1986; Roter et al., 2006; Smith & Larsen, 1984; Zuckerman, Larrance, Hall, DeFrank, & Rosenthal, 1979). Nonverbal behaviors communicate emotional information, such as joy, sadness, or anxiety, as well as agreement or turn taking in a conversation (Knapp & Hall, 2005). In general, physicians who are more emotionally expressive receive higher ratings in terms of patient satisfaction. Specific physician behaviors viewed favorably by patients include increased eye contact, less time looking at medical charts, forward leaning, open body posture, head nodding, use of hand gestures, maintenance of a closer interpersonal distance, and specific voice tones (Griffith, Wilson, Langer, & Haist, 2003; Hall, Roter, & Rand, 1981; Hall, Harrigan, & Rosenthal, 1995; Roter et al., 2006). In one study, nonverbal behaviors explained more variance in patient satisfaction than did verbal content, regardless of the type or severity of medical condition being discussed (Griffith et al., 2003).

Research evaluating nonverbal communication does not always show expected results. For example, although reduced interpersonal distance is usually associated with increased interpersonal satisfaction, *less* touch by a physician has been shown to be associated with greater patient satisfaction (Hall et al., 1995; Roter et al., 2006), possibly because touch may communicate power and dominance (Hall et al., 1995; Roter et al., 2006). Voice tone has also been associated with patient satisfaction in intriguing ways. Hall et al. (1981) found that patients were more satisfied with physicians who expressed a more anxious and irritated voice tone when this tone was coupled with sympathetic verbal content. The authors speculate that an anxious voice tone may express care and concern in this context.

Few studies have provided evidence that directly links nonverbal communication to health outcomes other than patient satisfaction, with two notable exceptions. In a prospective study (Ambady, Koo, Rosenthal, & Winograd, 2002), nonverbal behavior of physical therapists predicted patients' psychological and cognitive functioning at follow-up. In particular, poor eye contact and physical distancing were associated with worsened functioning, and greater facial expressiveness (e.g., smiling, nodding, and frowning) was associated with improved functioning. DiMatteo et al. (1986) also found that physicians who were rated as more nonverbally sensitive experienced fewer appointment cancellations that were not rescheduled by patients.

These findings highlight the potentially significant influence that nonverbal communication can have on outcomes. Specific nonverbal skills and behaviors that may influence outcomes are summarized in Table 7.2. Furthermore, studies show that although physicians do exhibit a broad range of nonverbal communication abilities, many physicians misread emotional distress cues and rate patients' emotional states more negatively than do their patients (Hall, Stein, Roter, & Rieser, 1999), suggesting that there is room for improvement. Although the findings in this section suggest ways in which nonverbal communication behavior can be improved, little work has been done to evaluate the effects of physician training on improving nonverbal communication skills. Such skills are typically absorbed at the individual level through one-on-one mentoring during clinical training rather than being included as part of the medical school curriculum. In the future, teaching and research should consider the important role that nonverbal communication plays in the development of a healing patient–physician interaction.

Table 7.2   Favorable and Unfavorable Nonverbal Communication Skills and Behaviors

Domain	Favorable	Unfavorable
Nonverbal Skills	Greater ability to decode nonverbal behaviors of others and to recognize their emotions accurately	Poor ability to decode (recognize) accurately the emotions of others
	Greater ability to transmit the intended emotional messages	Poor ability to encode emotional messages nonverbally
Nonverbal Behaviors	Eye Contact	
	Make direct eye contact	Make little eye contact
	Spend more time gazing at patient	Look at the medical chart
	Body Posture	
	Forward leaning	Backward leaning
	Open posture (arms open)	Closed arms and body
	Facial Expressivity	
	Smiling	Frowning
	Very expressive	Blank expression
	Gestures	
	Frequent head nodding	Lack of head nodding
	Frequent hand gestures	Lack of hand gestures
	Interpersonal distance	
	Closer distance	Greater distance
	Less touch	More touch
	Voice Tone	
	Emotionally expressive	Monotone
	More anxious	Less anxious/unconcerned

Verbal Strategies

Specific verbal behaviors can enhance patient-centered care and thereby potentially improve psychosocial communication (Roter et al., 1997). One study identified three physician communication behaviors that explained nearly 30% of the variance in patient satisfaction. These included use of more silence following patients' utterances, use of words similar to patients', and use of reflective interruptions or interruptions that were on topic with what patients were discussing. The fact that these three specific techniques accounted for nearly a third of the variance in satisfaction is impressive and suggests that their use is warranted (Rowland-Morin & Carroll, 1990). Later we describe in detail two more general approaches that a practitioner can use to facilitate patient-centered care.

Shared Decision Making

Shared decision making in the medical visit has evolved as a means to involve patients in decisions about their health and well-being. Medical encounters entail making decisions regarding diagnostic and screening tests, medication, and procedural treatments, as well as varied disease management strategies. Although for some medical conditions the most appropriate medical treatment is clear, for others, uncertainty prevails, and the incorporation of patients' values and preferences plays a salient role in the decision-making process. As noted previously, discussion of these values and preferences requires patients and physicians to communicate about psychosocial issues that influence patients' health.

Although researchers for the most part agree on why patients should participate in medical decision making, how best to involve them is less clear. In general, shared decision making is recommended because it helps patients to understand their condition, potential treatment options, and risks and benefits associated with each option. The shared decision-making process involves weighing patients' personal values and encouraging them to participate in making the final treatment decision (Sheridan, Harris, & Woolf, 2004). The textbox shows nine essential elements of shared decision making, as defined in a recent review (Makoul & Clayman, 2005) of published definitions of the concept.

Several methods have been developed to help patients explicitly clarify their values as they relate to available medical choices. For example, one method, social matching, presents patients with sample testimonials and asks them to align themselves with the options selected by other people they perceive as similar to themselves (Ubel, Jepson, & Baron, 2001). Rating, a second method, typically asks patients to rate the value they place on potential health states compared with the best and worst health states imaginable (Ryan et al., 2001). Rank ordering requires patients to rank a finite number of options from most to least favorable (Phillips, Johnson, & Maddala, 2002). For example, one clinic-based study examined how men decide whether to have a screening test for prostate cancer by combining the rating and ranking methods (Golin et al., 2006). Men watched an informational video about the test and were given five cards representing five aspects of the test: degree of accuracy of the PSA test, degree of certainty of treatment outcomes, need for knowing about having cancer, worry about side effects of treatment, and the magnitude of prostate cancer as a problem. For each of these characteristics, men were given two statements: one representing a value consistent with not wanting the test and the other a value consistent with wanting the test. Men were then asked to choose which one of the two statements best represented how they felt. For example, for the characteristic "*accuracy of PSA,*" men could choose either "I would only want to have the PSA test if it could tell me for sure if I do or don't have cancer," or "The fact that the PSA test doesn't give me a definite answer about whether I do or don't have cancer does not bother me; nothing in life is 100%." The cards were intended to make it easier for the men to discuss this potentially sensitive topic. After choosing a card for each of the five characteristics of the test, men were asked to rank the characteristics as most to least important regarding their decision to have a PSA test. Men receiving the intervention showed a greater increase in their desire to participate in medical decisions and were more likely to have a change in their intentions to get screened compared with men in the control group (Golin et al., 2006).

A variety of other values-clarification methods have been presented in the literature (Ryan et al., 2001; Schwartz & Bilsky, 1987), but additional studies would help determine which approaches are most helpful in aligning personal values with treatment choices. How best to understand and incorporate patients' values into medical decision making is indeed an emerging and understudied area (O'Connor et al., 2003); however, recent evidence suggests that although value clarification exercises do not necessarily increase perceived clarity of values, they tend to better align patients' medical choices with their personal values (O'Connor et al., 1999a, 1999b).

One barrier to implementing shared decision making in clinical settings is that it can be a time-consuming process, particularly when the decision involves complex tradeoffs; therefore, decision aids have been developed to facilitate the shared decision-making process. Such tools can provide information about the seriousness of a condition, treatment options, potential outcomes, and the pros and cons associated with each course of action (O'Connor et al., 2003) as well as helping patients to clarify their

---

Textbox 7.1   Nine Essential Elements of Shared Decision Making

Shared decision making occurs when:

1. The physician and patient define together the problem that needs to be addressed.
2. The physician and patient review together the options available to address the problem.
3. The physician and patient discuss the pros and cons of each option.
4. The physician provides knowledge and recommendations.
5. The physician helps the patient to discover his or her preferences through a process of values clarification.
6. The physician assesses the patient's understanding of the information reviewed.
7. The physician and patient discuss the patient's confidence to carry out what is required to implement the choice.
8. If a decision is to be deferred, the physician and patient make an explicit plan to defer.
9. The physician devises a plan to follow-up with the patient to assess the outcome of choices made.

Source: Data from Makoul, G. & Clayman M. L. (2005). An integrative model of shared decision-making in medical encounters. *Patient Education and Counseling*, *60*(3), 301–312.

---

values. Decision aids come in many forms, including written materials, decision boards, videos, interactive computer tools, and interactive sessions with a health educator. Two recent reviews (O'Connor et al., 1999a, 2003) also noted that some decision aid programs teach patients how to communicate with their doctors about their preferences and struggles. The use of decision aids can save the physician time and has been shown to improve patient knowledge, enhance patient satisfaction, reduce decisional conflict, and stimulate patients to play an active role in decision making about their healthcare (O'Connor et al., 1999a, 2003).

Motivational Interviewing

Motivational interviewing is another way that providers can learn about their patients' psychosocial situations and build long-term trust and rapport.

Originally developed to facilitate behavior change among problem drinkers, motivational interviewing has been adapted, often in abbreviated forms, to address a wide range of health behaviors including smoking cessation, diabetes management, intake of healthy fruits and vegetables, reduction of risky sexual behavior, and adherence to medication taking (Butler et al., 1999; Colby et al., 1998; Harding, Dockrell, Dockrell, & Corrigan, 2001; Kemp, Hayward, Applewhaite, Everitt, & David, 1996; Picciano, Roffman, Kalichman, Rutledge, & Burghuis, 2001; Resnicow et al., 2002; Rollnick, Butler, & Stott, 1997; Smith, Heckemeyer, Kratt, & Mason, 1997). Motivational interviewing is a style of counseling (Miller, 1996) based on the work of Carl Rogers (1987) and includes five key principles: (1) expressing empathy, (2) highlighting discrepancies between a patient's life goals and his or her current behavior, (3) avoiding argumentation, (4) accepting and dealing with resistance, and (5) supporting self-efficacy (Emmons & Rollnick, 2001; Kjellgren, Ahlner, & Saljo, 1995; Miller, 1996; Miller & Rollnick, 1991). One primary role of the provider using motivational interviewing techniques is to help patients recognize and resolve feelings of ambivalence about changing unhealthy behaviors (DiIorio et al., 2003; Emmons & Rollnick, 2001; Miller, 1996; Miller & Rollnick, 1991).

An important underlying principle of motivational interviewing (and a key component of patient-centered care) is that the provider must exhibit a genuine desire to understand the patient. Because this type of counseling takes the patient's perspective into account when making care plans, motivational interviewing can influence important patient outcomes. Specifically, motivational interviewing interventions have been shown to improve the following health outcomes: medication adherence among patients with psychosis (Kemp et al., 1996; Picciano et al., 2001) and HIV (Adamian et al., in press; DiIorio et al., 2003; Picciano et al., 2001), vegetable intake (Resnikow et al., 2001), weight loss among older women with diabetes (Smith et al., 1997), smoking cessation (Butler et al., 1999; Rollnick et al., 1997), and safe sexual practices (Kamb et al., 1998; Kelly & Kalichman, 2002; National Institute of Mental Health, 1998; Picciano et al., 2001; Rollnick et al., 1997). Furthermore, the motivational interviewing style allows patients to set the agenda for the session; in doing so, they become active participants in their care.

Although motivational interviewing is patient centered, it does allow providers to offer nonjudgmental, objective feedback to patients. To do so, however, providers must first listen deeply to their patients' concerns and the meaning that issues hold for patients. By reflecting back their own perceptions, the practitioner raises patients' awareness of discrepancies between their life goals and their current actions. By enhancing patients' self-efficacy, practitioners can provide support while moving patients toward change (Miller & Rollnick, 2002). For example, Textbox 7.2 presents the use of motivational interviewing in the case study of Ms. Bashford, a young woman living with HIV.

Several specific communication behaviors are present in high-quality motivational interviewing. These include using more statements (e.g., reflections) than questions and asking more open-ended than closed-ended

---

Textbox 7.2   Motivational Interviewing Case Study

Composite Case Study: Ms. Bashford, a 39-year-old African American woman who works as a real estate secretary, was diagnosed with HIV three years ago. A year ago, her doctor, Dr. Schaffer, recommended that Ms. Bashford begin taking medication to prevent disease progression; however, medication regimens for HIV are relatively costly, complex, and have significant side effects, yet patients must adhere very closely to the regimen to maintain its effect.

When she started the medication, the level of the HIV virus in Ms. Bashford's blood quickly became undetectable, indicating that the medication was working well; however, recently, the level of virus in Ms. Bashford's blood increased. Dr. Schaffer suspected that Ms. Bashford might not be taking her medication as directed and chose to use motivational interviewing techniques to address the issue. She knew that understanding Ms. Bashford's perspective and life challenges could help them develop strategies to improve her medication adherence. Dr. Schaffer also knew that if she were confrontational and prescriptive, Ms. Bashford might become resistant to taking her medication.

In discussions with Ms. Bashford, Dr. Schaffer assessed what it was like for her to take her medications in a typical day, how important taking the medication was to her, and how confident she felt that she could follow the recommendations. Through this process, they learned that although taking medication was very important to Ms. Bashford, side effects and the medication schedule made it difficult for her to stick with the regimen. In addition, she was afraid that taking the medication at work would reveal her HIV status to coworkers. By using motivational interviewing techniques, Dr. Schaffer helped Ms. Bashford raise her awareness of the importance that taking the medication had for Ms. Bashford and identify several strategies that would address her concerns and make it easier to stick with her regimen. Three months later, Ms. Bashford's virus level was undetectable, and she felt more satisfied with her decision and her relationship with her physician.

questions. Few studies have attempted to validate the specific communication behaviors most likely to affect outcomes and improve care. One exception is a study of a motivational interviewing program administered to HIV-infected patients (Thrasher et al., 2005) in which antiretroviral therapy adherence was positively associated with a greater ratio of reflections to questions and a greater number of affirming statements and negatively associated with closed-ended questions. More studies are needed that attempt to understand the mechanisms by which motivational interviewing can help physicians comprehend their patients' perspectives, build trust and rapport, and ultimately enhance health and healthy behaviors (Emmons & Rollnick, 2001).

NEXT STEPS: IDENTIFYING BARRIERS TO AND INTERVENTIONS FOR IMPROVING PROVIDER–PATIENT PSYCHOSOCIAL COMMUNICATION

Barriers to Psychosocial Communication Between Doctors and Patients

Although data exist indicating effective ways that physicians can communicate with patients, too often these practices are not carried out (Roter et al., 1997). Several studies have evaluated the barriers that physicians face in attempting to communicate about psychosocial issues. Some of the main impediments include lack of physician time, knowledge and training, physician discomfort, and sociodemographic characteristics of patient–physician dyads.

In one qualitative study of psychosocial communication with Latino patients (Shapiro, Hollingshead, & Morrison, 2002), physicians identified three major obstacles to engaging in culturally competent communication with patients about psychosocial issues: insufficient time, language barriers, and patient characteristics. Providers also felt that because many of their patients came from lower socioeconomic status backgrounds, they had greater problems maintaining continuity of care, making consistent communication a challenge. In contemplating solutions to cross-cultural communication barriers, doctors and patients both recommended changes in provider behavior, including developing language skills, learning to work with interpreters, acquiring personal knowledge of patients, maintaining an attitude of interest and respect, and improving general communication skills.

A study of patient–pediatrician interactions (Wissow et al., 2002) provides further evidence of how physician discomfort can serve as a barrier to psychosocial communication. In an analysis of 167 audio-taped interactions, physician utterances that discouraged patients from discussing psychosocial issues occurred in 77% of discussions that involved talking with parents about the use of corporal punishment as a parenting technique and in 34% of discussions that involved other psychosocial topics. These discouraging responses were related more to the type and acuity of the psychosocial topics than to doctor or patient characteristics.

In another study of audio-taped doctor–patient interactions, race served as barriers to disclosure of psychosocial information early in the parent–pediatrician relationship (Wissow et al., 2002). During initial visits, African American mothers made 26% fewer psychosocial statements than did white mothers; however, the physician's degree of patient centeredness was an important factor promoting psychosocial information giving for mothers, regardless of patient race or physician gender. Other studies have suggested physician gender to be an important factor related to patient-centered communication, finding that female physicians spend more time with their patients, are more likely to engage their patients in discussions of psychosocial issues, deal more often with feelings and emotions, and facilitate partnership and patient participation more effectively than do male physicians (Hall & Roter, 1998; Roter & Hall, 2001; Roter, Hall, & Aoki, 2002).

Taken together, these findings suggest that a variety of factors may impede physicians' use of patient-centered communication strategies and that many physicians may require extra support or training in order to discuss psychosocial issues with patients. Fortunately, several promising strategies for overcoming these barriers exist.

Overcoming Barriers to Psychosocial Communication: Training, Curriculum, and Organizational Strategies

Mounting evidence suggests that physicians can be trained to provide medical care that is more patient centered and takes into account the psychosocial and cultural context of patients' lives (Betancourt, Green, Carrillo, & Park, 2005; Brach & Fraser, 2000; Stewart et al., 2000). Curricular changes can enhance physicians' abilities to discuss psychosocial issues with a range of patients and improve the quality of patient care.

Educators have developed programs to enhance the communication of physicians in practice and have begun to incorporate such training into medical schools and residency programs. One innovative program at UCLA, called "Doctoring," trains medical students to give compassionate, humanistic, high-quality, and evidence-based care. Training occurs through a longitudinal, interdisciplinary curriculum that integrates traditional and experiential learning about psychosocial communication and uses interviews with simulated patients (Wilkes, Usatine, Slavin, & Hoffman, 1998). Findings of a recent review (Beach et al., 2005) also suggest that training providers in psychosocial communication can improve the knowledge, attitudes, and skills of healthcare professionals and the satisfaction of their patients; however, the impact on other patient outcomes, such as adherence and health, is less well established.

Kern et al. (2005) conducted an iterative evaluation as part of a national faculty development program. In this program, both experts and generalists taught psychosocial medicine while precepting medical students and residents in clinical settings. Using scientific evidence, educational theory, and experience, the authors developed consensus-based recommendations on the implementation of communication skills instruction for medical trainees, presented them in workshops, and revised them based on feedback from other experts and teachers. First, they identified evidence-based practices for addressing important common psychosocial situations including substance abuse, depression, anxiety, disorder, physical and sexual abuse, and posttraumatic stress disorder. Second, they developed a list of general steps that clinician educators could use to help educate trainees and improve their psychosocial care.

Evaluating physicians' and trainees' psychosocial communication skills and providing individually tailored feedback may also be an efficient and effective method for improving communication skills. Studies (Maynard & Heritage, 2005) have suggested that conversation analysis of audiotaped visits should be used by medical trainees to assess and improve (through feedback and teaching) their psychosocial communication skills. Conversation analysis takes a co-constructive and collaborative analytic approach, putting equal emphasis on the interactive communication behaviors of both physician and patient (Maynard & Heritage, 2005). In addition, Roter et al. (2004) found that the use of an innovative video-feedback technique combining evaluation and training significantly improved residents' patient-centered communication skills.

Although studied less often, efforts are also being made to train patients to be more active participants in their care and to assess the effects of such training on the therapeutic relationship and patient outcomes. In one study (Greenfield et al., 1985, 1988), mentioned previously, patients participated in a 20-minute session before their regularly scheduled visits, during which they were taught to read their medical record, ask questions, and negotiate medical decisions with their physicians. In a randomized controlled trial, researchers compared this intervention with a standard educational session of equal length. At follow-up, patients in the experimental group reported fewer physical limitations, preferred a more active role in medical decision making, and were as satisfied with their care as the control group. Those with diabetes also had greater control of their blood glucose. In O'Connor et al.'s (1999a, 2003) reviews of decision aids, a small proportion of tools studied included a coaching component that taught patients to communicate with their doctor. In a study among cancer outpatients who suffered from uncontrolled pain, those who underwent coaching for pain management skills and skills in communicating with doctors had greater improvement in their pain than did a control group (Oliver, Kravitz, Kaplan, & Meyers, 2001). More studies are needed to understand the combined effect of training both doctors and patients to communicate better with each other. In addition, systems level factors, such as duration of doctor visits, need to be addressed.

SUMMARY AND CONCLUSIONS

High-quality communication between health professionals and their patients is essential to the delivery of effective medical care. "Patient-centered care" has been identified as central to a variety of important outcomes including patient satisfaction, treatment adherence, and improved physiologic and health status outcomes. Patient-centered care requires that physicians communicate clearly and effectively with their patients and strive to understand their patients' beliefs, attitudes, emotions, cultural experiences, and the impact of illness on patients' lives. To achieve true patient-centered care, shared decision making about all aspects of disease management is needed, with a reciprocal communication process that involves shared input and responsibility. Patient-centered care also calls for a continued emphasis on "psychosocial communication," emphasizing awareness of and empathy with patients' emotional experiences. Research has shown that shared decision making and motivational interviewing are particularly valuable in facilitating patient-centered care. Shared decision making helps to assess and incorporate the patient's value system and to encourage the patient to participate in the decision-making process. Motivational interviewing helps providers learn about their patients' psychosocial situations and build long-term trust and rapport. Mounting evidence suggests that physicians can be trained in these and other approaches to better provide patient-centered care and that patients can be assisted to be more active participants in the medical care process. Although more research is needed, patient-centered communication strategies are beginning to show measurable improvements in patients' healthcare outcomes and quality of life.

REFERENCES

Adamian, M. S., Golin, C. E., Shain, L. S., & DeVellis B. (2004). Brief motivational interviewing to improve adherence to antiretroviral therapy: Development and qualitative pilot assessment of an intervention. *AIDS Patient Care and STDs, 18*(4), 229–238.

Ambady, N., Koo, J., Rosenthal, R., & Winograd, C. H. (2002). Physical therapists' nonverbal communication predicts geriatric patients' health outcomes. *Psychology and Aging, 17,* 443–452.

Balint, E., Courtenay, M., Elder, A., Hull, S., & Julian, P. (1993). *The doctor, the patient, and the group: Balint revisited.* London: Routledge.

Beach, M. C., & Inui, T. (2006). Relationship-centered care: A constructive reframing. *Journal of General Internal Medicine, 21*(Suppl 1), S3–S8.

Beach, M. C., Price, E. G., Gary, T. L., Robinson, K. A., Gozu, A., Palacio, A., et al. (2005). Cultural competence: A systematic review of health care provider educational interventions. *Medical Care, 43,* 356–373.

Beck, R. S., Daughtridge, R., & Sloane, P. D. (2002). Physician–patient communication in the primary care office: A systematic review. *Journal of the American Board of Family Practitioners, 15,* 25–38.

Bensing, J. M., Roter, D. L., & Hulsman, R. L. (2003). Communication patterns of primary care physicians in the United States and the Netherlands. *Journal of General Internal Medicine, 18,* 335–342.

Bensing, J. M., Verhaak, P. F. M., van Dulmen, A. M., & Visser, A. P. (2000). Communication: The royal pathway to patient-centered medicine. *Patient Education and Counseling, 39,* 1–3.

Bertakis, K. D., Roter, D., & Putnam, S. M. (1991). The relationship of physician medical interview style to patient satisfaction. *The Journal of Family Practice, 32,* 175–181.

Betancourt, J. R., Green, A. R., Carrillo, J. E., & Park, E. R. (2005). Cultural competence and health care disparities: Key perspectives and trends. *Health Affairs, 24,* 499–505.

Bosworth, H. B., & Voils, C. I. (2006). Theoretical models to understand treatment adherence. In H. B. Bosworth, E. Z. Oddone, & M. Weinberger (Eds.), *Patient treatment adherence: Concepts, interventions, and measurement* (pp. 13–46). Mahwah, NJ: Lawrence Erlbaum Associates.

Brach, C., & Fraser, I. (2000). Can cultural competency reduce racial and ethnic health disparities? A review and conceptual model. *Medical Care Research and Review, 57*(Suppl 1), 181–217.

Butler, C., Rollnick, S., Cohen, D., Bachman, M., Russell, I., & Stott, N. (1999). Motivational counseling versus brief advice for smokers in general practice: A randomized trial. *British Journal of General Practice, 49,* 611–616.

Colby, S. M., Monti, P. M., Barnett, N. P., Rohsenow, D. J., Weissman, K., Spirito, A., et al. (1998). Brief motivational interviewing in a hospital setting for adolescent smoking: A preliminary study. *Journal of Consulting and Clinical Psychology, 66*(3), 574–578.

DiIorio, C., Resnicow, K., McDonnell, M., Soet, J., McCarty, F., & Yeager, K. (2003). Using motivational interviewing to promote adherence to antiretroviral medications: A pilot study. *Journal of the Association of Nurses in AIDS Care, 14*(2), 52–62.

DiMatteo, M. R. (1998). The role of the physician in the emerging health care environment. *Western Journal of Medicine, 168*(5), 328–333.

DiMatteo, M. R., Giordani, P. J., Lepper, H. S., & Croghan, T. W. (2002). Patient adherence and medical treatment outcomes: A meta-analysis. *Medical Care, 40,* 794–811.

DiMatteo, M. R., Hays, R. D., & Prince, L. M. (1986). Relationship of physicians' nonverbal communication skill to patient satisfaction, appointment noncompliance, and physician workload. *Health Psychology, 5*(6), 581–594.

DiMatteo, M. R., Reiter, R. C., & Gambone, J. C. (1994). Enhancing medication adherence through communication and informed collaborative choice. *Health Communication, 6,* 253–265.

DiMatteo, M. R., Taranta, A., Friedman, H. S., & Prince, L. M. (1980). Predicting patient satisfaction from physicians' nonverbal communication skills. *Medical Care, 18,* 376–387.

Emmons, K., & Rollnick, S. (2001). Motivational interviewing in health care settings. opportunities and limitations. *American Journal of Preventive Medicine, 20,* 68–74.

Engel, G. L. (1977). The need for a new medical model: A challenge for biomedicine. *Science, 196,* 129–136.

Flocke, S. A., Miller, W. L., & Crabtree, B. F. (2002). Relationships between physician practice style, patient satisfaction, and attributes of primary care. *The Journal of Family Practice, 51,* 835–840.

Friedman, H. S., DiMatteo, M. R., & Taranta, A. (1980). A study of the relationship between individual differences in nonverbal expressiveness and factors in personality and social interaction. *Journal of Research in Personality, 14,* 351–364.

Frosch, D. L., & Kaplan, R. M. (1999). Shared decision-making in clinical medicine: Past research and future directions. *American Journal of Preventive Medicine, 17,* 285–295.

Gattellari, M., Butow, P. N., & Tattersall, M. H. (2001). Sharing decisions in cancer care. *Social Science and Medicine, 52,* 1865–1878.

Golin, C. E., Sheridan, S., Bunton, A., Schwartz, R., McCormack, L., Driscoll, D., et al. (2006, April). Evaluation of a prostate cancer screening shared decision-making (SDM) program that includes values clarification. Paper presented at the *Society of General Internal Medicine Annual Meeting*, Los Angeles.

Greenfield, S., Kaplan, S., & Ware, J. E., Jr. (1985). Expanding patient involvement in care: Effects of patient outcomes. *Annals of Internal Medicine, 102,* 520–528.

Greenfield, S., Kaplan, S. H., Ware, J. E., Jr., Yano, E. M., & Frank, H. J. (1988). Patients' participation in medical care: Effects of blood sugar control and quality of life in diabetes. *Journal of General Internal Medicine, 3,* 448–457.

Griffith, C., Wilson, J. F., Langer, S., & Haist, S. A. (2003). House staff nonverbal communication skills and patient satisfaction. *Journal of General Internal Medicine, 18,* 170–174.

Hall, J. A., & Roter, D. L. (1998). Medical communication and gender: A summary of research. *Journal of Gender Specific Medicine, 1,* 39–42.

Hall, J. A., Harrigan, J. A., & Rosenthal, R. (1995). Nonverbal behavior in clinician-patient interaction. *Applied & Preventive Psychology, 4,* 21–37.

Hall, J. A., Roter, D. L., & Rand, C. S. (1981). Communication of affect between patient and physician. *Journal of Health and Social Behavior, 22,* 18–30.

Hall, J. A., Stein, T. S., Roter, D. L., & Rieser, N. (1999). Inaccuracies in physicians' perceptions of their patients. *Medical Care, 37,* 1164–1168.

Harding, R., Dockrell, M., Dockrell, J., & Corrigan, N. (2001). Motivational interviewing for HIV risk reduction among gay men in commercial and public sex settings. *AIDS Care, 13,* 493–501.

Harrigan, J. A., & Rosenthal, R. (1986). Nonverbal aspects of empathy and rapport in physician–patient interaction. In P. D. Blanck, R. W. Buck, & R. Rosenthal (Eds.), *Nonverbal communication in the clinical context* (pp. 36–73). University Park, PA: Pennsylvania State University Press.

Institute of Medicine. (2001). *Crossing the quality chasm: A new health system for the 21st century.* Washington, DC: National Academies Press.

Kamb, M., Fishbein, M., Douglas, J. M., Jr., Rhodes, F., Rogers, J., Bolan, G., et al. (1998). Efficacy of risk-reduction counseling to prevent human immunodeficiency virus and sexually transmitted diseases: A randomized controlled trial. *Journal of the American Medical Association, 280,* 1161–1167.

Kaplan, R. M. (2004). Shared medical decision making: A new tool for preventive medicine. *American Journal of Preventive Medicine, 26,* 81–83.

Kelly, J. A., & Kalichman, S. C. (2002). Behavioral research in HIV/AIDS primary and secondary prevention: Recent advances and future directions. *Journal of Consulting and Clinical Psychology, 70,* 626–639.

Kemp, R., Hayward, P., Applewhaite, G., Everitt, B., & David, A. (1996). Compliance therapy in psychotic patients: Randomised controlled trial. *British Medical Journal, 312,* 345–349.

Kern, D. E., Branch, W. T. J., Jackson, J. L., Brady, D. W., Feldman, M. D., Levinson, W., et al. (2005). Teaching the psychosocial aspects of care in the clinical setting: Practical recommendations, general internal medicine generalist educational leadership group. *Academic Medicine, 80,* 8–20.

Kjellgren, K. I., Ahlner, J., & Saljo, R. (1995). Taking antihypertensive medication: Controlling or co-operating with patients? *International Journal of Cardiology, 47,* 257–268.

Knapp, M. L., & Hall, J. A. (2005). *Nonverbal communication in human interaction* (6th ed.). Belmont, CA: Wadsworth.

Kyngas, H., & Rissanen, M. (2001). Support as a crucial predictor of adolescents with a chronic disease. *Journal of Clinical Nursing, 10,* 767–774.

Leach, M. J. (2005). Rapport: A key to treatment success. *Complementary Therapies in Clinical Practice, 11,* 262–265.

Levinson, W., Gorawara-Bhat, R., & Lamb, J. (2000). A study of patient clues and physician responses in primary care and surgical settings. *Journal of the American Medical Association, 284,* 1021–1027.

Levinson, W., Roter, D. L., Mullooly, J. P., Dull, V. T., & Frankel, R. M. (1997). Physician–patient communication: The relationship with malpractice claims among primary care physicians and surgeons. *Journal of the American Medical Association, 277,* 553–559.

Makoul, G., & Clayman, M. L. (2005). An integrative model of shared decision-making in medical encounters. *Patient Education and Counseling, 60,* 301–312.

Maynard, D. W., & Heritage, J. (2005). Conversation analysis, doctor–patient interaction and medical communication. *Medical Education, 39,* 428–435.

Mead, N., & Bower, P. (2000). Patient-centeredness: A conceptual framework and review of the empirical literature. *Social Science and Medicine, 51,* 1087–1110.

Miller, W. R. (1996). Motivational interviewing: Research, practice, and puzzles. *Addictive Behaviors, 21,* 835–842.

Miller, W. R., & Rollnick, S. (1991). *Motivational interviewing: Preparing people to change addictive behavior.* New York: Guilford Press.

Miller, W. R., & Rollnick, S. (2002). *Motivational interviewing: Preparing people for change.* (2nd ed.). New York: Guilford Press.

National Institute of Mental Health Multisite HIV Prevention Trial Group. (1998). NIMH multisite HIV prevention trial: Reducing HIV sexual risk behavior. *Science, 280,* 1889–1894.

O'Connor, A. M., Rostom, A., Fiset, V., Tetroe, J., Entwistle, V., Llewellyn-Thomas, H., et al. (1999a). Decision aids for patients facing health treatment or screening decisions: Systematic review. *British Medical Journal, 319,* 731–734.

O'Connor, A. M., Stacey, D., Entwistle, V., Llewellyn-Thomas, H., Rovner, D., Holmes-Rovner, M., et al. (2003). Decision aids for people facing health treatment or screening decisions [electronic version]. *Cochrane Database of Systematic Reviews, 2,* CD001431.

O'Connor, A. M., Wells, G. A., Tugwell, P., Laupacis, A., Elmslie, T., & Drake, E. (1999b). The effects of an "explicit" values clarification exercise in a woman's decision aid regarding postmenopausal hormone therapy. *Health Expectations, 2,* 21–32.

Oliver, J. W., Kravitz, R. L., Kaplan, S. H., & Meyers, F. J. (2001). Individualized patient education and coaching to improve pain control among cancer outpatients. *Journal of Clinical Oncology, 19,* 2206–2212.

Phillips, K. A., Johnson, F. R., & Maddala, T. (2002). Measuring what people value: A comparison of "attitude" and "preference" surveys. *Health Services Research, 37,* 1659–1679.

Picciano, J. F., Roffman, R. A., Kalichman, S. C., Rutledge, S. E., & Burghuis, J. T. (2001). A telephone based brief intervention using motivational enhancement to facilitate HIV risk reduction among MSM: A pilot study. *AIDS and Behavior, 5,* 251–262.

Plato, & Emanuel, E. J. (Trans.). (1961). In E. Hamilton, & H. Cairns (Eds.), *Plato: The collected dialogues.* (pp. 720c–720e). Princeton, NJ: Princeton University Press.

Reeder, L. G. (1972). The patient-client as a consumer: Some observations on the changing professional-client relationship. *Journal of Health and Social Behavior, 13,* 406–412.

Resnicow, K., DiIorio, C., Soet, J., Ernst, D., Borrelli, B., & Hecht, J. (2002). Motivational interviewing in health promotion: It sounds like something is changing. *Health Psychology, 21,* 444–451.

Resnikow, K., Jackson, A., Wang, T., De, A. K., McCarty, F., Dudley, W. N., et al. (2001). A motivational interviewing intervention to increase fruit and vegetable intake through black churches: Results of the eat for life trial. *American Journal of Public Health, 91,* 1686–1693.

Rogers, C. (1987). The underlying theory: Drawn from experience with individuals and groups. *Counseling and Values, 32,* 38–46.

Rollnick, S., Butler, C., & Stott, N. (1997). Helping smokers make decisions: The enhancement of brief intervention for general medical practice. *Patient Education and Counseling, 31,* 191–203.

Roter, D. (2000). The enduring and evolving nature of the patient-physician relationship. *Patient Education and Counseling, 39,* 5–15.

Roter, D. L., & Hall, J. A. (1992). *Doctors talking with patients/patients talking with doctors: Improving communication in medical visits.* Westport, CT: Auburn House.

Roter, D. L., & Hall, J. A. (2001). How physician gender shapes the communication and evaluation of medical care. *Mayo Clinic Proceedings, 76,* 673–676.

Roter, D. L., Frankel, R. M., Hall, J. A., & Sluyter, D. (2006). The expression of emotions through nonverbal behavior in medical visits: Mechanisms and outcomes. *Journal of General Internal Medicine, 21*(Suppl 1), S28–S34.

Roter, D. L., Hall, J. A., & Aoki, Y. (2002). Physician gender effects in medical communication: A meta-analytic review. *Journal of the American Medical Association, 288,* 756–764.

Roter, D. L., Larson, S., Shinitzky, H., Chernoff, R., Serwint, J. R., Adamo, G., et al. (2004). Use of an innovative video feedback technique to enhance communication skills training. *Medical Education, 38,* 145–157.

Roter, D. L., Stewart, M., Putnam, S. M., Lipkin, M., Stiles, W., & Inui, T. S. (1997). Communication patterns of primary care physicians. *Journal of the American Medical Association, 277,* 350–356.

Rowland-Morin, P. A., & Carroll, J. G. (1990). Verbal communication skills and patient satisfaction: A study of doctor-patient interviews. *Evaluation & the Health Professions, 13,* 168–185.

Ryan, M., Scott, D. A., Reeves, C., Bate, A., van Teijlingen, E. R., Russell, E. M., et al. (2001). Eliciting public preferences for healthcare: A systematic review of techniques. *Health Technology Assessment, 5,* 1–186.

Schwartz, S. H., & Bilsky, W. (1987). Toward a universal psychological structure of human values. *Journal of Personality and Social Psychology, 53,* 550–562.

Shapiro, J., Hollingshead, J., & Morrison, E. H. (2002). Developing professional skills: Primary care resident, faculty, and patient views of barriers to cultural competence, and the skills needed to overcome them. *Medical Education, 36,* 749–759.

Sheridan, S., Harris, R., & Woolf, S. (2004). Shared decision making about screening and chemoprevention: A suggested approach from the U.S. preventive services task force. *American Journal of Preventive Medicine, 26,* 56–66.

Shorter, E. (1985). *Bedside manners.* New York: Simon & Schuster.

Smith, C. K., & Larsen, K. M. (1984). Sequential nonverbal behavior in the patient–physician interview. *Family Practice, 18,* 257–261.

Smith, D. E., Heckemeyer, C. M., Kratt, P. P., & Mason, D. A. (1997). Motivational interviewing to improve adherence to a behavioral weight-control program for older obese women with NIDDM: A pilot study. *Diabetes Care, 20,* 52–54.

Stanton, A. L. (1987). Determinants of adherence to medical regimens by hypertensive patients. *Journal of Behavioral Medicine, 10,* 377–394.

Stewart, M. (1995). Effective physician-patient communication and health outcomes: A review. *Canadian Medical Association Journal, 152,* 1423–1433.

Stewart, M., Brown, J. B., Donner, A., McWhinney, I. R., Oates, J., Weston, W. W., et al. (2000). The impact of patient-centered care on outcomes. *Journal of Family Practice, 49,* 796–804.

Szasz, P. S., & Hollender, M. H. (1956). A contribution to the philosophy of medicine: The basic models of the doctor-patient relationship. *AMA Archives of Internal Medicine, 97,* 585–592.

Thrasher, A. D., Golin, C. E., Earp, J. A., Tien, H., Porter, C., & Howie, L. (2005). Motivational interviewing to support antiretroviral therapy adherence: The role of quality counseling. *Patient Education and Counseling, 62,* 64–71.

Ubel, P. A., Jepson, C., & Baron, J. (2001). The inclusion of patient testimonials in decision aids: Effects on treatment choices. *Medical Decision-Making, 21,* 60–68.

World Health Organization. (2003). *Adherence to long-term therapies: Evidence for action.* Geneva, Switzerland: WHO.

Wilkes, M. S., Usatine, R., Slavin, S., & Hoffman, J. R. (1998). Doctoring: University of California, Los Angeles. *Academic Medicine, 7,* 32–40.

Wissow, L. S., Roter, D., Bausman, L., Crain, E., Kercsmar, C., Weiss, K., et al. (1998). Patient–provider communication during the emergency department care of children with asthma. *Medical Care, 36,* 1439–1450.

Wissow, L. S., Roter, D., Larson, S. M., Wang, M. C., Hwang, W. T., Johnson, R., et al. (2002). Mechanisms behind the failure of residents' longitudinal primary care to promote disclosure and discussion of psychosocial issues. *Archives of Pediatric and Adolescent Medicine, 156,* 685–692.

Zuckerman, M., Larrance, D. T., Hall, J. A., DeFrank, R. S., & Rosenthal, R. (1979). Posed and spontaneous communication of emotion via facial and vocal cues. *Journal of Personality, 47,* 712–733.

CHAPTER 8

Advocacy and Patient Literacy: What Healthcare Professionals Can Do to Help Patients Overcome Patient Literacy Barriers

Darren A. DeWalt and Michael P. Pignone

OBJECTIVES

- To understand the differences between reading ability and the broader concepts of literacy and health literacy
- To explore the links between literacy and health outcomes
- To assess interventions to improve health outcomes for people with low literacy
- To understand the role advocates can play in improving care for patients with low literacy

Patient literacy has emerged as an important factor in health and healthcare (Ad Hoc Committee on Health Literacy for the Council on Scientific Affairs, 1999; Dewalt, Berkman, Sheridan, Lohr, & Pignone, 2004; Institute of Medicine, 2004; Pignone, DeWalt, Sheridan, Berkman, & Lohr, 2005). The U.S. healthcare system is complex, and obtaining high-quality care is often predicated on patients' abilities to read, write, and process information at a sophisticated level; patients without these skills often find it difficult to function (Institute of Medicine, 2004). For example, the first step in acquiring healthcare—the process of selecting and enrolling in a health insurance plan—is difficult to comprehend, even for those with advanced education. The second step, gaining admittance into a clinic or emergency room, is also onerous, requiring patients to complete written forms, including clinical information about symptoms and medical history as well as contact and insurance information. After a patient is admitted, the complex, highly technical language used by healthcare providers assumes a working knowledge of medicine that many do not have. Few can retain all of their doctor's instructions, but patients who cannot benefit from written materials may have little choice; in the absence of an advocate, they are often left to piece together from memory a self-care strategy at home. In these ways, patients with low literacy may face great challenges at each step in the care process.

Literacy is an important topic for patient advocacy because low literacy affects a staggering number of people; over 90 million adults in the United States have only basic or below basic literacy skills (Kutner, Greenberg, & Baer, 2005). Furthermore, low literacy often has the greatest impact on those who are *already* facing significant barriers to healthcare access and quality: patients with low levels of education and income, those with chronic diseases such as diabetes that require complex self-management regimens, and those who know English as a second language or not at all. This chapter provides a context for advocacy interventions by further describing the problem of low literacy, including who is affected and at what points in the care process patients most often experience problems. This chapter also explores current advocacy efforts related to patient literacy.

Effective advocates recognize the literacy limitations of individual patients and help these patients navigate the system. Whether providers, family members, or volunteers, these advocates can assist patients with paperwork, employ strategies such as tape recording that reduce the need for reading, or provide verbal counseling and cues. At the same time, systems-level advocates are needed to adapt the healthcare environment to the needs of low-literacy populations. In this capacity, advocates may work to streamline paperwork, improve the readability of documents, and develop educational materials in easy-to-read or video formats. Given the magnitude of the problem of low literacy, no single intervention can completely address patients' needs. Professionals at all levels of the healthcare system, from care providers to administrators to researchers in health education, must join patients in an effort to create health-related materials and communication styles that better serve the entire population.

WHAT IS LITERACY?

A commonly used understanding of literacy, that is, "the ability to read and write" (*Oxford English Dictionary*, 2003), is far too limited a definition to capture the functional literacy needed to navigate everyday life. In 1991, Congress addressed some of these larger literacy issues through its National Literacy Act, which defined the concept as "an individual's ability to read, write, and speak in English, and compute and solve problems at levels of proficiency necessary to function on the job and in society, to achieve one's goals, and develop one's knowledge and potential" (Public Law 102-73, 1991). This definition suggests that literacy is about more than reading and writing for its own sake; it also includes the ability to identify information and apply that information toward problem solving. In short, from a functional standpoint, literacy involves analytic and decision-making processes above and beyond the ability to identify written words.

Given this term's range of meaning, literacy can be understood to exist along a continuum. As found in the 1992 National Adult Literacy Survey, few people in the United States are completely illiterate, yet millions cannot reliably obtain information from an article or document (U.S. Department of Education, 1992). Because of the stigma associated with low literacy, however, many adults with low literacy do not "self-identify" and instead report that they are able to read and write well without getting assistance from others. For this reason, many people who consider themselves "readers" actually score poorly on literacy tests (U.S. Department of Education, 1992). Thus, the term "illiteracy" as it is commonly understood rarely captures the difficulties people experience in obtaining and processing necessary information. For this reason, this chapter employs "low literacy" as the preferred term.

Literacy Levels in the United States: The 2003 National Assessment of Adult Literacy

The 2003 National Assessment of Adult Literacy (NAAL), the most comprehensive study of literacy in recent years, provides a glimpse into Americans' functional literacy skills (Kutner et al., 2005). The NAAL, which was administered to a national sample of over 19,000 adults, groups individuals' literacy skills into four levels: *below basic, basic, intermediate,* and *proficient* (Textbox 8.1). Those in the basic and below basic categories can generally be considered as having low literacy levels.

The 2003 NAAL reveals the overall impact of low literacy in the United States, with results indicating that 63 million American adults have only basic literacy skills and another 30 million have skills *below* basic literacy. Low literacy is particularly prevalent among certain populations: people without a high school degree, those from certain ethnic and racial minorities, those with multiple disabilities, and those 65 years old and older (Kutner et al., 2005). The impact of low literacy on people's daily lives is sobering. As the NAAL study suggests, an estimated 43% of U.S. adults lack the skills they need to complete insurance forms or credit applications independently (Comings, Reder, & Sum, 2001). By assessing adults' abilities to identify, comprehend, and apply information, the NAAL measures functional literacy. In doing so, low literacy is revealed as a common phenomenon that poses serious barriers to those seeking quality healthcare.

It is disheartening that the number of adults affected by low literacy in the United States has not improved much over time; results of the 2003 NAAL were essentially unchanged from the National Adult Literacy Study performed in 1992 (Kirsch, Jungeblut, Jenkins, & Kolstad, 2002). Determinants of literacy (e.g., the often poor quality of primary education, racial and social inequities, the unavailability and inefficiency of adult literacy programs) are numerous and complex, meaning that, even with NAAL data, researchers have not yet been able to pinpoint exactly why literacy scores are not improving. What *is* implicit in these findings, however, is a need for advocacy on many literacy fronts, particularly in healthcare. Indeed, because all healthcare consumers have a concrete and immediate need to prevent illness, obtain insurance, get well quickly, and manage chronic diseases effectively, healthcare professionals bear *de facto* responsibility for ensuring that communication strategies are, at the very least, adequate for those who cannot read well.

Health Literacy

Health literacy, a subset of overall literacy, exemplifies the significance of NAAL findings and why advocacy in this area is so critical. Similar to the NAAL's rather complex definition of functional literacy, all recent definitions of health literacy involve more than simply reading, writing, and

---

Textbox 8.1   The National Assessment of Adult Literacy

The National Assessment of Adult Literacy (NAAL), a study conducted in 1992 and in 2003 with a nationally representative sample, sought to determine how well American adults can read and comprehend written materials, a crucial ability for patients trying to navigate health systems and health-related materials. The NAAL survey assesses three components of literacy: ability to understand a text (prose literacy), ability to use written information to perform tasks (document literacy), and the ability to perform quantitative tasks such as adding. Participants are assigned a literacy level (below basic, basic, intermediate, or proficient) based on their ability to perform specific tasks such as understanding medical instructions, finding a place on a map, or calculating and comparing prices. Data collected on race/ethnicity, gender, age, language spoken before starting school, educational attainment, and employment status help put the overall findings in context and identify those populations especially struggling with issues related to low literacy.

The four levels of literacy used in the NAAL are described by the National Center for Education Statistics as follows (Kutner et al., 2005, p. 3):

> *Below Basic.* This category describes those with only the "most simple and concrete" abilities. At the very most, adults at this level can pick out information from written text and perform simple addition, such as adding numbers on a bank deposit slip. They may have trouble finding pieces of information or numbers in a lengthy text or finding two or more numbers in a chart and performing a calculation.
>
> *Basic.* Adults at this level can comprehend simple written passages and use numeric information to solve arithmetic problems requiring one step. Skills at this level include using a television guide to find what shows are playing at a particular time or comparing the list price of two products.
>
> *Intermediate.* This level describes adults who can read and understand more complex written passages, pick out numeric information from dense graphs or charts, and draw conclusions about an author's reason for writing. Those at the intermediate level can, for example, find a point on a map, use reference materials, and total the costs of a catalog order.
>
> *Proficient.* These adults can comprehend more demanding written passages and can think abstractly about the author's purpose in writing. Skills at this level include the ability to compare two editorial columns and to perform more complex arithmetic such as calculating the price per pound of a certain food.

The following is an abbreviated example of the kind of reading comprehension tasks NAAL participants were asked to perform.

Question 1 (ability to understand a text, or "prose literacy"): Refer to the article below to answer the following question. According to the brochure, why is it difficult for people to know if they have high blood pressure?

(continued)

Textbox 8.1   The National Assessment of Adult Literacy (continued)

TOO MANY BLACK ADULTS DIE FROM HIGH BLOOD PRESSURE WHAT CAN YOU DO? [Excerpt]

Have your blood pressure checked regularly

Unfortunately, high blood pressure is a silent killer and crippler. At least half of the people who have high blood pressure don't know it because symptoms usually are not present. The only way you can be sure is to have the doctor check your blood pressure. You should have your blood pressure checked at least once a year, especially if (1) you are black, (2) you are over 40, (3) members of your family or close relatives have high blood pressure or the complications of high blood pressure (stroke, heart attack, or kidney disease), or (4) you have frequent headaches, dizziness, or other symptoms that may occasionally be related to high blood pressure.

Correct answers to the survey question include "symptoms are not usually present" and "high blood pressure is silent."

Only 70% of level 2 (basic) respondents and 11% of level 1 (below basic) respondents were able to answer the question correctly. In addition to reading comprehension, NAAL participants are also asked to perform numeric calculations based on real world problems of varying degrees of difficulty and to derive information from different kinds of tables and other figures. For more examples of NAAL questionnaire items, see Kutner et al. (2005).

Source: Data from Author and Kutner et al., 2005.

---

arithmetic (Table 8.1). They also include a person's ability to act on health information or make decisions regarding health, with the World Health Organization definition going so far as to suggest that health literacy is critical to empowerment and personal advocacy (Nutbeam, 2000). These definitions do not capture all aspects of health literacy, yet they do identify skills that patients need in order to apply important health messages to their daily lives and to function well in the healthcare system.

Numerous studies documenting the link between low literacy and poor health outcomes have brought widespread attention to the issue of health literacy in recent years (Dewalt et al., 2004; Wolf, Gazmararian, & Baker, 2005). Low literacy has been associated with less health-related knowledge, less preventive care, poorer control of chronic illnesses, worse overall health status, lower adherence to medical regimens, and increased rates of hospitalization (Dewalt et al., 2004). (The majority of these studies

Table 8.1   Definitions of Health Literacy

Source	Definition
American Medical Association	"Health Literacy is a constellation of skills, including the ability to perform basic reading and numerical tasks required to function in the healthcare environment. Patients with adequate health literacy can read, understand, and act on healthcare information." (Ad Hoc Committee on Health Literacy for the Council on Scientific Affairs, 1999)
National Library of Medicine (NLM)/Healthy People 2010	"The degree to which individuals have the capacity to obtain, process, and understand basic health information and services needed to make appropriate health decisions." (Selden, Zorn, Ratzan, & Parker, 2000)
Institute of Medicine	Uses the NLM definition, but adds: a "shared function of cultural, social, and individual factors." (IOM, 2004)
World Health Organization	"Health literacy represents the cognitive and social skills which determine the motivation and ability of individuals to gain access to, understand and use information in ways which promote and maintain good health. Health literacy means more than being able to read pamphlets and successfully make appointments. By improving people's access to health information and their capacity to use it effectively, health literacy is critical to empowerment." (Nutbeam, 2000)

have been adjusted for other related factors such as socioeconomic status, race, and age.) For example,

- A survey of 2,923 adults found an association between low literacy and a decreased ability to perform day-to-day activities because of poor physical health and pain (Wolf et al., 2005).

- A prospective study of 2,512 older men and women found that those with low literacy had a 19.7% risk of death, whereas those with higher levels of literacy had only a 10.6% risk of death (Sudore et al., 2006).
- Among a sample of 182 patients with HIV/AIDS, those with low literacy were less able to adhere to medication regimens over a two day period (Kalichman, Ramachandran, & Catz, 1999).
- A study of asthma sufferers found that patients' reading abilities were strongly correlated with both their asthma management knowledge and technique (Williams, Baker, Honig, Lee, & Nowlan, 1998).

Although observational studies cannot prove a causal relationship between an exposure (low literacy) and an outcome (poorer health), the body of evidence documenting their association is substantial and suggests a number of possible pathways by which literacy could affect health outcomes. These findings compel further research and active involvement by organizations currently engaged in improving literacy through research and implementation of best practices (including the National Institutes of Health, the Joint Council on Accreditation of Healthcare Organizations, the American Medical Association, and the U.S. Department of Health and Human Services).

Given its range of meanings, developing measures for capturing health literacy levels presents a challenge. Yet quantifying health literacy can help researchers understand the relationship between health literacy and health outcomes. Measures used in research to date primarily test reading ability. To a lesser extent, these measures have occasionally tried to capture numeracy or quantitative skills; however, these skills are highly correlated with reading measures. As such, existing research documents the role of reading ability in health outcomes, but does not address the broader concepts often implied by the use of the term health literacy.

Research to date raises concerns about the role of patient literacy in healthcare. Studies clearly show that (1) many people are affected by low literacy and (2) low literacy is associated with worse health outcomes via a number of possible pathways (e.g., decreased ability to follow medication regimens, less access to care). Moreover, a number of vulnerable populations (e.g., African Americans, Hispanics, those with multiple disabilities, and those of retirement age) not only have lower literacy levels than other populations but also face significant healthcare barriers caused by socioeconomic status, age, or complex medical histories (Kutner et al., 2005). Separating literacy from higher order social determinants is important for researchers, yet advocates must keep in mind that low literacy is often only one of many risk factors for patients seeking high-quality healthcare, making advocacy efforts around raising literacy levels all the more crucial.

THE INTERSECTION OF LITERACY AND HEALTHCARE: OPPORTUNITIES FOR PATIENT ADVOCACY

The magnitude of literacy problems in the United States, combined with formidable literacy-related barriers in the healthcare system, means that many individuals will be unable to access high-quality healthcare until health systems take major steps toward reducing these barriers. As explored later, these barriers include problems related to accessing care, managing illness and, more generally, processing important pieces of health information.

Access to Care

Obtaining Health Insurance

One important feature of access to care is the availability of health insurance. For many Americans, obtaining and using health insurance require more than just the money to purchase the policy; they also require persistence and advanced literacy skills. Healthcare consumers must consider the relative merits of various insurance coverage options in light of both health and financial conditions, including sorting through exclusion clauses, deciding on whether a choice of providers is an important option, and determining whether to pay more in overall premium costs versus more in deductibles and co-payments. These decisions involve not only reading the fine print and determining what the different amounts are, but also weighing the cost of the insurance policy against the likelihood that one will need to seek care. These sorts of abstract comparisons are difficult, even for employed people whose benefits and human resources departments can assist in this process.

Not surprisingly, applying for special state or federal programs such as Medicaid and Medicare is especially difficult for those with low literacy. The combination of complex paperwork and the need to meet certain qualifications for these programs (see Chapter 2) means that patients often have difficulty understanding whether they are even eligible for such programs. Knowing where and how to apply is yet another challenge. Indeed, researchers have found that many qualified children are not enrolled in programs such as the state-based Children's Health Insurance Programs because of the onerous process of obtaining and completing the paperwork involved (Ross & Cox, 2005).

Patient advocates, long aware of the need to help patients access health insurance, have developed innovative state or local level programs to help individuals navigate the system. In the case of Children's Health Insurance Programs, California and several other states have initiated programs offering support services to help families determine whether they are eligible and how to fill out applications (www.healthyfamilies.ca.gov). At the same time, nonprofit advocacy coalitions such as the 100% Campaign are working to streamline the application process through strategies such as paperless income verification (www.100percentcampaign.org). Although these programs do not bill themselves as "literacy advocates," they do address literacy concerns. Providers and other health professionals can support patients with low literacy by helping them connect with these programs.

Finding a Provider

Even when a patient has health insurance, identifying a care provider can be difficult. Few high-quality resources exist for determining a good match between patient and provider, and thus, the process of choosing a physician or medical center may require significant literacy and information-seeking skills, including the use of websites, the yellow pages, or insurance plan directories. Here again, patient advocacy in this area often comes from individual providers, who give patients referrals, helping to connect them with quality services. In the absence of such personal advice, referral hotlines can help patients with low literacy find providers.

Knowing When to Seek Care

Understanding when to seek care and how to arrange care also demands literacy and includes several key steps:

1. A patient must possess health-related knowledge. (Should symptoms of pain with urination prompt a call or visit to one's provider?)
2. A patient must understand how to negotiate the healthcare system, or have at least a working knowledge of the system and an understanding of the process for accessing care. (Where do I go to get care? The emergency room? The health department?)
3. A patient must know whom to call on the phone in order to arrange a healthcare appointment. Understanding which providers are in a patient's network or which insurance plan accepts the patient and covers a particular situation requires searching manuals and/or the Internet. Finding information, a critical literacy skill, can be difficult. (How do I get an appointment with my doctor?)
4. A patient must acquire the information necessary to keep an appointment. After an appointment is made, patients may find it hard to read the appointment slip or may receive several cancellation or rescheduling notices. Keeping track of appointment times and responding to reminder notices require time management and calendar skills. Many patients with low literacy must also coordinate public transportation schedules to reach appointments, yet another obstacle. (How do I reach my appointment with the doctor?)

Highly literate patients may have no difficulty in negotiating these and far more formidable hurdles. After all, as argued in Chapter 4, many Internet-savvy patients are able to master sophisticated bodies of medical information, choose knowledgeably between several possible treatments, and negotiate with insurance providers to cover experimental protocols. Yet a health system that requires all patients to answer all of the previous questions without help wrongly assumes a high level of literacy on the part of the general population. The consequence of this assumption is that many people are discouraged from even gaining initial access to healthcare. In terms of patient advocacy, community-based efforts may be best suited for helping people determine whether they should seek care. Lay health advisor programs, for example, can help individuals seek and access appropriate care; in these programs, community members are

trained, usually in specific topics such as breast cancer screening or prenatal care, to assist others in gaining awareness of important health issues,
scheduling screening or treatment appointments, arranging transportation,
and even providing emotional support during the process (see Chapter 5).
For patients with an established care provider, an "advice nurse" who can
be contacted by telephone can also serve as an important resource.
Although these types of interventions are not literacy specific, they may
go a long way in helping people with low literacy access the care they
need.

Illness Management

Acute Illness Management

Addressing an acute illness often requires advanced literacy skills at a
time when patients' reading abilities may be compromised by a stressful situation and physical symptoms. Patients seeking care for an acute illness—
either in an outpatient setting or in the hospital—must interpret one or
several provider recommendations and apply them. Many years ago, medical recommendations often amounted to little more than advising a patient
to take a pill for a short period of time or instructions for rest and recuper-
ation. Now, with the enormous increase in the availability of therapies, recommendations may include several pills—each for a different purpose, with
a different schedule, and for different lengths of time. After a visit to the
doctor, a patient must negotiate with the pharmacy and understand and
organize the prescribed medications. A patient may also need additional
tests or a visit to a specialist to determine the appropriate care strategy.

The best patient advocates in the case of an acute illness are often the
patient's family members, friends, and healthcare providers, who can
assist the patient in collecting and processing information. Providers in
particular can employ communication styles that better support patients
with low literacy. For example, the American Medical Association emphasizes the importance of basic teaching principles, such as (1) using repetition, (2) increasing patient engagement by asking questions to assess
comprehension, and (3) decreasing reliance on print materials while
increasing use of spoken, recorded, or video instructions (Schwartzberg,
2003). When print materials *are* used, they should be appropriate for lower
literacy patients.

Chronic Illness Management

Chronic illnesses such as diabetes and HIV/AIDS require substantial information management skills, including complex self-management and attention to detail. Although people with low literacy can learn excellent self-management skills, the current healthcare system often relies on the patient's ability to read in order to develop these skills. Indeed, the overwhelming majority of health education materials appear in print, either online or in the form of pamphlets and other written materials. To cope with this challenge, patients who cannot read or who have low literacy may rely instead on a doctor's verbal instructions, a challenging assignment regardless of literacy skills. For example, providers frequently tell patients with heart failure to reduce their salt intake, weigh themselves every day, adjust their diuretic dose when their weight changes, and call the doctor for a variety of reasons. Learning these self-care strategies is not straightforward, especially when suggestions regarding the treatment of other illnesses such as diabetes and hypertension are offered to the patient in the same encounter.

As with acute illnesses, chronic illnesses often require advocacy from patients' family members and providers. Again, providers' abilities to communicate effectively is key. When providers adopt a more accessible, although not patronizing, communication style with patients who have low literacy levels, patients are more likely to retain needed information. Moreover, by recognizing that behavior change, regardless of literacy status, is often an incremental process and by eliciting patients' own health priorities, providers can help tailor patients' treatments to their needs, thereby reducing the demand on patients to sift through extraneous information (see Chapters 7 and 9).

Healthcare Transitions

The need to move patients from one healthcare facility to another is more common and more complex than in the past. Providers discharge patients from the hospital earlier and more readily transfer care to home health nurses, nursing homes, and outpatient practices. Patients are often discharged from the hospital with different medications and self-care regimens than they were using on admission. Although in recovery, the patient may still feel ill. The patient's weakened state may make the transition all the more challenging at a time when the need to communicate essential information about the condition to family members and other caregivers is greatest. Those with low literacy levels are at a particular risk because they are less able to rely on written instructions and are likely to have less knowledge of health-related terms and concepts. Again, providers can help minimize the patient's burden by communicating as clearly as possible (see Chapter 6) and by enlisting family members and friends to help in the transition process. At the systems level, hospital policies that increase the quality of discharge procedures can support these efforts.

General Information Processing

In addition to different points in the care process, certain types of paperwork are also challenging to patients with low literacy. These include the following.

Informed Consent

To protect patients, clinicians and researchers are required to obtain "informed consent" before performing procedures or admitting patients into a research study. This process involves telling patients about the risks and benefits of care or participation in a study as well as their rights as patients or research participants. Patients are most often asked to give consent by signing a written document. Too often, however, practitioners fail to ensure that informed consent is truly informed. This problem extends beyond those with low literacy; informed consent documents are difficult for most patients to read, and in some cases, researchers may not adequately explain the document verbally. Institutional review boards often specify standards for the readability of consent forms used in research studies, but consent forms for procedures or other therapies not involving research are often not held to these same standards and are sometimes dense and technically worded (see Table 8.2). As a result, patients may sign first and read later in order to receive treatment in a timely fashion. Health advocates can play a role in helping patients understand their options and choose the best course of action prior to signing the consent form and, on a policy level, by advocating for development of readable materials.

Table 8.2   Action Steps for Communicating Effectively with Patients with Limited Functional Health Literacy

- When designing all forms of written communication, keep the needs of the patient in mind.
- Write the way people talk.
- Use plain language.
- Define unfamiliar words.
- Use simple, specific, and direct sentences.
- Use the active voice.
- Follow a clear and logical structure when expressing ideas.
- Consider implicit and explicit messages.
- Be aware of diverse cultural backgrounds.
- Adapt policies and procedures to accommodate individuals with low literacy.
- Provide training in health literacy to all healthcare personnel.
- Invite people with low literacy to pilot test new programs and educational interventions.

Adapted from Rudd, September 2002 conference.

Medical Bills

Negotiating medical billing and payment systems requires both a great deal of effort and high literacy levels on the part of the patient. After obtaining healthcare, patients may receive multiple bills and statements from their providers and insurers, a prohibitively complex process for even the most literate person. From determining the actual amount of money owed to identifying discrepancies in the billing to sorting out deductibles, co-insurance, and co-payments to advocating for corrections, a patient must draw on a wide array of information-seeking, logic, and argumentative skills. Patient advocacy in this area is not as common, but may be provided through health advocacy organizations (see Chapter 15).

In summary, every step of accessing medical care requires sophisticated information processing skills, often in written form. Yet patients' abilities to read and use information related to healthcare varies greatly, with many unable to adequately understand healthcare communications. The health advocate, whether a family member, a provider, or a lay health advisor, may be in a position to bridge the gap between patients' reading abilities and the complex healthcare materials provided to them. This is an essential service. At the same time, however, advocacy at a system level can focus on streamlining paperwork, making reading materials more accessible, and developing health education alternatives to printed materials. These steps would help reduce the literacy demands placed on patients.

STRATEGIES AND TOOLS FOR ADVOCATES

Recognition of the high prevalence of low literacy is crucial for compelling the development of programs to mitigate its adverse effects. Failure of practitioners to consider the amount of information that patients can obtain and process effectively may result in disempowerment, disengagement, and consequently, worse adherence and poorer outcomes. Fortunately, strategies exist that can help to mitigate the effects of low literacy. This section reviews the importance of recognizing the problem, provides instruction in distilling information for patients to manageable levels, and suggests steps to improve the readability of documents designed by patients. These strategies are a starting point and have not been extensively evaluated. Research over the next several years will inform how practitioners and advocates can intervene most effectively to mitigate disparities caused by low literacy.

Recognizing the Problem

Most healthcare providers enter the profession to help people. After years of training, however, many have lost touch with the average person's ability to read and comprehend medical information. After recognizing the extent of low literacy throughout the population, health professionals need to gain awareness of how much they rely on medical jargon and then take steps to use simpler, more accessible language. Patient advocates can work with providers to help them develop patient-centered communication skills (see Chapter 6), identify promising strategies, and support individual patients to achieve better clinical outcomes. Patient advocates can also help to reform medical curriculums so as to break the cycle of poor communication (see Chapter 11).

Assessing Patients' Literacy Levels

Implicit in effective patient–provider communication is the provider's ability to judge where the patient lies on the literacy continuum. This assessment often happens informally when providers speak to patients and read the paperwork patients have completed. Researchers have also developed more formal assessments of reading level, usually in the form of written questionnaires such as the (1) Rapid Estimate of Adult Literacy in Medicine, which entails a word recognition test (Davis et al., 1993); (2) Test of Functional Health Literacy in Adults, which measures comprehension (Parker, Baker, Williams, & Nurss, 1995); and (3) Newest Vital Sign, which assesses functional literacy (Weiss et al., 2005). Whether providers should test the literacy level of individual patients is controversial; however, one study by Seligman et al. (2005) found that 94% of patients with low literacy felt that measuring health literacy and reporting it to the doctor was helpful. Yet some maintain that assessing literacy may alienate patients and strain the therapeutic relationship because of the stigma and potential embarrassment the test may hold for the patient as well as the time required to administer and score the surveys. Very little empirical evidence addresses the question of assessment by practitioners.

Distilling Information and Tailoring to Patients' Needs

Information is everywhere: Television, radio, the Internet, calls from telemarketers, the mail, and pamphlets all bombard consumers with messages. In this context, consumers must decide what information is valid and worthy of attention. Healthcare is no different. A provider could communicate with patients on a variety of health issues during any given encounter: how bodies function, the pathophysiology of disease, how different therapies work, and what behaviors should be modified. As individual consumers, we must decide what information is most important in our daily lives and consider which information is most immediately relevant. For example, knowing the pathophysiology of diabetes might not be the first thing a patient needs to know to bring the disease in check. Instead, learning how to follow a protocol for taking insulin might top the list. Similarly, learning and behavior change often happen incrementally, and thus, providers can learn to meet patients "where they are" by finding out what the patient already knows, what he or she is motivated to do, and by giving him or her the right amount of information at the right time and in the right format (see Chapters 6 and 8). Initially, providers should distill information, explaining what patients need to do and what they should look for in terms of symptoms. One potential role of the advocate is to tailor communication to the individual patient's needs and determine what information is critical for optimal adherence or decision making.

Improving the Readability of Documents

Improving the readability of health-related documents is another potential area for patient advocacy. Numerous studies have shown that standard patient education materials are written at grade levels that exceed the reading level of their intended audience. Complicated reading materials do not foster better care. In fact, incomprehensible materials are virtually useless; they are a waste of provider time and resources and are a source of frustration for patients.

Shaping patient-centered educational materials should begin with the language of the patient. Starting with words and phrases used by members of the target audience will give a much more useful point of view than the traditional expert-driven educational content. Pilot testing materials with the target audience or even engaging patients as co-developers is a wise practice in message development. By obtaining ideas and feedback from potential users and including language of the users in the materials, educators can better address the needs of the patient population. Doing so will also help ensure effective communication with other patients from a similar background.

Developers of health education materials can use a number of rules and assessments to increase the accessibility of their messages. Readable materials use shorter sentences and commonly understood words, maintain low text density by using "white space," and reinforce key points without providing extraneous information (Doak, Doak, & Root, 1996; Osborne, 2005). Several "readability" formulae are available to approximate the grade level of written materials, particularly prose documents (Textbox 8.1). (For example, this chapter is written at the 12th grade level according to the Flesch-Kincaid formula in Microsoft Word.) Table 8.3 offers a list of available readability formulae. Textbox 8.2 introduces a

Table 8.3   Commonly Used Readability Formulae in the Health Education Literature*

Name	Type	Reference
SMOG (Simple Measure of Gobbledygook)	Number of syllables and sentence length	McLaughlin (1969) and Doak et al. (1996)
Fry	Number of syllables and sentence length	Doak et al. (1996)
Flesch-Kincaid	Syllables, sentence length, active voice	Available in Microsoft Word
Lexile	Model-based and includes assessment of the commonness of words in the English language	www.lexile.com

*Numerous other formulae exist, and all are just a starting point for developing easy-to-read materials.

densely worded consent form and shows how using two readability formulae can help judge its accessibility.

After determining the readability score, materials should be subjected to a Suitability Assessment of Materials (Doak, Doak, & Root, 1996). This assessment addresses several aspects beyond readability, including cultural appropriateness, active voice, graphics, layout, and interaction. Ultimately, researchers should determine the usefulness of written materials by testing their clarity and comprehensibility for readers with a broad range of literacy skills, particularly those with limited literacy.

Different Media

Reforming written materials throughout our healthcare system would represent a major improvement in our efforts to communicate effectively with patients who have low literacy levels. Yet providing understandable, easy-to-read written materials may not be sufficient for producing desired outcomes. Patient advocates interested in health literacy should also consider using multiple forms of media to successfully reach the population

Textbox 8.2   Health Literacy and Readability

Each formula has its limitations, yet two relatively simple tests can help determine the "readability" of a text: the SMOG formula and the Flesch Kincaid Grade Level test. The easiest to hand calculate is the SMOG, a measure based on the number of words with three or more syllables in a series of 10 sentences. This number is plugged into a formula yielding a SMOG Score. A SMOG level of 10 means that most people will comprehend a given passage (National Literacy Trust, 2006).

The Flesch Kincaid Grade Level test determines the approximate grade level of a given text. Both tests use the total number of words, sentences, and syllables in a text (*Flesch-Kincaid Readability Test: From Wikipedia, the free encyclopedia,* 2006).

The process of informed consent is an essential piece of many clinical encounters; however, low literacy can limit patients' abilities to be fully informed about the procedures they are agreeing to undergo.

Below is a selection from a sample consent form. How readable is this consent form?

I understand that during the operation or procedure, it is possible for something unexpected to happen that may require that another or different operation or procedure be performed on me (the patient). If something unexpected happens during the operation or procedure, I hereby request and authorize my (the patient's) healthcare provider to do what is medically necessary and appropriate for me (the patient), including performing another or different operation or procedure.

I have discussed with my healthcare provider the possibility of administering blood or blood products before, during, or after the operation or procedure during my current admission or for the duration of planned treatment up to 1 year, as long as my medical condition and proposed treatment and associated risk have not changed.

I authorize and request medically necessary blood and blood products be given to me (the patient).

I do not authorize blood or blood products to be given to me (the patient). (The patient must also complete the Hospitals form "Refusal to consent to the use of blood and blood products.")

I have had an opportunity to ask questions and have those questions answered and have received sufficient information so that I have a general understanding of my (the patient's) medical condition, the nature of the operation or procedure, the benefits of the operation or procedure, the usual and most frequent risks of the operation or procedure, the risks and benefits of alternative treatment(s), and the prognosis of my (the patient's) condition with and without the operation or procedure.

(continued)

Textbox 8.2   Health Literacy and Readability (continued)

Words with three or more syllables are highlighted.

The SMOG score for this passage, based on six sentences, is 21 (18 if repeated words are counted only once). Compared with an entry level score of 9 to 10, this form is most appropriate for a highly literate patient.

Words with 3+ syllables = $60 \times 3 = 180$; select 169 (the closest number to 180 in the SMOG chart), then take the square root of $169 = 13$ and then add 8 for SMOG score = 21.

Running the calculation without word repetition = $33 \times 3 = 99 = 100$, square root of $100 = 10 + 8 =$ SMOG score = 18.

The following "Readability Statistics," including the Flesch-Kincaid Grade Level test, are provided by Microsoft Word after analyzing the above consent form:

Counts
Words	257
Characters	1354
Paragraphs	5
Sentences	7

Averages
Sentences per paragraph	1.4
Words per sentence	36.7
Characters per word	5.1

Readability
Passive Voice Sentences	14%
Flesch-Kincaid Grade Level	12.0

Although the estimates do not correlate precisely, the overall picture is the same. This consent form would not be considered readable for the majority of patients.

at large. The United States is now driven by visual media, with the average American watching more than four hours of television a day (Nielsen Media Research, 2000). Americans use written media less and less to meet their information needs. Because television is a primary source of information, capitalizing on video formats to transmit health information may be a good approach to "starting where the patient is." In the past, video formats have been expensive to develop and disseminate, but the emergence of digital technologies has lowered these costs, making it more feasible for literacy advocates to consider investing in nonprint media.

On a related note, patient advocates should be aware of special literacy issues related to health information on the Internet, the use of email, and other kinds of "e-health" (see Chapter 3). The personal computer and the Internet offer patients ease of access and the opportunity to obtain highly sophisticated medical information quite easily; however, even for those who can read well, navigating the Internet can be an overwhelming experience. Sorting through information requires advanced literacy skills and, not surprisingly, when it comes to looking for health information, a large education gap persists. Those with more education are more likely to look for medical and health advice online (Fox, 2005). Even so, very few people always check the source and date of the health information they find online, and moreover, those with less education are the least likely to follow a research protocol recommended by the Medical Library Association (Fox, 2006). In this context, patients with low literacy may need assistance in navigating the Internet effectively, and providers and other advocates can assist them by suggesting reputable, easy-to read sites and giving them tips for assessing a site's trustworthiness on their own. Because the Internet provides a self-paced way for patients to get information, it can be an invaluable tool, and literacy advocates should seek to help patients access and use the Internet and other e-health resources more successfully.

CAN ADVOCATES CHANGE THE HEALTH SYSTEM?

Creating a system that mitigates the effects of low literacy on health outcomes will require a conscious effort at every level of healthcare. Highly activated patients are already demanding accessible information, yet more needs to be done. Advocates can help communicate the needs of patients to providers and create a bridge between patients and the system. They can also raise clinicians' awareness of low literacy as a problem that they must address for their patients. Finally, patient advocates can help administrators recognize the importance of providing accessible health information for all patients. Such changes would help ensure that after patients have accessed the system, they are able to understand their treatment options and know how to adjust their self-care practices.

Research on the connection between literacy and health, although currently in an early stage, is also important; we have much to learn about why people with low literacy have poor health outcomes and how to overcome that association. Advocates undertaking literacy research can intervene to provide care to individuals, and they can contribute to studies that further our understanding of new methods for overcoming the barrier of low health literacy. Advocates have a responsibility to help patients realize their potential for navigating the health system and to empower individuals to seek appropriate health information. The work of literacy advocates in research can begin to convince clinicians and administrators that the problem of low literacy is widespread and that some effective solutions already exist.

As healthcare systems have gotten increasingly complex and as the abundance of information has continued to grow, the need for effective, accurate healthcare communication that reaches all patients is even more critical. The NAAL surveys show that literacy is not improving. As a result, the healthcare system must adapt to serve the needs of all patients. Patient advocates can be a major spur in helping to educate providers about the needs of low literacy populations, develop and test strategies to improve health communication for these patients, and serve as consultants in individual clinical encounters.

REFERENCES

Ad Hoc Committee on Health Literacy for the Council on Scientific Affairs, American Medical Association. (1999). Health literacy: Report of the Council on scientific affairs. *Journal of the American Medical Association, 281,* 552–557.

Comings, J., Reder, S., & Sum, A. (2001). *Building a level playing field: The need to expand and improve the national and state adult education and literacy systems.* National Center for the Study of Adult Learning and Literacy. Occasional paper. Retrieved October 30, 2006, from http://www.ncsall.net/fileadmin/resources/research/op_comings2.pdf#search=%22Building%20a%20level%20playing%20field%22.

Davis, T. C., Long, S. W., Jackson, R. H., Mayeaux, E. J., George, R. B., Murphy, P. W., et al. (1993). Rapid estimate of adult literacy in medicine: A shortened screening instrument. *Family Medicine, 25,* 391–395.

Dewalt, D. A., Berkman, N. D., Sheridan, S., Lohr, K. N., & Pignone, M. P. (2004). Literacy and health outcomes: A systematic review of the literature. *Journal of General Internal Medicine, 19,* 1228–1239.

Doak, C. C., Doak, L. G., & Root, J. H. (1996). *Teaching patients with low literacy skills* (2nd ed.). Philadelphia: Lippincott.

Flesch-Kincaid readability test: From Wikipedia, the free encyclopedia. (2006). Retrieved October 30, 2006, from http://en.wikipedia.org/wiki/Flesch-Kincaid_Readability_Test.

Fox, S. (2006. *Most internet users start at a search engine when looking for health information online. Very few check the source and date of the information they find. Pew Internet & American Life Project.* Retrieved February 19, 2007, from http://www.pewinternet.org/pdfs/PIP_Online_Health_2006.pdf.

Fox, S. (2005). *Health information online: Eight in ten users have looked for health information online, with increased interest in diet, fitness, drugs, health insurance, experimental treatments, and particular doctors and hospitals. Pew Internet & American Life Project.* Retrieved September 20, 2006, from http://www.pewinternet.org/pdfs/PIP_Healthtopics_May05.pdf.

Institute of Medicine, Committee on Health Literacy. (2004). In L. Nielsen-Bohlman, A. M. Panzer, & D. A. Kindig (Eds.), *Health literacy: A prescription to end confusion.* Washington, DC: National Academies Press.

Kalichman, S. C., Ramachandran, B., & Catz, S. (1999). Adherence to combination antiretroviral therapies in HIV patients of low health literacy. *Journal of General Internal Medicine, 14,* 267–273.

Kirsch, I., Jungeblut, A., Jenkins, L., & Kolstad, A. (2002). *Adult literacy in America: A first look at the findings of the national adult literacy survey* (3rd ed.). Washington, DC: U.S. Department of Education, National Center for Education Statistics.

Kutner, M., Greenberg, E., & Baer, J. (2005). *A first look at the literacy of America's adults in the 21st century: U.S. Department of Education: NCES 2006-470.* Retrieved October 29, 2006, from http://nces.ed.gov/pubsearch/pubsinfo.asp?pubid=2006470.

McLaughlin, G. H. (1969). SMOG grading: A new readability formula. *Journal of Reading, 12,* 639–646.

National Literacy Trust. (2006). *Readability: How to test how easy a text is to read.* Retrieved October 30, 2006, from http://www.literacytrust.org.uk/campaign/SMOG.html.

Nielsen Media Research. (2000). *2000 Report on Television* (p. 72).

Nutbeam, D. (2000). Health literacy as a public health goal: A challenge for contemporary health education and communication strategies into the 21st century. *Health Promotion International, 15,* 259–267.

Oxford English Dictionary, OED online. (2003). Retrieved July 16, 2006, from http://dictionary.oed.com.

Osborne, H. (2005). *Health Literacy from A to Z: Practical ways to communicate your health message.* Sudbury, MA: Jones & Bartlett.

Parker, R. M., Baker, D. W., Williams, M. V., & Nurss, J. R. (1995). The test of functional health literacy in adults: A new instrument for measuring patients' literacy skills. *Journal of General Internal Medicine, 10,* 537–541.

Pignone, M. P., DeWalt, D. A., Sheridan, S., Berkman, N., & Lohr, K. N. (2005). Interventions to improve health outcomes for patients with low literacy: A systematic review. *Journal of General Internal Medicine, 20,* 185–192.

Public Law 102-73, National Literacy Act. (1991). Retrieved October 30, 2006, from http://www.nifl.gov/public-law.html.

Ross, D. C., & Cox, L. (2005). *In a time of growing need: State choices influence health coverage access for children and families.* Retrieved September 30, 2006, from http://www.kff.org/medicaid/upload/In-a-Time-of-Growing-Need-State-Choices-Influence-Health-Coverage-Access-for-Children-and-Families-Report.pdf.

Schwartzberg, J. G. (2003). *Health literacy: Can your patient read, understand, and act upon your instruction?* Retrieved September 1, 2006, from http://www.rmf.harvard.edu/education-interventions/residents/dr-pt-relationship/health-literacy.aspx.

Selden, C. R., Zorn, M., Ratzan, S. C., & Parker, R. M. (2000). *Health literacy [bibliography online]. Current bibliographies in medicine; no. 2000-1.* Retrieved October 30, 2006, from http://www.nlm.nih.gov/pubs/cbm/hliteracy.html.

Seligman, H. K., Wang, F. F., Palacios, J. L., Wilson, C. C., Daher, C., Piette, J. D., et al. (2005). Physician notification of their diabetes patients' limited health literacy: A randomized, controlled trial. *Journal of General Internal Medicine, 20,* 1001–1007.

Sudore, R. L., Yaffe, K., Satterfield, S., Harris, T. B., Mehta, K. M., Simonsick, E. M., et al. (2006). Limited literacy and mortality in the elderly: The health, aging, and body composition study. *Journal of General Internal Medicine, 21,* 806–812.

U.S. Department of Education. (1992). *National Adult Literacy Survey (NALS).* Washington, DC: National Center for Education Statistics.

Weiss, B. D., Mays, M. Z., Martz, W., Castro, K. M., DeWalt, D. A., Pignone, M. P., et al. (2005). Quick assessment of literacy in primary care: The newest vital sign. *Annals of Family Medicine, 3,* 514–522.

Williams, M. V., Baker, D. W., Honig, E. G., Lee, T. M., & Nowlan, A. (1998). Inadequate literacy is a barrier to asthma knowledge and self-care. *Chest, 114,* 1008–1015.

Wolf, M. S., Gazmararian, J. A., & Baker, D. W. (2005). Health literacy and functional health status among older adults. *Annals of Internal Medicine, 165,* 1946–1952.

CHAPTER 9

Improving the Quality of Care Through Research: Measuring Patient Activation

Judith H. Hibbard

OBJECTIVES

- To show the role social science researchers can play in patient advocacy
- To discuss how clinical measures related to patient experience and involvement are important to advancing healthcare quality
- To illustrate how such measures are developed and incorporated into clinical practice, using the Patient Activation Measure as an example

Many patient advocates have described the need to shift the patient–provider relationship from a provider-directed model to a more patient-centered one. Quality healthcare, these advocates assert, requires a more egalitarian system, one in which clinicians tailor care to patients' values and preferences and in which patients themselves are actively involved in the care process. A great deal of uncertainty exists, however, about how to translate the abstract values of patient centeredness into day-to-day clinical practice. For example, what exactly does patient involvement entail? How can healthcare providers assess, or even increase, patients' "activation," or readiness, to participate in the care process? For that matter, how can providers evaluate their own ability to support such participation? If clinicians are to change their practice to achieve greater patient centeredness, they need specific objectives to aim for as well as the tools by which they can measure their success.

Toward this end, researchers in the social sciences are developing clinical measures of patient centeredness, and this chapter is an introduction to the process they use to define and evaluate concepts related to patient involvement. Using the Patient Activation Measure (PAM) as an example, we examine how researchers first establish the key components, or "domains," of a concept such as patient centeredness. In this case, the domain examined is patient activation. We then explain how researchers create scales so as to assess people's responses to that concept. Finally, we discuss how those scales are tested for validity and predictive value and then integrated into clinical practice. By relating this process, our intent is to show how researchers contribute to patient advocacy by creating measures that spell out the values of patient-centered care, allowing providers to analyze systematically the less biomedical aspects of diagnosis and treatment.

WHAT IS PATIENT ACTIVATION AND WHY IS IT IMPORTANT?

As Berwick (1999) emphasized in *Escape Fire: Lessons for the Future of Health Care*, information transfer is a key form of care. Patients need high-quality, just-in-time information to make good decisions about their health, particularly in an environment where many must manage chronic illnesses throughout their lives. Patients also frequently need support and guidance in managing those illnesses over time and in stressful situations. As Berwick (1999) has argued, "Time spent in building patients' skills in self-care is not a way to shift care; it *is* care." Yet many healthcare organizations perceive such skill-building efforts as overly time consuming; moreover, providers may themselves get discouraged by what they perceive as a small "return on investment" when they repeatedly encounter patients not prepared to act on the knowledge shared with them.

In this context, the concept of patient activation can help providers in meeting patients where they are with the information and support that will help those patients manage their chronic and acute illnesses. Briefly, patient activation describes patients' readiness, specifically their knowledge, skills, and confidence, to take part in the care process. Patients are more likely to make good decisions and take more actions to promote their own health if they are more engaged, informed, and feel confident that they can take care of themselves (Kaplan, Greenfield & Ware, 1989; Lorig, 1996; Lorig et al., 1999; Von Korff, Gruman, Schaefer, Curry, &

Wagner, 1997; Von Korff et al., 1998). Chronic disease patients in particular make many choices in their day-to-day lives that have major implications for their health and their need for care. They often must follow
complex treatment regimens, monitor their conditions, make lifestyle
changes, and make decisions about when they need to seek professional
care and when they can handle a problem on their own. Those who have
the skill and confidence to take on these challenges are better able to function and experience fewer health crises and functional declines (Lorig et
al., 1999). Thus, a key question for researchers to explore is how clinical
care systems can do a better job of encouraging patient activation.

WHAT DO PATIENTS NEED TO BECOME ACTIVATED?

Even though the benefits of involving patients in decisions about their
own care are becoming more widely recognized, interactions between
providers and patients appear to be still largely paternalistic, reinforcing a
passive role for patients (Roter et al., 1997). The difficulties of navigating
a highly complex delivery system have also served to reinforce feelings of
helplessness among patients. To take on a meaningful role in their own
care, however, patients need a sense of competence, a sense that they can
have some control over events related to their health and healthcare
(Bandura, 1991; Lorig, 1996).

Similar to physicians' discouragement when patients cannot follow recommended treatment regimens, interactions with physicians often solidify
patients' feelings of incompetence. For example, physicians often give
patients lengthy lists of what they must change about their lifestyles.
Being told to lose 20 pounds, start going to the gym, and take hypertension medication daily can be challenging for many, particularly those
chronic disease patients who have little understanding of what it means to
have a chronic illness, or that they must play a major part in managing it.
The list approach is unlikely to result in desired outcomes and is more
likely to result in feelings of embarrassment or inadequacy. Repeatedly
experiencing failure because of an inability to follow physicians' advice
demoralizes patients. What chronic disease patients need instead is a
series of successes that can build a sense of competence.

Using an approach tailored to an individual patient's knowledge and skill
level is one way to break the cycle of failure (see Chapter 6). Starting with
appropriate goals that fit patients' activation levels and working toward

increasing activation step by step, patients can experience small successes and steadily build up their confidence and skill for effective self-management (Bandura, 1991; Battersby, Ask, Reece, Markwick, & Collins, 2003). If clinicians had information on their patients' levels of knowledge and skills to self-manage, they could presumably be more effective by targeting self-care education and support to an individual patient's readiness to follow through with the recommended advice. If patients were asked to take steps that were reasonable, given their level of knowledge and skill, they would be more likely to succeed and build a sense of confidence and efficacy that could carry them forward to the next challenge.

WHY IS IT IMPORTANT TO MEASURE PATIENT ACTIVATION?

There are at least three reasons why it is essential to measure patient activation: (1) measurement is necessary to tailor care to individual patients' abilities and needs; (2) to be effective, clinicians need feedback on how they are doing at supporting patients in their self-management role; and (3) supporting patients' in self-management skills is part of high-quality care. Quality improvement in other areas of healthcare does not occur without first putting effective measurement systems in place (Institute of Medicine, 2004). Supporting patient self-management is no different. Indeed, the first Institute of Medicine Summit on Crossing the Quality Chasm (2004) suggested new directions in quality measurement consistent with the use of the PAM.

- First, measurement should focus on the patient, including patient experience and patient outcomes. Measurement could include intermediate outcomes, such as patient knowledge and skills for self-management, as well as the targeted health endpoints. By focusing on patient skills and knowledge, as well as health outcomes, providers explicitly acknowledge that patients are at the center of the care process and essential players in their own health outcomes.
- Second, measurement should be integrated into the care delivery process with the explicit purpose of improving the patient care being measured. By measuring intermediate patient outcomes, providers have an opportunity to improve care for the individual patient as well as assess quality across groups of patients.

- Finally, measurement should be longitudinal so as to capture what happens to patients over time and integrate it into the processes of care. If the patient's level of activation were treated as one of the vital signs taken at each visit, clinicians would acquire on a routine basis information critical to informing and tailoring patient care plans. Measuring patient activation at more than one point in time would allow providers to understand how care is affecting patients' experiences, their capabilities for self-management, and ultimately their quality of life, health, and ability to function.

THE DEVELOPMENT AND TESTING OF A PATIENT ACTIVATION MEASURE

A detailed description of the development and testing of the Patient Activation Measure (PAM) can be found in original publications (Hibbard, Mahoney, Stockard, & Tusler, 2005; Hibbard, Stockard, Mahoney, & Tusler, 2004). Here we provide a definition of the concept, together with an overview of our methods and findings and the research progression needed to determine the PAM's reliability and validity. We conclude with an assessment of the feasibility of using the PAM to guide care plans and as an evaluation tool to assess treatment success.

Progression of the Research

In order for a patient activation measure to be acceptable for use, a step-by-step developmental process is required. These steps include answers to the following questions:

1. Can a consensus among experts and patients on the definition of activation be developed?
2. Given a consensus definition, is it possible to measure patient activation? Is the measure reliable and valid? Is it reliable and valid for people with different chronic illnesses? What about for people who do not have a chronic illness?
3. Is the resulting measure predictive of important outcomes, such as disease-specific self-management behaviors, healthy behaviors, and health status and functioning?

4. Can activation levels be changed?
5. If activation levels are changed, do positive changes in activation result in improved health outcomes and reduced costs?
6. After a patient's activation level is known, what level-specific interventions will be most effective in moving patients to the next highest level?

Defining Patient Activation

The process of conceptually defining activation involved three steps: (1) a review of the literature, (2) systematic consultation with experts in the field using a "consensus method," and (3) consultation with individuals with chronic disease done through focus groups. The expert consensus process was carried out using an iterative mailed-out questionnaire. The expert panel did not see the responses of other members in the panel, but drew on their own expertise and experiences in rating the importance of different domains. Figure 9.1 shows areas of agreement among these three sources. The grid shows the domains derived from the literature included in the investigation. Domains identified as important by both patients and experts were: has the *knowledge* to self-manage and prevent declines; has the *skills* to self-manage, collaborate with provider, and prevent declines; and *believes patient is important in self-management, collaborating with provider, and preventing declines*. These domains served as the basis for the operational definition of patient activation (Hibbard et al., 2004). This is not to say the other areas are not important to activation, only that they were not identified as key components by both patients and experts.

Can Patient Activation Be Measured?

After we defined the concept of patient activation, we were able to begin the measurement process involved in creating the PAM. The tool is essentially a short questionnaire completed by patients that clinicians can use to assess a patient's level of readiness to participate in the care process. To create this tool, we developed a list of possible survey questions that captured the identified domains. For example, we developed and tested several items measuring self-management skills. We then conducted multiple

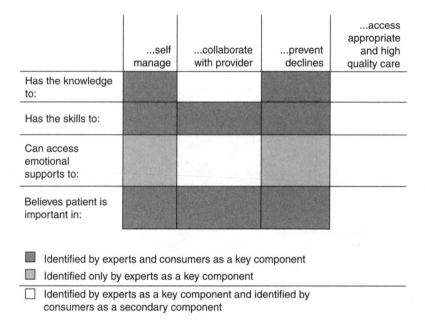

	...self manage	...collaborate with provider	...prevent declines	...access appropriate and high quality care
Has the knowledge to:				
Has the skills to:				
Can access emotional supports to:				
Believes patient is important in:				

■ Identified by experts and consumers as a key component
▨ Identified only by experts as a key component
□ Identified by experts as a key component and identified by consumers as a secondary component

Figure 9.1   Domains of Activation Measured

Source: From Hibbard, J. H., Stockard, J., Mahoney, E. R., & Tusler, M. (2005). Development of the Patient Activation Measure (PAM): Conceptualizing and measuring activation in patients and consumers. *Health Services Research, 39*(4): 1005–1026.

interviews to ensure that patients understood the items as intended. We excluded or edited items that were not well understood.

After the concept of patient activation was broken down into its parts, we ordered these pieces to create a ranking system, or "scale," that allowed us to rate patient activation levels from low to high. We used Rasch measurement, a probabilistic measurement model, to create an interval-level, unidimensional, Guttman-like scale from the ordinal data that emerge from survey questions (Rasch, 1960). The model is based on the idea that the data gathered conform to some reasonable hierarchy of "less than/more than" on a single dimension of interest. The measurement model calibrates the items in terms of activation difficulty. At the lower end of the scale, the items are easier to endorse; at the high end are items that are more difficult to endorse. Figure 9.2 shows the difficulty structure of the items in the measure.

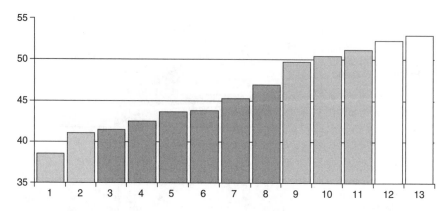

	Believes Active Role Important
1	When all is said and done, I am the person who is responsible for managing my health condition.
2	Taking an active role in my own health care is the most important factor in determining my health and ability to function.
	Confidence and Knowledge to Take Action
3	I am confident that I can take actions that will help prevent or minimize some symptoms or problems associated with my health condition.
4	I know what each of my prescribed medications do.
5	I am confident that I can tell when I need to go get medical care and when I can handle a health problem myself.
6	I am confident I can tell my health care provider concerns I have even when he or she does not ask.
7	I am confident that I can follow through on medical treatments I need to do at home.
8	I I understand the nature and causes of my health condition(s).
	Taking Action
9	I know the different medical treatment options available for my health condition.
10	I have been able to maintain the lifestyle changes for my health that I have made.
11	I know how to prevent further problems with my health condition.
	Staying the Course Under Stress
12	I am confident I can figure out solutions when new situations or problems arise with my health condition.
13	I am confident that I can maintain lifestyle changes like diet and exercise even during times of stress.

Figure 9.2   PAM with item scores and stages.

Source: University of Oregon, Judith H. Hibbard, Dr. P.H., 2004

The central mathematical property of measures resulting from Rasch models is called parameter separation. This term simply means that although the persons measured and the items of measurement are both located on the same equal interval scale, these two parameters are statistically independent of each other. Parameter separation is a key characteristic that sets the measurement model apart from other methods used in the social sciences. When the data fit the stringent requirements of the model, the resulting measure meets all of the requirements of scientific measurement (Smith, 1996). The resulting measure is a unidimensional and true interval yardstick; that is, the distance between the scores is equal, as on a ruler. Most social science measurement is not interval, but ordinal. For example, how would you rate your health: excellent, good, fair, or poor? This self-rated health question is an ordinal measure because although we know that there is an order to the responses we do not know the distance between the four possible responses, much less that they are equidistant from each other.

Rasch modeling has been used in educational achievement testing for some time (Wright & Masters, 1982; Wright & Stone, 1979), in part because the scales resulting from the models are particularly useful for measuring knowledge and skills. The Rasch method is beginning to be used in such diverse health-related areas as genetics and the measurement of vision disability (Massof, 2002). Because it can produce interval-level measures from ordinal data, the Rasch measurement approach is ideally suited to the development of a yardstick to assess the degree to which chronic disease patients have the necessary skills and knowledge to manage their health and healthcare effectively.

Are Patient Activation Scores Predictive of Behavioral and Health Outcomes?

Validity assessments, based on a national probability sample, indicate that the PAM is predictive of health status, healthcare use, and health behaviors. As measured by a standardized eight-item self-reported health measure (Ware, Kosinski, Dewey, & Gandek, 2001), those with higher activation report significantly better health and have significantly lower rates of emergency room visits and hospital nights (Mosen, Hibbard, Sobel, & Remmers, 2005). Those with higher activation scores are significantly more likely to exercise regularly, follow a low-fat diet, eat more fruits and vegetables, and not smoke (Hibbard et al., 2005). In addition, those with higher activation scores are significantly more likely to engage in consumer-savvy health behaviors, such as finding out about a new provider's qualifications or reading about possible side effects when taking a new prescription drug (Hibbard et al., 2004). Self-management behaviors associated with specific conditions are also significantly associated with measured activation levels. For instance, more highly activated diabetics are more likely to keep a glucose journal, and more activated arthritis patients are more likely to exercise. Among people with high cholesterol, those with higher activation scores are more likely to follow a low-fat diet (Hibbard et al., 2004). These findings indicate that the PAM, as a scale measuring patient activation, is a measure with a high degree of construct (predicts behavioral and health outcomes) and criterion (correlates with similar concepts) validity.

In addition, reliability assessments show that the PAM measure performs well for those both with and without chronic conditions. It is also stable across differing levels of health status. In addition, it shows consistent results across gender and different age groups, with a slight decline in its reliability in the oldest group (85 years or more). Finally, the measure's precision is stable across several different chronic illnesses (Hibbard et al., 2004). These findings suggest that the PAM measure can be reliably used to assess activation across a variety of population subgroups. Figure 9.2 shows the 13 items of PAM, its stages, and the difficulty structure of the scale.

The hierarchy of item difficulty implies that what is needed to increase activation depends on where the person is on the activation continuum. For example, those at the low end may lack the belief that they have an important role to play in their health and lack elementary knowledge about their condition and their care. Respondents scoring in the middle range of the scale tend to have the necessary knowledge for self-care, but appear to lack some of the skills and confidence needed to carry through on all that is required for effective self-care. Those scoring at the higher end of the scale largely possess the necessary knowledge, skills, and confidence, but may be derailed from their self-care course when they are under stress or encounter unexpected health events.

The findings from the testing and development phase indicate that the PAM appears to be a valid and reliable instrument to measure activation. The measure has strong psychometric properties and appears to tap into the developmental nature of activation. Because the measure is highly reliable at the individual level, it is possible to use it on an individual patient basis to diagnosis activation and individualize care plans. Moreover, because the measure maintains precision across different demographic and health status groups, it can also be used at the aggregate level to evaluate and compare the efficacy of interventions and healthcare delivery systems.

We conclude from this methodologic work that defining and measuring patient activation are possible (Hibbard et al., 2004, 2005) and that the PAM measure is predictive of important outcomes.

Can Activation Levels Be Changed?

We recently completed a study designed to assess whether people with chronic illness changed activation levels over time. The findings indicate that, over a 6-month period, some study participants stayed at the same level or declined in activation, and a small group increased in activation level. Those who increased in activation also improved their health behaviors. Those who declined or stayed stable in activation also stayed stable or declined in their health-protective behaviors. The findings indicate that activation levels are changeable and that when they change, these changes are followed by changes in behaviors in the same direction (Hibbard, Mahoney, Stock, & Tusler, 2005).

Thus, findings suggest that PAM scores can indeed be changed, and the change is related to subsequent behavioral improvements. The final two questions in the progression of research are these: If activation levels are changed, does the change result in better outcomes and reduced costs? After a patient's activation level is known, what are level-specific interventions that will be most effective in moving patients to the next highest level? Studies focusing on these last two questions are either just beginning or are in progress; no findings are available as yet.

HOW CAN THE PAM BE USED IN A CLINICAL SETTING?

Using the PAM to Tailor Individual Care Plans

PAM scores can provide insight into possible strategies for supporting activation among patients at different points along a continuum. Patients who score at the bottom of the measure may still believe that the doctor will "fix" them. Patients whose scores are somewhat higher but are still in the bottom half may understand that they must be involved in their care, but still lack basic knowledge about their conditions and the steps necessary for them to act effectively on their own behalf. Patients scoring in the bottom half of the measure likely need to work on self-awareness about their role in the care process and in gaining basic information about their own conditions.

Patients whose scores are in the upper half of the distribution are beginning to gain confidence in their ability to take on self-management behaviors and make lifestyle changes. At this stage, experiencing a series of small successes will likely build a sense of self-efficacy and increased activation (Battersby et al., 2003). Patients scoring near the upper end of the measure are likely to have made changes in their lifestyles but may still have difficulty maintaining them when new situations arise or when they are under stress. Thus, for those patients scoring in the upper half of the PAM, working on developing a sense of self-efficacy, either to achieve new skills or prevent relapse of skills already learned, is paramount. Patients who score higher still face challenges; however, they are more likely to do problem-solving, self-monitoring, and self-adjustments to their regimens. Here is how one chronic disease patient who scored in PAM stage 4 described what she thought it meant to manage her condition: "For myself, it means that I do whatever I need to do, which are the diet and exercise that have been recommended, and then I also do other things that I have found that help me feel better. . . . I'll go and ask questions to see if I need to change the things I am doing."

Attaining the basic knowledge and beliefs reflected in early stages of activation is likely necessary for building a sense of efficacy for the self-management tasks involved in the later stages. Logically, it would seem that patients need to pass sequentially through each of these stages on the way to becoming effective self-managers. These stages have some similarities with the stages of change in the transtheoretical model (Prochaska & DiClemente, 1983; Prochaska, Redding, & Evers, 1997). These are pre-contemplation, contemplation, preparation, action, and maintenance stages. The transtheoretical model emphasizes motivation and readiness to take action, but does not explicitly deal with issues of skill and knowledge acquisition. Furthermore, the transtheoretical model focuses on one behavior at a time and requires the development of a measurement tool specific to that behavior. The idea of tailoring interventions to the patient's stage is similar for both the patient activation and transtheoretical models.

Very likely a strategy that helps patients move from activation stage one (believing that the patient has an active role in chronic illness care) to activation stage two (having the confidence and knowledge to take action) will differ from what helps them move into stage three (taking action). That is, after a patient's score or stage is known, the next question to ask is, "What will help that patient move forward in activation?"

Pilot tests have shown some success with a paper and pencil approach to using the PAM scale. Because the items in the measure can be ordered by level of difficulty, providers can administer and then visually scan patient responses to observe when their answers begin to move away from "strongly agree." This approach does not require actually scoring the

When all is said and done, I am the person who is responsible for managing my health condition.	Strongly Disagree	Disagree	Agree	(Strongly Agree)
Taking an active role in my own health care is the most important factor in determining my health and ability to function.	Strongly Disagree	Disagree	Agree	(Strongly Agree)
I am confident that I can take actions that will help prevent or minimize some symptoms or problems associated with my health condition.	Strongly Disagree	Disagree	Agree	(Strongly Agree)
I know what each of my prescribed medications do.	Strongly Disagree	Disagree	(Agree)	Strongly Agree
I am confident that I can tell when I need to go get medical care and when I can handle a health problem myself.	Strongly Disagree	(Disagree)	Agree	Strongly Agree
I am confident that I can tell my health care provider concerns I have even when he or she does not ask.	Strongly Disagree	(Disagree)	Agree	Strongly Agree
I am confident that I can follow through on medical treatments I need to do at home.	Strongly Disagree	(Disagree)	Agree	Strongly Agree

Figure 9.3 Visual Scan Assessment of Patient Activation

responses, just visually scanning the responses. Clinicians can use this scan as an opportunity to begin a conversation with patients about the item where responses changed (Figure 9.3). For example, "I see you are less sure you can manage your medications. Let's talk about that." Using the PAM in this way can sharpen the specificity of a provider's interaction with an individual patient, increasing the probability that individual barriers and issues can be identified and dealt with. Using both the visual scan and the PAM score or stage together may be the most effective use of the measure. The "visual scan" approach is the easiest way to use the measure in a clinical encounter, particularly when electronic data collection is not an option. Because no scoring or date entry is involved, testing the efficacy of this "low tech" approach is also a priority.

Whether a PAM score is calculated or not, using the visual scan of the responses to the PAM can be valuable as a way to begin a discussion.

Clinicians have also paired this discussion with one that explores how the patients' health affects their quality of life. How does health keep patients from doing what they want to do? The clinician then uses the patient's responses on the PAM, the patient's priorities (based on the quality of life discussion), and clinical considerations to negotiate with the patient a reasonable and achievable goal. As Harry Laudermilk, a case manager with the Community Health Plan of Washington State, has observed, "In working with large numbers of persons with chronic disease(s), the PAM is able to reliably demonstrate [which] individuals need more case management interventions, education, and/or resources. It provides a timely, effective and efficient assessment while also providing specific areas for exploration in clinical interviews." The assumption is that patients will be more engaged in the process if the goal is designed to help them move toward achieving an outcome that they desire (Battersby et al., 2003; Delbanco, 1992). Although clinically appropriate, the goal may still represent a small step toward the patient's ultimate objective. Goals should be achievable and help patients develop a sense of competence as they experience a series of successes. Thus, not only should goals be clinically appropriate and represent steps toward outcomes that patients care about, but they should also be behaviorally appropriate. Behaviorally appropriate goals are ones that fit patients' levels of knowledge, skill, and confidence.

Pilot testing has also shown the value of using the PAM as one of the vital signs taken at every visit. First, patients have ups and downs. An acute episode, a new challenge related to a patient's condition, or other life stressors can lower a patient's sense of competence and therefore his or her PAM score. These setbacks are normal, but can also signal a need to adjust care plan goals. Second, regularly measuring PAM scores can provide a longitudinal assessment of an individual patient's progress. Finally, a provider can use PAM scores to look at progress across an entire class of patients. For example, a provider can ask, "Over the last year, how are the diabetic patients in my practice doing?" In these ways, patient activation measurement can provide feedback to clinicians about the efficacy of their efforts at supporting patient self-management.

Using the PAM to Manage Enrolled Populations

A measure of patient activation could possibly be used to manage entire patient populations. For example, delivery systems could stratify their

Table 9.1   Patient Segmentation Groups

1. Clinical risk factors high/PAM scores low	3. Clinical risk factors high/PAM scores high
2. Clinical risk factors low/PAM scores low	4. Clinical risk factors low/PAM scores high

(Highest risk   Lowest risk)

enrolled patient populations by both clinical indicators (e.g., blood pressure or cholesterol levels) as well as by their activation levels. Doing so would allow for early intervention with patients who have clinical risk factors and who lack the skills to self-manage, ideally intervening with patients before they move to a higher health risk group. Theoretically, patients could be segmented into four groups as shown in Table 9.1.

Health plans could then devise either group-level or individual-level interventions aimed at one or more of these patient segmentation groups. Many health plans already use segmentation strategies, most of which are based on resource consumption. To date, the strategies typically proposed for those in the high-risk group are some kind of care or disease management. Their efficacy, however, is uncertain. The efficacy of segmenting based on PAM (or patient knowledge and skill) is untested, but in theory could have an impact on outcomes and costs.

As we test the efficacy of different intervention approaches, we need to assess whether undesirable or unintended consequences result along with desired outcomes. Possible concerns might include labeling or stigmatizing patients or assuming that those low in activation stages are not able to change.

Data Collection

A strategy for collecting data from patients must be devised to use the PAM to either tailor individual care plans or manage enrolled populations. Studies using the PAM have employed telephone surveys, self-administered questionnaires, face-to-face interviews, and web-based surveys. To date, we have not observed any significant "mode effects" or differences in response related to the type of survey administered. For use in a clinical setting, a myriad of approaches for data collection is currently in use. A disease management company has programmed an interactive, automated voice-activated system for telephone data collection. Patients call a toll-free number, and an automated voice asks each of the PAM questions. Data collected in this fashion produces an electronic data file. Collecting data using a handheld computer tablet (the size of a writing pad) in the waiting room of clinics will soon be tested. This method also produces an electronic record that can then be integrated into an electronic medical file, printed out, or used for tracking or patient segmentation purposes.

How Does Measurement of Patient Activation Fit into Quality Improvement Efforts?

Engaging patients in their own care and including them as part of the care team are central tenets of the chronic care model (Bodenheimer, Lorig, Holman, & Grumbach, 2002; Von Korff et al., 1997). Patients receiving high-quality care should, over time, improve their self-management capability. As with other areas of healthcare performance, only through measurement can we determine how much caregiving has improved. Gains in patient activation can be viewed as an intermediate outcome of care. Furthermore, the processes of care that support patient activation, such as patient education, referrals, and coaching, need to be in place, and those processes need to be documented and measured. As Figure 9.4 indicates, quality-improvement activities require ongoing measurement of both the processes and intermediate outcomes of care in order to provide feedback on which to base improvements. After being established empirically, the links between the processes of care and outcomes do not need to be confirmed on an ongoing basis.

OTHER MEASURES OF PATIENT-CENTERED CARE

The PAM is beginning to be used in a wide range of clinical settings for a variety of purposes, including cardiac care, diabetes care, care for people with disabilities, disease management, hospital discharge planning, and obesity care. The PAM is also used in a number of research studies and to evaluate interventions aimed at groups of patients, including e-health ini-

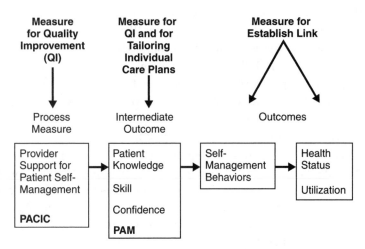

Figure 9.4 Measuring for Improvement at the System Level

Source: University of Oregon, Judith H. Hibbard, 2006.

tiatives. Yet the PAM is not the only measure healthcare researchers and medical practices are using to measure the processes of care. Other measures of patient-centered care currently being used include

- The Consumer Assessment of Healthcare Providers and Systems (CAHPS) family of survey instruments. These instruments measure patients' experiences in using healthcare. The surveys include information on patient access, how well patients understand the information they receive, and whether they are treated with respect and caring. Each of the surveys covers health maintenance organizations, ambulatory care venues, hospitals, nursing homes, and other healthcare facilities. The instruments are standardized so that consumers and providers can compare facilities, plans, and providers. The Consumer Assessment of Healthcare Providers and Systems instruments measure quality of care from the patient point of view.

- The health locus of control measure assesses the degree to which patients feel in control of their health. Health locus of control includes three subscales: a measure of internality (the degree to which one feels he is in control of his own health), a measure of externality or the influence of "powerful others" (the degree to which one feels that powerful others control his health, and a measure of chance (the degree to which one feels that chance events control his health) (http://www.vanderbilt.edu/nursing/kwallston/mhlcscales.htm).

- The Patient Assessment of Chronic Illness Care (PACIC), by Glasgow et al. (2005) measures patients' assessments of the degree to which the processes of care support their role as members of the healthcare team. Although both the PAM and the PACIC can be used as performance measures, the PACIC is a process measure, whereas the PAM assesses intermediate outcomes of care.
- Elwyns' OPTION (Observing Patient Involvement) scale assesses the extent and quality of shared decision making in clinical practice. The tool is intended for clinicians to use to evaluate shared decision making in their own practice. Although developed and tested in a general practice, the OPTION scale is generic enough for use in all types of consultations (Elwyn, 2001).

Next Steps

Although the PAM has strong psychometric properties, research is still needed to make it fully ready for use in different settings and with different populations. For example, PAM researchers are beginning to translate the measure into other languages. The degree to which the measure is valid and reliable in these translations and among different cultures is important in multicultural contexts. Although evidence indicates the measure is valid and reliable for different chronic illnesses, this observation requires further study. Replication studies of the measure with different populations in different settings are underway and will add to our understanding of these questions.

Research that tests interventions effective in encouraging and supporting patient advancement through the stages of activation described earlier is a high priority. Although there is a great deal of rhetoric about making healthcare more patient centered and engaging patients in the care process, moving beyond the rhetoric to action is unlikely to occur until measurement systems are in place that shine a light on what processes work and that provide actionable information. Integrating the measurement of patient activation into the processes of care, particularly for patients with chronic conditions, is one place to begin.

REFERENCES

Bandura, A. (1991). Self-efficacy mechanism in physiological activation and health-promoting behavior. In J. Madden, S. Matthysse, & J. Barchas (Eds.), *Adaption, learning and affect* (pp. 226–269). New York: Raven Press.

Battersby, M. W., Ask, A., Reece, M. M., Markwick, M. J., & Collins, J. P. (2003). The partners in health scale: The development and psychometric properties of a generic assessment scale for chronic condition self-management. *Australian Journal of Primary Health, 9,* 41–52.

Berwick, D. M. (1999). *Escape fire: Lessons for the future of health care.* New York: The Commonwealth Fund.

Bodenheimer, T., Lorig, K., Holman, H., & Grumbach, K. (2002). Patient self-management of chronic disease in primary care. *Journal of the American Medical Association, 288,,* 2469–2475.

Delbanco, T. L. (1992). Enriching the doctor-patient relationship by inviting the patient's perspective. *Annals of Internal Medicine, 116,* 414–418.

Elwyn, G. (2001). *Shared decision making: Patient involvement in clinical practice.* Nijmegen, The Netherlands: WOK.

Glasgow, R. E., Wagner, E. H., Schaefer, J., Mahoney, L. D., Reid, R. J., & Greene, S. M. (2005). Development and validation of the patient assessment of chronic illness care (PACIC). *Medical Care, 43,* 436–444.

Hibbard, J. H., Mahoney, E., Stock, R., & Tusler, M. (2005). *Can patient activation levels change?* New Perspectives Conference on Self-Management. Victoria, British Columbia, September 2005.

Hibbard, J. H., Mahoney, E. R., Stockard, J., & Tusler, M. (2005). Development and testing of a short form of the patient activation measure. *Health Services Research, 40*(6 Pt 1), 1918–1930.

Hibbard, J. H., Stockard, J., Mahoney, E. R., & Tusler, M. (2004). Development of the patient activation measure (PAM): Conceptualizing and measuring activation in patients and consumers. *Health Services, 39*(4 Pt 1), 1005–1026.

Institute of Medicine. (2004). In K. Adams, A. C. Greiner, & J. M. Corrigan (Eds.), *First annual crossing the quality chasm summit: A focus on communities.* Washington, DC: National Academy Press.

Kaplan, S. H., Greenfield, S., Ware, J. E. (1989). Assessing the effects of physician-patient interactions on the outcomes of chronic disease. *Medical Care, 27*(3 Suppl): s110–27.

Lorig, K. (1996). *Outcome measures for health education and other health care interventions.* Thousand Oaks, CA: Sage Publications.

Lorig, K. R., Sobel, D. S., Stewart, A. L., Brown, B. W., Jr., Bandura, A., Ritter, P., et al. (1999). Evidence suggesting that a chronic disease self-management program can improve health status while reducing hospitalization: A randomized trial. *Medical Care, 37,* 5–14.

Massof, R. W. (2002). The measurement of vision disability. *Optometry and Vision Science, 79,* 516–552.

Mosen, D., Hibbard, J. H., Sobel, D., & Remmers, C. L. (2005). Is patient activation associated with better outcomes for persons with diabetes? *American Public Health*

Association Annual Meeting and Exposition, Philadelphia, PA, December 2005. Retrieved on February 6, 2007, from http://apha.confex.com/apha/133am/techprogram/.

Prochaska, J. O., & DiClemente, C. C. (1983). Stages and processes of self-change of smoking: Toward an integrative model of change. *Journal of Consulting and Clinical Psychology, 51,* 390–395.

Prochaska, J. O., Redding, C. A., & Evers, K. E. (1997). The transtheoretical model and stages of change. In K. Glanz, F. M. Lewis, & B. K. Rimer (Eds.), *Health behavior and health education: Theory, research, and practice* (2nd ed.). San Francisco: Jossey-Bass.

Rasch, G. (1960). *Probabilistic models for some intelligence and attainment tests.* (Reprint with Foreword and Afterward by B. D. Wright, Chicago: University of Chicago Press, 1980 ed.). Copenhagen: Danmarks Paedogogiske Institut.

Roter, D. L., Stewart, M., Putnam, S. M., Lipkin, M., Jr., Stiles, W., & Inui, T. S. (1997). Communication patterns of primary care physicians. *Journal of the American Medical Association, 277,* 350–356.

Smith, R. M. (1996). Polytomous mean-square fit statistics. *Rasch Measurement Transactions, 10,* 516–517.

Von Korff, M., Gruman, J., Schaefer, J., Curry, S. J., & Wagner, E. H. (1997). Collaborative management of chronic illness. *Annals of Internal Medicine, 127,* 1097–1102.

Von Korff, M., Moore, J. E., Lorig, K., Cherkin, D. C., Saunders, K., Gonzalez, V. M., et al. (1998). A randomized trial of a lay person–led self-management group intervention for back pain patients in primary care. *Spine, 23,* 2608–2615.

Ware, J. E., Kosinski, J. E., Dewey, B., & Gandek, B. (2001). *How to score and interpret single-item health status measures: A manual for users of the SF-8 health survey.* Lincoln, RI: QualityMetric.

Wright, B. D., & Masters, G. N. (1982). *Rating scale analysis.* Chicago: Mesa Press.

Wright, B. D., & Stone, M. H. (1979). *Best test design.* Chicago: Mesa Press.

Strategy Three: Transforming Hospital and Medical Culture to Support Patient- and Family-Centered Care

After establishing the importance of the patient–provider relationship, the third section of this text adopts a wider lens to examine healthcare from a systems perspective. Patient advocacy in this context has traditionally focused on the issue of patient safety, where prominent health services research, as well as two reports by the Institute of Medicine, has demonstrated the urgent need for reform. Work in this area has emphasized the importance of macro-level factors such as organizational culture and methods of systems analysis, and patient advocates have responded by developing new models of care based on an appreciation for the importance of the healthcare environment.

In Chapter 10, Conway discusses the patient safety movement, chronicling its successes and its continued challenges. In a systems approach to reducing medical error, an effort is made to analyze how things work from top to bottom so that problems can be traced to environmental factors that can lead to errors. This chapter offers an overview of the patient safety movement, including the creation of the Institute for Healthcare Improvement, and focuses particularly on organizational changes leading to improved patient safety and experience.

In Chapter 11, Frampton and Gilpin introduce Planetree, a hospital-based model of patient-centered care founded as a nonprofit organization in 1978. Today, Planetree partners with hospital affiliates around the country to establish more personalized, holistic services than are offered by traditionally designed hospitals. For example, the model encourages hospitals to (1) increase communication and reduce errors by encouraging patients to read and write in their own medical records; (2) maximize patients' sense of well-being and control through architectural designs that provide well-planned, quiet, home-like spaces for families; and (3) make sure, through formal and informal mechanisms, that all employees can speak up about ideas for making care safer and more holistic. By increasing patients' leverage in a healthcare environment designed to speed healing, patients are more likely to participate in their own care, leading to greater patient satisfaction and better outcomes.

As many chapters in this book imply, changing hospital culture requires a concomitant change in medical schools. In Chapter 12, Sodomka, Moretz, and Zoppi examine patient advocacy efforts in medical education. Despite a growing demand for training in patient-centered care, strong barriers exist to such changes, including the culture of medical training programs that often champion biomedical rather than relational aspects of care. Even when students receive training in communication skills in the classroom, the so-called hidden curriculum, in which students adopt the modes and attitudes of their mentors, often militates against their formal classroom experiences and reinforces traditional physician-directed practices. Using the case of the Medical College of Georgia as an example, the authors discuss how hospital systems can successfully make the shift to training through a patient- and family-centered care model.

Chapter 13 offers a historical perspective on systems change through a discussion of the hospice and palliative care movements, which have long been at the forefront of debates surrounding health advocacy. With its philosophy of attending to all dimensions of a person (physical, emotional, and spiritual) and its emphasis on fostering patient self-determination, symptom control, and family connections, the hospice and palliative care movements have contributed significantly to our understanding of ways to operationalize patient-centered care. Winzelberg and Hanson's chapter summarizes the history of the hospice and palliative care movements in the United States, the problems they seek to address, the kinds of advocacy these movements have drawn on, and ethical issues surrounding their practice.

CHAPTER 10

The Contributions of Patient Advocacy in Patient Safety

James Conway

OBJECTIVES

- To introduce the history of the patient safety movement through the lens of patients and those who care for them
- To demonstrate the significant role that patient advocates have played in the evolution of the movement
- To illustrate the gaps that remain in partnerships with patient advocates, patients, and family members
- To showcase the leading edge of patient advocacy by individuals and organizations
- To affirm the resolve of a growing number of advocates for high-quality safe care 100% of the time

In little more than 10 years, remarkable advances have occurred in understanding the extent of error and in the application of safety science to healthcare. Those receiving and delivering care today have had a grandstand seat to the birth of a culture of safety. Many, including this author, have had the privilege of participating in this journey at an organizational, national, and international level. Many, including this author, have lost a family member—in my case a father—to preventable medical error (Textbox 10.1).

There are many ways to present a general introduction to patient safety, and the selected references (Table 10.3) serve this purpose well. The goal of this chapter, however, is not to repeat that exhaustive work, but instead to look at patient safety through the eyes of patient advocates. Included will be the stories and learning of those within and outside of healthcare. Referenced will be their tragedies, the harms they suffered, and their courage. Interwoven are the key elements, structures, and processes of the

Textbox 10.1   A Family Tragedy

It was August 1980 when the call came. "Jim, you need to come home. I think Dad is dead." As I rushed to the house, I couldn't fathom it . . . my father dead. He was a rock, rarely ill, a Boston policeman and always active. He was dead, and surprisingly, he had been to the hospital that day. He had had pain in his arm after clipping the hedges and my mother insisted that he go to the hospital. He was seen and given a prescription for medication. At home, he sat in his favorite chair, took his first pill, and died shortly thereafter. It didn't make sense. Because he was a retired cop, there was a quick police response. Because he had been recently diagnosed with prostate cancer, the medical examiner decided to waive the autopsy, but my sister and I, both working in healthcare, felt uneasy. Using our connections, we persisted. He was accepted as an ME case, and an autopsy was performed.

The autopsy noted my father had died of a heart attack, and there was evidence of a prior attack. There was a question about the medication he was on. At the request of my mother, my sister and I met with the president of the hospital where my father had been seen on the day he died. Her parents and my father had come from the same town in Ireland, and they had been at my father's wake. My mother wanted to know what happened that day in the emergency department, what care my father received, and whether there had been a problem. She didn't want to sue. The hospital had been good to us, and nothing would be gained from a suit.

An investigation was conducted, and we were informed of the results. The emergency department was busy the day my father was seen—so busy that the physician had only talked to him. Despite his presenting symptoms, no EKG or lab tests were ordered, and the physician had not even listened to his chest. He diagnosed my father's complaint as muscle pain from the hedge clipping. The muscle relaxant that he was given (when taken on top of the heart attack he had already had) had probably killed him. The hospital apologized, reviewed their practices, and engaged with the physician. We were told that if we wanted to sue, we could. We didn't, and we didn't realize how remarkable our experience in 1980 was— a story out of tragedy that was bound in trust and respect.

patient safety movement as well as barriers that limit further progress. Scattered throughout the chapter will be simple quotations from patients and family members heard over the years—simple yet profound in driving the tension for change.

Patient safety appeared on the national radar in 1995 when a cluster of high-profile, individual tragedies revealed widespread, systemic problems in our health system. Although data outlining extensive error and harm in healthcare had been published for years, this information went largely unnoticed outside of a few academic circles such as the anesthesia profession. Error and its extent remained a dark secret, a phenomenon considered a hidden cost of doing business. Affected patients and their family members, as well as patient advocates, knew errors happened, but if dealt with at all, incidents were treated confidentially and individually, with a primary goal of minimizing risk to organizations and professionals.

As this chapter shows, the safety-related tragedies of 1995 drastically changed this culture of silence. For the first time, healthcare's individuals, organizations, and systems were forced to confront publicly the enormous burden and legacy of error. The nation took notice, and those seeking to advocate on behalf of patients began to be given, or more often simply took, a license for action. Although the healthcare industry did not want to embrace this new accountability, it found itself forced to by the victims of harm.

Since the tragedies of 1995, there has been engagement, focus, and improvement by the public and the healthcare industry (Table 10.3). The Institute of Medicine (IOM) has issued seminal reports, the Joint Commission on the Accreditation of Healthcare Organizations (JCAHO) established new patient safety standards and requirements for disclosure, the National Quality Forum (NQF) has released a set of safe practices, the Institute for Healthcare Improvement (IHI) has led a campaign to save 100,000 lives (IHI, 2006), and the National Patient Safety Foundation (NPSF) enters its 10th anniversary year. Patients and consumer patient safety organizations have been strengthened in a partnership with healthcare to advance the safety agenda.

For all of the progress, there is still little cause for celebration as the suffering remains; the same tragedies that took place in 1995 continue to occur. Except by anecdote, feelings, and a few selected metrics, answering the question "Are we safer now than we were in 1995?" remains difficult. Do we believe we are safer? Definitely—just having the conversation, the tension, the spotlight, together with engaged patients and consumers ensures that change. Efforts that will improve safety are occurring around the world. Yet the rate of error remains much too high, and the toll of those injury rates is enormous. The changes underway have great potential but remain unfocused, and their outcomes are often unmeasurable. Eliminating harm will take the efforts of all in healthcare, working in partnership with patients and those who care for them. As the IHI's

100,000 Lives Campaign taught us, "Some is not a number, soon is not a time." We must set the goal for zero harm. Through the activism of those reading this chapter and book, the goal of eliminating harm, although lofty, is achievable.

HISTORICAL PERSPECTIVE

A Secret Discussion: A Pursuit of Academics and Radicals, an Expectation of Perfection

With a few notable exceptions, understanding of and attention to the field of patient safety in healthcare are very new. In more distant times, patient safety was mentioned anecdotally by Florence Nightingale (Nightingale, Reprinted 1987). The first "error reporting" may be traced to Emory Codman, a surgeon, who in 1913 made a practice of publishing an annual report of his hospital's medical errors so that patients could judge for themselves the quality and the outcome of his care. Despite his challenges to other hospitals to do the same, his practice appears to have been one of a kind (Neuhauser, 2002).

The modern patient safety movement began with concerted efforts in two areas: medication and anesthesia. In 1975, Michael Cohen began a lifelong journey to improve medication safety, establishing the Institute for Safe Medication Practice (Institute for Safe Medication Practices, 2006). A decade later, anesthesia professionals were prompted to address the issue of preventable medical error after a sensational television exposé raised public concern (Cooper, 2003). In response, leaders in anesthesia established the Anesthesia Patient Safety Foundation in 1985 with the mission to ensure that no patient would be harmed by the effects of anesthesia (Silker, 2006) (Textbox 10.2). Within 10 years, they have effected a significant reduction in anesthesia-related injury.

The work in anesthesia and medication safety went largely unnoticed by the rest of healthcare and the public and was rarely covered in the popular media. Healthcare through the 1990s seemed to talk about and celebrate only the stories of care, caring, discovery, technology, and innovation. Advocates such as Charles Inlander of the People's Medical Society (People's Medical Society, 2002), Arlene Salamendra of FAIR (FAIR, 2006), and Art Levin of the Center for Medical Consumers (2005) sought

Textbox 10.2 Anesthesia Patient Safety Foundation*

Patient safety in anesthesia was a topic for a few researchers starting in the 1950s but it was the face of the patient that brought energy to patient safety in anesthesia in the 1980s. On Thursday, April 22, 1982, ABC television aired a segment of the program 20/20 entitled, "The Deep Sleep, 6,000 will die or suffer brain damage." The announcer opened the program, "If you are going to go into anesthesia, you are going on a long trip, and you should not do it, if you can avoid it in any way. General anesthesia is safe most of the time, but there are dangers from human error, carelessness, and a critical shortage of anesthesiologists. This year, 6,000 patients will die or suffer brain damage." Following scenes of patients who had anesthesia mishaps, the program went on to say, "The people you have just seen are tragic victims of a danger they never knew existed—mistakes in administering anesthesia."

The 20/20 program was a watershed for anesthesia patient safety endeavors. In response, the American Society of Anesthesiologists established a new ASA committee, the Committee on Patient Safety and Risk Management. Among its first endeavors, the committee developed a series of patient safety videotapes. In 1984, Jeffrey Cooper, Richard Kitz, and Jeep Pierce hosted the first International Symposium on Preventable Anesthesia Mortality and Morbidity (ISPAMM), held in Boston with 50 anesthesiologists from the United States, Australia, Great Britain, South Africa, and Belgium attending. That international meeting has now been held every 2 years since. The Anesthesia Patient Safety Foundation (APSF) was established as an outcome of the Boston meeting. Their mission included:

• Fostering investigations that will provide a better understanding of preventable anesthetic injuries

• Encouraging programs that will reduce the number of anesthetic injuries

• Promoting national and international communication of information and ideas about the causes and prevention of anesthetic injuries

Why the improvement in anesthesia? It was the result of sustained focus, passion, and engagement, along with careful analysis and publication of the realities of practice. Reformers used clinical incidents, research and claims analysis, and specific activities and initiatives to detect and prevent mishaps. Furthermore, there were significant increases in the number and quality of anesthesia trainees as well as the development of better anesthesia techniques. Although patients and families have not been a major part of the anesthesia patient safety journey, a group of healthcare professionals advocating for the safety of the patients under their care has been central.

*This note draws heavily from the work of **Ellison C. Pierce, Jr., MD**, Associate Clinical Professor of Anaesthesia, Harvard Medical School, Chairman Emeritus, Department of Anaesthesia, Deaconess Hospital, Boston, MA, and the 34th Rovenstine Lecture to bring medical error issues forward, but they were dismissed as radical, dangerous foes of healthcare. Similarly, in academia, patient safety was an unstructured area of study for a very small group of researchers and clinicians (Leape et al., 1991, 1995). These early advocates raised concerns about errors and outcomes, publishing a small yet steady series of articles that went largely unnoticed.

In the 1980s and early 1990s, and no doubt before, some patients, family members, and patient advocates knew that medical error was a problem. They aired these issues in consumer and special interest patient groups; in Massachusetts, these included pediatric groups such as the Federation of Children with Special Needs, Children in Hospitals, and the Massachusetts Association of Parents of the Visually Impaired. Other states spawned similar organized responses. In those cases where advocates brought issues of injury or error to light, the issues were rarely moved forward by organizations, and when organizations did, they did so in secret.

For most practitioners, perfection was expected and even demanded under professional responsibility codes and according to the Hippocratic dictum of "first, do no harm." Additionally, physicians and organizations were worried about anything that increased their malpractice rates. Patients and families rarely had medical errors disclosed to them. Professionals and organizations were either unaware of adverse events or comfortable in the notion that "the family has been through a lot and there is nothing to be gained by telling them." Although hospital administrators might dismiss staff because of medical error, they rarely made changes at a systems level. Risk management in the early days was as aimed at mitigating financial exposure and not necessarily actual risk. Healthcare executives and clinicians did not understand the extent of error in their organizations and did not benefit from the application of safety science and high-reliability processes, already in use in nuclear power, aviation, naval operations, chemical plants, and manufacturing industries.

1995: A Face and Voice Comes to Patient Safety

In 1995 and 1996, a rash of high-profile medical errors captured the attention of the media and drew national recognition. These events (Belkin, 1997) included the following:

- University Community Hospital in Tampa, where a surgeon amputated the wrong leg of Willie King
- Sloan-Kettering Cancer Center in New York, where a neurosurgeon operated on the wrong side of the brain of the mother of a prominent Indian film star
- Butterworth Hospital in Grand Rapids, Michigan, where a surgeon, during a mastectomy, removed the wrong breast of a cancer patient
- Quincy Hospital in Boston, where a surgeon removed the wrong kidney from a patient after failing to check x-rays
- Martin Memorial Hospital in Florida, where an anesthesiologist injected Ben Kolb with a high dose of a concentrated form of epinephrine, killing him
- Herman Hospital in Houston, where Jose Martinez died from a 10-fold overdose of digoxin
- Dana-Farber Cancer Institute (DFCI) in Boston, where a fourfold overdose of chemotherapy led to the death of *Boston Globe* reporter, wife and mother, Betsy Lehman

The face of error, suffering, harm, and tragedy became visible in 1995, brought there by disclosures of organizations and/or discoveries by families and the media. Energy to do something about these problems came from angry and grieving patients, families, colleagues, friends, as well as agitated and frustrated regulatory and accreditation agencies. Each case was powerful. Together, they raised national questions, specifically, "What is going on in healthcare?" Newspapers throughout the country and world featured front-page, above-the-fold stories. They asked, "Why?" and specifically, "Why in good and often world-famous organizations?" Was this about incompetent, uncaring professionals or something bigger? Was this unique to these organizations, or did it signal a universal problem? Am I safe? Could it happen to me, to my mother, or to my child? What do we do about it?

These high-profile errors re-energized leaders who had long been laboring to shine a light on patient safety and adversity. These included surgeon Lucian Leape, MD, from the Harvard School of Public Health; Jeff Cooper, PhD, and Jeep Pierce, MD, of the Anesthesia Patient Safety Foundation; Dennis O'Leary, MD, of JCAHO; David Bates, MD, of the Brigham and Women's Hospital; Nancy Dickie, MD, then of the American Medical Association (AMA); Marty Hatlie Esq., of the NPSF; Don

Berwick, MD, from the IHI; John Nance from aviation and the media; and author Michael Millenson (1997).

In the mid 1990s, those directly harmed by medical error started to drive revolutionary change. These patient advocates emerged as leaders in safety, including the following: Ilene Corina, Long Island, NY; Jennifer Dingman, Pueblo, CO; Dan Ford, Oro Valley, AZ; Roxanne Goeltz, Lakeville, MN; Deborah Malone, RN, Denver, CO; Becky Martins, Warren, ME; Patti Hart O'Regan, Advanced Registered Nurse Practitioner, Port Richey, FL; and Arlene Salamendra, LaGrange, IL. Their stories are as tragic, powerful, and enabling as that of Betsy Lehman (NPSF, 2006). All of them told their terrible stories out of suffering and loss, with the goal of preventing such tragedies from happening again. Out of these courageous and tragic stories of courage, learning, and sharing, three organizational stories are recommended for further study: those at the DFCI (Conway et al., 2006a), the Martin Memorial Hospital (Haas, 2004), and the Herman Hospital (Belkin, 1997).

Patient Safety Is on the Table and Becomes Part of the Work

In 1996 an extraordinary event occurred: the first public conference dedicated to medical error and patient safety. The conference, called "Health Care: Developing a Prevention, Education and Research Agenda" (Annenberg Center for Health Services, 1996), was supported in part by Walter Annenberg, the communication guru, and was an unprecedented multidisciplinary gathering. Every sector of healthcare was represented— from patients and family members to practitioners, administrators, health plans, and regulators, plus researchers, ethicists, lawyers, risk managers, and quality-care professionals. This Annenberg meeting also marked the inception of the NPAF at the AMA.

The first conference was dedicated to Betsy Lehman, who had died from a preventable error at the DFCI. The agenda included updates about what had been learned from the deaths at DFCI, Herman Hospital, and Martin Memorial Hospital; introductions to safety science and management systems; reports on the 10 years of learning from the anesthesia profession; and presentations on medical error research and practice issues. Each attendee received a picture of Ben Kolb, the child who had died at the Martin Memorial Hospital. They were asked to hold it while the medical team, and family representatives told Ben's story, and the hospital's response to it. At that time, transparency about such issues was so unusual, and the discussion of error so rare, that many conference attendees would stop talking and stare when staff of the three aforementioned hospitals would walk in.

Representatives from these organizations had been invited to speak by respected healthcare leaders, and they had accepted, albeit with considerable trepidation. They agreed to speak for a number of reasons. Each had already received and was continuing to receive extensive media coverage; thus, preventing exposure was no longer an option. All were attempting to work closely with the patients and/or families, and they all knew that the tragedy that was bringing them into the spotlight was only part of the story. All wanted the nation to know that in the aftermath of these events, they had accepted responsibility and accountability. Everything was being done to prevent a similar tragedy from happening again, and they wanted to share lessons learned about the comprehensive systematic redesign they had initiated. Although many treated the staff from these organizations with distance, the majority rendered considerable support for the journey they were taking. National media attended the event, and considerable press coverage followed.

Although still "below the radar," safety efforts increased in the aftermath of the first Annenberg conference. The NPSF moved forward in bringing together key partners to understand what was necessary to support change and foster improvement. With the Second Annenberg Conference on Enhancing Patient Safety and Reducing Errors in Health Care in 1998 (NPSF, 1998), patients and families had become more fully integrated into the NPSF structure. Patients, families, and friends continued to "push forward" the faces of those who experienced preventable harm, and they were supported by leaders in the field. Yet, patient safety continued to struggle as a movement, and organizations and individuals specifically devoted to increasing safety were not ready to have patient advocates as active participants. A malpractice insurance crisis was sweeping the nation. Funds for social change were limited by foreign entanglements, and enormous barriers to transparency and risk-taking solutions remained. Healthcare professionals, well trained in the "silo mentality" of the individual contributor, struggled with the new focus on systems and shared responsibility.

In a report issued in 1998, the President's Advisory Commission on Consumer Protection and Quality in the Health Care Industry proposed creation of the NQF as part of an integrated national quality improvement agenda. In May of 1999, after a year of meetings by leaders from consumer, purchaser, provider, health plan, and health service research organizations, the NQF was incorporated. In October 1998, the JCAHO (2006) issued its Sentinel Event Policy and Procedures that required the reporting of errors reaching patients and causing significant harm or death. The extent of tragedy was becoming increasingly apparent, as were steps that could be taken to prevent it.

Locally, regionally, and nationally, groups including the American Medical Association, the American Hospital Association, the American Nurses Association, along with state hospital associations, began detailing their role to support and enhance safe practice. As one state example, in 1996 two very public preventable medication-related deaths led the Massachussetts Commissioner of Public Health to initiate formation in 1998 of the first statewide coalition focused on patient safety, the Massachusetts Coalition for the Prevention of Medical Errors (2006). The Massachusetts Hospital Association, with the help of the Institute for Safe Medication Practices, immediately performed an assessment of medication management practices across the state around the potential for harm. The results were sobering, and a series of best practices and an action plan were issued for the state (Massachusetts Hospital Association, 2001). Early on, patient advocates were members of these groups. NPSF and other groups, such as the JCAHO, AMA, and AHA, began accelerated efforts to educate citizens on patient safety. The influence of regional consumer groups such as PULSE began to grow. All of these efforts would dramatically accelerate when the IOM released its seminal report in December 1999.

The Gauntlet Is Laid Down, Structures Fall into Place, and Patient Safety and the National Healthcare Quality Agenda Get Underway

In 1998, the IOM was charged by Congress with issuing a series of reports on the safety and quality of the American Healthcare System. The first of these reports, released in December of 1999, *To Err Is Human: Building a Safer Health System* (IOM, 2000), by the Committee on the Quality of Health Care in America, opened with the death of Betsy Lehman. It announced the riveting numbers extrapolated from research performed years prior; somewhere between 44,000 and 98,000 deaths occur annually from medical errors in hospitals. Highlighted was the fact that there are more deaths in hospitals each year from preventable medical mistakes than there are deaths from motor vehicle accidents, breast cancer, or AIDS. A frenzy of media, policy, and legislation actions unfolded. The public was stunned, and although many were not surprised that these events had happened, most were amazed at the extent. Shortly after the report's release, President Clinton asked the Quality Interagency Coordination Task Force to analyze the problem of medical errors and patient safety and make recommendations for improvement within the government. The Report to the President on Medical Errors was published in February 2000 (Quality Interagency Task Force, 2000). The Agency for Healthcare Research and Quality was given a lead role in research related to patient safety, documenting the extent of the problem and the effectiveness of steps to reduce it.

Action in response to the IOM report came from many areas in addition to the federal government. The report recommended that large employers provide more market reinforcement for increasing the quality and safety of healthcare. The business community, frustrated over the slow pace of quality and safety improvement, realized that they could take "leaps" forward with their employees, retirees, and families by rewarding hospitals that implemented significant improvements in quality and safety. The Leapfrog Group (2006) was officially launched in November 2000. In 2001, the IOM issued its second report in the quality series, *Crossing the Quality Chasm: A New Health System for the 21st Century*. Six aims were established for healthcare system quality: safe, effective, patient centered, timely, efficient, and effective. With this report, having the patient and family as partners was not only the right thing to do, it became a required design element of any future system.

With increasing awareness of the problem of patient safety came a demand for disclosure. In 2000, the NPSF also issued their pivotal recommendation in *Talking to Patients about Health Care Injury: Statement of Principle*. NPSF recommended that all errors reaching the patient and causing harm or with the potential to cause harm be disclosed (NPSF, 2000). In 2001, the JCAHO, with an already well-articulated commitment to quality of care, issued a new patient safety accreditation standard requiring disclosure of unanticipated outcomes. Two years later, in 2003, the JCAHO began setting National Patient Safety Goals for the accelerated implementation of requirements that could not wait for the normal multiyear accreditation process. These accreditation requirements were unprecedented mandates for disclosure.

Over subsequent years, patient safety maintained its profile in politics. Within states, legislative agendas were full with quality and safety bills. Nationally, with considerable advocacy from their constituents, Congress, under the leadership of Kennedy, Grassley, Jeffords, and others, grappled with a national patient safety act (ultimately signed by President Bush after more than five years of discussion on July 29, 2005, as the Patient Safety and Quality Improvement Act of 2005) (109th Congress, 2005). Reports from the IOM, the World Health Organization (WHO), and others continue to be written, reinforcing the essential role of patients and families in the patient care and safety systems. A 2006 report from the IOM on preventing medication errors summarizes that the overall medication system cannot be fixed until it is organized around patients and those who care for them.

Throughout these years, more and more patient advocates emerged across the country—people like Sorrel King (Ayd, 2004) and Helen Haskell (Lieberman, 2004), Dale Micalizzi, Susan Sheridan, and Linda Kenney (Zimmerman, 2004).

The Journey Begins in Earnest

Accepting accountability for medical errors and the responsibility for building a safer system has emerged through the successive IOM reports, a national patient safety act, extensive legislation at the state level, pressure from Leapfrog and the business and legislative communities, the growing visibility of leadership, the powerful stories of organizations, and the active and growing voice of patients, family members, and staff. Today, a plethora of organizations emphasize safety. Consumers have become much more active, attending meetings of and working with provider and purchaser organizations. Take, for example, the following:

- Ilene Corina, a consumer representative and the president of PULSE (2006), has been appointed to the JCAHO Board of Directors.
- JCAHO has established a fully integrated patient and family advisory committee.
- Organizations such as IHI, in partnership with the Institute for Family-Centered Care, has brought forward strategies for including

patients and families (Conway et al., 2006b) at the organizational as well as microsystems level (Berwick, 2002).

- AHA (2005) declared that patient- and family-centered care is a major strategy for leadership and issued a tool kit supporting it to all hospitals in the country.
- The NPSF (2003) has published its *National Agenda for Action: Patients and Families in Patient Safety: Nothing About Me, Without Me.*
- The IHI in 2006 completed its innovative 100,000 Lives Campaign (Textbox 10.3).

Patient safety is also an important international topic and area of focus with considerable leadership provided from patients, families, and patient advocates. In October 2004, the WHO (2006a) launched the World Alliance for Patient Safety in response to a World Health Assembly Resolution urging WHO and member states to pay the closest possible attention to the problem of patient safety. The alliance raises awareness and political commitment to improve the safety of care and facilitate the development of patient safety policy and practice in all WHO member states. WHO's Patients for Patient Safety program is listening to the voice of the patient around the world through a series of workshops hosted in England and North America and South America. A critical byproduct of their early meeting in 2005 was the London Declaration, A Patient Manifesto (WHO, 2006b).

Patient-Centered Guidelines for Safety: Honoring Patient Expectations 100% of the Time

Through meetings sponsored by WHO, the IHI, and others, along with a review of the research and consultation with experts, a growing clarity has emerged of what patients and families expect of the healthcare system, and these expectations can be used to guide our work in reforming that system. Our patients expect 100% of the time to (IOM, 2006, p. 137):

- Be listened to, taken seriously, and respected as a care partner.
  - Have their family/caregivers treated the same.
  - Participate in decision making at the level they choose.

**Textbox 10.3   Leadership in Patient Safety:
The IHI 100,000 Lives Campaign**

On June 14, 2006, the Institute for Healthcare Improvement (IHI) announced that U.S. hospitals taking part in an unprecedented 18-month effort to prevent 100,000 unnecessary deaths by dramatically improving patient care had exceeded that goal. Hospitals enrolled in the 100,000 Lives Campaign have collectively prevented an estimated 122,300 avoidable deaths and, as importantly, have begun to institutionalize new standards of care that will continue to save lives and improve health outcomes into the future. Initiated by IHI in December 2004, the Campaign has enrolled more than 3,000 hospitals—representing an estimated 75% of U.S. hospital beds—and far surpassed the original enrollment goal of 2,000. The participating hospitals already engaged in a broad range of improvement activities pledged to implement up to six evidence-based and life-saving interventions:

- Deployment of rapid response teams at the first sign of patient decline
- Delivery of reliable, evidence-based care for acute myocardial infarction to prevent deaths from heart attack
- Prevention of adverse drug events (ADEs) by implementing medication reconciliation
- Prevention of central line infections by implementing a series of interdependent, scientifically grounded steps called the "Central Line Bundle"
- Prevention of surgical site infections by reliably delivering the correct perioperative antibiotics at the proper time and taking several other associated actions
- Prevention of ventilator-associated pneumonia by implementing a series of interdependent, scientifically grounded steps called the "Ventilator Bundle"

Highlights include:

- More than 50 healthcare organizations—state hospital associations, quality improvement organizations, or other healthcare entities, often working together—are serving as local field offices (or "nodes") for the campaign.
- More than 90 national partners—among them the American Medical Association, American Nurses Association, Centers for Disease Control and Prevention, Centers for Medicare and Medicaid Services and the Joint Commission on Accreditation of Healthcare Organizations—are actively involved, along with patient advocacy groups in supporting and promoting the campaign.

Textbox 10.3   Leadership in Patient Safety:
The IHI 100,000 Lives Campaign (continued)

- Nearly 100 hospitals that have demonstrated success with specific interventions are acting as "mentor hospitals," sharing their knowledge and experience with other hospitals aiming to achieve excellence in those areas.
- Hospitals and healthcare systems have begun to cooperate at unprecedented levels.

IHI expects to announce plans at its National Forum in December 2006 for the next stage of this healthcare improvement initiative. Simultaneously, IHI will work with expert groups and high-achieving facilities to explore new areas for hospital improvement that will be introduced in the next phase of the Campaign—complete with a new, ambitious aim for saving lives (Institute for Healthcare Improvement, 2006).

- Always be told the truth.
    - Have things explained to them fully and clearly.
    - Receive an explanation and apology if things go wrong.
- Have information communicated to all members of the care team.
    - Have their care timely and impeccably documented.
    - Have these records made available to the patient if requested.
- Have coordination among all members of the healthcare team across settings.
- Be supported emotionally as well as physically.
- Receive high-quality, safe care.

Challenges and Cautions in Patient Advocacy

As the history of the patient safety movement attests, patient advocates are significantly more engaged in patient safety than they were just five years ago; however, much remains to be done. Many in healthcare continue to have reservations when dealing with advocates. There is considerable concern over risk, transparency, unintended consequences, malpractice, the media, and the implications for broader public understanding of the fragility of much of healthcare practice. Clinicians and administrators, although interested in advancing the agenda in the name of quality patient care, want to do so in a way that is highly contained and patient focused as opposed to partnership and patient centered. Because of these challenges, maintaining a focus on the goals of patient advocacy is critical. These include increasing patient involvement, defining key terms and concepts, and understanding and pursuing culture change in medical organizations.

Increasing Patient Involvement

A recent study by Entwistle, Mello, and Brennan (2005) concerning patient education materials related to safety illustrates the pitfalls of many current safety initiatives. First, the researchers found that many healthcare organizations are creating materials without involving patients or families in the development process, resulting in materials that do not reflect most patients' experiences. Second, these materials often fail to give patients practical recommendations for protecting their safety. Third, some messages even suggest an inappropriate shifting of responsibility onto patients. For example, advice that involves directly challenging health professionals' actions appears to be particularly problematic for patients, many of whom are uncomfortable with the idea of questioning medical authority. Based on these findings, the researchers make recommendations that are applicable to many patient safety initiatives: (1) organizations should involve patients in program development, and (2) program planners must at the same time think carefully about who can and should take responsibility for change. Table 10.1 proposes several levels of quality based on those identified by the IOM's *Quality Chasm* report, ranging from environmental to organizational to microsystems (IOM, 2001; Berwick, 2002). These levels or domains may be used by program planners to guide thinking on patient involvement.

Defining Safety Terms and Concepts

Although the language of high reliability, human factors, and failure has been applied in other fields, healthcare has struggled with these concepts in the infancy of the patient safety movement. Considerable confusion existed around a range of words, including medical error, incident,

Table 10.1   Patient Advocate Engagement Across Patient Safety Domains

	Partnership Examples
Environment	• Efforts by WHO, JCAHO, IHI, NPSF, and CMS to integrate patient advocates fully in strategic and operational planning, task forces, and educational sessions • Inclusion of patient advocates on boards of trustees as in NPSF and JCAHO • Regional support groups for patients, family, and clinicians needing help after incidents • Inclusion in adverse event and near-miss reporting systems
Organizational	• Statement of commitment to partnerships • Patient and family advisory committees • Inclusion of patient advocates on patient safety and quality committees as well as in root cause analyses • Expectations and policies supporting ongoing communication, full disclosure, and apology • Participation in walk-rounds, patient-care unit rounds • Inclusion as faculty in new employee orientation, customer service training, clinical programs • Search committee members for new staff
Microsystems	• Family visiting in intensive care units at all times • Environment supports patient and family presence and participation as well as interdisciplinary collaboration • Participation on service design teams and operating committees
Experience of care	• Verifying medications before administration • Participating in joint care planning and goal setting • Evaluating the outcomes of care and quality of life • Activating rapid response teams

occurrence, slip, mistake, harm, adverse event, preventable adverse event. Growing clarity and consistency of use for key words are now emerging from the IOM, in glossaries, and in the work of researchers and clinicians, and this definitional process must continue if advocacy related to patient safety is to advance. Table 10.2 provides selected terms as well as their still-emerging definitions.

Fostering a Culture of Safety: The Case of Dana-Farber Cancer Institute (DFCI)

The nation's patient safety journey from 1995 has made many things clear. First and foremost, healthcare has learned that it cannot build a safe healthcare system by imploring staff to be safe and to deliver safe care. No matter how exceptional staff members are, they suffer from being human and are practicing in an increasingly more complex health system. Error will occur. Leadership must put in place culture and safety management systems that support safe practice. There are many definitions of such a culture of safety and the key ingredients of it (Botwinick, Bisognano, & Haraden, 2006). In this section, we view these concepts through the lens of DFCI. Their culture of safety journey provides context for others (Conway et al., 2006a).

DFCI understanding of a culture of safety is based in trust, respect, repentance, human rights, and forgiveness. Staff must be supported, enabled, and motivated to give their highest levels of performance. The culture must acknowledge the high-risk, error-prone nature of healthcare. Individual and shared acceptance of responsibility and accountability for safe delivery of quality care, risk reduction, and positive care outcomes must be ensured, and the approach must be systems based. All must be experts in looking for problems and must also inhabit a culture that supports and facilitates reporting and open communication about safety concerns in a fair and just environment. Assurance must be given that organizational structures, processes, goals, and rewards are aligned with improving patient safety. Finally, in a culture of safety, there is learning from errors and a sharing of stories.

DFCI has chronicled its patient safety journey extensively. On the 10-year anniversary of the overdose that killed Betsy Lehman, hospital leaders outlined the key learning that took place and elements that made their own journey possible. First and foremost, hospital leaders recognized that it is the responsibility of all leadership—governance, executive, clinical, and administrative—to drive patient safety by setting the vision and providing the will, ideas, and execution. Although organizations need content experts in areas

Table 10.2   Patient Safety Terms (Institute of Medicine)

Accident: An event that involves damage to a defined system that disrupts the ongoing or future output of the system.

Active error: An error that occurs at the level of the front-line operator and whose effects are felt almost immediately.

Adverse event: An injury resulting from a medical intervention. Referred to as preventable (due to an error) and nonpreventable (not due to an error).

Error: Failure of a planned action to be completed as intended or use of a wrong plan to achieve an aim; the accumulation of errors results in accidents.

Human factors: Study of the interrelationships between humans, the tools they use, and the environment in which they live and work.

Latent error: Errors in the design, organization, training, or maintenance that lead to operator errors and whose effects typically lie dormant in the system for lengthy periods of time.

Medical error: Any error in the care delivery process.

Medication error: Any error occurring in the medication use process

Mistakes: Incorrect choices. A mistake would be choosing the wrong diagnostic test or ordering a suboptimal medication for a given condition represent mistakes.

Patient safety: Freedom from accidental injury; ensuring patient safety involves the establishment of operational systems and processes that minimize the likelihood of errors and maximizes the likelihood of intercepting them when they occur.

Potential adverse event: Near miss or close call that does not reach the patient.

Quality of care: Degree to which health services for individuals and populations increase the likelihood of desired health outcomes and are consistent with current professional knowledge.

Slips: Failures of schematic behaviors, or lapses in concentration (e.g., overlooking a step in a routine task due to a lapse in memory, an experienced surgeon nicking an adjacent organ during an operation due to a momentary lapse in concentration). Forgetting to check the chart to make sure you ordered them for the right patient would be a slip.

System: Set of interdependent elements interacting to achieve a common aim. These elements may be both human and nonhuman (equipment, technologies, etc.).

such as quality, safety, and risk, the executives who are responsible for finance, development, and strategic planning must also lead quality and patient safety. To avoid being caught in the "arrogance of excellence," leadership must examine the realities of practice—the slips, errors, harm, suffering, and deaths along with the extraordinary stories of care, caring, and discovery that go on each day. They then must use the gaps between vision and reality to create the tension that drives the agenda for improvement.

The second element of key learning is the need for relentless vigilance at all levels of the organization by all staff every day to avoid risk, error, near misses, and harm. Every member of the team, including the patient and family, has a responsibility, and leadership must expect it and support these safety efforts.

Third, DFCI has found that hospitals must address the multiple victims of error: the patient, the family, and the staff. For 10 years, DFCI has disclosed medical error; it was the right thing to do, and no significant repercussions have occurred. Errors typically do not erode trust. In and outside of healthcare it appears clear: Far greater than the risk of disclosure is the risk of being found to have known something and not disclosed it. Also learned was the critical need to support staff at the sharp end of medical error; error and harm are overwhelmingly about bad systems and not bad people. When the worst nightmare happens and a patient is hurt, it is extremely traumatic for healthcare professionals. Much like the patient and family, they need support as well as inclusion in the process of finding out what happened, why, and what is being done to prevent it from happening again.

Fourth, hospital staff must listen to patients. A critical component in the death of Betsy Lehman was the fact that she herself felt that something was wrong; yet according to her family, no one listened to her. Up until the day before she died, Betsy was calling friends, asking for help from those on the outside because she felt that she was not mobilizing it from within. Betsy's death impressed on DFCI the importance of patient voice. Leaders in the institute realized that they could not undertake the massive redesign of its care systems without actively engaging patients and families—listening to their voices had to be a priority. Since 1996, patients and family members have been full partners, participating in all decision-making processes and committees (Ponte et al., 2003).

The fifth element of hospital culture change is the acknowledgment of the crucial role that the design of systems and application of technology play in support of safe practices. Leadership has a responsibility to put in place systems to support safe practice and to work closely with staff, patients, and families to ensure that they are the best they can be. These systems can range from electronic medical record and chemo-order-entry systems to smart pumps, access management systems, and streamlined processes for medication management. Over the last 10 years Dana-Farber, excellent but not perfect, has achieved high levels of safety performance, dramatic increases in volume, and little clinician turnover. Systems, guidelines, algorithms, and standard operating procedures were crucial to the achievement of these milestones.

Finally, DFCI learned that the organization chart could not dictate how it delivered care. Healthcare is populated by extensive silos around nurses, pharmacists, physicians, and other clinicians, with the organizational chart more often getting in the way of care than not. The emphasis must switch from an individual to a team responsibility for care, and the patient and families are members of the team.

Table 10.3 Resource List: Selected Patient Safety Books, Articles, and Organizations

---

Books not cited in text:

Berntsen, K. J. (2004). *The patient's guide to preventing medical error.* Westport, CT: Praeger

Boss, P. (2000). *Ambiguous loss.* Boston: Harvard University Press.

Gawande, A. (2002). *Complications: A surgeon's notes on an imperfect science.* New York: Metropolitan Books.

Gerteis, M., Edgman-Levitan, S., Daley, J., & Delbanco, T.L. (Eds.) (2002). *Through the patient's eyes: Understanding and promoting patient-centered care.* San Francisco: Jossey-Bass.

Gibson, R., & Singh, J. P. (2003). *Wall of silence: The untold story of the medical mistakes that kill and injure millions of Americans.* Washington, DC: LifeLine Press.

Reason, J. T. (1997). *Managing the risks of organizational accidents.* Aldershot, Hants, England: Ashgate.

Wachter, R. M., & Shojiana, K. G. (2004). *Internal bleeding: The truth behind America's terrifying epidemic of medical mistakes.* New York: Ruggedland Press.

Youngberg, B. J., & Hatlie, M. J. (2003). *The patient safety handbook.* Sudbury, MA: Jones and Bartlett.

(continued)

Table 10.3   Resource List: Selected Patient Safety Books, Articles, and Organizations (continued)

Articles not cited in text:

Blendon, R. J., DesRoches, C. M., Brodie, M., Benson, J. M., Rosen, A. B., Schneider, E., et al. (2002). Views of practicing physicians and the public on medical errors. *New England Journal of Medicine, 347,* 1933–1940.

Gallagher, T. H., Waterman, A. D., & Garbutt, J. M. (2006). U.S. and Canadian physician's attitudes and experiences regarding disclosing errors to patients. *Archives of Internal Medicine, 166,* 1605–1611.

Harvard Hospitals. (2006). *When things go wrong.* Retrieved October 26, 1996, from http://www.macoalition.org/documents/respondingToAdverseEvents.pdf

Leape, L. L. (1994). Error in medicine. *Journal of the American Medical Association, 272,* 1851–1857.

U.S. Patient Safety Organizations not cited in text:

Name/Acronym		Website	Description/Mission
Agency for Healthcare Research and Quality	AHRQ	www.ahrq.gov	The lead federal agency charged with improving the quality, safety, efficiency, and effectiveness of healthcare for all Americans.
Center for Medical Consumers	CMS	www.medicalconsumers.org	Nonprofit founded to provide access to accurate, science-based information for consumers and to hold medicine more accountable.
Consumers Advancing Patient Safety	CAPS	www.patientsafety.org	Consumer-led nonprofit organization formed to be a collective voice for individuals, families, and healers who wish to prevent harm in healthcare encounters through partnership and collaboration.
Institute for Healthcare Improvement	IHI	www.ihi.org	Nonprofit organization that seeks to accelerate change in healthcare by cultivating promising concepts for improving patient care and turning those ideas into action.
Institute for Safe Medication Practices	ISMP	www.ismp.org	Nonprofit organization that works closely with healthcare practitioners and institutions, regulatory agencies, professional organizations, and the pharmaceutical industry to provide education about adverse drug events and their prevention.
Institute of Medicine	IOM	www.iom.edu	Independent federal agency that provides unbiased, evidence-based, and authoritative information and advice concerning health and science policy to policy makers, professionals, leaders in every sector of society, and the public.

(continued)

Table 10.3   Resource List: Selected Patient Safety Books, Articles, and Organizations (continued)

U.S. Patient Safety Organizations not cited in text:

Name/Acronym		Website	Description/Mission
the Accreditation of Healthcare Organizations	JCAHO	www.jcaho.org	Joint Commission on Nonprofit that provides healthcare accreditation and related services that support performance improvement in healthcare organizations.
The Leapfrog Group	Leapfrog	www.leapfroggroup.org/	Voluntary program aimed at mobilizing employer purchasing power to alert America's health industry that big leaps in healthcare safety, quality, and customer value will be recognized and rewarded.
Medically Induced Trauma Support Services	MITSS	www.mitss.org	Nonprofit that supports, educates, trains, and offers assistance to individuals affected by medically induced trauma.
National Patient Safety Foundation	NPSF	www.npsf.org	Nonprofit established as a central voice to improve safety through research, dissemination of best practice, education, and collaboration among all partners in the healthcare system.
National Quality Forum	NQF	www.qualityforum.org	Not-for-profit membership organization created to develop and implement a national strategy for healthcare quality measurement and reporting. Established as a public-private partnership, the NQF has broad participation from all parts of the healthcare system.
Persons United Limiting Substandards and Errors	PULSE	www.pulseamerica.org	Nonprofit support group and organization working to improve patient safety and reduce the rate of medical errors in this country using real life stories and experiences. Members and participants are encouraged to use their experience to educate the community and advocate for a safer healthcare system.
Partnership for Patient Safety	P4PS	www.p4ps.org	Nonprofit offering programs and services from a patient-centered perspective to advance the reliability of healthcare systems worldwide.
The SorryWorks Coalition		www.sorryworks.net	Nationwide group of doctors, patient advocates, lawyers, and insurers that promotes full-disclosure as a middle ground solution to the medical malpractice crisis.

CLOSING COMMENTS

Safety of patients and freedom from harm remains an elusive and an ongoing goal of healthcare. The journey is underway and accelerating. It has been fueled by many errors and the stories of those hurt, by research and by safety science, and most importantly by the relentless efforts of those who advocate for patients and families from within and outside of the healthcare industry. Reaching a successful outcome will require listening to patients and those who advocate for them, taking them seriously, and respecting them as care partners.

REFERENCES

109th Congress. (2005). *Patient safety and quality improvement act of 2005.* Retrieved October 24, 2006, from http://www.govtrack.us/congress/bill.xpd?bill=s109-544.

American Hospital Association, Institute for Family Centered Care. (2005). *Strategies for leadership: Patient and family centered care.* Retrieved December 12, 2005, from http://www.aha.org/aha/key_issues/patient_safety/resources/patientcenteredcare.html.

Annenberg Center for Health Services. (1996). Examining errors in health care: Developing a prevention, education and research agenda. Rancho Mirage, CA.

Ayd, M. A. (2004, Spring/Summer). *A remedy of errors: Johns Hopkins Medicine.* Retrieved October 24, 2006, from http://www.hopkinsmedicine.org/hmn/S04/feature1.cfm.

Belkin, L. (1997, June 15). How can we save the next victim? [Electronic version]. *New York Times,* p. 28. Retrieved August 8, 2000, from http://query.nytimes.com/gst/fullpage.html?res=9C04EFDF173FF936A25755C0A961958260&sec=health&pagewanted=print database.

Berwick, D. M. (2002). *Escape fire: Lessons from the future of health care (overview of book published by the Commonwealth Fund, New York).* Retrieved January 27, 2005, from http://www.cmwf.org/publications/publications_show.htm?doc_id=221609.

Berwick, D. M. (2002). User's manual for the IOM's 'Quality Chasm' report: Patients' experiences should be the fundamental source of the definitin of 'quality.' *Health Affairs, 21*(3): 80–90.

Botwinick, L., Bisognano, M. & Haraden, C. (2006). *Leadership guide to patient safety: Institute for Healthcare Improvement.* Retrieved from http://www.ihi.org/IHI/Results/WhitePapers/LeadershipGuidetoPatientSafetyWhitePaper.html.

Center for Medical Consumers. (2005). *Working to protect your rights: Helping you make informed decisions.* Retrieved September 4, 2006, from http://www.medicalconsumers.org/index.html.

Conway, J., et al. (2006a). *Key learning from the Dana-Farber Cancer Institute's ten-year patient safety journey.* Retrieved August 8, 2006, from http://www.dfci.harvard.edu/pat/patient/patient-safety/docs/journey.pdf#search=%22key%20learning%20dfci%20patient%20safety%22.

Conway, J., et al. (2006b). *Partnering with patients and families to design a patient- and family-centered health care system: A roadmap for the future: A work in progress. Institute for Family-Centered Care and Institute for Healthcare Improvement.* Retrieved October 24, 2006, from http://www.ihi.org/IHI/Topics/PatientCenteredCare/PatientCenteredCareGeneral/Literature/PartneringwithPatientsandFamilies.htm.

Cooper, J. (2003). An accidental life: Patient safety and biomedical engineering. In R. J. Kitz & H. Ali (Eds.), *This is no humbug! Reminiscences of the Department of Anesthesia at the Massachusetts General Hospital: A history* (pp. 377–420). Ashland, OH: Atlas Books.

Entwistle, V. A., Mello, M. M., & Brennan, T. A. (2005). Advising patients about patient safety: Current initiatives risk shifting responsibility. *Joint Commission Journal on Quality and Patient Safety, 31,* 483–494.

FAIR. (2006). *FAIR is an Illinois statewide organization committed to "FAIR" consumer practices.* Retrieved September 4, 2006, from http://www.network54.com/Forum/21098/page-3.

Haas, D. (2004). Moving beyond blame to create an environment that rewards reporting. In B. J. Youngberg & M. J. Hatlie (Eds.), *Patient safety handbook* (pp. 415–421). Sudbury, MA: Jones and Bartlett.

Institute for Healthcare Improvement. (2006). *IHI announces that hospitals participating in 100,000 lives campaign have saved an estimated 122,300 lives (June 14, 2006, Press Release).* Retrieved October 26, 2006, from http://ihi.org/NR/rdonlyres/1C51BADE-0F7B-4932-A8C3-0FEFB654D747/0/UPDATED100kLivesCanpaignJune14milestonepress release.pdf.

Institute for Safe Medication Practices. (2006). *About ISMP.* Retrieved October 24, 2006, from http://www.ismp.org/about/Default.asp.

Institute of Medicine. (2000). In L. T. Kohn, J. M. Corrigan, & M. S. Donaldson (Eds.), *To err is human: Building a safer health system.* Washington, DC: National Academy Press.

Institute of Medicine. (2001). *Crossing the quality chasm: A new health system for the 21st century.* Washington, DC: National Academy Press.

Institute of Medicine, Committee on Identifying and Preventing Medication Errors. (2006). In P. Aspden, J. Wolcott, J. L. Bootman, & L. R. Cronenwett (Eds.), *Preventing medication errors: Quality chasm series.* Washington, DC: National Academies Press.

Joint Commission on the Accreditation of Healthcare Organizations. (2006). *Sentinel event policy and procedure.* Retrieved October 24, 2006, from http://www.jointcommission.org/SentinelEvents/PolicyandProcedures/.

Leape, L. L., Bates, D. W., Cullen, D. J., Cooper, J., Demonaco, H. J., Gallivan, T., et al. (1995). Systems analysis of adverse drug events. ADE prevention study group. *Journal of the American Medical Association, 274,* 35–43.

Leape, L. L., Brennan, T. A., Laird, N., Lawthers, A. G., Localio, A. R., Barnes, B. A., et al. (1991). The nature of adverse events in hospitalized patients. Results of the Harvard Medical Practice study II. *New England Journal of Medicine, 324,* 377–384.

Leapfrog Group. (2006). *The Leapfrog Group fact sheet.* Retrieved October 24, 2006, from http://www.leapfroggroup.org/about_us/leapfrog-factsheet.

Lieberman, T. (2004, November). *Fatal mistakes (AARP bulletin).* Retrieved October 24, 2006, from http://www.aarp.org/bulletin/yourhealth/a2004-10-27-fatal_mistakes.html.

Massachusetts Coalition for the Prevention of Medical Errors. (2006). *Home page.* Retrieved October 24, 2006, from http://www.macoalition.org/.

Massachusetts Hospital Association. (2001). *Massachusetts Hospitals taking steps to prevent medication errors.* Retrieved October 24, 2006, from http://www.mhalink.org/public/news/2001/2001-02-17.cfm.

Millenson, M. L. (1997). *Demanding medical excellence: Doctors and accountability in the information age.* Chicago: University of Chicago Press.

National Patient Safety Foundation. (1998). *Enhancing patient safety and reducing errors in health care (1998 conference archive).* Retrieved October 24, 2006, from http://www.npsf.org/congress_archive/1998/1998.html.

National Patient Safety Foundation. (2000). *Talking to patients about health care injury: Statement of principle.* Retrieved October 24, 2006, from http://www.npsf.org/html/statement.html.

National Patient Safety Foundation. (2003). *National agenda for action: Patients and families in patient safety: Nothing about me, without me.* Retrieved October 26, 2006, from http://www.npsf.org/download//AgendaFamilies.pdf.

National Patient Safety Foundation. (2006). *Patient and family advisory committee biographies.* Retrieved August 8, 2006, from http://www.npsf.org/html/pfacbios.html.

Neuhauser, D. (2002). Ernest Amory Codman MD. *Quality & Safety in Health Care, 11,* 104–105.

Nightingale, F. (Reprinted 1987). *Notes on nursing: What it is, and what it is not.* New York: Buccaneer Books.

People's Medical Society. (2002). *Charles B. Inlander.* Retrieved August 8, 2006, from http://www.peoplesmed.org/charlesb.html.

Ponte, P. R., Conlin, G., Conway, J. B., Grant, S., Medeiros, C., Nies, J., et al. (2003). Making patient-centered care come alive: Achieving full integration of the patient's perspective. *Journal of Nursing Administration, 33,* 82–90.

PULSE. (2006). *Home page: Persons United Limiting Substandards and Errors in health care.* Retrieved October 24, 2006, from http://www.pulseamerica.org/index.htm.

Quality Interagency Task Force. (2000). *Report to the President on medical affairs.* Retrieved October 24, 2006, from http://www.quic.gov/report.

Silker, E. S. (2006). *APSF history overview.* Retrieved August 8, 2006, from http://www.apsf.org/about/brief_history.mspx.

World Health Organization. (2006a). *World alliance for patient safety.* Retrieved October 24, 2006, from http://www.who.int/patientsafety/en/.

World Health Organization. (2006b). *London declaration, A patient manifesto.* Retrieved October 26, 2006, from http://www.who.int/patientsafety/patients_for_patient/London_Declaration_EN.pdf.

Zimmerman, R. (2004, May 18). *Doctors' new tool to fight lawsuits: Saying I'm sorry.* Retrieved October 26, 2006, from http://www.mc.vanderbilt.edu/root/vumc.php?site=CPPA&doc=3270.

CHAPTER 11

Planetree, a Hospital Model for Patient-Centered Care

Susan B. Frampton and Laura Gilpin

OBJECTIVES

- To illustrate the role that hospitals, as organizations with distinct cultures and policies, play in patient care
- To identify aspects of traditional hospital models that detract from patient involvement and patient safety
- To contrast these models with more patient-centered ones, using Planetree as an example
- To impart strategies, challenges, and lessons learned about organizational change

For decades, patients have been speaking out about the need to personalize, humanize, and demystify the healthcare experience. The emergence of healthcare consumerism, fueled in part by the aging of the baby boomer generation, expanded access to information afforded by the Internet, as well as growing direct costs to consumers for their care, has increased demands for a safer, more patient-centered experience. The leading private and government healthcare agencies shaping policy around a patient's hospital experience have begun to push for the adoption of a more personalized approach to medical care. To that end, they have developed guidelines for a shift in organizational culture. As a case in point, *Crossing the Quality Chasm*, the seminal publication by the Institute of Medicine (2001), included "patient centeredness" as one of its top priorities for hospital quality improvement (see Chapter 1).

This chapter explores how hospitals can be transformed at the organizational level to support patient-centered care. What are the policies and practices that impact patient centeredness? What is organizational culture, and how can it be changed to be more responsive to patients' needs and priorities? How can organizations determine what is most important to patients and hospital staff in the first place? By understanding the organizational dimensions of patient centeredness, patient advocates can bring about structural changes that improve the environment in which healthcare is delivered as well as the policies that govern patient–provider interactions.

The Planetree hospital model is a comprehensive approach to patient centeredness that introduces a broad range of organizational-level factors that patient advocates have targeted. This chapter discusses the Planetree philosophy and the model's major components as well as the most relevant challenges to organizational culture change. These challenges include the growing complexity of medical information; increasing choices in treatment approaches and options, reduced staff time for teaching, and a history of paternalism in the physician–patient relationship. In this context, ensuring that patients are engaged and educated about their conditions is about more than simply improving patient satisfaction scores. Organizational change is essential if we are to increase patient safety and improve quality health outcomes and is, therefore, a priority for every healthcare organization.

WHAT IS ORGANIZATIONAL CULTURE AND WHAT IMPACT DOES IT HAVE ON PATIENT CARE?

An organization's culture is its "personality," manifesting the shared values that guide how people do their work and interact with each other (Kane-Urrabazo, 2006, p. 188). As explored in other chapters (see Chapters 3 and 12), hospitals in the United States have traditionally been characterized by a culture that values the biomedical and technological aspects of care as well as the authority of medical providers, especially physicians. Critics of the U.S. healthcare system often identify this culture as one of the barriers to patient safety and patient involvement in care. The primacy of the biomedical orientation, they believe, together with attempts at cost-saving payment structures such as managed care, has resulted in increasingly hurried and impersonal medical encounters that discourage patients from becoming participants in the care process (see Chapter 6). This chapter illustrates how aspects of traditional hospital culture have shaped patient care, and contrasts that tradition with a culture that cultivates patient-centered values of collaboration, social support, and personalization.

Authoritarian Versus Collaborative Approaches

As many proponents of patient-centered care have pointed out, hospital environments have traditionally been designed around the needs and schedules of healthcare providers, rather than those of patients (Berwick & Kotagal, 2004; Edgman-Levitan, 2003). In particular, physicians, as highly trained professionals, are regarded as authorities in the hospital setting. At the interpersonal level, the prestige afforded to these professionals has often resulted in a paternalistic relationship between physicians, who are regarded as decision makers, and patients, who are encouraged to "follow doctors' orders." The imbalance of power between physicians and patients manifests itself at the organizational level as well. Physicians are supported by a wide array of policies and practices that facilitate their work and ensure their access to information. Charting systems, for example, allow physicians to keep careful notes on their patients' progress. Organizational resources such as medical libraries enable them to perform case-specific research. Historically, however, patients and their families have rarely had easy access to these sources of information. Even though patients now can and do turn to the Internet as an important storehouse of medical knowledge (see Chapter 4), this resource depends on the initiative and research skills of the patient; it has not been, until recently, a resource typically provided for patients by hospitals. As a result, patients are less likely to participate in the care process than physicians, and rarely can they do research on their illness in the same way physicians can. Patient advocacy at the organizational level involves changing hospital culture to give patients the tools they need to learn about their conditions and participate collaboratively with physicians in their care plans.

A collaborative culture is also important in recognizing the important advocacy role other hospital staff, in addition to physicians, can play in patient care. In focus groups, patients often recount how one caring person listened to or supported them, even if only briefly, at a difficult time and dramatically changed their experience. For example, patients have been known to state that the person who listened or seemed most caring was a hospital housekeeper. Indeed, as Donald Berwick notes in his essay *Escape Fire: Lessons for the Future of Health Care*, what his wife, Anne, identified first among "the most impressive moments of help" during a long hospital stay was a housekeeper "who every evening would come into her room and, while cleaning, talk about her children and ours" (1999, p. 22). From a patient's perspective, the title or job description of the hospital employee is of less importance than the fact that the employee is providing support. For this reason, ensuring that all hospital staff, housekeepers included, perceive themselves as "caregivers" can help produce a culture of trust, one in which patients' needs are communicated in a timely, compassionate, and collegial fashion.

An excellent example of the importance of involving support staff as advocates was illustrated at one hospital when a housekeeper went beyond the scope of her position to engage with a patient who seemed in need of conversation. During the interaction, the patient revealed his fear about a surgery scheduled for the next day; his brother had died because of an undetected familial risk factor during what the patient believed was a similar procedure a year before. The patient had not revealed this important information to the anesthesiologist, surgeon, or any of the nursing staff. By sharing this knowledge with the nursing staff, the housekeeper may have played a vital role in gathering significant data that helped keep this patient safe.

Emphasis on Technical and Biological Aspects of Healthcare Versus Psychosocial Aspects and Social Support

In addition to a "top-down" approach, hospital culture is also known for favoring biomedical aspects of care. Test results pointing to biological determinants of illness are often emphasized over psychosocial aspects of care that can be uncovered through patient interviews (see Chapter 7). Providers have been pushed increasingly into the role of technicians rather than caretakers, and economic pressures have only exacerbated this imbalance. Physicians' heavy case loads leave them little time for interpersonal interaction with patients (see Chapter 6). A result of this technology-driven culture, patients often receive only one kind of care, such as a pharmaceutical intervention, when they could benefit from a whole range of treatments, including psychological counseling, social support via support groups, complementary and alternative medicine, and spiritual or cultural practices. At the organizational level, patient advocates can work to change hospital culture by educating providers about the importance of these practices and helping connect patients to appropriate complements to traditional medical care.

Perhaps even more importantly, however, because the goal is more ubiquitous, is advocacy for a hospital culture shift that encourages family members and friends to provide social support to patients. Research has shown that those who are socially isolated or have few social connections are at significantly greater risk of dying (Reynolds & Kaplan, 1990). Many other studies report findings that loneliness, isolation, and lack of social ties contribute to other illnesses and premature death (Berkman, Leo-Summers, & Horwitz, 1992; Blazer, 1982; Wiklund et al., 1988). Several mechanisms through which the health-promoting effects of social networks take place have been proposed; social support may help patients maintain healthier eating and sleeping patterns, interact more effectively with their physicians, or experience less stress, possibly decreasing the production of hormones such as cortisol and prolactin as well as lowering blood pressure (Kamarck, Manuck, & Jennings, 1990; Lepore, Mata, & Evans, 1993; Spiegel, 1993).

Despite much research recognizing the importance of social support in facilitating the healing process (Edgman-Levitan, 2003), hospital policies and design often limit who may visit patients and for how long, especially in emergency and critical care environments, where patients are in most need of regular contact (Berwick & Kotagal, 2004). These policies are not primarily in the best interests of patients and families, although often justified on those grounds. Rather, they are a convenience for providers and a means of efficiency for hospitals (see Chapter 12). Furthermore, the resistance to changing these practices comes primarily from nurses and physicians (Berwick & Kotagal, 2004; Edgman-Levitan, 2003).

Standardization and Convenience for the Hospital Versus Personalization and Comfort for Patients

A third way to improve hospital culture is by reducing unnecessary standardization in the healthcare environment. Obviously, many aspects of healthcare, such as the process of giving medication, require that guidelines be established and strictly followed. In other areas, however, such as times when patients can eat and sleep, rules may be less important than ensuring patients' comfort. Patients have been known to liken their stay in a hospital to a prison experience. After entry, they are processed through a system that replaces their personal clothing with drab uniforms, fastens numbered identification bracelets to their wrists, and assigns them to cramped rooms with strangers for roommates. They are told who can visit and at what time, when they will eat and what, when they will wake up, and when they will go for treatments. They are often deprived of needed sleep in the name of uniform guidelines, and woken in the middle of the night for routine tasks that could be scheduled during waking hours. These practices are particularly disruptive for those experiencing the mental anguish that often attends a critical illness or frightening diagnosis. In order to help make patients feel more comfortable and cared for, advocates, including administrators and physicians, can work to make hospital practices and policies more flexible to allow for greater personalization in healthcare to the extent possible.

Many nurses as well as other staff do advocate for patients, but hospital staff members may pay a significant price for doing so. Advocating for a patient sometimes means challenging the healthcare system or breaking established norms. In hospitals across the country, for example, nurses often must break the rules around who can visit and when to allow family members, or even a patient's beloved pet, to be with them at the bedside outside of posted visiting hours. In short, in many hospitals, personalizing healthcare puts nurses in a difficult situation. Being a good caregiver from the patient's perspective may mean being a troublesome employee from management's perspective.

In an organization that supports personalization of care, nurses and other caregivers no longer have to bend or break rules to support their patients' needs. Take the real-life example, for instance, of an acutely ill patient who requested to go to a family reunion in another state. He felt that, because of his prognosis, he would never have another opportunity to visit with his entire family. Despite his unstable condition, the patient threatened to leave the hospital against medical advice to attend the event. Rather than argue with or ignore him, the nurses and his physician worked together to make the necessary arrangements for the patient to travel. The physician contacted a physician at the location of the family reunion so that the appropriate care could be provided if needed. Nurses arranged for portable oxygen and worked with the family to provide for other needs. The patient attended the reunion with no ill effects. He returned to the hospital grateful and happy. He was eventually well enough to be discharged and died of his illness several months later.

Fearing resistance from the hospital administration or feeling that it was not part of their job description, some staff might not have gone to these lengths to advocate for a patient. In this case, the hospital had guidelines for signing patients out of the hospital against medical advice, but it had no policies for helping patients travel with the consent of their providers. Yet because hospital administration had adopted a patient-centered environment, where staff were empowered to advocate for patients, fears about breaking the rules took a back seat to creative problem solving. Staff worked out a solution for the patient because it gave them satisfaction to do so and because their organization not only supported but celebrated their creative approach to meeting a patient's needs.

As the previous examples imply, changing hospital culture to embody a more patient-centered ethos may involve a number of interventions. First, stakeholders must be encouraged to embrace a new set of values, and these values must be communicated to all hospital staff in an unambiguous way. Second, these values can then be used to guide hospital administrators as they develop new policies and practices, including decisions about hospital design and regulations (see profile on Cincinnati Children's Hospital in Chapter 3). In particular, providing patients with the information, tools, and skills that they need to be actively involved in their own care is key. Hospitals have an important role to play in giving patients access to health information, particularly permission to view their own medical records. Finally, organizational-level change involves supporting the individual-level advocacy of patients' family members and healthcare providers. When a hospital's culture is based on collaboration and a belief in the efficacy of social support and personalization, patients are more likely to receive safe and supportive care called for in the IOM's *Crossing the Quality Chasm* (2001).

THE PLANETREE MODEL: A COMPREHENSIVE APPROACH TO PATIENT CENTEREDNESS

Because of their size and complexity, changing the nature of hospital environments presents unique challenges. To achieve lasting change, an intervention needs to have an impact on the beliefs and practices of a large number of employees across an extremely diverse range of work responsibilities. These widespread changes cannot be accomplished on a person-by-person basis, but instead require an organizational cultural shift. One approach to delivery that has been instrumental in bringing about cultural transformation to hospitals is the Planetree model of patient-centered care. Developed in 1978 by a patient in response to several disturbing encounters with the healthcare system, Angelica Thieriot and a group of visionary thinkers created an approach that emphasized the human aspects of the care delivery experience. The Planetree model, focusing on integrating the patient's perspective into hospital policies and practices, has now been adopted by a growing number of hospitals, clinics, and long-term care facilities across the United States, Canada, and Europe.

Taking its name from the sycamore, or planetree, under which Hippocrates taught his students, the Planetree organization focuses on dramatically changing the way healthcare is delivered. Planetree promotes the evaluation of everything in the hospital setting from the perspective of the patient. All aspects of the organization's protocols, practices, and procedures are evaluated based on whether they enhance or detract from personalizing the patient experience. In particular, hospitals adopting the Planetree model ensure that appropriate information is available to patients and their advocates, thereby enabling them to be actively involved in their care experience.

Planetree's original focus was on provision of information. Along these lines, in 1981 in San Francisco, the organization established one of the country's first consumer health resource centers. The Resource Center, a place where the public had access to medical and health information, provided a library of over 2,000 health books and medical texts, a clipping file of current medical research, a catalogue of referral groups and agencies, and a bookstore. Based on the success of this first effort, Planetree has grown to include an entire range of organizational interventions. Major components include professional development, patient education, hospital design, policy development, and programs that encourage social support and family involvement.

Education and Training for Hospital Staff

Changing a hospital's culture means changing the values that guide the work of hospital staff. Planetree has focused extensively on creating a framework for organizational change by engaging hospital staff through a combination of initiative teams and experiential retreats. Staff teams are organized around various aspects of patient-centered care and focus on bringing about change in specific policies and practices that impact the patient experience. The core components of the Planetree model serve as the foundation for each of the initiative teams. These components include:

- Human interactions. This component involves not only providing nurturing, compassionate, personalized care to patients and families, but also creating an organizational culture that supports and nurtures staff.
- Access to information and education. Planetree's emphasis on patient and family education is carried out through such strategies as customized information packets and collaborative care conferences. The open chart policy enables patients to read and write in their medical records. Patients can keep their medications at the bedside and assume responsibility for their administration, where possible. In addition, a variety of educational materials are made available to patients' families and the community through consumer-friendly health resource centers.
- Participation of family and friends. The Care Partner Program, which will be described in more detail later in the chapter, provides education and training that assists family participation in the care of patients while hospitalized and at home after discharge. Volunteer care partners are available for those patients who are alone.
- Architecture and healing design. Facility design focuses on efficient layouts that support patients and their families. Domestic aesthetics, art, and warm, home-like designs are emphasized. Architectural barriers that inhibit patient control and privacy and that interfere with family participation are removed. The design of a Planetree facility provides patients and families with spaces for both solitude and social activities, including libraries, kitchens, lounges, activity rooms, chapels, and gardens. Comfortable space and accommodations are provided for families to stay overnight.
- Caring touch. Therapeutic full-body or chair massage may be provided for patients, families, and staff. Internship programs for massage therapists and training for volunteers to give hand and foot rubs are also available and help keep costs minimal. Families, as part of the Care Partner Program, can also be taught to give massages to loved ones while in the hospital and at home.

- Nutrition and wellness. Kitchens on the floor encourage families to prepare favorite foods or meals for loved ones and also serve as gathering places, thus helping to create spontaneous support groups. Cooking demonstrations and classes are provided by nutritionists and volunteers.

- Arts and entertainment. Music, storytellers, and funny movies create an atmosphere of playfulness in the Planetree model. Artwork in patient rooms and treatment areas adds to the ambiance. Volunteers work with patients who would like to create their own art, whereas involvement from artists, musicians, poets, and storytellers from the local community helps expand the boundaries of the healthcare facility.

- Spirituality. Chapels, gardens, and meditation rooms provide opportunities for reflection and prayer; chaplains are seen as vital members of the healthcare team.

- Integrative therapies. To meet the growing consumer demand for complementary and alternative medical therapies, Planetree has instituted heart disease referral programs, mind/body medicine interventions such as meditation and healing guided imagery, therapeutic massage, therapeutic touch, Reiki, acupuncture, Tai Chi, and yoga.

- Healthy communities. Working with schools, senior centers, churches, and other community partners, Planetree affiliates include the health and wellness of the larger community into their missions.

- The retreat process. Intensive educational experience for all hospital employees is designed to sensitize staff to the patient's perspective and to encourage supportive interactions with each patient.

In an effort to meet patients' needs, some hospitals have tried to identify generic behaviors or interactions, such as listening to patients, that are perceived to be beneficial. This approach misses the central point of the Planetree concept, which is to recognize each patient as a unique individual and, to the extent possible, develop care plans based on the expressed preferences of that individual. Although Mr. Jones may wake up at 5:00 a.m. ready for breakfast, Mrs. Smith may be accustomed to staying awake until 2:00 a.m. and prefer to sleep until noon. Many hospitals support task- or procedure-specific training for front-line staff, but this more extensive approach to understanding and advocating for the individual patient's perspective has traditionally been viewed as an unacceptable expense. The

Planetree model, however, underscores the long-term value of personalization and encourages staff to question all hospital routines from a patient perspective, in an atmosphere of acceptance and openness to looking at things differently. Creating that atmosphere hinges on the messages and modeling provided by organizational leadership; therefore, leaders are typically engaged in the culture change process prior to the staff's involvement. This approach assists leaders in understanding how to support their employees' involvement.

An example of how culture change efforts can have an impact on staff and patient experience comes from Northern Westchester Hospital. A staff member there, on seeing the exhausted state of a family member watching at the bedside of a seriously ill patient, recalled from a previous conversation that the woman played the piano. In an effort to help reduce the strain on the family member, the staff member mentioned the availability of a grand piano in the hospital lobby and invited her to play. The visitor did just that. As she was playing, a housekeeper dusting in the lobby paused to listen and then ducked into the gift shop. When the music stopped, the housekeeper approached the pianist to tell her that her hands were "a gift" and to offer her a bottle of lotion she had bought "to protect that beautiful gift." The gestures of both staff members might be perceived as unnecessary "extras" in many hospital environments. In the Planetree model, however, such gestures signal a hospital culture that has internalized an ethos of respect for how socially supportive efforts can improve morale and speed healing (see Chapter 7).

Patient Education and Involvement

Patients should be given many opportunities to learn about their specific diagnoses and needs. Information packets provided by the Planetree Health Resource Center include basic medical information, wellness literature, and support group listings. Information about complementary therapies, such as massage or stress management, is also available to those interested. The original Planetree Health Resource Center has become a model for hundreds of consumer health libraries across the country. The Center even developed a consumer cataloging system known as the Planetree Classification Scheme that continues to be used by health resource centers around the world (Ford & Gilpin, 2003).

Access to health and medical information was just the beginning of Planetree's vision for personalizing healthcare. The Planetree philosophy stresses that one of the most valuable resources for learning to be a partner in one's care is the patient's own medical chart. Patients are encouraged by their nurses to read their charts daily, ask questions, discuss findings, and participate in decisions affecting their care. In some Planetree hospitals, patients are also encouraged to write patient progress notes, which become a permanent part of their medical chart if so desired. In this way, hospitals can establish procedures that encourage patient participation.

Hospital Design

The architectural design of most hospitals isolates patients, placing barriers between staff, patients, and families. Despite the extensive research on the importance of social support referred to earlier (Reynolds & Kaplan, 1990; Taylor, Repetti, & Seeman, 1997), poor design continues to contribute to restricted access and social isolation. Insufficient space in patient rooms and waiting areas is common, and a lack of confidentiality in areas where only curtains separate patients is an accepted rationale for prohibiting family presence.

Although hospitals may not have the resources to completely redesign their physical plant, even subtle changes to interiors and finishes can encourage social connectedness. For example, research has shown that visits to patients by family and friends were longer in carpeted patient rooms as opposed to patient rooms with hard surface flooring (Harris, 2000). Furniture arrangements can also have an effect on social interactions (Melin & Gotestam, 1981). Perhaps the most symbolic environmental element of the separation between patients and caregivers is the centrally located nursing station. This segregated area is often designed with high imposing counters, glass partitions, and limited entry points. The message to patients and families is clear: Keep out! Although research has shown that contact with caring individuals during times of stress is beneficial to health (Kamarck et al., 1990; Lepore et al., 1993), in most places, hospitals have yet to integrate these findings into their facilities' designs.

As renovations or building projects are conducted, Planetree works with hospitals to use these opportunities to transform the typical hospital environment into a physical space that truly promotes healing and learning, as well as patient and family participation. Standard barriers between staff and patients are removed, leaving open workspaces that encourage interactions and communication. Relaxing colors are used, and lounges are created to be welcoming places where patients, families and friends can interact, share a meal, or watch a movie together. Many lounges also serve as satellite resource centers, providing health information in a convenient location close to patient care areas. Many of these spaces are equipped with Internet access for patient and family use.

Whenever possible, Planetree medical units are constructed to include a kitchenette where patients and family members are encouraged to prepare meals or store food they bring from home. The kitchenette is routinely stocked with a variety of healthy snack foods, available at all times of the day or night, when hospital cafeterias may be inaccessible. Design elements such as these are of critical importance in providing personalized care and in encouraging family involvement.

Patient-Centered Policies

In addition to hospital design, the Planetree model focuses on transforming hospital policies so that they are more conducive to positive interactions between patients, their families, and hospital staff. Family visitation policies are a prime example. Restrictive visitation policies are still in place in many hospitals that not only limit the hours of visitation, but limit who may visit as well. In an effort to address common patient experiences of anxiety, fear, and loneliness while hospitalized, the patient's family and friends are encouraged to spend as much time as possible with the patient. Visiting hours in most Planetree hospitals are unrestricted, and children are permitted to visit. Overnight accommodations, either in the patient's room or on a sofa bed in a nearby lounge, are offered to family members who want to spend the night.

Programs That Support Family Involvement

Family involvement is also encouraged through formalized programs. For example, many Planetree hospitals have implemented a simple program called "Care Partners" that has become one of the best improvement strategies for involving and supporting family members and friends. When patients are admitted to the hospital or as part of the pre-admission workup, they are asked to identify a family member or friend who will be their primary caregiver or support person. This care partner is usually a spouse or close relative, but can also be a friend or even someone hired to help. Care partners are identified by name in the chart and given buttons or name tags, making it easy for hospital staff to identify them. With information and training provided by nurses and other hospital staff, they are encouraged to assist with care and enhance communication with the healthcare team, and their role as patient advocates is reinforced.

Care partners are supported in a variety of ways to help them care for patients. At some Planetree hospitals, they are served meals along with the patient or given discounted meal tickets for the cafeteria. In many facilities, they can stay in the room with the patient 24 hours a day if they choose to. They are also given other sources of support, such as discounted parking and hotel rooms, to encourage their involvement.

Care partners participate to whatever extent they and the patient wish. Many care partners use the opportunity to learn and practice the caregiving skills that may be needed when the patient goes home. Tube feedings, dressing changes, and helping to position patients are among the many skills that care partners often learn. Those not interested in providing hands-on care may help support the patient emotionally, bringing in favorite music or cooking a special meal.

Perhaps the most meaningful part of the program is that care partners are encouraged to be active participants in the care process. As a part of their orientation, they are advised to speak up with their questions and to challenge anything that does not seem right, such as unexpected tests or procedures, unexplained medications, or adverse reactions. They are respected and vital partners in the care of the patient and work closely with the staff to ensure quality care. After a care partner program is established, most staff nurses find these family caregivers to be a valuable and time-saving asset in addressing patients' needs.

Common reactions of family members empowered to participate as care partners are summed up by one family member's comment: "I was the primary caregiver for my husband before he was admitted to the hospital, and I will be when he goes home. I know his needs better than anyone else possibly could. It's been wonderful to have the staff acknowledge this and let me participate in his care."

Stress Reduction and Complementary and Alternative Therapies

Acknowledging the role of stress in disease causation today, Planetree hospitals actively educate patients about avenues for reducing and coping with the stress of their illness in their daily lives. Staff members and volunteers who specialize in guided imagery, visualization, and massage therapies provide these services at no charge, creating a more holistic hospital stay that addresses healing modalities often overlooked or devalued in traditional hospital environments.

Medicine draws on the body's resources to heal. To enhance this healing process, Planetree affiliates focus on the need to nurture the resources within each patient. Incorporating the mind and spirit into this process aids healing more completely, whether via access to the arts, music, or spiritual support services. Patient rooms may be decorated with artwork featuring nature themes. Portable CD players and a large selection of musical and relaxation options are made available, as are comedy movies and selections of books on tape. Chaplains, chapels, meditation rooms, labyrinths, and other ethnically appropriate spiritual supports are provided in an attempt to engage the spiritual resources of each patient. The Planetree model looks at every aspect of the patient experience, from the patient's perspective, and strives to create healing environments in what are often high-tech, biomedically oriented intimidating settings.

The many components of the Planetree model—from professional development to patient education to hospital design—demonstrate the wide range of interventions possible at the organizational level.

Hospitals vary greatly by size, function, location, and culture, and for this reason, each Planetree project is specifically tailored to the strengths and challenges of the hospital in question. The example in Textbox 11.1 helps shed light on culture change efforts supported through the Planetree model.

The Business Case for Planetree

The level of individualized care provided to patients through the Planetree model may lead many administrators to shy away from adoption, fearing sticker shock. Yet labor costs between hospitals adopting the Planetree model and those that do not are roughly comparable (Charmel, 2003). Higher nurse staff ratios are not the norm on Planetree units, and

Textbox 11.1   A Planetree Success Story: Northern Westchester Hospital

Northern Westchester Hospital considers clinical excellence and service quality as the twin pillars of its Planetree Program. It is the definition of those values, however, that sets Northern Westchester apart from hospitals with traditional quality of care approaches. Maria Hale, Vice President for Patient Advocacy and Service Excellence, explains that most of the hospital's efforts to sensitize staff members to meeting patients' needs begin with the question, "If I were in that bed, what would I want?"

"Our approach," she said, "reminds staff and volunteers that each patient is a unique human being whose needs may be completely different from the patient in the next room. The important thing is to find out what the patient wants. What is special for him or her? We teach people to ask and then to listen—really listen—to the answer. And we give them the authority to act on what they hear."

Planetree retreats are mandatory for everyone who works at the hospital, from housekeepers to transport staff to nurses, volunteers, and physicians. The overriding purpose, explains Hale, is "to reacquaint ourselves with why we went into healthcare. We share stories about what brought us to this field. At the retreats, through a series of interactive exercises, we experience the feelings of vulnerability, loss of power, and anxiety that our patients feel. We want everyone who works in our hospital to have empathy and compassion front and center in their minds so that day-to-day tasks don't overtake what matters most."

One family member's comments in a letter to the hospital capture what the Planetree model hopes to accomplish through its culture change efforts: "When I brought my son to Northern Westchester Hospital, it wasn't for a specific nurse but for an attitude which encompasses the facility. Every employee I met had the same drive to make my son's stay better. This attitude was seen in every nurse, physician, dietician, and housekeeping personnel. I would like to congratulate you on an institution which strives for excellence not only in patient care, but in personal care." Similarly, another family member observed in a focus group that "the level of compassion—and I must repeat this word, because there is no other more suitable—the compassion shown to my mother was extraordinary and went far beyond what could be expected of any human. This compassion will not be forgotten for as long as I live."

supplemental paid staff members are rarely necessary. Many elements of the Planetree model are delivered by existing staff members or through volunteers. The most significant cost increase associated with adoption of the Planetree model is staff training; however, training costs never exceed 1% of operating costs. What is more, because Planetree affiliates have such high staff retention rates, significant savings are achieved by minimizing staff turnover (Textbox 11.1).

MEASURING ORGANIZATIONAL CHANGE: THE ROLE OF CULTURE AUDITS

There is little question that we can improve the quality of the patient experience by listening to patients' perceptions of their own needs, but understanding what patients want and why they feel the way they do can be a challenging task in the complicated arena of healthcare. Planetree applies the tools used in other business settings to gather data on customer opinions that are particularly important for undertaking culture change initiatives. These tools include regularly administered satisfaction surveys and focus groups with patients, families, and staff. This evaluation serves as a "cultural audit" and is essential for tracking an organization's progress, as well as a review and evaluation of the physical environment.

When applying a business model to healthcare, many "customers" must be recognized, and all must be engaged and solicited for their perspectives if culture change is to take place. These include not only patients and their families, but front-line staff, managers, hospital volunteers, physicians, board members, and administrators. Reviewing satisfaction data collected from these groups over time and identifying trends and issues are good places to begin. Conducting in-depth focus groups and interviews gives administrators a clearer understanding of key problems and opportunities for fixing them. All of these data are needed in designing appropriate interventions, suggesting targeted initiatives, and developing educational programs for staff. This process ensures that all constituencies are heard, that their ideas and issues are addressed up front, and that buy-in with cultural transformation activities will be well supported. Using an outside source such as Planetree, which partners with but does not own hospital franchises, to conduct focus groups and analyze the data gathered is key to obtaining objective, unbiased results, as it is extremely difficult for organizational "insiders" to resist the common phenomenon of selective listening and interpretation.

Patient Satisfaction

In addition to focus groups, another avenue for obtaining information directly from patients about their hospital experiences are phone and mailed surveys sent to recently discharged patients. Many questions asked on a typical patient satisfaction survey solicit the patient's perceptions about the manner in which care was delivered. How friendly and courteous was the staff in various departments? How caring were the nurses? How willing were nurses to answer questions? How well were family members kept informed? Rarely do patient satisfaction surveys ask questions asked about the medical care itself. Was the surgical procedure performed correctly? Did you receive the correct medications? Were falls prevented? Instead, these sorts of questions about the quality of the medical care are usually tracked through incident reports, performance improvement measures, and reviews of adverse patient outcomes. In the absence of asking patients such questions about the quality of their care, current patient satisfaction surveys, subjective though these measures are, are the best indicator of how well patients feel heard and supported.

The first study of patient satisfaction at a Planetree site was conducted by the University of Washington. In this randomized, controlled trial of 618 patients hospitalized between 1986 and 1990, patient outcomes on the Planetree unit were compared with those on other medical–surgical units. Planetree patients were found to be significantly more satisfied with their hospital stay, their nursing care, the support they received, the environment, and the education that they were given. Planetree patients reported more involvement in their care during their hospitalization. Although there were few differences in health outcomes between Planetree patients and those in the control group, Planetree patients reported better mental health status and role functioning initially after discharge. Costs were found to be the same (Martin et al., 1998).

Other Planetree sites have also measured patient satisfaction using a variety of instruments. Stamford Hospital of Stamford, Connecticut, found that patient satisfaction on their inpatient units after implementation of patient-centered approaches to care increased on their surveys from the 18th to the 75th percentile in just 18 months. Satisfaction with the emergency department went from the 44th percentile to the 89th in the same time period. Griffin Hospital, in Derby, Connecticut, found that patient satisfaction increased from 83% to 97% during the four-year period in which Griffin fully implemented the Planetree model throughout the hospital. The hospital has maintained these extremely high levels of satisfaction over the past decade, and their performance on the Hospital Consumer Assessment of Healthcare Providers and Systems (HCAHPS) survey, a nationally standardized patient satisfaction tool created by the Center for Medicare and Medicaid Services, has been as impressive. Staff to patient ratios remained the same, and cost per discharge was unchanged, demonstrating that delivering high-quality patient-centered care does not have to cost more.

Budget-conscious administrators often have the misconception that supportive interactions require more staff or more time and are therefore more costly. Although labor costs are a substantial part of any hospital budget, more personalized interactions themselves add nothing to the budget. Listening to patients or answering their questions costs nothing. It could be argued that negative interactions—alienating patients, not advocating for their needs, limiting their sense of control, restricting family visits—can be very costly in lost patient revenues and even litigation (see Chapter 20). Angry, frustrated, or frightened patients may be combative, withdrawn, and less cooperative, requiring far more time than it would have taken to interact with them initially in a positive way.

Staff Satisfaction

Although the importance of patient satisfaction cannot be overemphasized, staff satisfaction with their work is also a key indicator of an organization's health (see Chapter 15). Many hospitals monitor patient satisfaction every month, but staff satisfaction may be measured only every few years, if at all. Planetree was created to address how patients experience healthcare, but it became immediately clear that patient satisfaction and staff satisfaction go hand in hand (see Chapter 15).

Research conducted by Press Ganey Associates (2003) in 18 hospitals found an extremely high correlation between employee and patient satisfaction. Although Planetree is often referred to as "patient centered," it is equally as focused on nurturing caregivers. Many nurses (who represent approximately 70% of the employees in most hospitals) as well as other staff choose to work in healthcare for the opportunity it affords to advocate for their patients' needs.

Fortunately, Planetree has found that most caregivers want to give the kind of care patients want to receive. At Griffin Hospital, a 160-bed community hospital in southern Connecticut, 75% of new clinical staff cite the hospital's model of care (Planetree) as their reason for choosing to work at Griffin. This hospital, a Planetree affiliate for over 15 years, has found that creating an environment that is better for patients (as measured by their 97% patient satisfaction rating) is also better for staff. Fortune Magazine has rated Griffin for seven consecutive years (2000 to 2006) as one of the "100 Best Places to Work" in America.

Another reason that staff satisfaction is vital is that hospitals are now competing not only for patients but for staff as well. According to figures from the U.S. Department of Health and Human Services, the current nursing shortage is estimated to become a national crisis by 2010, and it is not only nurses who are in short supply. Many regions of the United States are also in need of pharmacists, physical therapists, and radiology and ultrasound technologists. As a result, staff satisfaction is receiving the attention that it has always been due but rarely gotten.

The importance of retaining and recruiting highly qualified staff cannot be overstated. The economic impact alone can be staggering given that the estimated cost of recruiting, hiring, and training one nurse is as high as $64,000 (Nursing Executive Center, 1999). In the United States, nursing turnover rates fluctuate between 12% and 20% and in some regions are up to 35% (Nursing Executive Center, 1999), but the human cost may be even higher as the baby boomers age and find that hospitals are unable to care for them without adequate staff. State-of-the-art medicine is nothing in the absence of qualified people to deliver the care and serve as advocates for patients.

Creating Communication Channels Between Hospital Staff and Administrators

Two-way communication (being informed and being heard) is another interaction that contributes to staff satisfaction and is vital to organizational change. When staff members are informed, they are better able to participate in creating a work environment in which they can serve as patient advocates. A structure needs to be established that solicits their input and encourages their ideas and solutions.

To be most effective, communication needs to be two ways (i.e., staff want to be kept informed but also need an opportunity to be heard). Having a "voice" in how care is delivered and having opportunities to participate create an environment in which staff can be the patient and family advocates they want to be. It is a misconception that the benefit of staff input is simply to win their support and buy-in. The opinions, ideas, suggestions, and creative solutions of caregivers are tremendous assets in creating a healing environment for patients and an optimum working environment for staff. As a case in point, staff in the emergency department of a large urban hospital recommended and received support for adding rocking chairs to each treatment room. This simple addition created a soothing outlet for agitated patients and family members, as well as a more compassionate place for grieving families to hold their children, in some situations for the last time.

Good leadership is vital in creating an environment that supports staff participation. Traditionally, the role of management was to serve as key problem solvers and then to direct staff to accomplish those tasks. In a patient-centered environment, front-line employees, those who work most closely with patients and their families, are empowered to find solutions most appropriate to the patients' needs. Good leaders must therefore become champions of staff, recognizing them not only for their clinical skills but also for their creative problem solving. Good leadership includes advocating for staff so that staff can fill the role of patient advocate.

CONCLUSION

Most Americans agree that fundamental change is needed in the healthcare system. Many would like to see a safer, more transparent, and more personalized system that invites patients and their families into the experience in a meaningful and respectful manner. There are significant ways that we can change hospital culture to benefit patients. Perhaps the most powerful is to move the system toward one in which patients become equal partners in their own healthcare, families are fully integrated into caregiving, and hospital staff members are supported and engaged in a meaningful dialogue about quality improvement. The power of patient advocacy at the organizational level cannot be overestimated. When organizations embrace a patient-centered culture, patients feel that they have advocates and can *be* advocates, that they are heard and understood, and that they are truly cared for. At that point, patient-centered care becomes a reality.

REFERENCES

Berkman, L. F., Leo-Summers, L., & Horwitz, R. I. (1992). Emotional support and survival after myocardial infarction: A prospective, population-based study of the elderly. *Annals of Internal Medicine, 117,* 1003–1009.

Berwick, D. M. (1999). *Escape fire: Lessons for the future of health care.* New York: The Commonwealth Fund.

Berwick, D. M., & Kotagal, M. (2004). Restricted visiting hours in ICUs: Time to change. *Journal of the American Medical Association, 292,* 736–737.

Blazer, D. G. (1982). Social support and mortality in an elderly community population. *American Journal of Epidemiology, 115,* 684–694.

Charmel, P. A. (2003). Building the business case for patient-centered care. In S. Frampton, L. Gilpin, & P. Charmal (Eds.), *Putting patients first* (pp. 193–204). San Francisco: John Wiley & Sons.

Edgman-Levitan, S. (2003). Healing partnerships: The importance of including family and friends. In S. Frampton, L. Gilpin, & P. Charmel (Eds.), *Putting patients first* (pp. 51–70). San Francisco: John Wiley & Sons.

Ford, C., & Gilpin, L. (2003). *Informing and empowering diverse populations: Putting patients first* (p. 32). San Francisco: John Wiley & Sons.

Fortune Magazine Online. 100 Best Companies to Work For 2007: Full List. Retrieved February 5, 2007, from http://money.cnn.com/magazines/fortune/bestcompanies/2007/full_list/.

Harris, D. (2000). *Environmental quality and healing environments: A study of flooring materials in a healthcare telemetry unit.* Unpublished dissertation, Texas A&M University, Department of Architecture.

Institute of Medicine, Committee on Quality of Health Care in America. (2001). *Crossing the quality chasm: A new health system for the 21st century.* Washington, DC: National Academy Press.

Kamarck, T. W., Manuck, S. B., & Jennings, J. R. (1990). Social support reduces cardiovascular reactivity to psychological challenge: A laboratory model. *Psychosomatic Medicine, 52,* 42–58.

Kane-Urrabazo, C. (2006). Management's role in shaping organizational culture. *Journal of Nursing Management, 14,* 188–194.

Lazarou, J., Pomeranz, B. H., & Corey, P. N. (1998). Incidence of adverse drug reactions in hospitalized patients: A meta-analysis of prospective studies. *Journal of the American Medical Association, 279,* 1200–1205.

Lepore, S. J., Mata, A. K., & Evans, G. W. (1993). Social support lowers cardiovascular reactivity to an acute stressor. *Psychosomatic Medicine, 55,* 518–524.

Martin, D. P., Diehr, P., Conrad, D. A., Davis, J. H., Leickly, R., & Perrin, E. B. (1998). Randomized trial of a patient-centered hospital unit. *Patient Education and Counseling, 34,* 125–133.

Melin, L., & Gotestam, K. G. (1981). The effects of rearranging ward routines on communication and eating behaviors of psychogeriatric patients. *Journal of Applied Behavior Analysis, 14,* 47–51.

Nursing Executive Center. (1999, February 11). A misplaced focus: Reexamining the recruiting/retention trade off. Washington, DC: The Advisory Board Company.

Ornish, D. (1998). *Love & survival: The scientific basis for the healing power of intimacy.* New York: HarperCollins.

Press Ganey Associates. (2003). Undeniable: Patient and employee satisfaction linked. Retrieved on January 31, 2007, from http://www.pressganey.com/scripts/news.php?news_id=84.

Reynolds, P., & Kaplan, G. A. (1990). Social connections and risk for cancer: Prospective evidence from the Alameda County study. *Behavioral Medicine, 16,* 101–110.

Spiegel, D. (1993). *Living beyond limits: New hope and help for facing life-threatening illness.* New York: Times Books.

Taylor, S. E., Repetti, R. L., & Seeman, T. (1997). Health psychology: What is an unhealthy environment and how does it get under the skin? *Annual Review of Psychology, 48,* 411–417.

Wiklund, I., Oden, A., Sanne, H., Ulvenstam, G., Wilhelmsson, C., & Wilhelmsen, L. (1988). Prognostic importance of somatic and psychosocial variables after a first myocardial infarction. *American Journal of Epidemiology, 128,* 786–795.

Williams, R. B., Barefoot, J. C., Califf, R. M., Haney, T. L., Saunders, W. B., Pryor, D. B., et al. (1992). Prognostic importance of social and economic resources among medically treated patients with angiographically documented coronary artery disease. *Journal of the American Medical Association, 267,* 520–524.

CHAPTER 12

Confronting the Hidden Curriculum in Medical Education: The Challenge Faced by Patients, Families, Educators, and Administrators in Changing Medical School and Hospital Culture

Kathy Zoppi, Patricia Sodomka, and Julie Moretz

OBJECTIVES

- To identify historical and cultural factors that have contributed to the hidden curriculum in medical education
- To describe the ways in which the culture of medicine works against integration of patient- and family-centered care into the biomedical environment of medical education
- To describe the economic, educational, and historical barriers to changing the learning environment for medical students and residents
- To identify and describe models of care that provide alternatives to traditional biomedical provider-centered healthcare, including competency-based education, patient- and family-centered care, and relationship-centered care

In recent years, practitioners have developed an appreciation that healthcare professionals must change their approach from an overemphasis on technical capability to a perspective that emphasizes partnership between patients and providers. Patients, families, caregivers, and now patient advocates are raising their voices about their desire for seamless and transparent healthcare, and medical schools are listening. As a result, medical students are now coached in communicating more effectively with patients and their families and in the value of adopting a compassionate, responsive "bedside manner."

Moreover, a brief overview of recent reforms shows that medical schools and certifying organizations are putting muscle behind their call for change. Medical students must now pass a national test measuring their grasp of effective communication principles. Specifically, the National Board of Medical Examiners requires that students be graded on their clinical skills, including taking medical histories, writing chart notes, communicating clearly with patients, and performing physical exams. In addition, the Accreditation Council on Graduate Medical Education, which accredits residency and fellowship specialty education, requires all training programs to demonstrate that graduates are competent in communicating and developing relationships with patients and families. Many specialty groups are including clinical skills examinations in their board recertification programs. Although no clinical certification can ensure compassion and responsiveness, today's medical students are expected to possess and demonstrate proficiency in communicating with patients (Cheshire, 2004).

Despite these improvements, many patients, families, and patient advocates continue to express concern that practicing physicians fail to grasp fully how central communication is to the effective practice of medicine (Moore, 1997; *Through the Patient's Eyes*, 2002). This chapter posits several reasons why communication and relational problems between patients and physicians persist, even among newly trained clinicians. Specifically, despite meaningful curricular changes in many medical schools, most graduating students finish their training having more thoroughly imbibed a biomedical model rather than a patient- or family-centered model of care (see Textbox 12.1 for brief definitions; see also Chapter 3). This chapter explores the ways in which the biomedical model of care is conveyed to students, even as it suggests strategies for achieving crucial changes through three major mechanisms. These three areas of change are the following: modifications to the formal medical school curriculum to support patient- and family-centered care modalities; focusing greater attention on the lessons students absorb through the intense mentoring and modeling process that begins in year three of medical school, lessons that often reinforce a biomedical model of care; and implementing broader changes in the culture of teaching hospitals themselves.

VIGNETTE: THE BIOMEDICAL MODEL

The resident, fellow, four medical students, and the attending physician hovered in the hallway outside Mr. Johnson's room to discuss his case. Inside, the patient lay connected to life support, one leg amputated just below his knee cap. Given his recent episodes of tachycardia (abnormally rapid beating of the heart) and the swelling around the "good" parts of his brain, the healthcare team concluded that no medical or technical options remained for this middle-aged, African American man. At 9:20 a.m., after a 15-minute conference in the hall, the group entered the dimly lit room. One by one, they circled the patient with their backs to his wife, who sat

---

Textbox 12.1   Definitions: Types of Healthcare

Biomedical provider-centered care: An approach to healthcare based on a technical assessment of the patient's disease state from the perspective of the provider. The focus of care is on accurate diagnosis and appropriate medical treatment and only secondarily consideration of the patient's social or psychological status.

Patient-centered care: "Providing care that is respectful of and responsive to individual patient preferences, needs, values and ensuring that patient values guide all clinical decisions" (Institute of Medicine, 2001).

Patient- and family-centered care: "An approach to planning, delivery and evaluation of health care that is grounded in mutually beneficial partnerships among patients, families and health care providers" (Institute for Family-Centered Care).

Relationship-centered care: An approach to patient care that emphasizes interdependence within relationships among caregivers, patients, and the healthcare system. Improvements to relationships and outcomes are emphasized.

quietly in the corner of the room. The click-click-click of the ventilator and the steady rise and fall of the patient's chest gave way to the discussion that was inevitable. From across the bed where her husband lay, the attending doctor addressed the patient's wife. "Mrs. Johnson, I think you understand where we are right now. Have you talked with the rest of your family?" Almost in unison, the group of healthcare professionals turned their eyes to her. Mrs. Johnson hesitated. She wanted to make sure that she did understand. She wanted to know how long it would take for him to die after the ventilator was removed. She wanted to hear them say that they had done everything. She wanted to know if he could hear her voice, even now. Instead, she asked, "Is he in pain?" After answering her question, the group quietly exited the room. It was 9:45 a.m. Only five minutes had elapsed since the encounter began.

Reactions to Vignette

This vignette, which illustrates a typical experience on rounds in an academic medical center, also reflects a biomedical model of care. The technical aspects of care were available and delivered to the patient; however, the patient's ultimate needs and those of his family went beyond what could be conveyed by a biomedical intervention. The clinicians failed to make a meaningful connection with Mrs. Johnson as she faced her husband's impending death, leaving her alone in her grief. In this context, how would such an interaction have differed had the medical team approached the encounter from a patient- or family-centered orientation as defined and explored in Chapter 3? Some issues to consider in this context include the following:

- Although the attending physician did appropriately use Mrs. Johnson's name during this brief conversation, at no time was the group introduced to her. Although it was certain that she knew the attending physician and possibly the resident, the rest of the medical team members were not acknowledged or introduced as students. In a patient- and family-centered model, members of the healthcare team respect the patient and family by knocking on the door and introducing themselves. This simple courtesy can help foster more inclusion in discussion and shared decision making.

- Additionally, the attending physician should have considered his or her physical proximity to the patient or family member when communicating. Rather than standing above the patient from across the room, a better approach would have had the attending physician seated beside Mrs. Johnson to establish eye-level contact during this difficult conversation.

- Medical situations such as Mr. Johnson's are difficult to discuss with the family, yet a positive outcome can occur, even when the patient dies, if the family feels that care was delivered in a genuinely compassionate manner. In this case, the care offered did not provide a connection or any real empathic moments for Mrs. Johnson. Given Mrs. Johnson's situation, it would have been appropriate to ask her if another family member, or even the hospital chaplain, might be helpful for her to see.

- The care team's avoidance of end-of-life issues left Mrs. Johnson without the opportunity to ask questions. At no time did the team discuss next steps to take in her husband's care from Mrs. Johnson's perspective. The patient- and family-centered care model encourages collaboration and support throughout the entire healthcare experience and is not truncated with the announcement of a prognosis.

BIOMEDICAL/PROVIDER-CENTERED CARE VERSUS PATIENT- AND FAMILY-CENTERED CARE

As suggested in the vignette, one of the challenges in achieving widespread adoption of patient- and family-centered care and in cultivating its "linchpin" skill, high-quality communication, is that the culture of American medicine remains primarily driven by the biomedical sciences. Primary care specialties do increasingly support patient and family-focused approaches, yet these specialties are also the least powerful entities, politically and financially, in most academic centers, where the bulk of early training occurs (Ludmerer, 1999). Moreover, medical education still takes place in an environment where much of the teaching is done by basic science faculty not specifically trained as medical educators and by clinical faculty whose own education may not have included training in psychosocial and communication sciences. Thus, despite the commitment of many programs to patient- and family-centered methods, the culture that surrounds students still emphasizes a biomedical and physician-focused model of care.

Historically, the biomedical model has placed more value on technical proficiency than on communication skills (Candib, 1995; Ludmerer, 1999); its aim is the identification of pathological bases of diseases and their cures. In traditional biomedical model hospitals and practices, patients' problems are generally confined to signs, symptoms, and diagnoses and the workload parceled out by specialty. Coordination of the patient's care by multiple providers often happens through the chart, nursing staff, or family members so that aspects of care under this model frequently fall through the cracks. Providers analyze data and define treatment plans, usually without patient or family input, before conveying these plans in efficient, often impersonal ways to family members who will be expected to carry them out.

Even for well-trained physicians, the goal of meeting patients' emotional needs has been secondary or seen as the domain of nurses, social workers, or counselors. Time constraints on physicians in training affect their willingness to work with patients and families on the details of care or management after a situation does not require technical focus. In this way, patients often become the "object" of care. In turn, families are visitors, peripheral to the tasks of care in the hospital, especially if those tasks are technical or procedural. Once released from the hospital or physician's care, however, patients and families are expected to manage technical follow-up care at home day to day, usually with minimal training in what can be complex procedures (see Chapter 8).

In contrast, a patient- and family-centered system focuses on identifying and using the strengths of the patient and his or her family as problem-solving partners in successfully managing the particular healthcare situation. Agents in a patient- and family-centered system look for opportunities to offer choices and to support dialogue where all parties can reach common ground (Stewart et al., 2003). A patient- and family-centered care philosophy recognizes that patients and families have important knowledge no one else on the team has (e.g., how an individual reacts to medication, how severe the patient's chronic illness is, the extent of support in the home) and that providers cannot access this expertise unless they ask. Ideally, information is transparent and flows freely in this system so that documentation in the record is written in ways that patients and families can read, understand, and contribute to. Patients' emotional needs are recognized and supported. With this approach, flexibility is paramount, with all caregivers encouraged to use discernment when applying policies to individual patient situations (see Chapter 11). The emphasis on building partnerships among patients, their families, and healthcare professionals empowers patients, increasing their sense of well-being and control over their own care (Institute for Family-Centered Care).

A HISTORICAL PERSPECTIVE ON PATIENT-CENTERED CARE

Despite the benefits of the relationship-centered care model, the continual need for reform demonstrates how difficult it is to overcome ingrained patterns to achieve true culture change. As early as the 1950s, a number of educators called attention to the goal of preserving what Michael Balint, a British psychoanalyst, called "the humane" within technical biomedicine. When Balint used the term "the doctor as drug," for example, he was trying to direct general practitioners' attention to the healing potential of their interpersonal relationships with patients (Balint, 2000). Similarly, George Engel, a University of Rochester internist, was among the first physician educators to write about the biopsychosocial model of care (Engel, 1977). As the movement to focus attention on humanism in the medical school curriculum gained ground in the 1970s, ethicists like Edmund Pellegrino (1999) emphasized how training in the humanities, particularly ethics, could give physicians a better understanding of their role in society and help them recognize the ways in which a narrow focus on science and its application did not serve the patient.

As part of this general reform movement, social scientists began to study interactions between patients and clinicians. They found that much of the communication process between patients and their providers was physician centered—that is, physicians held most of the power in interactions by defining the agenda, controlling the topic, interrupting the patient's narrative, or focusing the discussion on the medical topics physicians identified, rather than on concerns patients raised (Beckman & Frankel, 1984; Marvel, Epstein, Flowers, & Beckman, 1999). This tendency led researchers at the University of Western Ontario's Department of Family Medicine to posit another model, patient-centered care (Stewart et al., 2003). The term *patient centered* implied that a patient's needs, agenda, and concerns should come first and that physicians should adapt to these needs as they develop relationships with patients. As an outgrowth of this concept, in 1994, a group of national advisors on health professionals' education reviewed recommendations to bring medical education in line with the social missions of health professions (Tresolini & The Pew-Fetzer Task Force, 1994). They coined the term "relationship-centered care," a concept meant to capture the reciprocal, interdependent nature of patients, physicians, and the social good. This concept appealed to a network of educators who broadened the term beyond its initial focus on patient–physician education to embody a set of approaches to patient care, family interactions, administration, and organizational design (Beach & Inui, 2006; Miller, 2004; *Partnerships in Health Care*, 1998; Suchman et al., 2004; Tresolini & The Pew-Fetzer Task Force, 1994). Candib (1995), building on the work of these colleagues, also analyzes the ways in which relationship-centered and biomedical approaches to care are part of a "gendered" discourse in which biomedical approaches are perceived as adhering to a more masculine coda while relational approaches are often perceived as a more feminized expression of care.

CURRICULUM REFORM TO SUPPORT
PATIENT-CENTERED CARE

Throughout the 1990s, and especially with the publication of the Institute of Medicine report *Crossing the Quality Chasm* in 2001, the idea of cultivating a culture of patient- and family-centered care with good communication at its core has gained traction in the U.S. medical system. Many family physicians and general practitioners already recognize the need to improve communication skills with their patients (Ashbury, Iverson, & Kralj, 2001), while leaders in health communication have agreed on central elements of effective communication (Makoul, 2001). Strong models for medical interviewing are available (Frankel & Stein, 1999), and evidence suggests that patient care centered on strong communication leads to better health outcomes (Griffin et al., 2004; Ong, de Haes, Hoos, & Lammes, 1995; Stewart et al., 2000). Moreover, high-quality communications courses have already been developed to meet these needs. Evidence for their effectiveness comes from Smith et al. (1998) and Maguire (1999), both of whom have demonstrated long-term outcomes on real clinical practices for students who receive training in patient-centered communication skills. In particular, successful communication courses focus on specific patient–physician communication skills identified by Roter (2000), including information giving, question asking, partnership building, rapport building, and socioemotional talk (2000) (see also Chapter 7).

Of course it is not enough simply to provide information and training; there also needs to be a way to evaluate student learning. Competency-based education and assessment have been promoted in medicine as one way to ensure that physicians and other providers are skilled in domains beyond strictly biomedical areas of expertise, including not only communication but self-awareness and ethics as well (Addison, 1989; Leach, 2002). Competency-based education requires not just that these elements be part of a curriculum but that students demonstrate acquired skills, knowledge, and attitudes as outcomes of training (Epstein & Hundert, 2002). Used in other industries to assess performance, the concept of competency-based education was first applied to undergraduate medical education by faculty at Brown University Medical School in the 1990s. The competency-based curriculum initiated at Indiana University in 1996 requires that students be evaluated according to several dimensions, including clinical skills, using science, life-long learning, professionalism, social and cultural context, communication, self-awareness, and ethics (Shank & Zoppi, 2001; Zoppi & Epstein, 2002). Skills in these areas are assessed through feedback from patients, peers, and faculty and in simulated tests that use standardized patients (i.e., patient educators who have been trained to provide students with feedback about their medical skills) (Zoppi & Epstein, 2001). Other medical schools are beginning to implement similar competency-based curricula, but currently, the entity that accredits undergraduate medical education (the Liaison Committee on Medical Education) does not have a method for assessing these programs as part of school accreditation.

Together with these reforms, different schools use a variety of methods to help place the patient's voice at the center of the educational experience. Most schools use standardized patient education as a teaching method that gives student neophytes the opportunity to perform mock interviews and physical examinations. Recently, in fact, the National Board of Medical Examiners implemented standardized patient exams for medical students as a required part of the board exams taken by fourth-year students to demonstrate clinical skills.

Trained standardized patients are reliable and valid evaluators of medical student interviewing and physical examination skills (Williams, Hall, Supiano, Fitzgerald, & Halter, 2006); however, they do not perfectly mimic the dynamics in a typical patient encounter. Most simulations consist of one-physician, one-patient scenarios, which do not do justice to the complexity of real patient care settings where family, friends, and other health-care professionals all have an influence. Students are rarely taught and evaluated on how to handle working with several people at the same time, and these skills are seldom assessed with the instruments most commonly used to evaluate communication (Schirmer et al., 2005).

At least two medical schools—the University of Rochester and East Tennessee State University—represent the exception to this general rule. At the Indiana University School of Medicine, family medicine residents, under the supervision of both marriage and family therapists as well as their peers, deliver health and psychosocial counseling to patients (Dankoski, Pais, & Zoppi, 2003). This training includes working with the residents' own patients and the patients' family members. Although such programs result in trainees more skilled in family-centered approaches to care, such supervision is expensive, labor intensive, and not common. At Indiana University's Riley Hospital, a program using patients and family as faculty educators has been developed as part of pediatrics training for students and residents (Zoppi & McKegney, 1997). Including family members as teachers, however, is not a model widely applied to the entire curriculum.

THE HIDDEN CURRICULUM: WHAT ARE WE REALLY TEACHING IN YEAR 3 AND BEYOND?

In the best-case scenario, as described previously here, students in their first two years of medical school are currently being trained to build relationships with patients and their families and enhance their interpersonal skills; however, although lessons learned in the classroom are critical, skills-building courses have only a limited impact if they are not reinforced in other settings. Yet this is not usually the case. In their third and fourth years of training, students rotating through busy patient care units often encounter a biomedical approach to medical care that conflicts with their earlier training (Levinson, Gorawara-Bhat, & Lamb, 2000; Marvel et al., 1999). For students who are, in part, following rules as a way of mastering medical knowledge, their entry in year 3 into a fast-paced, "no mistakes allowed" environment where they are subaltern to many makes it challenging for them to feel confident in adapting rules to specific patients and family situations (Haas & Shaffir, 1987).

In analyzing this dynamic, medical educators Thomas Inui and Frederick Hafferty have coined the term "the hidden curriculum" (Hafferty, 1998; Inui, 2003) to describe "the commonly held understandings, customs, rituals, and taken-for-granted assets of what goes on in the life-space we call medical education" (Hafferty, 1998). This includes all the teachings students experience "on the job" during their clinical rotations under the guidance of senior medical faculty. Not surprisingly, teachers at the bedside may provide more powerful guidance to students about "the way it's *really* done" than does the overt curriculum espoused by classroom professors (Haidet & Stein, 2006). This real-time learning may overshadow principles espoused by classroom professors in students' early years (Hafferty & Franks, 1994).

In contrast to the overt curriculum, which may feature formal courses and units on communication and patient-centered care, the "hidden curriculum" emphasizes the biomedical model. Thus, although the overt curriculum focuses on training students in the technical application of evidence-based biomedicine, the hidden curriculum includes key lessons about how to treat team members, other professionals, and patients in the actual context of care. The overt curriculum trains medical students in gathering history data from patients in a nonevaluative manner, but the hidden curriculum models strategies for quickly determining when a patient is really in pain or exaggerating, whether a person requesting pain medication is really in need, and how to streamline approaches to gathering such information (Hafferty, 1998; Levinson et al., 2000; Marvel et al., 1999). In short, the future skills of practicing physicians are shaped, for better or worse, by their informal experiences of learning, teaching, and observations of patient care while in the later years of graduate training.

Several factors contribute to the influence of the hidden curriculum. In the third year of medical school, students are transformed from mostly passive learners participating in lecture classes or group discussions to doctors in training, working long hours on clinical rotations in hospitals or in outpatient clinics, with limited time for reflection. With this shift to the clinic, students are learning to function in a time-pressured environment, even as they are expected to master more technical medical knowledge and skills. At this point, the realities of teaching and learning in a hierarchical team can shift students' focus from the patients to the supervisors who evaluate their work. A student trained in patient-centered communication techniques, for example, might encounter her preceptor, an established physician who has guided students for many years. He may urge the student to "just get the important information in three minutes and meet back to discuss it right away." In turn, the student may well feel that she has little choice but to get the work done as prescribed by her mentor.

Equally important, medical education has traditionally been a highly hierarchical process, with teams working in a command and control structure. Ultimate authority for decisions about patient care typically rests with the most senior member of the team. As documented in a landmark participant observational study, such a hierarchical structure can lead surgical trainees (Bosk, 2003; Institute of Medicine, 2000) to avoid discussion of problems in patient care. These cultural practices hinder learning and work against the straightforward, blame-free discussion of medical errors identified by the Institute of Medicine as key to improving healthcare quality. Given the enormous impact of observational learning in the later years of medical school, attempts to influence the practice of medicine through curriculum reform must explicitly confront the hidden curriculum if they are to be effective.

To address the hidden curriculum while improving the experience of care for patients, some teaching hospitals are beginning to make changes in the clinical learning environment. Such culture change is essential, not only to give learners a seamless educational experience but also to address the myriad problems in healthcare itself. The Agency for Healthcare Research and Quality now tracks specific questions to measure "patient centeredness" because of its specific association with outcomes, including morbidity, mortality, and cost (Agency for Healthcare Research and Quality website). Yet, as explored through the case example below, changing a healthcare environment often takes systemic approaches over and above curricular change, including a committed leadership, community involvement, and even architectural ingenuity.

Confronting the Hidden Curriculum by Changing the Clinical Setting: The Case of Medical College of Georgia

In the course of developing a new children's hospital in the early 1990s, the Medical College of Georgia, the health sciences university for the University System of Georgia, began exploring concepts of patient- and family-centered care. Institutional leaders supported a commitment to patient- and family-centered care as a core concept of the new Children's Medical Center, which opened in 1998. Several factors converged to make this new hospital, with its "new" approach to patient care, a reality. A group of oncology nurses proposed adopting a patient-centered care model as a way for health professionals to partner better with parents and enhance outcomes for young patients. Although hospital leadership was initially receptive to this idea, real change happened when one of the authors, the mother of a child with heart disease, challenged hospital visitation restrictions. This mother wanted to be with her son in the pediatric intensive care unit after his multiple heart surgeries and wanted to be an active partner in her child's care. Instead, she and her husband were caught in a restrictive healthcare system and, like other parents, were met with by a system of barriers.

Thanks in part to Daniel and his parents, this family's hospital underwent a transformation (Textbox 12.2). Before 1998, the hospital's policies were designed to accommodate healthcare professionals and existing systems. Parents were escorted out of the pediatric intensive care unit during nursing shift changes so as not to get in the way. Clearly, parents were considered outsiders and could only "visit" their child during specified times during the day. Although the healthcare team provided excellent medical care, a major piece was missing—the parents and families who were instrumental to a patient's healing.

As the MCG Children's Medical Center administrators and staff began to partner with families, staff came to realize that the existing culture surrounding medical care was inflexible. Through the exchange of perspectives among parents, staff, and faculty, all parties came to understand that the "rules" governing visitations actually interfered with the ideals of patient care. If parents were the "experts" in their children's lives, then they were valuable partners in the care process itself, not just distant observers of a technical care system.

Institutional leaders committed themselves to making patient- and family-centered care a core concept of their new Children's Medical Center of the Medical College of Georgia and commissioned a team of parents to work as partners in what would result in an exceptional facilities design. More than 20 parents and children worked with architects and hospital staff to ensure that the space provided a healing environment. Although facility design can be costly, leaders at MCG recognized that by involving families they could avoid poor design features that would hinder effective care in the long run. As it turned out, features that were important to parents, such as providing sleeping accommodations for them in their children's rooms, could be easily and inexpensively achieved. The end result

Textbox 12.2   A Mother's Story: A Case Example of Patient- and Family-Centered Care in Action

We watched intently as the tall technician stood on a box, his hands clasped together, vigorously pumping Daniel's chest. The lights were brilliant over our son's body, but we couldn't see his face. The faces of the medical team surrounding Daniel glistened under the OR lights—the beads of sweat, the determination, the puffed chests from holding their own breath, hushed tones, the whispered pleas, "Come on, Daniel."

Over the clicks of the machines that pumped fluids into Daniel's young body, my weary mind flashed back to those early days in the PICU. I recalled how we used to arrive at the hospital at 6 a.m. to be with Daniel. Most days, we found ourselves in a waiting room while the medical team made their rounds. We might wait as long as three or four hours only to be escorted out if another sick child was brought into the unit or it was time for nursing shift changes. As supportive and loving as our medical team was, hospital policy and procedures did not support family presence. But why did I have to leave my son's bedside? Why couldn't I hear what was said as decisions were made about him? More than that, why weren't we asked to participate in this discussion? Why was I treated as a visitor when I was the mommy?

Over time, we would come a long way from those early days as "visitors" to active participants in Daniel's care. Eventually, Daniel would undergo 12 heart-related surgeries and ultimately a heart transplant. Over the years, we watched and participated in the transitioning of our hospital to a patient- and family-centered care environment.

Most of us will never have to make a choice to watch our child die. I did. I asked to be at Daniel's side as his doctors worked furiously to revive him. We had just learned that our 14-year-old son's heart stopped during a heart catheterization procedure that he had undergone many times. Soon, Daniel was put on ECMO, a lifesaving device that pumps his blood outside his body so his heart and lungs could rest. He would need all his strength to get through the night and to withstand yet another heart transplant. I could see how sick Daniel was, yet at the same time, I rejoiced that he had made it this far. Although he was still unconscious, our family took turns sitting by his bedside, talking to him, and praying for his recovery.

As I held Daniel's IV-laden and bruised hand, I remembered a meeting I had attended just a week before his catheterization. I was advocating for parents to have the choice to be present during a code, a procedure, or anesthesia induction before surgery. I just didn't expect it to be my own son's code. Two days later, with our family and medical team encircling his bed and the early morning sun shining on the brilliant red strands of his hair, our beloved Daniel died. I realize that had it not been for the patient- and family-centered care philosophy embraced by our hospital, we would not have been with Daniel at the most critical time of his life and death.

Source: Created by Julie Moretz.

of this collaborative process was a children's hospital with an award-winning architectural design as designated by Modern Health Care (Croswell, 2000, p. 28; Pinto, 1997, p. 54).

Since the initial construction of the children's hospital in 1998, leaders at MCG continue to ensure that the concept of partnering with families and patients is an integral part of program and policy development. A hallmark of this health system's program is the way it includes more than 130 patients and family members recommended by various healthcare professionals to serve as advisors on hospital committees. The active Family Advisory Council, consisting of parents and grandparents, works together with the Children's Advisory Council for ongoing input into hospital services through the eyes of their youngest patients. As the culture shifted to this patient- and family-centered care environment, patient satisfaction benchmarks rose, with scores reaching a continuous 95th percentile and above on the Press Gainey measurement tool. Market share grew by 40% during this time period, and discharge volume increased 83% in the same period.

Medical College of Georgia Health System institutional leadership sought to extend the culture change to the adult medical center. The first successful pilot was conducted in the Neurosciences Center and quickly proved itself a nationally recognized model of care. This 20-bed unit opened in December 2003 with 10 universal intensive care unit beds, an open visitation policy, a family resource area, and organized patient advisors who interviewed all potential staff before they were hired to work on the unit. Outcomes proved successful, with a 50% decreased length of stay, a 62% decrease in medication errors, improvements in nurse retention (the RN vacancy rate dropping from 7.5% to 0%, with a waiting list of registered nurses), and dramatic improvements in patient satisfaction measures, which jumped from the tenth to the 95th percentile by Press Gainey measures.

One neurology resident's comments help illuminate why the changes made at MCG were so successful:

> When I began my internship, one of the first things I learned when caring for either a child or a patient whose illness prevented them from communicating well is that the best source of knowledge regarding the patient's condition is the family. As a medical student, I was often intimidated by the family, afraid they would ask me questions about their loved one's illness that I would be unable to answer. As I became more comfortable around patients as well as their families, I realized

that the history of what had brought the patient to me was nearly as valuable as the physical exam. In patient- and family-centered care, where family members are always welcome, I am able to perform my job as a physician much more easily as I have access to the family's perspective. . . . Often, just asking a mother what her thoughts are on what may be going on with her child can give me insight into what she is most worried about; this gives me the opportunity to discuss these fears with her. I have learned to examine patients in a compassionate manner, as there are nearly always family members looking on. This helps me remember to value the patient's privacy, and it also gives me the opportunity to discuss my findings with the family, which often eases their minds and makes them feel like they are being informed of all that is occurring in the care of their loved one.

In addition to these major changes in hospital culture and function, a family faculty was developed in 2002 to co-teach alongside the professional faculty in all five schools (medicine, nursing, allied health, dentistry, and graduate studies). A formal evaluation process of the impact of this type of collaborative teaching is under development, although student and professor surveys alike indicate high ratings in every session from students participating in this method of teaching. The institution has implemented its first baseline culture survey to measure attitudes and perceptions regarding patient- and family-centered care across the entire university. Institutional leadership has committed to implementing patient- and family-centered care principles systemically and to aligning its collective mission and values with these principles throughout its entire operation (Textbox 12.3).

CONCLUSION

The theories and examples described throughout this chapter imply that in order to achieve widespread adoption of patient- and family-centered care models across the United States, reform efforts cannot be limited to formal curricular improvements in medical schools. Biomedical approaches to care are deeply ingrained in most teaching hospitals and clinics (Roter et al., 1997), meaning that curricular reforms in medical schools are likely to have only a modest influence on how care is deliv-

---

Textbox 12.3   Key Learning Lessons from Patient Advisors for the Healthcare System

Over a 13-year period, leaders at the medical school and teaching hospital have learned the following lessons from patient advisors:

1. It is often small things that are most important: "If you are going to put windows in the waiting room of the Cancer Clinic make sure there is a heat source nearby, . . . we are all cold from our chemotherapy treatments" (Patient advisor, Oncology Center).
2. "Women getting mammograms don't want a test on Friday and lose sleep all weekend waiting for results" (Patient advisor, Breast Health Center).
3. Cardiology patients want a sense of competence, confidence, and security in receiving heart care. There are no generic spaces and no generic patients (cardiologist).
4. "We want to know what medications we are taking in the hospital; we want to know, if any error touches us, whether harm occurred or not; we want a list of medications that follows us wherever we go in the hospital" (patient advisor, MCG Health Partners).
5. "When patient advisors are in the room, we gain perspective and insight that is unavailable to us by any other means" (nurse manager).
6. "Patients hold the true knowledge of how our system works. Staff are isolated in their unique functions and duties; patients are the system's thinkers and teach staff how systems really do function" (social worker, adult medical center).

---

ered on a grand scale. Instead, reforms need to extend to all levels of the learning environment, from the classroom to mentoring relationships to the culture of teaching hospitals themselves (Haidet, Kelly, & Chou, 2005; Haidet & Stein, 2006). Achieving such changes is no small challenge, but if relationship-centered care cannot be made to work on the hospital units where patients, families, and providers live and practice, then it does not stand much of a chance of developing at all. As illustrated by the case of the Medical College of Georgia, culture change in both the classroom and the clinical care setting increases the likelihood that students *and* patients will encounter providers who embrace and model relationship-centered practices with strong communication skills at its core. These are ideas whose time has come.

REFERENCES

Addison, R. (1989). Covering over-reflecting during residency training: Using personal and professional development groups to integrate dysfunctional modes of being. In M. J. Little, & J. E. Middling (Eds.), *Becoming a physician* (pp. 87–110). New York: Springer-Verlag.

Agency for Healthcare Research and Quality. (2006). *AHRQ home page.* Retrieved October 31, 2006, from http://www.ahrq.gov.

Ashbury, F. D., Iverson, D. C., & Kralj, B. (2001). Physician communication skills: Results of a survey of general/family practitioners in Newfoundland. *Medical Education Online, 6,* 1–11. Retrieved November 2, 2006, from http://www.med-ed-online.org/res00014.htm.

Balint, M. (2000). *The doctor, his patient, and the illness* (2nd ed.; millennium reprint ed.). Edinburgh, Scotland: Churchill Livingstone.

Beach, M. C., & Inui, T. (2006). Relationship-centered care: A constructive reframing. *Journal of General Internal Medicine, 21*(Suppl 1), S3–S4-8.

Beckman, H. B., & Frankel, R. M. (1984). The effect of physician behavior on the collection of data. *Annals of Internal Medicine, 101,* 692–696.

Bosk, C. L. (2003). *Forgive and remember: Managing medical failure* (2nd ed.). Chicago: University of Chicago Press.

Candib, L. M. (1995). *Medicine and the family.* New York: Basic Books.

Cheshire, W. P. (2004). *Benchmarking bedside manner in medical education.* Retrieved October 31, 2006, from http://www.cbhd.org/resources/healthcare/cheshire_2004-09-17.htm.

Croswell, C. L. (2000). 2000 design awards. *Modern Healthcare, 30,* 27–34, 36, 38.

Dankoski, M. E., Pais, S., & Zoppi, K. A. (2003). Popcorn moments: Feminist principles in family medicine education. *Journal of Feminist Family Therapy, 15,* 55–73.

Engel, G. L. (1977). The need for a new medical model: A challenge for biomedicine. *Science, 196,* 129–136.

Epstein, R. M., & Hundert, E. M. (2002). Defining and assessing professional competence. *JAMA, 287,* 226–235.

Frankel, R. M., & Stein, T. (1999). Getting the most out of the clinical encounter: The four habits model. *Permanente Journal, 3,* 79–88.

Griffin, S. J., Kinmonth, A. L., Veltman, M. W., Gillard, S., Grant, J., & Stewart, M. (2004). Effect on health-related outcomes of interventions to alter the interaction between patients and practitioners: A systematic review of trials. *Annals of Family Medicine, 2,* 595–608.

Haas, J., & Shaffir, W. (1987). *Becoming doctors: The adoption of a cloak of competence.* Greenwich, CT: JAI Press.

Hafferty, F. W. (1998). Beyond curriculum reform: Confronting medicine's hidden curriculum. *Academic Medicine, 73,* 403–407.

Hafferty, F. W., & Franks, R. (1994). The hidden curriculum, ethics teaching, and the structure of medical education. *Academic Medicine, 69,* 861–871.

Haidet, P., Kelly, P. A., & Chou, C. (2005). Characterizing the patient-centeredness of hidden curricula in medical schools: Development and validation of a new measure. *Academic Medicine, 80,* 44–50.

Haidet, P., & Stein, H. F. (2006). The role of the student-teacher relationship in the formation of physicians. The hidden curriculum as process. *Journal of General Internal Medicine, 21*(Suppl 1), S16–S20.

Institute for Family-Centered Care. *FAQ (frequently asked questions)*. Retrieved October 31, 2006, from http://www.familycenteredcare.org/faq.html.

Institute of Medicine. (2000). *To err is human: Building a safer health system*. Washington, DC: National Academy Press.

Institute of Medicine. (2001). *Crossing the quality chasm: A new health system for the 21st century*. Washington, DC: National Academy Press.

Inui, T. S. (2003). *A flag in the wind: Educating for professionalism in medicine*. Washington, DC: Association of American Medical Colleges.

Leach, D. C. (2002). Competence is a habit. *JAMA, 287*, 243–244.

Levinson, W., Gorawara-Bhat, R., & Lamb, J. (2000). A study of patient clues and physician responses in primary care and surgical settings. *JAMA, 284*, 1021–1027.

Ludmerer, K. M. (1999). *Time to heal: American medical education from the turn of the century to the era of managed care*. Oxford, UK: Oxford University Press.

Maguire, P. (1999). Improving communication with cancer patients. *European Journal of Cancer, 35*, 2058–2065.

Makoul, G. (2001). Essential elements of communication in medical encounters: The Kalamazoo consensus statement. *Academic Medicine, 76*, 390–393.

Marvel, M. K., Epstein, R. M., Flowers, K., & Beckman, H. B. (1999). Soliciting the patient's agenda: Have we improved? *JAMA, 281*, 283–287.

Miller, W. (2004). The clinical hand: A curricular map for relationship-centered care. *Family Medicine, 36*, 330–335.

Moore, P. L. (1997). Patients unhappy, AHA/Picker say. *Profiles in Healthcare Marketing, 13*, 37–41.

Ong, L. M., de Haes, J. C., Hoos, A. M., & Lammes, F. B. (1995). Doctor–patient communication: A review of the literature. *Social Science & Medicine, 40*, 903–918.

Partnerships in health care: Transforming relation process. (1998). In A. L. Suchman, R. J. Botelho, & P. Hinton-Walker (Eds.), Rochester, NY: University of Rochester Press.

Pellegrino, E. D. (1999). The origins and evolution of bioethics: Some personal reflections. *Kennedy Institute of Ethics Journal, 9*, 73–88.

Pinto, C. (1997). 1997 design awards. *Modern Healthcare, 27*, 47–48, 50–62.

Roter, D. (2000). The enduring and evolving nature of the patient–physician relationship. *Patient Education and Counseling, 39*, 5–15.

Roter, D. L., Stewart, M., Putnam, S. M., Lipkin, M., Jr., Stiles, W., & Inui, T. S. (1997). Communication patterns of primary care physicians. *JAMA, 277*, 350–356.

Schirmer, J. M., Mauksch, L., Lang, F., Marvel, M. K., Zoppi, K., Epstein, R. M., et al. (2005). Assessing communication competence: A review of current tools. *Family Medicine, 37*, 184–192.

Shank, J. C., & Zoppi, K. (2001). The well-trained resident in behavioral medicine. *Clinics in Family Practice, 3*, 127–138.

Smith, R. C., Lyles, J. S., Mettler, J., Stoffelmayr, B. E., Van Egeren, L. F., Marshall, A. A., et al. (1998). The effectiveness of intensive training for residents in interviewing: A randomized, controlled study. *Annals of Internal Medicine, 128*, 118–126.

Stewart, M., Brown, J. B., Donner, A., McWhinney, I. R., Oates, J., Weston, W. W., et al. (2000). The impact of patient-centered care on outcomes. *Journal of Family Practice, 49*, 796–804.

Stewart, M., Brown, J. B., Weston, W. W., McWhinney, I. R., McWilliam, C. L., & Freeman, T. R. (2003). *Patient-centered medicine: Transforming the clinical method* (2nd ed.). Abingdon, UK: Radcliffe Medical Press.

Suchman, A. L., Williamson, P. R., Litzelman, D. K., Frankel, R. M., Mossbarger, D. L., Inui, T. S., et al. (2004). Toward an informal curriculum that teaches professionalism: Transforming the social environment of a medical school. *Journal of General Internal Medicine, 19,* 501–504.

Through the patient's eyes: Understanding and promoting patient-centered care. (2002). In M. Gerteis, S. Edgman-Levitan, J. Daley, & T. L. Delbanco (Eds.) (1st paperback ed.). San Francisco: Jossey-Bass.

Tresolini C. P., & The Pew-Fetzer Task Force. (1994). *Health professions education and relationship-centered care.* San Francisco: Pew Health Professions Commission.

Williams, B. C., Hall, K. E., Supiano, M. A., Fitzgerald, J. T., & Halter, J. B. (2006). Development of a standardized patient instructor to teach functional assessment and communication skills to medical students and house officers. *Journal of the American Geriatrics Society, 54,* 1147–1152.

Zoppi, K., & Epstein, R. M. (2001). Interviewing in medical settings. In J. Gubrium, & J. Holstein (Eds.), *Handbook of interview research* (pp. 355–383). Thousand Oaks, CA: Sage Publications.

Zoppi, K., & Epstein, R. M. (2002). Is communication a skill? Communication behaviors and being in relation. *Family Medicine, 34,* 319–324.

Zoppi, K., & McKegney, C. (1997). The difficult clinical interview. In M. Mengel, & W. L. Holleman (Eds.), *Fundamentals of clinical practice: A patient-centered approach.* New York: Plenum Medical Book Co.

CHAPTER 13

Advocacy for Improving End-of-Life Care: A 30-Year Healthcare Cultural Revolution

Gary S. Winzelberg and Laura C. Hanson

OBJECTIVES

- To explain how patient advocacy efforts from families and ethicists resulted in the legal precedents and tools that protect patient autonomy for those who are incapacitated
- To describe how the development of hospice and palliative care have created better systems for providing quality end-of-life care
- To illustrate the efforts of clinicians to create patient-centered models of care and to increase professional education in end-of-life care
- To identify future directions for end-of-life care advocacy

She was already transformed by her disease. Her face was drawn and pale, eyes closed with fatigue, and her belly tense with fluid. Every other day a physician drew fluid from her abdomen. Despite this repeated procedure, it continued to accumulate and crept inevitably up into her lungs.

Her husband sat near her bedside every day, touching her hand or bringing her small comforts. Both of them seemed quiet and reserved, and he rarely burdened her with questions or small talk. In his admission note, the physician noted that they were Christian Scientists who had violated church teaching to come here, once prayer had failed to heal her ovarian cancer.

On the day when oxygen and fluid removal could no longer satisfy her need to breathe or relieve the pain in her abdomen, she was moved to an intensive care unit (ICU). Her husband followed her bed as it was rolled down the hall, but as is customary, he was not allowed to come into the ICU while the doctors and nurses "worked on her." Over the next several hours, she lay under cover of sterile drapes as an arterial line was placed in her arm, a central line in her neck, and a breathing tube inserted into her throat.

Her husband called back every 30 minutes or so, asking whether he could see his wife. Each time the nurse reported that the doctors were still working and that he would need to wait. His expression grew more pained, but he never protested. Finally, after hours of effort, his wife died. The doctors stepped away, and a nurse escorted him back to her room where he again sat, quietly touching her hand. He did not say anything more.

The need to improve the quality of care for dying patients in the United States has been evident for more than three decades. In this country, most people die from chronic incurable illnesses such as cancer, heart failure, and emphysema. Many dying patients receive inadequate symptom management (SUPPORT Principal Investigators, 1995) and yet receive life-prolonging treatments even if they prefer care that maximizes comfort (Teno, Fisher, Hamel, Coppola, & Dawson, 2002). Most Americans die in hospitals or nursing homes despite an expressed desire for death at home (Pritchard et al., 1998). Family caregivers are also affected—one in five leaves employment to provide in-home care, and many experience physical and psychological stress while caring for a loved one (Covinsky et al., 1994). In addition, families are financially impacted, as one third report spending a majority of their savings to cover medical costs of end-of-life care (Covinsky et al., 1994; Schulz & Beach, 1999). Physicians and other health professionals receive little training in managing end-of-life care symptoms and communicating with patients and families about treatment decisions.

Although the goal of ensuring that all dying patients receive quality care has not yet been accomplished, patient advocacy efforts in the fields of law, healthcare delivery and financing, health services research, and professional education have all made important contributions to improving end-of-life care nationally. Each effort considered individually represents an evolutionary change in this country's healthcare culture; however, taken together, patient advocacy activities have resulted in a system-level revolution in the care of individuals at the end of life. For example, patient advocacy in end-of-life care has led to:

1. The development of advance directives that promote autonomy and patient-centered care through respect for decision-making preferences and the right to refuse life-prolonging treatments.
2. The creation and growth of hospice and palliative care to provide dying patients with alternatives to disease-oriented treatments offered in hospitals.
3. The growth of health services research defining the scope and severity of end-of-life care deficiencies and identifying care areas most in need of system-level change.
4. The support of end-of-life care research, education, and clinical program development by national professional organizations, private foundations, and the National Institutes of Health.
5. The recognition of palliative care as a distinct health profession specialty that relieves suffering and improves quality of life for patients with advanced illnesses and their families (Morrison & Meier, 2004). In turn, this recognition has led to a great expansion of the number of physicians and nurses with clinical end-of-life care expertise.

This chapter analyzes these five dimensions of end-of-life advocacy, suggesting that the field of end-of-life care may serve as a model for how patient advocacy as a whole can accomplish its aims. Specifically, the end-of-life movement offers models for how advocates may transform grassroots efforts to improve healthcare across the spectrum from individuals' lives to system-level reforms that hold promise for satisfying patient and family priorities. This chapter also addresses the impact and limitations of these initiatives and considers future directions for patient advocacy as the health system seeks to meet the challenges of providing quality end-of-life care to an aging population.

LEGAL ADVOCACY

The roots of patient advocacy in end-of-life care grew from the public response to the proliferation of life-saving medical treatments in the 1960s. The adoption of these new treatments not only prolonged patients' lives but also prolonged the deaths of those left uncured. Patients survived illnesses that previously would have been fatal with interventions such as cardiopulmonary resuscitation, mechanical ventilation, kidney dialysis, and tube feeding. The first end-of-life care advocates were family members of patients incapacitated by acute, unexpected brain injuries who sought to represent their loved ones' wishes by discontinuing their life-sustaining treatments.

The names of Karen Ann Quinlan and Nancy Cruzan may not be as familiar to Americans as that of Terri Schiavo, yet the plights of these other two young women challenged the legal and medical communities to better define the rights of patients and their families to control the use of medical treatments. These three young women—Quinlan in the 1970s, Cruzan in the 1980s, and Schiavo in the 1990s and 2000s—were kept alive in persistent vegetative states through life-sustaining medical treatments. Their circumstances came to the public's attention as the ethical dilemmas faced by their families evolved into legal conflicts regarding cessation of life-sustaining treatments.

For many Americans, the Quinlan, Cruzan, and Schiavo cases epitomize the core problem with end-of-life care: dying patients who are unable to communicate their preferences are kept alive using medical technologies they may not want while they are powerless to determine their treatment. The conflicts involving these women have helped solidify the right of dying patients to determine their medical decisions, either themselves, or through prior expression of wishes and the voices of surrogate decision makers. This principle of patient autonomy promoted through patient advocacy is now well-ingrained within the healthcare system. Yet, as this section shows, these three well-known cases and the issues they raised produced mixed results and, moreover, overshadowed other important, effective efforts to improve respect for patient preferences through advance care planning.

The Karen Ann Quinlan Case

The first end-of-life care case to gain national notoriety involved Karen Ann Quinlan, a young woman in a persistent vegetative state resulting from a drug overdose in the early 1970s. The right of a capable patient to make medical decisions, even decisions that could hasten death, was not in question; however, as with Ms. Quinlan, most life-sustaining treatment withdrawal decisions affect incapacitated patients (Hanson, Danis, Mutran, & Keenan, 1994). Both her physicians and parents sought to make medical decisions for Ms. Quinlan, and a legal conflict ensued when her physicians questioned whether her parents, who were not considered her guardians since she was over the age of 18, had the right to request that the mechanical ventilator assisting her breathing be removed.

A 1976 New Jersey Supreme Court decision granted her parents authority to serve as their daughter's guardians, after which they were legally able to order that their daughter's ventilator be removed. The court supported the parents' request for decision-making authority based on the principle of "substituted judgment," meaning that they could best represent the decisions that Ms. Quinlan would have made if conscious. This decision recognized patients' decision-making autonomy even when incapacitated through the use of a surrogate decision maker, usually a spouse or blood relative. This surrogate is responsible for enacting the patient's stated wishes before becoming incapacitated or using his or her best judgment when explicit instructions were not given.

The Quinlan case demonstrated the need for patients to have loved ones who could represent their treatment preferences if they became incapacitated. In response, ethicists began to promote advance care planning and developed advance directives as mechanisms for patients to specify treatment preferences and select preferred decision makers in advance of any condition associated with decision-making incapacity. The use of a living will—a document to record treatment preferences for use in future illnesses—was first proposed at the time of the Quinlan case (Bok, 1976) to establish an individual's end-of-life care treatment preferences. During the same time, the "do not resuscitate" or DNR order was implemented at Beth Israel Hospital in Boston as a unique physician order, designed to prevent unwanted cardiopulmonary resuscitation attempts in the event of a cardiac arrest (Rabkin, Gillerman, & Rice, 1976).

The Nancy Cruzan Case

While the Quinlan decision fostered the creation of advance directives, the case of Nancy Cruzan, a young woman in a persistent vegetative state after suffering a brain injury in an automobile accident, encouraged their use nationally in the late 1980s. Ms. Cruzan's parents requested removal of her feeding tube, but their request was denied by the Missouri Supreme Court based on inadequate evidence of her preferences. In 1990, the U.S. Supreme Court affirmed the state's position, ruling that individual states could establish standards regarding the "clear and convincing" evidence necessary to establish an incapacitated patient's treatment preferences. In a later state court hearing, further evidence of her preferences was presented, and the feeding tube was withdrawn.

The Cruzan case led to national and state legislation on advance directives following the particular legal support the Supreme Court decision gave to patients' designations of healthcare proxies (Annas, 1990). In the year after the Cruzan decision, the U.S. Congress enacted the Patient Self-Determination Act, requiring all healthcare facilities receiving federal funding to ask patients on admission if they have an advance directive and to provide patients with help in completing a directive if requested. Over the next two decades, all states established laws specifying the process for making decisions on behalf of incapacitated patients, determining which evidence is required to discontinue life-sustaining measures and when advance directives will be granted legal authority.

The Patient Self-Determination Act and the dissemination of advance directives transformed early legal advocacy for individual patients into a national standard for fostering communication within the healthcare system and for respecting patients' treatment preferences. Although disagreements between families and physicians remain inevitable (Breen, Abernethy, Abbott, & Tulsky, 2001), the Quinlan and Cruzan decisions resulted in a general acceptance among health professionals that families have a critical role in assisting with end-of-life care decision making when patients become incapacitated. This acceptance, in turn, allows for clinical rather than legal decision making to resolve these conflicts in nearly all cases.

Most recently, the legal conflict between the parents and husband of Terri Schiavo, another young woman in a persistent vegetative state, gained national attention in 2005. After years of tube feeding, Ms. Schiavo's husband requested removal of this form of life-sustaining treatment, but her parents objected. Ms. Schiavo was assessed many times by physicians, and her case was repeatedly reviewed by local courts, which consistently sided with Mr. Schiavo; however, in 2005, the conflict in the case was magnified by public involvement on both sides. First, state legislators in Florida and later the U.S. Congress enacted laws attempting to prolong Schiavo's life (Annas, 2005). Eventually, Ms. Schiavo did have her feeding tube removed and died under the hospice care she had long received. Her case serves as a reminder that advance directives can have an important role in end-of-life care decision making. Ms. Schiavo's protracted legal dispute would likely have been avoided if she had signed a living will or formally designated her husband as her healthcare proxy.

Limitations of Legal Advocacy

Endorsement of patient autonomy and its exercise through advance directives have been major benefits of legal advocacy. Despite the utility of advance directives in individual cases, however, their overall impact on improving end-of-life care quality has been limited. Less than half of seriously ill patients complete advance directives, and use of advance directives is less common for people in ethnic and racial minority groups (Winzelberg, Hanson, & Tulsky, 2005). In addition, advance directives are not always available at the time decisions must be made, and their language may not be relevant to all medical circumstances (Winzelberg et al., 2005).

Advance directives appeal to patients who seek to protect themselves against undesired life-sustaining treatments and are willing to designate a specific surrogate decision maker. Compared with white patients, individuals from racial and ethnic minority groups are more likely to request continuation of life-sustaining treatments and therefore are less likely to complete a living will or designate a proxy decision maker. They also may be more accustomed to making decisions as a family and feel uncomfortable deciding on a healthcare proxy as this legalistic standard forces them to choose one decision maker among their loved ones.

Beyond Advance Directives

Since their inception, there have been multiple attempts among patient advocates to modify advance directives to increase their use and impact on end-of-life care decisions. Initiatives that have been successful include community-based efforts to increase advance care planning. In La Crosse, Wisconsin, a relatively homogeneous community with a defined set of healthcare services, a community-based group developed the Respecting Choices initiative to promote completion of advance directives. Implementation of the Respecting Choices program was associated with almost complete consistency between patients' actual treatment decisions and their previously documented preferences and may have reduced hospital care at the end of life (Hammes & Rooney, 1998).

In the state of Oregon, public attention to advance directives was catalyzed by the debate around legalization of physician-assisted suicide. Healthcare providers, ethicists, and patient advocates recognized that public support for assisted suicide reflected a broader desire to improve patient control over circumstances of dying. This group designed a universal and portable set of end-of-life treatment orders that was binding regardless of the patient's healthcare setting. The Physician Orders for Life-Sustaining Treatment Program (POLST) is a physician's order regarding end-of-life treatment. It is available to patients in all settings, but has primarily been used to increase documentation of nursing home residents' treatment preferences. A majority of Oregon nursing homes and hospices voluntarily participate in this program, with one study suggesting that no patients received unwanted intensive care, mechanical ventilation, or cardiopulmonary resuscitation (Tolle, Tilden, Nelson, & Dunn, 1998). The successes of both the Respecting Choices and POLST programs have led other communities and states to implement these initiatives (Oregon Health & Science University, 2005).

Although establishing patients' rights to make end-of-life care treatment withdrawal and withholding decisions has been the central focus of legal advocacy during the past 30 years, some advocates have sought to expand dying patients' rights to include access to physician-assisted suicide. Oregon is presently the only state that has legalized physician-assisted suicide. The effect of patients' rights to physician-assisted suicide on their end-of-life care experience remains both uncertain and controversial. Some patient advocates assert that the availability of physician-assisted suicide increases patients' control over their dying experience. Other advocates raise concerns that patients will choose physician-assisted suicide because of the unavailability of quality end-of-life care. Oregon's experience suggests that few dying patients request physician-assisted suicide and an even smaller number of patients actually complete their suicides (Hedberg, Hopkins, & Kohn, 2003).

Legal advocacy has served to raise public awareness of the need to ensure protection for patients' end-of-life care decision-making rights and develop mechanisms such as advance directives to promote the healthcare system's respect for patients' treatment preferences at the end of life. Other forms of advocacy are required to move beyond the limits of advance directives.

> In the hospital, the patient, his family, and his physicians all acknowledged that his heart disease could no longer be improved with medication or surgery. He had received several stents to open blocked arteries, had been in the ICU a few times for intensive management of medication, and still his heart kept failing.

Long ago, when his heart attacks first began, he had prepared a living will in anticipation of the worst. His wishes were that, in the face of incurable and terminal illness, no further life-sustaining treatments should be used. His fondest wish at this time was to be made comfortable at home; however, his doctors simply couldn't imagine it. How could all of the careful medication titration take place? Who in his family had the strength to lift him in and out of bed? And what would happen when those potentially agonizing final moments came—wouldn't the family panic and call 911?

HEALTHCARE DELIVERY AND FINANCING ADVOCACY

Despite the attention given to the Quinlan, Cruzan, and Schiavo cases and physician-assisted suicide debate, most end-of-life care decisions are made at the bedside among patients, families, and health professionals and occur without significant rancor or requests for hastened death. Fortunately, the vast majority of families with an incapacitated loved one do not experience intense conflict or legal action. For this large majority of patients and their families, quality of end-of-life care is about the capabilities and resources of the healthcare system rather than the presence or absence of a binding legal document, such as an advance directive. In parallel to efforts surrounding legal rights, patient advocates have championed care delivery and financing reforms during the past 30 years to address concerns that the healthcare system serves dying patients poorly. Callahan (2005) described the development of a schism in medicine in the 1970s between those who considered death an enemy and advocated for increasing research to cure diseases, as exemplified by President Nixon's war on cancer, and those who recognized that death was unavoidable and sought to promote terminally ill patients' comfort and quality of life.

Traditional health services emphasize cure and prolonged survival, but may not always match the needs and preferences of patients living with incurable chronic illness. Diseases such as cancer and heart disease became chronic conditions that patients could live with for months or even years before their deaths; however, disease treatments such as chemotherapy and heart disease medications are not taken without consequences. Patients may experience pain and other physical symptoms related to their underlying incurable illnesses and to the treatments keeping them alive. The course of disease from diagnosis to death has become longer, with increased time spent in recurrent hospitalizations and functional dependency.

Hospice

Hospice began as a community-based response by advocates seeking an alternative to hospital-based deaths. In the United States, the objective of hospice's founders was that patients should receive pain relief, comfort, and supportive care in the face of terminal prognoses and, whenever possible, die at home (Foley, 2005). Hospice focuses on caring rather than curing and provides dying patients and their families with expert symptom management and psychosocial support. Hospice also offers bereavement services for patients' loved ones.

The creation of the Medicare hospice benefit in 1982 transformed hospice from a sporadic community-based initiative into a national program offering a patient- and family-centered care model. This transformation has yielded contradictory effects. On the one hand, the use of hospice services by dying patients has steadily expanded as Medicare, Medicaid, and private insurance all include hospice as a covered benefit. Families of dying patients express greater satisfaction with pain and symptom control and quality of terminal care when patients enroll in hospice (Baer & Hanson, 2000; Teno et al., 2004). In 2004, almost one million patients annually were enrolled in a hospice program, representing approximately one third of all adult deaths (National Hospice and Palliative Care Organization).

Although insurance coverage has expanded access, hospice eligibility criteria and service limitations have created barriers to its use by some patient populations (Lorenz, Asch, Rosenfeld, Liu, & Ettner, 2004). Patients must relinquish some care options on joining a hospice program. In particular, they are not permitted to receive disease-specific treatments intended to cure or prolong life. In addition, physicians are required to confirm that the patient has six months or less to live if the terminal disease follows an expected progression. Despite enabling patients to die at home, hospice programs are only able to provide limited home-based services, and patients must therefore have a primary caregiver. Hospice programs are responsible for all of the patients' medications, medical equipment, and nursing services although Medicare reimburses them per patient day rather than by the services provided. Although the regulations prohibiting curative treatment and requiring a six-month-or-less diagnosis were designed to reduce costs and prevent misuse of the benefit, patients must sometimes choose between discontinuing hospice or foregoing treatments that could promote comfort and quality of life such as blood transfusions or palliative radiation.

These eligibility criteria and service limitations have meant that historically hospice has disproportionately served terminally ill patients with cancer who have family to care for them at home or those who live in a nursing home. Doctors have difficulty formulating prognoses for any terminal illness (Christakis, 1999), although many cancers have a more predictable progression compared with diseases such as dementia or heart disease. Since 2004, however, noncancer diagnoses such as end-stage heart disease, dementia, and lung disease have made up a majority (54%) of hospice admissions (National Hospice and Palliative Care Organization).

Palliative Care

The growth of hospice programs during the past 20 years has contributed to culture change within the healthcare system, although it has become clear that hospice cannot be the only end-of-life care program given its current utilization barriers. Palliative care emerged during the past decade as a largely hospital-based initiative that complements hospice (Morrison & Meier, 2004). Although there is not a single definition, the World Health Organization describes palliative care as an approach, which improves the quality of life of patients and their families facing life-threatening illness, through the prevention, assessment, and treatment of pain and other physical, psychosocial, and spiritual problems (Billings, 1998). Although palliative care and hospice share the same commitment to excellent symptom management and patient- and family-centered care, palliative care functions as an evaluation and management clinical service. Interdisciplinary palliative care teams deliver care regardless of stage of disease or prognosis. Palliative care services may be delivered concurrently with delivery of disease-specific treatments.

Hospital-based palliative care programs have dramatically expanded since the late 1990s (Morrison, Maroney-Galin, Kralovec, & Meier, 2005).

The percentage of U.S. hospitals offering palliative care services increased from 15% in 2000 to 25% in 2003, and there has been additional growth since. Palliative care programs are not equally distributed across the United States. Hospitals are more likely to have established programs if they are located in New England, have an academic affiliation with a medical school, and/or are large in size. The Veterans Administration (VA) has made palliative care an organizational priority and provided funding for VA hospitals throughout the country to develop palliative care services. In addition, palliative care programs help hospitals meet accreditation standards established by the Joint Commission on Accreditation for Healthcare Organizations (JCAHO) (Center to Advance Palliative Care, 2004). JCAHO accredits all U.S. hospitals, and hospitals' recognition that palliative care satisfies accreditation criteria will likely promote continued development and expansion of palliative care programs.

The development and growth of palliative care have also been fostered by several advocacy organizations formed during the past 10 years to address the needs of dying patients and their families. The Center to Advance Palliative Care provides technical assistance to hospitals in the process of forming palliative care programs. Caring Connections, a program of the National Hospice and Palliative Care Organization, provides individuals with end-of-life care resources. Both Center to Advance Palliative Care and Caring Connections have been funded by the Robert Wood Johnson Foundation as part of its grant-making strategy to enhance end-of-life care professional education, institutional change, and public engagement (Welsfeld, Miller, Gibson, & Schroeder, 2000). Other foundations that have provided significant support to promoting quality end-of-life care include the Project on Death in America of the Open Society Institute and Soros Foundation, the Fetzer Foundation, the United Hospital Fund, the Aetna Foundation, and the Greenwall Foundation.

CLINICAL RESEARCH ADVOCACY

Many examples of patient advocacy come from individuals working outside of the healthcare system to effect changes within the system. End-of-life care advocacy is one example in which health professionals have promoted reforms through research initiatives to demonstrate poor quality care and test innovative healthcare delivery.

Study to Understand Prognoses and Preferences for Outcomes and Risks of Treatment

The Study to Understand Prognoses and Preferences for Outcomes and Risks of Treatment (SUPPORT) was a remarkable endeavor that greatly raised awareness among health professionals, policy makers, and the public about the need to improve end-of-life care (Welsfeld et al., 2000). SUPPORT galvanized patient advocacy in end-of-life care by demonstrating the extent of care quality deficiencies affecting seriously ill hospitalized patients and the ineffectiveness of a nursing intervention to improve care (SUPPORT Principal Investigators, 1995). Conducted from 1989 to 1994 and funded by the Robert Wood Johnson Foundation, physician-researchers examined the hospitalizations of almost 10,000 patients admitted with one of eight terminal diseases to five geographically distinct teaching hospitals. These diseases included cancer, heart failure, and emphysema.

Many patients who participated in SUPPORT died either during their initial hospitalization or in subsequent months. Half of the dying patients experienced moderate to severe pain in their final days according to their families, whereas other symptoms such as shortness of breath also occurred commonly. More than one third of patients who died spent 10 or more days in an ICU, and less than one half of physicians knew when their patients preferred to avoid a cardiopulmonary resuscitation attempt. As a result, many patients received care that was inconsistent with their treatment preferences, especially if they preferred a comfort-focused approach (Teno et al., 2002).

After learning of these care deficiencies, the SUPPORT investigators designed an intervention based on the assumption that greater communication of patient treatment preferences would change care. Trained nurses interviewed patients and their family members and placed information regarding prognosis and treatment preferences in the medical record; however, this approach did not significantly change patients' hospital experiences in pain management, treatment decision making, or cost of care.

Although SUPPORT did not demonstrate how to improve the care of dying patients in U.S. hospitals, the more than 200 papers published using SUPPORT data quantified the need to improve end-of-life care. In addition, the failure of the intervention phase, modeled on advance directives, raised new questions and promoted innovation in interventions other than advance directives to improve care for dying patients. Multiple national professional organizations such as the American Medical Association (1996) and the Institute of Medicine (1997) affirmed this need and proposed an agenda for reforming clinical practice.

Beyond SUPPORT

An essential part of this agenda was moving beyond advance directives to increase end-of-life research, amplify professional education in end-of-life care, and further develop patient-centered models of care. Clinical researchers expanded their approaches, using the methods of social science to develop a patient- and family-centered model of quality end-of-life care. Interdisciplinary teams of investigators used focus groups, interviews, and national surveys to better understand patient, caregiver, and healthcare provider perspectives regarding end-of-life care quality (Singer, Martin, & Kelner, 1999; Steinhauser & Clipp et al., 2000; Steinhauser & Christakis et al., 2000), including factors contributing to the quality of physicians' care (Curtis et al., 2001).

These efforts have helped explain why the SUPPORT study found that symptom management, physician knowledge of patient care preferences, and appropriate use of life-prolonging technologies were not necessarily most important to patients or their families.

One national survey asked respondents to rate the importance of 44 end-of-life care quality attributes (Steinhauser & Christakis et al., 2000). Twenty-six attributes were rated as important by more than 70% of patients, bereaved family members, and health professionals, including pain and symptom management, preparation for death, achieving a sense of completion, decisions about treatment preferences, and being treated as a "whole person." Some items were rated more highly by patients than physicians, such as being mentally aware, having funeral arrangements planned, not being a burden, helping others, and coming to peace with God.

From an advocacy perspective, this survey demonstrates both areas of consensus that may be promoted as practice standards and areas of variation in defining end-of-life quality that might require more individualized and culturally sensitive approaches. Patient-centered research consistently endorses the importance of pain control and patient and family input into critical treatment decisions. Notably, patients and families are unified in advocating for improved physician communication regarding their end-of-life care concerns and decisions. They identify physician communication as important to end-of-life quality (Curtis et al., 2001) and express dissatisfaction with how physicians currently communicate (Hanson, Danis, & Garrett, 1997; Teno et al., 2004).

In another survey, almost one third of bereaved family members in a national survey wanted but did not have contact with a physician, lacked information to prepare them for what to expect during their loved one's dying processes, and reported inadequate emotional support from physicians (Teno et al., 2004). One quarter of the family members desired greater involvement in their loved one's end-of-life care decisions. Desires to die at home and concerns related to spiritual care and family involvement are best handled with sensitivity toward patients' and families' heterogeneous priorities. In 2005, the National Consensus Project published practice guidelines for palliative care after convening health professional and patient advocate groups to review existing evidence. These consensus guidelines will be applied in future policy and education efforts to promote best care practices for dying patients (National Consensus Project for Quality Palliative Care, 2006).

HEALTH PROFESSIONAL EDUCATION ADVOCACY

Programs such as Education on Palliative and End-of-Life Care and End-of-Life Nursing Education Consortium train practicing physicians, nurses, and other professionals in core end-of-life care competencies as well as prepare them to become educators within their own hospitals and practice settings. This "train-the-trainer" model recognizes that end-of-life care specialists cannot meet the demand for physician education themselves to achieve the goal of improving care quality on a national level. The training modules of End-of-Life Nursing Education Consortium's core curriculum are summarized in Table 13.1 (Fox et al., 1999).

Another component of the agenda, endorsed by national organizations, has been to increase end-of-life care education and training for medical and nursing students and trainees. The development and growth of palliative care as a medical and nursing specialty parallel the expanding number of palliative care programs in U.S. hospitals. There are currently 2,145

Table 13.1   End-of-Life Care Terminology

Advance care planning: A broad term that encompasses the different aspects of planning for end-of-life care, including discussions in which patients, families, and clinicians explore goals of care in the context of current health and potential health declines; discussion of treatment options; completion of an **advance directive** document that articulates those wishes.

Advance directive: A legal document, such as a **living will** or **healthcare proxy**, that specifies a patient's preferences for care in particular situations and that is used if and when a patient is incapacitated.

Do not resuscitate (DNR) order: This is a written physician's order that prevents the healthcare team from initiating cardiopulmonary resuscitation (CPR) in the event that a patient's heart stops. The success of CPR is extremely low in persons who are already approaching the end of life.

Healthcare proxy (or "power of attorney"): This is an advance directive that designates and authorizes a family member, loved one, or other trusted individual to make medical decisions for an incapacitated patient.

Hospice: End-of-life care that provides comfort and support for patients near the end of life as well as their families. In general, hospice is provided at a patient's home where it aims to make the patient comfortable through **symptom management** and psychosocial support after curative treatment has stopped. To receive hospice, a physician must state that if the disease follows its normal progression, the patient's death may be expected within six months. It is paid for by Medicare and private insurance.

Living will: An **advance directive** that guides a patient's family and healthcare team, explaining the medical treatment the patient wishes to receive if incapacitated.

Palliative care (or "palliative medicine"): An approach to life-threatening illness that improves the quality of life of patients and their families through the prevention, assessment, and treatment of pain and other physical, psychosocial, and spiritual problems. It is generally provided in hospitals, functioning as an evaluation and management clinical service. Interdisciplinary palliative care teams deliver care regardless of stage of disease or prognosis. Palliative care services, unlike **hospice**, may be delivered concurrently with disease-specific curative treatments.

Physician-assisted suicide: This process is where doctors assist terminally ill patients in taking their own life. The physician does not *directly* cause the patient's death but enables the patient to choose the time and circumstances of his or her

(continued)

Table 13.1   End-of-Life Care Terminology (continued)

own death. In Oregon, the only state where physician-assisted suicide is legal, the law requires patients to be 18 or older, a resident of the state, capable of informed consent, diagnosed with a terminal illness that will lead to death within six months, and not suffering from depression or another mental disorder, based on the assessment of two physicians.

Physician orders for life-sustaining treatment (POLST): The POLST form is a physician's order form that is a kind of **advance care planning** in that it is a way of summarizing an individual's wishes regarding life-sustaining treatment. Started in Oregon, where it is primarily used in nursing home settings, it has been adopted in other states. The form is intended for any individual with an advanced life-limiting illness and is portable from one care setting to another.

Symptom management: Care given to improve the quality of life of patients who have a serious or life-threatening disease. The goal of symptom management is to prevent or treat as the symptoms of the disease, such as pain or breathlessness, and side effects caused by treatment.

physicians certified by the American Board of Hospice and Palliative Medicine (American Board of Hospice and Palliative Medicine, 2006). The number of physician fellowship training programs in palliative medicine is increasing, and standards for accreditation of these programs were recently established. In June 2006, the American College of Graduate Medical Education recognized Hospice and Palliative Medicine as a new discipline for medical training, and in the fall of 2006, the American Board of Internal Medicine will sponsor Palliative Medicine as a new subspecialty certification. These steps toward professional training, recognition, and certification reinforce support for future education and training.

Other initiatives have focused on documenting needs for improved education for health professionals (Billings & Block, 1997). For example, textbooks published during the past few decades provided detailed information about the diagnosis and treatment approaches to terminal diseases but gave little if any attention to their prognoses (Christakis, 1999) and expected course during patients' final days or weeks.

FUTURE ADVOCACY DIRECTIONS

Substantial changes in the care of dying patients have occurred during the past 30 years, yet additional reforms will be needed to ensure that patients receive high-quality end-of-life care consistent with their values and supportive of their families' needs:

1. **Communication skills to support advance care planning.** The flexibility of advance care planning should be increased to better address the priorities of an increasingly multicultural and aging population (Winzelberg et al., 2005). Many patients and physicians alike currently associate advance care planning with completing an advance directive. Yet this perspective does not serve the majority of patients who do not complete a directive. Physicians should inform or reassure patients that written documents are only the beginning of communication about good medical decisions, and in order to accomplish this goal, there must be improved health professional training in communication skills, with a focus on eliciting patients' care preferences, quality-of-life perceptions, and desired level of family decision-making involvement. Tables 13.2 and 13.3 summarize communication approaches with either capable patients or families of incapacitated patients that place advance directives in the context of the physician's commitment to understanding and respecting the patient's decision-making priorities (Annas, 2005).

2. **Policy reforms for hospice.** The Medicare hospice benefit should be redesigned to increase utilization among patients with noncancer diagnoses and a less certain trajectory toward death. Eligibility should no longer be based solely on prognosis but rather on confirmation of a patient's irreversible functional decline associated with an incurable disease. Although hospice use for patients with a noncancer diagnosis has been increasing (National Hospice and Palliative Care Organization), the prognosis estimate requirement has had the unintended effect of disproportionate hospice use for cancer patients. This has been due in part to the increased difficulty of prognostication in patients in diseases such as dementia, congestive heart failure, and emphysema (Fox et al., 1999). In addition, hospice programs' resources to provide home services should be expanded to enable patients without a full-time caregiver to remain at home.

Table 13.2 End-of-Life Nursing Education Consortium: Core Curriculum Training Modules

1. *Nursing care at the end of life.* Overview of death and dying in America, principles and goals of hospice and palliative care, dimensions of and barriers to quality care at the end of life, concepts of suffering and healing, role of the nurse in end-of-life care.

2. *Pain management.* Definitions of pain, current status of and barriers to pain relief, components of pain assessment, specific pharmacological, and nonpharmacological therapies, including concerns for special populations.

3. *Symptom management.* Detailed overview of symptoms commonly experienced at the end of life, and for each, the cause, impact on quality of life, assessment, and pharmacological/nonpharmacological management.

4. *Ethical/legal issues.* Recognizing and responding to ethical dilemmas in end-of-life care, including issues of comfort, consent, prolonging life, withholding treatment; euthanasia, and allocation of resources; and legal issues including advance care planning, advance directives, and end-of-life decision making.

5. *Cultural considerations in end-of-life care.* Multiple aspects of culture and belief systems, components of cultural assessment with emphasis on patient/family beliefs about roles, death and dying, afterlife, and bereavement.

6. *Communication.* Essentials of end-of-life communication, attentive listening, barriers to communication, breaking bad news, and interdisciplinary collaboration.

7. *Grief, loss, bereavement.* Stages and types of grief, grief assessment and intervention, and the nurse's experience with loss/grief and need for support.

8. *Achieving quality care at the end of life.* Challenge for nursing in end-of-life care, availability and cost of end-of-life care, the nurse's role in improving care systems, opportunities for growth at the end of life, concepts of peaceful or "good death," "dying well," and dignity.

9. *Preparation and care for the time of death.* Nursing care at the time of death, including physical, psychological, and spiritual care of the patient, support of family members, the death vigil, recognizing death, and care after death.

Source: Fox, 1999.

Table 13.3   Physician End-of-Life Communication Approach with Capable Patients

1. Identify whether the patient has completed an advance directive.
2. Inquire about the patient's motivations for completing or not completing an advance directive.
3. Assess the patient's desire for decision-making control.
4. Express commitment to understand the patient's treatment preferences and care goals.
5. Make treatment recommendations after listening to the patient's care goals and values.
6. Identify the patient's preferred surrogate decision maker(s).
7. Ask the patient to specify any individual who should be excluded from the decision-making process if the patient lacks decision-making capacity.
8. Discuss the patient's ideal division of decision-making responsibility between the physician and family if the patient becomes incapacitated.

Source: Annas, 2005.

Table 13.4   Physician End-of-Life Communication Approach with Family Caregivers for Incapacitated Patients

1. Identify families who prefer to use a strict substituted judgment standard.
2. For other families, present substituted judgment as one of the factors to consider when making decisions.
3. Discuss decision-making factors considered important by the family. Factors may include the patient's preferences, perceived quality of life, safety, and the family's interests such as caregiver burden.
4. Assess the family's need for specificity of medical information.
5. Empathize with families' caregiving burden.
6. Present decisions as a shared responsibility between the physician and family.
7. Make treatment recommendations after discussing the patient's needs and family's concerns.
8. Give families permission to choose palliative care.

Source: Annas, 2005.

3. **Insurance reforms for palliative care.** The Centers for Medicare and Medicaid Services should lead other insurers to expand reimbursement for hospital-based palliative care programs. Palliative care consultations currently do not generate sufficient revenue for the programs to be self-sustaining and therefore must rely on hospital support, private donations, and foundation grants to exist.

   Although patients and families value quality communication, physicians are not presently reimbursed for the time required for comprehensive advance care planning discussions. Both physician communication training programs and policy changes to allow adequate reimbursement for communication time are needed.

4. **Healthcare systems reform for chronic disease care.** The redesign of the hospice benefit and increased reimbursement of palliative care services are two components of an overall strategy to change the healthcare system from an acute care to a chronic care model (Lynn, 2001). A chronic care model would better address the needs of dying patients and their families by providing additional resources for quality outpatient primary physician care, home, and nursing home care so that the hospital would not be viewed as the only option when disease exacerbations occur.

5. **Palliative care programs for long-term care settings.** Nursing homes have increasingly become patients' site of death as hospital length of stay shortens and patients' care needs prevent them from returning home. There should be increased focus on improving end-of-life care quality for patients in nursing homes, ideally through advanced training and innovative programs rather than punitive regulation. Families are least satisfied with nursing homes among all death sites (Hanson et al., 1997; Teno et al., 2004). Many patients with advanced dementia cannot be cared for at home and require nursing home care during their final months to years. The need for quality end-of-life care in nursing homes will therefore persist.

6. **Education and communication skills to support cultural competency.** The needs and preferences of dying patients from racial and ethnic minority groups should be further evaluated and addressed. African Americans, Latinos, and others are less likely than Caucasian patients to complete advance directives and enroll in hospice while they are more likely to request continuation of

life-sustaining treatments. Ensuring that racial and ethnic minority patients receive end-of-life care consistent with their preferences should be a priority as future end-of-life care reforms are pursued.

CONCLUSION

Patient advocacy has promoted the significant advances that have been made in the care of dying patients during the past 30 years. Patients' families served as the first end-of-life care advocates as they sought to protect their loved ones' autonomy and right to choose surrogate decision makers. Families continue to this day to advocate for dying patients' needs at their bedsides in hospitals, nursing homes, and their own homes; however, advocates for quality end-of-life care now include individual health professionals trained to provide hospice and palliative care, their national organizations, and private foundations.

To continue the progress that has been made during the past 30 years for patient- and family-centered care at the end of life through providing quality end-of-life communication, decision making, symptom management, and care delivery to dying patients, there must be ongoing advocacy efforts in future years. These efforts will help ensure that the healthcare system is able to address the needs of dying patients and their families.

RESOURCES

American Academy of Hospice and Palliative Medicine
http://www.aahpm.org
A palliative care physician membership organization provides conferences and other tools to assist health-care providers who treat patients at the end of life.

American Board of Hospice and Palliative Medicine (ABHPM)
http://www.abhpm.org
A national organization that promotes training standards and provides the certification examination in palliative medicine.

Caring Connections
http://www.caringinfo.org
Information for individuals on family caregiving, serious illness, hospice and palliative care, grief, and loss. State-specific advance directives available to download.

Epidemiology of Dying and End of Life Experience (EDELE)
http://www.edeledata.org
Organized access for providers, health policy experts, and advocates to search
health services and epidemiologic data on end-of-life care in the United States.

End of Life/Palliative Education Resource Center (EPERC)
http://www.eperc.mcw.edu
Online site with peer-reviewed educational resources, including materials on
communication and end-of-life decision making.

Growth House, Inc.
http://www.growthhouse.org
Online information clearinghouse for all information related to end-of-life care.

Hospice and Palliative Nurses Association (HPNA)
http://www.hpna.org
Professional nursing organization that promotes hospice and palliative nursing
practice and research and provides extensive educational opportunities for all
levels of nursing from nursing assistants to advance practice nurses.

National Citizens' Coalition for Nursing Home Reform (NCCNHR)
http://www.nccnhr.org
A grassroots consumer/advocate organization that provides information and
leadership on federal and state regulatory and legislative policy development
and models and strategies to improve care and life for residents of nursing
homes and other long-term care facilities.

Palliative Care Education Resource Team for Nursing Homes (PERT)
http://www.swedishmedical.org/pert
Online educational resources to expand training in palliative care for nursing
home staff.

Physician Orders for Life-Sustaining Treatment (POLST)
http://www.ohsu.edu/ethics/polst/index.shtml
Innovative advance care planning documentation developed in Oregon.

REFERENCES

American Board of Hospice & Palliative Medicine. *Home page.* Retrieved July 31, 2006,
from http://www.abhpm.org.

American Medical Association, Council on Scientific Affairs. (1996). Good care of the
dying patient. *Journal of the American Medical Association, 275,* 474–478.

Annas, G. J. (1990). Nancy Cruzan and the right to die. *New England Journal of Medicine,
323,* 670–673.

Annas, G. J. (2005). "Culture of life" politics at the bedside: The case of Terri Schiavo. *New England Journal of Medicine, 352,* 1710–1715.

Baer, W. M., & Hanson, L. C. (2000). Families' perception of the added value of hospice in the nursing home. *Journal of the American Geriatrics Society, 48,* 879–882.

Billings, J. A. (1998). What is palliative care? *Journal of Palliative Medicine, 1,* 73–81.

Billings, J. A., & Block, S. (1997). Palliative care in undergraduate medical education: Status report and future directions. *Journal of the American Medical Association, 278,* 733–738.

Bok, S. (1976). Personal directions for care at the end of life. *New England Journal of Medicine, 295,* 367–369.

Breen, C. M., Abernethy, A. P., Abbott, K. H., & Tulsky, J. A. (2001). Conflict associated with decisions to limit life-sustaining treatment in intensive care units. *Journal of General Internal Medicine, 16,* 283–289.

Callahan, D. (2005). Death: "The distinguished thing." *Hastings Center Report, 35*(Suppl), S5–S8.

Center to Advance Palliative Care. (2004). *Crosswalk of JCAHO standards and palliative care: With PC policies, procedures and assessment tools.* Retrieved September 15, 2006, from http://www.capc.org/support-from-capc/capc_publications/JCAHO-crosswalk.pdf.

Christakis, N. A. (1999). *Death foretold: Prophecy and prognosis in medical care.* Chicago: University of Chicago Press.

Covinsky, K. E., Goldman, L., Cook, E. F., Oye, R., Desbiens, N., Reding, D., et al. (1994). The impact of serious illness on patients' families. *Journal of the American Medical Association, 272,* 1839–1844.

Curtis, J. R., Wenrich, M. D., Carline, J. D., Shannon, S. E., Ambrozy, D. M., & Ramsey, P. G. (2001). Understanding physicians' skills at providing end-of-life care perspectives of patients, families, and health care workers. *Journal of General Internal Medicine, 16,* 41–49.

Foley, K. M. (2005). The past and future of palliative care. *Hastings Center Report, 35*(Suppl), S42–S46.

Fox, E., Landrum-McNiff, K., Zhong, Z., Dawson, N. V., Wu, A. W., & Lynn, J. (1999). Evaluation of prognostic criteria for determining hospice eligibility in patients with advanced lung, heart, or liver disease. *Journal of the American Medical Association, 282,* 1638–1645.

Hammes, B. J., & Rooney, B. L. (1998). Death and end-of-life planning in one midwestern community. *Archives of Internal Medicine, 158,* 383–390.

Hanson, L. C., Danis, M., & Garrett, J. (1997). What is wrong with end-of-life care? Opinions of bereaved family members. *Journal of the American Geriatrics Society, 45,* 1339–1344.

Hanson, L. C., Danis, M., Mutran, E., & Keenan, N. L. (1994). Impact of patient incompetence on decisions to use or withhold life-sustaining treatment. *American Journal of Medicine, 97,* 235–241.

Hedberg, K., Hopkins, D., & Kohn, M. (2003). Five years of legal physician-assisted suicide in Oregon. *New England Journal of Medicine, 348,* 961–964.

Institute of Medicine, Committee on Care at the End of Life. (1997). In Field M. J. & Cassel C. K. (Eds.), *Approaching death: Improving care at the end of life.* Washington, DC: National Academy Press.

Lorenz, K. A., Asch, S. M., Rosenfeld, K. E., Liu, H., & Ettner, S. L. (2004). Hospice admission practices: Where does hospice fit in the continuum of care? *Journal of the American Geriatrics Society, 52,* 725–730.

Lynn, J. (2001). Perspectives on care at the close of life. Serving patients who may die soon and their families: The role of hospice and other services. *Journal of the American Medical Association, 285,* 925–932.

Morrison, R. S., Maroney-Galin, C., Kralovec, P. D., & Meier, D. E. (2005). The growth of palliative care programs in United States hospitals. *Journal of Palliative Medicine, 8,* 1127–1134.

Morrison, R. S., & Meier, D. E. (2004). Clinical practice: Palliative care. *New England Journal of Medicine, 350,* 2582–2590.

National Consensus Project for Quality Palliative Care. (2006). *Home page.* Retrieved July 31, 2006, from http://www.nationalconsensusproject.org.

National Hospice and Palliative Care Organization. *Home page.* Retrieved July 31, 2006, from http://www.nhpco.org/templates/1/homepage.cfm.

Oregon Health & Science University, Center for Ethics in Health Care. (2005). *Physician orders of life-sustaining treatment paradigm.* Retrieved July 31, 2006, from http://www.ohsu.edu/polst.

Pritchard, R. S., Fisher, E. S., Teno, J. M., Sharp, S. M., Reding, D. J., Knaus, W. A., et al. (1998). Influence of patient preferences and local health system characteristics on the place of death. *Journal of the American Geriatrics Society, 46,* 1242–1250.

Rabkin, M. T., Gillerman, G., & Rice, N. R. (1976). Orders not to resuscitate. *New England Journal of Medicine, 295,* 364–366.

Schulz, R., & Beach, S. R. (1999). Caregiving as a risk factor for mortality: The caregiver health effects study. *Journal of the American Medical Association, 282,* 2215–2219.

Singer, P. A., Martin, D. K., & Kelner, M. (1999). Quality end-of-life care: Patients' perspectives. *Journal of the American Medical Association, 281,* 163–168.

Steinhauser, K. E., Christakis, N. A., Clipp, E. C., McNeilly, M., McIntyre, L., & Tulsky, J. A. (2000). Factors considered important at the end of life by patients, family, physicians, and other care providers. *Journal of the American Medical Association, 284,* 2476–2482.

Steinhauser, K. E., Clipp, E. C., McNeilly, M., Christakis, N. A., McIntyre, L. M., & Tulsky, J. A. (2000). In search of a good death: Observations of patients, families, and providers. *Annals of Internal Medicine, 132,* 825–832.

SUPPORT Principal Investigators. (1995). A controlled trial to improve care for seriously ill hospitalized patients: The study to understand prognoses and preferences for outcomes and risks of treatments (SUPPORT). *Journal of the American Medical Association, 274,* 1591–1598.

Teno, J. M., Clarridge, B. R., Casey, V., Welch, L. C., Wetle, T., Shield, R., et al. (2004). Family perspectives on end-of-life care at the last place of care. *Journal of the American Medical Association, 291,* 88–93.

Teno, J. M., Fisher, E. S., Hamel, M. B., Coppola, K., & Dawson, N. V. (2002). Medical care inconsistent with patients' treatment goals: Association with 1-year Medicare resource use and survival. *Journal of the American Geriatrics Society, 50,* 496–500.

Tolle, S. W., Tilden, V. P., Nelson, C. A., & Dunn, P. M. (1998). A prospective study of the efficacy of the physician order form for life-sustaining treatment. *Journal of the American Geriatrics Society, 46,* 1097–1102.

Welsfeld, V., Miller, D., Gibson, R., & Schroeder, S. A. (2000). Improving care at the end of life: What does it take? *Health Affairs, 19,* 277–283.

Winzelberg, G. S., Hanson, L. C., & Tulsky, J. A. (2005). Beyond autonomy: Diversifying end-of-life decision-making approaches to serve patients and families. *Journal of the American Geriatrics Society, 53,* 1046–1050.

Strategy Four:
Making Consumers' Voices
Heard in Policy and Law

Patient advocacy aims to ensure lay people have a voice in a healthcare system traditionally dominated by the values, beliefs, and practices of health professionals and, increasingly, business interests. The initial two strategies in this book focus largely on ways to engage patients in discussion and decision making during a medical encounter, while the third focuses on ways that organizational change will support these and other, related, aims. Another important goal of health advocacy, however, is to respond to the patient or consumer's perspective through policy and law. This section of the text accordingly explores the ways advocates concerned with improving healthcare can participate in decision making at the policy level through activism, ombudsman programs, organizational change, and political lobbying.

Chapter 14 chronicles the emergence of the consumer health advocacy movement as a significant force in health care. Tomes traces the uneasy balance between medical authority and the patient-consumer's "power of the purse," and shows how the rise of a managed healthcare economy has taken power from both parties. The future of consumer advocacy may lie in translating the successes of disease-specific advocacy efforts in areas such as breast cancer into support for reform of a more structural nature that could address inequities in access and quality that plague the current system.

In Chapter 15, Holder and Frank recount the successes and challenges of grassroots advocacy efforts in the area of long-term care, using the work of the National Citizens' Coalition for Nursing Home Reform (NCCNHR) as an example. The long-term care movement offers a unique perspective on political factors that contribute to social problems and the skill sets needed to affect change at the state and federal levels of policy. The chapter also explores both the strengths and limitations of grassroots organizations in general while making a case for including constituents in policymaking.

In Chapter 16, Davenport-Ennis examines ways in which nonprofit organizations can inform healthcare policy. This chapter describes the Patient Advocate Foundation (PAF) and its sister organization, National

Patient Advocate Foundation (NPAF), both established in 1993. PAF is a national patient services organization that provides counseling and legal support to patients who need assistance in resolving issues of debt crisis, job retention, and insurance matters caused by serious illness. Simultaneously, these cases are rigorously documented in databases that provide valuable information about different populations' current advocacy needs. These data are then used by the NPAF, a nonpartisan lobbying organization responsible for legislative and policy reform measures designed to improve patients' access to care and allow for appropriate treatments at the state and federal levels. This chapter introduces the politics and economics of health care and suggests ways nonprofit organizations can learn from business models.

In Chapter 17, Michaels and Collyar discuss the emergence of research advocacy. For the past four decades, lay people have sought to gain influence on the targets and methods of medical research. Thanks in part to HIV and breast cancer activists, consumers are now participating in review boards for many research endeavors. "Research advocates" have not only had an impact on the way research is carried out, they have also influenced decisions about research funding at the local, state, and national levels. Applying "embodied health movement theory," the authors examine strategies advocates have used to transform their "lived experience" into motivation for systemic change. They conclude by considering future implications for research advocacy, including the dangers inherent in trying to institutionalize a consumer movement.

CHAPTER 14

Did Patient/Consumers Cause the Healthcare Crisis? Historical Talking Points for the 21st Century Patient Advocate

Nancy Tomes

OBJECTIVES

- To become familiar with the history of patient empowerment and advocacy movements in the United States
- To identify the historical factors and trends that helped produce the consumer health movement that began in the 1970s
- To understand why some aspects of that movement have succeeded while others have failed
- To appreciate the challenges that patient advocates face in the 21st century United States

Over the last 50 years, significant changes have taken place in the conception of the patient's role in healthcare. Whereas before the 1960s an ethos of "patients should be seen but not heard" prevailed in American medicine, nowadays, it is widely accepted that patients should take an active role in their own healthcare. In the "best practices" definition of this model, patients and doctors own different forms of expertise. Patients are recognized as uniquely knowledgeable about the impact of their illness on their bodies and lives. Physicians offer a scientific expertise grounded in their lengthy medical training and clinical experience. Together, they review the probable benefits and risks associated with different treatments so that patients may choose the ones most likely to result in the outcomes they want. Being treated as a responsible party, patients are more likely to cooperate with the treatment plan and to achieve the best possible clinical results.[1]

Patients themselves played a critical role in developing this new collaborative model, both as participants in organized social movements and as individuals pressing for change. As this chapter shows, patients have never been as subservient as they were often portrayed in traditional sociological theory; like Mark Twain's death, the extent of their passivity and subordination in the past has been greatly exaggerated.[2] Inspired by the civil rights movement, a vocal minority of them began to question the "be seen but not heard" ethos. Starting in the 1960s, patient advocates combined democratic political traditions with popular consumer economics to develop a strong grassroots critique of medical authority. This new activist sensibility emerged in many different places, in movements concerned with women's health, disability rights, and the environment.[3]

Physicians, not surprisingly, initially responded to activist demands for change with skepticism and even hostility. Although many doctors saw patient education as a useful tool in securing therapeutic compliance, their conception of themselves as "captains of the healthcare team" did not allow for patients to take the helm. Yet gradually physician opposition to the idea of patient empowerment softened as they came to appreciate the ethical arguments for informed consent and realized that patient-initiated changes—for example, letting partners in the birthing woman's delivery room or having a lumpectomy over a radical mastectomy—resulted in superior therapeutic outcomes (Katz, 1984; Leavitt, 2003; Lerner, 2001).

Now, almost 40 years after its genesis, the patient-as-partner model has clearly changed medical practice in important ways. Among the legacies of patient-led initiatives are measures as diverse as legal abortion, living wills, hospice care, patients' bills of rights, lumpectomies, toxic waste superfunds, revised rules for experimental clinical trials, and a vast array of consumer health information and education resources (see Table 14.1). Patients' well-being, as measured by their health needs and outcomes, figures more prominently in clinical and policy decision making than ever before (see, e.g., Institute of Medicine, 1999, 2001).

These developments would seem to confirm the 1970s optimism that the fragmenting, alienating tendencies of modern medicine could be overcome by better educated, more empowered patients. As Ivan Illich argued in *Medical Nemesis* (1975, p. 35), probably the most influential of the 1970s critiques of medicine, patients' growing "will to self-care" and

Table 14.1 Achievements and Weaknesses of the Consumer Health Movement

A. Achievements
- Procedures for gaining informed consent for medical treatment
- Stronger oversight of drug safety and efficacy
- Improved labeling and instructions for drugs
- Increased protection of patient privacy
- Greater efforts to prevent discrimination against the mentally and physically disabled
- Reforms of medical education designed to improve physician communication skills and increase sensitivity to gender, race, ethnic, and class differences
- Fairer procedures for involuntary commitment of people with mental disabilities

B. Weaknesses
- Inherent inadequacies of consumer model to address problems of the poor and uninsured
- Fragmentation of efforts among many different disease "causes" and factions
- Ease with which other stakeholders co-opt rhetoric of empowerment (forcing the American Medical Association to allow doctors to advertise, loosening of FDA restrictions on direct to consumer advertising of prescription drugs)

determination to shape their own destinies would lead to a redistribution of information and power and ultimately result in better healthcare for all.[4]

Yet even the most committed advocates of patient-centered medicine (of which I count myself one) have to admit that expanding patients' roles, in both policy formulation and clinical decision making, has not been a magic cure-all for modern medicine. Advocates' faith that empowered patient–consumers could lead the way toward a more equitable, cohesive, and effective system of healthcare has been tested in recent years. Although considerable advances have been made in the last 50 years, patient-centered medicine is still far from a reality. As recent studies show, many patients still do not receive the treatments recommended for their illnesses. Rates of misdiagnosis and medical error remain high, and spending on individual medical care still far outstrips the resources devoted to population-based forms of disease prevention (Burris, 1997; Institute of Medicine, 1999).

Meanwhile, the achievements of the more patient-centered approach appear in danger because of the seemingly unmanageable cost and fragmentation of healthcare services. Despite varied efforts at cost containment—managed care, managed competition, and now consumer-driven healthcare—healthcare costs continue to rise, testing the willingness of tax payers and employers to subsidize them. As of 2006, over 16% of Americans lack any form of health insurance. A political stalemate has developed over whether these problems should be addressed by more privatization and market-oriented measures or by more direct governmental regulation of the healthcare system (Schlesinger, 2005).

For patient advocates, these are especially perilous times because the newly visible "patient consumer" provides such a tempting scapegoat for the persistent ills of the American healthcare system. Because patients now have a greater role in making their healthcare decisions, their actions naturally figure more centrally in explanations for the healthcare crisis.

One view tends to present the patient/consumer as the villain of the piece, portraying consumer irrationality as the root cause of both poor health quality and inefficiencies in healthcare. More so than any developed nation in the world, so we are told, American consumers get what they want in healthcare and other aspects of life. If those choices disappoint, patient–consumers have only themselves to blame. Affluence has bred an unhealthy lifestyle, whose expensive-to-treat ravages might be lessened if only Americans could control their appetites and make simple changes in their daily behavior: eat smaller portions, walk a few more steps, and give up those cigarettes.

Similarly, patients with unrealistic expectations have fueled the demand for ever better, more expensive, more malpractice-proof treatments. With their healthcare heavily subsidized by third-party payers—employers, state governments, and federal programs such as Medicare and Medicaid—Americans have no idea what their healthcare really costs. As a result, they resist paying their fair share of the burden, trying instead to pass it along to employers or the government. According to this line of argument, the solution to the healthcare crisis is a simple one: make American consumers more directly responsible for their healthcare choices, make them pay what their care really costs, and limit their ability to sue for malpractice (see, e.g., Pipes, 2004).

In contrast, other analysts have developed what might be termed the consumer-as-victim model. This interpretation stresses the unhealthy structural and cultural incentives built into the American way of life, mainly to benefit large corporations. Huge advertising and marketing budgets help fuel the sales of unhealthy products, from Big Macs to cigarettes, whereas heavily promoted modern technologies, from automobiles to the Internet, foster the decline in physical exercise. The American way of life is structured, deliberately as well as unconsciously, to promote unhealthy behaviors, and only the fortunate, because of superior genes or will power, can resist its blandishments.

Similarly, the American healthcare system is designed primarily to protect the profitability of the "medical industrial complex" and only secondarily to treat patients effectively. If the consumer health movement has failed, it is because powerful lobbying groups have co-opted its language to advance their own economic interests. Efforts to rationalize and coordinate the healthcare system do not succeed because those changes might disrupt what is an extremely profitable sector of the postindustrial service-oriented economy.

Which interpretation is right? Are consumers villains or victims? Anyone hoping to advocate on behalf of patients today needs a good answer to those questions, but unfortunately, the answer is not a simple one. As with every such dichotomy, truth can be found in both positions. In a nation of 300 million, plenty of people are making poor choices about their lifestyles and medical care, and Americans do have a very fuzzy sense of who pays what for their healthcare. At the same time, when it comes to making poor choices, Americans get considerable encouragement from powerful corporations interested in preserving their profits; nor is there any doubt that the major stakeholders described by Ehrenreich and Ehrenreich in 1970 as the "medical industrial complex"—organized medicine, private insurance companies, hospitals, the pharmaceutical industry, medical device manufacturers, and the like—still have far more political clout in policy making than do groups organized to advocate on behalf of patient–consumers.

Faced with this complicated reality, it is tempting to revert to reductionist arguments, to indulge in established rituals of doctor or patient "bashing," or to rail against managed-care companies and the pharmaceutical industry. Yet for patient advocates in the 21st century, it is crucial to avoid the tendency to oversimplify the obstacles they face. Pushing ahead in the cause of patient-centered medicine requires a historically grounded, sophisticated understanding of how the current state of gridlock and frustration came to be. To that end, this chapter presents a brief and selective history of the consumer health movement of the last 40 years, aimed at understanding why the model of "patient as partner" has succeeded in some respects and failed in others.

It is an irony that in the United States, with its deep-seated allegiance to individual rights, the sacredness of choice and personal responsibility for health has produced a healthcare system that is more fragmented, expensive, and uneven in quality and access than those of its Western European peers. How do we explain that puzzle?

Certainly, if we start with American medicine circa 1850, this outcome was not at all apparent. Patients in our great-great-grandmothers' era probably had a better working relationship with their physicians than we do today. Granted, the medicine that doctors had to deliver a century and a half ago did not "work" as well as ours. Yet the healing partnerships of this older era had some equitable features that are worth reflecting on.

Before the late 1800s, when a new laboratory model began to remake the science of medicine, what is now termed the "competence gap" between healer and patient was much smaller than it is now. As Charles Rosenberg (1979) argued in a now classic exposition of the healing relationship, physicians and lay people shared a similar model of cause and effect regarding illness and its treatment. As learned men, doctors had a greater command of that model, yet it was not thought beyond patients' abilities to comprehend.

The economic and social context of 19th century healthcare reinforced patients' power vis-à-vis physicians'. Americans had a long tradition of medical self-help; every community had a range of domestic healers, most of them women, who offered a large repertoire of home remedies to be tried before seeking a doctor's help. After patients decided to consult a doctor, they exercised considerable "power of the purse." Prior to the introduction of third-party payment in the mid-20th century, physicians relied on patient fees for their livelihood; dissatisfied patients could and did withhold payment for services they thought inferior. Nineteenth century Americans also commonly practiced what a later generation would call "doctor shopping," a practice made easier by the revocation of medical licensing laws in the wake of the American Revolution. In the early 1800s, the spirit of "every man his own doctor" prevailed, and healing sects proliferated, much to the dismay of the "regular" physicians, the antecedents of our modern doctor (Tomes, 2006b).

The 19th century was no patients' paradise, however. By modern standards, the treatments available were often ineffective and even dangerous; aseptic surgery was not introduced until the 1870s, and the discovery of antibiotics would come only in the 1940s. Moreover, being white, native born, and property owning were requisites of good medical service. Then (as now), poor, recent immigrants, and people of color had little "power of the purse" to exercise and thus received worse treatment than their more affluent counterparts.

Within these significant limitations, Americans who were "free, white, and 21" exercised considerable autonomy in their health affairs. As Rosenberg (1999) noted, "Fee paying patients did not need to be 'empowered'—to use late twentieth-century jargon; they were empowered by their family's social position, by their often sophisticated knowledge of medical thought and practice, by their ability to judge a physician's character and competence, and—perhaps most importantly—by their ability to pay the fees that constitute the physician's sole source of income" (Rosenberg, 1999, p. 208).

In short, the mid-1800s represent the one and only point in American history where there existed a truly free market in medical services, in the sense that it was directed primarily by consumer choices and regulated by open competition over price, type, and quality of service. After the Civil War, that free-market medical economy began to close down, not because consumers were unhappy with it, but because physicians sought its end.

After the late 19th century bacteriological revolution, which identified the microbial agents of killer diseases and allowed for safer forms of surgery, the medical profession successfully pressed for reinstatement of medical licensing laws. Between the 1870s and the 1920s, state after state passed new medical practice acts that vested licensing in the hands of physicians themselves. Simultaneously, "regular" physicians—forerunners of today's modern doctor—undertook a thorough reorganization of medical education, linking it more closely to hospital training, a move designed to increase the value of the medical license (Starr, 1982).

This professionalizing process did not proceed without patients' resistance. In fact, the first systematic efforts to define a set of "patients' rights" outside of medicine's own ethical codes occurred in those areas of medicine where the new balance of power between doctor and patient was most evident. The rise of surgery fueled the expansion of medical malpractice law, as patients disappointed with surgeons' services sought redress with the help of another group of experts, namely lawyers and judges. The expansion of mental hospitals prompted growing protests against a draconian involuntary commitment process. What is usually regarded as the first "patients' rights" initiative in the United States developed as an effort to protect the diminishing rights of mental patients (see Textbox 14.1). Finally, patients used their political influence to make sure that the new medical licensing laws recognized the value of alternative healing traditions, such as homeopathy and osteopathy, that they valued (Tomes, 2006b).

Still, by the early 1900s, the regular medical profession, led by a newly reorganized American Medical Association, had gone far toward securing what 1970s critics would term the "medical monopoly." In the view of early 20th century physicians, it was a benevolent despotism; they exercised their expanded powers for the patients' own good. As Kenneth Ludmerer has described it (1985), the Progressive era saw a new "social contract" between physician and the patient/public, in which a more scientific, effective medical profession was given substantial authority to regulate its own credentials and conduct; in return, the profession promised to enforce professional standards that ensured physicians would always put patients' well-being before their own economic interest.

During the same time period, a different model of "consumer protection" evolved in the regulation of health-related products. Starting in the late 1800s, city and state governments began to regulate the production of foods and medicines because, if improperly made or falsely advertised, such goods could literally kill the unwary consumer. As such goods were increasingly made by national companies operating across state lines,

---

Textbox 14.1   The First Patient Advocate: Elizabeth Packard (1816–1897)

Elizabeth Packard was a housewife committed to an Illinois asylum by her clergyman husband, who objected to her unorthodox views on religion. With the assistance of friends, she obtained a writ of habeas corpus, which protects against imprisonment without due process, and won her release from her husband's bondage. After leaving her husband, Packard supported herself by selling her memoirs, titled *A Modern Persecution*, and used the funds to lobby on behalf of American asylum inmates (Packard, 1973, 1875). She visited almost 30 states, helping to pass over 20 so-called Packard laws, which established more stringent requirements for involuntary commitment and safeguarded inmates' rights to communicate with the outside world.

pressure built for a national system of food and drug inspection. After a hard-fought battle, pitting lay reformers and physicians against food manufacturers and proprietary drug companies, the United States Congress passed the Pure Food and Drugs Act of 1906, the first major piece of modern consumer protection. A few years later, Congress created the Federal Trade Commission, which assumed oversight over consumer advertising as part of its policing of fair business practice (Hilts, 2003).

Thus, by the 1920s, the free market medicine of the mid-1800s had been replaced by a more regulated medical economy. The new medical licensing laws ensured that only certain individuals, meeting a uniform standard of scientific education, could practice medicine. They and they alone qualified as the patients' "trusted intermediaries," guiding them in the choice of lifestyle and treatment. Similarly, new food and drug regulations sought to guarantee a minimal level of product safety. Sellers no longer had the "right" to peddle dangerous products with deceptive advertisements. Even if they wanted to, patients could not buy drugs laced with opium or patronize an abortionist because those choices were "unsafe." This contraction of free choice was widely portrayed as in the patient/consumer's own good, and in many ways it was: Drugs laced with opium came off the market, and medical charlatans promising phony cancer cures found it harder to practice.

Yet the new healthcare economy did not work perfectly, especially from the patient–consumers' point of view. As the "competence gap" between doctor and patient widened, the process of choosing a doctor and understanding his bill grew more confusing. From the 1920s onward, medicine rapidly became more specialized; patients had to negotiate increasingly complex healthcare hierarchies characterized by different kinds of doctors (e.g., internists, cardiologists, neurosurgeons) and related health professionals (public health nurses, dietitians, physical therapists), not to mention the many alternative healers who continued to practice (chiropractors, osteopaths, herbalists). While working strenuously both to upgrade doctors' education and to restrict their competitors, the American Medical Association and its state societies found it difficult to stop economic practices, such as fee splitting and unnecessary surgery, by which doctors colluded in overcharging patients. Even more distressingly, medical societies found it difficult to discipline impaired and incompetent members (Tomes, 2007).

Meanwhile, regulators were hard pressed to keep unsafe drugs off the market, to expunge misleading health claims from advertisements, and to ensure that all trusted intermediaries looked out for their patients' interests first. By the late 1920s, it was not hard to find evidence that the quality of information people had to make choices about drugs or doctors was flawed, that plenty of bad products and misleading ads got through the regulatory screening, that people's "wise choices" about their health were fatally compromised by a high volume of commercial influences, and that doctors did not always perform well as their patients' trusted intermediaries (Tomes, 2007).

The defects of the new medical economy came to the forefront of public debate during the Great Depression. One focal point for discussion was the findings of the Committee on the Costs of Medical Care, the first large-scale social scientific survey of medical care in the United States. In the series of studies published in the early 1930s, the Committee on the Costs of Medical Care produced evidence that physicians were not meeting their end of the "social contract," that many areas of the country had too few doctors and hospitals, that too many families could not afford the rising cost of medical care, and that the medical profession was not responding to these problems effectively, largely because of its inflexible commitment to fee-for-service practice (Falk, Rorem, & Ring, 1933).

Also during the 1930s, determined groups of consumer advocates pointed out that, with the limited legal and fiscal resources allotted to the Food and Drug Administration (FDA) and the Federal Trade Commission (FTC), regulators could not keep products harmful to American health off the market. Widely read exposés such as Kallet and Schlink's *100,000,000 Guinea Pigs* (1933) (Textbox 14.2) and Ruth deForest Lamb's *The American Chamber of Horrors* documented the dangerous wares slipping through the regulatory net: drugs laced with unhealthy substances, cosmetics that blinded their wearers, and foods packed with impurities (Jackson, 1970).

In general, the rethinking of the American economy precipitated by the Great Depression produced a new predisposition to look at that economy from consumers' points of view. As part of what political scientists have termed the New Deal broker state, the "consumer interest" emerged as an important counterpoint to the growing power of big business, big labor, and big government. Federal agencies created new roles for so-called consumer representatives (usually professionals and academics), and in response to consumer pressure, the U.S. Congress considered various new forms of consumer protection (Cohen, 1998).

Textbox 14.2   A Depression-Era Best Seller: Kallet and Schlink's *100,000,000 Guinea Pigs*

To help sort worthwhile from useless products, Arthur Kallet and F.L. Schlink founded Consumers' Research in 1930 to develop consumer ratings and in 1933 published the best seller *100,000,000 Guinea Pigs: Dangers in Everyday Foods, Drugs, and Cosmetics*. This book presented a shocking exposé of the unsafe products that federal regulation and voluntary industry guidelines were allowing to go on the market, such as Koremlu, a depilatory made with thallium, which poisoned its users, and Radithor, a cancer cure laced with radium. The book's success inspired more "guinea pig" books in the 1930s, focusing on products related to women's hygiene, food and nutrition, and children's health. The consumer guide has remained a popular form of health information ever since.

In the healthcare realm, the new consumer consciousness of the 1930s resulted in two big political initiatives: campaigns to create some form of government-sponsored health insurance and to increase the regulatory powers of the FDA and the FTC over the safety of food, drugs, and cosmetics. Although the majority of Americans favored some governmental assistance with health insurance, the American Medical Association's arguments that any deviation from private fee-for-service medicine represented a step toward "socialized medicine" carried the day, and health insurance never became part of the New Deal package of social welfare services (Engel, 2002; Gordon, 2003).

The second initiative was more successful. After years of gridlock, the U.S. Congress did finally vote in 1938 to strengthen the FDA and FTC, largely because of the 1937 tragedy in which over a hundred people died after taking the new sulfa "wonder drug" sulfanilamide suspended in a liquid buffer containing a chemical similar to antifreeze. Although more business friendly, especially in its handling of advertising, than consumer advocates had hoped, the legislation strengthening the FDA and FTC laid the foundation for greater oversight of prescription drugs (Hilts, 2003).

With the coming of World War II and then the Cold War, what little traction organized health consumer lobbies had achieved in the Depression-era New Deal disappeared. To ward off further discussion of national health insurance, organized medicine decided to promote the expansion of private medical insurance, in particular the doctor-sponsored Blue Cross and Blue Shield programs, as a way to cover rising hospital expenses.

Meanwhile, the U.S. Congress proved generous in funding medical infra-structure through the Hill Burton Act, which used taxpayer dollars to build hospitals, and through the National Institutes of Health, which funneled money into basic and clinical science research, from 4 million dollars in 1947 to 400 million dollars in 1960 to 28 billion dollars today. This mas-sive underwriting of medical progress came with no strings attached: no mechanisms for system coordination, much less cost control or quality assurance (Schlesinger, 2005; Starr, 1982).

The "space age" medicine symbolized by the modern antibiotic and the new cardiac care unit further widened the distance between doctors' and patients' knowledge base. As employers began slowly to assume the costs of healthcare due to pressure from labor unions and competition for executive employees, important decisions about what procedures to subsidize, at what price, shifted to insurance companies, who deferred to physicians' judgments about what constituted a "reasonable" charge (Starr, 1982). Simultaneously, the pharmaceutical revolution produced a bounty of new "wonder drugs" that patients could only obtain by seeing a physician (Tomes, 2005).

Yet despite the dazzling accomplishments of space age medicine, patient consumers in the 1950s showed clear signs of restiveness. To be sure, as opinion polls repeatedly showed, most Americans were impressed by med-ical science and trusted their personal physicians. Yet the same polls showed strong distrust of organized medicine's economic motives and resentment over the skyrocketing cost of hospital care and prescription drugs. Starting in the 1950s, newspapers and mass-market magazines began to carry arti-cles critical of modern medicine; as the business periodical *Fortune* declared in 1954, "The doctor is off his pedestal" (Tomes, 2007).

The sharpening tone of criticism also reflected the changing size and structure of the healthcare economy. Although physicians continued to present themselves as small businessmen, their fast growing incomes and hospital-based practices gave the profession an increasingly corporate look, and so did the profession's growing enmeshment with the pharma-ceutical industry, one of the fastest growing sectors of the postwar U.S. economy. Driven by the rapid pace of scientific discovery and technolog-ical innovation, as well as new third-party paying systems, a new kind of "medical industrial complex" could be seen emerging in the 1950s and 1960s, far removed from the old family doctor celebrated by Norman Vincent Peale and others. In the new field of medical sociology, academ-ics began to worry that the "whole patient" was being lost in an increas-ingly impersonal, highly fragmented, and potentially dangerous healthcare system (Freidson, 1970). As Robert Wilson described the hospitalized American in the first edition of *The Handbook of Medical Sociology*, published in 1963, "He is a stranger and afraid," adrift in a technological system that left him "less able to mobilize his own recuperative powers" (Wilson, 1963, p. 292).

These concerns led to major changes in the 1960s. In 1962, in the wake of another drug tragedy, this time involving the sedative thalidomide, the U.S. Congress approved another major overhaul of the FDA, this one to ensure greater care in the clinical testing of prescription drugs before their release to the public (Hilts, 2003). A few years later, in 1965, the federal government finally entered the business of national health insurance, although only for certain groups: Medicare for older people and Medicaid for low-income consumers, but again, the new federal funding simply poured more money into the established channels of healthcare delivery without any mechanisms to ensure cost or quality control. Thus, the reforms of the 1960s only accelerated the expansion of the "medical-industrial complex" (Ehrenreich & Ehrenreich, 1970).

The generation of Americans coming of age in the 1960s faced this new landscape in an increasingly critical frame of mind. The civil rights, free speech, and antiwar movements caused young people to question all forms of authority, including that of physicians. They were also influenced by a broadening conception of consumers' rights, in particular "the right to safety, the right to be informed, the right to choose, and the right to be heard," enumerated in John F. Kennedy's famous 1962 consumer bill of rights (Preston & Bloom, 1986, p. 38). In the turbulent 1960s, patient dissatisfaction with the healthcare system soon went from the simmering to the boiling point.

Again, psychiatry proved to be an early forcing ground for a new patients' rights sensibility. Ex-patients launched a radical "mental patients' liberation movement" centered on ideas of self-help and independent living (Tomes, 2006a). People with physical disabilities pressed for similar goals, going to court to secure accessible buildings and an end to workplace discrimination (Shapiro, 1993). Led by groups such as the Boston Women's Health Collective, second-wave feminists made the male doctor's dismissive treatment of the female patient a symbol for the plight of patients as a whole (Morgen, 2002; Weisman, 1998) (Textbox 14.3). Last, but not least, the welfare rights movement called attention to the systematic neglect and abuse of low-income and non-Caucasian patients, especially in inner city neighborhoods (Piven & Cloward, 1979).

Textbox 14.3   The Boston Women's Health Collective

The "second wave" women's movement that began in the 1960s played an especially important role in shaping the consumer health movement. Perhaps the most important exemplar of this feminist critique was the Boston Women's Health Collective, a group of women living in the Boston area who met at a women's conference in the late 1960s. To free women from male medical domination, the BWHC urged women to take their health care into their own hands. A newsprint pamphlet, first published in 1970, evolved into the classic *Our Bodies, Ourselves*, first published by Simon and Schuster in 1973 and as revised over the years, still a bestseller.

Led by activists who had read the works of medical critics such as Barbara Ehrenreich, Thomas Szasz, and Ivan Illich, these new patient-led initiatives mounted a vigorous assault on medical paternalism, symbolized by the concept of a "patient's bill of rights" (Textbox 14.4). In search of alternatives to the traditional model of the passive patient, activists experimented with different terms—client, consumer, even victim—for themselves. Eventually "consumer" prevailed as the most commonly used shorthand for these new style patients, who were determined to participate as fully as possible in making choices about their healthcare (Tomes, 2006b).

This idea of consumer empowerment expanded not only in clinical settings but also in policy arenas. Harkening back to New Deal concepts of the broker state, the architects of the "Great Society" programs of the 1960s believed that citizen/consumer oversight was the key to better functioning government. Starting in the mid-1960s, many federal programs made inclusion of consumer representatives on their planning boards a prerequisite for receiving federal funding. This principle reached its fullest articulation in the National Health Planning and Resources Development Act of 1974, which promised to ensure "planning with teeth," that is, to give consumer interests more clout vis-à-vis other interest groups (Checkoway, 1981).

We now arrive back at the observations with which this chapter began: For all its seeming promise, the transformative potential of the health consumer movement to bring about sweeping structural changes ran into serious obstacles. For just at the point patient activists began to assert themselves, the healthcare system began to change in ways that limited not only physicians' autonomy but also their own.

Rising healthcare costs triggered powerful responses, first by the federal government and then by private employers, to reign in the power of medical decision making. These efforts to make medicine more cost-effective ran counter to the need to sustain the profitability of specific healthcare industries. The clash between opposing objectives—reduce costs but maintain profit levels—led to what McLean and Richards (2004) have dubbed healthcare's "Thirty Years' War." As the latest in cost-containment strategies would be introduced—HMOs, DRGs, capitation plans, and the like—they would be quickly undercut by stakeholders' adjustments designed to protect their bottom lines (Schlesinger, 2005).

As the "Thirty Years' War" unfolded, patient advocacy groups found themselves courted by all the major stakeholders, as the latter realized that appealing to "the consumer interest" could be a useful political strategy. Groups organized specifically to promote patient interests became players in policy circles as never before (Textbox 14.4), yet on the whole, organizations created primarily to represent patient/consumer interests remained smaller and more fragmented than other stakeholders involved in healthcare policy debates. Meanwhile, groups with diametrically opposed objectives adopted the rhetoric of health consumerism to justify their own interests, resulting in a confusing array of supposedly consumer-friendly policies (Tomes, 2007).

The end result has not been a simple shift in the see-saw in which physicians' power went down as patients' influence went up. Rather, recent changes have left both doctor and patient with less direct say in the overall structuring of therapeutic choice. In the current economic climate, neither doctor nor patient can act as fully autonomous agents; their ability to function as therapeutically or economically "rational" actors is limited by a highly managed healthcare economy over which they have limited control.

As a consequence, patient-initiated requests tend to be realized only if some more powerful stakeholder sees that request as useful to its own agenda. Patient empowerment is thus refracted through an increasingly complex set of economic and political alliances. For example, requests for more drug information in the 1970s led to more drug advertising in the 1980s and 1990s (Tomes, 2005); at the same time, longstanding public interest in expanding government-sponsored health insurance programs has been ignored (Schlesinger, 2005).

This selective uptake of consumer demands is critically linked to the power of the purse issue, in that the better insured and more affluent the consumer, the more likely his or her preferences will be honored.

Textbox 14.4   The Patient's Bill of Rights: Two Generations

In the late 1960s, welfare rights organizers became indignant about the abuse of poor patients in urban hospitals and began to pressure the American Hospital Association to adopt a "patient's bill of rights." In 1973, the American Hospital Association approved and adopted a "Patient's Bill of Rights," which held that the patient has the right to:

1. Considerate and respectful care.
2. Obtain from his or her physician complete current information concerning diagnosis, treatment, and prognosis in terms the patient can be reasonably expected to understand.
3. Receive from his or her physician information necessary to give informed consent prior to the start of any procedure and/or treatment.
4. Refuse treatment to the extent permitted by law and to be informed of the medical consequences of his or her action.
5. Every consideration of his or her privacy concerning the medical care program.
6. Expect that all communications and records pertaining to his or her care should be treated as confidential.
7. Expect that within its capacity a hospital must make reasonable response to the request of a patient for services.
8. Obtain information as to any relationship of his or her hospital to other healthcare and educational institutions insofar as care is concerned. The patient also has the right to obtain information as to the existence, by name, of any professional relationships among individuals who are treating him or her.
9. Be advised if the hospital proposes to engage in or perform human experimentation affecting care or treatment. The patient has the right to refuse to participate in such research projects.
10. Expect reasonable continuity in care.
11. Examine and receive an explanation of bills regardless of source of payment.
12. Know what hospital rules and regulations apply to his or her conduct as a patient. (Condensed from Countryman and Gekas, 1980)

In 1998, an Advisory Committee on Consumer Protection and Quality in the Health Care Industry, appointed by President Bill Clinton, adopted a "Consumer Bill of Rights and Responsibilities," which is summarized here. In 2001, Senators John McCain and Edward Kennedy introduced legislation calling for a similar "bill of rights" to be enacted into law. As of the fall of 2006, the U.S. Congress has been unable to agree on the wording of such a patients' bill of rights.

(continued)

Textbox 14.4   The Patient's Bill of Rights: Two Generations
(continued)

Patients' Bill of Rights, adopted 1998

I. Information Disclosure
You have the right to receive accurate and easily understood information about your health plan, healthcare professionals, and healthcare facilities. If you speak another language, have a physical or mental disability, or just do not understand something, assistance will be provided so that you can make informed healthcare decisions.

II. Choice of Providers and Plans
You have the right to a choice of healthcare providers that is sufficient to provide you with access to appropriate high-quality healthcare.

III. Access to Emergency Services
If you have severe pain, an injury, or sudden illness that convinces you that your health is in serious jeopardy, you have the right to receive screening and stabilization emergency services whenever and wherever needed, without prior authorization or financial penalty.

IV. Participation in Treatment Decisions
You have the right to know all your treatment options and to participate in decisions about your care. Parents, guardians, family members, or other individuals that you designate can represent you if you cannot make your own decisions.

V. Respect and Nondiscrimination
You have a right to considerate, respectful, and nondiscriminatory care from your doctors, health plan representatives, and other healthcare providers.

VI. Confidentiality of Health Information
You have the right to talk in confidence with health care providers and to have your healthcare information protected. You also have the right to review and copy your own medical record and request that your physician amend your record if it is not accurate, relevant, or complete.

VII. Complaints and Appeals
You have the right to a fair, fast, and objective review of any complaint you have against your health plan, doctors, hospitals, or other healthcare personnel. This includes complaints about waiting times, operating hours, the conduct of health care personnel, and the adequacy of healthcare facilities.

Source: Countryman and Gekas, 1980, pp. 4–7.

Conversely, those who have little or no money or insurance coverage have little or no consumer power. As scholars have long noted, consumer-oriented social movements historically have worked best for affluent, educated, white Americans and worst for the poor, working class, aged, and non-Caucasian (Tomes, 2006b). The same disparities noted earlier in describing the free market medical economy of 19th century America still exist in the managed medical economy of the 21st century.

So where does that leave the patient advocate of today? Other chapters explore the challenges and possibilities of the current scene in more detail. Let me conclude here with some brief observations about the historical problem of patient/consumer "choice." We must begin with the recognition that, in the words of Scott Burris, "rational choosers start with a heavily inscribed slate"—that is, the specific choices available to doctor and patient "depend on the social options available to the chooser and, more deeply, on the way in which different options are socially constructed" (Burris, 1997, p. 1608). Thus, long before they ever reach the patient/consumer, the available choices have been whittled down and weighted in favor of other stakeholders' interests.

As this history makes clear, the "slate of choices" available to patients reflects medicine's increasing centrality in a post-industrial service economy, where it represents a spectacularly successful profit sector. Meanwhile, health and body issues have become so central to the formation of individual identity that choices concerning them are guaranteed to be both diverse and fiercely contested: For example, the health choices of the Caucasian male heterosexual conservative will differ from those of the African American lesbian liberal. In these ways, at the same time, late modern culture excels at churning up new wants and desires, the certainty of science, much less religion, differentiating the authentic from the inauthentic need has been made all the more difficult (Williams & Calman, 1996).

One response to that difficulty is to focus on the process of choice itself: to regulate more closely the choices and risks available and to ratchet up expectations that individuals choose "wisely"—even as the standards for what constitutes a wise choice get harder and harder to determine. This highly fraught process of choosing takes place in the context of an aggressive consumer-oriented economy that seeks to direct consumer awareness and desires toward the newest and most profitable choices. One force making for increased tension is the greater latitude given health-related marketing and advertising, which, as we saw earlier, were introduced in the late 1970s and 1980s as consumer-friendly measures. To take the prescription drug example, for both doctor and patient, the use of prescription drugs is embedded in a complex system of marketing and advertising. Pharmaceutical promotions to physicians (detailing, free samples, educational events) help shape the physicians' perceptions of available options; media coverage and direct-to-consumer prescription drug advertisements (at least in the United States) shape patients' articulations of symptom and expectation. The principle of rational prescribing—giving the right medicine in the right dose at the right time—overlaps and may conflict with the principles of rational marketing—ensuring a growing volume of sales for a specific company's brand of prescription drug (Tomes, 2005).

The recourse to rationality misses the significance of the many "irrational" impulses that motivate both doctor and patient. Both parties bring to the medical encounter unconscious and conscious motives: beliefs, assumptions, wishes, and desires that do not fit neatly into the category of efficacy (see, e.g., Metzl, 2003). Showing a patient the latest results from a large-scale study of a drug or procedure does not necessarily dampen the hope that the therapy might work for this specific individual. Strong economic incentives make it all too easy for physicians to recommend the latest drug or treatment. The fact that the vast majority of healthcare spending occurs in the last year of life underlines how complex these decisions are (Hoover, Crystal, Kumar, Sambamoorthi, & Cantor, 2002).

As a good example of what sociologists call the "perpetuation of doubt" problem (Williams & Calman, 1996), attempts to apply scientific methods to clarify the value of different treatments, as in evidence-based medicine, run up against competing systems of determining authenticity and value that may undercut legitimacy in the eyes of at least some patients.[5]Are doctors' choices shaped by pharmaceutical marketing practices less valid than ones shaped by reading the latest Cochrane review? Are patient choices based on drug ads less valid than choices based on consulting the latest edition of *Worst Pills, Best Pills* (Wolfe, Sasich, & Lurie, 2002)? Answering those questions requires not simply becoming more statistically literate but also becoming more reflective about the cultural complexities involved in the process of choosing itself.

One obvious solution is to limit the number of choices available by determining and enforcing "best practices" guidelines, a strategy consistent with modern decision science, which finds that too many choices are paralyzing. In other words, doctors and patients would do better with shorter menus featuring only the best choices, surely a sensible suggestion (Schwartz, 2004). But the closing down of choice has to be conducted with scrupulous attention to *how* and *by whom* this is done; for either doctors or patients to give up certain choices, they have to be reassured that the slate of options is being inscribed in *their* best interests, not in the interests of some third-party stakeholder. Most patient advocates would agree that in setting practice guidelines physicians should be the senior partners. By professional training and experience, they are the most logical group to judge among alternatives, discarding some and promoting others. But to exercise their crucial roles on patients' behalf as "learned intermediaries" and trustworthy agents, they have faithfully to demonstrate their credentials for superior choosing: by agreeing on scientific standards of value, by distancing professional judgments from commercial pressures, and by including patient representatives as close advisors in the process of structuring healthcare choices.

A case in point is the evidence-based medicine movement. Evidence-based medicine, defined as "the conscientious, explicit and judicious use of current best evidence in making decisions about the care of individual patients," represents a creative wedding of expert collaboration, information technology, and sophisticated statistical analysis. In the last decade, it has gained great popularity as a new conception of the scientific "gold standard" that is seemingly firewalled from both bad science and commercial influence. It is a classic example of the kind of "late modern" rationality identified by sociologists in the Giddens-Beck school: a technologically sophisticated approach to therapeutic choice that attempts to minimize risk by better understanding and predicting it.

As critics immediately recognized, evidence-based medicine had the potential to perpetuate a hierarchical conception of information in which patients' goals and expectations come last. Cochrane groups and other evidence-based medicine initiatives were initially set up as collaborations between researchers and clinicians, not between doctors and patients. In the pyramid figures often used to illustrate the ordering of medical information, sources close to the patient tended to be at the bottom (Mead & Bower, 2001). In response to these criticisms, evidence-based groups have begun in recent years to extend the concept of collaboration to include consumers. Yet the challenges to making these collaborations work remain daunting on many fronts. As Hilda Bastian noted in the *Cochrane News* in

January 1998, "Involving consumers is something that is easier said than done—especially when everyone's time and resources are stretched." For this involvement to be more than "an ad hoc or token activity," she noted, "there needs to be a systematic plan and approach—and someone has to be responsible for seeing it through."

The dissemination and acceptance of evidence-based guidelines to lay audiences also involves a challenge, inasmuch as their credibility depends on a level of statistical sophistication of risk and risk reduction that is beyond even many physicians. On that score, physicians today are probably better prepared than they were 40 years ago to acknowledge the statistical basis of modern risk calculation. In comparison, lay people rarely get any systematic introduction to the same issues, a lacuna that leaves them open to influence from dubious opinion makers. Given the high degree of economic and statistical "illiteracy" revealed in popular surveys, it is unlikely that most people comprehend the statistical reasoning behind the risk assessment of drug treatments of the sort that led to the withdrawal of some Cox 2 inhibitors, a family of prescription drugs designed to reduce inflammation, from the market.

Likewise, the larger economics of healthcare are hard to understand, in part because they are extraordinarily complex and in part because they are the subject of intense intellectual and ideological debate. Again, if people do not score well on economic "literacy tests" about common economic facts such as the differences between adjustable and fixed rate loans, are they likely to understand the risks involved in the privatization of medical savings accounts or the economic concept of "moral hazard"? To sum up, making good choices is hard work for which most of us are both underprepared and undersupported. All parties involved need better guidance in negotiating the healthcare challenges of the 21st century.

Collective collaborations, in which trusted intermediary groups seek credible treatment guidelines, grounded in good science and vetted by both medical and patient representatives, and conducted behind firewalls that minimize for-profit market influences, seem the more promising route for the future. In the United States, where a high degree of medical specialization exists, the logical place for such discussions is the level of medical specialties and their relevant associated patient advocacy groups. In many areas of medicine, especially those having to do with serious, chronic threats to health such as cancer, those alliances between medical groups and advocacy groups have, in fact, developed over the last 20 years (see Chapter 17) and have made promising strides toward defining common objectives (Lerner, 2001). The field of mental health offers a particularly striking example in which collaborative inter-actions among patient/consumer groups, policy makers, and clinical researchers have replaced the hostile exchanges of the 1970s with good results (Tomes, 2006a).

The challenge is to combine these networks into larger political alliances to press for points of common interest. As this chapter suggests, patient advocates have succeeded more easily in securing specific changes in treatment than they have in stimulating deep seated structural changes. The latter objective is obviously much harder to realize, yet absolutely essential for future progress. Historical experience suggests pursuit of these much needed changes will be difficult and frustrating.

In the face of those challenges, I urge readers of this collection to do the following: to accept the complexity of the issues involved and to reject overly simplistic models of victims and villains, to "think globally and act locally" by combining activism around specific issues and dis-ease problems with political actions focused on more structural change, to work hard at finding common ground with other advocacy groups, both of patients and of health professionals, and to strive to overcome the limitations of conventional consumer empowerment when it comes to the health needs of the poor and unpopular. These strategies offer the best hope for fully realizing the benefits of collaboration between doc-tor and patient, surely as worthy a goal in the early 21st century as it was in the 1970s.

ENDNOTES

1. For a good summary of the contrasts between the old and new models of patient care, see Mead and Bower, 2001.
2. "The reports of my death are greatly exaggerated," quipped Mark Twain on reading the premature obituary of himself in the *New York Journal*.
3. There is as yet no synthetic history of this consumer health revolution. Hamilton (1982) provided a good survey from the perspective of the early 1980s; Halpern (2004) and Tomes (2006a) provided more recent overviews.
4. Other influential 1970s discussions of the emergence of the medical "monopoly" are Jewson (1976), Freidson (1970), Zola (1972), Ehrenreich and English (1973), and Szasz (1960).
5. For a good discussion of evidence-based medicine, see Williams and Calman (1996, especially pp. 1614–1615).

REFERENCES

Bastian, H. (1998). Planning consumer participation in review groups. [Electronic version]. *Cochrane News, 12.* Retrieved May 15, 2005, from http://www.cochrane.org/newslett/ ccnews12.pdf.

Boston Women's Health Book Collective. (1973). *Our bodies; ourselves.* New York: Simon and Schuster.

Burris, S. (1997). The invisibility of public health: Population-level measures in a politics of market individualism. *American Journal of Public Health, 87,* 1607–1610.

Checkoway, B (Ed.). (1981). *Citizens and health care: Participation and planning for social change.* New York: Pergamon Press.

Cohen, L. (1998). The new deal state and the making of citizen consumers. In S. Strasser (Ed.), *Getting and spending: European and American consumer societies in the twentieth century* (pp. 111–125). New York: Cambridge University Press.

Countryman, K. M., & Gekas, A. B. (1980). *Development and implementation of a patient's bill of rights in hospitals.* Chicago: American Hospital Association.

Ehrenreich, B., & English, D. (1973). *Complaints and disorders: The sexual politics of sickness.* Old Westbury, NY: Feminist Press.

Ehrenreich, J., & Ehrenreich, B. (1970). *The American health empire: Power, profits, and politics.* New York: Random House.

Engel, J. (2002). *Doctors and reformers: Discussion and debate over health policy, 1925–1950.* Columbia, SC: University of South Carolina Press.

Falk, I. S., Rorem, C. R., & Ring, M. D. (1933). *The costs of medical care: A summary of investigations on the economic aspects of the prevention and care of illness.* Chicago: University of Chicago Press.

Freidson, E. (1970). *The profession of medicine: A study of the sociology of applied knowledge.* New York: Dodd, Mead.

Gordon, C. (2003). *Dead on arrival: The politics of health care in twentieth-century America.* Princeton, NJ: Princeton University Press.

Halpern, S. (2004). Medical authority and the culture of rights. *Journal of Health Politics, Policy and Law, 29,* 835–852.

Hamilton, P. A. (1982). *Health care consumerism.* St. Louis: C. V. Mosby.

Hilts, P. J. (2003). *Protecting America's health: The FDA, business, and one hundred years of regulation.* New York: Knopf.

Hoover, D. R., Crystal, S., Kumar, R., Sambamoorthi, U., & Cantor, J. C. (2002). Medical expenditures during the last year of life: Findings from the 1992–1996 Medicare current beneficiary survey. *Health Services Research, 37,* 1625–1642.

Illich, I. (1975). *Medical nemesis: The expropriation of health.* New York: Pantheon.

Institute of Medicine. (1999). In L. T. Kohn, J. M. Corrigan, & M. S. Donaldson (Eds.), *To err is human: Building a safer health system.* Washington, DC: National Academy Press.

Institute of Medicine, Committee on Quality of Health Care in America. (2001). *Crossing the quality chasm: A new health system for the 21st century.* Washington, DC: National Academy Press.

Jackson, C. O. (1970). *Food and drug legislation in the New Deal.* Princeton, NJ: Princeton University Press.

Jewson, N. (1976). The disappearance of the sick man in medical cosmology, 1770–1870. *Sociology, 10,* 225–244.

Kallet, A., & Schlink, F. J. (1933). *100,000,000 guinea pigs: Dangers in everyday foods, drugs, and cosmetics.* New York: Grosset & Dunlap.

Katz, J. (1984). *The silent world of doctor and patient.* New York: Free Press.

Lamb, R. D. (1936). *The American chamber of horrors; the truth about food and drugs.* New York: Farrar & Rinehart.

Leavitt, J. W. (2003). What do men have to do with it? Fathers and mid-twentieth-century childbirth. *Bulletin of the History of Medicine, 77,* 235–262.

Lerner, B. H. (2001). *The breast cancer wars: Hope, fear, and the pursuit of a cure in twentieth-century America.* New York: Oxford University Press.

Ludmerer, K. M. (1985). *Learning to heal: The development of American medical education.* New York: Basic Books.

McLean, T., & Richards, E. (2004). Health care's "thirty years war": The origins and dissolution of managed care. *New York University Annual Survey of Law, 60,* 283–328.

Mead, N., & Bower, P. (2001). Patient-centeredness: A conceptual framework and review of the empirical literature. *Social Science and Medicine, 51,* 1087–1110.

Metzl, J. (2003). *Prozac on the couch: Prescribing gender in the era of wonder drugs.* Durham, NC: Duke University Press.

Morgen, S. (2002). *Into our own hands: The women's health movement in the United States, 1969–1990.* New Brunswick, NJ: Rutgers University Press.

Packard, E. P. W. (1973, 1875). *Modern persecution, or, insane asylums unveiled.* (Reprint of the 1875 ed. published by Case, Lockwood and Brainard, Hartford. ed.). New York: Arno Press.

Pipes, S. (2004). *Miracle cure: How to solve America's health care crises and why Canada isn't the answer.* San Francisco: Pacific Research Institute.

Piven, F. F., & Cloward, R. A. (1979). *Poor people's movements: Why they succeed, how they fail.* New York: Vintage Press.

Preston, L., & Bloom, P. (1986). Concerns of the Rich/Poor consumer. In P. Bloom & R. Smith (Eds.), *The future of consumerism* (pp. 37–57). Lexington, MA: Lexington Books.

Rosenberg, C. E. (1979). The therapeutic revolution: Medicine, meaning, and social change in nineteenth-century America. In M. J. Vogel, & C. E. Rosenberg (Eds.), *The therapeutic revolution* (pp. 3–25). Philadelphia: University of Pennsylvania Press.

Rosenberg, C. E. (1999). Codes visible and invisible: The twentieth-century fate of a nineteenth-century code. In R. B. Baker (Ed.), *The American medical ethics revolution: How the AMA's code of ethics has transformed physicians' relationships to patients, professionals, and society* (pp. 207–217). Baltimore, MD: Johns Hopkins University Press.

Schlesinger, M. (2005). The dangers of the market panacea. In *Healthy, wealthy, and fair: Health care and the good society* (pp. 91–134). James A. Moore and Lawrence R. Jacobs, Eds. New York: Oxford University Press.

Schwartz, B. (2004). *The paradox of choice: Why more is less.* New York: HarperCollins.

Shapiro, J. P. (1993). *No pity: People with disabilities forging a new civil rights movement.* New York: Times Books.

Starr, P. (1982). *The social transformation of American medicine.* New York: Basic Books.

Szasz, T. S. (1960). *The myth of mental illness.* New York: Harper and Row.

Tomes, N. J. (2005). The great American medicine show revisited. *Bulletin of the History of Medicine, 79,* 627–663.

Tomes, N. J. (2006a). The patient as a policy factor: A historical case study of the consumer-survivor movement in mental health. *Health Affairs, 25,* 720–729.

Tomes, N. J. (2006b). Patients or health care consumers? Why the history of contested terms matters. In R. Stevens, C. Rosenberg, & C. Burns (Eds.), *Public health and public policy* (pp. 83–110). New Brunswick, NJ: Rutgers University Press.

Tomes, N. J. (2007). *The patient paradox.* Manuscript in preparation.

Weisman, C. S. (1998). *Women's health care: Activist traditions and institutional change.* Baltimore, MD: Johns Hopkins University Press.

Williams, S. J., & Calman, M. (1996). The "limits" of medicalization? Modern medicine and the lay populace in "late" modernity. *Social Science and Medicine, 42,* 1609–1620.

Wilson, R. (1963). Patient-practitioner relationships. In H. Freeman, S. Levine, & L. Reeder (Eds.), *Handbook of medical sociology* (pp. 273–295). Englewood Cliffs, NJ: Prentice-Hall.

Wolfe, S. M., Sasich, L. D., & Lurie, P. (2002). *Worst pills, best pills: A consumer's guide to avoiding drug-induced death or illness.* New York: Pocket Books.

Zola, I. (1972). Medicine as an institution of social control. *Sociological Review, 20,* 487–504.

CHAPTER 15

Advocacy for Residents in Long-Term Care: Lessons and Challenges

Elma L. Holder and Barbara Frank

OBJECTIVES

- To identify essential elements of successful advocacy and key characteristics of effective advocates using the nursing home reform movement in the United States
- To illustrate that successful advocacy takes many forms and uses strategies based on the advocate's skills and experiences and based on the situation in which the advocacy is needed
- To demonstrate that because social issues are complex and deeply embedded within health settings, advocacy can be equally complex, multifaceted, adaptable, and persistent
- To show the interdependency between local, state, and national advocacy, individual and systemic advocacy, professional and volunteer advocacy, advocacy working within the system collaboratively, and confrontational advocacy working outside the system
- To emphasize the importance of building coalitions and incorporating all stakeholders in order to achieve advocacy goals

Every day, 1.6 million people in America wake up in a nursing home (Walshe & Harrington, 2001). Whether they are there for a short stay or for the rest of their lives, while in a nursing home, they are dependent on the kindness and competency of caregiving staff to meet their physical, mental, and emotional needs. The care they get today is better than it was 40 years ago, when nursing home advocacy efforts began in earnest, but for the most part, it is still far from what any of us would want for our loved ones or ourselves. The improvements experienced by today's nursing home residents are the result of decades of hard work by many in the long-term care system—volunteer and professional advocates, courageous people inside and outside of government, practitioners, researchers, reporters, and many others (Gudzowsky & Feinberg, 1995). A primary lesson of this chapter is that no one can do it all alone. The hallmark of nursing home reform advocates' effectiveness has been their continuous work with all parties in the system, drawing on different stakeholders' wisdom, hearing out their concerns and experiences, and relying on their energies, innovations, and convictions in moving good care forward (Hawes, 1996; Horn & Griesel, 1977; Institute of Medicine [IOM], Committee on Improving Quality in Long-Term Care, 2001).

Social issues such as nursing home care are complex, embedded as they are in larger social and fiscal policies. The quality of nursing home care is directly related to Medicaid and Medicare payment and oversight practices and is affected by social issues related to race, class, age, and gender (National Citizen's Coalition for Nursing Home Reform [NCCNHR], 1983; Stone, 2000). Not one effort alone could have led to the reforms that have occurred, and efforts over decades have not yet brought about universal improvement.

This chapter tells the story of advocates' work in improving long-term care and, by so doing, illustrates valuable lessons about effective advocacy in many settings. Some advocates have taken direct action to draw attention to abhorrent conditions; others have devised new approaches to improve care and enforce standards. These advocates have pushed and partnered with nursing home providers both to hold them accountable and to support them in their efforts to innovate and improve. Indeed, the nursing home reform movement, particularly as it manifested in organized citizen advocacy and the long-term care ombudsman program, provides a good basis for understanding the range of advocacy strategies undertaken through grassroots organizing and how such organizing can shape policy making, monitoring, and implementation.

In addition, this chapter describes the interplay between local, state, and national advocacy, that is, how advocates built a nationally supported, locally based system to give representation and assistance to vulnerable individuals who needed help to get good care. It also portrays how this national network drew and continues to draw on experiences of individual residents and their advocates to inform national and state policy development and implementation. Whether taking a stand against poor nursing home care or partnering with practitioners to bring about better practices, effective advocates adhere to several key principles to be illustrated in this chapter. These include do your homework; keep your constituents' perspective and well-being at the center of your thinking; be honest and direct; seek and contribute to the development, implementation and monitoring of solutions; speak truth to power; persevere; and bear witness to other people's suffering.

ORIGINS OF NCCNHR

"Grassroots" citizen advocates have played an important role in long-term healthcare reform since the beginning. These "kitchen table" advocates are ordinary people, called to action by moral conviction, who have

> **Advocacy Lesson 1**
> Change happens incrementally, over time.

learned to engage in the political process, work in coalitions, garner media attention, and represent the needs of their loved ones. In 1968, as Marion Ballentine visited her retired school teacher friends living in nursing homes in Spokane, Washington, she realized that some staff among those caring for her friends had little training in care for older persons, were overwhelmed by working short staffed, and were exhausted from working multiple jobs to make ends meet. She saw that in order for her friends to receive good care, the nursing assistants needed more support to improve their abilities, opportunities, and daily work experiences. She gathered her retired colleagues around her kitchen table, and together they learned about state policies related to nurse aide qualifications, training, and pay. Over many years, they worked to upgrade training requirements and wages, learning how to support their cause effectively at the state capital. Nursing assistants often met in Ms. Ballentine's home, where she taught and supported them and their cause (NCCNHR, n.d.).

Their group, Citizens for the Improvement of Nursing Homes, helped found the NCCNHR, which will be profiled in greater detail throughout this chapter; the original group also influenced NCCNHR's development of its first issue paper, "The Plight of the Nurse Aide in America's Nursing Homes: An Obstacle to Quality Care for Nursing Home Residents," published in 1978. That paper called for action to improve pay, benefits, qualifications, training, opportunities, and working conditions for nursing assistants. As is detailed more fully later here, in 1987, NCCNHR combined the advocacy of its grassroots members with the efforts of dozens of national organizations to enact a federal nursing home reform law that requires all nurse aides to receive a minimum of 75 hours of training. Across the country, this requirement became the national standard. Certified nursing assistants were no longer hired off the street and placed in a position to care for people without training in how to do so.

WHY ADVOCACY IS NEEDED IN LONG-TERM CARE

In the 40 years since Marion Ballentine gathered friends around her kitchen table, much has improved through a range of advocacy initiatives, all building on each other; yet serious problems remain.

The Current Situation

Advocacy continues to be crucial in long-term care settings because of the vulnerability of the people served. Older persons and persons with disabilities are susceptible to a host of serious problems (Carlson, 1999; Consumer Consortium on Assisted Living, 2002; Crescenzo, 2003; Lieberman & Rudder, 2005; Rudder & Lieberman, 2005). They frequently face multiple, complex health conditions that leave them frail and with limited mobility. Communication problems such as hearing loss, visual impairments, and speaking difficulties make it hard for many to communicate their needs or advocate for themselves. Social isolation and lack of support from family, friends, or social groups are common. Likewise, impediments such as mental confusion, depression, dementia, and Alzheimer's disease make it challenging to ensure the provision of good care. This complex web of physical, social, and emotional factors contributes to isolation and vulnerability, making it hard for nursing home residents to speak for themselves, vote with their feet, or seek help from others (Lombardo, Fogel, & Robinson, 1995). In this context, advocacy helps individuals get good care and receive benefits that they are entitled to, such as Medicare, Medicaid, rehabilitation and disability, mental health, and legal services.

Government studies over the past 40 years have documented major quality-of-care problems in nursing homes. For a sample of these studies, one need only review Senate and House Committee on Aging and General

Accounting Office reports. Problems experienced by nursing home residents run the gamut from horrific abuse and neglect to the slow wasting away caused by loneliness, isolation, depersonalization, and despair. When nursing homes are short staffed, residents often go without basic assistance with meals, drinks, toileting, exercise, bathing, and meaningful activity. Residents can develop pressure ulcers, contractures, and experience declines in their mobility and ability to function independently (IOM, 2001; U.S. General Accounting Office, 1997).

In addition, many residents live in a state of "psychic despair" from the experience of living in a state akin to homelessness (Carboni, 1987). Many nursing homes adhere to tight schedules in which staff wake people according to the task list instead of their individual preferences, bring them trays of food as they come up from the kitchen rather than when and what they want to eat, and toilet and turn people by the clock rather than by their needs. These problems represent the failure of the long-term care system as a whole to provide individualized care that supports people to continue to thrive physically and emotionally to the extent possible given their medical conditions (Elon, 1992; Harrington, Carillo, & Crawford, 2004). Over the years, advances in understanding about best practices have helped caring practitioners make improvements (Center for Excellence in Assisted Living, n.d.). Advocates have been in the forefront of disseminating these practices and embedding them into laws, regulations, and governmental oversight activities.

Nursing home staff members represent another disenfranchised group, with their own vulnerabilities (Wilner & Wyatt, 1999). They are all too often plagued with barriers that prevent good care. Staff shortages are common, resulting in exhausting work schedules (Bates, 1999; Harrington et al., 2004). Most workers receive minimal wages with few benefits, lack proper supervision and training, and go without necessary equipment and supplies to provide appropriate care. Traditional command and control approaches to management depersonalize staff, and institutionalized care systems set a deadening pace that dehumanizes caregiving. For these reasons, the long-term care advocacy movement has always taken a dual approach, working for the rights of residents even as it seeks to improve working conditions for those who provide care (Assisted Living Work Group, 2003; Association of Health Facility Survey Agencies et al., 2003).

Although most people think of nursing homes when there is talk of long-term care, essential care and services extend far beyond the nursing home. Services encompass outpatient medical and healthcare for chronic conditions, home care, assisted living, and board and care, as well as long-term hospitalization and rehabilitation. Patient advocacy is needed in each of these arenas. This chapter centers on advocacy for residents living in nursing homes, but the approaches, methods, tools, and skills needed for advocacy cut across the spectrum of long-term care venues and indeed, are applicable to healthcare advocacy in many programs and settings (Grant, 2003).

Barriers to Reform

Some individual level problems can be readily solved through advocacy. Yet systems reform is an important aspect of long-term care advocacy and is a much more arduous process. A plethora of crucial state and national laws and regulations help protect residents in long-term care. For example, federal and state laws now guarantee residents' rights and require a comprehensive assessment and plan of care, directing nursing homes to "provide care and services to attain or maintain the highest practicable physical, mental, and psychosocial well-being of each resident."[1] Ample evidence, however, documents that regulatory agencies, state and national, have failed to implement these public standards in a manner that achieves enduring change to benefit patients or (to use the preferred term) residents.

A case in point is the chronic understaffing that plagues the majority of nursing homes in the country (Harrington et al., 2004; NCCNHR, 2003a). Without payment for adequate staff, livable wages, and better working conditions, nursing homes will continually be short staffed, making it impossible for them to meet the requirements for residents' quality of care and quality of life (Marks, 1996). At the same time, however, requiring nursing homes to staff to a level that would fully meet residents' needs would necessitate an infusion of public funds on a scale that few states would consider. The effectiveness of government enforcement of standards is intertwined with its willingness to commit the level of public resources needed to support good care (U.S. General Accounting Office, 1997).

Sometimes, even when regulations are vigorously enforced, they may inadvertently contribute to problems rather than solving them. This arises in part because of sometimes contradictory requirements, as when enforcement of safety procedures trumps quality of life concerns. For example, the life safety code may be cited to prevent some residents from bringing their own furniture into rooms; in other instances, a nurse's aide may discourage residents from trying to move in an effort to prevent them from falling. Although such responses to resident independence may appear overly controlling, practitioners and facilities are held accountable for safety first and foremost, a policy often achieved at the expense of other important resident concerns. Nursing homes face serious consequences when a resident suffers a fall yet restraining residents to prevent them from attempting to stand up (and thereby preventing them from falling) leads many to lose their ability to walk altogether. The emphasis on safety backfires if regulators penalize falls in a way that promotes immobility. In short, operational issues are not always worked out ahead of time when new requirements are implemented, meaning that providers are sometimes held to conflicting standards (Dobkin, 1989; Wilson, 1993).

Organizational Resistance

Another obstacle that advocates face is habitual resistance and opposition to change by providers of care. Most health professionals and paraprofessionals, often providing treatment under adverse working conditions, strive hard to give good care. As a result, it can be emotionally difficult for caregivers to accept the reality that bad care exists, even in the face of conditions they would find unacceptable if they or their families were the victims.

Even though protective laws and regulations are established through an arduous public process involving all stakeholders, as this chapter illustrates, the long-term care industry as a whole denies the necessity of many laws and regulations, particularly when confronted with strong enforcement action for standards violations.

Opposition has different origins. Many nursing home staff members often feel scathed by each report of poor care and unappreciated for their earnest efforts. Some experience new regulations as another burden that does not positively affect their caregiving. For some owners, particularly larger corporations, opposition can result from business interests. Although nursing home owners sign a public contract accepting responsibility to provide good care to beneficiaries, they and their stockholders also expect profits in an explosively expensive healthcare system. Seventy-five percent of U.S. nursing homes are propriety, with net profits averaging only 2.2% (Scully, 2003). Needed changes, such as increased nurse-staffing levels, are often ignored in this context. A corporation's regional vice president may, for example, routinely call each facility for a report on daily census without giving similar attention to staffing levels, except to ensure that the facility is not "over budget." Corporate owners drive decision making to such an extent that some reward senior management with large end-of-year bonuses for keeping staffing, food, and other costs down, and even though corporate owners argue that they must maintain these practices to meet their bottom line, they also have numerous ways of reaping financial advantage before profit through related operations, leasing arrangements, and support of corporate operations. Taken together, these practices have a significant impact on quality of care (Bates, 1999; Harrington, 2001; HCIA & Arthur Anderson LLP, 1998).

Keeping this thorny framework of issues in mind when studying long-term advocacy affords a window into the serious and difficult work for people who, whether by choice or by necessity, become advocates. The challenges of combining individual problem solving with systemic advocacy emerge in many settings. This review of how they have been handled, successfully and unsuccessfully, in the context of long-term care, can provide guidance for other advocacy fields as well as long-term care.

THE ARC OF LONG-TERM CARE ADVOCACY: THE EARLY DAYS

Records of legislative committees and governmental agencies dating back to the 1950s document public concern about the delivery of healthcare to America's elderly and citizens with disabilities. At that time, nursing home care was governed by an uneven patchwork of state requirements. In many states, staff could be hired off the street with no training. Nursing home residents were at risk of fire, often found in states of neglect and sometimes abuse. Professional oversight of medical care was inadequate in many cases, and attention to quality of life was left to the resourcefulness of individual providers and family members. In the absence of federal regulations, homes ran the

Advocacy Lesson 2

Establishing national standards and systems is key. They provide a set of expectations for consumers, providers, and owners, and they provide the mechanisms for pursuing good care.

gamut from warm, loving care environments to places where people were left in their own urine and feces, moaning alone in their beds and chairs. Early reform activities (only later to be labeled *advocacy*) were motivated by individual and family complaints, usually made to elected representatives and government agencies and often broadcast by the media.

Reports of poor care and neglect of the elderly in institutions in the 1950s galvanized early professionals in the field of aging to champion a movement for national nursing home standards. Although these early efforts resulted only in voluntary standards (U.S. Department of Health, Education and Welfare, 1963), the document produced was the first to articulate a minimum threshold of acceptable care and would serve as the basis for later advocacy efforts.

Another notable effort to improve healthcare for older people was the public campaign to achieve Medicare and Medicaid. National organizations, such as the National Council of Senior Citizens, AARP, and the National Council on the Aging, drew on several important advocacy tools—effective public speaking and legislative lobbying—to convince political leaders that government-supported nursing home services were a needed resource. In the end, both Medicare and Medicaid provided funding for regulated nursing home care. At the same time, as a mechanism for ensuring good care, the programs included the proviso that state regulatory agencies must have facility owners sign contracts promising to provide good care according to publicly adopted standards. Following on the heels of the advent of Medicare and Medicaid, citizen advocacy groups began to address concerns related to nursing home care in their communities. The public standards of care became a reference point for their efforts.

ENTER CONSUMER ACTIVIST RALPH NADER

As a specialized field, consumer advocacy for nursing home reform emerged in the mid-1960s through the work of Ralph Nader. In 1969 Nader supported a group of college students and young professionals to conduct intensive research on turbulent issues in nursing homes. After a 1970 hearing of the U.S. Senate Special Committee on Aging, the Nader report, *Old Age: The Last Segregation*

Advocacy Lesson 3

Regulatory systems benefit from citizen groups or ombuds programs that help ensure enforcement of standards.

(Townsend & Nader, 1971), received wide publicity that led to a public outcry for reform.

In the following year, the president, in a major address, announced an eight-point nursing home reform program that called for stronger enforcement, training for personnel, and the formation of a government-funded demonstration ombudsman program. This third initiative was the brainchild of Dr. Arthur Flemming, an educator and statesman who served as Advisor on Aging to President Nixon. Recognizing that government standards alone could not ensure good care, Flemming oversaw development of a demonstration program that relied on citizens themselves to monitor and resolve problems in nursing homes. In the Scandinavian model, the ombudsman is a neutral party who weighs all factors surrounding a case to determine whether a government action or program harmed a citizen and, if so, serves as mediator in efforts to find a solution. Yet Dr. Flemming recognized that nursing home residents needed a different model. He designed the ombudsman program to provide advocacy for residents, recognizing that by virtue of their condition and their environment, they could not always advocate for themselves.

The three-year ombudsman demonstration project, started in 1972, eventually came to be housed in the Administration on Aging. Later, Congress made the ombudsman program a mandatory part of every state's services to its elders (1978 Amendments to the Older Americans Act). Comprehensive amendments in 1987 required each state ombudsman to engage in individual and systemic advocacy on behalf of nursing home residents without willful interference on the part of individuals or organizations hostile to their work; state ombudsmen were also required to support the development of citizen groups as well as resident and family councils (IOM, Division of Health Care Services, 1995).

FORMATIVE YEARS OF THE OMBUDSMAN PROGRAM COINCIDE WITH ENTRÉE OF CITIZEN ADVOCACY

Besides spurring legislative and government action, the 1970 Nader report inspired consumers in many states to organize advocacy groups. Hundreds of older persons responded to Nader, validating his group's assessment of poor nursing home conditions and the need for reform. Significantly, respondents urged Nader to include older volunteers in his consumer work on nursing homes. These recommendations led Nader to launch the Retired Professional Action Group in 1971 as part of his nursing home reform campaign (Townsend & Nader, 1971). At about the same time, developments such as the first national standards for nursing home care and the initiation of Medicare and Medicaid requirements for nursing home coverage led Nader's group to realize that consumer action at such an opportune moment could help bring about sweeping changes. To achieve its aims, the group adopted effective strategies from Nader's other advocacy work: (1) "do your homework" by identifying and documenting consumer experiences and initiatives around the country, (2) get a seat at the table with government agencies and others, and (3) use documented public concerns to refocus policy makers' and business interests' attention and priorities (see Chapter 16).

Providers had been involved from the beginning in government efforts to develop national Medicare/Medicaid regulations, but achieving consumer representation in these government deliberations was a struggle. In fact, the Retired Professional Action Group was the first to do so. Although they were able to make some headway representing resident concerns, they did not, at that point, have the leverage to significantly influence the rule-making process. Final regulations issued in 1972 therefore lacked standards that would mandate minimum nurse staffing levels. Unable to achieve its original aims, the organization used its national presence to generate vocal criticism of areas where the regulations fell short and set about increasing its negotiating power.

In 1972, Maggie Kuhn, with her retired professional friends, launched the premier National Gray Panther movement, an organization that successfully influenced policy on aging issues. Nader, inspired by Kuhn's work, led the Retired Professional Action Group to merge with the Gray Panthers in 1973. Nader's studious, fact-based approach, combined with Kuhn's energizing organizing abilities, proved a potent force for nursing home reform. Elma Holder, of the Retired Professional Action Group, worked with Kuhn to start the Gray Panther's Long-term Care Action Project. This project focused immediately on networking with advocates all over the country, an effort that resulted in a "Citizens' Action Guide to Nursing Home Reform" (Horn & Griesel, 1977). This foundational document, later published in book form as *Nursing Homes: A Citizen's Action Guide*, identified common issues related to residents' rights, staffing needs, poor food quality, and inadequate rehabilitative and medical services. At the same time, it guided readers to public resources and community strategies for tackling these issues. The guide helped build a national

Advocacy Lesson 4

Seize the day; use opportune moments to advance your aims and expand your agenda.

movement by underscoring individual advocacy groups' common mission and by sharing advocacy information and strategies.

At about the same time, in 1974, the Senate Special Committee on Aging responded to problems in nursing homes through the first in a series of reports on "Nursing Home Care in the United States: Failure in Public Policy" (U.S. Senate, Special Committee on Aging, 1974).[2] Coming in the wake of a devastating *New York Times* series on poor care in New York City's nursing homes, together with other publications documenting the grim realities of America's nursing homes (Butler, 1975; Mendelson, 1974; Moss & Halamandaris, 1977; Tulloch, 1975), this report substantiated concerns of rampant neglect and abuse.

Given this context, the local organizing activities of the newly formed Long-Term Care Action Project paid off in a national advocacy opportunity in June 1975. At that point, the American Health Care Association, in an effort to reach out to consumer groups, sponsored a meeting on "Participative Management in Nursing Homes." Holder and Kuhn made a strategic decision to use the gathering as an opportunity for consumer groups to unite and present themselves as a critical mass. On the day before the meeting, about 20 persons from citizen groups dedicated to nursing home reform strategized participation in this industry meeting and developed a platform of issues of common concern. By the end of the day, the attendees had formed the NCCNHR. By coming in to the American Health Care Association meeting as a united front, the groups were able to gain attention for their concerns. They even held a press conference before the meeting. For the first time, and at the American Health Care Association's own venture, a vanguard of newly united consumers expressed its views and demands for change to the nursing home industry.

Although begun as an ad-hoc organization, the needs NCCNHR addressed early on and the infrastructure that it was able to create (it has maintained a core membership of local and state groups) have translated to its success over a 30-year period. One key to the organization's strength has been its drive, not just to identify poor outcomes for residents, but to trace those problems to their roots and then focus their advocacy on those root causes. NCCNHR's first platform included the poor,

Advocacy Lesson 5

Focus advocacy on root causes, not just poor outcomes.

negligent, and abusive care witnessed by consumers. Yet the organization's members were also vividly aware of the link between poor working conditions and poor caregiving. NCCNHR's inaugural research resulted in a report presented to government officials and legislative committees in 1978 entitled "The Plight of the Nurse Aide in America's Nursing Homes: An Obstacle to Quality Care for Nursing Home Residents." This report made the case that, until workers' needs were addressed, nursing home staff would not be able to meet residents' needs (NCCNHR, 1978).

The NCCNHR also understood the importance of public standards of care—that they provide the framework for consumer expectations, provider guidelines, and the resources advocates can bring to bear on the system. Other early advocacy work therefore focused on developing regulations for nursing homes certified to receive payment from Medicare and Medicaid. The biggest battles were then and continue to be fought over attempts to adopt acceptable levels of nurse staffing and nurse aide training. Given that labor costs make up over 70% of the daily cost of nursing home care, these concerns also lie at the heart of the financial issues faced by corporate owners and government funders.

Another way in which advocates achieved legislative reform was by using the strategy of testing a law's efficacy in several states before proposing its adoption at the national level. For example, several novel regulations for resident rights were adopted by states in the 1970s as a result of a similar law's success in Minnesota. Examples include the right to have visitors for a minimum number of hours per day; the right to access one's medical records; and the rights to vote, to complain, to refuse treatment, and to manage one's own personal funds. These might today seem to be basic rights; in the 1970s, however, they were not guaranteed for every resident. Advocates had to work to secure them. The consumer group Nursing Home Residents' Advocates (now the ElderCare Rights Alliance) persuaded a number of states to adopt the regulation. Through this method, the new practice became widely accepted and, moreover, demonstrated the need for across-the-board requirements after some states failed to comply voluntarily with the guidelines. Based on this state experience and consumer advocacy nationally, the federal government issued residents' right regulations in 1980.

> **Advocacy Lesson 6**
>
> Demonstrating benefits of regulations in several states first can build support for national regulation.

Before the residents' rights regulations were even implemented, advocates learned just how tenuous a victory can be. In 1981, a new federal administration, believing that regulation interfered with market forces, announced that the residents' rights regulations and other protections would be rescinded. Because NCCNHR's representatives had approached the rule-making process with thoughtfulness and integrity, they had achieved strong credibility within the government agency. Government staff members shared crucial documents detailing the new administration's plan. In turn, NCCNHR provided the agency with comprehensive evidence documenting the continued need for these regulations and rallied supporters and the media to protest the proposed change of course. NCCNHR summarized and simplified the federal requirements so that their impact could be understood by the general public.

Advocacy Lesson 7

Working with integrity, even with adversaries, strengthens an organization's credibility, which is its lifeline.

As news accounts spread, individuals around the country called for the latest information, as did reporters, Congressional staff, and representatives of national organizations. Nursing home practitioners at that time were also gravely concerned. Doctors, nurses, social workers, administrators, and other nursing home staff called in to NCCNHR for information and guidance on action. NCCNHR was able to enlist national organizations representing these practitioners in a joint effort with the national network of ombudsmen and citizen groups to stop nursing home deregulation. NCCNHR's strategy of bringing local experience to the national scene and bringing national information to local individuals paid off. The administration was forced to change its position, announcing publicly that it "would not turn back the clock" on nursing home reform.

To prevent further damage to the regulations and to maintain the energy generated by its successful organizing efforts, NCCNHR seized the opportunity to help strengthen and improve the existing standards. NCCNHR used both the information provided by callers across the country, and the relationships developed through this process. This effort brought together over 60 organizations, including industry representatives. A hallmark of NCCNHR's strategy, initiated at that time and continued throughout its history, was to seek common ground among all stakeholders. Groups representing providers, practitioners, consumers, and labor worked through points of contention and hammered out agreements. They found, as they listened to one another, that they had more in common than they realized.

In the end, they collectively endorsed a plan that would result in stronger protections for residents and improvements in nursing home care (NCC-NHR, 1983, 1986). In addition, the group process helped build a strong working relationship among all parties.

In advocacy that takes the long view, each gain is a building block to the next (Hardcastle, Wenocur, & Powers, 1997). The consensus report addressing regulatory reform, presented in 1982, persuaded Congress to initiate a study of possible nursing home improvements. Because the national for-profit provider association, which had favored the proposals to deregulate federal oversight, had not sup-ported the consensus document, long-term care advocates used industry representatives' resist-ance to support not just another study, but a study designed to produce recommendations

Advocacy Lesson 8

Take the long view.

from the most respected of sources, the National Academy of Sciences IOM. In the meantime, Congress halted deregulatory efforts by inserting into the FY 83 budget bill a moratorium on government action on nursing home regulation, pending the study's completion.

NCCNHR played an active role throughout the 2-year IOM study, gathering information from local advocates to influence national work. It did so not only through staff contributions but, in keeping with its historic approach of drawing directly on its constituents, by facilitating direct contact between committee members and nursing home residents and their advocates. It has been a matter of principle for NCCNHR always to involve many nursing home residents directly in its day-to-day work as well as in its leader-ship structure. The organization convinced the IOM to convene one of its study sessions with representatives of consumer groups and actual nursing home residents and to commission papers researching consumer and resident

Advocacy Lesson 9

Always seek out and include the voice of your constituency.

involvement and concern. This process provided committee staff with a mountain of documented history they could not ignore.

Moreover, to help the committee fulfill its charge of understanding factors necessary to achieve quality care, NCCNHR itself engaged in a 12-month research study that resulted in the report "A Consumer Perspective on Quality Care: The Residents' Point of View" (1985). For this study, NCCNHR conducted intensive group interviews with more than 400 residents of nursing homes in 15 different localities, asking them to define quality care based on their experiences. A national symposium followed, attended by committee members, researchers, practitioners, advocates, and 12 nursing home residents who had participated in the study. After hearing first hand from residents about their experiences, the committee actually reframed its final report and recommendations in a fundamental way that reflected what it had learned from listening to residents.

Advocacy Lessons 10 and 11

Do not let good reports gather dust; seek common ground, achieve consensus among all stakeholders.

Released in spring 1986, the IOM report "Improving the Quality of Care in Nursing Homes" confirmed the need for strengthening nursing home regulations and provided recommendations for new mechanisms and practices to support better care. In response to what the committee had learned from residents, it also embraced each individual's quality of life as an essential component of quality care (IOM, 2001). The report signaled a turning point for NCCNHR. Instead of fighting *against* abuse and neglect, the group now had something to fight *for*, thanks to the authoritative IOM report outlining positive practices in nursing home care. In addition, instead of simply opposing government deregulation, NCCNHR could now advocate for proven regulatory practices.

Shortly after the IOM report was published, the study director personally challenged NCCNHR staff to prevent it from gathering dust. Moreover, Congress indicated that, before it could put IOM recommendations into law, interest groups needed to work out a policy consensus. Congressional allies did not want to be caught in the cross-fires of counter-lobbying efforts. As a response to both challenges, NCCNHR organized the *Campaign for Quality Care*. Representatives of over 50 national organizations representing older persons, industry, labor, and major professional groups came together regularly to discuss the IOM recommendations and develop agreement on how they should be translated into laws, regulations, and operational practices. In order to pass substantial legislation in Congress, they had to work through their differences and achieve consensus, a true challenge with so many different perspectives and interests represented. NCCNHR was able to ensure that everyone "had a seat at the table" and to reach consensus by challenging the group to put residents' needs at the center of its deliberations. As a result, the venture was a success.

THE 1987 NURSING HOME REFORM LAW: A PREMIUM TOOL FOR ADVOCACY

The report produced by the *Campaign for Quality Care in 1987* addressed long-standing areas of concern and debate about care delivery and oversight. It included consensus recommendations on 12 critical issues such as nurse staffing, nurse aide training, residents' rights, resident assessment and care planning, and enforcement. At the core of the recommendations from the IOM committee and the *Campaign for Quality Care* was a mechanism for supporting "individualized care." This process of assessment, care planning, and care delivery would also provide a focal point for inspections centered on care each individual resident received. The plan represented a revolution in nursing homes by affirming the right of each individual to good care, and it was endorsed by all parties. Once again, NCCNHR sought not only to set a standard of care but also to put in place a means for it to be implemented.

NCCNHR and its colleagues presented their consensus document in a joint briefing to members of Congress, signaling to legislators that support for this legislation would be a win for everyone. In previous legislative efforts, consumer and provider groups met separately with Congressional staff to present opposing viewpoints. Now they met together to present shared positions. As the debate over enactment ensued, the coalition partners worked together steadfastly and in an unprecedented manner and achieved a landmark public law.

> *Advocacy Lesson 12*
> Develop laws that allow citizens to help enforce standards.

The preeminent national *Nursing Home Reform Law* (OBRA, 1987) was achieved in December 1987, when it was secured as Title III of the Social Security Act. The law is an outstanding document, promising quality of care, quality of life, resident rights, best-care practices in the use of restraints, proper nutrition and hydration, and other critical healthcare issues. Furthermore, it holds promise for strong enforcement of these standards, making it one of the best possible tools for advocacy.

By ensuring, through law, that all residents must have a comprehensive care plan based on their healthcare needs and customary living habits, the advocacy movement elevated individual consumer concerns to the forefront of provider practice and government oversight. Before the law's enactment, nursing homes focused on and were judged by how their systems looked on paper. Now inspectors would look at care outcomes and care systems (Hawes, 1996).

The law also provided tools for advocacy. Previously, many residents and families who had sought to organize support for their concerns had faced intimidation and resistance from nursing homes. They also had found it difficult to access information about care decisions, let alone be a part of the decision-making process. Through this law, nursing homes were and are required to grant ombudsmen access to residents and their records (details about the impact of ombudsman programs on nursing home residents and on systemic reform are discussed in a later section). Residents and families are free to organize councils and to provide recommendations for change without retaliation; moreover, although it is not perfected in practice, nursing homes are required to support these efforts. Residents and family members (or their representatives) have the right to participate in resident assessment and care planning. The process has come full circle; individual long-term care experiences helped inform development of federal regulations that now, in turn, help bolster local advocacy efforts and improve individual experiences.

CITIZEN ADVOCACY AT THE LOCAL AND STATE LEVELS

Although collective citizen advocacy achieved a national nursing home reform law, it takes local advocacy to bring the law into reality for individual residents. Advocates provide education to members of their communities, represent their concerns to governmental entities, and push for enactment and enforcement of state level laws and regulations. They continually seek training to develop their basic advocacy skills: public speaking and communication, coalition building, media utilization, legislative monitoring and lobbying, utilization of the legal system, and effective fundraising. In the Nader tradition, citizen advocacy groups do their homework. At every stage of their work, education is a cornerstone of effective advocacy. Advocates need to know how a long-term care facility operates and to understand the mechanics of regulatory and legislative systems. They must have a basic knowledge of geriatric healthcare conditions and special precautions to prevent common, serious problems (inadequate nutrition and hydration, pressure sores, restraints, falls, overmedication, and immobility). They need to understand effective resident care planning and assessment, how to care for people with Alzheimer's disease, and how to identify and prevent negligence and abuse. As a matter of fact, advocates are often in a position to participate in the education and training of nursing home staff by providing important caregiving information and by facilitating sharing of best practices among providers.

Citizen advocacy groups can be found in many states throughout the country. The snapshots in Table 15.1 depict the wide range of local advocacy activities.

Most of these state-level groups focus to varying extents on public education, constituent development, and policy advocacy. Through policy forums, research, and testimony, they capture consumer experience and bring it to the policy debate. Some advocates work to make systems responsive to consumers; others go beyond the government, through lawsuits, or by supplementing information available to consumers. Many meticulously gather information and document their experiences. All find that enacting laws is never the end of the story. Monitoring and pressing for their implementation are ongoing efforts.

OMBUDSMAN PROGRAMS

Growth and Development 1975–2005

The ombudsman program, discussed earlier in the chapter, has had a major impact on improving conditions in nursing homes. More specifically, it provides a formal mechanism by which advocates are able to get involved with monitoring nursing home care and enforcing standards (Hunt, 2004a). As mentioned earlier, this innovative program began in 1974 when the Administration on Aging determined, through an extensive evaluation, that ombudsman programs were urgently needed to serve as advocates in resolving problems on behalf of nursing home residents. The Administration on Aging put muscle behind this program in 1975 by offering funds for every state to establish a statewide ombudsman program. Because of its effectiveness and because advocates were successful in demonstrating that effectiveness, in 1978, Congress made the program mandatory for every state through amendments to the Older Americans Act (Table 15.2).

Federal law gives ombudsmen major support and direction. State governments must ensure that program employees have access to long-term care facilities and their residents and, with the permission of a resident or

Table 15.1   Examples of Local Advocacy Initiatives Supporting Long-Term Care Reform

California Advocates for Nursing Home Reform (CANHR)

• Provides consumers with specific information about facility care based on state inspection reports.

• Provides extensive, consumer-friendly public survey information.

• Trains its network of family councils to use information effectively.

• Monitors the state's regulatory system by participating on state boards and committees; brings consumer viewpoint to policy discussions.

• Alerts constituents when proposals needing consumer action are underway.

• Educates consumers so they are knowledgeable about good care.

• Provides public education courses on topics such as pain management with older persons, end-of-life care, prevention of abuse, neglect, and exploitation.

• Produces a newsletter that informs readers of facilities' inspection reports.

• Provides onsite training to nursing home staff in about 30 cities, highlighting resident rights training.

Arkansas Advocates for Nursing Home Residents (ANNHR)

• Provides members with latest education on care-giving issues; updates members on legislative/governmental affairs.

• Monitors nurse staffing levels in Arkansas nursing homes to ensure standards are maintained.

• Raises public awareness of living conditions for residents by achieving regular attention from local media.

• Has achieved higher nurse-staffing standards in Arkansas through forming coalitions with other powerful consumer groups, documenting need, and generating active member participation.

Texas Advocates for Nursing Home Residents (TANHR)

• Organizes and trains family representatives to set up family councils that can hold facilities accountable for their care practices.

• Educates and trains family members on common care problems.

Table 15.2   The Role of the Ombudsman

Ombudsmen are paid staff and citizen volunteers who receive training to carry out a set of duties that rely on strong diplomacy and negotiating skills. Namely, ombudsmen receive and investigate complaints made by or on behalf of residents and then represent residents' interests in working to resolve them either by negotiating solutions with the staff and management of a facility, by referring complaints to the official licensure agency, or even by assisting residents in obtaining information about potential legal action. Additionally, the Older Americans Act requires each state Ombudsman office to have a full-time Ombudsman and to

1. Prepare an annual report of problems found and provide recommendations for changes in laws, regulations, and policies based on these problems.
2. Analyze and monitor development and implementation of local, state, and federal laws and recommend needed changes.
3. Provide information to public agencies, legislators, and others about problems and concerns of persons living in facilities.
4. Provide staff and volunteers with training; promote development of citizen organizations to participate in the ombudsman program.
5. Establish a statewide reporting system and procedures to ensure that resident files are confidential unless written permission is granted by the resident or the individual's legal representative or by court order.

resident's legal guardian, grant access to review residents' medical and social records. If a resident is unable to consent to the review and has no legal guardian, the ombudsman must be given appropriate access to the resident's records. In addition, all states must prohibit retaliation by a long-term care facility when and if any resident or employee files a complaint with or provides information to the ombudsman office. They must also ensure that program representatives are not liable for the good faith performance of official duties (NCCNHR, 2003b).

Today, thousands of paid and volunteer ombudsmen in every part of the country resolve tens of thousands of resident complaints (Office of Inspector General & U.S. Department of Health and Human Services, 2003). In addition to individual complaint resolution, they also work on legislative and policy issues and broker coalitions that support improved practices. They augment public enforcement efforts by their personal regular presence in nursing homes while also challenging the public enforcement system to be more responsive to nursing home residents' concerns.

The ombudsman programs serve as an official entity that bridges government action and citizen concerns. The programs work closely with citizen groups that in turn extend the reach of ombudsman programs. As demonstrated by the ombudsman program, government oversight of industries can be strengthened when coupled with local citizen action (National Association of State Long Term Care Ombudsman Programs, 2003).

State and Local Models

Ombudsman programs conduct various types of advocacy at both the state and local levels, including supplying decision makers with essential information about resident life in nursing homes, supporting residents in self-advocacy, pursuing legal strategies to address systemic problems, and supporting fundamental and system changes in the organizational culture of nursing homes (see Table 15.1) (National Association of State Units on Aging, 2002; Wheaton, n.d.).

Examples of Ombudsman Programs That Support Residents in Self-Advocacy

- The Barren River District Ombudsman Program (Kentucky) hosts annual meetings where residents of long-term care gather to discuss needs and concerns.
- A program in Connecticut hosts annual forums with presidents of resident councils to help guide their legislative agenda; it also provides their resident councils with training.
- State and local ombudsman programs in Minnesota, Massachusetts, and Maryland have established and provide support to family councils.

Examples of Ombudsman Programs Pursuing Legal Strategies to Address Systemic Problems

- The Washington State Ombudsman Program, with resident councils of Washington, filed suit against the Center for Medicaid and Medicare Services. They objected to new regulations that would permit hiring of "feeding assistants," a move that they believed side-stepped the mandated minimum levels of training required for nursing assistants (Center for Medicare Advocacy, 2004).

- Several state ombudsman programs partnered with Medicare fraud control units to train ombudsmen to identify billing fraud.
- Oklahoma's ombudsman program worked cooperatively in the late 1990s with federal crime agencies to investigate fraud and corruption among regulatory officials there. This scandal, leading to the imprisonment of one government official and a notorious nursing home owner, helped spearhead major legislative reforms in Oklahoma (Houser, 2003).

Examples of Ombudsman Programs Promoting Organizational "Culture Change"

- Using models produced by the Pioneer Network and other culture change experts (Action Pact Inc., 2001; Frank, 2000; Kuhn, 1991; Lustbader, 2000; Misorski, 2004; Quality Partners of Rhode Island, 2005; Weiner & Ronch, 2003), several state programs have worked to change the institutional culture of nursing homes. Ombudsmen team with practitioners to train management and staff on transforming nursing home care and systems to be person-centered instead of task-oriented.
- A number of ombudsman programs have taken up workforce retention and staffing as a key to improving the organizational culture. They have worked with Department of Labor resources, provider groups, and community colleges to provide educational opportunities in the workplace. Activities also include efforts to improve wages and benefits for staff and to bring more inclusive and supportive management approaches into practice (Estes, Hunt, Goldberg, Lohrer, & Nelson, 2004a).

In many states, state and local ombudsman programs help establish and/or work in close partnership with citizen advocacy groups (Hunt, 2001). Depending on circumstances, each organization assumes different roles; however, ombudsman programs and advocacy groups are not at all shy about monitoring one another and help to keep each other accountable for their advocacy work on behalf of nursing home residents. Some ombudsmen situated within state government experience limits in their ability to advocate for changes in state laws and rely on citizen advocates to represent residents' interests in the legislative process (O'Connor, 2002). In some cases, ombudsmen work within the system, attending government committee meetings, whereas citizen advocates press their cause from outside the system, through media, letter writing, public events, and other forms of advocacy (Hunt, 2004b, 2004c; NASOP, 2000).

ADVOCACY BY CONSUMERS AND OMBUDSMEN OFTEN INITIATES MAJOR REFORM CAMPAIGNS

Abundant documented evidence demonstrates that local, state, and national level advocacy by ombudsmen and citizen advocates has had a significant impact in improving long-term care (Estes, Zulman, Goldberg, & Ogawa, 2004b; Hedt, 2004). Major accomplishments that have been achieved over time through advocacy have included

- **Increasing**
  - Nurse staffing levels
  - Restraint-free care
  - Proper use of medications
  - Family and advocate access to residents and facilities
  - Effectiveness of advocates and ombudsmen
  - Consumer participation in governmental processes to regulate long-term care
  - Corporate accountability to state and federal governments

- **Improving**
  - Workers' condition
  - Nutrition and hydration for residents
  - Consumer access to information and education
  - Access to legal representation for residents harmed in long-term care
  - Conditions in nursing homes through transformational change in facility culture, management, and systems of service delivery

- **Establishing**
  - ○ Rights of residents and family members
  - ○ Resident and family councils
  - ○ Resident assessment and care planning
  - ○ Quality indicators for nursing homes
  - ○ Avenues to enforce laws and regulations

- **Preventing**
  - ○ Abuse, neglect, and exploitation of long-term care residents
  - ○ Medicaid cutbacks in benefits for residents
  - ○ Government program and policy that would weaken the national law (NCCNHR, n.d.)

Every one of these arenas is replete with examples of outstanding advocacy. The list demonstrates the breadth and complexity of advocacy work and the reality that all significant change happens incrementally. Each of these areas has required work over several decades, and all continue to present ongoing challenges.

In the states and at the national level, citizen advocates and ombudsmen have been the prime players in initiating action on issues that concern residents and their families (Burger, 1996). The progressive body of work on restraints, resident assessment and care planning, malnutrition and dehydration, nurse staffing, and culture change can all be traced to introductory action by advocates (Holder, 1985). Their effectiveness in all of these spheres is largely due to their exceptional information gathering, research, and monitoring as well as their dissemination efforts (Hedt, 2004; IOM, 1995). Multiple high-quality "how-to" manuals guide family members in getting good care for loved ones and advocating for high-quality care for others on a broader scale (Fish-Parcham, 2001; Grant, 2002; Lieberman, 1995; NCCNHR, 1998; Smetanka, 1997). It also reflects the close relationship advocates have developed with researchers in gerontology and healthcare as well as with healthcare professional groups.

As a case in point, in the mid-1980s, the NCCNHR focused its annual meetings on training advocates on resident assessment and care planning so that when the IOM recommended a comprehensive assessment and care planning process, advocates understood it well and could support its proper implementation in their communities. In that same time period, NCCNHR's annual meetings introduced advocates to practitioners at the forefront of removing physical and chemical restraints. Ombudsmen replicated these training programs in their own states, joining a national movement to "Untie the Elderly." This interplay of local and national advocacy allows the NCCNHR and other organizations to bring local issues to national attention and to provide local groups with national education that can have a powerful impact in their local communities.

CONCLUSION: FINAL THOUGHTS ABOUT ADVOCACY

Ample evidence in the literature shows that hundreds—indeed thousands—of older persons and others with chronic disabilities have suffered harm in long-term care. Current records (from regulatory inspections, legislative reports, research studies, and routine reports from ombudsmen and advocates) affirm that poor care, neglect, abuse, and exploitation continue to exist (NCCNHR, 1997; Walshe & Harrington, 2001). Although this is not true in every long-term care setting in every community, it is commonplace and cannot be ignored. At the same time, thousands of nursing home staff members go to work every day with good hearts and intentions, some without the tools and support to care well, and others to caring environments that allow the most humane caregiving. Advocates face the challenge of speaking the truth about both the daily problems and the caring efforts because both are true.

In this context, work on important issues such as long-term care can be highly controversial, even downright confrontational. Although being an advocate requires perseverance, it does not mean one has to be an unrelenting adversary. Advocates are challenged to be open to the experiences and perspectives of those they may see as opponents. The best advocates for residents in long-term care place a high value on being honest, fair, and civil in their approach to advocacy. They must be open to allies from any quarter and prepared to speak the truth in every direction. In the end, for real change to succeed, people must grow in their understanding of one another.

This chapter has focused on advocacy for residents in nursing homes by describing the progress of a social change movement from the kitchen table to the United States Congress. More broadly, however, this chapter has attempted to highlight that lessons learned in this arena are applicable to all healthcare advocacy efforts. Without advocacy in this arena or in virtually all arenas where health and welfare are at stake, living conditions would not improve. Some advocates are drawn to this work by personal experience, others by a commitment to make a difference. When they work well—by doing their homework, being sound in their judgment, keeping the person they are advocating for in the center of their thinking, and working more for a win–win than just a win—they make a world of difference.

Julie Trocchio, who led the efforts of the nursing home industry during the era when the Nursing Home Reform Law was being developed and enacted, gave a gift to these authors at the end of that great campaign. It was a commissioned cartoon that depicted her lying in her bed with sheep jumping over it. The sheep had our names as lead advocates who had at one time been her adversaries and with whom she had partnered to pass this landmark law. The caption read, "I sleep better knowing you are here."

ENDNOTES

1. Federal Nursing Home Reform Act from the Omnibus Budget Reconciliation Act of 1987.
2. This report contains nine supporting papers covering abuse, drug misuse, lack of medical care and nursing staff, nursing home fires, mental health, lack of access for minorities, and profits.

REFERENCES

Action Pact Inc. (2001). *Culture change now! Creating community in long-term care.* (Periodical, vol. 1). Retrieved November 16, 2006, from http://www.culturechangenow. com/mag-ish1.html.

Assisted Living Work Group. (2003). *Assuring quality in assisting living: Guidelines for federal and state policy, state regulation, and operations (a report to the U.S. Senate Special Committee on Aging, April 2003.)* Retrieved November 15, 2006, from http://www.aahsa.org/alw/intro.pdf.

Association of Health Facility Survey Agencies, Center for Medicare Advocacy, National Association for Regulatory Administration, National Association of Local Long-Term Care Ombudsmen, National Association of State Ombudsman Programs, National Citizens' Coalition for Nursing Home Reform, National Committee to Preserve Social Security and Medicare, et al. (2003). *Policy principles for assisted living (presented to the U.S. Senate Special Committee on Aging, April 2003).* Retrieved November 15, 2006, from http://www.ltcombudsman.org//uploads/PolicyPrinciplesforAL0403.pdf.

Bates, E. (1999). *The shame of our nursing homes: Millions for investors, misery for the elderly. (In The Nation, March 29, 1999 issue, pp. 11–19).* Retrieved November 15, 2006, from http://www.thenation.com/doc/19990329/bates.

Burger, S. (1996). *Nursing homes: Getting good care there.* San Luis Obispo, CA: American Source Books.

Butler, R. (1975). *Why survive? Being old in America.* New York: Harper & Row.

Carboni, J. T. (1987). *Making it home (Carboni quoted within presentation by Quality Partners of Rhode Island).* Retrieved November 15, 2006, from http://www.sdaho.org/ Convention/2006/Handouts/B%20&%20F%20Making%20it%20HOME.pdf.

Carlson, E. M. (1999). Looking behind the facade of assisted living (within chapter on residential care facilities). *Long-term care advocacy.* Newark, NJ: LexisNexis.

Center for Excellence in Assisted Living. (n.d.). *Assisted Living Quality Summit 2004.* Retrieved on November 15, 2006, from http://www.theceal.org.

Center for Medicare Advocacy. (2004). *Resident Councils of Washington vs. Thompson. (lawsuit regarding CMS regulations for feeding assistants in nursing homes filed by the Center for Medicare Advocacy; update December 2004).* Retrieved November 16, 2006, from http://www.medicareadvocacy.org.

Consumer Consortium on Assisted Living. (2002). *Choosing an assisted living facility: Considerations for making the right decision* (2nd ed.). Retrieved November 15, 2006, from http://www.metlife.com/WPSAssets/94678680301027365983V1FPDF13.pdf.

Crescenzo, J. (2003). In R. Smith (Ed.), *Choosing assisted living: What you need to know.* Falls Church, VA: Consumer Consortium on Assisted Living.

Dobkin, L. (1989). *The board and care system: A regulatory jungle.* Washington, DC: American Association of Retired Persons, Consumer Affairs Program Department.

Elon, R. (1992). Abuse and neglect of elderly persons living in nursing homes: Prevention and intervention. *Journal of Medical Direction, 2,* 76–80.

Estes, C. L., Hunt, S., Goldberg, S., Lohrer, S. P. & Nelson, M. (2004a). *Enhancing the performance of local long-term care ombudsman programs in New York State and California project (web reference to the toolkit is a 2006 product from the research project).* Retrieved November 16, 2006, from http://www.ltcombudsman.org/uploads/ EstesToolkit06.pdf.

Estes, C. L., Zulman, D. M., Goldberg, S. C., & Ogawa, D. D. (2004b). State long term care ombudsman programs: Factors associated with perceived effectiveness. *The Gerontologist, 44,* 104–115.

Fish-Parcham, C. (2001). *Designing a consumer health assistance program, Publication No. 01-106.* Retrieved November 16, 2006, from http://www.familiesusa.org/assets/ pdfs/guide200127e7.pdf.

Frank, B. (2000, May). *Ombudsman best practices: Supporting culture change to promote individualized care in nursing homes.* Retrieved November 16, 2006, from http://www.ltcombudsman.org/uploads/CultureChangeMay01.pdf.

Grant, R. (2002). *A family caregiver's guide to long-term care (prepared for the Ombudsman Program at the Legal Assistance Foundation of Metropolitan Chicago).* Retrieved November 16, 2006, from http://www.ltcombudsman.org/ombpublic/ 49_346_4234.cfm.

Grant, R. (2003). *Translating nursing home ombudsman skills to assisted living: Something old, something new.* Retrieved November 15, 2006, from http://www.ltcombudsman.org//uploads/TranslatingNHtoALAdvocacy0303.pdf.

Gudzowsky, N., & Feinberg, J. (1995, December). Regulation of nursing facilities in the United States: An analysis of resources and performance of state survey agencies. *Consumers Union.*

Hardcastle, D. A., Wenocur, S., & Powers, P. R. (1997). Chapter 12: Using the advocacy spectrum. *Community practice: Theories and skills of social workers.* New York: Oxford University Press.

Harrington, C. (2001). Regulating nursing homes: Residential nursing facilities in the United States. *BMJ, 323,* 507–510.

Harrington, C., Carillo, H. & Crawford, C. S. (2004). *Nursing facility staffing, residents, and facility deficiencies: 1997 through 2003.* Retrieved November 15, 2006, from http://www.nursinghomeaction.org/public/245_1267_9316.cfm.

Hawes, C. (1996). *Assuring nursing home quality: The history and impact of federal standards.* Commonwealth Fund. New York.

HCIA, & Arthur Anderson LLP. (1998). *The guide to the nursing home industry.* Baltimore, MD.

Hedt, A. (2004). [Review of the book: Doing good for the aged: Volunteers in an ombudsman program]. *Contemporary Gerontology, 10.*

Holder, E. (1985). Organizing for change in long-term care facilities. *Public concerns, community initiatives: The successful management of nursing home consumer information programs: Based on the proceedings of a United Hospital Fund conference held November 2 and 3, 1984.* Carol Ewig & John Griggs, eds. New York: United Hospital Fund of New York.

Horn, L., & Griesel, E. (1977). *Nursing homes: A citizen's action guide.* Boston: Beacon Press.

Houser, E. (2003, April). *Appendix V: Systems advocacy in the LTCOP: Within conference proceedings and recommendations: The long-term care ombudsman program: Rethinking and retooling for the future.* Retrieved November 16, 2006, from http://longtermcare.state.wi.us/home/whitepaper03_FINAL.pdf.

Hunt, S. S. (2001). *Joining forces for residents: Citizen advocates and long-term care ombudsmen (summary of a session at the 2000 annual meeting of the National Citizens' Coalition for Nursing Home Reform).* Retrieved November 16, 2006, from http://www.ltcombudsman.org/ombpublic/49_352_1001.cfm.

Hunt, S. S. (2004a). *Equipping long-term care ombudsmen for effective advocacy: A basic curriculum: The history and role of the ombudsman program and the aging process (manual and compact disk available from NCCNHR).* Retrieved November 16, 2006, from http://www.ltcombudsman.org/ombpublic/251_1508_8733.cfm.

Hunt, S. S. (2004b). *Equipping long-term care ombudsmen for effective advocacy: A basic curriculum.* Retrieved November 16, 2006, from http://www.ltcombudsman.org/ombpublic/251_1508_8733.cfm.

Hunt, S. S. (2004c). *Equipping state long-term care ombudsmen for their leadership role: A self-study guide.* Retrieved November 16, 2006, from http://www.ltcombudsman.org/ombpublic/251_1508_8733.cfm.

Institute of Medicine, Committee on Improving Quality in Long-Term Care. (2001). In G. S. Wunderlich and P. Kohler (Eds.), *Improving the quality of long-term care.* Washington, DC: National Academy Press.

Institute of Medicine, Division of Health Care Services. (1995). In J. Harris-Wehling, J. C. Feasley, & C. L. Estes (Eds.), *Real people, real problems: An evaluation of the long-term ombudsman programs of the Older Americans Act.* Washington, DC: National Academy Press.

Kuhn, M. (1991). The wisdom and triumph of growing old. In M. Kuhn, C. Long & L. Quinn (Eds.), *No stone unturned.* New York: Ballantine Books.

Lieberman, T. (1995, August–October). Nursing homes: When a loved one needs care (three part series). *Consumer Reports.* Vol. 60, issue 8, p. 521; Vol. 60, issue 9, pp. 591–597; and Vol. 60, issue 10, pp. 656–662.

Lieberman, G., & Rudder, C. (2005). *Resident's guide for assisted living: Maintain your independence, choice and control.* Retrieved November 15, 2006, from http://www.assisted-living411.org/ltcccbuttons/documents/residentsguide_forweb.pdf.

Lombardo, N. E., Fogel, B. S., & Robinson, G. K. (1995). Achieving mental health of nursing home residents: Overcoming barriers to mental health care. *Journal of Mental Health and Aging, 1,* 165–211.

Lustbader, W. (2000). The pioneer challenge: A radical change in the culture of nursing homes. In L. S. Noelker & Z. Harel (Eds.), *Quality of care and quality of life in nursing homes* (pp. 185–203). New York: Springer.

Marks, D. T. (1996). People at risk: Neglect in nursing homes. *Trial, 32,* 60–62.

Mendelson, M. A. (1974). *Tender loving greed: How the incredibly lucrative nursing home "industry" is exploiting America's old people and defrauding us all.* New York: Knopf.

Misorski, S. (2004). *Getting started: A pioneering approach to culture change in organizations.* Retrieved November 16, 2006, from http://www.pioneernetwork.net.

Moss, F. E., & Halamandaris, V. J. (1977). *Too old, too sick, too bad: Nursing homes in America.* Germantown, MD: Aspen Systems Corp.

National Association of State Long Term Care Ombudsman Programs. (2000, October). In National Citizen's Coalition for Nursing Home Reform (Ed.), *Guidance for long-term care ombudsman program participation in developing consumer advocacy programs,* NCCNHR, Washington, DC.

National Association of State Long Term Care Ombudsman Programs. (2003, April). *The long-term care ombudsman program: Rethinking and retooling for the future. Proceedings and recommendations ("The Bader Report").* Retrieved November 16, 2006, from http://longtermcare.state.wi.us/home/whitepaper03_FINAL.pdf.

National Association of State Units on Aging. (2002, April). *Long-term care ombudsman program: A summary of state enabling statutes.* Retrieved November 16, 2006, from http://www.ltcombudsman.org/ombpublic/49_346_3987.CFM.

National Citizen's Coalition for Nursing Home Reform. (n.d.). *Two decades of advocacy for long term care consumers: Time chart of significant achievements 1975–1995.* NCCNHR, Washington, DC.

National Citizen's Coalition for Nursing Home Reform. (1978, February). *The plight of the nurse aide in America's nursing homes: An obstacle to quality care for nursing home residents (a working paper presented to HEW/HCFA officials).* NCCNHR, Washington, DC.

National Citizen's Coalition for Nursing Home Reform. (1983). *Principles for a federal regulatory system: A report to the Health Care Financing Administration, HHS.* NCC-NHR, Washington, DC.

National Citizen's Coalition for Nursing Home Reform. (1985). *A consumer perspective on quality care: The residents' point of view.* Retrieved November 16, 2006, from http://www.nccnhr.org/pdf/resident_pers.pdf.

National Citizen's Coalition for Nursing Home Reform. (1986). *Report to Congress on 12 consensus policy positions for a national nursing home reform law.* NCCNHR, Washington, DC.

National Citizen's Coalition for Nursing Home Reform. (1997). *The high cost of poor care: Information brief.* NCCNHR, Washington, DC.

National Citizen's Coalition for Nursing Home Reform. (1998). *Family education and outreach: Final report (Project period October–December 1997).* Retrieved November 16, 2006, from http://www.nccnhr.org/pdf/Report598.pdf.

National Citizen's Coalition for Nursing Home Reform. (2003a). In S. Burger (Ed.), *Nursing home staffing: A guide for residents, families, friends, and caregivers.* Washington, DC.

National Citizen's Coalition for Nursing Home Reform. (2003b). *A residents' rights tool kit 2003: 24/7: Residents' rights around the clock.* Retrieved November 16, 2006, from http://www.ltcombudsman.org/ombpublic/49_781_2746.cfm.

O'Connor, P. (2002). *Ombudsmen often feel powerless in efforts to blow the whistle (published October 15, 2002 in the St. Louis Post-Dispatch, series: Neglected to death: Preventable deaths in nursing homes.).* Retrieved November 16, 2006, from http://www.stltoday.com/stltoday/news/special/neglected.nsf/0/C4F143DEF2D0FF128 6256C5400018654?OpenDocument.

Office of Inspector General, & U.S. Department of Health and Human Services. (2003). *Nursing home complaints: 1996–2000.* Retrieved November 16, 2006, from http://oig.hhs.gov/oei/reports/oei-09-02-00160.pdf.

Quality Partners of Rhode Island. (2005). *News links.* Retrieved November 16, 2006, from http://www.qualitypartnersri.net/cfmodules/objmgr.cfm?CID=110&Y2005=1&OBJ= News&MID=110&PMID=110&CLEAR=&.

Rudder, C., & Lieberman, G. (2005). *Thinking of moving to an assisted living residence? A guidebook for finding choice and independence.* Retrieved November 15, 2006, from http://www.ltccc.org/news/documents/alguidepotresfinal.pdf.

Scully, T. (2003). *Health care industry market update: Nursing facilities (May 20, 2003, publication from the Centers for Medicare and Medicaid services).* Retrieved November 15, 2006, from http://www.cms.hhs.gov/CapMarketUpdates/Downloads/ hcimu52003.pdf.

Smetanka, L. O. (1997). *Where do I go from here? A guide for nursing home residents, families and friends on consulting an attorney.* Washington, DC: National Citizen's Coalition for Nursing Home Reform.

Stone, R. I. (2000). *Long-term care for the elderly with disabilities: Current policy, emerging trends, and implications for the 21st century.* Retrieved November 1, 2006, from http://www.milbank.org/reports/0008stone/index.html.

Townsend, C., & Nader, R. (1971). *Old age: The last segregation.* New York: Grossman Publishers.

Tulloch, G. J. (1975). *A home is not a home: Life within a nursing home.* New York: Seabury Press.

U.S. Department of Health, Education and Welfare. (1963). *Nursing home standards guide: Recommendations relating to standards for establishing, maintaining, and operating nursing homes.* Public Health Service, Division of Chronic Diseases, Nursing Homes and Related Facilities Program.

U.S. General Accounting Office. (1997). *Long-term care: Consumer protection and quality-of-care issues in assisted living (report to the Honorable Ron Wyden, U.S. Senate).* Retrieved November 15, 2006, from http://www.gao.gov/archive/1997/he97093.pdf.

U.S. Senate, Special Committee on Aging. (1974). *Nursing home care in the United States: Failure in public policy* (No. 93-1420). Washington, DC: U.S. Government Printing Office.

Walshe, K., & Harrington, C. (2001, May). *The regulation of nursing facilities in the U.S.: An analysis of resources and performance of state survey agencies. Prepared for the Henry J. Kaiser Family Foundation, Grant no. 95-2394A.*

Weiner, A. S., & Ronch, J. L. (2003). *Culture change in long-term care.* New York: Haworth Social Work Practice Press.

Wheaton, S. (n.d.). *Current lists of state and local LTC ombudsmen: National Ombudsman annual report data.* Retrieved from http://www.aoa.gov/ltcombudsman and http://www.ltcombudsman.org.

Wilner, M. A., & Wyatt, A. (1999). *Paraprofessionals on the front lines: Improving their jobs-improving the quality of long-term care (an AARP conference background paper presented in September 1998).* Retrieved November 15, 2006, from http://www.paraprofessional.org/publications/pps_frontlines_esum.pdf.

Wilson, K. B. (1993). Developing a viable model of assisted living. In P. Katz, R. L. Kane, & M. Mazey (Eds.), *Advances in long-term care.* New York: Springer.

CHAPTER 16

Access to Healthcare: Using Data from a Nonprofit Advocacy Practice to Drive Policy Change

Nancy Davenport-Ennis

OBJECTIVES

To understand key strategies of successful organizations, including:
- Developing of rigorous data collection systems that support effective program planning, evaluation, fund raising, and lobbying efforts
- Cultivating of and collaborating with a board of directors
- Developing of a business model to ensure an organization's future solvency
- Securing access to key state and federal committees to help influence policy decisions
- Engaging in coalition building to change state and federal policies

Many chapters in this text refer to barriers, particularly health insurance problems, that may prevent patients from obtaining the healthcare services they need. This chapter delves more deeply into this topic, exploring problems such as billing disputes and denials of preapproval for treatments. Across the United States, nonprofit organizations have formed to address such problems at the individual and the policy levels. This chapter spotlights a pair of organizations, the Patient Advocate Foundation (PAF) and the National Patient Advocate Foundation (NPAF), that are structured to do both simultaneously.

PAF is a national patient services organization that provides counseling and legal support to patients who need assistance in resolving issues of debt crisis, job retention, and insurance matters caused by a serious illness. These cases are rigorously documented in databases that provide valuable information about different populations' current advocacy needs. These data are then used by NPAF, a nonpartisan lobbying organization, in its efforts to improve patients' access to care and appropriate treatments at the state and federal levels through legislative and policy reform. This chapter is important in introducing the politics and economics of healthcare and for suggesting concrete ways nonprofit organizations following a business model can have an impact in this arena.

A CHRONICLE OF PATIENT NEED: ANATOMY OF URGENCY

Vignette 1

Not long ago, a young man stepped into the PAF lobby asking to meet with a case manager. In that meeting, he indicated a simple bump on his shoulder, diagnosed that very day as an advanced Ewing's sarcoma that threatened the loss of his arm and possibly his life. Uninsured, this college-degreed professional, at the beginning of his career, faced a stark reality: without insurance, his options for treatment were minimal at best and completely unavailable at worst. His income, possession of a car, and recent purchase of a home disqualified him from enrolling in his state's Medicaid program, while his cancer diagnosis, as a pre-existing condition, disqualified him from enrolling in private insurance. Even before his diagnosis, his limited budget and short time in the workforce had hampered his ability to purchase insurance. In his case, a PAF case manager served as a mediator with both the young man's employer and an insurer. The case manager negotiated a successful insurance enrollment. Care was provided, and the young man's limb and likely his life were saved. Today, in addition to a successful career, he is an ardent advocate for having young adults recognize insurance enrollment as a necessity, not an option.

Vignette 2

A child diagnosed with a rare brain tumor needed immediate surgery. The child's oncology treatment team recommended transferring her to another nationally-known research hospital for surgery so she could benefit from a leading neurosurgeon with a record of successful pediatric brain operations. Yet the child's insurer denied the transfer. The recommended facility was not part of the health plan's preapproved network, making treatment there potentially more costly to the health plan than it would have been if carried out in the referring hospital. Insurance companies often define preapproved facilities as only those within a limited geographic service area. Care prescribed for beneficiaries that falls outside this predefined service area is not covered. The receiving hospital, Duke University Medical Center, contacted PAF to intervene with the primary and referral hospitals, the family's insurer, employer, parents, and physicians from both institutions. Within 24 hours, PAF was able to arrange the child's transfer to the recommended facility with full insurance benefits. PAF also provided air-lift services for the child and her parents through Angel Flight (a free air transportation service to specialized healthcare facilities), and today, that child is enjoying an active, independent life.

Vignette 3

A widowed senior citizen diagnosed with advanced terminal cancer decided after consultation with her physician and family members to move from the northeastern United States to the southeast to be near her daughter during the last months of her life. Medicare informed the woman that her insurance carrier did not offer services in her daughter's state. Hence, if she moved, she would lose her healthcare benefits. To resolve this impasse, PAF helped the woman enroll in a Medicare plan in her daughter's state, establish residency there, and terminate her enrollment in the state where she was presently living. The patient was able to spend the final months of her life with her daughter, with insurance benefits provided by Medicare.

Each of these cases from the PAF files illustrates fractures in the healthcare system associated with insurance coverage. Every day, U.S. healthcare consumers confront complicated access, delivery, and reimbursement dilemmas that impede the initiation of recommended care. In turn, these delays may result in progression of disease, debilitation, and premature death. As underscored by research reported to the Kaiser Commission on Medicaid and the Uninsured (Rowland, 2004), inadequate health insurance influences when and whether individuals seek necessary medical care, how much debt they accrue when they do obtain care, and ultimately, their health outcomes. Specifically, according to one Kaiser Commission Report, insurance may help reduce mortality rates by 10% to 15%, improve annual earnings by 10% to 30% (depending on the measure and specific health conditions), and even increase educational attainment (Rowland, 2004).

Despite these social benefits, the high cost of healthcare and insurance has serious negative consequences for many. According to one study, of the 1.46 million American families who filed for bankruptcy in 2001, around half cited medical reasons as their primary source of financial difficulties (Himmelstein, Warren, Thorne, & Woolhandler, 2005). Indeed, in 2001, an estimated 1.9 to 2.2 million Americans experienced medical bankruptcy. Moreover, over three quarters of those whose illnesses led to bankruptcy had insurance at the onset of their illness (Himmelstein et al., 2005). Often these families confront losses in cross-generational assets (e.g., grandparents intervene financially to support adult children undergoing cancer treatments, or adult children pay for their aging parents' treatment).

Even having insurance, however, does not guarantee access to healthcare in the United States. A recent Rand Institute for Civil Justice and Rand Health study (2004) reported that insurers initially denied 75% of preservice appeals for surgical procedures, office consultations, and diagnostic tests. These data suggest that having insurance does not guarantee patients' access to needed care; it simply provides individuals with access to initiate a care-seeking process and an opportunity to negotiate favorable resolutions when confronted by obstacles to care.

As discussed in Chapter 2, the U.S. healthcare system is, for the most part, conceived of a free-market enterprise; it provides access to healthcare in direct proportion to an individual's personal insurance benefits and ability to underwrite gaps in coverage. Most working-age adults in the United States receive their insurance coverage through employers. For those 65 and older, the United States offers safety net programs through Medicare, funded and regulated at the federal level. Medicaid programs, which provide coverage for poor families with children, are regulated principally by states, but are funded collaboratively by both states and the federal government. Not surprisingly, covered services can vary widely from state to state.

This snapshot of access to care in the United States is made all the more complex when considered in light of the nation's socioeconomic, cultural, educational, ethnic, and geographic diversity. Rates of medical procedures in the United States vary significantly by race, even when controlling for insurance status, income, age, and severity of conditions (Institute of Medicine, 2002a). These racial and ethnic disparities are intensified by economic and cultural divides that are partly responsible for 46 million Americans being uninsured (Collins, Davis, Doty, Kriss, & Holmgren, 2006). Hispanics, closely followed by African Americans, constitute the largest uninsured ethnic groups (Doty & Holmgren, 2006). The number of *underinsured* Americans has also been increasing sharply with the erosion of employer-based benefits as well as increased cost sharing for Medicaid recipients (Edwards, Doty, & Schoen, 2002; Ku & Broaddus, 2005).

Although public hospitals and emergency departments are "providers of last resort," many Americans who lack health insurance often do not get the care they need (Kaiser Commission on Medicaid and the Uninsured, 2006). The consequences of being uninsured for working-age adults with cancer, diabetes, HIV/AIDS, heart and kidney disease, mental illness, traumatic injuries, and heart attacks are profound (Hadley, 2002; Kaiser Commission on Medicaid and the Uninsured, 2006). When the uninsured are hospitalized, as one report noted, they "experience higher rates of death in the hospital, are likely to receive fewer services, and are more likely to experience substandard care and resultant injury than are insured patients" (Institute of Medicine, 2002b, p. 87).

In the face of these major access problems, several organizations have sprung up to attempt to restructure private insurance and Medicare. The three previous vignettes illustrate the role of one national nonprofit organization, PAF, in providing direct services to healthcare consumers, both insured and uninsured, whose healthcare coverage does not ensure initial or sustained access to medical treatment for chronic, life-threatening, or debilitating illnesses. In relating PAF's history, this chapter also explores the value to nonprofit organizations of collecting data that can help influence state and national policies, as illustrated by the activities of PAF's sister organization, the NPAF. In describing these two foundations, the chapter highlights how nonprofit organizations structured along business model lines can have a measurable impact on healthcare outcomes.

INSURANCE REFORM EFFORTS NATIONALLY, 1996–2006

Exploring the work of nonprofits such as PAF and NPAF requires a basic understanding of insurance reform efforts at the national level. Over the past 10 years, these efforts have sought to address two major issues: patient access to quality care and ballooning healthcare expenditures. To improve access and quality of care, health system reformers have focused on establishing consumers' right to insurance portability, guaranteeing consumers' entitlement to maintain coverage at the same cost, even when moving from one health plan to another, as often happens with a change in employment. In a separate set of efforts aimed at curtailing rising costs, lawmakers have recommended changes in how the Centers for Medicare & Medicaid Services (CMS), as a government healthcare purchaser, determine levels of provider reimbursement and payment for services.

The Health Insurance Portability and Accountability Act

In the same time period, two massive reform efforts have also altered the healthcare landscape for both the public and private sectors. The Health Insurance Portability and Accountability Act (HIPAA), passed in 1996, required greater administrative simplification, initiated a Medicare Integrity Program to prevent fraud and abuse, and mandated health insurance portability. HIPAA's most dramatic impact, however, came in the area of privacy and security of healthcare-related information. Gone are the days when individual hospitals or medical practices could decide on their own which patient information they would keep or destroy. Under HIPAA, healthcare entities are now restricted in how and with whom they can share personally identifiable health information.

Another important aspect of HIPAA was its amendment to the Employee Retirement Income Security Act (ERISA). This amendment required insurance providers to guarantee continued health insurance coverage of qualified individuals even after those individuals changed jobs. Other features of the amendment include a six-month look-back period (meaning that insurers can "exclude" coverage for illnesses diagnosed up to six months before and twelve months after a consumer enrolls) and a requirement that pre-existing condition exclusions be offset by a period of certified credible coverage. Provisions such as these are meant to limit insurers' ability to deny coverage and to lessen the risk of losing coverage associated with changes in employment.

The Medicare Prescription Drug Improvement and Modernization Act

Several federal laws other than the 1996 HIPAA have also had significant impacts on health coverage. The Medicare Prescription Drug

Improvement and Modernization Act of 2003, also known as MMA, included provisions intended to combat waste, fraud, and abuse through payment reform in the Medicare program. The MMA also authorized a much debated outpatient prescription drug coverage program known as Medicare Part D, implemented in January 2006. Finally, MMA revised the Medicare-managed care program, now known as Medicare Advantage, so that patients over age 65 could receive broad insurance coverage, including enrollment in preferred provider organization plans, private fee-for-service plans, and Medicare specialty plans.

Other Reform Efforts

Several other federal initiatives in the past 10 years have advanced patient-centered healthcare. In 1997, President Clinton created the Advisory Commission on Consumer Protection and Quality in the Health Care Industry, which produced the influential Consumer Bill of Rights and Responsibilities (President's Advisory Commission, 1998). This document covered such topics as information disclosure, choice of providers and plans, access to emergency services, participation in treatment decisions, respect and nondiscrimination, confidentiality of health information, complaints and appeals, and consumer responsibilities. Although this effort did not result in significant federal insurance reforms, the Consumer Bill of Rights has served as a blueprint for many states and providers who went on to adopt the principles advocated by the Advisory Commission.

Other recent reform efforts have focused specifically on patient access issues. In the past, patients for whom standard treatment had failed or who had suffered from an illness for which no clear standard treatment existed were asked to pay for the cost of experimental treatments on their own. Yet in 2000, President Clinton issued an Executive Memorandum directing Medicare both to reimburse providers for the cost of routine care for patients participating in clinical trials and to promote Medicare beneficiaries' participation in such trials. Similarly, the Breast and Cervical Cancer Prevention and Treatment Act of 2000 gave states the option to provide medical assistance through state Medicaid programs to eligible women screened for and found to have breast or cervical cancer (106th Congress, 2000). Finally, in June 2005, President Bush signed the Patient Navigator bill into law (Mendendez, 2005). This act authorized a $25 million demonstration program (yet to be funded) that would link patient navigator outreach efforts to existing screening programs (Patient Navigator Outreach and Chronic Disease Prevention Act, 2005).

PAF AND NPAF

Despite the major legislative efforts summarized above, care-seeking still takes place in a context of fragmented, piecemeal healthcare coverage that leaves an increasing number of people uninsured or underinsured. Furthermore, in the current political/social environment, little support exists for comprehensive solutions to this problem (Oberlander, 2003). Change is slow, as documented by Congress's failure to pass the Patient Bill of Rights championed by former President Bill Clinton from 1996 through 1999. Other agenda items outside the healthcare arena, including the Iraq war, redirect domestic funding to international security initiatives. Recent reductions in the National Cancer Institute's research budget, despite the combined advocacy of One Voice Against Cancer (2005), a coalition of 57 groups, illustrate this point. For the foreseeable future, few expansions of either the federal or state safety net programs will take place, even as state Medicaid programs are reduced and physician reimbursement through pay-for-performance initiatives is expanded.

In such a cost-cutting environment, healthcare advocacy organizations can make significant contributions. Yet the initial investment in these non-profit initiatives requires not just talent and organizational skill, but an almost unifocal devotion to the mission as well. The establishment and especially the growth of PAF and the NPAF illustrate this point. Both foundations were established in April 1996 as a result of the friendship between Cheryl Grimmel and the founder of PAF and NPAF, Nancy Davenport-Ennis (this chapter's author), and John Ennis, her husband. Grimmel, a mother of a 12-year-old son, was diagnosed with stage IV metastatic breast cancer at the age of 31. She was given no options for treatment to slow the advance of the disease. Yet through direct intervention by Davenport-Ennis, Grimmel was enrolled in a clinical trial to receive a bone marrow transplant at the Duke University Medical Center, where Davenport-Ennis had been treated in 1993 and 1994 for breast cancer. Grimmel's physicians estimated that the intervention extended her life three years. The Ennis's battled financially and personally to resolve Grimmel's medical and social service needs, seeking to have her health plan reverse its denial of benefits for the clinical trial treatment.

Ultimately, together, the Ennis and Grimmel families spearheaded the fundraising of $210,000 to pay off Grimmel's medical bills.

During those three years, Davenport-Ennis initiated passage of legislation in Virginia to improve benefits coverage for women seeking to enroll in clinical trials for evolving breast cancer therapies. She established a task force comprised of nurses, physicians, attorneys, social workers, healthcare reporters, and state legislators specializing in healthcare. The legislation they helped spur was passed in 1994 in Virginia (House Bill 240) and was later adopted in 17 additional states. The Cheryl Grimmel experience, one echoed by many other women, illustrated the desperate need for patients to have daily access to case managers who could resolve obstacles to healthcare access, debt crisis, and job discrimination because of illness.

Ten years later, in 2006, PAF had an annual operating budget of six million dollars, has recently added 4450 square feet to the 10,000 square foot space they originally occupied, and employed a 76 member, full-time, paid staff with an annual staff growth rate of 28% and a retention rate of 98% (PAF, 2005). Additionally, PAF has 162 national healthcare attorneys who provide pro bono services to patients referred by PAF for mediation with health plans. The latter number suggests the high degree of personal commitment PAF employees feel toward the organization's mission and shows the potential for volunteers to make meaningful contributions toward improving healthcare access when given a compelling reason and a well-structured opportunity.

PAF's approach to problem solving for patients and family members confronting medical debt and acute medical access issues has been documented widely, including, most recently, in *Business Week* (Tergesen, 2005), *Prevention Magazine* (Harrar, 2002), *Reader's Digest* (Gower, 2004; Topolnicki, 2000), *Wall Street Journal* (Dockser-Marcus, 2003, 2004; Landro, 2000), *New York Times* (Bereson, 2005), and *USA Today* (Appleby, 2005). Each time an article appears, PAF experiences a burst of new clients searching for ways to gain access to treatment or overcome problems with medical debt.

DATA GATHERING AND ITS IMPACT ON NON-PROFIT ORGANIZATIONS

PAF directly assisted over 4.1 million patients in 2005 (PAF, 2005). Yet even as PAF's case management staff members offer patients immediate relief through mediation and intervention, they also collect data from each caller. Data collected include patient demographics as well as diagnosis, insurance status, whether the caller has public or private insurance, site of care, and current status of treatment and disease progression. Additionally, problems blocking patients' access to treatment are recorded, including radiology services, pharmaceutical agents, surgical intervention, home healthcare, hospice, and early detection and prevention services. Specific insurance issues are documented, including denial of benefits requiring an appeals process, coding and billing errors, disputes that block continued access to treatment, coordination of benefits disputes between co-insurers of the beneficiary, and expedited enrollment of patients into public programs such as Social Security Disability Benefits, Medicare, and Medicaid as well as private, ecumenical community programs that provide assistance to patients. The resulting Patient Data Analysis Report (PDAR), scrubbed of personal identifiers and published by the PAF annually, is used not only by PAF for planning and improving its services, but also by its sister organization, NPAF, to influence state and federal policy.

USE OF DATA TO IMPROVE PROGRAMS AND SERVICES

After years of collecting data, PAF has identified the following categories as areas of need and in some cases has responded with programmatic initiatives: (1) access to pharmaceuticals, (2) preauthorizations, and (3) billing disputes.

Access to Pharmaceuticals

PAF's Patient Data Analysis Reports confirm findings from national studies about consumers' difficulties in purchasing pharmaceuticals. Specifically, as illuminated in PAF's annual data report, in 2005, 27% of patients contacting PAF for assistance were covered by Medicare, 16% by Medicaid, 38% by private insurance, typically through employers, and 21% were uninsured. Escalating co-payments for prescribed medications (which can range from 10% to 75% of their cost) are driving PAF callers to skip or split pills and to choose between food and medicine, as others have confirmed. Data also reveal that 40% of PAF's inquiries involved a lack of access to pharmaceutical agents; of these callers, 35% could not make insurance co-payments. Twenty-one percent had no pharmacy benefits. Twenty-six percent had plans requiring them to use generic drugs only, even when no generic medications were available for their condition, and 15% needed access to a drug not included in their plan's approved formulary.

Capturing data such as these help a nonprofit like PAF be more responsive to the needs of the populations it serves. Based on the above findings, for example, PAF launched a new initiative, its Co-Pay Relief Program (CPR), in October 2004. The program provides cash co-payment assistance for pharmaceuticals to medically and financially qualified patients on a first-come, first-served basis. Payments are made directly to pharmacies and/or medical practices that then provide drugs to the patients. The program is funded through national donations at no cost to consumers. The data collected from callers help the PAF document the extent of the problems consumers confront in paying for prescription medications, while undergirding the foundation's increasingly successful efforts to win grants and gifts from large donors.

Preauthorizations

Preauthorization is typically sought for complex therapies, new medical devices, or drugs newly approved by the Food and Drug Administration but not yet part of a health plan's formulary. Usually these requests are denied at point of service. Resolving these denials often takes months. In December 2004, for instance, Good Morning America profiled a PAF client diagnosed with late stage non-Hodgkin's lymphoma. Despite the fact that the protocol recommended by this client's physician was routinely used to arrest this disease, the client's insurer denied preauthorization. According to the health plan, recommended treatment could not be offered to anyone over age 60. The patient, a professional woman who had just turned 60 the previous week, spent six months seeking to overturn the denial before contacting PAF. By involving the employer's senior leaders, PAF was able to negotiate a reversal of the denial. Unfortunately, however, by the time the denial was reversed, the woman's disease had advanced to a terminal condition, and the therapy was no longer effective. Delays in medication approval cost people their lives every day. Often, patients simply stop trying to gain access to treatment once a preauthorization has been denied.

Billing Disputes

Consumers confronting billing disputes can spend hours trying to reach the correct insurance company representative. PAF records document many patients who try for months to reach billing representatives, with many patients placed on hold in excess of an hour or who get busy signals for days. Economic ramifications include missing work time as patients spend hours on the phone. Based on an audit of its patient records, PAF found that over half its interventions in billing disputes result in reimbursement to patients. The largest overpayment reimbursed to a PAF patient to date was $70,000, with the average return in the $15,000 to $20,000 range. These are not insignificant figures.

USE OF DATA TO INFLUENCE STATE AND FEDERAL POLICY

Collecting data can have other powerful uses as well. Access to data from its sister organization, PAF, allows NPAF to document and report on national-level trends as, for example, when it identified a high number of denials and long delays in appeals processes connected to bone marrow and stem cell transplants. These data help NPAF make a strong case when it intervenes directly in policy issues. In 1999, for example, when Florida's Medicaid program announced plans to withdraw reimbursement for products routinely used by cancer patients, NPAF used data from PAF's PDAR files to intervene directly with the governor's office. Other state and national organizations and agencies joined forces with NPAF, resulting in restoration of Medicaid benefits to Floridian transplant patients. More broadly, PAF data include patients from every state in the United States. The foundation has helped sign media and testimony releases, allowing PAF patients to be interviewed by national media and/or included as witnesses in policy debates at both state and federal levels. These contributions provide faces, voices, and stories that more vividly help make the case for wider access and more humane, patient-centered insurance policies.

Another example of NPAF's use of data to lobby for policy change comes from 2003. In that year, Iowa's John Deere Health Plans instituted a policy requiring all drugs to be sent directly to beneficiaries' homes, including cancer chemotherapy products that needed special climate control conditions (Lewin Group, 2003). In response to this cost-cutting proposal, physicians declined to accept the risk for infusing chemotherapy of unknown origin or of unclear chain of custody or product composition. This situation resulted in state-wide interruption of infusion therapy to cancer patients. Through the Lewin Group, NPAF commissioned a survey of 3,000 Iowans' attitudes toward "brown-bagging" of cancer products, with 2,880 survey participants responding unfavorably to the direct mail process (2003). NPAF invited physician representatives from Iowa, national patient advocacy groups, and national provider organizations with offices in Iowa to join NPAF in presenting the survey results to senior representatives of the American Association of Health Plans, a national trade association of health insurers. The American Association of Health Plans then intervened with John Deere Health plans, helping to restore the previous delivery system in less than two months (see Textbox 16.1).

ROLE OF BOARDS OF DIRECTORS IN NONPROFIT ADVOCACY ORGANIZATIONS

Determining the structure of a nonprofit health advocacy organization takes much planning, yet many resources are available to assist the advocate in that endeavor. The nonprofit case examples discussed throughout

---

Textbox 16.1   Advocacy Businesses in Medical Billing and Insurance Negotiation

The problem of healthcare access is not the interest of nonprofit organizations alone; in recent years, many for-profit businesses have sprung up to help patients navigate the healthcare system. Offering an array of services, companies may (1) audit patients' bills so as to ensure accuracy, (2) negotiate insurance disputes, and/or (3) provide counseling services to help clients understand their medical bills and insurance benefits. These businesses differ from nonprofits such as PAF in that their services are offered for a price, and companies may employ any number of payment structures to collect their fees. Some require the purchase of an ongoing membership, whereas others work on a fee-for-services basis. Still others operate on a percentage of fees recovered for the patient. Medical Billing Advocates of America is a general referral site for businesses such as these. It is beyond the purview of this chapter to spotlight individual businesses, but their existence as a group is important in confirming patients' need for advocacy.

this chapter illustrate this point well. PAF is a 501-C3 nonprofit direct patient services organization; NPAF is a 527 policy organization established to remove barriers to healthcare access through regulatory reform and legislative initiatives. Both follow a model that relies heavily on the advice of active and diverse boards of directors. PAF's board was originally culled from colleagues who had collaborated in 1994 with Davenport-Ennis on the Virginia State Task Force to broaden coverage for women enrolling in clinical trials for breast cancer therapies. Similar to that task force, PAF's board contains elected officials, research and clinical oncologists, healthcare lawyers, and patient advocates (see www.patientadvocate.org for a complete listing of original and current board members).

As illustrated by PAF's experience, a board of directors can play a pivotal role in the growth, innovation, and effectiveness of an organization. At PAF, the executive board of directors was charged with supporting fundraising and national branding initiatives. The attorneys on the board helped expand PAF's network of 27 volunteer healthcare attorneys who serve patients at no charge; today, that network consists of 162 attorneys. Similarly, oncologists on the board inform PAF of current legislative issues that may limit access to care, as, for example, in the previously mentioned case of lack of reimbursement for clinical trials care. To ameliorate this problem, PAF hired the services of its companion policy organization, NPAF, to join efforts by legislators in Washington seeking passage of the Patient Bill of Rights. Although the Patient Bill of Rights was ultimately defeated, President Clinton, in the final days of his presidency in 1999, used an executive order to mandate coverage for clinical trials reimbursement for patients in the Medicare system. This initiative, a direct result of the Patient Bill of Rights campaign, resulted in many states passing legislation between 2002 and 2004 addressing specific components of the Patient Bill of Rights. Additionally, many private insurers in the United States voluntarily added coverage benefits for phase III and phase IV clinical trials to their plans.

Nonprofits such as PAF and NPAF are aided by their flexible and creative approach to leadership, adapting to circumstances as needed. In 1997, for example, PAF added a scientific board of directors, consisting of three highly respected oncologists. These physician board members review medical protocols for those patients who request support in seeking reimbursement; they clarify the evolving therapies NPAF is asked to support in state and federal initiatives, and they provide testimony when appropriate. For example, testimony from PAF's scientific board, together with patients' experiences documented through the foundation's database, enabled PAF to make its voice heard before FDA oncology drug advisory committees.

FOLLOWING A BUSINESS MODEL

Many nonprofits help to ensure their success by subscribing to the same principles that undergird successful profit-making companies. These include (1) a collaborative short- and long-term planning process; (2) commitment to managing an implementation plan by measuring quality and outcomes; (3) implementing a constant review process that helps the organization respond flexibly to changes in the marketplace, staff, supporters, and outside influences; and (4) vigilantly focusing on income diversification and resource management through strict accounting systems.

Short- and Long-Term Planning

In the case of PAF, short- and long-term planning usually begin with a summary of the past year's activities in the context of a historic review of the organization. New program needs are typically identified by trends noted in the PDAR. For example, this process illuminated the need in 2001 for PAF to establish its national Hispanic/Latino Outreach Initiative and in 2002 to establish the African American Outreach program, focused on educating this population on early warning signs of specific diseases and steps they could take to prevent illness. In another example, in 2003, 40% of PAF's callers sought assistance with co-payments. In response to these data, PAF opened the previously described Co-Pay Relief (CPR) Program. In the same year, PAF also initiated its Senior Services Division in response to passage of the 2003 Medicare Modernization Act. Each of these programs was created in response to needs identified through data PAF had collected from its clients. Each initiative was developed with careful planning for staff recruitment, English and Spanish language materials development, and identifying short- and long-term financial resources to fund the initiative.

Measuring Quality and Outcomes

In another example of sound business practices, PAF strategically defines goals and objectives for each service area and develops an action plan for measuring the outcomes and management of daily services they offer. PAF's chief program officer collaborates with department leaders to define performance expectations and develop instruments to measure their achievement. This team educates staff about goals and measures, including individual performance evaluations for employees. Employees know that an external quality control officer at PAF randomly audits both open and closed cases of all PAF case managers and co-pay relief call counselors. Employees are informed of the evaluation standards and review process. These audits provide the foundation for corrective actions, as appropriate, and for merit raises and performance bonuses where these are called for. Each PAF program reports specific daily and monthly goals to the leadership in a consistent, well-defined process.

Resource Management

PAF's CPR is an example of how strict accounting practices and resource management can allow a nonprofit to make the most of its resources. For example, when the CPR got started, PAF created software that gave the accounting department daily reports on such line items as (1) total dollars allocated for newly approved patients each day by disease type, (2) total dollars expended per day per disease type per patient, and (3) total number of dollars re-allocated to the master disease account per day as a result of the death of patients whose funds were no longer needed. This accounting system, with its reporting outcomes, provides clear direction to each employee. It also serves as a management tool for managers responsible for motivating and overseeing exemplary performance of a small overextended staff.

Income Diversity

Income diversity is essential for ensuring that a nonprofit organization continues to serve its mission and constituents. PAF income is developed through a corporate development department with leadership by the chief development officer and a team of marketing, contract, and grant specialists. Together, the team has diversified income to include funding through earmarks from the U.S. Congressional budget, multiyear Centers for Disease Control grants, grants and contracts for services with both the Susan G. Komen and Lance Armstrong Foundations, grants from multiple state healthcare programs for the underserved, and grants through independent foundations researched by PAF development staff for specific projects. Additional revenue sources include an annual gala and auction, single-donor direct-mail programs, and programmatic funding. PAF also applies for independent unrestricted grants for direct patient services and support of the CPR. In 2005, PAF's annual operating budget was 5.9 million dollars, with total programmatic funding approaching 20 million dollars. Development of a responsible, multiperson accounting team managed by a hands-on chief operating officer with direct accountability to the CEO and the finance committee of the board of directors helps to ensure donors that funds contributed to the organization's mission are handled in a manner consistent with the intent of the donation.

As distinct from PAF, funding for the activities of NPAF requires a development team that negotiates annual dues for membership in the NPAF Policy Consortium. This consortium convenes twice annually in Washington to examine current regulatory and legislative priorities that may have common points of interest to its members and to negotiate research dollars for the Global Access Projects. GAP is a research collaborative, described later in this chapter, whose members are interested in completing unbiased, independent research projects. NPAF also obtains funding through contracts with its sister organization, the PAF, to represent its interests at both the federal and state levels.

The axiom "keep the old while adding the new" is imperative when building a nonprofit's base of supporters. New nonprofits are wise to find common ground among their members and develop their goals collaboratively, with mutual respect for missions beneficial to all participants. Being creative while listening to new ideas are two processes that PAF seeks to nurture daily.

TOOLS FOR SUCCESS

Aside from the structure and business model practices, several key tools are instrumental in the success of a nonprofit health advocacy organization. These are collaboration, a clear visioin, and development of key stakeholder partners who are both committed to a common cause and who embrace similar ideas about process and implementation.

Collaboration

Collaboration with other nonprofits can be instrumental in bringing attention to a problem, passing legislation, and making sure that areas of need are covered. In the case of NPAF, productive alliances have helped all stakeholders amplify their voices. In 2004, for example, NPAF established the Global Access Project, a research collaborative comprised of 40 stakeholder organizations, including national physician groups, national nursing and social worker organizations, nonprofit patient advocacy organizations, and pharmaceutical companies interested in completing unbiased, independent research projects. To date, six research projects costing a total of $2.5 million have been completed, with funding contributed by Global Access Project stakeholders. All research decisions and processes have been managed by the Lewin Group, contracted by NPAF to ensure independence of study design and reporting. Studies completed to date have analyzed:

- Clinical trials accrual trends in the United States (Heilig, Strouse, & Hassett, 2005)
- The history of coding and billing within the Centers of Medicare and Medicaid to define reimbursement inequity areas (Moran, Suter, Shostak, Kirby, & Braid, 2004)
- Cost of the preparation of chemotherapeutic therapies in both independent clinic settings and hospital pharmacies to document unreimbursed services (University of Utah, 2005)
- A geographic study of sites of oncology care in the United States in free-standing clinic and hospital settings (Dalton, 2005)
- A follow-up mapping study of oncology care locations to illustrate changes in delivery-of-care sites and to define the impact of changes on such special populations as older, culturally diverse, and underserved patients (Dalton, 2005)

Nonprofit members of the Global Access Project used data and information from these studies in multiple ways. They found them particularly useful, however, in their lobbying efforts with legislators on the subject of healthcare realities in the United States. The U.S. Government is the single largest insurer in the country through its health plan vendors (see Chapter 2). NPAF's studies particularly resonated with members of the three legislative committees with jurisdiction over the CMS: the House Ways and Means Committee, the House Energy and Commerce Committee, and the Senate Finance Committee. These committees have authority to define the scope of services provided by CMS to the 42 million beneficiaries in its Medicare program, 51% of whom have incomes below 200% of the poverty level (Kaiser Family Foundation, 2005).

By producing these studies, NPAF provided decision makers with data on which to base their decisions on improving access to healthcare. For example, the coding method study (Moran et al., 2004) has resulted in CMS's Medicare Coverage Advisory Committee's decision to increase the number of billing codes available to providers so that they could be reimbursed for newly defined service areas. Additionally, the unreimbursed cost of chemotherapeutic preparations study (University of Utah, 2005) resulted in a 2005 proposal by CMS to increase reimbursement to physicians to help offset the $36.00 to $44.00 cost documented per preparation. By reimbursing oncologists for the full range of services they offer, NPAF is helping to ensure patients' continued access to community physicians. Compression of reimbursement to providers can result in reduction of services or access.

Like all nonprofits with a service mission, patient advocacy nonprofits such as PAF often find themselves in competition with each other in seeking funding from the same sources. Nevertheless, leaders at PAF have also found that working collaboratively with a united voice results in greater improvements for all, as demonstrated by the annual odyssey to Capitol Hill to procure research dollars for the National Institutes of Health research funding.

A Seat at the Table

A seat at the table is an additional tool that provides nonprofits with the opportunity to shape future healthcare delivery systems, products, and processes. Today, PAF occupies a seat as a member of the Director's Consumer's Liaison Group advising the director of the National Cancer Institute on how to actively engage the patient advocacy community through a new website (http://ncilistens.cancer.gov/). Additionally, PAF provides advice to many states on improved access to care as they develop Medicaid programs and independent community initiatives.

NPAF also has a goal of gaining membership in or access to important federal committees or decision makers, for example, through its work as a member on the American Health Information Technology Community, appointed by the Department of Health and Human Services. Most recently, Davenport-Ennis has co-chaired an American Health Information Technology Community subcommittee charged with seeking national consensus on recommendations for creating a personal health records system that will be affordable, portable, safe, secure, and ubiquitous. In another example of gaining access to decision makers, in 2004, at the request of Senator Bill Frist, Senate Majority Leader, NPAF produced a white paper, in collaboration with PAF staff, directed at practical solutions for improving coverage of the U.S. uninsured population. The result was *The Uninsured: Voices of Despair* (PAF, 2004). This report is updated regularly for members of Congress to use in legislative deliberations on this problem. The report's recommendations range from expanding existing safety net programs, to developing tax credits for employers offering health insurance to employees, to tax credits for low-income workers so that they can purchase independent policies. NPAF has also collaborated with staff members of key Congressional committees to carry out research, review draft language for bills when invited, provide amendment language, and negotiate with elected officials to encourage sponsorship of key advocacy legislation (see Textbox 16.2)

Textbox 16.2   Personal Reflections of Nancy Davenport-Ennis

As the first-born daughter in our family in which my mother was a director of nurses at our largest community hospital and my father was the owner of a car dealership in North Carolina, my life was one of awareness of those much less fortunate than we were. Daily conversations at home focused on how to improve the lives of others. After graduating from college with my English degree in hand and a high school teaching position waiting, I declined the invitation to move to Texas to earn a doctorate in sociology; however, the desire to leave the world a better place than when I arrived was firmly planted in my soul.

(continued)

Textbox 16.2   Personal Reflections of Nancy Davenport-Ennis
(continued)

My early professional years included teaching English to high school juniors and seniors until the birth of my first child, Beth, at which time, I took a 10-year sabbatical to be a full-time mother to Beth and her sister, Fran, born four years later. Community and church service filled those years with political activism and volunteerism.

I re-entered the professional arena when I became a North Carolina real estate broker and residential contractor in 1979. Invited to become a regional trainer for Century 21 of the Carolinas, I directed training of agents and brokers in North and South Carolina before accepting a similar position in Vienna, Virginia. There I became the director of education for Century 21 of the Mid-Atlantic Region, which included Virginia, Maryland, Delaware, and Pennsylvania. Three years after joining Century 21, I was invited to become the national director of New Homes Sales and Marketing, nationally headquartered in Irvine, California.

In 1986, marriage to my husband, John H. Ennis, relocated our family to Hampton, Virginia, where I began a career as an independent consultant and national speaker in the new home construction industry and real estate community. It was in this role that I developed educational materials for all types of learners and wrote books for diverse audiences.

In 1993, that world changed with my first diagnosis of breast cancer. A quick trip to surgery in December 1993 at Duke University Medical Center for a mastectomy was barely a blip on a very busy schedule; however, a subsequent diagnosis of cancer in the opposite breast six months later, with a second mastectomy in May 1994, made a permanent impression. Life is short. My own belief was that God had been very good to me in my lifetime. I knew I needed to give back, but did not have a clear plan of action until I met Cheryl and began our journey with her.

As that journey developed, it became clear that my life's mission was twofold. First, I wanted to establish a foundation that would resolve healthcare access issues for patients confronting loss of life, dignity, and security. My objective was to offer a program of professional services that would relieve patients and their loved ones of responsibility for fighting business issues at the same time that they were trying to survive cancer treatment and recapture wellness. Additionally, I felt a moral responsibility to document each life experience statistically so that the pain and passion of each patient could be used to make life better through policy and regulatory reform for countless patients. The result was the establishment on April 4, 1996, of the Patient Advocate Foundation and National Patient Advocate Foundation. The opportunity to address audiences nationally removed any fear of failure as I contemplated building two organizations from the ground up with limited resources.

(continued)

Textbox 16.2   Personal Reflections of Nancy Davenport-Ennis
(continued)

What is more, the two organizations established in 1996 as a result of these experiences included family members on the staff from the beginning. My husband joined me as a co-founder of both PAF and NPAF even as he continued to pursue his own career. In 2000, he became chief development officer for PAF. That same year, I also recruited both my daughters to PAF full time, one as chief program officer, the other as chief operating officer, following several years during which they had volunteered their time in the evenings, on weekends, and in summers, even as they pursued careers in other professions.

A fundamental reality we accepted early on was that failure often provided the seeds of future success. An example was our first attempt at publishing. When our draft was reviewed by the project's financial supporters, they recommended a rewrite with collaborative support from an attorney well versed in health advocacy publications. Our ability to remain appreciative of their advice as we began the eight-month rewrite process resulted in our best selling publication to date, "Managed Care Answer Guide" (Groom & Khanna, 1997), nine years after its publication. As a result of that first experience, PAF has published six texts, including the *National Financial Resource Directory: A State by State Guide to Resources* (PAF, 2002), purchased by CMS for Senior Health Insurance Program Services counselors and distributed to more than 6,000 social workers with Medicaid, Social Security, and community hospitals and clinics. PAF case management staff wrote all six publications in collaboration with PAF Board members. In 2001, PAF established a formal publications committee that reviews requests for new publications, evaluates the need, assigns priorities, and sets and attains annual production goals. Publications are available in English and Spanish, can be accessed online at www.patientadvocate.org, and are distributed to patients at no charge.

For me, the greatest motivator and sustainer in my advocacy endeavors has been my faith in God. With my faith in His direction, together with the love and support of my family, and the passion and gifts of insight, service, and vision of PAF and NPAF's board of directors and staff members, the path to success, although often difficult, has never been uncertain.

The tools to success for both foundations lie with the many volunteers who have demonstrated the commitment and made significant sacrifices so that our vision could become a reality. My husband and children made sacrifices, as did I, but they were always made knowing that the future for the patients we served would be improved if our mission could succeed. Each opportunity we viewed as a blessing and each challenge as an opportunity to learn. A balance of blessings and challenges keeps us humble, focused, and engaged with others to find success.

CONCLUSION

PAF and NPAF are innovative organizations that embody values of the broader patient advocacy movement in several ways. First, the organizations represent the work of a dedicated individual who, with the help of her supporters, has translated her personal experience of advocacy into broader efforts that have affected the lives of many; simply put, the work of Davenport-Ennis shows how much patients and their loved ones have to offer as reformers of the healthcare system. Second, the organizational structure of PAF and NPAF acknowledges the need for a two-pronged approach to patient advocacy, one that helps individual patients resolve their difficulties in navigating the healthcare system while addressing the policy-level factors causing those difficulties. This close coordination of purpose helps to ensure that neither branch loses touch with the other. Third, PAF and NPAF may reflect a growing sophistication among advocates, as they increasingly use both data to drive their interventions and business knowledge to inform their organizational structure and activities. In these ways, PAF and NPAF serve as excellent case studies for students of patient advocacy, offering insight into the role advocacy organizations can play in providing direct services as well as enacting patient-centered policies.

ACKNOWLEDGMENTS

Life affords us many opportunities to make contributions that improve the lives of others in this world. This chapter is the result of my association with many people through the years who have contributed to the body and character of services that PAF and NPAF have provided to Americans since 1996. Board of director members, employees, community financial supporters, including Mayor Joe Frank and the city of Newport News, VA, pharmaceutical and medical community national foundations, the Centers for Disease Control, the federal government through an annual earmark, and individual donors, are each to be acknowledged. Their belief in and support of our mission made this chapter possible.

Special thanks go to Fran Castellow, chief operating officer of PAF, for her editing and research documentation as well as her oversight and implementation of PAF's growth during the last five years; Donna McQuistan, director of patient services, for research citations as well as information on other U.S. organizations that provide audit services of consumer medical bills; Diana O'Brian, JD, regulatory attorney of NPAF, who contributed both research assistance and the section entitled, "Insurance Reform/Efforts Nationally, 1996–2006"; Melynda Obergfell, my friend and executive assistant who identified articles in national publications featuring PAF and NPAF as well as for her administrative support through this process; Beth Darnley, chief program officer of PAF, who selected specific patient cases for this chapter and, who since 2000, has implemented the majority of programs at PAF; Leah Arnett, board secretary of both PAF and NPAF, for her collaboration and extensive fact checking.

Without the love and support of my husband, John H. Ennis, devoting my life's work to advocacy through the establishment and development of both PAF and NPAF simply would not have been possible. Similarly, his unselfish gift of sacrificing our personal time together so that this chapter could be written ensured its completion. Indeed, the chapter reflects the work of everyone at PAF and NPAF past and present who contributed to our visions, strategic planning, and implementation in service to others.

References

Appleby, J. (2005, April 29). Medical costs prove a burden even for some with insurance. *USA Today.* Retrieved March 9, 2007, from http://www.usatoday.com/money/industries/health/2005-04-28-medical-bills-usat_x.htm.

Bereson, A. (2005, July 12). Cancer drugs offer hope, but at a huge expense. *New York Times.* Retrieved March 9, 2007, from http://www.nytimes.com/2005/07/12/business/12cancer.html?ex=1278820800&en=1eb889752ca5eb49&ei=5088.

Breast and Cervical Cancer Prevention and Treatment Act of 2000; Public Law 106-354. (2000). Retrieved November 19, 2006, from http://www.cdc.gov.libproxy.lib.unc.edu/cancer/nbccedp/bccpdfs/publ354-106.pdf.

Collins, S. R., Davis, K., Doty, M., Kriss, J. L., & Holmgren, A. L. (2006). *Gaps in health insurance: An all-American problem.* Retrieved November 19, 2006, from http://www.cmwf.org/publications/publications_show.htm?doc_id=367876.

Dalton, K. (2005, January). *Geographic access to care study: Cecil G. Sheps Center for Health Services Research, University of North Carolina at Chapel Hill.* Retrieved November 19, 2006, from http://www.npaf.org/pdf/gap/unc_study.pdf.

Dockser-Marcus, A. (2003, March 12). Sorry only half of that surgery is covered. *Wall Street Journal,* p. D1.

Dockser-Marcus, A. (2004, September 7). Price becomes a factor in cancer treatment. *Wall Street Journal,* p. D1.

Doty, M. M., & Holmgren, A. (2006). *Health care disconnect: Gaps in coverage and care for minority adults: Findings from the Commonwealth Fund biennial health insurance survey (2005).* Retrieved November 2, 2006, from http://www.cmwf.org/publications/publications_show.htm?doc_id=386220.

Edwards, J. N., Doty, M. M., & Schoen, C. (2002). *The erosion of employer-based health coverage and the threat to workers' health care: The Commonwealth Fund.* Retrieved November 2, 2006, from http://www.cmwf.org/publications/publications_show.htm?doc_id=221528.

The Employee Retirement Income Security Act of 1974; Public Law 93-406, 88 Statute 829. (1974).

Gower, T. (2004, February). *Blindsided (in Reader's Digest, pp. 94–98).* Retrieved November 19, 2006, from http://www.rd.com/content/openContent.do?contentId=27598.

Groom, C. D., & Khanna, V. (1997). *Managed care answer guide (Patient Advocate Foundation).* Retrieved November 19, 2006, from http://www.patientadvocate.org/pdf/pubs/mc_answer-guide.pdf.

Hadley, J. (2002, May 10). *Sicker and poorer: The consequences of being uninsured (publication no. 20020510).* Retrieved November 19, 2006, from http://www.kff.org/uninsured/20020510-index.cfm.

Harrar, S. (2002). Win the insurance war. *Prevention, 54,* 44.

Health Insurance Portability and Accountability Act of 1996; Public Law 104-491. (1996).

Heilig, F., Strouse, D., & Hassett, N. (2005). *Adult cancer clinical trials in the community setting: A baseline study to examine patient accrual.* Retrieved November 19, 2006, from http://www.npaf.org/pdf/gap/sept_2004/aspen_031405.pdf.

Himmelstein, D. U., Warren, E., Thorne, D., & Woolhandler, S. (2005). MarketWatch: Illness and injury as contributors to bankruptcy (W5-63-W5-73). *Health Affairs, Suppl Web Exclusives* (January–June). Retrieved November 19, 2006, from http://content.healthaffairs.org/cgi/reprint/hlthaff.w5.63v1.

Institute of Medicine. (2002a). In Smedley, B. D., Stith, A. Y. and Nelson, A. R. (Eds.), *Unequal treatment: Confronting racial and ethnic disparities in health care.* Washington, DC: National Academy Press.

Institute of Medicine, Committee on the Consequences of Uninsurance. (2002b). *Care without coverage: Too little, too late [electronic version of report brief available: http://www.iom.edu/Object.File/Master/4/160/Uninsured2FINAL.pdf].* Washington, DC: National Academy Press.

Kaiser Commission on Medicaid and the Uninsured. (2006). *The uninsured, a primer: Key facts about Americans without health insurance.* Retrieved November 2, 2006, from http://www.kff.org/uninsured/upload/7451-021.pdf.

Kaiser Family Foundation. (2005). *Medicare at a glance.* Retrieved November 2, 2006, from http://www.kff.org/medicare/upload/1066-08.pdf.

Ku, L., & Broaddus, M. (2005). *Out-of-pocket medical expenses for Medicaid beneficiaries are substantial and growing: Center on Budget and Policy Priorities.* Retrieved November 2, 2006, from http://www.cbpp.org/5-31-05health.htm.

Landro, L. (2000, July 7). National group goes to battle for patients fighting their insurers. *Wall Street Journal,* p. B1.

Lewin Group. (2003). *Patient advocate foundation survey: Patient and consumer views of brown bagging and mandatory vendor imposition.* Retrieved November 2, 2006, from http://www.anco-online.org/NPAFBB.pdf.

Medicare Prescription Drug Improvement and Modernization Act of 2003; Public Law 108-173. (2003).

H.R. 1812: Patient Navigator Outreach and Chronic Disease Prevention Act of 2005. (2005). Retrieved March 9, 2007, from http://www.govtrack.us/congress/bill.xpd?bill=h109-1812.

Moran, D., Suter, K., Shostak, D., Kirby, K. & Braid, M. (2004). *Practice expense reimbursement for cancer care services: Methodology evaluation & assessment of alternative policies: Final report September 23, 2004: The Moran Company.* Retrieved November 19, 2006, from http://www.npaf.org/pdf/gap/moran_study.pdf.

Oberlander, J. (2003, August 27). The politics of health reform: Why do bad things happen to good plans (p W3-391-W-3-404)? *Health Affairs, Suppl Web Exclusives* (July–December). Retrieved November 19, 2006, from http://content.healthaffairs.org/cgi/reprint/hlthaff.w3.391v1.

One Voice Against Cancer. (2005). *Home page.* Retrieved November 19, 2006, from http://www.ovaconline.org/.

Patient Advocate Foundation. (2002). *National financial resource directory: A state by state guide to resources* (2nd ed.). Retrieved November 2, 2006, from http://patient.cancerconsultants.com/StateGuide.pdf.

Patient Advocate Foundation. (2004). *The uninsured: Voices of despair.* Retrieved November 19, 2006, from http://www.patientadvocate.org/pdf/uninsured_report.pdf.

Patient Advocate Foundation. (2005). *Annual report 2005.* Retrieved November 2, 2006, from http://www.patientadvocate.org/pdf/annual_2005.pdf.

President's Advisory Commission on Consumer Protection and Quality in the Health Care Industry. (1998). *Consumer bill of rights and responsibilities.* In *Quality first: Better health care for all Americans (Appendix A).* Retrieved November 1, 2006, from http://govinfo.library.unt.edu/hcquality/final/append_a.html.

Rand Institute for Civil Justice and Rand Health. (2004). *Inside the black box of managed care decisions: Understanding patient disputes over coverage denials* (Rand, RB-9030). Retrieved March 28, 2006, from http://www.rand.org/pubs/research_briefs/RB9039/index1.html.

Rowland, D. (2004, March 9). *Uninsured in America (publication No. 7048, Kaiser Family Foundation, Washington, DC).* Retrieved November 19, 2006, from http://www.kff.org/uninsured/7048.cfm.

Tergesen, A. (2005, October 24). Your guide to the medical maze (pp. 120–122 in print edition). *Business Week.* Retrieved November 19, 2006, from http://www.businessweek.com/magazine/content/05_43/b3956131.htm.

Topolnicki, D. (2000, December). What to do if your insurer says no. *Reader's Digest New Choices Magazine,* pp. 43–47.

University of Utah, Pharmacotherapy Outcomes Research Center. (2005, February 9). *Documentation of pharmacy cost in the preparation of chemotherapy infusions in academic and community-based oncology practices.* Retrieved November 19, 2006, from http://www.npaf.org/pdf/gap/utah_study.pdf.

CHAPTER 17

Research Advocacy in Traditional Research Settings: Questions of Influence and Legitimacy

Margo Michaels and Deborah Collyar

OBJECTIVES

- To be able to define research advocacy
- To be familiar with a historical context and framework for reviewing lay people's involvement as research reviewers
- To review current efforts in cancer research advocacy
- To reflect on the legitimacy and influence of research advocates
- To be able to envision a future in which advocates
  - Are selected through a systematic process and trained appropriately
  - Have a meaningful, clearly defined role
  - Enjoy widespread acceptance from the research community

Many scholars mark the mid-1980s as the start of effective research advocacy in the United States, a point at which lay people became active in the research arena and started to change the "politics of biomedical research" (Dresser, 2001, p. 10). At that time, leaders within the gay rights movement—frustrated and anguished at the death of so many loved ones from AIDS—pushed both medical researchers and government agencies to take at least three steps: ease the rules governing patients' access to investigational medications, speed approval of promising drugs such as AZT to the market, and alter research priorities to conform more closely to publicly stated needs. These recommended changes sparked intense controversy.

445

Researchers and even many members of the lay public expressed anxiety about the politicization of science and what they feared could be the erosion of scientific standards. Today, however, many perceive it as a given policy that "communities affected by a disease have a voice, and must be consulted" in research (Schmalz, 1993, p. 58). How did we get from there to here? This chapter provides a historical overview and a framework through which to view lay people's involvement in research activities in the United States. These are followed by an overview of current efforts in cancer research advocacy, together with observations made through interviews with several cancer research advocates.[1] The chapter ends by raising a series of questions about the role, legitimacy, and influence of advocates in research. Because cancer research advocacy has been particularly successful over the past 20 years, the chapter focuses specifically on the direct influence of cancer advocates in deciding what research should be undertaken and funded and how that research should be done.

DEFINITIONS

Research advocates[2] are lay persons who work to influence clinical, behavioral, and basic science research directly. Mostly volunteers affected by a disease, research advocates seek not only to change *how* research is conducted but also to influence decisions about *what* research should be funded.

Research advocates participate in the research process at a number of levels. On the individual level, they can teach new patients about clinical trials, represent research participants with trial investigators, and facilitate information exchange between patients and scientists. On a community level, they can serve on a hospital's institutional review board. When they promote research or lobby for increased governmental funding, they are operating on a system or policy level (Chapters 1 and 19; Dresser, 1999). This chapter focuses specifically on one aspect of system or policy change: the participation of cancer advocates in deciding what research should be funded and how it should be done. The chapter explores five different types of activities currently pursued by advocates, namely

- Serving on the committees (scientific merit review panels) that make funding decisions about what research to support
- Advising on the scope of research programs and suggesting new research questions

- Helping design studies that optimize patient participation
- Raising funds to sponsor advocates' own research
- Facilitating more effective information exchange between scientists and patients

Many within the research community continue to harbor misgivings about the presence of research advocates. Some scientists feel that advocates have a single-minded focus on treatments and cures and may give short shrift to the kinds of basic research that may eventually lead to clinical applications (Dresser, 2001; Gross, 1991). Others express concern that advocates on review panels have the potential to disrupt voting or scoring of proposals, thereby delegitimizing the peer review process. Still others fear that advocates can waste researchers' time, bring an "agenda" or "too much emotion" to what researchers see as an objective process, and/or lack sufficient experience to speak to essential issues of scientific merit (Agnew, 1999; Andejeski et al., 2002a). Despite these concerns, research advocates have made a strong case for the ways their presence can improve the merit review process. Among other benefits, advocates can

- Inspire scientists to pursue research opportunities that might not have been obvious to those lacking knowledge of the disease experience (e.g., studies that examine how to prevent co-morbidities such as lymphedema, fatigue, or depression)
- Provide insights on the accuracy, clarity, and readability of clinical trial consent forms
- Improve plans for recruitment, retention, outreach, and follow-up of study participants by identifying culturally appropriate recruitment plans, educational messages, or potential incentives for participation
- Contribute a patient, family member, or research participant perspective to a proposed study so that a "real-life" perspective on benefits, risks, and quality of life are adequately communicated to scientists
- Remind scientists about the ultimate purpose of biomedical research, that is, to produce concrete health benefits for real people rather than the more limited aim of funding elegant research leading to interesting journal articles (Agnew, 1999; Andejeski et al., 2002a; Dresser, 2003)

Finally, some observers have suggested that the mere presence of advocates in the room during the scientific review and deliberation process has prompted reviewers to consider the impact of their decisions on patients themselves. One advocate noted that she was surprised to learn that many scientists on review panels were not aware of the patients' experiences, including symptoms that typically result from various treatments. As she observed, "I know our participation in these panels was invaluable—from both the perspective of the scientists and the survivors involved" (National Breast Cancer Coalition Fund [NBCCF], 1996–1998). The sense of urgency an advocate can create by serving on review panels is echoed by one high-ranking government official, who commented that "science can sound so beautiful, but . . . when the woman sitting next to you has metastatic . . . cancer, it draws you into thinking 'what can I get out the door here and now?'" (Lieutenant Colonel Kenneth A. Bertram, MD PhD, then director of Congressionally Directed Medical Research Programs, as quoted in Haran). These "in the room" dynamics cannot be quantified, but are clearly important to all involved in the process.

RESEARCH ADVOCACY AS A SOCIAL MOVEMENT

Historians have charted the rise in cultural authority demonstrated by the medical profession during the first half of the 20th century (see Chapter 14). Although other legal, political, and social forces contributed to this trend, the medical profession itself has played a major role in the healthcare policies, laws, and norms around healthcare that curtailed patients' access to information and decision making (Starr, 1982). As a response to this highly controlled health and medical culture, social movements of the 1960s and 1970s—self-help, women's health, and patient rights—advocated for the right of all people to be informed, involved, and active in their own healthcare. Regardless of the focus, their goal was to promote greater equality, collegiality, and accountability in the relationship between patients and doctors and to grant consumers as much control over and participation in their care as possible. These movements helped prompt changes in laws and regulations as well as in attitudes, values, and practices in both the healthcare system and society at large (Gartner & Reissman, 1984; Ruzek, 1978).

As a way of explaining how these social movements change people's experience of disease and can transform the healthcare system, sociologists have described various types of health social movements, which they define as collective challenges to medical policy and politics, belief systems, research, and practice. In general, health social movements are large-scale efforts to democratize how and what kinds of scientific knowledge in medicine and public health research gets produced and disseminated. Health social movements challenge political powers, professional authority, and personal and collective identity, redefining disease from a personal trouble to a public issue (Brown & Zavestoski, 2004; Brown et al., 2004). Although the medical profession draws its authority from the competitive selection of its members and the rigor of training required, health social movements posit that, as a group, those who have experienced an illness have a unique authority that must be respected in all aspects of research and policy.

Of the several different types of health social movements postulated, the most germane to research advocacy is probably the embodied health movement, a social movement characterized by its drive to legitimize a personal understanding and experience of illness. Its participants are lay people and citizens' organizations that challenge science on multiple levels, including etiology, diagnosis, treatment, and prevention in order to make medical establishments more responsive to their concerns (Brown & Zavestoski, 2004). Embodied health movements have three major identifying traits. They introduce the personal experience of illness as part of a social movement; they challenge existing medical and scientific knowledge and practice; and, somewhat paradoxically, they often involve collaborations among activists, scientists, and healthcare professionals (Brown et al., 2004). Research advocacy meets all three criteria of being an embodied health movement in that it introduces lay people's lived experience into the research process. These experiences provide movement members with a form of knowledge unavailable to other actors on the scene, a form of knowledge that "lends moral credibility to the mobilised [*sic*] group in the public sphere and scientific world" (Brown et al., 2004). In turn, this credibility legitimizes the roles lay people play in research activities.

Disease can transform the advocacy experience, yet the reverse is true as well. Politicization of disease can alter the disease experience, particularly by establishing a new role for survivors who wish to contribute to social change. As traced by an embodied health movement perspective, individual circumstances alone do not shape the disease experience; rather, politics, culture, social relationships, access to information, and institutional practices shape the experience as well. Furthermore, sick people can play a part in influencing these determinants (Klawiter, 2004). This perspective differs significantly from Parsons' (1951) theory of illness, dominant in the early days of medical sociology. Parsons described a "social contract" in which the patient acquired benefits (e.g., getting sympathy from others) from entering a passive sick role as long as that illness was "certified" by a physician. In contrast, the disease experience understood within an embodied health movement framework emphasizes a different social contract, one in which the patient assumes an active role. Here, individuals reject both the primacy of the physician's certification and the benefits of the passive sick role. Instead, they adopt the language and attitude of empowerment, learning more about their disease and treatment options and focusing outward on activity to challenge standard medical and scientific practice.

The ways in which both the lay public and health professionals now understand, think about, and fund health-related endeavors has changed significantly in the last 20 years. In large part, this shift in thinking is due to collective efforts described here as embodied health movements. By participating in research activities, advocates are taking part in a social movement that is significantly altering the way scientific research is conducted in the United States today.

RESEARCH ADVOCACY IN THE 1980S: PEOPLE WITH HIV/AIDS

Consumer movements of the 1960s and 1970s encouraged people to seek changes in the healthcare system and in self-care; yet by and large, these efforts did not extend to the area of medical research (Epstein, 1996). Advocacy for HIV/AIDS treatment was the first to target the relationship patients had with researchers and policy makers (Gross, 1991; Marshall, 1993). Through their combined efforts, AIDS advocates were able to persuade government officials to ease rules governing access to investigational medications, join scientific teams in designing research protocols, and serve on review panels deciding which research proposals should be funded (Dresser, 1999).

How were AIDS activists able to accomplish these aims? As the number of people with AIDS grew during the 1980s, gay white men (primarily) began to organize social service, case management, and self-help organizations to address the needs of those infected with HIV. In the early years, advocates' efforts dealt primarily with issues of care-taking and end-of-life care. Later in the decade, people with AIDS began to look outward, focusing on access to treatment and clinical trials. New drugs were slow to go through the established Food and Drug Administration (FDA) approval process. In the meantime, those suffering from the disease had no alternative but to hope for drugs to be approved or enroll in a clinical trial, given that *usual* care was ineffective at extending life. In this context, AIDS advocates began to argue against standard randomized clinical trials whose focus on seeking "pure" subjects and clean data was "killing people" (Epstein, 1989). Instead, they insisted on "a revolution in clinical trial design" so that research could "do a better job of meeting people's needs" by altering stringent approval standards to speed the development of new treatments (Epstein, 1989).

Initially, these advocates' pleas fell on deaf ears. Researchers and policy makers felt they knew, by objective standards, the optimal course of research. By 1987, however, one of the most influential groups in the HIV/AIDS movement, the AIDS Coalition to Unleash Power (ACT-UP), was organized. One of ACT-UP's initial goals was "the encouragement of well-funded research that was publicly accountable to the community it hoped to serve" (ACT-UP, 1993). Although some activists pursued acts of protest and civil disobedience, others advocated for specific research and treatment initiatives while challenging traditionally accepted scientific protocols. They educated themselves about drug development and clinical research, challenged the regulation and design of clinical trials, organized "treatment action groups," and advocated for community-based research. They also made the case that, as people with the disease, their perspective on research and treatment was valuable. By educating themselves on details of scientific protocols, HIV/AIDS advocates felt they stood on an equal footing with credentialed experts (Epstein, 1989, p. 38; Gamson, 1989). For the first time, disease victims were "transformed into activist/experts" with a distinct role in both research and science policy (Schmalz, 1993, p. 58).

By blurring the boundaries between experts and lay people, these early research advocates helped bring about many changes in the practice of AIDS research, including randomized clinical trial design at the National Institute of Health's AIDS Clinical Trials Group.[3] Although some scientists initially referred to the early advocates as a "violent threat" to research (Fedor, 1991, 1992), over time, alliances made between scientists and lay persons helped them find common ground. In a watershed event in 1989, the Institute's Anthony Fauci decided to open the AIDS Clinical Trials Group meetings to the public and invited community representatives to become full members (Epstein, 1996). The Group's recommendations formed the basis of federal legislation enacted in 1992 that changed how the National Institutes of Health (NIH) coordinated its AIDS research funding (Marshall, 1993).[4]

Advocates also encouraged regulatory reforms such as the "fast-track" approval process, which the FDA adopted in 1992 to expedite approval of drugs for the treatment of life-threatening diseases. Furthermore, they helped foster acceptance of special and compassionate-use exceptions and advocated successfully for programs that provided experimental drugs for seriously ill patients before FDA approval. Efforts such as these helped foster mutual recognition and collaboration among advocates and scientists, an outcome that would profoundly affect their cooperation in the years to follow. Along the way, AIDS research advocates were the first outsiders to become effective participants in the "most professional of enclaves, the world of scientific research" (Jonsen & Stryker, 1991).

RESEARCH ADVOCACY SINCE THE 1990S: WOMEN WITH BREAST CANCER

The success achieved by AIDS activists had a powerful influence on the newly emerging breast cancer advocacy movement of the 1990s. Up until the early 1970s, breast cancer was frequently seen and experienced as a humiliating but invisible disease veiled in stigma and shame. Support groups that emerged in the 1970s helped make the disease less private, a trend that gained further credibility from efforts of famous women like Betty Ford, Happy Rockefeller, and reporter Betty Rollin, public figures who spoke openly about their disease. At the same time, books, magazines, and organizations began to suggest that there was not just one "right answer" with regard to medical treatment and that the "science" of medicine might not be so rational after all (Marieskind & Ehrenreich, 1975; Ruzek, 1978). Rose Kushner started a one-woman crusade to question the scientific rationale behind what were, at the time, standard medical procedures—the Halsted radical mastectomy, for example, and the one-step biopsy/mastectomy. Kushner's efforts were among the first patient challenges to conventional breast cancer treatment (Lerner, 2001; Montoni & Ruzek, 1989).

By the late 1980s, breast cancer support groups began to look outward, as AIDS groups had done before them, to focus on problems with access to and funding for screening, insufficient funding for scientific research, ineffective or questionable treatment regimens, and the absence of public awareness about the disease.

By 1991, many breast cancer groups began focusing on ways to help transform breast cancer from a private problem for individual women to a public problem that required federal involvement in the areas of treatment and research (Ferguson & Kasper, 2000). Adopting strategies learned from ACT-UP, these groups called attention to the inadequate funding allocated to breast cancer research in light of the high breast cancer death rates in the United States. Several groups joined together to form the National Breast Cancer Coalition (NBCC), an organization that would prove influential in promoting a role for advocates in the research process.

Throughout the 1990s, breast cancer advocates' influence grew rapidly, from the beginning involving collaborations with scientists and healthcare professionals. First, NBCC convened its own "research hearings" on breast cancer research during which top researchers, attracted by the possibility of bringing public attention to the cause, discussed where and how additional dollars should be allocated to the under-funded area of breast cancer research (Marshall, 1993). Nationally, NBCC successfully lobbied Congress in 1992 to allocate funds to the U.S. Department of Defense's Congressionally Directed Medical Research Programs to develop a new breast cancer research program. Around the same time period, another group of advocates helped create the state-funded California Breast Cancer Research Program.

These early efforts helped set the stage for the growing influence of research advocates in many types of cancer research.[5] Often, however, similar to the example of advocacy around HIV/AIDS, scientists and advocates in the breast cancer arena were dubious about the impact of these efforts. As one advocate described the situation,

> [In the beginning] . . . there was evident trepidation on the scientists' part [to include patient advocates in research]: they thought patient advocates could never understand the science they conducted, assumed advocates would slow down their research process. . . . Similarly, patient advocates were quite skeptical about [scientists'] commitment to speed up research projects, to apply relevant patient needs to their science and to develop new agents on a timely basis." (Collyar, 2005, p. 75)

Despite these tensions, cancer research advocates have continued to gain influence across a broad range of activities and in a variety of settings, including government agencies, foundations, and research institutions. These include participating in the peer review process, shaping calls for research and designing studies, and sponsoring research. As Advocate 1 noted, "One of the best benefits we offer to scientists is the question 'why do it that way?' . . . We . . . bring a sense of urgency and focus on results that don't exist in the traditional academic approaches."

PARTICIPATING IN THE GRANT REVIEW PROCESS

The NIH spends over 5.6 billion dollars on cancer research and control each year (FY 2005, NIH website). To determine how those dollars are spent, the NIH uses peer review study sections, small panels of 15 to 25 experts charged with weighing the scientific merit of federal grant applications. Once the exclusive domain of scientists, these study sections started to change in the early 1990s, when select cancer advocates began to be invited to participate. Today, peer review committees within at least one institute of the NIH—the National Cancer Institute (NCI)—sometimes include advocates in its peer review process (NIH & NCI, 2003).

Advocates' participation on study sections is often limited to topic areas perceived as directly applicable to consumers' interests, such as community outreach, recruitment and retention, epidemiology, and clinical trials, rather than on the technical merits of the application. One exception to this norm has been the previously mentioned U.S. Department of Defense, Congressionally Directed Medical Research Programs (2006). Since its inception in 1992, this program has included consumers[6] as full members on all review and advisory panels. Its Breast Cancer Research Program, moreover, was the first to include consumer reviewers on every review and advisory panel, including those reviewing basic science proposals.

Despite initial concerns that advocates would disrupt the peer review process, the Department of Defense's early evaluation of its consumer participation policy found that consumers on the panel proved otherwise. All members felt that having consumers on review panels was beneficial and did not have drawbacks (Andejeski et al., 2002a, 2002b). As one scientist told Fran Visco, then president of the NBCC, "I've come to realize that you want what we want . . . the best science" (Haran, 2001). As an indicator of research advocates' increased acceptance in this milieu, in 1997, the Institute of Medicine commended the program for advocates' involvement in the peer review process and "the unwavering respect and advocacy for this program among breast cancer advocacy organizations nationwide" (IOM, 1997).

The Department of Defense incorporates advocates in each of its seven research programs.[7] The agency noted that advocates "help the scientists understand the human side of how the research will impact the community and allow for funding decisions that will reflect the concerns and needs of patients as well as the clinicians who treat them" (Department of Defence, Breast Cancer Research Program, 2006). As a concrete illustration of advocates' impact, one scientist recalled his experience of evaluating a proposed study that was initially intriguing to the scientists on the review panel. The advocates resisted, saying that "because the perceived benefit was marginal, no one in their right mind would undergo it" (Agnew, 1999). It was through their influence that the study was not favorably evaluated.

SHAPING RESEARCH AND DESIGNING STUDIES

Advocates not only review proposed research but also work with scientists to *develop* research studies. Specifically, advocates play an increasingly visible role in NCI-funded Cancer Cooperative Groups. Most clinical cancer research conducted in the United States is designed and implemented through 10 cooperative groups, large networks of investigators and institutions working together to conduct clinical research. Beginning in 1994, two cooperative groups[8] began to invite patient advocates to join their committees. By doing so, the groups hoped advocates would help improve protocol development and implementation of new trials by offering their insights into potential patient experiences. For example, Advocate 1 brought attention to potential problems with accrual to the study that required patients to undergo painful endometrial biopsies every three months. "I told them, look, I want to see this trial accrue patients too, but you're not going to get the patients you need with the number and types of tests you want to do in this study!"

Despite the inclusion of approximately 100 research advocates in all 10 cooperative groups (Advocate 2), the alliance between advocates and scientists remains tenous, and the exact role of the advocate remains poorly defined. One advocate's interaction with a scientist underscores the blurred nature of the role: "He told me 'I'm glad you're serving on the committee. Advocates help us accrue more patients to our studies.' 'No,' I told him. 'We're helping to make the studies more accruable'" (Advocate 3). Another advocate summed up her perception, shared by many, that they are still an afterthought rather than integral members of the review committee: "We bring an experiential viewpoint to the scientific discussion and offer suggestions to make study designs friendlier to patients, from forming the concept to the accrual of patients. But [the doctors] often don't see [our role] that way, and they don't call us in until they're having problems with enrollment." (Advocate 4).

Even as advocates have made inroads into how medical research is conceived, conducted, and funded, many see their work as encompassing a much broader agenda than simply contributing to the status quo. Are we "taking a seat (at the table)," asks one advocate, "or redesigning the table itself?" (Brenner, 2000). In many cases, advocates do seek to "redesign the table," including calling for (1) more of a focus on behavioral, social, and environmental contributions to disease instead of what they see as a restrictive biomedical approach and (2) enhanced efforts to (a) further increase access for advocates participating in all types of research, (b) bolster low rates of participation in research by minorities and older persons, (c) analyze research results by gender, assuming that women and men are both studied in equal numbers, and (d) continue questioning approaches to prevention, chemoprevention, screening, or treatment where the risks or toxicities have questionable benefit (Rosser, 2000).

In addition to participating in programs created by others, advocates have also created programs in which *they* determine how they will be involved in a research process. For example, through its Clinical Trial Initiative, NBCC members attempt to work with research organizations to improve trial design and monitoring, increase trial access and accrual, educate the medical community and consumers, and promote initiation of breast cancer trials. In a widely cited effort, NBCC worked on an important Phase III clinical trial of the drug Herceptin (indicated for the treatment of certain types of breast cancer), helping to design an expanded access program and working with grassroots organizations to raise awareness about the trial (Bazell, 1998; Shak et al., 1998). The organization worked with the study sponsor on all aspects of the trial, from protocol design to outreach to oversight, and these efforts led to record accrual (Visco, 1998). Despite the success of these efforts, however, such partnerships have not been common in recent years.

SPONSORING RESEARCH

Research advocates have also sought to supplement government research funding with privately raised funds. Motivated by a personal health tragedy, several survivors and their families have started influential, often highly visible foundations promoting a research agenda to investigate causes and cures in cancer (see Table 17.1). Despite the fact that these groups were initiated by advocates themselves, advocate participation in their own grant review process is inconsistent.

The broad range of research advocacy activities undertaken by cancer advocates clearly fits the definition of an embodied health movement as articulated by Brown et al. (2004). The efforts of research advocates continue to blur the boundaries between experts and lay people, challenging established review procedures while simultaneously seeking collaboration with scientific experts. What remains to be seen, however, is the impact of these efforts on the direction, reach, and future outcomes of research, indeed the actual strength of research advocates' influence on research success.

Table 17.1   A Selection of Private Nonprofit Organizations Funding Cancer Research

---

- American Cancer Society
- Susan G. Komen Breast Cancer Foundation*
- The Lance Armstrong Foundation*
- Avon Foundation Breast Cancer Crusade*
- Cancer Research and Prevention Foundation
- Breast Cancer Research Foundation
- National Colorectal Cancer Research Alliance
- The V Foundation for Cancer Research

* The website explicitly states the group's use of research advocates in grant review.

THE ADVOCATE ROLE: ASSESSING QUALIFICATIONS, SELECTION, LEGITIMACY, AND TRAINING

Dresser suggested that if advocates are to be ethically involved in the research process, the system itself must ensure fairness, transparency, training, clear definition of role, and meaningful integration into the larger research process (see Table 17.2). Given the disparate ways in which the advocate role is defined—or not defined at all—it is questionable whether the growing opportunities for research advocacy could ever meet these ethical criteria.

The Role of the Advocate: "Stick to Human Subject Concerns?"

As public institutions develop more opportunities for people to participate in research advocacy activities, many within the advocacy community have begun to debate the need for universal standards and what such standards might mean.

What does it mean to "provid[e] the patient perspective in the assessment of scientific excellence" (NIH, NCI Guide, 2003, p. 18) or to "evaluate proposals from the unique perspective of a survivor?" (U.S. Department of Defense, Congressionally Directed Medical Research Programs, 2006). How does one define the singular community an advocate represents? Advocate 3 suggests three roles or "hats" for advocates:

Table 17.2   Suggested Essential Components of a System that Seeks to Include Research Advocates

1. A clearly defined advocate role, one universally implemented and accepted by all
2. Training to help advocates make ethical judgments about research studies
3. A fair and open selection process
4. Meaningful implementation of the advocate role so that advocates do not just take token seats in the room

Source: Dresser, 1999.

(1) helping scientists see a potential study through the eyes of a study participant, (2) representing the lay community's priority on meaningful changes in treatment and quality of life, and (3) being a "marketing expert" who considers whether a study's recruitment and retention plan, as well as whether its outreach and education plans, are culturally appropriate and realistic. Others describe a different set of roles. Andejeski defines an advocate's role as that of *interpreter*, validating the importance of federally supported scientific research, as *educator*, teaching others about the complexities of living with a disease, and as *ally*, focusing on the importance of the research process in finding cures for disease (Andejeski et al., 2002a; Charles & DeMaio, 1993).

As these varying definitions illustrate, delineating a clear set of roles for research advocates has proven challenging. Explicit or implicit organizational policies attempt to define boundaries for advocate involvement in scientific review to be all topic areas or only those of "consumer interest" (Schwarcz, Brown, Greenbaum, Kayden, & Trumbull, 1981; Advocates 5 and 6). One advocate summed it up this way: "What we (the consumer advocates) are looking for is the relevance of the proposal to finding the causes, prevention, or detection of . . . cancer. Our responsibility is to bring up the human side of the problem" (Advocate 5). Another advocate considers her role as going beyond assessing relevance: "When I conveyed legitimate concerns regarding points they hadn't considered, they began to really appreciate my participation in the process (see Textbox 17.1).

Also important in a definitional sense is determining exactly how an advocate should provide the *patient perspective* in helping assess the scientific excellence of a piece of research. In most instances, the role is self-defined. Yet despite the benefits of such flexibility, many advocates serving on committees seek clearer role definition and greater support. To fill this need, several cooperative groups have formed committees to determine advocates' responsibilities and to share strategies for gaining greater influence. For example, in one cooperative group, advocates developed a 13-point review form called "IMPACT" that has been effective in guiding advocates through their review of concepts and protocols (American College of Radiology Imaging Network, 2004) (see pp. 474–77).

Textbox 17.1   Competencies, Skills, and Knowledge Research Advocates Need to Master to Function Effectively in Their Roles

Skills

- Ability to apply scientific concepts and knowledge to analyze complicated proposals in both written and verbal forms.
- Ability to objectively reflect on the impact of research for individual patients and for the patient community, rather than for oneself. *An advocate must be able to represent a group of patient experiences, not just his/her own situation.*
- Ability to reflect, question, and respond without becoming defensive.
- Self-confidence to ask questions of physicians and scientists and to disagree with them when necessary.
- Ability to network beyond her own area of expertise or organization.
- Ability to maintain focus on why advocates are there (i.e., make people's lives better, not self-aggrandizement).

Knowledge

- Basic clinical concepts (screening, treatment, staging, prognosis).
- Basic science concepts (cellular behavior, genetics).
- Epidemiological concepts (incidence and prevalence, risk, study design, randomization).
- Basic statistics (p value, confidence interval, odds ratio, risk ratio).
- Key aspects of community outreach and accessible communication and education strategies.
- Ethical principles of research as outlined in the Belmont report.
- How new treatments are developed (from laboratory to phase 3 study to FDA approval).
- The culture, function, and procedures of the peer review process.

Skills, Knowledge, and Experience

Beyond experience with the disease, what qualifications enable a patient advocate to adequately provide the patient perspective on proposed scientific research?

Requiring advocates to have specific competencies before participating in research activities and how they would acquire such competencies remain controversial. Most advocates agree that the illness experience alone is not enough to make them effective. Effective training is critical for avoiding several common missteps. Advocates may, for example, preface their comments with self-deprecating remarks ("I'm just a survivor, but . . ."), limit their analysis to a singular focus ("I didn't see the box checked indicating this proposal concerns human subjects"), or verbalize a global effusiveness ("even if the proposal is poorly planned, we should recommend it for funding because I know patients need this service"). Advocates themselves emphasized their own need for training, as when one said: "When I first started reviewing concepts and protocols, I didn't know what to look for, or what was most important. . . . I just started looking for typos! . . . We have such an important role, but there's no mechanism to help prepare us. . . . *They* [doctors] go to eight years of school, but *we* just got cancer" (Advocate 6). Advocate 2 noted, "To be effective, I think you've got to know enough science to critically examine proposals from a patient perspective. It's a very delicate balance, and you need a lot of practice." It is clear that, in addition to understanding scientific principles, advocates need to have the ability to listen objectively, possess some degree of resonance with the scientific research objectives as well as the advocacy community's goals, have an empathetic understanding that all disease experiences will differ despite the commonality of disease itself, and have ties with a legitimate constituency or community with whom to share information.

In their effort to master these skills and scientific knowledge, many research advocates end up with extensive knowledge about the disease as they go through a process dubbed "expertification" (Epstein, 1996, p. 13). Some teach themselves via the Internet, journal articles, and medical texts; others by working with scientists or by getting informal guidance from their constituents; still others by taking positions according to their own beliefs about what would be best for patients (Dresser, 1999).

In addition, many advocates participate in training programs that focus on different aspects of scientific literacy, a precedent set by the NBCC in 1995. A 4-day course, Project LEAD (NBCCF, 1996–1998) is one of the only independent advocate training programs unaffiliated with any research or funding entity. It was the first science training course designed to help advocates influence research and public policy processes (see Textbox 17.2). The course has now trained over a thousand advocates and is often cited as an exemplar by others in cancer advocacy (NBCC, 2006). One advocate explained the benefits of the LEAD training to her work. "I wouldn't have been able to review . . . grant proposals had I not been through . . . training. I didn't have any scientific knowledge base, and I wouldn't have known what to expect from a peer-review panel" (NBCCF). Now over 10 years old, the course is well-respected by scientists and policy makers (see Textbox 17.2).

Some agencies also provide training for advocates accepted to their review committees. For example, the U.S. Department of Defense pairs novice advocates with experienced consumer review panel members, sends orientation materials, and arranges brief orientation sessions on peer review. In 2003, the NCI began a new training program to prepare its selected advocates to participate effectively in the NCI peer review process.

Textbox 17.2   Focus on Project LEAD® (Leadership Education and Advocacy Development)

Participants in Project LEAD:

- Learn the language and concepts of science
- Discover how to critically appraise scientific literature
- Acquire study skills necessary to remain educated on scientific aspects of breast cancer
- Study how breast cancer research decisions are made
- Become familiar with the wide range of consumer advocacy opportunities
- Gain confidence to speak up, ask questions, and find common ground with scientists

The course includes the following subjects:

- Basic science, such as the biology of cancer, basic genetics, the roles of DNA, RNA and proteins, and development of cancer at the molecular level
- Basic epidemiology and biostatistics, such as descriptive studies, analytic studies, clinical trials, causality, meta-analysis, and screening
- Leadership and advocacy development skills and how to participate effectively in the scientific community as a breast cancer advocate

Source: Data from NBCC

Selection Process: Questions of Fairness, Representation, and Legitimacy

When cancer advocates first started to serve on national advisory committees, they were appointed by program administrators who felt they would provide an important perspective. To ensure fairness in selection and to screen out candidates who might be ill prepared at best or disruptive at worst, many public institutions have instituted some type of application process. The criteria on which advocates are screened varies greatly, bringing the legitimacy of the process, and the advocates themselves, into question. For example, the NCI selects its pool of consumer advocates from a large group of applicants whose applications are reviewed by NCI staff and outside advocates.[9] After being accepted into the pool, the scientific review administrator, whose function is to run all aspects of the review panel, decides if advocates should be on a panel and who those advocates should be. In contrast, the Department of Defense requires a letter of nomination from an advocacy group before the interested individual can submit an application and be invited for an interview. Advocates are then selected by former advocate participants and Department of Defense officials.

Recent scholarship on research advocacy is divided over whether benefits of a rigorous selection process outweigh potential drawbacks. Some suggest that a formal process carries with it the possibility that insiders will "hand-pick or co-opt known [persons]" in an effort to avoid the "prolonged debates, open conflicts, surprise moves and efforts to reset the agenda" that unknown advocates might be willing to engage in (White, 2000). On the other hand, careful selection can help committees avoid the uneven quality, and even lack of legitimacy, of lay representatives in research. Solving these problems is important. Left unaddressed, their consequences may have the unintended effect of delegitimizing the role of research advocates (Dresser, 1999).

Representation

Research advocates' presence in formerly restricted arenas such as scientific panels and review groups gives communities a voice. This is an important outcome. Once there, however, what mechanisms can help ensure that advocate voices are heard? Even the best educated cancer advocates are often muscled out of discussions "dominated by the scientific reviewers and other study section members" (Brenner, 2000). This type of participation risks devolving into tokenism. In other words, the panels can seem to legitimate and affirm the role of advocates while actually maintaining scientists' control over an established process (White, 2000).

In another process that could undermine the work of advocates, institutionalizing the role could have the paradoxical effect of making advocates "insiders" who are unwilling to challenge others on the panel. "There's been some changes in 'generations' of advocates. The first wave (myself included) knocks down the doors and demands inclusion and respect. The second wave is invited in, and often waits to be asked. The third wave thinks it's always been this way, and doesn't want to rock the boat!" (Advocate 1).

As research advocates are preferentially selected and transformed into "professional advocates," new questions arise. Among them are the following: Will advocates continue to remain outsiders, and if so, how will that outsider status manifest itself? Under what circumstances are advocates more likely to be co-opted ("lapdogs vs. watchdogs")? Do research advocates still have a constituency if they no longer have contact with actual patients? Do they have legitimacy without that contact?

The research advocate's job is a demanding one. Although some are able to do this work on their own time, outside of their paid employment, many choose to make advocacy their full-time job, whether paid or unpaid. Given this commitment, the ways in which advocates actually represent patients or other public constituencies are vitally important. In interviews with advocates for this chapter, some mentioned that they no longer had any contact with patients currently being treated for cancer. In one of the few published studies on the impact of community representatives in research conducted in the early 1990s, most advocates came from a "voluntary sector elite" (i.e., mostly professional volunteers). Only a few consult their organizations about the work they are doing; many have no specific mandate from an organization to participate as consumer representatives (Jewkes & Murcott, 1998). Moreover, the mere existence of a rigorous selection process naturally attracts those individuals or organizations with the time and resources to commit to these efforts. Given that the ultimate purpose of research advocacy is to provide an ordinary patient perspective to research, it may be that current advocacy efforts have not yet reached their goal. This shortcoming may require research funders to reconsider mechanisms that promote fairness when advocates do participate, including possibly remunerating research advocates for their time (Dresser, 1999).

MAKING A DIFFERENCE

This chapter has assumed that research advocates have had an impact on the development and implementation of research studies. Certainly ad hoc reports suggest that the peer review process has seen qualitative improvements, with both scientists and advocates generally perceiving that advocates' presence has enhanced the research process. Interviews done for this chapter reveal that advocates experience some satisfaction with their role and that they perceive that their influence in scientific peer review committees is growing. Yet no standardized evaluation has been completed to determine the impact of advocates' influence on any specific study. We do not yet know exactly how consumer involvement has changed the processes and outcomes of research (Williamson, 2001). An evaluation designed to measure advocates' impact would need to compare the variation in scoring between advocates and scientists, as the Department of Defense has done, but it would also need to consider the penetration of the advocates' voice in the discussion and the perceptions of both advocates and scientists about the entire process. Considering patient recruitment and retention in studies subject to strong advocate review would also be important (see Textbox 17.3).

Textbox 17.3   An Advocate's Perspective

The entire peer review process . . . was very inspiring to me as a patient. It allowed me to learn more about my disease, and to see how much progress medical research has already made in finding a cure. More importantly, it demonstrated how much more work is needed. I was impressed by the number of people involved in research that were requesting funding and by the quality of their work. I was even more impressed by the individuals who were serving on the peer review panel with me. After each session, I was told by many of the scientists that (we) were an inspiration to all of the scientists on the panel . . . that we helped them see the importance of what they are doing. My reply was that they were an inspiration to me. The intelligence and commitment of everyone on the panel—all extremely dedicated to finding a cure—have convinced me that there will soon be a cure for CML. David Cranmer, Chronic Myeloid Leukemia Survivor (Department of Defense, Congressionally-Directed Medical Research Programs, 2006)

Source: DOD, CDMRP, 2006

THE FUTURE OF RESEARCH ADVOCACY AS AN EMERGING HEALTH MOVEMENT

The research advocate's role will likely continue to evolve over time. If this is the case, some important questions need to be answered. Will research advocates become increasingly sophisticated so that professional advocates are the norm rather than the exception? Will more ordinary people with a disease who have never been advocates feel more empowered to engage in the emerging health movement of research advocacy, or will the role be reserved for an elite few? From the point of view of institutions, will the selection process for advocates become more open or more exclusive? As research advocates become increasingly institutionalized into the scientific arena, the following questions need further examination:

- Will institutionalization diminish the initial reform goals of the research advocacy movement?
- Will the movement remain predominately reformist (i.e., seeking to modify existing institutions), or will activists push for fundamental changes in social, political, and economic structures (Brenner, 2000)?
- As research advocates are transformed into professionals, how can they continue to have a "constituency," especially if they no longer have contact with patients? What can be done to ensure that all people, not just the elite, have an opportunity to serve as research advocates?
- As research advocates are transformed into professionals and are preferentially chosen to take part in activities, how do they remain loyal to their roots while also leveraging expertise gained through experience?
- Do advocates need to be "certified?" If so, what are the tradeoffs inherent in enforcing a formal requirement?

Any research endeavor that includes advocate review should be congratulated. After all, despite its benefits, this inclusion can make review more cumbersome and time consuming. Nevertheless, this "place at the table" is not enough and should not be accepted as such. We must ensure that the role is a meaningful one, that advocates have appropriate training, that they are selected fairly, and that their constituency is clear. Only by addressing these concerns can we ensure the ongoing success of the movement.

RESOURCE LIST

Programs

NCI Consumer Advocates in Research and Related Activities Program

The NCI Consumer Advocates in Research and Related Activities (CARRA) program was created to integrate the perspective of people affected by cancer into NCI's programs and activities. CARRA members participate in activities that focus on the scientific merit of proposed research and the communication of research results.

Web: http://carra.cancer.gov/

E-mail: ncicarra@mail.nih.gov

Phone:
CARRA Coordinator: 301-451-3321
CARRA Program Development Manager: 301-451-3393
Office of Liaison Activities: 301-594-3194

U.S. Mail:
Consumer Advocates in Research and Related Activities (CARRA)
Office of Liaison Activities
6116 Executive Boulevard, Suite 220
Bethesda, MD 20892-8324

Department of Defense Congressionally Directed Medical Research Programs

The office of the Congressionally Directed Medical Research Programs (CDMRP) manages Congressional Special Interest Medical Research Programs (CSI) encompassing breast, prostate, and ovarian cancers, neurofibromatosis, military health, and other specified areas. Consumers provide a broad perspective of disease-related issues important to their consumer community. For more information about consumer involvement, contract the Congressionally Directed Medical Research Programs at

ATTN: Consumer Recruitment
1077 Patchel Street
Fort Detrick, MD 21702-5024

Phone: 301-619-7079

Fax: 301-619-7792

E-mail: cdmrp.consumers@det.amedd.army.mil

http://cdmrp.army.mil/

U.S. Food and Drug Administration Cancer Liaison Program

The Cancer Drug Development Patient Consultant Program incorporates the perspective of cancer patient advocates into the drug development process, allowing them an opportunity to participate in the FDA drug review regulatory process.

The Patient Representative Program recruits, assesses, and selects patient representatives to serve as members of advisory committees.

For more information, contact:
JoAnn Minor
FDA Office of Special Health Issues
Cancer Liaison Program
301-827-4460

Education Network to Advance Cancer Clinical Trials

The Education Network to Advance Cancer Clinical Trials (ENACCT) is the only national organization devoted solely to implementing and evaluating clinical trial educational efforts. Its mission is to identify, implement, and validate innovative approaches to cancer clinical trials education, outreach, and recruitment to improve outcomes for all. ENACCT offers high-quality, fee-based services that enhance the capacity of organizations conducting cancer clinical trials outreach, education, and recruitment. In addition, ENACCT seeks to

- Influence the inclusion of appropriate cancer clinical trial education as a top national priority.
- Become a national leader in the development and delivery of the highest quality community-focused clinical trials education programs for healthcare providers, patients, and the public.
- Use our programs to critically evaluate cancer clinical trials education approaches to determine the most effective approaches.
- Help stimulate a research agenda on promising areas of inquiry.

1010 Wayne Avenue Suite 770
Silver Spring, MD 20910
http://www.enacct.org
E-mail: info@enacct.org

ADVOCATE PROFILES

Margo Michaels, Executive Director, President and Founder

Before founding ENACCT, Margo Michaels spent 10 years as Education Branch Chief at the NCI, where she developed programs to educate cancer advocates, community leaders, and healthcare professionals about policy and science issues related to cancer and cancer clinical trials education. She developed NCI's Clinical Trial Ambassador Program, NCI's Clinical Trial Education Series, and the Clinical Research: Affiliates Funding Trials (CRAFT) program at the Susan G. Komen Breast Cancer Foundation in Dallas, TX. She was the Director of the NBCC's Project LEAD in the late 1990s. Ms. Michaels has extensive experience in project management, outreach, partnership development, and creation of educational materials. She holds an M.P.H. in Health Behavior and Health Education from the University of North Carolina School of Public Health. She notes that at least five sentences from this chapter come directly from her "prescient masters paper" she wrote in 1993 on activism in breast cancer and HIV/AIDS.

Deborah Collyar

Deborah has been a leader in cancer patient advocacy since 1991 and has paved the way for patient advocate involvement for all cancers in research. In 1996, she founded Patient Advocates in Research, a national network of cancer patient advocates.

From 1992 to 2003, Ms. Collyar created and managed the first successful model that incorporated patient advocates into a multidisciplinary research program through the UCSF Breast SPORE Advocacy Core. This group was fully integrated into basic science, epidemiology, and clinical science aspects of the program.

She was one of the first patient advocates in an NCI-funded cooperative group (Cancer and Leukemia Group B-CALGB) and has since developed advocate programs for CALGB, North Central Clinical Trials Group, and the American College of Surgery Oncology Group and has provided input to the American College of Radiology Imaging Network.

Ms. Collyar has also served on the Department of Defense Breast Cancer Research Program's Integration Panel and many American Society of Clinical Oncology (ASCO) and NCI committees and program review panels. She was the only patient representative on the NCI Board of Scientific Counselors.

Ms. Collyar is a two-time breast cancer survivor and lives in California.

ENDNOTES

1. Quotes were obtained in one of three ways: (1) From individual interviews conducted with four different research advocates, 2005–2006. Advocate interviews took place at two meetings: the C-3 Colorectal Cancer Coalition Training, January 2006, San Francisco CA; and the Radiation Therapy Oncology Group Semi Annual Meeting, January 2006, Miami FL. (2) From discussions with individual advocates, cited as Advocates 1–6 in chapter text, not on the reference list. (3) From the National Breast Cancer Coalition Fund's Project LEAD UPDATE 1996–1998, for which one author (Michaels) served as project director.
2. Many terms are used to describe research advocates. In this chapter, the terms "research advocate," "advocate," "patient advocate," and "consumer" are used interchangeably, according to how they are named or how they name themselves. Some cancer research programs only consider those who have had cancer as eligible to serve on these committees.
3. The AIDS Clinical Trials Group is part of the National Institute of Allergy and Infectious Disease.
4. The NIH Revitalization Act of 1993 strengthened the NIH Office of AIDS Research, requiring it to undertake a comprehensive evaluation of all NIH-sponsored AIDS research and set priorities for AIDS research.
5. Notably, people affected by prostate cancer and ovarian cancer formed new groups that took their lead from the work of breast cancer advocates.
6. Consumers are explicitly defined as breast cancer survivors whose experience, augmented by the experiences of others from the group who nominated the advocate, provides a perspective that complements scientific expertise.
7. The six other research programs besides breast cancer include prostate cancer, ovarian cancer, neurofibromatosis, tuberous sclerosis complex, chronic myelogenous leukemia, and the prion diseases.
8. The Eastern Cooperative Group (ECOG) and the Cancer and Leukemia Group B (CALGB).
9. These individuals are screened through an NCI program, Consumer Advocates in Research and Related Activities (CARRA), created to integrate the perspective of people affected by cancer into NCI's programs and activities.

REFERENCES

ACT-UP (AIDS Coalition to Unleash Power). (1993). *Fact sheet.* New York.

Agnew, B. (1999). NIH invites advocates into the inner sanctum. *Science, 283,* 1999–2001.

American College of Radiology Imaging Network. (2004). *Patient advocacy committee.* Philadelphia, PA.

Andejeski, Y., Breslau, E. S., Hart, E., Lythcott, N., Alexander, L., Rich, I., et al. (2002a). Benefits and drawbacks of including consumer reviewers in the scientific merit review of breast cancer research. *Journal of Women's Health and Gender-Based Medicine, 11,* 119–136.

Andejeski, Y., Bisceglio, I. T., Dickersin, K., Johnson, J. E., Robinson, S. I., Smith, H. S., et al. (2002b). Quantitative impact of including consumers in the scientific review of breast cancer research proposals. *Journal of Women's Health and Gender-Based Medicine, 11,* 379–388.

Bazell, R. (1998). *HER-2: The making of Herceptin, a revolutionary treatment for breast cancer.* New York: Random House.

Brenner, B. (2000). Sister support: Women create a breast cancer movement. In A. Kasper & S. J. Ferguson (Eds.), *Breast cancer: Society shapes an epidemic* (pp. 235–254). New York: St. Martin's Press.

Brown, P., & Zavestoski, S. (2004). Social movements in health: An introduction. *Sociology of Health and Illness, 26,* 679–694.

Brown, P., Zavestoski, S., McCormick, S., Mayer, B., Morello-Frosch, R., & Gasior Altman, R. (2004). Embodied health movements: New approaches to social movements in health. *Sociology of Health and Illness, 26,* 50–80.

Charles, C., & DeMaio, S. (1993). Lay participation in health care decision making: A conceptual framework. *Journal of Health Politics, Policy and Law, 18,* 881–904.

Collyar, D. (2005). How have patient advocates in the United States benefited cancer research? *National Review of Cancer, 5,* 73–78.

Department of Defense, Breast Cancer Research Program. (2006). *Department of Defense, Congressionally Directed Medical Research Programs: Breast cancer.* Retrieved October 25, 2006, from http://cdmrp.army.mil/bcrp/default.htm.

Department of Defense, Congressionally Directed Medical Research Programs. (2006). *Department of Defense, Congressionally Directed Medical Research Programs: Home page.* Retrieved October 25, 2006, from http://cdmrp.army.mil.

Dresser, R. (1999). Public advocacy and allocation of federal funds for biomedical research. *Milbank Quarterly, 77,* 257–274.

Dresser, R. (2001). *When science offers salvation: Patient advocacy and research ethics.* New York: Oxford University Press.

Dresser, R. (2003). Patient advocates in research: New possibilities, new problems. *Washington University Journal of Law and Policy, 11,* 237–248.

Epstein, S. (1989). Democratic science? AIDS activism and the contested construction of knowledge. *Socialist Review, 21,* 35–64.

Epstein, S. (1996). *Impure science: AIDS, activism, and the politics of knowledge.* Berkeley: University of California Press.

Fedor, M. (1991). AIDS, advocacy and activism. *Nursing and Health Care, 12,* 515.

Fedor, M. (1992). AIDS, advocacy & activism. *Nursing and Health Care, 13,* 12–13.

Ferguson, S. J., & Kasper, A. (2000). Introduction: Living with breast cancer. In A. Kasper & S. J. Ferguson (Eds.), *Breast cancer: Society shapes an epidemic* (pp. 1–24). New York: St. Martin's Press.

Gamson, J. (1989). Silence, death and the invisible enemy: AIDS activism and social movement newness. *Social Problems, 36,* 351–367.

Gartner, A., & Reissman, F. (1984). *The self-help revolution.* New York: Human Sciences Press.

Gross, J. (1991, January 7). Turning disease into political cause: First AIDS and now breast cancer. *New York Times,* p. A12.

Haran, C. (2001). *Three's company: The Army, women with cancer and the medical community have joined forces (article printed in January 2001 issue of MAMM magazine).* Retrieved October 25, 2006, from http://cdmrp.army.mil/pubs/articles/threescompany.htm.

Institute of Medicine, Committee to Review the Department of Defense's Breast Cancer Research Program. (1997). *A review of the Department of Defense's Breast Cancer Research Program.* Washington, DC: National Academy Press.

Jewkes, R., & Murcott, A. (1998). Community representatives: Representing the community? *Social Science & Medicine, 46,* 843–858.

Jonsen, A. R., & Stryker, J. (1991). *The social impact of AIDS in the United States.* Washington, DC: National Academy Press.

Klawiter, M. (2004). Breast cancer in two regimes: The impact of social movements on illness experience. *Sociology of Health and Illness, 26,* 845–874.

Lerner, B. H. (2001). *The breast cancer wars: Hope, fear, and the pursuit of a cure in twentieth-century America.* New York: Oxford University Press.

Marieskind, H. I., & Ehrenreich, B. (1975). Toward socialist medicine: The women's health movement. *Social Policy, 6,* 34–42.

Marshall, E. (1993). The politics of breast cancer. *Science, 259,* 616–617.

Montoni, T., & Ruzek, S. (1989). The emergence of breast cancer treatment policy. *Research in Sociology of Health Care, 6,* 3–32.

National Breast Cancer Coalition. (2006). *Home page.* Retrieved October 25, 2006, from http://www.natlbcc.org.

National Breast Cancer Coalition Fund (NBCCF). (1996–1998). *Project LEAD update.*

National Institutes of Health. (2006). *Estimates of funding for various diseases, conditions, research areas (chart).* Retrieved August 16, 2006, from http://www.nih.gov/news/fundingresearchareas.htm.

National Institutes of Health, & National Cancer Institute. (2003). *NCI consumers' guide to peer review.* Bethesda, MD.

Parsons, T. (1951). *The social system.* London: Routledge & Kegan Paul.

Rosser, S. (2000). *Controversies in breast cancer research: Breast cancer: Society shapes an epidemic* (pp. 245–270). New York: St. Martin's Press.

Ruzek, S. B. (1978). *The women's health movement: Feminist alternatives to medical control.* New York: Praeger.

Schmalz, J. (1993, November 28). Whatever happened to AIDS? *New York Times,* p. 58.

Schwarcz, S. L., Brown, T., Greenbaum, L. M., Kayden, H. J., & Trumbull, R. (1981). Nonscientist participation in the peer review process: Is it desirable? Is it implementable? Who are the nonscientists who should become involved? A panel discussion. *Annals of the New York Academy of Sciences, 368,* 213–228.

Shak, S., Bales, R., Baughman, S. A., Curd, J. G., Fuchs, H. J., Perry, C., et al. (1998). Genentech and breast cancer advocacy. *Breast Disease, 10,* 61–64.

Starr, P. (1982). *The social transformation of American medicine.* New York: Basic Books.

Visco, F. M. (1998). *President of the National Breast Cancer Coalition on the Genetech HER2 clinical trial: May 16, 1998.* Retrieved on March 3, 2007, from http://www.natlbcc.org.

White, D. (2000). Consumer and community participation. In G. L. Albrecht, R. Fitzpatrick, & S. C. Scrimshaw (Eds.), *Handbook of social studies in health and medicine* (pp. 465–480). London: Sage.

Williamson, C. (2001). What does involving consumers in research mean? *QJM: Monthly Journal of the Association of Physicians, 94,* 661–664.

Appendix 1   Project IMPACT Review Form (Used for Preliminary Protocol Concept Development, Protocol Concept Submission, Protocol)

* Sections 8.3 and 8.5 are to be completed upon review of the drafted protocol.

Review Statement:

Please indicate your overall level of support for the document in review: enthusiastically support, support, support with reservations, cannot support. Include elements of the review (positive/negative) that you feel are especially important for presentation to the steering committee.

1.0   Introduction/Background: Why Is This Study Important?

1.1   In layman's terms, what is the question/hypothesis being asked by the trial?

1.2   What is the value of the answer to patients? Will having the answer help patients live longer/live better? If yes, how?

1.3   How long will it take to complete the trial, and will the answer to the question be relevant when the trial is completed?

1.4   Does the trial fit into a strategic plan or initiative such as NCI Progress Review Group recommendations or American College of Radiology Imaging Network committee plan?

1.5   These first questions are addressed in many places on the American College of Radiology Imaging Network forms. If you see inconsistencies between sections or revisions, identify them here.

2.0   Study Hypothesis

2.1   Define the specific hypothesis and indicate what kind of study it is (screening, diagnostic, staging, image-guided treatment, treatment response).

3.0   Study Design/Protocol Development

3.1   How does the study design compare with standard of care (i.e., number of procedures and cost to patients)?

3.2   Do you feel that demands on patients are reasonable when compared with standard of care?

(continued)

**Appendix 1   Project IMPACT Review Form (Used for
Preliminary Protocol Concept Development, Protocol Concept
Submission, Protocol)** (continued)

3.3 Are correlative studies (which will lead to future research
     questions) included? Why or why not?
3.4 Will this study be conducted in community settings? Do you
     think that it will work in a community setting?
4.0 Rationale/Study Objective
4.1 What are the formal trial endpoints, and how do they compare
     with the goals in the hypothesis? For example, if the hypothe-
     sis states that the trial will increase survival, but the endpoints
     do not include survival, why not?
5.0 Eligibility
5.1 Who's included and excluded from the trial? Do you think that
     the trial population is representative of the patient population?
6.0 Preliminary Statistical Design
6.1 If the trial examines more than one treatment, are participants
     randomized to a single treatment, or is crossover allowed
     whereby participants may receive some or all of the treatments
     being studied? Why or why not, and do you agree with the
     trial design?
7.0 Competing Protocols
7.1 Do you have any additional comments about possible compet-
     ing protocols or possible partnerships with other cooperative
     groups, industry, or institutions?
8.0 Feasibility
8.1 Do you think patients will be interested in enrolling? (Yes/No)
8.2 Do you think the numbers expected to enroll are reasonable?
     (Yes/No)
8.3 Does the protocol include a section regarding the monitoring
     of accrual goals and plans for corrective actions should accrual
     fall short of the target? (Yes/No)
8.4 Are there specific aspects of the trial that you think will make
     accrual more difficult?

(continued)

Appendix 1   Project IMPACT Review Form (Used for Preliminary Protocol Concept Development, Protocol Concept Submission, Protocol) (continued)

8.5 Diversity:
   a. Does the protocol include a section regarding the accrual of a diverse population to this study? (Yes/No) See Appendix II for sample protocol language.
   b. Will any of the eligibility requirements make it difficult for diverse populations to qualify for this trial? (Yes/No)
   c. Will the trial be open at sites where diverse populations receive care? (Yes/No)

9.0 Schema/Flowchart
9.1 Is the schema designed in a patient-friendly form?
   a. Reading left to right, not top to bottom? (Yes/No)
   b. Can a calendar be overlaid? (Yes/No)

10.0 Informed Consent Process
10.1 Does the protocol describe the informed consent process to be used and not just include a form? (Yes/No)
   a. Supplemental patient materials? (Yes/No)
   b. Training for Clinical Research Associates and physicians? (Yes/No)
   c. Follow-up materials? (Yes/No)
10.2 Is the informed consent based on the 03.04.04 NCI template? (Yes/No)
   a. All study requirements are in bulleted format? (Yes/No)
   b. All procedures have clear explanations? (Yes/No)
   c. Study schema is clear and in calendar format? (Yes/No)
10.3 What happens in the event of an injury: Who pays? Is this clear?
10.4 What grade level is the informed consent written at? What provisions are made for people with limited reading ability?
10.5 Any correlative study sections (i.e., tissue or quality of life) should be at the end of the main consent, but before the signature page. Do any tissue consent pages have separate sections to
   a. Enroll in this study? (Yes/No)
   b. Use patient's tissue for future studies? (Yes/No)
   c. Contact/do not contact patient? (Yes/No)

(continued)

Appendix 1   Project IMPACT Review Form (Used for Preliminary Protocol Concept Development, Protocol Concept Submission, Protocol) (continued)

10.6 Adequate confidentiality safeguards: Can researchers link back to patient outcomes while still maintaining confidentiality? How?

11.0 Communication Plan

11.1 Has a communication plan been identified? (Yes/No)

11.2 Have needed communication/recruitment materials been identified? (Yes/No)

11.3 Does the communication plan include a campaign specifically targeted to minorities? (Yes/No)

11.4 Has a timeline been established for production and distribution? (Yes/No)

11.5 Record any suggestions for additional communication materials/strategies.

12.0 Dealing with Results

12.1 What is the plan to communicate trial results to patients and healthcare professionals? Does this seem appropriate/adequate?

13.0 Other Comments (add anything else you feel is relevant):

Strategy Five: Advancing Education and Professional Roles in Advocacy

Patient advocacy, often perceived as a modality practiced within established professions, is slowly developing its own distinct vocabulary, theories, and strategies. Indeed, people from a variety of professional backgrounds have begun to examine and practice advocacy as the primary focus of their work. As different practitioners start to coalesce, however, intense debates have arisen concerning the role of credentialing and training programs. This section therefore examines the trade-offs of professionalization as well as what can be done to maintain a respect and appreciation for the lived experience of patients. Chapters in this unit explore training programs for advocates as well as some of the professional roles they may assume, including patient representatives, clinicians, community organizers, and attorneys.

In Chapter 18, advocacy educators from two prominent graduate programs share the theory that undergirds their core curricula and delineate some of the core components of their respective programs. Of particular importance is a theoretical model demonstrating the progression advocacy often takes from an experience in self-advocacy to a dedication to public advocacy. Recognizing that health advocacy is a calling to many practitioners, Hurst et al. use case studies as teaching tools, thereby facilitating students' transitions from personal to political advocacy and helping them find their place in the wide spectrum of advocacy work.

In Chapter 19, Renneker and Stritter examine the emergence of a subspecialty in healthcare, the clinical advocate who researches therapy options, resolves conflicts between providers and patients, and presents a fresh look at how advocates can professionalize as advocates. With 15 years of experience in working with hundreds of patients, two physicians recount the experiences that led them to leave their traditional medical practices and embark on a professional experiment that would allow them to connect with patients in more meaningful ways. Through case studies, the authors describe the problems they have encountered as well as solutions they have been able to offer.

In Chapter 20, Morrison describes the role of attorneys in patient advocacy at the individual and systems levels, focusing in particular on problem-solving methods such as mediation and coaching that offer promising alternatives to litigation.

CHAPTER 18

Educating For Health Advocacy in Settings of Higher Education

Marsha Hurst, Martha E. Gaines, Rachel N. Grob,
Laura Weil, and Sarah Davis

OBJECTIVES

- To understand the value of health advocacy education in the context of professional legitimacy and practice quality
- To understand the purpose and historical underpinnings of health advocacy education
- To identify the benefits and limitations of two models of advocacy education: the stand-alone degree program and the complementary transdisciplinary model
- To identify key themes of health advocacy education and how these resonate in practical applications
- To clarify ethical, procedural, and practical tensions inherent in health advocacy work and the role of formal education in preparing advocates to deal with these tensions

I was a critical care nurse for 27 years, and I loved nursing. But I always wanted to do more. I was active in quality assurance, risk management, and clinical trials. Before the [Sarah Lawrence Health Advocacy] program, I thought of myself as an RN. After the program, I thought of myself as a researcher and advocate who wanted to commit to providing better healthcare for consumers. The program assisted my transition from being a nurse to being a different kind of professional with a different set of skills.

Sarah Lawrence College Health Advocacy Program M.A., 2000,
Patricia Banta, RN

What health advocacy intervention is appropriate when a hospitalized patient's spiritual beliefs seem to conflict with all hospital regulations? What factors should a health advocate consider when a client appears to be making inappropriate demands based on unreasonable expectations? How does a health advocate foster recognition of a community's strengths and build coalitions to capitalize on those assets?

This chapter explores the benefits of formal health advocacy[1] training in higher education settings for a variety of stakeholders, including the individuals who engage in such professional training, those on whose behalf they act, and the broader healthcare arena in which they operate. Section 1 explores the history and purpose behind educational health advocacy programs. Section 2 highlights the specifics of two successful educational advocacy programs—their evolution, structure, student body composition—and outlines the method underscoring the themes, models, and theories explored in the curricula. Section 3 uses case studies to demonstrate key themes in advocacy education. The concluding section addresses challenges and lessons learned from our experiences of educating for advocacy and our vision for the future of health advocacy education.

FORMAL HEALTH ADVOCACY EDUCATION: HISTORY AND PURPOSE

History[2]

Educating specifically for health advocacy grew out of the patient rights movement of the 1970s. During this era, a "rights-based" approach provided the foundation of much social action. The approach extended to groups (e.g., women) who sought to assert their right to autonomy and voice in their own medical care; it also extended to advocates for the poor who were the focus of the Great Society programs of the Lyndon Johnson years. The initial inspiration for a patient bill of rights came from the National Welfare Rights Organization. In 1970, the National Welfare Rights Organization list of patients' rights was incorporated into the accreditation standards for hospitals, becoming the basis for the Patient Bill of Rights adopted by the American Hospital Association in 1972 (Rothman, 1997) (see also Chapter 14).

Patient advocacy, as a hospital-based practice, grew out of this patient rights movement; advocates were needed to protect and enhance patient rights at a time when hospital stays were long, and acute conditions—heart disease, stroke, and cancer—contributed to the boom in hospital growth. The broader field of health advocacy, which extends beyond the hospital setting, also has earlier roots in the voluntary organization sector of society, where early health advocates typically advocated for a cause instead of for an individual or group. They were activists in social movements, voluntary associations (including civic organizations), women's associations and labor organizations, and in the early disease-specific nonprofits such as the American Cancer Society (1913[3]) or the March of Dimes (1938[4]).

In the first decades of the 20th century, these health advocates came to their work through other professional routes. They were social workers, attorneys, public health nurses, or doctors. They were the progressive era "new women" of Hull House and the Children's Bureau, the American Association for Labor Legislation leaders of the movement for national health insurance before World War I, and the nurses who worked with Lillian Wald to advocate for indigent and worker health care through visiting nurse services.

In the early years, three critical elements were primary in developing a health advocacy profession: association, credentialing, and education. In 1971, under the auspices of the American Hospital Association, the Society for Healthcare Consumer Advocacy[5] was founded as an association of mainly hospital-based patient advocates, without the autonomy characteristic of a profession. These early hospital-based advocates believed some credentialing was important, but discussions foundered on the topic of educational requirements. Moreover, history suggests that Society for Healthcare Consumer Advocacy's tie to the American Hospital Association may also have contributed to the death of the credentialing effort, as credentialing would have challenged the hegemony of the hospital as employer. In response, with her colleagues, Ruth Ravitch, a founder of the pioneering patient advocacy program at Mt. Sinai Hospital in New York City, decided to separate education from the more controversial credentialing. They turned to an academic environment (at Sarah Lawrence College) to develop a graduate professional education curriculum independent of the hospital "industry."

In the history of virtually every profession, there is a period in which a diverse group of practitioners works in various ways to "consolidate authority" (Starr, 1982, pp. 79–144). For medicine, this moment of coalescence is recognized in the Flexner Report (1910), which rated medical schools and gave a major boost to the American Medical Association leadership; however, for some professions, consolidation never happens. Indeed, more than two decades ago, in 1984, former Congressman (FL) Paul Rogers (1986) noted in a volume on Advocacy in Health Care, "Advocacy in health care is a calling many of us have pursued—one way or another—for many years. And yet, it has not attained the full status of an independent profession" (p. 1). He expressed the hope that the emerging master's program in Health Advocacy at Sarah Lawrence College would help accomplish this goal.

Education for advocacy has been slow to develop but is now gaining momentum. The master's program in Health Advocacy at Sarah Lawrence College was founded in 1980 to create an educational foundation for students interested in careers in health advocacy (Ravitch, 1981). In 2001, after several years of planning and teaching a patient advocacy course, the Center for Patient Partnerships of the University of Wisconsin joined the arena with a graduate-level educational model that builds on the culture of professionals applying their skills toward activism to achieve social change. The center offers advanced and specialized advocacy training and education to students in a range of related professional disciplines (e.g., medicine, nursing, pharmacy, social work, and law). A certificate program in healthcare consumer advocacy to formally complement students' professional degrees is in development. In the fall of 2004, Stanford School of Medicine developed a Patient Advocacy Program for undergraduate premedical and health policy students to enhance patient care at area clinics primarily serving underserved populations. Cleveland State University also began offering a continuing education Patient Advocacy Certificate Program in 2004 for practicing professionals, and the University of North Carolina at Chapel Hill School of Public Health taught its first course in patient advocacy to public health, pharmacy, nursing, and occupational therapy students, as of the 2006–2007 academic year.

Purpose

As patients and communities have become mobilized, they have demanded access to high-quality health advocacy. Consumers' increased demands are attributed to their increased dissatisfaction with the limitations of a scientifically-oriented medical model and specialization in health fields. Both these forces have increased the number of disparate provider contacts, reduced time spent with each provider (Ravitch, 1986), overshadowed humanistic dimensions of care, and weakened the provider/patient relationship. As a result, consumers struggle to have their "voice" included within medical narratives (Balshem, 1993), be the center of concern in healthcare interventions (beneficiaries of patient-centered care), and have their values considered in medical decision making.

As these patients and their families navigate complex health systems, they demand—and deserve—high-quality care and often require highly skilled, unbiased representatives to assert their interests (Annas, 2004). Groups and communities also help them from health advocacy, which successfully moves health agendas forward by garnering resources, pursuing legislative solutions and building coalitions. The existence of formal health advocacy educational programs both signals that long-term health system transformation is essential and produces a cadre of skilled health advocates to address patients' and communities' immediate concerns, whether as hospital-based patient representatives, community organizers, or nonprofit leaders.

The formal education of advocates is not without some resistance, however. Many health advocates derive inspiration and legitimacy from their own personal advocacy experiences, and for this reason, some view formal training and credentialing with apprehension. They fear that such measures might be barriers to advocacy for those with great experiential knowledge but little access to formal training. The challenge for advocacy educators is to honor personal experience while still valuing the benefits of formal education, which include skill building, the generation of new knowledge, and the development of codes of ethics and the futhering of social justice.

Formal education creates a forum for skill acquisition, yet most important for health advocacy, it provides methods to build advocates' capacity, enhance systemic impact, and develop a symbiosis between those new to the field and its educators. It also provides legitimacy to an emerging profession. Historically, professions have gained legitimacy through imposing and controlling educational requirements and structuring education around a defined body of knowledge and conventions of practice (Friedson, 1970; Starr, 1982).

Acquisition of this defined body of knowledge generally enhances the effectiveness and capacity of the professional. Educating for health advocacy is to being an advocate as educating for medicine is to being a doctor: effective health advocates must garner the tools of their trade and the expertise to use them effectively. In addition, health advocacy skills can be complementary: A doctor educated in both medicine and advocacy could be a skilled doctor and an effective health advocate. In some respects, the practice of any profession can be performed by skilled, knowledgeable, and ethical nonprofessionals, exclusionary regulations notwithstanding. Nevertheless, advocates, like other service providers, benefit from aspects of professionalization. Those benefits include adherence to professional ethics, participation in an intellectual community, and connection to the growth and accumulation of knowledge a profession provides.

Benefits, however, also accrue to consumers and patients who look to professionalization as one standard they can use to verify the skills of their advocates. Health advocates aim to enhance the power of the patients or clients and the communities they serve. A recognized educational credential is an important step in that direction. Students who receive their advocacy education as part of another professional degree program have the dual credentials of the health advocacy specialty and the primary professional degree.

Because educational settings are centers of research, writing, and dialogue, graduate programs provide a focal point for the collection, formulation, and dissemination of knowledge in the field of patient and health advocacy. In institutions of higher education, the construction of new knowledge and challenges to existing knowledge can proceed relatively insulated from the pressures of stakeholders and shareholders alike.

In addition, health or patient advocacy education may maintain a focus on social justice, a purpose which is usually integral to advocacy goals and thus embedded in its structure and content. Formally educated health advocates are taught to understand the patient's experience of illness, help define their care needs, and contextualize that patient's problem within a larger social justice framework. They learn to understand the complexities of care in the mixed public–private system of the U.S. healthcare system (see Chapter 2) and analyze how social inequities are reproduced in both the health services and health status of individuals and communities.

EXISTING ADVOCACY PROGRAMS: STRUCTURE, STUDENTS, AND CURRICULUM

> The most beneficial feature of the Center for Patient Partnerships is its interdisciplinary nature; patients are provided with advocacy which meets their complex, multifaceted needs in a holistic way. At

the same time, student advocates learn how to work with professionals in other disciplines on behalf of clients—this is an essential skill in the "real world" after law school.

Center for Patient Partnerships, Patient Advocacy Clinical,
UW-Law School Graduate Anthea Hasler, 2006

Program Structure

The structures of formal health advocacy education differ on a variety of measures: where their academic homes are, how broad-based their programs are, and whether they offer degrees. Atul Gawande (2002), in his essay "The Computer and the Hernia Factory," described a group of Canadian surgeons who do nothing but hernia operations and get much better results than other surgeons despite lacking the advanced qualifications of American surgeons. "Paradoxically," writes Gawande, "this kind of super-specialization raises the question of whether the best medical care requires fully trained doctors" (2002, p. 31). As with medicine or any other profession, advocacy also raises questions of how much value is added through additional education and where to draw the difficult line between breadth and depth, technical skill and knowledge.

The differences in the two graduate-level programs that currently offer formal higher education in patient advocacy in the United States—Sarah Lawrence College Health Advocacy Program and Center for Patient Partnerships, University of Wisconsin-Madison—underscore the tension Gawande raises and suggests that there is no one "right" approach to advocacy education. Sarah Lawrence's master's program is comprehensive and theoretical, providing students with a graduate-level degree specific to health advocacy. The Center's program, in contrast, does not issue a degree (a certificate program is pending), supplements other professional education, and with its primary clinical service learning approach, is practical and hands-on in its method. The Sarah Lawrence Program broadly introduces students to all forums and forms of health advocacy (see Table 18.1), whereas the Center's program focuses primarily on patient advocacy. This distinction between the broader perspective of "health advocacy," which includes a policy and class-based focus, as opposed to applied, case-based "patient advocacy" as a part of structured advocacy training, is a central difference between the two programs. The Sarah Lawrence program is a stand-alone program, whereas the Wisconsin

Table 18.1   Major Characteristics of Two Higher Education Programs for Health Advocacy

	Sarah Lawrence College Health Advocacy Program	Center for Patient Partnerships, University of Wisconsin-Madison
Type	Dedicated Master of Arts Program	Interdisciplinary Center–Certificate Program pending
Approach	Comprehensive	Supplementary
Curriculum	Interdisciplinary courses and multidisciplinary curriculum; social science and humanities-based; three required internships; optional capstone project/thesis	Primarily clinical/service learning with complementary substantive courses in patients' rights and consumer issues in healthcare
Founded	1980	2001
Faculty	Fourteen full- and part-time instructors; working health advocates and scholars from a range of disciplines	Five full- and part-time instructors, broad collaboration with affiliated faculty, practicing professionals, and national advocacy leaders
Students	Twenty-five to 35 students, some part time and some full time; mix of people changing careers and younger more recent college graduates	Per semester: 8 to 12 clinical students, 20 to 25 students from various disciplines (e.g., medicine, law, nursing, pharmacy, industrial engineering, social work) enrolled in courses
URL	http://www.slc.edu/grad_healthadvocacy.php	www.patientpartnerships.org

program is an interdisciplinary effort of the schools of law, medicine, and nursing. Although their structures are disparate, they share kindred missions, motivations, and historical contexts.

Students

Many students of health/patient advocacy are engaged in advocacy work for themselves or others before they ever enter a formal educational setting. They have cared and advocated for self, family, and friends; read widely; made difficult decisions; fought battles with insurers; and navigated the barriers of access and availability deeply embedded in the American healthcare system. They seek advanced education to deepen their understanding of advocacy issues and enhance their effectiveness as change agents, and their life experiences make them exceptional candidates for our programs. Others come because of a different kind of commitment to service, including undergraduate service learning programs, political action, or social justice work. For these students, hands-on experience has combined with fascination and frustration in the healthcare system to kindle a passion to advocate on behalf of others.

Many who come to advocacy are professionals or students in related fields such as law, medicine, or nursing. These students often seek to develop the tools to apply their passion for social justice to health advocacy work on behalf of others within their home professions. Some students pursue higher education to change the setting they advocate in—such as a move from the private realm to the legislative arena. Self-trained advocates already in the workforce may pursue formal advocacy education to fill gaps in their knowledge or to gain professional recognition or affirmation.

In fact, no matter what their primary motivation, most students have had their own individual, family, or community experience with healthcare. In this respect, they often differ from other professional students in their motivation to make the personal political. Perhaps most important, they have the boldness to embrace a professional identity that is their own creation—an identity that, as one student put it, can be "morphed into what you want to do with it" and used "to go in so many different directions" on behalf of patients, families, and communities.

> I worked for a year in an administrative capacity in a labor and delivery unit and found out that there was a lot horribly wrong with the healthcare system. I saw a lot of inequities. That's when I got interested in health advocacy. When I read about [the health advocacy field], I thought, "This is exactly what I want to do—to change the health care system." My education as an advocate didn't give me all the answers I was looking for because there isn't one fix. There's no one answer, but it gave me the tools and exposure to situations that are real and to people who have made some changes in the system. Then you have to carve out a path for yourself to see where you want to advocate and how.
>
> *Sarah Lawrence College Health Advocacy Program Graduate*
> *Omega Bugembe, M.A. 2004*

The Curriculum: Multidisciplinary and Disciplinary Components

Core advocacy coursework builds students' expertise in the substance and theory of advocacy and health systems transformation; that is, students have an opportunity to explore the various roles advocates fill both within and outside the healthcare systems, the paid or volunteer employment opportunities they have in a broad range of settings, the geographic, disease-specific, or otherwise delineated populations they serve, and the range or breadth of their service. As illustrated in Figure 1, courses in the Sarah Lawrence College program introduce specific examples of how advocacy is practiced. For instance, how do advocates influence individual decisions or community-level initiatives to restore, preserve, or enhance health? What interventions might advocates bring to the research process, beginning with the formulation of research questions and agendas and ranging through the design and implementation of studies and the dissemination and interpretation of results? How do we influence the media from both within and outside its mainstream? What are the points of commonality, difference, and intersection between health advocacy and the disability rights movement? Feminism? Environmental advocacy? Both programs have a hands-on component that exposes students to advocacy in action: field work at Sarah Lawrence and direct patient advocacy clinical work at Wisconsin.

There is no standard textbook or how-to manual one can turn to for quick comprehensive training in the fundamentals of health advocacy. Because its range of expression is so broad, educating advocates is a decidedly interdisciplinary process. The educational process in advocacy is also highly interactive, as interpersonal skills and the development of an effective advocacy style—the deliberate choice of a particular affective manner or method of engagement—are just as crucial for advocates as substantive and procedural knowledge.

Complementing this interdisciplinary "core" base for health advocacy is a strong knowledge base that is either multidisciplinary (as at Sarah Lawrence College) or disciplinary (as at the Center for Patient Partnerships at the University of Wisconsin-Madison). In the former model, courses build on perspectives from many disciplines and several traditions for constructing knowledge. The course content is focused on health and illness, particularly those aspects that raise issues or experiences important for advocates to understand. For example, a course on health economics may teach students about prescription drug pricing and the power of the pharmaceutical industry in influencing health policy on this issue, providing a context for understanding the experience of an individual consumer or patient faced with unaffordable drug costs.

In the disciplinary model, the program provides courses addressing topics of health systems change and patients' rights to complement its central interdisciplinary clinical learning experience. The program draws students enrolled in related graduate programs such as public policy, health systems engineering, pharmacy, public health, social work, nursing, medicine, and law. Wisconsin students complete their advocacy education by supplementing the Center's clinical program and courses with relevant courses offered in their home (and other) disciplines.

Health advocates need a strong knowledge base and specific skills to be effective. The self-contained master's program can teach them about related disciplines, including the value of the way a specific discipline structures knowledge and disciplinary-based tools to access that knowledge. In contrast, a center that engages graduate students from a range of disciplines draws on the depth of each discipline's training and then enriches that core with educational and practical experience in the interdisciplinary nature of advocacy issues and patient needs. In so doing, it highlights the value of a holistic approach to health care for patients and their families.

The Curriculum: Attentiveness to "Voice"

Health/patient advocates are distinguished from other professionals by their attentiveness to "voice," the experiences and perceptions of real people as they struggle with issues related to health and healthcare. In this tradition, the individual is always at the center of attention when educating for advocacy (see Table 18.2). We begin by focusing on the experiences and perspectives, needs and strengths, history, and aspirations individuals themselves articulate. We then examine how "voice" is heard, silenced, ignored, or answered by the care systems and social structures that frame health and illness.

When a patient is the focus of health advocacy, we make sure our approach is "patient centered" by "consciously adopt[ing] the patient's perspective" (Gerteis, Edgman-Levitan, Daley, & Delbanco, 1993, p. 5). In other words, our approach is "respectful of, and responsive to, individual patient preferences, needs, and values" (Institute of Medicine, 2001, p. 6). We teach cultural awareness and competency (Abraham, 1993; Fadiman,

1997) and respect for personal, familial, and community values in decision making (Davis & Gaines, 2006; Fadiman, 1997; Giller, 2005).

In our effort to approach advocacy education by starting with the person, we make sure that the actual person whose life is affected by any given advocacy intervention is solidly in front of us from the outset. To do this, the Center for Patient Partnerships' clinical patient advocacy program uses both value-centered decision-making models (Davis & Gaines, 2006) and "opening moments," interview techniques. These client-centered techniques use open-ended questioning, attentiveness, and other encouraging linguistic strategies that enable the client to both frame the discussion and provide a complete response. This approach is critical as clients usually reveal critical information at the beginning of an interview (Gellhorn, 1998, pp. 344–350). In the Health Advocacy graduate program, attention to the patient's voice is threaded through all courses, with two courses, "Illness Narratives" and a semester-long workshop course on communication as a core advocacy competency, organized explicitly around this focus. Patient voice has also been the subject of faculty retreats and development. In both programs, case studies, field work, clinical courses, classroom exercises, and exposure to speakers ensure that we keep our eye trained on that person throughout.

A THEMATIC APPROACH

Connecting the substance and theory of advocacy with disciplinary knowledge from many sources is a number of themes that arise repeatedly in the course of health advocacy work across roles, positions, and arenas of action. These themes have emerged from years of advocacy and educating for advocacy (see Table 18.2). For example, as illustrated in the later case studies, we treat the power and plurality of culture and identity as a theme iterated throughout advocacy work and the discipline-based bodies of knowledge. One way we highlight this theme is by examining advocacy issues in clinical research today. There is mounting pressure from funding agencies to include minority populations among the subjects, or as the focus, of study (National Institutes of Health, 2001). Health advocates working in research arenas need to be sensitive to the politics of this "inclusivity," the collective experience and history of various minority groups who have been used as unwilling or unwitting subjects by medicine in the past (Jones, 1993), the importance of advocating with (as distinguished from

Table 18.2   Themes Central to Patient and Health Advocacy (Health Advocacy Program, 2005)

- *Case and Class/Systemic*: advocacy on behalf of individuals compared with groups or systems, and how these two overlap and intertwine
- *Agency*: the role of representation in client/advocate relationships; awareness of "on whose behalf" an advocate is intervening
- *Voice*: how the "voice" of patients/individuals and advocates is heard, silenced, ignored, or answered within care systems and social structures that frame health and illness
- *Psychological and Social*: psychological and social dimensions of health and healthcare and the relationship between the two
- *Health Improvement Models*: asset/strength-based approaches to health improvement and promotion and problem/deficit-based models, including treatment and pathology-based intervention
- *Collaboration and Specialization*: collaboration, specialization, and the relationship between the two across the spectrum of care
- *Culture and Identity*: self-identification with groups (ethnicity, socioeconomic status, nationality, sexual orientation) and how this identity is perceived and used by oneself and by others
- *Autonomy and Self-determination*: the tension between acting for others and building capacity in others so they may act for themselves
- *Legal and Human Rights*: the concept of rights and its importance as an underpinning for advocacy
- *Power*: who has it, how it is exercised, and how it is acquired and shifted—in understanding both the status quo and the potential for change
- *Models of Knowledge*: competing paradigms (e.g., scientific knowledge, personal narratives, culturally based understanding), standards for establishing "truth" about causality, and how these models impact health, healthcare, and advocacy
- *Representation and Legitimacy*: the importance of representation (including media coverage) in shaping opinion, experience, and advocacy efforts

advocating for) a community as it defines its own relationship to research, and the ethical conflicts inherent in conducting research among vulnerable third-world populations (Kass, Dawson, & Loyo-Berrios, 2003).

Later in this chapter we explicate these themes through case examples, just as we do in our classrooms. At the same time, these case studies illustrate the range of activities in which health advocacy students may engage.

USING CASES TO EDUCATE ADVOCATES: UNDERSCORING KEY THEMES

The examples given here elucidate how Sarah Lawrence College and the Center for Patient Partnerships use case studies in health advocacy education. These cases underscore the ways in which critical themes in health advocacy connect disciplines, tie individuals (e.g., patients, advocates, health workers, family members, and community members) to the larger population, and provide conceptual threads that help students situate each case within a coherent framework. In turn, this case-based framework structures advocacy across institutional and community settings, issues, and patient/consumer experiences.

All cases illustrate the intertwined nature of individual and systemic advocacy even though some focus on individuals and some on change processes at the community level.

Each case highlights themes important to health advocacy and is situated in a unique advocacy framework. Health advocacy students read the cases with a view toward addressing a number of questions, including the following: What is the relevance of settings, issues, and experiences? How does each case emphasize the role of health advocates in creating micro and macro change? How does the case highlight themes that form the core of interdisciplinary work in health advocacy?

The use of the case study model is particularly effective in the context of teaching about health advocacy in the direct care setting. Health advocates (e.g., patient representatives, hospital social workers, community health law attorneys) are often called in when a situation occurs that has no precedent and apparently conflicts with normal hospital procedures or challenges accepted constructs. It is in these situations that case examples can be most useful, in effect providing precedent where none existed.

CASE STUDY 1

End of Life, Multicultural Sensitivity: Buddhist Tradition and Hospital Protocol

The following is a case that illustrates the needs of a particular patient, his "family" (mindful of the many ways one can define family), other patients on the unit, and hospital staff. The case explores themes of agency (on whose behalf an advocate might be intervening), voice (whose needs are being expressed and what drivers are involved), and models of knowledge (i.e., culturally based understanding and power within an institutional setting). Students are guided to see beyond the presenting issues to understand the larger implications of their advocacy on behalf of an individual or group. The case provides an opportunity to explore a variety of advocacy interventions and to recognize the potential impact of these interventions on the legitimate needs of other stakeholders.

> A Mandarin-speaking older Buddhist monk was near death from end-stage neurologic disease in the Medical Intensive Care Unit. He had no biological family but was surrounded by loyal and devoted disciples, who took turns at his bedside. Some of the members of this congregation spoke English, although with varying degrees of proficiency.
>
> According to one disciple, the monk had expressed a desire to forgo treatment and feeding with the goal of accepting death from his underlying disease. This disciple also informed the clinical unit staff that when the monk expired, according to Buddhist tradition, his body must be left undisturbed for a period of three days. The prognosis, according to the care team, was grave, with clinical deterioration and death likely expected within several days. The care team contacted the patient advocate for assistance.

Class discussion should be designed to tease out several advocacy issues involved in this case and to prioritize how they would be addressed. Of primary importance was to determine how the patient himself saw his situation, what he needed and wanted, and what relevant rights, if any, were involved. A discussion of the concepts of voice and agency can illustrate the potentially conflicting goals of those involved: Did hospital staff contact the patient advocate in order to further their own goals? What might those goals be? On whose behalf is the disciple speaking? Might there be a subtext to his statements different from the expressed words? For whom does the advocate work? What conflicts are inherent in the relationship between the advocate and the institution? Who should speak for the patient if he is not able to speak for himself?

> Ultimately, with the services of an interpreter, the patient was interviewed without his disciples present. He was alert, oriented, and capable of understanding the impact of the decisions he was making. He clearly expressed an understanding of his clinical status and clearly stated that he wished to abstain from further medical intervention and

was prepared for death. He wished to limit his intake of nourishment to only that which was comfortable. He was offered the opportunity to name a specific surrogate decision maker from among his disciples, but he demurred, stating that he could not single out one person to act for him. His explicit wishes regarding refusal of artificially provided food and fluids as well as further medical intervention were clearly documented in his medical record.

This case challenges our concept of "family" and provides an advocacy opportunity: to help staff and other affected patients understand that this man's "family" was not biological but, rather, was comprised of his religious community. Advocates must learn that although the regulatory legitimacy of surrogate decision making may not encompass this nonbiological relationship (absent an advance directive), hospital staff still need to recognize the significance of the relationships involved and ensure they are honored. The case also provides an opportunity to discuss patients' rights: autonomous decision making, the right to refuse treatment and interventions, and surrogate decision making within the context of local laws and federal regulations (see Chapter 13).

The advocate discussed with the patient his spiritual needs regarding the time following his physical death. He corroborated his disciples' statements regarding Buddhist belief about the length of time required to allow the spirit to leave the body. The staff explored how he would be accommodated given that three days was not really an option in a hospital setting. Clearly, he no longer required the life-extending resources of the intensive care unit. Options included returning to the temple—his home—with hospice care to support his disciples in caring for him until his death, or remaining in the hospital hospice unit. This second option would entail a shortened time his body could remain undisturbed. He opted for a 24-hour period of undisturbed time on the hospice unit after his death. He was comfortable with this resolution, and his "family" accepted his decision.

Additional advocacy issues became evident as the case unfurled, including the needs of other patients in the ICU, those waiting for scarce intensive care beds, and the discomfort of hospital staff and patients with a deceased patient remaining on the unit for an extended period.

When he was transferred to the hospice unit, nearby patients and their family members were approached one by one and informed that there would be quiet chanting for a 24- to 36-hour period as the monk approached death and his spirit began its journey. Patients and family members who were uncomfortable were accommodated with room changes. Unit staffing was assigned according to each individual's level of comfort with the situation. The air temperature in the room was adjusted after death to slow decomposition of the corpse. The death and the following religious process unfolded without incident. All in all, the experience was spiritually uplifting to those involved. It was also a valuable opportunity for the staff to learn about the spiritual and cultural needs of one particular individual and his community and how hospital procedures could be modified to meet those needs without undue disruption.

We have established that there are, at minimum, four stakeholders in this scenario: the patient, his "family," the hospital staff, and other patients. Advocacy must foster awareness of all these groups' needs and motivations and craft interventions that do not, if possible, create additional or disproportionate burdens for any of the stakeholders. One could argue that an additional stakeholder is the health advocate herself—a person with internal biases, needs, and an agenda. An integral element of the curriculum is to help advocacy students recognize the importance of self-awareness and self-reflection. Other skills/knowledge required for managing this case include expertise in end-of-life decision-making regulations, familiarity with requirements and resources for meeting the needs of people with limited English proficiency, effective mediation among stakeholders, and understanding relevant hospital protocols. It is most important that each of the stakeholders perceives that the advocate is fair and effective. This requires that the advocate understand the values and limitations of various advocacy styles.

CASE STUDY 2

Building Capacity, Enabling, and Disempowering: The Case of a "Simple Phone Call"

Use of the case study model is also effective as a complement to supervised "service learning." Student patient advocates will experience clients with varying educational levels, medical knowledge, capacities (mental, physical, emotional), and support systems. Students also approach advocacy through the infrastructure of their own experiential knowledge and belief systems. The use of case studies during intensive orientation sessions allows students and educators alike to identify challenges that may emerge during a formal advocacy relationship.

The following case illustrates several themes: autonomy and self-determination, that is, the tension between acting for others, and building capacity so they may act for themselves; voice, that is, whose needs are being expressed; and representation and legitimacy, that is, the importance of representation in shaping opinion, experience, and advocacy efforts. In an effort to help students see beyond their initial gut instincts and understand the larger implications of their advocacy on behalf of an individual, the case provides an opportunity to explore one's fears about advocacy work and identify potential biases that could influence advocacy.

> "Bob," a very bright and well-educated law student in his early 30s—returning to school after a brief teaching career—became a student patient advocate at the Center for Patient Partnerships. Bob was assigned to work with a man in his early 60s, "Kenneth," who had been diagnosed a couple of months earlier with multiple myeloma. In their initial phone contact, Bob learned that Kenneth's medical care was progressing and that he had no insurance coverage issues. On his own, Kenneth had recently completed an application for Social Security Disability Insurance (SSDI) payments but felt uncertain about what to do next—whether he should send it in then or wait until he was unemployed longer.

Class discussion should parse the several advocacy issues involved in this case and assist students in identifying the needs and motivations of the client. Listening to the client's voice and empathizing with his perspective are key. Why was Kenneth applying for SSDI? How did he feel about being unable to work? What were the effects of his treatment on his energy level or ability to concentrate? Who represents his support system?

> Kenneth had a toll free number that he could call, but he felt confused and overwhelmed by the thought of this phone call and asked Bob, his patient advocate, to make the phone call. Bob told his supervisor that he found it "a bit ridiculous" that Kenneth had asked him to "make a simple phone call." Bob felt Kenneth was being too dependent.

This case challenges advocates to be honest about their true feelings for clients. How do you advocate for someone you do not respect or connect with? Having identified biases, how do you overcome them? How do you overcome your own feelings of helplessness when confronted by another's feelings of being overwhelmed? How can you employ empathy and listening skills to move beyond your own perception of a situation. Do you agree with Bob's characterization of the phone call as "simple"? "Simple" to whom? What strategies could Bob employ to empathize with Kenneth? A face-to-face meeting was encouraged.

> Soon after, Bob met Kenneth face to face for the first time. Kenneth brought his disability application for Bob to look over, and they strategized about what to do next. Kenneth explained to Bob what information he felt was needed from the Social Security Administration. He also explained that he thought it was important to have a representative assist him with the application and call on his behalf; he believed this added legitimacy to his claim of disability. Bob used this opportunity to ask Kenneth about his illness experience and find out how Kenneth felt about not working, and he therefore learned how hard it was for Kenneth to talk to his kids about being sick. After their meeting, Bob made the phone call, got the information about how to proceed, and helped Kenneth complete and file the necessary paperwork.

Advocates regularly encounter the tension between autonomy and self-determination: how much to do *for* clients and how much to teach them to do for themselves. This distinction is at the heart of the difference between advocacy that builds capacity and advocacy that disempowers. Over time, a clients' problems may evolve; they might change and so does their ability to advocate for themselves. With coaching and a little time, some clients naturally become effective self-advocates. Others get sicker, more tired, and more daunted by the challenges of illness. Skilled advocates are vigilant about not crossing the line where advocacy threatens empowerment. What are the signs of disempowerment? How can an advocate know when she is doing too much? Kenneth felt that having an advocate would offer legitimacy. Under what circumstances is it valuable to have representation? Are there circumstances where representation of one individual can disempower others or even a class of people?

CASE STUDY 3

Hearing the Voice of Residents and Assessing Community Strengths in Yonkers, New York

This third case study is used to explore community advocacy with students in the classroom setting. It is an important example of how case studies highlight the dilemmas and processes of groups as well as individuals. A community-level case study challenges students to begin with a series of questions about how "community" itself should be defined, thus raising issues of case and class differentiation. This case also highlights the themes of collaboration and specialization, culture and identity, and asset-based versus problem/deficit-based approaches to advocacy work.

> The Early Childhood Initiative (ECI), a community collaborative with more than 60 public and private organizational partners as well as a number of involved residents, conducted a two-year, city-wide needs assessment that culminated with publication of the *Yonkers Early Childhood Data Book: Building on Our Strengths, Meeting Our Challenges* (Yonkers Early Childhood Initiative, 2000). The ECI data book project relied on a deliberately strengths-based approach to community needs assessment in order to re-conceptualize the idea of "need" in Yonkers. The *process* of researching and producing the data book made the collaborative more inclusive, built trust and respect among members from a wide array of cultural and ethnic backgrounds, and facilitated meaningful forms of participation by residents. The *product*—an award-winning book distributed to agencies, individuals, and political leaders in Yonkers, Westchester, New York State, and beyond—gave members of the collaborative an opportunity to showcase the hard work already accomplished by community institutions in the city while at the same time effectively positioning Yonkers to compete successfully for grants and other resources.

In class discussion, specific aspects of the data book and particular quotes from it are used to highlight course themes as well as why it has proved such an effective advocacy tool. For example, students are asked to identify what they think may be evidence of an asset-based or deficit-based approach in the book. How are data, photographs, illustrations, and recommendations organized to represent the present state in Yonkers?

As noted in the data book's introduction, the ECI made a conscious decision to look "for data that shows what is working well in Yonkers, along with data that will increase our understanding of unmet needs" (p. 3). To highlight the strengths and challenges approach, each of the data book's five chapters concludes with a list of strengths ("We can be proud that . . ."), followed by a list of challenges ("We must continue trying to . . ."). These summaries of things Yonkers can be proud of—more than 40 of them all told—range from improvements in measurable outcomes (e.g., "We can be proud that hospitalizations for asthma management are vastly decreased because of the school/hospital partnership" [p. 116]), to public sector initiatives, to generalizations about what the people in the city are trying to accomplish. In addition, 18 "Spotlight On" features in the book highlight block initiatives and programs that work in Yonkers. Data illustrating positive impact are included for each, as are lively photographs illustrating the initiative or program, narrative descriptions, and testimony from residents, staff, and/or community leaders about what's working well and why.

This case also raises important issues of collaboration and of voice. Are residents speaking for themselves, or are experts speaking about them? Whose voice dominates the narrative of the book? Examples highlighted in class discussion might include some of the many quotes featured in the book in bolded, pullout format titled "A Parent Speaks" or "Yonkers Parents Speak." For example, many quotes offer candid advice to service providers (e.g., "All new parents need the reassurance that they're doing the right thing" [p. 125]). Others provide concrete suggestions for making the city more hospitable for families with children, observations about what parents know works for kids, or testimony about what is difficult about parenting in Yonkers.

The data book development process helped the ECI build mechanisms for ongoing and meaningful participation of "community representatives." In contrast to much of the more purely conceptual groundwork community that collaboratives must undertake in their early days, this process involved concrete tasks meaningful to community representatives (e.g., gathering data, advising on layout and presentation, and obtaining and selecting photographs to include in the book). It also resulted in a tangible product—the data book itself. After it was complete, the data book immediately became a recruiting tool for soliciting the participation of new community representatives in ECI.

The concrete nature of the data book is useful in the classroom just as it is in the community. Students are encouraged to think about the balance between "process" and "product" that must be maintained when working on advocacy initiatives with groups of people. They also explore what it really takes to "make room at the table" for individuals who are participating in the collaborative as residents rather than as professionals, including discussion of the painful struggles ECI encountered in this process, especially with respect to issues of culture and identity. Unpacking the power dynamics inherent in situations where participants have different kinds of influence and status leads to rich discussion. Likewise, discussing how community members can participate in the construction of knowledge highlights how group advocacy can contribute to a new view of the "facts" about a city and its residents.

THE FUTURE OF HEALTH ADVOCACY EDUCATION: LESSONS LEARNED AND INFORMED NEXT STEPS

From the health advocate educator perspective, the rewards of the educational process itself complement the social importance of the work. These rewards include the challenge of teaching in a continually evolving field, which necessitates regular revision of curricula and teaching methods to incorporate new ideas. The health advocacy education field presents other ongoing challenges. We grapple with the demands of instructor-intensive, customized, experiential, and reflective learning. We operate in the margins of established disciplines with our interdisciplinary approaches. We stress the value of student advocates' own personal histories and experiences while keeping central the patient's voice. This last issue requires conscientious mentoring in both classroom and practicum/internship settings because students' transition from their own particular experience to advocating for others, who may or may not share that experience, can be difficult.

Advocacy educators in programs that complement structured professional education in medicine or law recognize the need to nourish advocacy-inclined students so that their advocacy orientation is not stifled and to reinforce their instinct that advocacy skills are important to future practice. Educators in dedicated programs grapple with how to prepare future professionals who will be advocating for consumers, patients, and families, but may be paid by institutions or providers who put their own interests first.

As described throughout this chapter, educating for advocacy evokes several tensions: the balancing act between disempowering and building capacity in clients; the cost that must be borne when another player intervenes in existing relationships between health systems stakeholders and those they serve; and the reality that advocacy may extend privilege and resources to the highly vocal few, thereby perpetuating a privilege-based system rooted in economic class, education, and "voice." Attempting to resolve or avoid these tensions creates an overly simplistic and possibly stagnant field of study. Indeed, because the healthcare system itself is complex and contradictory, teaching students about the unsettling aspects of healthcare—tensions, complexities, contradictions, inequities of race and class, mixtures of public and private coverage and care—is central to the mission of advocacy education. In this way, students see advocacy as essential in navigating our existing healthcare system, but also as playing a critical role as an agent for positive future change in that very system. Patient and health advocates are especially needed in the United States where no legal right to nonemergency healthcare exists (Annas, 2004). This situation creates a permanent state of unmet needs for many who seek healthcare (Abraham, 1993; May & Cunningham, 2004). In addition, even where the means for legal redress exists, as in malpractice litigation and insurance contract disputes, only a tiny fraction of patients who have cause for action take that step (Localio et al., 1991) (see Chapter 20).

Health advocacy has not yet been formalized as a profession. Increasingly however, job descriptions exist for health advocates by many names (e.g., hospital social worker, patient representative, ombudsman) and across many settings (e.g., hospitals, government social service providers, non-profit and for-profit free-standing advocacy organizations, and the halls of Congress). In addition, many doctors, pharmacists, nurses, attorneys, health educators, and other professionals see health advocacy as an integral part of their jobs. Graduates of advocacy programs incorporate advocacy skills as they occupy these formal advocacy jobs. They do so alongside an army of extraordinary advocates with no formal advocacy education.

Those of us who educate for health advocacy value formal education. At the same time, we believe that a plurality of advocates strengthens the field. Included in this plurality are those who identify advocacy as their core activity and those who see advocacy as an essential secondary component of other work. Future professionalization should preserve this fruitful tension while prioritizing the protection of health consumers.

Professionalism still evokes heated debate among patient and health advocates. Although health advocacy is not yet a formal profession, education is core to skilled professionals. Still, there remains a tension between the importance of education and standards on the one hand and the organic development of a consumer advocacy movement on the other. Health advocacy was born from the passionate commitment of men and women who saw injustice in the healthcare system and took action to redress it. Today a powerful group of "kitchen table advocates" demonstrate how passion and expertise—often on behalf of an affected family member—are critical to advocacy. Successful professionalization must acknowledge the plurality of health advocates: those at their kitchen tables, independent health advocates, and healthcare professionals who incorporate skilled advocacy into their daily work.

Although efforts to professionalize health advocates may provide a means to enhance and certify proficiency and expertise, many also express fear that this process could lead to marginalization of some health advocates. We remain committed to preserving the rich, passionate diversity of advocacy in the United States. At a conference in early 2006, we embarked on a future where the diversity of roads to becoming an advocate and the value of structured education in helping map those roads and disseminate this information to others can be honored together.

ENDNOTES

1. Health advocacy and patient advocacy are related concepts whose precise relationship is still under debate. Generally speaking, however, health advocacy is a broader concept that includes patient advocacy as well as an interest in health determinants outside of healthcare settings.
2. Health Advocacy Program materials.
3. Founded as the American Society for the Control of Cancer.
4. Founded as the National Foundation for Infantile Paralysis.
5. Founded as the National Society of Patient Representatives.

REFERENCES

Abraham, L. K. (1993). *Mama might be better off dead: The failure of health care in urban America.* Chicago: University of Chicago Press.

Annas, G. J. (2004). *The rights of patients: The authoritative ACLU guide to patient rights.* Carbondale, IL: Southern Illinois University Press.

Balshem, M. (1993). *Cancer in the community: Class and medical authority.* Washington, DC: Smithsonian Institution Press.

Davis, S., & Gaines, M. E. (2006). *Advocating for patients: A guide for students and volunteers working at the center for patient partnerships.* Unpublished manuscript.

Fadiman, A. (1997). *The spirit catches you and you fall down: A Hmong child, her American doctors, and the collision of two cultures.* New York: Farrar, Straus, and Giroux.

Friedson, E. (1970). *The profession of medicine.* New York: Dodd, Mead & Co.

Gawande, A. (2002). *Complications: A surgeon's notes on an imperfect science.* New York: Metropolitan Books.

Gellhorn, G. (1998). Law and language: An empirically based model for the opening moments of client interviews. *Clinical Law Review, 4,* 321–358.

Gerteis, M., Edgman-Levitan, S., Daley, J., & Delbanco, T. L. (1993). Introduction: Medicine and health from the patient's perspective. In M. Gerteis, S. Edgman-Levitan, J. Daley, & T. L. Delbanco (Eds.), *Through the patient's eyes: Understanding and promoting patient-centered care* (pp. 1–15). San Francisco: Jossey-Bass.

Giller, C. A. (2005). *Port in the storm: How to make a medical decision and live to tell about it.* Washington, DC: Regnery.

Institute of Medicine, Committee on Quality of Health Care in America. (2001). *Crossing the quality chasm: A new health system for the 21st century.* Washington, DC: National Academy Press.

Jones, J. H. (1993). *Bad blood: The Tuskegee syphilis experiment.* New York: Free Press.

Kass, N., Dawson, L., & Loyo-Berrios, N. I. (2003). Ethical oversight of research in developing countries. *IRB, 25,* 1–10.

Localio, A. R., Lawthers, A. G., Brennan, T. A., Laird, N. M., Hebert, L. E., Peterson, L. M., et al. (1991). Relation between malpractice claims and adverse events due to negligence: Results of the Harvard Medical Practice Study III. *New England Journal of Medicine, 325,* 245–251.

May, J. H., & Cunningham, P. J. (2004). Tough trade-offs: Medical bills, family finances and access to care. *Issue Brief (Center for Studying Health System Change), 85,* 1–4.

National Institutes of Health, Office of Extramural Research. (2001, October). *NIH policy and guidelines on the inclusion of women and minorities as subjects in clinical research—amended.* Unpublished manuscript. Retrieved May 25, 2006, from http://grants2.nih.gov/grants/funding/women_min/guidelines_amended_10_2001.htm.

Ravitch, R. (1981). Where have we been? (speech on October 21, 1981). *10th Annual Meeting and Conference of the National Society of Patient Representatives.* Detroit, MI.

Ravitch, R. (1986). Patient advocacy. In J. Marks (Ed.), *Advocacy in health care: The power of a silent constituency* (pp. 51–60). Clifton, NJ: Humana Press.

Rogers, P. G. (1986). Milestones in public interest advocacy. In J. Marks (Ed.), *Advocacy in health care: The power of a silent constituency* (pp. 1–7). Clifton, NJ: Humana Press.

Rothman, D. (1997). *Beginnings count.* New York: Oxford University Press.

Starr, P. (1982). *The social transformation of American medicine.* New York: Basic Books.

Yonkers Early Childhood Initiative, Julia Dyckman Andrus Memorial, & Surdna Foundation Inc. (2000). *Yonkers early childhood data book 2000: Building on our strengths, meeting our challenges.* Yonkers, NY: Early Childhood Initiative; Health Yonkers Initiative.

CHAPTER 19

Clinical Advocacy– Clinicians Advocating for Patients and Families Facing Complex, Life-threatening Illnesses

Mark Renneker, Gwendolyn Stritter, and Paul Jentes

Physicians have an obligation to promote their patients' welfare in this increasingly complex healthcare system. This entails forthrightly helping patients to understand clinical recommendations and to make informed choices among all appropriate care options. It includes management of the conflicts of interest and multiple commitments that arise in any practice environment, especially in an era of cost concerns.

American College of Physicians, *Ethics Manual*, 5th Edition, 2005

OBJECTIVES

- To discuss the key principles of clinical advocacy
- To analyze ways in which clinical advocacy is conceptualized and practiced among physicians
- To describe situations in which clinical advocacy can improve a patient's medical care
- To examine barriers to clinical advocacy and weaknesses associated with this type of practice
- To seek ways to provide gold standard optimal healthcare for all patients

Clinical advocacy is a practice in which providers devote themselves to helping patients and their families navigate complex medical problems. Acting much like consultants, these advocates use their "insider" perspective and extensive medical knowledge to provide intensive, one-on-one services; for example, they may research treatment options, help patients resolve problems with their care providers, or negotiate with insurers to make sure patients receive the coverage to which they are entitled. Clinical advocacy is a recent development, an area with few practitioners and almost no supporting literature. Yet, even as this textbook goes to press, the number of non-profit and for-profit practices offering such care has increased markedly, suggesting that patients and providers both are dissatisfied with results achieved by "standard care" and are willing to go outside established systems to give and receive optimal care. Because of the pioneering nature of their work, this chapter's authors offer a personal account and analysis of starting and running their clinical advocacy practices.

The basis of this chapter is optimism, a belief that no matter how desperate or hopeless a patient's situation may appear there is always more that can be done. This may require spending the time to identify the nature and extent of the problems, looking exhaustively for new treatment strategies, and, most importantly, seeking ways to overcome obstacles preventing patients from having access to those ideas and treatments. Potentially, many types of clinicians could engage in this process, including physicians, nurses, psychologists, health educators, social workers, and health plan managers. Nonclinicians, such as Internet researchers, self-educated family members, and other lay people, may also be effective in these roles. This chapter, however, focuses on the role of physicians in performing clinical advocacy work with patients who are suffering from complex, life-threatening illnesses and are not currently being well served by the healthcare system. Dissatisfied patients are common in today's medical practices. One survey showed that about 35% of all American adults do not trust doctors to do what is best for patients some or most of the time (Henry J. Kaiser Family Foundation, 1999). Another poll showed that 5% of all patients do not trust their doctors at all (WSJ Online/Harris Interactive, 2004). Clinical advocacy addresses this problem by beginning where "standard care" leaves off. It seeks the ideal of the "gold standard"—truly optimal, comprehensive, no stone left unturned, pull-out-all-the-stops healthcare. Through six case studies from the practice of two physicians currently working as clinical advocates, this chapter presents strategies and techniques used in clinical advocacy; a practice analysis then explores characteristics of the patient population currently using clinical advocacy services. The chapter attempts to place clinical advocacy in a larger context, reviewing the sparse medical literature and professional statutes available. It concludes with a distillation of basic philosophical and foundational principles (i.e., lessons learned) important for those who might be interested in pursuing clinical advocacy as a profession.

PROFILE 1: THE MEDICAL EQUALIZER, BY MARK RENNEKER, MD, MPH

It could have been due to the "Healthcare Is a Right, Not a Privilege" mantra of my inner-city family medicine training program (at San Francisco General Hospital, the University of California—San Francisco's Family Medicine Residency) or possibly the undue influence of television shows like "The Equalizer" (a 1980s noir drama featuring undercover agents battling injustice on behalf of vulnerable people). Whatever the impetus, I ran a classified ad in the *San Francisco Chronicle* for one week at the start of October 1988. "Trapped in a Medical Nightmare and Need Help?" it read, "Call THE MEDICAL EQUALIZER, a physician specializing in advocating for you, resolving unsolvable cases, and in-a-jam 2nd opinions."

I placed this ad as a quasi-experimental measure of what I had begun to observe all around me: patients, rich and poor, increasingly dissatisfied and struggling with the healthcare system. For whatever reason, I had found I was good at getting such patients "unstuck" and wondered whether I might forge a practice doing just that. The ad targeted patients whose medical problems were so complex and their experiences with the medical system so disastrous that they had quite literally given up and were now so desperate they would actually answer such an ad.

About 20 calls came in over the first week; a few of them were crank calls, but the rest were from people with truthful and compelling stories. In my view, much could still be pursued on their behalf. I tried out various strategies: seeing some patients in person, talking with others on the phone, reviewing patients' records, talking with their doctors, finding and analyzing relevant published literature, and calling experts around the country. Some I helped considerably, others less so, but each seemed less burdened by frustration and quite grateful for my efforts.

My position with those initial patients was and remains that I would not provide treatment, only advocacy and case-specific research, education, and guidance. I quickly learned that an entirely different clinical strength came from tying my hands as a treating physician—it was now much easier to focus on the entire patient and not just his or her acute disease process. I discovered other unexpected outcomes as well:

- Most of the work was best accomplished over the phone.
- These cases required inordinate amounts of time (10 to 20 hours in a week as compared with the fraction of an hour I had spent in the past as a general practitioner).
- The need for such services was pervasive, as suggested by the calls from patients elsewhere in the country.
- People were entirely willing to pay out-of-pocket on a time-spent basis—as with a lawyer—for my services.

Because most insurance companies would not pay for such consultations, I worked out a sliding-fee scale to keep my services accessible.

In the early 1990s, I rented a house to serve as my office, hired an office manager, and subcontracted with an expert in searching for medical information. To avoid becoming like so many too-busy doctors, with not enough time for each patient, I established a "lifeboat" rule: no more than one new case per week. With no further advertising, my practice as a clinical advocate grew quickly, primarily via word of mouth through friends, family, colleagues, and, in particular, the patients I worked with. I took an all-comers approach, even if I had never heard of a patient's disease. My promise to patients was not my expertise concerning every condition; it was my skill in finding, evaluating, and accessing experts, research, and ideas about any disease, together with my commitment to follow through on every lead. Because I was a family physician, I felt comfortable with virtually every kind of patient—pediatric, adolescent, adult, obstetric, geriatric, hospice—and trusted myself handling problems from any specialty. In addition, my generalist's training had been inherently advocacy based and taught me never to leave patients to fend for themselves with specialists.

Now, 15 years later, I have worked with hundreds of patients and families, spanning an immense variety of medical problems and advocacy issues. In that time, about 50 non-physicians (mostly computer maven types) and 30 physicians have sought me out with a serious interest in becoming either a researcher or a clinical advocate. They hoped to have me train them or at least wanted to observe my practice, but mainly due to the exigencies of my time and not wanting to shift to a training focus, I chose to meet with very few—about 15 or so, and only half of those more than once. Of these, three physicians actually became clinical advocates, all of them after completing a minimum of three months of training with me plus a period of ongoing teaching–supervision of their cases. Only one of those three, Gwen Stritter, MD, established a full-time clinical advocacy practice, a trajectory that she had pursued even before learning of my work.

PROFILE 2: A DIFFERENT PATH, BY GWENDOLYN STRITTER, MD

After finishing my anesthesia residency at Stanford University Hospital in 1989, I followed several top residents in joining a new anesthesia group at Kaiser San Jose, where I was soon appointed director of their Pain Management Unit. There, I honed my patient-centered style of practice, becoming known for helping patients maneuver through the Kaiser system. I was favorably impressed with The Permanente Medical Group. The doctors themselves, rather than the health plan, decided what services would be covered, and as a non-profit organization, Kaiser Health Plan did not expend valuable resources paying shareholder profits and excessive executive payrolls.

In the early 1990s, however, a paradigm shift occurred in the healthcare industry. In their fight for market share, for-profit HMOs steeply cut the cost of their premiums with little regard for the effects on patient care. To stay in business, Kaiser Health Plan had to cut its premiums, too. Initially, I compensated for the loss of resources imposed by the cuts by spending extra, unpaid time with patients, but as the healthcare economic crisis deepened and the patient load increased, my practice style proved unsustainable.

Around this time, my father was diagnosed with metastatic cancer. Having no training in cancer diagnosis and treatment, I trusted the local oncologists to do their best to advise and treat him. Soon enough, it became clear that my father needed a medically savvy advocate. His oncologist did not research my father's unusual cancer, nor did he explain his treatment choices in sufficient detail. There were significant delays in responding to abnormal lab reports. Finally, I realized that although the oncologist meant well, his large caseload and busy office hours prevented him from giving my father first-rate medical care. I had to become my father's clinical advocate: to educate him about his cancer, to guide him through the healthcare maze, and to "watch his back" as it were. Because he lived across the country, in North Carolina, this became my first experience with telephone-based advocacy. By the time he died in 1994, my father's experiences had deepened my own commitment to practicing patient-centered medicine.

By the late 1990s, I decided to start a new kind of medical practice, one based on advocacy and case-intensive research. My goal was to provide the highest level of medical information to all of my patients. In 2000, I resigned my position at the Permanente Medical Group to design and implement this vision. On learning in early 2001 that Mark Renneker was engaged in the type of practice I envisioned developing myself, I spent the next 11 months under his tutelage, gaining from what he had learned in his 10 years of high-level clinical advocacy. I spent several days per month at his office listening to his consultations, doing research for the cases (literature searches, phone calls, etc.), and gradually taking on cases under his supervision.

I encountered several hurdles along the way. Because I had been trained as a specialist, I felt comfortable with anesthesia and pain management cases, less so with primary care cases and oncology, a field in itself. With Mark's guidance, I gained mastery in these areas, intensively reading textbooks and journals as well as attending numerous conferences. I also realized that I needed to discard many interview techniques learned in my previous, fast-paced practice (e.g., lack of open-ended questions, leaving no time for addressing the patient's agenda) and returned to the more patient-centered interview style I had originally learned in medical school. The third hurdle in establishing an independent practice proved the hardest. My first two years in practice were devoted to my cases and refining the art of clinical advocacy. Most patients were people I knew or referrals from Mark. I also had to spend time on business aspects of the practice, including increasing my visibility in the community as a physician advocate. Now, five years later, I have a very satisfying, fully functioning clinical advocacy practice.

CASE EXAMPLES

The following case examples illustrate the range and types of interventions required of clinical advocates, the kinds of problems patients confront when seeking high-quality treatment and guidance, and the goals and outcomes of clinical advocacy.

Case 1: Physician Obstructionism

An older woman admitted to a hospital with a hip fracture was diagnosed with Alzheimer's disease; the doctor told the woman's middle-aged son that she needed to go into a nursing home. Beyond this initial assessment, the doctor was unwilling to talk to the son. Having seen his mother behaving normally the week before, the son found it hard to believe the doctor's diagnosis and felt that if he could just get his mother back into her own home she would probably be fine. The son wanted an outside physician to double check the diagnosis and to look for ways to help her return home as soon as possible.

The clinical advocate's response (Mark Renneker): After speaking with the son, I contacted the doctor to see whether I could get a better understanding of the conflict. The doctor told me that after he transferred the mother to the nursing home he would no longer be caring for her. Furthermore, he thought the son was a "jerk." I found out that the doctor had not done a dementia workup or brain scan, nor had he referred her to a neurologist, even though these are reasonable steps when diagnosing Alzheimer's disease. "Why bother?" he said. "She's got it. Believe me." I didn't believe him and helped the son realize that this physician was not serving his mother well. I arranged for other physicians to evaluate her. Her "Alzheimer's" disappeared as soon as she was treated for the urinary tract infection her original doctor had missed. She was home within a week, and I found a good geriatrician to care for her in the future.

Case 2: Wrong Cancer Diagnosis

A 27-year-old intern was diagnosed with a rare thymus cancer and was treated by her residency director, also an oncologist. She underwent surgery to remove part of her lung and then received radiation and chemotherapy. She had read that these tumors often recur and consulted me to see whether she should receive additional treatment.

The clinical advocate's response (Mark Renneker): With all cancer diagnoses, particularly rare ones, I advocate for confirmation of the pathological diagnosis. Was the evaluation thorough? The physician stressed the accuracy of the diagnosis; she had even sent the biopsy specimen to an internationally known pathology department for a second opinion. However, I located their report, which she had not obtained, and found that it raised the possibility of a different kind of cancer, a lymphoma. I recommended send-ing all the surgical specimens to a third, neutral pathology department for a comprehensive analysis. It turned out to have been a lymphoma; the surgery and radiation therapy had been unnecessary, the chemotherapy of the wrong type. Her doctor never apologized to her and opposed (unsuccessfully) her wish to receive a newer combination of chemotherapy as recommended by M.D. Anderson Cancer Center in Houston, Texas.

Case 3: Too Little Time

A patient with metastatic cancer had not responded to several different chemotherapy regimens. After asking her oncologist about experimental treatment protocols available at other cancer centers, he bluntly told her he was too busy to investigate for her. If she were able to find one herself, he would be happy to refer her. She asked me to investigate on her behalf.

The clinical advocate's response (Mark Renneker): The National Can-cer Institute keeps an up-to-date, nearly complete listing of experimental pro-tocols. Although it is readily available to physicians and patients, it is difficult to navigate, with some drugs identified by nothing more than a number and with most treatments evaluated by very little published material. Each clini-cal trial, moreover, includes a maze of inclusion and exclusion criteria. In these situations, the advocate must find and examine all available literature related to a potential treatment in order to make an informed treatment deci-sion. The patient and I worked through all the possibilities, and I called the investigators for more information. Of the best-looking options, the patient chose one, and her doctor provided the appropriate referral to the hospital where the clinical trial was being performed.

Case 4: Managed Care

A 57-year-old psychotherapist with metastatic lung cancer researched various ways that her cancer care could be improved. On finding some options, she was devastated to learn from her HMO's oncologists that her insurance would cover only standard care. She felt that she would soon die if she followed that course and sought my advice and support.

The clinical advocate's response (Mark Renneker): We discussed all treatment options. She found the courage to leave her HMO and go to an integrative cancer care program elsewhere in the country, although she had to mortgage her house to do so. There she received the same types of chemotherapy that she would have received from her HMO, but given by a circadian-rhythm based technique known as chronomodulation (combined with intravenous nutrients). She was also treated with comprehensive complementary therapies, such as psychological, physical, and nutritional care. She soon became cancer free and later won in arbitration against her HMO, which had to reimburse her for her medical care as well as for emotional damages. Although she later died of recurrent disease, she had more than tripled her expected length of survival.

Case 5: Implementing the Latest Research

A 55-year-old author was diagnosed with squamous cell cancer of the back of the tongue with metastases to the neck and lung. His academic oncologist recommended a standard chemotherapy regimen, indicating a 30% to 40% chance of partial or complete remission. The patient wanted to know whether any newer, better treatments were available.

The clinical advocate's response (Gwendolyn Stritter): This man contacted me just before the annual meeting of the American Society for Clinical Oncology. At that meeting, I sought information on new treatments. One such treatment, which combined standard chemotherapy with a recently approved targeted therapy, showed a greater than 80% response rate, with little difference in toxicity. The oncologist, however, refused to consider this new treatment. Citing the protocol's newness, he convinced the patient to proceed with standard chemotherapy. Within six weeks, the patient was near death. The cancer had progressed dramatically. The oncologist said that he had nothing more to offer, predicting that the patient would likely live only a few more weeks. I helped find the patient a different oncologist, one who was comfortable using the newer drug. The patient soon achieved a durable partial remission (10 months at present). He is again writing.

Case 6: Incomplete Patient Evaluation

A 48-year-old man suffered severe abdominal pain for a year and a half. More than 10 physicians, including some at a prestigious medical center, had seen him. His numerous blood tests, CT scans, MRI scans, x-rays, "scopes," and ultrasounds gave no clues to the cause of the problem. Two surgical procedures and 14 different medications did not help. His doctors said there was nothing more they could offer and that he would have to learn to live with the pain. He was anxious and depressed and had not worked for nearly a year.

The clinical advocate's response (Gwendolyn Stritter): This patient had a two-inch stack of medical records. After careful review, it was apparent that the pain most likely originated from the abdominal wall muscles. They had been damaged by a muscle tear after lifting an extremely heavy piece of furniture. Unfortunately, none of his physicians had evaluated him for it. I wrote a two-page case summary and sent it to the treating physician along with a letter requesting a pain clinic referral to evaluate for abdominal muscle pain. Within two weeks, the client had returned to work and his pain and depression had greatly abated.

PRACTICE ANALYSIS

As demonstrated by these case studies, clinical advocacy involves helping patients map out the entire range of treatment options so they can choose the path that best serves them. A practice analysis reveals additional information about what clinical advocacy entails as well as what kinds of patients may seek out such services. Since 1993, all new patients to Renneker's practice have completed questionnaires asking them about their medical experiences to date, perceptions of their physicians, attempts to engage in self-advocacy, and use of self-care and complementary and alternative medicine (CAM). A retrospective chart analysis of all new patients to this practice in 1996 and 2002 revealed several findings. Results of this analysis, together with Renneker's observations about their significance, appear later.

Comments on Table 19.1: Patient Demographics

Of the 68 patients included in the combined analysis, more than half were female (59%). About two thirds resided in California, and nearly half had 16 or more years of education. About one third of the patients (or referring family members) were health professionals or held other advanced degrees. The average patient age was 53. Most (59%) had cancer; others suffered from chronic pain (12%), neurologic problems (9%), and rheumatic or endocrine

Table 19.1   Baseline and Demographic Information

Gender	
Male	28 (41%)
Female	40 (59%)
Total	68

Age	Average (Range)
Male	48 (22–82)
Female	57 (6–89)
Total	52.5 (6–89)

Location of patients	
Bay Area	31%
California (not Bay Area)	32%
Out of state	34%
Out of the country	3%

Types of cases	
Cancer	59%
Chronic pain	12%
Neurologic	9%
Rheum/endocrine	7%
ENT	3%
Gastrointestinal	3%
Congenital	3%
Other/unusual	4%

Number of physicians seen before consulting Dr. R.	
Average (range)	7 (1–30)

Level of education (years)	
0–12	10%
13–16	42%
16+	48%
Average level completed	16
Patients whose referring family member held PhD/MD/JD or advanced graduate degree	31%

Consecutive new patients seen by Dr. R: 1996 (*N* = 30) and 2002 (*N* = 38); total *N* = 68.

issues (7%). Most patients believed that they had received suboptimal care and knew that more options remained. "In fact," Renneker stated, "they were often emphatic about these issues during the first appointment."

Comments on Tables 19.2–19.4

Tables 19.2, 19.3, and 19.4 include data from the 2002 chart analysis ($N = 38$).

Patients' Relationship with Their Physicians

More than half of these patients reported ongoing involvement by a primary care physician. Most had a positive view of their doctors and reported extremely or reasonably good communication. Women were more likely to report poor communication than men. Although many physicians did not perform literature searches, provide patients with in-depth information about their disease, or consult with non-local physicians or specialists, patients reported that 75% of physicians responded to specific requests for additional information when asked. Most patients reported good relations with their physicians, yet nearly two thirds expressed hopelessness about their condition, suggesting the need, in Renneker's words, for a *hope history*. "What was the patient told, by whom? When did the patient begin to feel the absence of hope?" Renneker makes the point that what he calls "false hopelessness" (i.e., unwarranted hopelessness) needs to be "treated" before going any further; otherwise, patients may not be able to engage fully in thinking about and deciding on the range of treatment possibilities that are likely to emerge as the case proceeds.

Before contacting Renneker, patients had been coping with their health-care issues for approximately 30 months and had seen an average of seven other physicians. Most patients waited four months after submitting applications to Renneker's Clinic for a first appointment.

Mode of Consultation

Almost all (95%) consultations were conducted by phone. One benefit of telephone communication in Renneker's practice is the greater flexibil-

Table 19.2   Patient Interaction with Primary Care Doctor

Patient currently has a primary care doctor

Yes	68%

Percent of above where the primary care doctor is still involved

Yes	62%

Patients' views of their doctor

Positive	63%
Neutral	13%
Negative	24%

Communication with doctor primarily in charge of the case

Extremely good	38%
Reasonably good	35%
Not very good	27%

Communication level by patient gender	*Males*	*Females*
Extremely or reasonably good	1	9*
Not very good	16*	11

Did doctor honor patient request to do more work on their case?

Yes	75%
No	25%

Has doctor done a medical literature search for the patient?

Yes	19%
No	47%
I doubt it	10%
I do not know	24%

Did doctor provide patients with articles or in-depth information about their conditions?

Yes	21%
No	79%

Did the patients' doctors consult with physicians/specialists outside their local medical community?

Yes	21%
No	40%
I doubt it	26%
I do not know	13%

* Value significant at $P < .05$
Consecutive new patients seen by Dr. R: 2002 ($N = 38$).
Source: Data from The Porrath Foundation

Table 19.3   Patient Self-Advocacy

Had the patient done personal research?	
Yes	90%
No	10%

Did patient request that the doctor do more work on the case?	
Yes	53%
No	47%

Is the patient interested in complementary and alternative (CAM) therapies?	
Yes	95%
No	5%

Number of CAM therapies used	
Average (range)	4 (0–13)

* Value significant at $P < .05$
Consecutive new patients seen by Dr. R: 2002 ($N = 38$).

Table 19.4   Patient Interaction with Physician Clinical Advocate

Length of time patient had lived with the medical condition before consulting Dr. Renneker (months)	
Average (range)	30 (0.1–180)

Number of doctors seen before consulting Dr. Renneker	
Average (range)	7 (1–30)

Time from application to first appointment (months)	
Average (range)	4.1 (1–7)

Appointment Location	
By phone only	95%
In office	5%

(continued)

Table 19.4 Patient Interaction with Physician Clinical Advocate
(continued)

People "present" during appointment	
Patient and family	50%
Patient alone	37%
Family alone	13%

Billing rate	
Average (range)	$180 ($0–$400)

Length of ongoing consultation to date (months)	
Average (range)	12 (1–28)

Total hours worked on case by Dr. Renneker	
Average (range)	10.6 (1–52)

Additional specialists consulted by Dr. Renneker for the case	
Average (range)	2.2 (0–8)

Consecutive new patients seen by Dr. R: 2002 (*N* = 38).

ity afforded to all parties, including family members who want to be part of conference calls. Although convention holds that face-to-face contact between patient and physician is necessary to build trust and facilitate communication, recent research on telephone care for those suffering from depression suggests otherwise (Simon, Ludman, Tutty, Operskalski, & Von Korff, 2004). A degree of intimacy can often be established in phone conversations that cannot always be achieved in face-to-face encounters. They surmise that patients' increased openness may be due to the relative anonymity of the phone exchange; a similar phenomenon may also operate with talk radio or Internet blogs. Clinical advocacy rarely requires physical examinations; rather, it usually entails reviewing voluminous records of exams that have already been conducted. Examining the patient only becomes necessary when clear inconsistencies or missing information cannot be resolved with further evaluation by the patient's own physicians.

Family Involvement

In half of the cases, both the patient and family members were present for the consultation. Too often in medicine, family members and close friends sit helplessly on the sidelines, wanting to help, but not knowing what to do or having their efforts rebuffed by physicians; however, as described in Chapters 3, 4, 7, and 9, Renneker and Stritter also report that "extraordinary things can occur when family members take on active roles on behalf of their loved ones," even tasks as simple as tracking down records or scans.

In a small number of cases (13%), patients did not participate in the phone consultations, usually because they were in the hospital or too ill to communicate. Such circumstances frequently involved end-of-life cases, where the pressing issues related to withholding treatment, living wills, pain control, grieving, and hospice care. Even as such circumstances "cried out" for a clinical advocate, they also challenged the practitioner to determine, ethically, whom he was working for. As Renneker observes, "In some instances, patients actually need to be protected from their families." This is especially true in cases where the dying patient wishes to discontinue medical treatment, but the family is reluctant to comply.

Information Seeking

Patients who contacted Renneker had often done some self-advocacy, with half the patients having asked their physician to do more work on their case. Most (90%) had conducted personal research, with men significantly more likely than women to have done so. Recent findings confirm Renneker's observations about the kinds of assistance patients need from their physicians. Namely, patients are drowning in excess information, need help separating wheat from chaff, and want reassurance that their searches have been thorough and that they have understood what they have read (Chapter 4). These cases usually focus on teaching the patient or family member how to search for, interpret, and act on medical reports and literature. These cases usually allow the advocate to identify and alleviate the fears of patients or families who are afraid to do their own research for fear of finding out that they have an incurable condition or a short time to live (something Renneker calls Unwanted Prognosis Syndrome).

CAM Use

Consistent with other studies, many patients were already using CAM or were interested in doing so (Barnes, Powell-Griner, McFann, & Nahin, 2002; Eisenberg et al., 1993, 1998). Up to two thirds of patients who use alternative medicine do not tell their physicians about their CAM use; many fear that their physicians "won't understand." Others report that their physicians have never inquired about their CAM use (D'Arcy, 1991, 1993; Eisenberg et al., 1998). These data suggest that physicians tend to be uninvolved in this aspect of care, yet physician clinical advocates should be prepared to research, discuss, and monitor patients' use of CAM therapies as rigorously as they do mainstream or experimental therapies. Even physicians who do not object to CAM use but who remain uninvolved in this aspect of the treatment may be seen as abdicating their responsibility to protect the patient. Lack of communication about this issue could, at a minimum, represent an undue burden for the patient and, at worst, compromise the patient's treatment.

Affordability

In this analysis, patient incomes ranged from less than $10,000 to several million dollars per year. Rates ranged from pro bono to $400 per hour, depending on the client's income level. The average rate in 2002 was $180 per hour. It is Renneker's experience that those with less money often seem more fully engaged in their cases and more eager to gain self-advocacy skills.

Time

The resource that patients and families most often need is time. In this survey, consultations lasted an average of 12 months, required an average total of 10.6 hours, and involved consultations with two additional specialists. This time investment does not include time spent on behalf of each patient by other physicians.

CLINICAL ADVOCACY MEDICAL LITERATURE REVIEW

To our knowledge, no peer-reviewed studies of clinical advocacy practiced by physicians have been published. We believe this to be an important area of future research, particularly with regard to the potential impact of physician patient advocacy on cost effectiveness and quality of care. Despite the lack of published work in this field, most physician organizations have issued statutes or codes outlining the physician's responsibility to advocate as well as to heal. These codes provide guidance for the clinical advocate. For example, the American Medical Association Code of Ethics states that "[t]he relationship between patient and physician is based on trust and gives rise to physicians' ethical obligations to place patients' welfare above their own self-interest and above obligations to other groups, and to advocate for their patients' welfare. Similarly, the same Code of Ethics also states that, [w]ithin the patient–physician relationship, a physician is ethically required to use sound medical judgment, holding the best interests of the patient as paramount" (American Medical Association, 2004). Many medical subspecialties and state medical boards refer to the American Medical Association codes as guidelines for their physicians. Some even have their own codes (see Textbox 19.1); however, none has a formal mechanism for assessing or reviewing physician compliance with these guidelines (see Textbox 19.1).

The last five years have seen increasing efforts to train health professionals as advocates, primarily for cancer patients. The Center for Mind-Body Medicine, in Washington, DC, offers an annual "CancerGuides" course to train healthcare providers in the use of complementary approaches for cancer patients. The Porrath Foundation for Patient Advocacy, in Beverly Hills, California, offers continuing medical education courses to train primary care providers, psychiatrists, and psychologists as professional cancer patient advocates (Bernay, 2001). Their course objectives outline a comprehensive advocacy approach, regardless of disease type (see Textbox 19.2).

CONCIERGE MEDICINE

Concierge or boutique medicine, a type of medical practice that began to emerge in the 1990s, shares several significant features with clinical advocacy. Both may be seen as a response to physicians' growing discontent with shortened doctors' appointments and curtailed medical services. In contrast

---

Textbox 19.1   Excerpts from Professional Codes of Physician Conduct

1. The neurological surgeon and the patient, and patient's family, when appropriate, shall be involved in dialogue so the joint medical decision-making process will be in keeping with the patient's philosophy and desires. *American Association of Neurological Surgeons, Code of Ethics*
2. The patient–physician relationship and the principles that govern it should be central to the delivery of care. These principles include beneficence, honesty, confidentiality, privacy, and advocacy when patients' interests may be endangered by arbitrary, unjust, or inadequately individualized institutional procedures. *American College of Physicians Ethics Manual, 2005*
3. Patient trust is fundamental to the relationship thus established. It requires that . . . the physician be an advocate for needed medical care, even at the expense of the physician's personal interest. *North Carolina Medical Board; Position Statement: The Physician–Patient Relationship*

RESOURCES

American Association of Neurological Surgeons Code of Ethics
http://ethics.iit.edu/codes/coe/neuro-code.html
Accessed May 22, 2006

American College of Physicians
Snyder, Lois & Leffler, Cathy for the Ethics and Human Rights Committee, American College of Physicians. (2005). *Ethics Manual*, 5th ed. *Annals of Internal Medicine, 142*, 570.
http://www.annals.org/cgi/reprint/142/7/560.pdf
Accessed May 22, 2006

North Carolina Medical Board
Position Statement: The Physician-Patient Relationship
http://www.ncmedboard.org/
Select "For Physicians" and then "Board Position Statements"
Accessed May 22, 2006

---

to clinical advocacy, which is organized on a fee-for-service basis, concierge practices require patients to pay an annual fee, ranging from $900 to $20,000 on top of the regular cost of office visits, procedures, etc. (Hoffman, 2001). The primary emphasis in these practices is on wellness and preventive care, with an annual physical exam and screening included. In return for the fee, physicians agree to limit their practice to a manageable number of patients, usually around 600. They offer longer time slots and same-day appointments, no voice mail, and 24-hour access via telephone or personal pager (Hoffman,

---

Textbox 19.2   Selected Skills for Professional Cancer Patient Advocates from Training Materials Produced by the Porrath Foundation

• Understanding the diagnosis, informing family and friends, and noting how illness might affect family, lifestyle, and work decisions
• Researching and choosing a medical team
• Arranging or attending meetings with cancer specialists
• Helping to determine treatment
• Understanding and managing treatment options and getting strategically prepared for new treatments on the horizon
• Gathering a complementary medicine team to provide mind/body support while patient undergoes traditional treatment
• Helping with rehabilitation and being alert to recurrence
• Providing palliative care (referral to hospice and end-of-life care)
• Referring patients to resources that can help with insurance and finances
• Cutting through hospital red tape

The Porrath Foundation
http://www.porrathfoundation.org/
Accessed on May 22, 2006

2001). Some doctors convert their practices entirely to concierge patients while others continue to treat both members and nonmembers (Hoffman, 2001). Physicians may also accompany patients to appointments with specialists, visit them in hospitals or nursing homes, or even conduct home visits. Most concierge doctors accept third-party payer reimbursement for services not covered through the concierge agreement.

Physicians' availability, time, and preventive counsel are what patients pay for when they subscribe to these plans. MDVIP, for example, provides organization, structure, and technical support for its 103 member physicians located in 15 states (MDVIP, 2006). Patients pay $1,500 to $1,800 per year for an annual physical exam, regular preventive screening and lab work, a personalized wellness plan, a medical record on CD-ROM, and a personal patient website. Most MDVIP doctors practice internal medicine, although some are specialists as well.

Concerns about concierge medicine as the province of the wealthy focus on the idea that, rather than aiming their energy and leadership abilities at fixing an ailing system, such providers opt to practice the kind of medicine they believe in, albeit at a price many patients cannot afford

(Hoffman, 2001). At the same time, many concierge physicians offer reduced rates and pro bono services for those who need them, although no formal study has yet documented the extent of reduced fee care provided in the average concierge practice.

More broadly, a tiered approach to healthcare based on socioeconomic status has long been present in the United States. Those with excellent health insurance have access to significantly more healthcare resources than those without. Many physicians working in private hospitals or clinics are shielded from bearing the full brunt of that reality by institutional practices (i.e., patients are screened and their financial resources assessed even before they see the physician). Nevertheless, by virtue of working within these systems, providers also contribute to inequities in healthcare delivery. The trade-off concierge practitioners live with is the recognition that the care they offer is not available to all; at the same time, they are able to offer the best care for every individual they work with, and if they wish, they are also able to provide such care to those who cannot afford the full cost of those services.

Both types of practices (clinical advocacy and concierge medicine) share important features in terms of their client base and in their efforts to provide optimal medical care to a limited number of patients; however, whereas concierge medicine is intended as a "one stop shop" that provides patients with significant face time with the primary care physician, clinical advocacy does not provide treatment. Instead, it offers advocacy, case-specific research, and education to patients with complex life-threatening illnesses who have exhausted all other resources. Clinical advocacy extends, but does not supplant, the medical team.

LESSONS LEARNED: BECOMING A CLINICAL ADVOCATE

In recent years, there has been an upsurge in interest among physicians and others wanting to engage in clinical advocacy. What follows is guidance for starting such a practice, gleaned from Renneker, and now Stritter's years of practice in this area.

Taking the Patient's Side

The starting point for this work must always begin with emotionally going where the patient is—doing everything possible to understand all patients' feelings, fears, confusion, frustrations, hopes, and desires, as well as their physical symptoms and suffering. The primary allegiance is to the patient, less so to the medical profession. Moreover, what family members want often differs significantly from what a patient wants. Although all aspects of such complex situations must be explored, the patient's decisions must guide the advocate, even if the advocate does not agree with those decisions. A case in point is this: A patient may decline chemotherapy even when it has the best track record of all available cancer treatment options. In this situation, the clinical advocate must work very hard to leave "no stone unturned" in the search for effective non-chemotherapy treatments that the patient will accept.

At the same time, family members are too often relegated to the sidelines and are frustrated by how little physicians involve them. When patients themselves cannot jointly analyze medical information because of their illness, another family member may be delighted to become the designated "research hound" for the family.

Putting the Patient in Charge

Clinical advocacy's overriding goal is to put patient and families in charge of their overall case. Doing so generally requires working in two realms: bringing about a considerable elevation in patients' knowledge of their condition and helping them learn how to direct their physicians more effectively. Strength in one realm begets strength in the other. As patients come to realize that they possess as much valuable information about their own problems as their doctors do, they gain the confidence to participate more equally with their physicians in case planning and decision making. One indication that a case is going well happens when the patient and family increasingly direct the clinical advocate in what they want done (i.e., patient-directed consultation). This shift may be a prelude to patients taking greater control over their own cases and sharing in decision making with their doctors.

Helping patients communicate with their physicians is an important part of the clinical advocate's role. The advocate invests significant amounts of time in preparing patients to talk with their physicians and debriefing them following these encounters, often helping patients to see their own role in troubled communication. "Physician humanizing" can help patients understand that their physicians are also bound by limitations, also entitled to feeling doubt and fear, hurt and insecurity, grief, and loss.

Working with Other Clinicians

In addition to being empathic to patients, a clinical advocate must be empathic toward physicians, recognizing their many constraints, frustrations, and generally good intentions. A patient may sometimes need to seek a new physician (Dr. Laurens White, a now-deceased San Francisco oncologist, used to regularly intone: "It can be highly therapeutic to fire your doctor!"), although this is rarely necessary. Even the suggestion of changing doctors can be traumatic for patients; most are very dependent on and fear offending their physicians. When possible, working within a patient's existing structure of caregivers results in the best emotional outcomes. When possible, and in keeping with the goal of having patients gain more control over their own case, the patient or family, rather than the clinical advocate, should request any needed improvements. When clinical advocates must intervene directly, a nonconfrontational strategy helps build bridges between patient and physician. Physicians who have been in a difficult relationship with a patient or family are often greatly relieved to talk about it with a colleague, want to improve matters, and are usually quite receptive to suggestions for how to do so. Those physicians who are not open to such possibilities are in the minority and probably do deserve to be fired.

A Generalist Approach

Clinical advocates, like most health professionals, often try to avoid getting involved with cases in areas outside their expertise, yet frequently the opposite is needed. One of the clinical advocate's greatest strengths may lie in what he or she does not know. Because they have recently learned about the disease themselves, clinical advocates are uniquely equipped to teach patients, helping to guide them through the conceptual steps they need to master in order to understand their condition.

OBSTACLES AND CHALLENGES

The work of clinical advocacy is not without obstacles and challenges. These include dealing with legal situations, investigating CAMs, and negotiating various forms of communication technology and insurance bureaucracy.

Litigation

Although the term "patient advocate" has traditionally referred to legal advocacy for patients, a clinical advocate should be wary of entanglement in legal proceedings, whether this involves gathering information for a malpractice suit or giving expert testimony. Rare is the malpractice suit that is therapeutically beneficial to a patient. Rather, getting involved with legal proceedings often diverts time as well as physical and emotional energy away from care-seeking options, even as it tends to heighten, not lessen, the patient's anger and frustration. In addition, the advocate often winds up working mainly with attorneys rather than the patient or family, writing or giving dispositions that are then shaped and used by attorneys, often in ways not intended by the clinical advocate. These processes can have the effect of undermining the relationship between the advocate and the patients and families as the advocate often ends up, or appears to end up, more on the lawyer's "side" and distanced from the patient. This does not mean, however, that a clinical advocate should avoid nudging an insurance company or HMO to cover a patient or negotiating with these entities after they have refused coverage and arbitration is underway. Alternatively, as suggested in Chapter 20, clinical advocates may refer those seeking legal remedies to mediators.

CAMs

Most clinicians are either open to or dismissive of integrating mainstream medicine with CAM. Yet a clinical advocate must be a fence straddler on this issue, maintaining a broad openness toward all forms of healing. The nature of the clinical advocate's work—to seek out all possibly useful treatments for a patient—requires an ability to keep an open mind.

Communication Technologies

Less obvious barriers to clinical advocates include the invidious nature of voice-mail trees, the often inferior quality of e-mail versus verbal communication, and the pervasive and anonymous control of insurance companies' medical review boards over any procedure or test that is not "evidence based" or "standard of care." The methods of the clinical advocate depend on his or her ability to interact in nonconfrontational, non-legally threatening ways, and to do this an advocate needs to seek out human or professional connections wherever possible.

PHYSICIAN VERSUS NON-PHYSICIAN ADVOCATES

Although this chapter has addressed physicians as clinical advocates, non-physicians may also be successful in this profession. Traditionally, the major difference between physicians and non-physicians in this field concerns access; physicians can more easily negotiate "locked doors" in the medical system, such as speaking with other physicians, getting phone calls returned, and having records sent to them (HIPPA regulations notwithstanding), but those barriers are beginning to come down; a more level playing field among clinicians and lay people makes the possibility of non-physician advocacy more feasible than in the past.

The most appropriate advocate is someone who knows a patient's medical history and condition and can speak of and for the patient. This role is not necessarily limited to physicians. Depending on the case and the institution, advocates may come from a range of backgrounds, including nurses, nurse practitioners, physician assistants, health educators, health advocates, psychologists, social workers, and others. Initially, non-physician clinical advocates may feel more comfortable working within a system they are familiar with, such as their university or HMO. Later, they may feel confident in extending their range. Ideally, few differences should exist between what a physician and a non-physician clinical advocate can accomplish.

CONCLUSION

The physician clinical advocate represents a recent response to fractured health systems in the United States and addresses concerns patients are currently voicing about the care they receive. The strength of physician clinical advocates is their ability to invest significant amounts of time in responding to the unique needs of each patient. They provide patients with tailored education about specific conditions as well as training in how to negotiate the medical system and communicate effectively with their other doctors. The goal of the clinical advocate is not to work against the patient's other providers but instead to leave no options unexamined—to do the research, consult with experts, and hunt down information so that patients receive gold standard care.

REFERENCES

American Medical Association. (2004). "The patient-physician relationship" code of medical ethics: Current opinions with annotations, 2004–2005. *Section E -10.015.* Chicago, IL.

Barnes, P., Powell-Griner, E., McFann, K., & Nahin, R. (2002). Complementary and alternative medicine use among adults: United States. *CDC Advance Data Report, 343,* 1–19.

Bernay, T. (2001). Becoming a professional cancer patient advocate: A new market practice for primary care physicians. *Western Journal of Medicine, 175,* 342–343.

D'Arcy, P. F. (1991). Adverse reactions and interactions with herbal medicines: Part 1: Adverse reactions. *Adverse Drug Reactions and Toxicological Reviews, 10,* 189–208.

D'Arcy, P. F. (1993). Adverse reactions and interactions with herbal medicines: Part 2: Drug interactions. *Adverse Drug Reactions and Toxicological Reviews, 12,* 147–162.

Eisenberg, D. M., Davis, R. B., Ettner, S. L., Appel, S., Wilkey, S., Van Rompay, M., et al. (1998). Trends in alternative medicine use in the United States, 1990–1997: Results of a follow-up national survey. *Journal of the American Medical Association, 280,* 1569–1575.

Eisenberg, D. M., Kessler, R. C., Foster, C., Norlock, F. E., Calkins, D. R., & Delbanco, T. L. (1993). Unconventional medicine in the United States. Prevalence, costs, and patterns of use. *New England Journal of Medicine, 328,* 248–252.

Henry J. Kaiser Family Foundation. (1999, October). Race, ethnicity and medical care: A survey of public perception and experience. *Topline Report.*

Hoffman, W. (2001). *Fed up, some doctors turn to "boutique medicine" from the October 2001 ACP-ASIM Observer.* Retrieved May 22, 2006, from http://www.acponline.org/journals/news/oct01/new_model.htm.

MDVIP. (2006). *MDVIP frequently asked questions.* Retrieved October 18, 2006, from http://www.mdvip.com/NewCorpWebSite/AboutUs/AboutMDVIP/FrequentlyAsked Questions.aspx.

Simon, G. E., Ludman, E. J., Tutty, S., Operskalski, B., & Von Korff, M. (2004). Telephone psychotherapy and telephone care management for primary care patients starting antidepressant treatment: A randomized controlled trial. *Journal of the American Medical Association, 292,* 935–942.

WSJ Online/Harris Interactive. (2004). Health-care professionals, pharmacies, hospitals gain the public's top trust. *Health Care Poll, January 28, 2004.*

CHAPTER 20

Using the Law to Strengthen the Patient's Voice

Virginia L. Morrison and Nicola B. Truppin

OBJECTIVES

- To examine traditional methods, including legislation and litigation, that lawyers have used to date to advocate for patients
- To appreciate the limits of these traditional methods for achieving patient and healthcare professional satisfaction, strengthening the patient–caregiver partnership, or improving healthcare quality and patient safety
- To introduce theory for how legal tools can be used to achieve individual and system change
- To present alternatives to traditional methods, including collaborative strategies such as mediation and preventive law, useful in advocating for patients

Lawyers and people in related disciplines (this chapter refers to them as "problem-solving professionals") play a vital role in patient advocacy. Within the healthcare, policy, and legal systems, they complement other patient advocates by contributing access to seats of power and supplying expert influence for prevention, access to care, and redress of harm. When advocacy is carried out in partnership with these individuals, the results are amplified and strengthened.

Legal or other problem-solving professionals who use the tools of the legal profession use a range of traditional and alternative legal strategies. Historically, lawyers have achieved and enforced legal rights for patients through litigation, legislation, and regulation, as well as by representing patients in several lesser known arenas. Traditional legal advocacy methods have real benefit, but they can also fail to meet important patient[1] needs, and they can even have negative, unintended consequences. They can create a backlash effect, undermining the patient–provider relationships, communication, and treatment they were meant to preserve. With over a million healthcare injuries in the United States annually (Institute of Medicine [IOM], 2006), it is clear that traditional legal strategies are not enough to protect patients from harm; indeed, some argue that they have little, or even a negative, effect on making patients safer. Moreover, when a patient is harmed, society often expects her to use the court system for redress, but difficult access, limited success, and the system's inability to meet a variety of nonfinancial needs can make it an unsatisfactory venue. It is also not clear that adversarial methods actually motivate individual or system change so that future patients are protected.

Of course, not all patients' legal needs spring from an injury. Patients also need access to benefits and high quality care, respectful delivery of reliable information, and inclusion in individual and policy-level decisions. Legal problem-solving professionals strengthen the patient's voice in these ways, as well.

Because traditional legal methods incompletely address medical–legal needs, advocates have joined healthcare practitioners and patients to seek creative, effective solutions that address a range of patient needs. Preventive and collaborative methods hold great promise for achieving these objectives. These partnerships promote systems thinking to prevent injuries and, ultimately, to prevent legal, social, and healthcare crises. Practices that emphasize problem solving and fostering of relationships lay the foundation for shifting cultural norms toward greater responsibility on the part of all stakeholders for safety and patient-centered care. Indeed, as we argue in this chapter, a more flexible approach, one that employs a variety of methods, is more effective in responding to the complexities of the healthcare system as legal patient advocacy evolves.

TRADITIONAL LEGAL AVENUES

Legal work in litigation, legislation, and regulation created the structure on which patient advocates rely to establish and enforce rights. As U.S. cultural norms shifted away from unquestioning acceptance of medical authority in the 1960s and 1970s (Scott, 2003), legal methods helped to set baseline expectations for doctors' and institutions' obligations to patients. For example, in the 1970s, the law established norms of clinical and relational behavior, formally recognizing that patients are entitled to information, participation in decision making, and quality standards. Later, in the context of technological, economic, and social change, legal mechanisms served as a check on excesses. In California, for example, the law stopped insurers from using reimbursement practices to discharge women too soon after giving birth. Another California law set solvency standards to prevent patients from being stranded when health plans suddenly went out of business.[2] As we discuss later here, different traditional legal methods can serve different purposes in protecting patients.

LITIGATION

Most individual lawsuits (or "litigation" or "tort law") are aimed at helping correct for losses, usually by substituting money for financial and other kinds of losses. Tort law is meant to ensure that the patients are, ultimately, no worse off than if they had not been injured. If a lawsuit establishes a new principle, it also creates rights for others. Thus, tort law is the source for medical malpractice standards and for informed consent requirements.[3] Tort law also led to requirements that forced managed care companies to accept certain providers into their networks, thereby protecting patient choice; tort law also banned "gag rules" that prevented clinicians from discussing certain treatment options with patients (Rodwin, 2003) (see Table 20.1).

Lawsuits also can serve the greater public good through class action suits. Such "impact litigation" focuses on benefits that may accrue to much larger groups. Health Law Advocates, for example, is a Boston non-profit law firm affiliated with the patient advocacy organization Health Care for All. The partnership works to ensure healthcare access for society's most vulnerable members (Health Law Advocates, 2006). For instance, in 2005, the firm proved that low-income children had problems accessing Massachusetts' Medicaid dental services. As part of the settlement, the groups collaborated with the Medicaid dental program to send families regular notices about the importance of oral health, increase the number of participating dentists, and simplify the reimbursement process. The court appointed a practicing dentist to oversee adherence to and effectiveness of the agreement, which is expected to result in appropriate and timely dental services for 500,000 minors.[4]

Table 20.1   Some Healthcare-Related Rights

Healthcare rights are created by federal or state statute, regulation, or court decision.[5] They can vary regionally. Here are some of the most well-established rights for patients:

- Make an informed decision to accept or refuse treatment, even if it will shorten life
- Have treatment that is as skillful and careful as is commonly offered by practitioners in the same field and geographical area ("standard of care")
- Express treatment preferences ahead of time using advance directives and to name a surrogate decision maker if the patient becomes unable to make healthcare choices
- Have detailed information before deciding whether to participate in research and be free from coercion when deciding whether to join or remain in a study
- Review a patient's own medical records and maintain her privacy by giving or withholding permission for access to them
- Receive screening and stabilization for an emergency condition without hospitals delaying to inquire about patients' ability to pay

LEGISLATION

The other arena most commonly associated with legal practice is legislation. Lawyers write bills, lobby to pass them, and play an active role in drawing up the regulations needed to implement laws. In healthcare, some laws aim to ensure a baseline of patient safety, such as California's law mandating a maximum patient-to-nurse ratio for hospital care.[6] Some laws regulate clinical care; New Jersey, for instance, requires practices to screen and educate new mothers about postpartum depression.[7] To ensure equity, Massachusetts mandates minimum, low-cost, portable health insurance for all individuals.[8] Various other state laws require insurance coverage for certain conditions, such as biologically based mental illnesses and medically necessary speech therapy.[9] The Federal Women's Health & Cancer Rights Act of 1998 mandates certain benefits if a woman chooses reconstructive surgery after a mastectomy (U.S. Department of Labor). Federal law requiring many health plans to have patient grievance processes is also designed to advance fairness (see Textbox 20.1).[10]

Textbox 20.1   What Else Do Lawyers Do?

Although lawyers' most recognized work is in court and legislatures, some other traditional legal arenas include

- *Arbitration*: Arbitration is much like a trial before a judge, with an individual or panel hearing evidence and issuing a decision. The rules governing arbitration are more flexible, and the time and costs tend to be less than going to court.
- *Administrative hearings*: Some government agencies have administrative law judges who are subject matter experts and hold hearings to decide claims by patients or others.
- *Transactional law*: Lawyers can benefit patients by supporting nonprofits in writing contracts, setting up business structures, negotiating deals, and managing regulatory compliance.

THE NEED FOR NEW APPROACHES

Despite the gains in healthcare rights, there is an increasing gap between what advocates hope to gain and what can be achieved through litigation, legislation, and regulation. Regulatory agencies are not staffed for close scrutiny of the facilities they oversee (see Chapter 15). Healthcare professionals often throw their hands up in exasperation when confronted by the volume, complexity, and even conflicts among laws, regulations, and accreditation requirements (Hetzler, Morrison, Gerardi, & Sanchez Hayes, 2006). Individual lawsuits do little to effect system change. Moreover, they do not truly solve an injured patient's problem because, when placed on the defensive, providers withhold the very information and acknowledgment that patients are seeking when they sue. Lawsuits cannot require an apology, a corrective treatment, or a change in care delivery.

Threats to patient safety remain pervasive, and the limitations of the litigation and regulation system are too great to continue to rely on them as the primary source of patient protection. Scholarship from diverse fields, as well as evidence culled from the personal experience of advocates and patients, demonstrates the need for new approaches as an adjunct to more traditional adversarial legal methods.

PATIENT SAFETY IS STILL A PROBLEM

In the healthcare community, patient safety concerns date back at least to the late 1970s (Millenson, 1999, 2003, p. 104).The issue exploded into public consciousness with the 2000 IOM report (2000), *To Err Is Human*, which presented the alarming statistic that as many as 98,000 patients may die annually in U.S. hospitals from error, and untold numbers of patients suffer injuries and close calls in hospitals and other treatment settings (Leape, 2000).

The IOM report galvanized public and industry attention (see Chapter 10). Dozens of organizations formed to advance patient safety. Vast federal dollars funded research; the Agency for Healthcare Research and Quality oversaw $84 million in patient safety research in 2005 alone. Most hospitals adopted patient safety initiatives. Yet, disturbingly, the injury numbers remain high. As recently as 2006, the IOM estimated that at least 1.5 million preventable, serious medication errors take place annually (IOM, 2006). Patient safety leaders issue increasingly impatient critiques about the lack of progress in reducing injuries.[11]

After patients have been harmed during treatment, injury may be compounded by insult. Consider the case of a well-known patient safety advocate:

> Linda went to a highly respected hospital for an ankle replacement, her nineteenth operation for congenital clubfeet. Within seconds of receiving an injection of local anesthetic, Linda had a grand mal seizure and went into cardiac arrest. She was resuscitated, rushed into cardiac surgery, and then spent 10 days in intensive care. By accident, the anesthetic had gotten into Linda's circulation and had threatened her life.
>
> During Linda's hospitalization, she was told nothing about what had happened; when she did ask, she was told that she was allergic to the anesthesia. The absence of communication shook her trust. No one in the hospital offered support to her husband; no one acknowledged what a horrible event it had been for Linda and her family. The anesthesiologist, Rick, was devastated that he was unable to talk with Linda, despite repeated tries, as he was told to leave communication to the hospital risk management team.
>
> Months later, finding herself in an increasingly fragile state and with her family still suffering, Linda wrote to the hospital to suggest offering support for patients and families like hers. She received two "cold and uncompassionate" letters from administrators in response.

She says, "If I had ever been angry about this incident, it was after I received those two letters. I could appreciate why some patients want to sue . . . to get letters like this . . . it felt like being victimized twice. (MITSS, 2006a)

A great deal of patient safety work has emphasized error prevention. Its central premise is "systems thinking," the idea that the vast majority of healthcare errors and injuries result from breakdowns in care delivery processes and that the most effective harm prevention comes from thoroughly examining actual and potential errors and aggressively addressing the systemic root causes (IOM, 2000). Efforts have included clinician hand hygiene campaigns to reduce infection, a host of medication safety initiatives, new team operations, "patient safety rounds" for hospital leaders to learn about latent safety problems, and evidence-based guidelines for specific health conditions such as preventing pneumonia or treating heart attacks (Brennan, Gawande, Thomas, & Studdert, 2005; Sachs, 2005; U.S. Department of Health and Human Services, 2006).

Although not immediately evident, an equally critical area in the patient safety arena is how patients are treated after a healthcare injury. Less adversarial and more collaborative relationships among patients, healthcare professionals, and lawyers after harm can meet patient needs *and* have powerful effects on organizational attempts to prevent future injuries. On the other hand, an organization's failure to treat an injured patient with respect, honesty, and compassion may further traumatize the patient. Clinicians become additional victims when they are prevented from communicating with their patients after something goes wrong (Wu, 2000). Linda's case and thousands like it challenge our current methods for responding to patient injury and raise new questions. What kinds of patient needs should we be trying to meet? What legal methods can help?

WHAT DO PATIENTS NEED?

Results of research investigating what injured patients want demonstrate a remarkable consistency. As early as 1994, Vincent found that patients "wanted greater honesty, an appreciation of the severity of the trauma they had suffered, and assurances that lessons had been learnt from their experiences" (Vincent, Young, & Phillips, 1994). Many look for an apology. These desires surface in virtually every major discussion of the topic, with some adding that patients do not want to suffer financially because of the injury (Joint Commission on Accreditation of Healthcare Organizations, 2005, p. 27).

Coping with medical harm is a process. Loss accompanies injury; patients may grieve the loss of a person, independence, physical function, sense of self, or the trusting relationship with a doctor. Grieving includes confronting the loss; reflecting on the person, ideal, or object lost; and, finally, detaching from what was lost (Stroebe & Stroebe, 1991).

Authors also note patients' need for others to recognize and validate their views (Shuman, 1996). In addition, patients need resolution. Some patients focus on justice—particularly looking to symbolically correct the moral and power imbalance that results when one person harms another (Shuman, 1996, pp. 447–449, 456). People may turn to the legal system to meet these needs; however, the more we know about patients' experiences, modern functioning of the legal system, and psychology, the more we see that litigation and regulation fail to fulfill many patients' hopes for healing.

Accreditation bodies, licensing boards, and most other regulatory agencies act to protect patients on a broad scale but are not designed to be responsive to individual patients. They do investigate complaints, but they do not inform patients about results. Some do not even interview the patient. The National Practitioner Data Bank collects information meant to be indicators of unsafe practice, but the public cannot search that information source (National Practitioner Data Bank).

As to the court system, for many patients, access is illusory. Media coverage of sensational cases gives the impression that medical malpractice suits are everywhere. The truth is that the vast majority of people with real claims cannot or do not sue. Multiple studies of potential medical malpractice claims, and of other types of personal injury, all show that 90% to 99% of injured people with legitimate claims do not sue (Localio et al., 1991; Studdert et al., 2000; U.S. Department of Commerce, 1978). In the widely quoted Harvard Medical Practice Study, one analysis concluded that less than 1% of patients had suffered an injury the researchers believed was caused by negligence, and only 1.53% *of those patients* (as a weighted average) filed malpractice claims (Localio et al., 1991).

One reason that most people do not sue for medical malpractice undoubtedly is that people do not know how to access attorneys. "The elderly and the poor are particularly likely to be among those who suffer negligence and do not sue, perhaps because their socioeconomic status inhibits opportunities to secure legal representation" (Studdert et al.,

2000). Moreover, after being approached, attorneys accept very few cases. To win, the patient must have sustained damages that others recognize. The professional must have been at fault, and the patient must be able to demonstrate these conditions within the rules of the court. In the meantime, an attorney must gamble at least $20,000 to $30,000 of his own funds on out-of-pocket costs. Experienced lawyers estimate that they accept only 7% of the cases presented to them by patients (Rice, 2000). In particular, the adversarial system leaves out those whose injury costs less than $50,000 (Shuman, 1993, 1996).

Most patients who do sue do not receive the benefits promised by the tort system. At least 90% of lawsuits settle before trial.[12] This ends the process before a patient is able to hear any judgment or validation of his individual case (Sebok, 2003). The actual payment comes from an insurer who is not at fault.[13] Little wonder, then, that any sense of vindication, of justice, or of righting an imbalance can seem missing or hollow (Shuman, 1996, pp. 434, 438).

As Professor Anthony Sebok of Brooklyn Law School writes:

> Only 2% of all federal civil cases were decided by a trial. And there is every reason to believe that the state systems would reveal the same story, if only there were enough resources to perform a similar survey. . . . What good is a tort system in which the vast majority of disputes are handled outside of trial? Do plaintiffs feel satisfaction at the end of a process that is essentially bureaucratic? Do culpable defendants come away feeling chastised, and deterred? Do defendants who did nothing wrong feel vindicated? Common sense tells us the answer to all of these questions, sadly, is no." (Sebok, 2003)

There is literature arguing both for and against the therapeutic value of lawsuits (Ehrenzweig, 1953; Owen, 1976), but we see both trial and settlement as poor vehicles for meeting most needs patients have expressed. These needs are explored in greater detail later here.

Financial

Litigation is best suited to repaying a patient's loss of money. Any amount won is meant to "make patients whole," that is, put them back in the position they would be in if the injury had never happened.[14] However, the idea that a patient can walk away from a lawsuit feeling as though money has been restorative after the reality of emotional damage and broken trust seems dubious at best. Moreover, most injured patients do not win; some data show only 27% of patients succeed at trial (Cohen, 2004). As Gawande has put it, when the number who do not sue is added to the equation, "Fewer than 1 in 100 deserving families receive any money. The rest get nothing: no help, not even an apology" (2005).

Validation

In contrast to what one might expect, the patient's need for validation may actually be undermined throughout the litigation process. Testimony is subject to strict rules of evidence, and patients say these constraints prevent them from fully telling their stories. The patient's credibility and perceptions are constantly challenged. Even if the lawsuit is successful, these limitations can diminish the sense that justice was done.

Grieving

Because pursuing a lawsuit can easily require five years, litigation may prolong the grieving process (Shuman, 1993). By keeping the loss alive for the purposes of gathering evidence and preparing effective arguments, litigation prevents patients from taking the critical step of detaching from the loss (Shuman, 1996, pp. 452–453).

Information

Stories abound in the patient safety literature about injured patients who were not told what happened (Gibson & Singh, 2003; Gilbert, 1995). Patients report feeling forced to sue to find out these crucial details (Gibson & Singh, 2003). There are legal mechanisms that require information to be produced, but attorneys acknowledge they use silence to force patients to use an expensive and time-consuming procedure until a court requires the release of information. In these cases, the information comes sporadically, in disjointed pieces, and with no guarantee that it will ever form a coherent explanation of the events leading to the injury (Hetzler, 2005).

Acknowledgment of Responsibility and Apology

When everything a healthcare professional says or does has the potential to be used against him or her in an adversarial process, it tends to silence even those who feel responsibility and compassion. After patient safety efforts revealed the vital need for an apology, the legal and healthcare communities sought to use language carefully to acknowledge the patient's experience but not admit legal responsibility. Several states passed laws reinforcing this approach.[15] Although the laws were meant to encourage apologies, they are not clear about how providers can apologize without those words being used against them in court.

As a result, professionals are still very cautious when it comes to acknowledging responsibility. Sometimes they use statements such as, "I am sorry that this happened to you," an often suggested refrain; however, scholars say an apology such as this falls far short of what the situation requires. We expect an apology to acknowledge responsibility, express remorse, offer to repair the wrong, and promise not to repeat it (Lazare, 2004; Scher & Darley, 1997; Taft, 2005). Without these elements, researchers find that many people consider this kind of expression no better than saying nothing at all; in fact, it can "exacerbate the very injury that prompted the disclosure" (Robbennolt, 2003; Taft, 2005) (see Textbox 20.2).

In the case discussed earlier about Linda and her doctor, Rick, an extraordinary twist occurred. Despite everything he was told, Rick wrote Linda to explain what had happened and to apologize. Linda found that, after six months, she wondered whether Rick was suffering and wanted to call to forgive him. During the phone call, she felt that Rick was more honest with her than anyone else in the hospital had been and that forgiving him gave her the ability to move on in her life. She told him she knew that

---

Textbox 20.2 Apology

Healthcare, legal, and legislative experts continue to debate what kind of apology should be made and at what time. Here are some things to keep in mind:

- Merely saying "I'm sorry" is *not* an admission that you are legally liable.
- Using careful language can sound insincere and self-protective and can therefore backfire by leaving the patient feeling insulted instead of apologized to.

it had been an accident and did not blame him. Rick says it was the best phone conversation he had ever had, that it lifted the burden he had been carrying. Both said they felt free to move forward with their lives.

Harm Prevention and Social Change

As part of their emotional resolution, many patients want to ensure that what happened to them will not happen to others. Perhaps the impetus comes from a need to make sense out of a senseless situation and fulfills the need to *do* something when so much seems out of control. The drive to protect others is captured poignantly by Sorrel King, the mother of a toddler who died in medical care:

> Josie was 18 months old. She had brown eyes and light brown hair. She loved to dance and had just learned to bounce on the trampoline. . . . Josie died from severe dehydration and misused narcotics. Careless human errors. On top of our overwhelming sorrow and intense grief we were consumed by anger. They say anger can do one of two things to you. It can cause you to rot away or it can propel you forward. . . . Tony and I decided that we had to let the anger move us forward. We would do something good that would help prevent this from ever happening to a child again. . . . My precious memories and everlasting love for Josie give me this strength, and I will not rest until we make something good come from her senseless death. I will not rest until hospitals become safer places. (Josie King Foundation, 2003)

With a charge this compelling, how should advocates accomplish it? What changes individual behavior in hospital settings? What changes social norms in these situations? Adversarial methods have worked to establish standards, and it is appealing to believe that their power will force individual provider change. Conventional wisdom has it that tort law deters unsafe behavior, but such claims have never been demonstrated (Shuman, 1993). In fact, good evidence in the psychological literature and from empirical observation suggests that adversarial methods actually work *against* changing behavior (Shuman, 1993).

Although we cannot cover all motivations for change in one chapter, a few are worth highlighting. We start with the most basic but deeply influential idea: People do not like being told what to do. If they follow dictates, they do so because the rules legitimize their own values (Shuman, 1993); otherwise, we have all seen people avoid or work around a rule, implementing only the bare minimum of the requirement.

The less we require people to draw on their own morality, the less they are able to do so. In a heavily regulated system, regulations "crowd out" internal motivation for trustworthy conduct, replacing it with narrow compliance, usually only to the extent people perceive the regulation will be enforced (Hall, 2004a; Leape & Berwick, 2005). Likewise, the more people are separated from their sense of responsibility for equity the more it weakens individuals' sense that it is up to them to behave with equity (Walster, Berscheid, & Walster, 1973, pp. 151, 164).

A system that relies almost exclusively on punishment to enforce behavior also undermines patients' abilities to trust healthcare professionals. That trust is based on what is believed about a provider's intentions as much as results and skills (Hall, 2004a). Malpractice awards, licensing discipline, and regulations signal to patients that providers' intentions are unreliable, that they must be *forced* to engage in trustworthy behavior (Hall, 2004a). Although there is undoubtedly a need for these processes in some situations, an overarching punitive approach sets people up for perpetual struggle and undermines *patients'* abilities to work toward partnership.

Major schools of psychology tell us that punishment, or its threat, does little to generate desired behavior. Behavioral change theory and social learning theory give more credence than other theories to negative reinforcement, but it only works if it is immediate and consistent. Neither of these conditions is met in the tort or licensing systems, as actions are taken so rarely and penalties, if any, are imposed years after the conduct (Shuman, 1993). Worse, threat of punishment only creates short-term behavior change (Shuman, 1993). In our natural response, we behave more safely initially, but this behavior diminishes over time and is often replaced only by anxiety. Nowhere is this clearer than in health professionals' reactions to malpractice suits and regulation (Shuman, 1993).

Litigation also commonly fails to create system change. In torts, tradition says that a judge or jury can almost never order a hospital or a professional to change how care is delivered. Although organizations now commonly examine what led to an injury—called "root cause analysis"—litigation and licensing fears can still color the discussion so that participants focus on defending their actions rather than examining unsafe processes. This focus limits the creativity needed for effective problem-solving and stifles the willingness to share information with patients and other hospitals. This climate denies the patient the chance to know that some good came out of his suffering. For example, it would not be unusual for a hospital to decide to separate medications with similar packaging on pharmacy shelves to reduce the chance of providing the wrong one, but never tell the patient whose injury led to the change.

Providers as well as patients have reason to fear that they will not be treated fairly by the current tort system. Because expertise and professional community are so important to providers' identities, lawsuits strike them as an "assault on their professional competence or morality that become defining themes in their lives" (Gerardi, 2005; Shuman, 2000). Furthermore, because payment amount is based on the patient's injury, settlements or judgments can be huge when clinicians have very little fault and vice versa. These paradoxes feed a sense that the system is arbitrary and that providers may be blind sided at any time. Much has been made of the practice, labeled "defensive medicine," of ordering tests and procedures out of litigation fears rather than medical judgment; however, defensive medicine is just one symptom of the more widespread problem of professionals' inability to believe that the legal system will protect them from arbitrary punishments and unfair accusations about their competence and integrity. Adversarial methods are much more likely to reinforce shared beliefs that courts, regulators, and patients are arbitrary, threatening, and untrustworthy, thus creating entrenched practices rather than promoting change.

THE IMPORTANCE OF TRANSPARENCY

Within a complex medical system, injuries may be inevitable. Healthcare professionals must grapple, ethically and socially, with putting the ideals of transparency into practice, and legal advocates must support them in this effort. Transparency, the concept of making information visible and accessible, is essential to safety in several ways. Open communication invites caregivers and patients to offer information necessary for safe care decisions. Transparency is critical for identifying where systems break down and for expressing empathy, respect, and partnership to patients who are affected.

Many commentators note that, for the shift to systems thinking to be successful, cultural norms must change within healthcare settings as well as in society's view of healthcare practice (Schyve, 2005). Adversarial methods "seem insufficient to do the job of transforming cultures, where the deeper solutions lie" (Leape & Berwick, 2005). For transformation, individuals and institutions need to address "beliefs relat[ing] to the norms, values, and practices that constitute the culture" of healthcare practice (Gallagher et al., 2006). Organizations need to actively cultivate this culture change; otherwise, individual efforts will atrophy in an adversarial environment. True accountability will only be achieved when the traditional response to injuries, often labeled "shame and blame," is replaced by openness to discussing actual and potential errors in combination with commitments to change practices within the individual's control. To influence this cultural shift, healthcare leaders must use more collaborative efforts, taking into account the needs of all stakeholders, and disseminate change through social networks (Morrison, 2005). Later here, we discuss emerging trends that show how some organizations are attempting to accomplish this goal.

PREVENTION AND COLLABORATIVE PROBLEM SOLVING

In view of the limitations of traditional legal methods, approaches are evolving to better fit the needs of patients and healthcare organizations. Some lawyers, mediators, and legally sophisticated patient advocates have rejected adversarial processes in favor of using legal knowledge and skills as problem-solving tools. These methods bring stakeholders together, often in collaborative processes, to protect patients, advance their interests, and ultimately, effect systemic change. In doing so, two trends emerge: using law for prevention and collaborative problem solving.

Preventive Methods

Civil law is designed to be reactive, to be used only when injury has occurred; however, innovative lawyers are challenging that assumption, seeking to prevent legal and healthcare problems before they occur or become a crisis (Stolle, Wexler, Winick, & Dauer, 2000). This might mean anticipating the effects of a legal choice before it is made and offering counseling to prevent litigation or other legal problems. It might mean taking actions to lessen the severity of an existing legal problem. Preventive methods certainly require creative problem solving, looking at remedies more varied and holistic than winning a rights-based argument (Barton & Cooper).

Helping Patients Navigate the System

Problem-solving professionals sometimes intervene before the issue crystallizes into a legal problem. In the case of insurance assistance programs, consumer health assistance programs and ombudsman programs help those with all types of health insurance as well as the uninsured (Health Assistance Partnership, 2006a). For example, some programs ensure that Medicaid and State Children's Health Insurance Program beneficiaries know their rights and can exercise them. State health insurance assistance programs "provide information, referrals, and counseling to Medicare beneficiaries and their caregivers on a wide range of health access and insurance matters" (Health Assistance Partnership, 2006b). With patients gaining benefit from this legal support, many health access, service, and coverage issues can be prevented.

Legally sophisticated advocates use their knowledge to assist patients in obtaining healthcare services and appropriate coverage (O'Hanlon, 2004). Pennsylvania-based Healthcare Advocate and Massachusetts-based Health Navigator Partners, for example, help patients navigate the healthcare system by assisting with coordination of care, finding the right providers for an illness, helping patients understand their benefits, and attempting to resolve disputes with insurers (Health Advocate, Inc., 2006; Health Navigator Partners, LLC, 2006). An advocate who understands the complex health system, the law, and the interaction between them can ensure that patients negotiate the system more efficiently, making certain that correct actions are taken and correct treatments are approved. This problem-solving approach works with insurers and providers in a nonadversarial way to ensure that patients can access the care and benefits to which they are entitled.

Medical–Legal Partnerships

Medical–legal partnerships employ a multifaceted approach to treating disease by combining healthcare interventions with social work and legal strategies to address the social conditions that cause or exacerbate poor health. For example, infestation or mold in housing can worsen asthma, so an attorney may negotiate with a landlord to improve housing standards. Similarly, the medical–legal team can address inadequate nutrition by helping families apply for public benefits or appeal a denial, as fewer than 50% of eligible families receive their entitled benefits in some states (Barnickol, Hirschman, & Justicz, 2005, p. 41).[16] A legal intervention can also help stabilize homes threatened by issues of violence, immigration-related concerns, or job worries.

Begun at Boston Medical Center and expanded to more than 20 states, medical–legal partnerships work through multidisciplinary teams of physicians, nurses, social workers, and attorneys; some also integrate medical residents and law students (Tames, Tremblay, Wagner, Lawton, & Smith, 2003; Westphal, 2006; Zuckerman, Sandel, Smith, & Lawton, 2004). Partnerships are located in hospitals and clinics, allowing families direct access and easy referrals. Lawyers negotiate for families and represent them in court and administrative hearings. Health and legal professionals streamline documentation for benefits and appeals, participate in clinical rounds, develop advocacy protocols, and educate clinicians in advocacy options and techniques. They also educate families about exercising rights for themselves.

Initially concentrating on children's health, medical–legal partnership sites serve families as a whole and also consider applications related to elder care, prisoners re-entering the community, and homeless populations (Curran, 2006). With legal associations estimating that nearly half of all low- and moderate-income U.S. households face a serious legal issue each year (Cantril, 1996, p. 4), the social and public health implications are deep and broad.

Collaborative Methods

Another significant trend in the evolution of legal patient advocacy is the emergence of a variety of methods based in collaboration. These processes generally recognize the patient as a whole person and attempt to serve a range of patient needs.

Dialogue

Practitioners of dialogic processes bring specific structures to group conversations with the aim of increasing understanding and generating collective reflection (Isaacs, 1999). "Dialogue is a process that enables people . . . to talk deeply and personally about some of the major issues and realities that divide them" (National Coalition for Dialogue & Deliberation, 2006).

Dialogues are powerful, transformational experiences that often lead to both personal and collaborative action (Heierbacher, n.d.). They help participants examine their own perspectives and biases and work to dispel stereotypes and build trust. Dialogue may be used to foster innovative ideas, impact policy, transform conflicts, and build collaboration. Louise Diamond (2006), President Emeritus of the Institute for Multi-Track Diplomacy, wrote the following: "In dialogue, the intention is not to advocate but to inquire; not to argue but to explore; not to convince but to discover."

The Wosk Centre for Dialogue in Vancouver, the Health Care Ethics Consortium of Georgia, and the Georgia State University Center for Law, Health & Society collaborated to convene structured dialogues in healthcare communities. Participants represented healthcare professions, government, unions, patients, conflict resolution professionals, attorneys, spiritual leaders, educators, and risk managers. The dialogues increased awareness of common values and goals and sought to incorporate patients' views into healthcare delivery (Healthcare Ethics Consortium of Georgia, 2005; Morris J. Wosk Centre for Dialogue, 2004).

Coaching

First developed as an intensive one-on-one means to improve executives' leadership skills, coaching has been extended to help people analyze and understand conflict, to plan better approaches to anticipated conflict, and to learn to prevent it (Brinkert, 2006). Coaching has useful application in legal patient advocacy collaborations. The Center for Patient Partnerships, a patient advocacy program at the University of Wisconsin-Madison (see Chapter 18), is one program incorporating conflict coaching into a range of patient advocacy practices. Run jointly by an attorney and healthcare clinical and policy professionals, the center coaches patients in conflict management principles and accompanies patients to healthcare appointments to help with reframing medical conversations (Gaines, 2005; Gaines & Sanford-Ring, 2004).

Ombuds

Ombuds programs provide advisors who act as intermediaries between patients and insurers or healthcare facilities. One well-established program, the Long-term Care Ombudsman, is found in all states. The ombuds inform patients about long-term care facilities and quality-of-care standards and handle complaints about the facilities (see Chapter 15).[17] The ombuds program has handled an increasing number of complaints about residents' rights, care, and quality of life since 1996. The primary issue—exceeding three quarters of all complaints annually—is nursing home residents' care (U.S. Department of Health and Human Services, 2005). In 2004, 287,824 complaints were filed nationwide, 77% of which were resolved to the satisfaction of the person complaining.

Although many ombuds programs assist the working poor and uninsured, some assist patients regardless of income level. In Massachusetts, for example, the Managed Care Ombudsman intervenes in disputes between patients and insurance plans and helps residents understand their rights in the claims review processes at each health plan (National Conference of State Legislatures, 2006). As part of the Office of Patient Protection, the ombud has no enforcement power, but refers legal violations to the Division of Insurance (Massachusetts Department of Public Health, 2006).

Disclosure Programs

Legal problem-solving professionals are partnering with clinicians and administrators to design better ways to respond when patients have been harmed during treatment. Joint Commission on Accreditation of Healthcare Organizations and four states mandate that patients be told about such events.[18] The question becomes how to serve patients' needs in these conversations. Disclosure, that is, the truthful and open revealing of information about what happened to cause an injury or death, holds great promise for addressing events in less emotionally wrenching and time-consuming ways. In contrast to their litigious reputation, some lawyers and risk managers have been at the forefront of the disclosure movement (American Society for Healthcare Risk Management, 2003; Kraman & Hamm, 1999). The practice can be seen as a meaningful step toward accountability.

Many health systems have implemented disclosure policies and processes, with most attempting to meet patient-identified needs. The Veterans Affairs Medical Center in Lexington, Kentucky, was the first to widely publicize its regular practice of disclosure (Kraman & Hamm,

1999). The University of Michigan Health System, Minneapolis Children's Hospital, Children's Healthcare of Atlanta, National Naval Medical Center, and Kaiser Permanente are among the most prominent organizations using a patient-centered approach to disclosure (Children's Healthcare of Atlanta, 2004; Children's Hospitals and Clinics of Minnesota, 2006; Hall, 2004b; Herlik, 2006; Houk, 2002; National Naval Medical Center, 2006). These programs tend to emphasize contact within hours or days of the harm by employees trained in disclosure principles and dispute resolution.

The programs are the very essence of patient-centered care (IOM, 2001). These conversations enable immediate acknowledgment of harm and its effects and offer support to the patient. The patient receives information, and staff may apologize and acknowledge responsibility. Commonly, staff will also assure the patient that they will investigate possible causes of the harm and stimulate efforts to prevent this event from recurring (IHI Forum, 2006).

In response to a 2002 law requiring that patients be informed about serious medical events, the Project on Medical Liability in Pennsylvania was created to investigate ways to address patient safety while also addressing increasing medical malpractice insurance premiums. Among other things, researchers explored ways to integrate the disclosure conversation into a wider context (Liebman & Hyman, 2004). One model provides widespread introductory training in conflict resolution skills for doctors and administrators. It calls for developing a core group of trained communication experts to help other healthcare professionals prepare for disclosure conversations. The model encourages early mediation, debriefing disclosure conversations, support for clinicians, and improving patient safety with the information learned.

As the practice of disclosure matures, some malpractice insurers are joining the effort, encouraging their own staff and insured physicians to have forthright conversations (COPIC Companies, 2006; CRICO/RMF, 2006). Industry leaders include Physicians Reimbursement Fund, in San Francisco, and COPIC, in Colorado (COPIC Insurance Company, 2004; Lee, 2005).

Data are limited, but suggest that patients are less likely to sue because they feel fairly and honestly treated and supported during appropriate disclosure conversations (COPIC Companies, 2004; Herlik, 2006; Houk, 2002; Kraman & Hamm, 1999). Four healthcare organizations or insurers report handling nearly 7,000 events in this holistic way. Of these, less than

1% of patients went on to file suit (COPIC Companies, 2004; Herlik, 2006; Houk, 2002; Lee, 2005). The University of Michigan has seen its number of annual lawsuits cut in half since it began using this approach (Hall, 2004b). These reports are consistent with empirical research documenting that an apology with acknowledged responsibility helps injured people feel more sympathy and less anger, making them more willing to forgive the people who harmed them (Robbennolt, 2003). Moreover, a holistic disclosure helps injured patients more quickly; two of the medical centers found that the average time to resolution is now 1 to 1.5 years, rather than the 5 years a court case typically takes (Hall, 2004b; Hetzler, 2005). Some patients even report that relationships with their caregivers were restored (MITSS, 2006b).

Mediation

Mediation is a confidential, problem-solving, dispute-resolution process. It is especially well-suited where issues are complex, a relationship is damaged, and emotions and stakes are high, such as when patients are harmed during treatment (Liebman & Hyman, 2004).

Mediators' backgrounds may be in law, behavioral health, or related fields. A growing number of lawyers are introduced to mediation in their training, with 43% of American law schools offering mediation instruction, including 31 mediation clinics for practical experience (University of Oregon School of Law, 2006). Most mediators, however, begin practice after a specialized 30- to 40-hour course, and only Florida formally licenses mediators (see Textbox 20.3).

Facilitative mediation can be used at any point, optimally before anyone has decided a lawsuit is necessary. The mediator works to protect fairness and neutrality, structuring the conversation to get at the issues important to each participant and to help people get their messages through to each other. The participants are responsible for deciding what they expect of each other and what they will agree to do (Association for Conflict Resolution, 2003). There is no limit on the types of solutions that can be explored. These might include safer practices, public education campaigns, patient input into hospital operations, or other measures meaningful to the patient. One child was crushed at missing her birthday party because she remained hospitalized after a healthcare injury. In disclosure-related discussions, the organization agreed to pay for a new celebration,

---

Textbox 20.3   Some Mediation Terms

Facilitative mediation: An impartial person, the mediator, facilitates a negotiation between disputing parties. The mediator has no power to impose a settlement. The mediator "works with disputing parties to help them explore settlement, reconciliation and understanding among them. . . . The primary responsibility for resolution of disputes rests with the parties" (Association for Conflict Resolution, 2003; Beach, 2004; Fisher & Ury, 1991).

Principled or interest-based negotiation: "Method of negotiation that focuses on satisfying the mutual interests of the parties to a dispute, rather than on haggling and trying to prevail over each other's negotiating stances." Interests are the needs, desires, concerns, and fears that motivate people to take the stances they do (Lind et al., 1990).

Textbox endnotes: mediation (North Carolina Standards of Professional Conduct, 1999), styles (McDermott & Obar, 2003), principled (Fisher & Ury, 1991; Yarn, 1999)

---

a gesture that met the patient's needs much more than a large sum of money (Beach, 2004).

Psychologists have found that, when people are in a position to sue, process is even more important than outcomes (Lind et al., 1990, pp. 953, 955). In particular, injured people want to be accorded dignity, trust, and participation. If these are present, injured people are more inclined to believe that an outcome was fair (Lind et al., 1990, pp. 953, 955). Although some argue that litigation provides these features, our experience shows that procedural limits on patient testimony, the difficulty in obtaining required information from professionals, and the general climate of distrust severely limit the value of litigation.

Mediation, on the other hand, is organized around these very principles, and its structures are designed to foster participation, dignity, and trust. Although researchers are just beginning to explore this link, initial studies support this claim. The New York City Project for Mediating Malpractice Cases conducted detailed evaluations after mediating serious injury and wrongful death claims against New York City hospitals (Hyman & Schechter, 2006). Interviewed patients were satisfied with the outcomes. They were even more satisfied with the mediation process—whether they settled or not—and they focused on the extent to which they were treated with respect. Where the patient received an apology, all but one of the cases settled. Similar results were apparent in a study of mediation for disclosing healthcare injuries (Liebman & Hyman, 2005). These studies support the importance of apology and illustrate how mediation can create a climate where apologies can be offered and accepted. Although the field needs much more research, these initial studies suggest that the intended benefits will be borne out in practice.

Patients can access mediation through private mediators and some hospitals. Some hospitals encourage mediation as the first approach to patient care disputes. Abington Memorial Hospital and Drexel University College of Medicine in Pennsylvania, Johns Hopkins Health System in Baltimore, and Methodist Hospital in San Antonio are among those requesting that a patient agree, on elective admission to the hospital, to mediate any concerns related to the care received before initiating a lawsuit (ECRI, 2005). The nonmandatory agreements help hospitals promote communication when something goes wrong in a patient's care. According to Drexel's General Counsel, in the two years that Drexel has used mediation for early intervention and as a settlement venue for lawsuits, plaintiffs' attorneys are more likely to request a conversation before they send a formal demand letter or file suit (Oxholm, 2006).

Medicare is on the leading edge in offering mediation as a national program (Morrison, 2005). Each state has a Quality Improvement Organization (QIO) responsible for much of Medicare's daily operations, including providing incentives to improve care and responding to patient complaints. QIOs offer mediation as one option for patients, drawing on a panel of independent mediators and providing advisors to support and educate patients.[19]

COLLABORATIVE LAW

Even when working within traditional adversarial structures, forward-thinking attorneys are making legal processes more person-centered through collaborative law, an approach that has been successful in other fields (Fasler, 2005a). In this approach, the parties hire attorneys expressly to use interest-based negotiation with the goal of reaching a fair settlement. All agree to share information openly and to consult the same experts. If there is no settlement, none of the attorneys and experts can be involved in any subsequent lawsuit (Fasler, 2005b; Fuller, 2004). Experience shows that individuals know best what terms they can live with, and they prefer to control that decision rather than handing it over to someone else.

A variant on this practice is well-established at Children's Healthcare of Atlanta, where attorneys and risk managers are forthcoming with information and conduct interest-based negotiations and mediation instead of, or early in, the litigation process. Decisions are made with an eye toward serving patients' needs consistent with institutional values (Hetzler, 2005).

CONCLUSION

Although the law has served as an invaluable tool in establishing the field of patient advocacy and in moving patients toward a more equal role in healthcare decision making, its limits are being tested. Very few patients access the legal system. Traditional legal processes often fall short of meeting patients' needs and can inhibit individual and cultural change. At the same time, a growing number of professionals are using legal knowledge to develop preventive, less adversarial advocacy. Using a range of collaborative methods, they advance problem-solving, therapeutic relationships, trust, and respect.

These methods treat patients as whole persons. Some approaches, including medical–legal partnerships and consumer health assistance programs, endeavor to prevent medical and social crises by proactively helping patients navigate the healthcare and legal systems. Other methods, including dialogue, coaching, ombuds, disclosure programs, mediation, and collaborative law, integrate patients into policy making and problem solving. These innovations model a more holistic approach that practitioners and patient advocates may draw on as they design patient-centered models of care.

Healthcare is too complex and human motives are too varied to offer a single, clear-cut prediction of how healthcare legal advocacy will develop going forward. Yet the signs pointing to change are extraordinary. We know of innovative practices in every U.S. region, including rural settings and urban ones, community hospitals and prestigious universities, practice groups, law firms, and mediation centers (Medical Legal Partnership for Children, 2006; Morrison, 2005). For advocates to connect these pockets of innovation to form a foundation for cultural change, there are several key points to appreciate.

As with any change, awareness must come first. As people become cognizant of these options, they will begin to ask questions: Will this work in my situation? Can it be done without spending too much time and money? Is it consistent with my values? People must feel confident that their willingness to participate in more preventive, less traditional methods will not ultimately be used against them. To foster the growth of these approaches, proponents must address these questions for patients and healthcare professionals.

According to diffusion of innovation theory (Oldenberg & Parcell, 2002), system change begins when a small number of early adopters try new methods. If the methods prove to be effective, these individuals will spread the change by influencing their peers. Especially in healthcare, where social networks are key, leveraging early adopters' influence will be critical to ensuring more widespread adoption of nonadversarial problem solving. Patient advocates can serve as a bridge, connecting patients to early adopters and educating patients about the value of these approaches.

Context is critical. In order for nonadversarial approaches to take hold, proponents must address the concerns of administrators, insurers, the traditional legal community, healthcare professionals' communities, and families. Each has the capacity to support or scuttle innovative problem-solving mechanisms.

The need for data is great. There is very little empirical data about whether lawsuits and regulations generate meaningful change, and much less about the effect of preventive and collaborative methods. After researchers measure which methods are and are not effective for which populations and under what conditions, study results will drive the creation and implementation of new and meaningful processes. Measures will need to address intangibles such as whether important psychic needs were served and whether the patient–provider relationship was restored, as well as the more typical endpoints of health outcomes and preservation of legal rights.

With experience in different problem-solving approaches, individuals will be better equipped to choose the most effective method for the situation. Healthcare providers, legal advocates, and patients will work alongside each other to solve issues, make policies, and change the system, and stereotypes and mistrust should begin to recede, along with the anxiety that blocks effective partnering. As patients come to be seen as problem-solving partners and the healthcare system adopts more approaches to preventing and resolving conflict, we expect the next generation of legal patient advocates will draw on this broad repertoire to enhance patients' health and dignity.

ENDNOTES

1. Throughout this chapter, we use the term "patient" to mean patients, their families, and others close to them.
2. CA H&S § 1367.62; CA H&S § 1347.15.
3. See, e.g., Cobbs v. Grant, 8 Cal.3d 229 (1972) and Salgo v. Leland Stanford, Jr., University Board of Trustees, 317 P.2d 170 (1957).
4. United States District Court, District Of Massachusetts, Civil Action No. 00-10833-RWZ, Healthcare For All, Inc., et al. v. Governor Mitt Romney, et al., Memorandum of Decision, July 14, 2005, & Judgment, February 3, 2006; Press Statement HCFA dated August 31, 2005; First Joint Report on Proposed Remedial Program.
5. Regarding informed consent, see, e.g., Cobbs v. Grant, 8 Cal.3d 229 (1972); regarding refusing treatment, see, e.g., Cruzan v. Director, MDH, 497 U.S. 261 (1990); regarding advance directives, see, e.g., CA Prob §§ 4600 et seq; NC Gen Sess §§ 32A-16 et seq; HI Rev Stat §§ 327E-3 et seq; KY Rev Stat §§ 311.623 et seq; Patient Self-Determination Act of 1990, 42 USC 1395 cc; regarding participation in research, see, e.g., Protection of Human Subjects 45 CFR § 46.116 et seq; Protection of Human Subjects 21 CFR 50.20 et seq; Protection of Human Subjects in Medical Experimentation Act, CA H&S §§ 24170-24179.5; regarding privacy and medical records, Health Insurance Portability and Accountability Act of 1996, Pub L 104-191; regarding emergency treatment, Emergency Medical Treatment and Active Labor Act, 42 U.S.C. 1395 dd.
6. CA H&S § 1276.4 and 22 CCR 70217 (statute, and regulation interpreting it, providing detailed specifications of maximum nurse-to-patient ratios and minimum staffing and licensure levels in many types of hospital units).
7. N.J. STAT. ANN. § 26:2-176 (requiring licensed healthcare professionals providing prenatal care and birthing centers to include postpartum depression education and treatment resources and all such professionals providing postnatal care to repeatedly screen new mothers for symptoms).
8. MASS. SESS. LAWS ch. 58 (2006)
9. CA H&S § 1367.62 (requiring any healthcare service plan providing maternity coverage to pay for at least 48 hours of hospitalization after vaginal delivery and 96 hours of hospitalization after caesarean section, unless a shorter time is mutually agreed by the woman and her physician); http://www.mass.gov/doi/Bulletins/bulletins_01_03.html (speech therapy); http://www.mass.gov/doi/Legal_Hearings/211_37.pdf (211 CMR 37.00 infertility benefits); Massachusetts Mental Health Parity Law Chapter 80 of the Acts of 2000: http://www.mass.gov/doi/Bulletins/bulletins_00_06.html; Women's Health and Cancer Rights Act, 29 U.S.C. 1185b.
10. Employee Retirement Income Security Act of 1974, 29 CFR Part 2560, Rules and Regulations for Administration and Enforcement; Claims Procedure; Final Rule.
11. See, e.g., Lawrence, D. M. (2005), remarks at 8th Annual National Patient Safety Foundation Patient Safety Congress, May 12, 2005, San Francisco, California.
12. See, e.g., Report of the Proceedings of the Judicial Conference of the United States 4–5 (March 12, 1991).
13. Hensler, D. R., et al. (1991). *Compensation for Accidental Injuries in the United States* 107-08, 175 (90% of compensation for accidental injury is paid by insurance or government program).

14. Restatement (Second) of Torts § 901; Harper, F.V., et al. (2d ed. 1986). *The Law of Torts* §25.1, 493.
15. California Evidence Code § 1160 (West 2004); Massachusetts General Laws Annotated. ch. 233, § 23D (2004); Texas. Civil Practice & Remedies. Code § 18.061 (Vernon 2004); Colorado Revised Statute § 13-25-135 (2004); GA§ 24-3-37.1 (2005); Ohio Revised Code Annotated § 2317.43 (Anderson 2005); Oklahoma Statute Annotated tit. 63, § 1-1708.1H (West 2004); Or. Revised Statute § 677.082 (2003); Wyoming Statute Annotated § 1-1-130 (Michie 2004).
16. Only 22% of eligible Project Access families were receiving benefits and only 3% of control families.
17. Older Americans Act of 1965; Pub. L. 89-73, July 14, 1965, 79 Stat. 218 (42 U.S.C. 3001 et seq). By 1978, the act required all states to establish a program. See the National Long Term Care Ombudsman Resource Center site at http://www.ltcombudsman.org/default.cfm.
18. Joint Commission on Accreditation of Healthcare Organizations Standard RI.2.90; Florida Statute Annotated § 395.1051 (West 2005); N.J. Statute Annotated § 26:2H-12.25(d) (2004); Nevada Review Statute 439.835 (2003); Pennsylvania Statute Annotated tit. 40, § 1303.308 (2004).
19. As of this writing, serious injuries or death and substantive quality-of-care complaints are not considered appropriate issues for the QIO mediation program.

REFERENCES

American Society for Healthcare Risk Management. (2003). *Disclosure of unanticipated events: The next step in better patient communication (first of three parts).* Retrieved November 4, 2004, from http://www.ashrm.org/ashrm/resources/files/Disclosure.Pt1.pdf.

Association for Conflict Resolution. (2003). *Frequently asked questions about conflict resolution.* Retrieved April 16, 2006, from http://www.acrnet.org/about/CR-FAQ.htm.

Barnickol, L., Hirschman, J., & Justicz, J. (2005). *Report on the findings and recommendations of project access: A medical, legal and case management collaboration (June 2000–December 2004).* Retrieved August 11, 2006, from http://mlpforchildren.org/files/Project%20Access%20Final%20Report.pdf.

Barton, T. D., & Cooper, J. M. *Preventive law and creative lawyering: Multi-dimensional lawyering.* Retrieved August 17, 2006, from http://www.preventivelawyer.org/content/pdfs/Multi_Dimensional_Lawyer.pdf.

Beach, A. (2004). *Personal communication with Ann Beach, Vice-President of Medical Affairs, Children's Healthcare of Atlanta, March 2004.*

Brennan, T. A., Gawande, A., Thomas, E., & Studdert, D. (2005). Accidental deaths, saved lives, and improved quality. *New England Journal of Medicine, 353,* 1405–1409.

Brinkert, R. (2006). Conflict coaching: Advancing the conflict resolution field by developing an individual disputant process. *Conflict Resolution Quarterly, 23,* 517–527.

Cantril, A. H. (1996). *Agenda for access: The American people and civil justice: Final report on the implications of the comprehensive legal needs study: Forward (sic) and executive summary: Consortium on legal services and the public, American Bar Asso-*

ciation. Retrieved November 10, 2006, from http://www.abanet.org/legalservices/downloads/sclaid/agendaforaccess.pdf.

Children's Healthcare of Atlanta. (2004). *Module I: Disclosure of unanticipated events.* Retrieved February 3, 2005, from http://www.choa.org/default.aspx?id=1656.

Children's Hospitals and Clinics of Minnesota. (2006). *What we've learned: Stories and milestones from the patient safety journey.* Retrieved May 13, 2006, from http://xpedio02.childrensmn.org/stellent/groups/public/@web/@aboutus/documents/policyreferenceprocedure/072550.pdf.

Cohen, T. H. (2004). *Medical malpractice trials and verdicts in large counties, 2001: Bureau of Justice Statistics Civil Justice Data Brief.* Retrieved August 17, 2006, from http://ojp.usdoj.gov/bjs/pub/pdf/mmtvlc01.pdf.

COPIC Companies. (2006). *3Rs program.* Retrieved May 9, 2006, from http://www.callcopic.com/home/what-we-offer/coverages/medical-professional-liability-insurance-ne/physicians-medical-practices/special-programs/3rs-program.

COPIC Companies. (2004). *COPIC's 3Rs program (newsletter), vol. 1, issue 2, October 2004.* Retrieved February 3, 2005, from http://www.callcopic.com/resources/custom/PDF/3rs-newsletter/vol-1-issue-2-oct-2004.pdf.

COPIC Insurance Company. (2004). *Participation manual for physicians and other providers, version 1.6, San Francisco, CA. Unpublished.*

CRICO/RMF. (2006). *Home page.* Retrieved May 9, 2006, from http://www.rmf.harvard.edu/.

Curran, M. (2006). *Comments at the Medical–Legal Collaboration Conference, April 28, 2006. Madison, WI. Unpublished.*

Diamond, L. (2006). *Quick reference glossary: Entry for dialogue.* Retrieved August 30, 2006, from http://thataway.org/index.php/?page_id=499.

ECRI. (2005). *Mediation fits a culture of patient safety (within risk and quality management strategies 20, mediation and arbitration, p 10).* Retrieved November 13, 2006, from http://www.ecri.org/MarketingDocs/RiskQual20.pdf.

Ehrenzweig, A. A. (1953). A psychoanalysis of negligence. *Northwestern University Law Review, 47,* 855–866.

Fasler, K. (2005a). *Medical malpractice: A proposal for the selected use of collaborative law as an alternative to the current legal process.* Unpublished manuscript.

Fasler, K. (2005b). *A niche of its own: The use of collaborative law in medical malpractice cases.* Unpublished manuscript.

Fisher, R., & Ury, W. (1991). *Getting to yes: Negotiating agreement without giving in.* New York: Penguin Books.

Fuller, K. (2004). *Collaborative law: What is it? Why do it?* Retrieved April 26, 2006, from http://www.collaborativelaw.us/articles/How_It_Works.pdf.

Gaines, M. E. (2005). *Telephone interview with Martha Gaines, Director, Center for Patient Partnerships, University of Wisconsin-Madison (February 2005). Madison, WI. Unpublished.*

Gaines, M. E., & Sanford-Ring, S. (2004). *Alchemy: Medical mediation at its best in Focus on Patient Safety: A newsletter from the National Patient Safety Foundation, vol. 7, issue 4, pages 1–3.* Retrieved November 13, 2006, from http://www.npsf.org/download/Focus2004Vol7No4.pdf.

Gallagher, T. H., Waterman, A. D., Garbutt, J. M., Kapp, J. M., Chan, D. K., & Dunagan, W. C., et al. (2006). U.S. and Canadian physicians' attitudes and experiences regarding disclosing errors to patients. *Archives of Internal Medicine, 166,* 1605–1611.

Gawande, A. (2005). The malpractice mess. *New Yorker, 81,* 62–71.

Gerardi, D. (2005). The culture of healthcare: How professional and organizational cultures impact conflict management. *Georgia State University Law Review, 21,* 857–890.

Gibson, R., & Singh, J. P. (2003). *Wall of silence: The untold story of the medical mistakes that kill and injure millions of Americans.* Washington, DC: Lifeline Press.

Gilbert, S. M. (1995). *Wrongful death: A medical tragedy.* New York: W. W. Norton.

Hall, M. (2004a). Law, medicine, and trust: Therapeutic jurisprudence's application to healthcare law. *Stanford Law Review, 55,* 463.

Hall, S. (2004b). *U-M docs say sorry, avert suits (article in the Detroit News, May 12, 2004, p 1c 6).* Retrieved November 13, 2006, from http://www.sorryworks.net/media5.phtml.

Health Advocate, Inc. (2006). *Home page.* Retrieved May 12, 2006, from http://www.healthadvocate.com/main.asp.

Health Assistance Partnership. (2006a). *Home page.* Retrieved April 14, 2006, from http://www.healthassistancepartnership.org/index.html.

Health Assistance Partnership. (2006b). *State Health Insurance Assistance Programs (SHIPs).* Retrieved April 14, 2006, from http://www.healthassistancepartnership.org/ship-locator/ships.html.

Health Law Advocates. (2006). *About HLA.* Retrieved April 9, 2006, from http://www.hla-inc.org/index.php.

Health Navigator Partners, LLC. (2006). *Home page.* Retrieved May 12, 2006, from http://www.healthnavigatorpartners.com.

Healthcare Ethics Consortium of Georgia. (2005). Managing conflict ethically: Collaboration in bioethics and health law, April 13–14, 2005. Decatur, GA. Conference co-sponsored by Georgia State University College of Law's Center for Law, Health, and Society and Healthcare Ethics Consortium of Georgia. In Decatur, GA. Unpublished.

Heierbacher, S. (n.d.). *What are dialogue and deliberation?* Retrieved August 30, 2006, from http://thataway.org/index.php/?page_id=490.

Herlik, A. (2006). Doing the right thing: How to implement the Healthcare Ombudsman/Mediator (HCOM) role. *CRICO-RMF/Kaiser Conference: Seize the Moment: Reaching Excellence in Patient Safety.* Boston, MA. Unpublished.

Hetzler, D. C. (2005). Subordinate claims management: Resolution focus from day one. *Georgia State University Law Review, 21,* 891–909.

Hetzler, D., Morrison, V., Gerardi, D., & Sanchez Hayes, L. (2006). Curing conflict: A prescription for ADR in healthcare. *Dispute Resolution Magazine-Journal of American Bar Association, Dispute Resolution Section,* 5–7.

Houk, C. (2002). *The internal neutral: Why doesn't your hospital have one?* Retrieved April 24, 2006, from http://www.mediate.com/articles/houk.cfm?nl=3.

Hyman, C. S., & Schechter, C. B. (2006). Mediating medical malpractice lawsuits against hospitals: New York City's pilot project. *Health Affairs, 25,* 1394–1399.

IHI Forum. (2006). *Summary of presentation given at the December 2005, Institute for Healthcare Improvement National Forum: Patient expectations: 100% of the time.*

Reflections of patients and family voices (see pdf pp. 177–178.). Retrieved November 13, 2006, from http://www.naph.org/naph/Fellows06/PresentationsSession2.pdf.

Institute of Medicine. (2000). In Kohn L. T., Corrigan J. M., and Donaldson M. S. (Eds.), *To err is human: Building a safer health system*. Washington, DC: National Academy Press.

Institute of Medicine. (2001). *Crossing the quality chasm: A new health system for the 21st century*. Washington, DC: National Academy Press.

Institute of Medicine, Committee on Identifying and Preventing Medication Errors. (2006). In Aspden P., Wolcott J., Bootman J. L., and Cronenwett L. R. (Eds.), *Preventing medication errors: Quality chasm series*. Washington, DC: National Academies Press.

Isaacs, W. (1999). *Dialogue and the art of thinking together: A pioneering approach to communicating in business and in life*. New York: Random House.

Joint Commission on Accreditation of Healthcare Organizations. (2005). *Healthcare at the crossroads: Strategies for improving the medical liability system and preventing patient injury (p. 27 on pdf)*. Retrieved June 28, 2005, from http://www.jointcommission.org/NR/rdonlyres/167DD821-A395-48FD-87F9-6AB12BCACB0F/0/Medical_Liability.pdf.

Josie King Foundation. (2003). *Sorrel's speech to IHI conference, October 11, 2002*. Retrieved August 13, 2006, from http://josieking.org/speech.html.

Kraman, S. S., & Hamm, G. (1999). Risk management: Extreme honesty may be the best policy. *Annals of Internal Medicine, 131*, 963–967.

Lazare, A. (2004). *On apology*. New York: Oxford University Press.

Leape, L. L. (2000). Institute of medicine medical error figures are not exaggerated. *Journal of the American Medical Association, 284*, 95–97.

Leape, L. L., & Berwick, D. M. (2005). Five years after *To err is human:* What have we learned? *Journal of the American Medical Association, 293*, 2384–2390.

Lee, G. (2005). *Personal communication with George Lee, CEO, Physicians Reimbursement Fund (January 2005)*.

Liebman, C. B., & Hyman, C. S. (2004). A mediation skills model to manage disclosure of errors and adverse events to patients. *Health Affairs, 23*, 22–32.

Liebman, C. B., & Hyman, C. S. (2005). *Medical error disclosure, mediation skills, and malpractice litigation: A demonstration project in Pennsylvania*. Retrieved November 13, 2006, from http://www.pewtrusts.com/pdf/LiebmanReport.pdf.

Lind, E. A., Maccoun, R. J., Ebener, P. A., Felstiner, W. L., Hensler, D. R., Resnick, J., et al. (1990). In the eye of the beholder: Tort litigants' evaluations of their experiences in the civil justice system. *Law & Society Review, 24*, 953–996.

Localio, A. R., Lawthers, A. G., Brennan, T. A., Laird, N. M., Hebert, L. E., Peterson, L. M., et al. (1991). Relation between malpractice claims and adverse events due to negligence: Results of the Harvard Medical Practice Study III. *New England Journal of Medicine, 325*, 245–251.

Massachusetts Department of Public Health, Office of Patient Protection. (2006). *Annual report 2004*. Retrieved April 13, 2006, from http://www.mass.gov/?pageID=eohhs2terminal&&L=4&L0=Home&L1=Researcher&L2=Insurance+(including+MassHealth)&L3=Managed+Care+Protections+and+Grievances&sid=Eeohhs2&b=terminalcontent&f=dph_patient_protection_r_annual_reports&csid=Eeohhs2.

McDermott, E. P., & Obar, R. I. (2003). *What's going on: What really happens in the mediation of charges before the EEOC (Remarks at the American Bar Association Section of Dispute Resolution Annual Spring Conference, March 20–22, 2003, San Antonio,*

TX). Retrieved August 17, 2006, from http://www.conflict-resolution.org/sitebody/acrobat/ABASan_Antonio_final.pdf.

Medical Legal Partnership for Children. (2006). *Home page*. Retrieved September 14, 2006, from http://mlpforchildren.org/.

Millenson, M. L. (1999). *Demanding medical excellence: Doctors and accountability in the information age*. Chicago: University of Chicago Press.

Millenson, M. L. (2003). The silence. *Health Affairs, 22*, 103–117.

MITSS, Medically Induced Trauma Support Services. (2006a). *Home page reference to videotape of Linda Kenney and Rick Van Pelt, MD*. Retrieved on October 25, 2006, from http://www.mitss.org/index.html.

MITSS, Medically Induced Trauma Support Services. (2006b). *Patients and family*. Retrieved May 10, 2006, from http://www.mitss.org/Patients_files/Patients.htm#Patients%20and%20Family%20Members.

Morris J. Wosk Centre for Dialogue. (2004). *Conference website: Creative conflict management in healthcare, March 24–26, 2004*. Retrieved April 1, 2006, from http://www.healthdialogue.org.

Morrison, V. L. (2005). Heyoka: The shifting shape of dispute resolution in healthcare. *Georgia State University Law Review, 21*, 931–963.

National Coalition for Dialogue & Deliberation. (2006). *Home page*. Retrieved August 30, 2006, from http://www.thataway.org.

National Conference of State Legislatures. (2006). *Managed care state laws for ombudsman, report cards and provider profiles*. Retrieved April 23, 2006, from http://www.ncsl.org/programs/health/hmorep2.htm.

National Naval Medical Center. (2006). *Healthcare mediator home page*. Retrieved April 16, 2006, from http://www.bethesda.med.navy.mil/Patient/Patient_Support_Services/organizational_Ombudsman.aspx.

National Practitioner Data Bank. *Querying and reporting*. Retrieved August 30, 2006, from http://www.npdb-hipdb.com/queryrpt.html.

North Carolina Standards of Professional Conduct. (1999). In D. H. Yarn (Ed.), *Dictionary of conflict resolution*. San Francisco: Jossey-Bass.

O'Hanlon, L. H. (2004). *Companies offer help negotiating medical system (in the Boston Globe, April 6, 2004)*. Retrieved November 10, 2006, from http://www.boston.com/news/science/articles/2004/04/06/companies_offer_help_negotiating_medical_system/.

Oldenberg, B., & Parcell, G. S. (2002). Diffusion of innovations. *Health behavior and health education: Theory, research and practice* (pp. 312–334). San Francisco: Jossey-Bass.

Owen, D. G. (1976). Punitive damages in product liability litigation. *Michigan Law Review, 74*, 1257–1281.

Oxholm, C. (2006). *Conversation with Carl Oxholm III, Senior Vice-President and General Counsel, Drexel University College of Medicine, August 30, 2006*.

Rice, B. (2000). *How plaintiffs' lawyers pick their targets (in Medical Economics, vol. 8, p. 94)*. Retrieved August 9, 2006, from http://www.memag.com/memag/content/printContentPopup.jsp?id=124124.

Robbennolt, J. K. (2003). Apologies and legal settlement: An empirical examination. *Michigan Law Review, 102*, 460–489.

Rodwin, M. A. (2003). *Consumer voice in managed care: An alternative for promoting accountable healthcare: Investigator Awards in Health Policy Research, issue 8, page 3.* Retrieved November 9, 2006, from http://www.iahpr.rutgers.edu/rwjf/downloads/research_in_profiles_iss08_aug2003.pdf.

Sachs, B. P. (2005). A 38-year-old woman with fetal loss and hysterectomy. *Journal of the American Medical Association, 294,* 833–840.

Scher, S. J., & Darley, J. M. (1997). How effective are the things people say to apologize? Effects of the realization of the apology speech act. *Journal of Psycholinguistic Research, 26,* 127–140.

Schyve, P. M. (2005). *Advances in patient safety: From research to implementation (vol. 2 of AHRQ publication nos. 050021 from the Agency for Healthcare Research and Quality, Rockville, MD).* Retrieved May 13, 2006, from http://www.ahrq.gov/qual/advances/.

Scott, W. R. (2003). The old order changeth: The evolving world of health care organizations. In S. S. Mick & M. E. Wyttenbach (Eds.), *Advances in health care organization theory* (pp. 23–29). San Francisco: Jossey-Bass.

Sebok, A. (2003). *The corrosive effect of the politicization of tort reform: What Newsweek's "Lawsuit Hell" didn't tell you.* Retrieved May 6, 2006, from http://writ.news.findlaw.com/sebok/20031215.html.

Shuman, D. W. (1993). The psychology of deterrence in tort law. *Kansas Law Review, 42,* 115–116.

Shuman, D. W. (1996). The psychology of compensation in tort law. In D. Wexler & B. Winick (Eds.), *Law in a therapeutic key* (pp. 433–465). Durham, NC: Carolina Academic Press.

Shuman, D. W. (2000). When time does not heal: Understanding the importance of avoiding unnecessary delay in the resolution of tort cases. *Psychology, Public Policy, and Law, 6,* 880–897.

Stolle, D., Wexler, D., Winick, B., & Dauer, E. (2000). Integrating preventive law and therapeutic jurisprudence: A law and psychology-based approach to lawyering. *Practicing therapeutic jurisprudence: Law as a helping profession* (pp. 5–44). Durham, NC: Carolina Academic Press.

Stroebe, M., & Stroebe, W. (1991). Does "grief work" work? *Journal of Consulting and Clinical Psychology, 59,* 479–482.

Studdert, D. M., Thomas, E. J., Burstin, H. R., Zbar, B. I., Orav, E. J., & Brennan, T. A. (2000). Negligent care and malpractice claiming behavior in Utah and Colorado. *Medical Care, 38,* 250–260.

Taft, L. (2005). Apology and medical mistake: Opportunity or foil? *Annals of Health Law, 14,* 55–94.

Tames, P., Tremblay, P., Wagner, T., Lawton, E., & Smith, L. A. (2003). The lawyer is in: Why some doctors are prescribing legal remedies for their patients, and how the legal profession can support this effort. *Boston University Public Interest Law Journal, 12,* 505–527.

University of Oregon School of Law. (2006). *List of law school offerings related to dispute resolution (Electronic directory maintained through ongoing collaboration with the ABA Section of Dispute Resolution and the University of Oregon School of Law).* Retrieved August 17, 2006, from http://www.law.uoregon.edu/aba/.

U.S. Department of Commerce. (1978). *Interagency task force on product liability: Final report* (No. 212-13). Washington, DC: National Technical Information Service.

U.S. Department of Health and Human Services, U.S. Administration on Aging. (2005). *Long-term care ombudsman report FY 2004.* Retrieved August 17, 2006, from http://www.aoa.gov/PROF/aoaprog/elder_rights/LTCombudsman/National_and_State _Data/2004nors/2004%20Ombudsman%20Report%20final.pdf.

U.S. Department of Health and Human Services. (2006). *Hospital compare, a quality tool for adults including people with Medicare.* Retrieved May 1, 2006, from http://www.hospitalcompare.hhs.gov.

U.S. Department of Labor, Employee Benefits Security Administration. *Your rights after a mastectomy . . . Women's Health & Cancer Rights Act of 1998.* Retrieved August 31, 2006, from http://www.dol.gov/ebsa/publications/whcra.html.

Vincent, C., Young, M., & Phillips, A. (1994). Why do people sue doctors? A study of patients and relatives taking legal action. *Lancet, 343,* 1609–1613.

Walster, E., Berscheid, E., & Walster, G. W. (1973). New directions in equity research. *Journal of Personality and Social Psychology, 25,* 151–176.

Westphal, S. P. (2006). *Lawyers help patients solve problems (Wall Street Journal, April 11, 2006, page D3).* Retrieved November 10, 2006, from http://development.bmc.org/site/pp.asp?c=flLVJhP8H&b=960975.

Wu, A. W. (2000). Medical error: The second victim: The doctor who makes the mistake needs help too. *British Medical Journal, 320,* 726–727.

Yarn, D. H. (1999). In D. H. Yarn (Ed.), *Dictionary of conflict resolution.* San Francisco: Jossey-Bass.

Zuckerman, B., Sandel, M., Smith, L., & Lawton, E. (2004). Why pediatricians need lawyers to keep children healthy. *Pediatrics, 114,* 224–228.

Conclusion

CHAPTER 21

Patient Advocacy: A Bridge to Improving Healthcare Quality

Jo Anne L. Earp, Katie Emmett, and Elizabeth French

OBJECTIVES

- To identify the aims of patient advocacy and the methods used to achieve those aims
- To define who is an advocate and introduce a new association for health advocates
- To review and synthesize the preceding chapters around five central themes
- To understand that collaboration, coalitions, and compromise are central advocacy approaches
- To appreciate the ways in which patient advocacy presents ethical dilemmas even as ethics undergirds all of advocacy

With this final chapter, we revisit our purpose in light of chapters that have come before; we make connections between authors and articulate themes, assess what we have accomplished and possibly neglected, and look to the future. Through the preceding 300 plus pages, we have sought to define and understand this nascent field, patient advocacy. In doing so, our attempt was to achieve at least four larger order aims, aims that cut across chapters and that we explore in greater depth in this summary chapter.

AIMS 1 AND 2: ADVOCACY'S PLACE IN HEALTHCARE AND AS A SUBJECT OF STUDY

Throughout this book, we have been building a case for the *place* of advocacy in healthcare, both as it appears in formalized roles (research advocates, hospital-based patient advocates, heads of nonprofits) and as a dimension of other roles (the patient, caregiver, provider, health educator, social worker, lawyer, researcher, or journalist as advocate). In other words, we explore *who is an advocate* and what his or her significance is in health-related areas. Second, and connected to this first purpose, we make an implicit case for the importance of advocacy as a *stand-alone subject*, one that needs to be conceptualized, studied, and taught as a separate dimension from other topics in healthcare. As the chapters in this book demonstrate, patient advocacy manifests itself across roles and exerts significant power at all levels of our healthcare system. Yet it has been understudied as a subject in its own right. By focusing on this topic in an extended work, we hope to stimulate thought, discussion, and research on this complex subject.

AIM 3: WHAT WE ADVOCATE FOR

Soon after we began working on this project, one of our colleagues, pointing to our distinguished contributors, urged us to use this book as a "call to arms." We chose to go a different route, attempting to record the forms of advocacy we identified and how different actors and collectivities use these forms of advocacy to achieve their aims. Yet in the end, we could not, nor did we want to, disentangle ends from means. Thus, we did not separate the advocacy methods we examined from the measures we were advocating for. This point brings us to our third aim. Through the chapters we have chosen and helped to shape, we make a case about *what kinds of changes we as participants in a social movement need to advocate for*. These include the following:

1. Accessible, affordable healthcare that takes into account the whole person
2. The central place of good communication as a defining factor in high-quality care
3. The ability of individual patients and consumers to contribute substantively to the care they receive and to the health-related policies that get adopted
4. The *necessity* of having patients and families contribute to that care and those policies if healthcare is ever going to be as safe and humane as the public expects it to be

We may yet deliver that call to arms. If we do, these four goals will be at its core. In the meantime, sketching out avenues of effective advocacy may increase the likelihood that the eventual delivery of that manifesto will have its intended impact.

AIM 4: DEFINING PATIENT ADVOCACY AS A SET OF METHODS

In 2003, Carolyn Clancy, director of the Agency for Healthcare Research and Quality, asked in a plenary talk at the Patient Advocacy Summit at the University of North Carolina, "Do we need an army of good advocates, or a better system in which advocates are not necessary?" As William Roper responds in his forward and as we argue throughout this chapter and book, we need both. By this do we mean that we need advocates to shepherd patients through our healthcare system one by one? No. That would be a terrible waste of resources. Do we mean training people in effective approaches to getting good solutions adopted, even as those same people may help protect and advocate for individuals? Yes. Do we mean raising public awareness of the need to be assertive, to ask questions, and to adopt information-seeking habits when it comes to health? Undoubtedly. In other words, taken together, these chapters aim to show that defining a problem, gathering data, and developing good solutions are critical steps. Yet they are not enough. To work on a broad scale, solutions need advocates—to overcome inertia, to change people's minds, to show that a business case can be made for an ethical position, and for many other reasons. This book addresses many of the methods that help advocates do just that. In doing so, it fills a major need for analyzing just how these processes happen.

OMISSIONS

As a first-time effort to define patient advocacy and review its methods, we have undoubtedly overlooked important dimensions, even as we may have given short shrift to others. We apologize for these oversights and hope that they will be a catalyst for further assays into this subject. One topic we did not discuss, for example, is the importance of narrative in patient advocacy. Researchers and academics put a premium on the appeal to logic and data in their presentations of evidence, and for good reasons. Among others, they want to avoid being manipulated by unsupported appeals to emotion, to show that they are canny about the ways vulnerability can be deployed as a weapon to influence public opinion, and because they want readers to trust that they are not promulgating hidden, unsupported agendas. As Grob and Hurst have pointed out (2005), only after advocates strategically used the story of Ryan White (a child and a hemophiliac) did Congress allocate significant funds for HIV/AIDS research, despite the vigorous efforts of ACT-UP and other gay-rights organizations. This example remains interesting for how it sheds light on the possibly exploitative uses of innocence together with the public's conflicted response towards stigmatized groups such as HIV-positive gay men. The narrative is also significant in the way it reinforces received ideas of how some victims are more worthy than others.

Despite the potentially suspect uses of narrative, almost every chapter includes one or more cases or vignettes in which patients interact with providers or other healthcare entities. By foregrounding individual narrative, we inevitably spotlight a tension, seen throughout the book, between the value of data and measurement ("what gets measured is what gets done") and the fact that we are discussing real people, real lives. Human beings underpin the data we collect. We do not overstate our claims to say that many have suffered and died needlessly because they could not access healthcare, because of faulty communication, because of poor quality or for other systemic problems. In the absence of data, a powerful story, told thoughtfully at the right moment and in the right place, can give researchers, clinicians, patients and policy makers a push in the right direction—hence, the need for narratives. They imprint the emotional texture of people's lived experiences on readers' minds. They communicate urgency. They point to problems that need to be quantified and traced to their source. As important, the emotional quality of patients' and healthcare workers' experiences are at the nerve center of advocacy. Even though data give advocates leverage in making their arguments, individual experience is the fuel that drives them to up-end their organizations, knock on doors, work late for months and years, and try every strategy they know to increase awareness and inspire change.

ADVOCACY AND ETHICS

As this discussion of a major omission in our book implies, patient advocacy, as a set of methods and a set of actors, is highly charged by the ethical issues that define its core. Therefore, in addition to surfacing and synthesizing some of the book's major themes, this chapter also briefly reprises the question of who in this fledgling field can meaningfully be called an advocate. We overview those values, qualities, and characteristics that help unite a diverse set of advocacy initiatives around common goals and beliefs about what is important. We conclude by examining the ethical obligations of patient advocates and the conflicts that arise when competing agendas intersect. As we aim to make clear, patient advocacy is a force in healthcare, an area that involves a complex set of skills and a highly attuned ethical sensibility.

Although progress is slow and obstacles can be formidable, the culture of delivering medical care has begun to be transformed; increasingly, the emphasis is on treating people, not disease. Thousands of individuals, whether patients, providers, caretakers, nonprofit administrators, or educator/researchers, are already making a difference. Advocacy, or the social movement that is changing the culture of healthcare delivery from medicine-driven to relationship-centered care, is not restricted to any one level of the ecological framework (see Chapter 1) or one type of change agent. Patient advocates, whether healthcare providers (Chapter 10), lay persons (Chapter 14), or organizations, such as the Joint Commission on Accreditation of Healthcare Organizations (Chapter 20), the National Citizens' Coalition for Nursing Home Reform (Chapter 15), the National Breast Cancer Coalition (Chapter 17), or the Accreditation Council for Graduate Medical Education (Chapters 6 and 13), have taken the lead in mobilizing public opinion about patient safety. They have taken the lead as well on issues of equity, training, and communication so as to better serve patients, families, *and* providers. Patient advocacy is a subject whose time has come.

WHO IS AN ADVOCATE?

The defining feature of a patient advocate is someone whose primary goal is to act in the best interests of patients, often those who are not able to advocate for themselves. Beyond this basic definition of role, patient advocacy has many faces. Patients, friends, and family members work alongside healthcare providers as advocates. As often as not, individuals may fall into multiple categories, both personal and professional. What sets advocates apart from others in their personal or professional lives is their cognizance of their role; they self-identify as advocates and consciously seek ways to fulfill this identity.

These self-identified advocates represent a dizzying array of affiliations. Some are front-line providers of healthcare services; others are associated with a nonprofit or grassroots organization. Some focus on specific diseases such as HIV/AIDs or breast cancer (Chapters 5 and 17), on particular life stages, such as childhood (Chapter 3) or end of life (Chapter 13), or on a specific community or population such as the National Citizen's Coalition for Nursing Home Reform (Chapter 15). Some work with individual patients (Chapter 7), whereas others lobby legislators, write laws, and work for policy change (Chapters 16, 17, and 20). Some advocacy organizations seek to reform the healthcare system so as to prevent future problems, whereas others attempt to meet the needs of patients today who have been ill-served by the current system or have suffered the effects of a discriminatory past (Chapter 5). Although organizations usually tend to specialize in some way, even on global issues such as ensuring health insurance coverage of the 46 million people in the United States who are uninsured in 2006 (Chapter 2), some perform more than one function. For example, although the Patient Advocacy Foundation provides direct services to patients negotiating insurance claims, its sister organization, the National Patient Advocacy Foundation, works to achieve legislative reforms across a wide set of access issues (Chapter 16).

Lest we run the risk of making the advocacy community sound like one big happy family, the preceding chapters, together with this essay, show the ways in which it is not. These chapters demonstrate why it may be controversial to yoke a physician and a family member together and call them advocates in the same sentence. So-called kitchen table advocates, burned by their experiences with the healthcare system, their expertise often discounted or dismissed, frequently come to mistrust the interests of physicians, researchers, and administrators, suspecting that the "bottom line" or the next research article may take precedence over their needs. Similarly, physicians, researchers, and administrators, all of whom may self-identify as advocates, may feel that "kitchen tablers" do not adequately recognize the constraints they work under—the 20 other patients with needs as dire as theirs, the need to balance the books at the end of the year, the need to solve question x before tackling solution y. In these circumstances, it is easy to vilify entire professions.

Despite these formidable problems, as editors, we have chosen to pitch a big tent, to conceptualize patient advocacy as it manifests across the spectrum, from the family member who has been radicalized to start her own education program or citizen advocacy organization (Maggie Hoffman and Project DOCC in Chapter 3 and Marion Ballentine and NCNNHR in Chapter 15) to the administrator who has set in motion dramatic changes in his or her hospital (Jim Conway at Dana Farber in Chapter 10 and Pat Sodomka at Medical College of Georgia in Chapter 12). This big tent approach is not without its pitfalls. Doubtless some readers will throw our book across the room for too much doctor bashing ("How many times do the authors need to tell us docs won't take the time to communicate well with their patients!"), whereas others will throw it across the room for having let physicians "off the hook" with our repeated expressions of sympathy about the constraints of the seven-minute appointment. Yet we have run these risks deliberately, if not always elegantly, in the belief that showing the tradeoffs associated with insider or outsider status can help all advocates approach these issues from less dualistic positions. In doing so, our intent is to build trust among all stakeholders, thereby leveraging the strengths each position has to offer.

PROFESSIONALIZATION

The diversity of approaches to advocacy, together with the divisions between insider/professional advocates versus outsider/kitchen-table advocates, has deterred attempts to professionalize patient advocacy. Vexing questions about the advantages and disadvantages in developing patient advocacy as a profession span the gamut. Should standards be developed, competencies specified, credentials required? Will such a response exclude those who have gained their expertise through lived experience rather than formal training? Are professional and lay advocates two different species or simply two variants of the same entity?

A quick look at the difference in approaches—top-down/professional versus bottom-up/kitchen table—can suggest where and why tensions inhere in this discussion. William Roper, former director of the Centers for Disease Control and Prevention as well as of the Health Care Financing Administration (the forerunner of the Centers for Medicare and Medicaid Services), favors a university-based center for consumer health advocacy that will address these questions through evidence-based research. The Agency for Health Care Research and Quality (AHRQ), the lead federal agency for ensuring that research about healthcare gets adopted by practitioners, has established a Center for Quality Improvement and Safety, whose mission includes convening agenda-setting workshops, disseminating information, developing outcome and performance evaluation measures, and facilitating the setting of standards (Leape & Berwick, 2005). The Institute for Health Care Improvement in Boston (http://www.ihi.org/ihi), the Leapfrog Group (http://www.leapfroggroup.org/), and the National Quality Forum in Washington, DC (http://www.qualityforum.org/) are other organizations that have committed themselves to responding to the safety and quality problems identified in the 1999 Institute of Medicine report, *To Err Is Human* (Levin, 2005). The 100,000 Lives Campaign is one example of a program designed to target six specific risk areas (preventing central line infections and adverse drug events, for example) and in the process save a hundred thousand lives (Levin, 2005). During the first 18 months of the campaign (between December 2005 and June 2006), the Institute for Health Care Improvement estimates that 122,300 lives were indeed saved in the 3,000 hospitals across the United States currently enrolled in the program (Institute for Healthcare Improvement, 2006). Of course, the Institute of Medicine, with its ground-breaking set of reports on patient safety and health disparities written by prestigious panels of experts, as well as with less well-known write-ups than *To Err Is Human* (Institute of Medicine, 1999) and *Crossing the Quality Chasm* (Institute of Medicine, 2001), such as those on *Health Literacy* (Institute of Medicine, 2004), *Pay for Performance* (Institute of Medicine, 2007), and *Who Will Keep the Public Healthy?* (Institute of Medicine, 2003), is a leader in giving voice to the principles that underlie both patient safety and healthcare equity as social movements.

Given these "Goliaths" of healthcare advocacy with their powerful positions and organizations, high levels of credibility, and comparatively large budgets, what can kitchen-table advocates accomplish on their own, often working in isolation without credentials, and armed primarily with personal experience and charisma, both of which are often discredited? In this daunting environment, where can such advocates gain a foothold if they want to make a difference? As described in the Health Advocates Association (HAA) (see Textbox 21.1), a small group of patient advocacy thinkers and practitioners hosted a two-day meeting in the spring of 2006 to discuss the need for an organization, tentatively called the Health Advocates Association, that would help bring individual advocates together— from those working out of their homes to those heading up major organizations.

Conveners argued that a professional society could help define and shape the direction of the field, give individual advocates working in the

Textbox 21.1   Health Advocates Association

A small group of Health Advocates came together in April 2006, at the Shelter Rock Retreat Center in Manhasset, Long Island, to determine whether there was a need for a professional association of Health Advocates. Reservations, questions, and possibilities were debated during the two-day retreat.

Background

At least two specific events precipitated the Shelter Rock retreat. The first were two Patient Advocacy Summit meetings organized by the Department of Health Behavior and Health Education in the School of Public Health at the University of North Carolina at Chapel Hill in November of 2003 and again in March of 2005. At these meetings, issues of credentialing, professionalization of advocates, development of competencies for the field, and tensions between "lay" and "professional" advocates arose repeatedly.

The second precipitating event was a meeting at the Genetic Alliance conference in Washington, DC in July 2005. Numerous members of the Genetic Alliance had requested a society or association of health advocates to be both an umbrella organization, offering "lay advocates" benefits and networking, as well as a resource connection for training opportunities.

Why a Health Advocates Association Now

The group spent time in the early part of the Shelter Rock retreat defining who is now doing health advocacy and the various kinds of work such advocates do. Attendees agreed that definitions were not standardized and that terms currently in use—for example, patient advocate versus health advocate; consumer versus patient—can be problematic or even divisive. Advocates occupy a wide range of positions in the workforce (paid and volunteer) and advocacy may involve playing many roles.

The group agreed that central to all advocacy is functioning as a **change agent**, either by directly causing productive change in healthcare or by empowering others to do the same. Health advocacy includes direct service advocacy (working with or for individuals or families), legislative or policy advocacy, research advocacy, community-based advocacy (working with or for a geographically defined group), population-based advocacy (working with or for a group defined on the basis of a shared illness experience or other characteristic), or education advocacy.

The working name for the proposed association is **Health Advocates Association**. It will be an organization comprised of individual health advocates, not of health advocacy organizations.

(continued)

Textbox 21.1   Health Advocates Association (continued)

After extensive debate on whether an association of Health Advocates would be useful to advocates and to the public, those present at Shelter Rock Retreat Center agreed that such an organization would not only be useful, but necessary, for the following reasons. It would:

- Help health advocates be leaders in defining the direction of a profession that is showing definite signs of coalescing
- Provide infrastructure to marshal the power of a common voice and a way to be heard by the media
- Build an association "born and raised" by health advocates rather than by a more narrowly constituted group
- Help answer the questions, "Where do you go if you want to be a patient advocate?" and "How *do* you become an advocate?"
- Provide an answer to people already in the field who ask, "Where is the professional voice of Health Advocacy?"
- Better protect the public by equipping advocates to do their jobs in ethical, competent ways

Common Ground: What "Professional" Health Advocates Share

The Shelter Rock group agreed that an essential function of the retreat was to define principles, values, competencies, professional ethics, and strategies affirmed by all health advocates, regardless of position, role, or background. Principles affirmed by the group included the need to promote equity and justice while advocating for health, to work on behalf of others, and to maintain hope in the face of challenges. Later here are the group's conceptualization of values and competencies.

Values
Health advocates should be guided by a responsibility and commitment to
1. Respect the context, values, and preferences of each person, group, and community served
2. Be an agent of productive, positive change
3. Idealism and achieving the "impossible dream"
4. Finding, using, and sharing the best quality knowledge available
5. Serving both the individual and the group
6. Promoting and protecting patient rights
7. Personal transparency about motives, limitations, and conflicts of interest
8. Multiple pathways for attaining health advocacy credentials

(continued)

Textbox 21.1   Health Advocates Association (continued)

Competencies

Health advocates should possess the ability and capacity to

1. Identify and support each person, group, and community, taking into account and respecting their context, history, values, and preferences
2. Build capacity for others (patients, families, support networks, organizations)
3. Ably, fairly, and honestly "represent" others
4. Communicate effectively
5. Facilitate access to support
6. Know personal limits
7. Understand how the healthcare system works
8. Recognize and disclose conflicts of interests

Pathways to Professionalism

The Shelter Rock group reaffirmed that the purpose of the association was to provide essential resources and support to everyone who wanted to be an advocate. Although the group agreed that credentialing is necessary in order to protect the public and create an articulated professional core for the health advocacy profession, they were emphatic that *the pathways to eventual credentialing through the association must be flexible and inclusive.* Such pathways might include direct experience (survivor, family member, etc.), formal education, career or professional experience, training or mastery of a body of knowledge, independent or self-designed study.

Some of the benefits of membership in the HAA could be a journal, a website, health insurance and pension plans, opportunities for networking; mentoring for new health advocates, seeing the commonalities among advocates, and identifying workshops and educational opportunities.

"wilderness" a home, and help ensure that high-quality advocacy was delivered. Yet given the dangers of professionalization, of sidelining kitchen-table advocates through the very formation of a professional body, why organize? Perhaps our previous sketch of major change organizations offers a window into why. "Top downers"—physicians, administrators, researchers, other professionals—can express their advocacy inclinations through many engines. "Kitchen tablers" rarely have these options and, moreover, often express intense frustration that their experiences, their *hundreds* of stories recounting deaths and injuries, never seem to be enough to change a paradigm. Their efforts show the ways that insiders have difficulty *seeing* the evidence they are presented with because they have difficulty believing in the underlying *thesis* of these advocates, i.e., that our health systems do not deliver high-quality care despite the best efforts of hundreds of care providers. For that thesis to get accepted by insiders, it seems, an advocate still needs credentials and a powerful position; it requires the voice of a Don Berwick, physician at Harvard, his wife the casual victim of dozens of medical oversights and errors, rallying his profession and starting the influential Institute for Healthcare Improvement. In other words, we are revisiting the power of roles and credentials in advocacy. As desirable as Berwick's outcome has been, it probably does not salve the frustration on the part of many kitchen tablers that the stories they offer are not enough to jump start research and change mindsets. In this context, professionalizing can offer a place to gain strength in numbers, among other benefits.

Eventually the organizers hope that the HAA will provide networking opportunities and paths to training for advocates as well as represent patient advocacy to society as a whole and particularly to those individuals newly identifying themselves as advocates. HAA meeting participants also view the association as a way to distinguish between corporate organizations whose patient representative services are limited to those who can pay and nonprofit models of patient advocacy, which usually attempt to be more broadly inclusive, at least of their own constituencies. Fledgling though the Health Advocates Association is, organizers unanimously endorsed advocacy as a necessity for *all* patients, not as a luxury for the few.

While believing that some form of credentialing is probably desirable in order to confer legitimacy and protect consumers, association organizers sought to define this aspect flexibly. As is clear from the HAA principles, values, and competencies, any endorsement of credentialing would recognize the value of life experience as well as more formally gained knowledge and skill sets. Essentially, those who signed on to the HAA statement view standards not as a way to exclude lay people but as a means to establish credibility and confer recognition and status on lessons learned from life. Requirements for HAA membership would likely need to be approved by the community health advocates on whose behalf the society is being established.

As the previous discussion and HAA textbox seek to demonstrate, defining patient advocates in binary or exclusionary terms can lead to a diminution of the field. Advocates fall within a broad spectrum of personal and professional experiences. Depending on their background and the circumstances eliciting their advocacy efforts, advocates gain some perks and lose others. Marginalizing one form of advocacy as "less than" another because of the advocate's place within or outside a system can discourage highly capable individuals from getting involved. Just as advocates are needed at every level of the ecological framework (Chapter 1), a diversity of backgrounds helps us collectively think through new strategies and apply pressure from all angles.

THEMES/VALUES IN ADVOCACY

Although the diversity of this young field may challenge readers to perceive it as a field at all, an awareness of several key concepts can help unify advocates working in different contexts. The five themes highlighted in this chapter and the values associated with each emerge repeatedly throughout this text. As advocates from a multitude of backgrounds tell their stories, the consensus is clear: we need patient-centered care that is accessible for everyone. The ability to communicate effectively is vital and a skill that both patients and providers must work to master. The problems in our healthcare system are both pervasive and entrenched; thus, innovative approaches must be applied to achieve broad social change.

Patient-Centered Care

Patient-centered care is guided by a patient's goals, preferences, and needs. In order to deliver patient-centered care, providers must know their patients. This "knowing" may involve learning about the person's history, cultural context, or religious faith. It may require becoming aware of the person's family relationships, social context, and home environment. In the case of end-of-life care, it means knowing a patient's wishes for his or her own death. As Winzelberg and Hanson point out in Chapter 13, these may be specified prior to an acute illness in the form of an advance directive, living will, and/or durable power of attorney; however, they also may not be. When a person has slipped into a coma, it is too late to inquire about preferences. Thus, providers must take initiative when working with this population if they want to be able to deliver care that is informed and directed by the patient's wishes. At the end of life, a simple conversation can prevent months and years of anguish.

Patients are not the only ones who need care. In a medical crisis, families need care too. The boundaries of this function, however, are not easy to decipher. In Chapter 3, Seyda et al. assert that family-centered care should be the goal we are seeking to achieve in medicine. For example, a doctor practicing family-centered care will recognize the importance of listening to the observations and concerns of a patient's mother, daughter, or spouse. Although close family members are not usually experts in medicine, they are intimately familiar with what is or is not normal behavior for their loved ones. This perspective is especially important in situations in which the patient is a child but certainly applies for many adults as well, especially for those too ill to speak for themselves. Broadly defined, family plays a role in the current and future care of the majority of patients, regardless of age. Although this concept may be an axiom for some medical care providers, for others, it could involve a significant shift in mindset and hence the need for a different kind of training.

Indeed, as Donald Berwick points out, interactions are not the by-products, or the price, of care but care itself. As he puts it in his seminal work, *Escape Fire*: "Time spent in building patients' skills in self-care is not a way to shift care, it *is* care. Access to information is desirable not because it improves care or supports compliance but because it is a form of care" (2002, p. 51). As of 2004, we were spending 1.9 trillion dollars annually on healthcare expenditures in the United States (Smith, Cowan, Heffler, Catlin, & the National Health Accounts Team, 2006). According to Berwick, there is no better way to invest our healthcare dollars than in building relationships. Many families who felt that their concerns were not heard when coping with illness would agree.

Patient-centered care modalities are vital for protecting patients while in the hospital or facing acute illness, yet they also lead to better care for patients managing chronic disease. Building on this theme, Hibbard implicitly argues in Chapter 9 that fostering an activated patient population should be a central aim of patient advocacy. The theory behind patient activation is that patients who come to their appointments educated, prepared, and engaged will have more successful interactions and make better use of their time with physicians than those who have not "done their homework." Although obvious, it bears pointing out that no provider, not even a family caretaker, will spend as much time with the chronic condition as does the patient him or herself. Where possible, therefore, the patient should be the source of all control.

Patient activation, as Hibbard describes it (Chapter 9), is a crucial concept because of the primary role of self-management in treating chronic disease (Bodenheimer, Lorig, Holman, & Grumbach, 2002). In healthcare interactions, Berwick asserts that, "Control begins in the hands of the people we serve. If we caregivers wish to take it, we must ask. If a patient denies control, then we must accept their will as a matter of right. We are not hosts in our organizations so much as we are guests in our patients' lives" (2002, p. 54). As guests, clinicians have much to offer their patients, yet patients need the opportunity to make decisions for themselves. This technique both respects patients' agency and helps motivate patients to follow through with care plans. This delicate balance is negotiated in the context of relationships. Indeed, accountability to quality care means placing a premium on social interactions, making relationships central not only with patients but also with their families, who are often the ones who help acutely or chronically ill individuals care for themselves and cope with their illnesses.

In Chapter 6, Lown and Kalet seek to show readers the complexities of providing relationship-centered care from the clinician's perspective. In their view, echoing many kitchen-table advocates, more attention should be paid to the interaction between the doctor, the patient, and the relationship formed between them over time. Their chapter illustrates what care looks like when physicians serve as advocates for their patients. It also highlights the many reasons why offering such care is challenging and the changes that need to take place in medical education and residency training in order to create a more hospitable environment for delivering relationship-centered healthcare. An individual physician will find it difficult to implement tools like the Macy Model of physician–patient communication (see Chapter 6) without institutional support; delivery of relationship-centered care requires significant healthcare system change in addition to recognition of its importance.

Planetree hospitals provide one example of facilities that are designed from the ground up with the needs of patients and families in mind (Chapter 11). They have abolished visiting hours, making it possible for family members to remain with loved ones 24 hours a day. They have provided sleeping accommodations and access to kitchens so that family members have a place to sleep and prepare food. Blood draws and bathing are scheduled with the best interests of patients, rather than the medical care system, in mind. Designated caretakers (often family members) receive training while the patient is still in the hospital so that they can be skilled and knowledgeable resources for the patient following discharge. Hospitals also provide patients and family members with educational materials related to the condition in question and tailored to the needs and abilities of the individual. These innovations and many others help create a patient- and family-centered hospital stay, at the same time encouraging patients and families to take an active approach to their care rather than thinking "the doctor is going to fix me." As a result, the Planetree model of hospital care has taken a quantum leap forward in institutionalizing care that begins and ends with the goal of meeting the needs of patients and families.

Based on evaluations and national rating systems, staff at Planetree hospitals find these accommodations to patients and families acceptable, although more evidence on this point would provide a stronger business case for the Planetree model specifically and patient-centered care in general. A strong business case is what concept such as Planetree needs behind it if it is going to achieve wide adoption. Just as some hospitals are making safety profitable as a product line, the idea of treating people rather than diseases will gather adherents if it is valued not only by the public but by the corporate sector, too.

Integral to the Planetree philosophy is the recognition that satisfied staff members are likely to deliver better care. Indeed, it makes sense that healthcare settings where employees enjoy working are more likely to be facilities where patients and families feel comfortable. Although more research in this area would be useful, as is true of virtually all the areas covered in this book, preliminary evidence suggests that when staff needs and concerns are addressed, often those of patients and families are as well.

Healthcare Should Be Accessible for Everyone

Many obstacles to obtaining healthcare in the United States are addressed in this text. In Chapter 2, Silberman identifies a primary barrier—lack of health insurance—for a significant portion of the nation's population. She points out that the absence of insurance is not a random phenomenon; several categories of people regularly fall through the healthcare coverage cracks. It is ironic that even though the United States has an employer-based insurance system, large majorities of the uninsured either have full-time jobs or are in families with someone who is working full-time. Although the federal government provides some health benefits for low-income people, individuals and families must meet stringent requirements in order to qualify for them. For example, Medicaid restrictions make it virtually impossible for adults under 65 years of age with no dependents to qualify for coverage, regardless of how poor they are. Similarly, because the State Children's Health Insurance Program, which serves as a backup system for children living slightly above the poverty line, is funded by federal block grants, states are forced to freeze benefits when the money runs out, even if eligible children have not been covered. These gaps, deficits, and irrationalities in insurance coverage place heavy burdens on workers, families, individuals, children, employers, and taxpayers in the United States and highlight the frayed nature of the so-called healthcare safety net in America.

People from certain racial and ethnic backgrounds as well as those living in rural areas or with disabilities also struggle to obtain adequate health services. For example, although black women are less likely than white woman to get breast cancer, they are more likely to die from it because they tend to be diagnosed at later stages. Earp and Moore, in Chapter 5, describe an intervention designed to address breast cancer disparities for black women living in rural counties in North Carolina. The North Carolina Breast Cancer Screening Program selected and trained "natural helper" lay health advisors within these counties to educate their communities about breast cancer and encourage women to get screened (Earp, Altpeter, Mayne, Viadro, & O'Malley, 1995). The program not only made women aware of their risk for breast cancer but also provided information about and transportation to free screening for those without a regular healthcare provider. The beauty of the natural helper lay health advising model is that it empowers women who have already gained the trust and respect of their peers to provide counsel on health-related concerns (Bishop, Earp, Eng, & Lynch, 2002).

Those who do have access to a provider may still encounter obstacles in obtaining appropriate care because of language and literacy issues. In Chapter 8, DeWalt and Pignone discuss the gap between the information and educational materials that are regularly provided to patients and the average person's ability to comprehend them. The use of sophisticated medical jargon may be technically accurate, but it is not an effective means of communicating if patients do not understand it. The authors point out that research study consent forms are frequently written in language far beyond the grade level required for general comprehension. Language barriers and the limited availability of interpreter services for nonnative English speakers can place low-literacy patients in danger of receiving inadequate or inappropriate care. Moreover, the persistence of literacy and language barriers suggests a larger problem. The lack of awareness among physicians about what their patients do and do not understand is likely to impede their ability to create individually tailored, patient-centered care plans for them. Similarly, a lack of awareness of their patients' literacy and other language barriers (e.g., English-as-a-second-language speakers) or lack of awareness of strategies for working with such patients may lead to poor medical history taking as well (Duggan, Geller, Cooper, & Beach, 2006).

Communication Is Key

Many health system problems that patients encounter are the result of communication failures rather than negligence or lack of medical expertise. Indeed, in examining all sentinel events, the Joint Commission on Accreditation of Healthcare Organizations (JCAHO) reports that communication issues are the most frequently identified root cause, present in more than 60% of all cases (2006). Rather than simply developing new technology, we need *more* and more effective communication among doctors, nurses, patients, and families.

Patients are ready for this change; from the recent Kaiser Family Foundation survey (2006), it appears that patients are becoming more informed and are feeling more empowered, especially around the issue of medical errors. A proposed fee change announced by the Centers for Medicare and Medicaid Services (CMS) would institutionalize the value that quality-care experts place on communication by paying physicians for the time they spend with patients, advising and assisting them in managing their health. If the proposed revisions in physician work "relative value units" are adopted, Mark McClellan, former CMS administrator, predicts that doctors will be reimbursed "for giving [Medicare] patients the help they need to manage illnesses more effectively" (CMS, 2006). A change such as this creates a positive financial incentive for providers to spend more time talking with patients.

In addressing the issue of patient safety and medical errors in Chapter 10, Conway draws attention to this major killer in our nation's hospitals by highlighting specific patients and families who have suffered and died as a result of medical errors. Similar to the case we make early in this chapter about the uses of narrative in patient advocacy, Conway implies that health-care providers need to more deeply internalize the impact of their errors by seeing the victims of those errors in their full humanity. Only then, Conway suggests, can clinicians be convinced of the ways effective communication strategies can help to avoid these tragedies in the first place. Indeed, Champions of Change, a national symposium held in September 2006 to highlight healthcare reform efforts and introduce the PBS documentary series *Remaking American Medicine*, demonstrates that stories are integral to organizational change through their effect on public opinion. In fact, it has been suggested that perhaps every hospital board of trustees meeting should open with a discussion of a recent case (McClellan, 2006).

Although errors that result in medical harm to the patient may be the easiest to document, errors resulting from miscommunication between a patient and physician often do not come to light. More subtly, communication styles (and by extension advocacy) may differ depending on whether patients are in an acute, inpatient situation or whether they are at home, in the process of coping with a chronic disease or condition. In a hospital-based situation, effective communication between patients, families, and clinicians can immediately save a life. Alternatively, for patients with chronic conditions, effective communication with clinicians can help them manage their condition, protect them from further harm, and keep them out of the hospital. In Chapter 7, Golin et al. describes strategies that can be used in a medical setting to help physicians and patients understand one another better. For example, motivational interviewing (MI) is a technique initially developed for use with patients struggling with alcohol and substance abuse. Since then, short MI versions have been developed to better fit the clinical office setting and has been used effectively in a variety of different medical contexts (Emmons & Rollnick, 2001).

Much of treating chronic disease is linked to behavior and thus depends on a patient's ability to make lifestyle changes. So few, if any, of these necessary changes can take place within the confines of the medical visit. MI's intent is to help patients set the agenda for a visit with the provider based on the health issues the patient feels ready to address. The theory behind the MI approach is that it aids patients in pursuing their own goals rather than those suggested by an outsider and overcoming barriers constraining their efforts to change. In this context, the physician serves as a counselor, motivating patients to achieve goals *they* decide on together, rather than dictating to patients what they should or should not do.

Patients do not necessarily need to wait for the doctor to make the first move; they can take the initiative as well. For example, many patients have found other forms of support to supplement the limited time they have in clinical visits. As Ferguson observes in Chapter 4, detailed information (including text, graphics, figures, tutorials, photographs, and video footage) about many disease topics is available to patients and their families online. Many times, these resources have been created, edited, or compiled by individuals who suffer from the same condition, often ensuring that the information provided is relevant and easy to understand. Moreover, patients can find much more than just information on the web. E-mail from friends, chat rooms, and Internet support groups provide a vital source of encouragement and hope for patients and their families as well as some of the most cutting-edge information available. As a resource, the Internet is especially valuable for those with rare conditions who may not be able to connect with other patients locally. Although the digital divide exists, technological compatibility across devices such as cell phones, television, and computers is likely to narrow that divide in the future.

Education Is Not Just for Patients

Although the need to provide patients with medical information is an essential component of advocacy and one that is emphasized throughout this text, patients are not the only ones who need education. Aspects of medical school curricula and hospital culture that create distance between doctors and patients or contribute to cynicism and mistrust on all sides also need to be examined. In Chapter 12, Zoppi, Sodomka, and Moretz talk about physicians' need for patient information, and not just the typical data gathered from a history and physical. Reform efforts are currently underway to prepare medical students to work with patients more effectively, to train them according to standards of cultural and psychosocial excellence as well as clinical and technical expertise. Some training institutions are even bringing in patients and family members as faculty, inviting them to play a more formalized role in medical education. The hope is that programs such as these will teach doctors to view their patients more holistically, to see them as human beings in a complex environment rather than simply as disease states or malfunctioning organs. Programs such as Project DOCC or the Families in Resident/Student Teaching program underscore the importance of each patient's history and trajectory, emphasizing that an individual's story expands far beyond his or her medical record. The goal of healthcare is not only to help people recover from acute illnesses or injuries but also to help them live longer, higher quality lives, even when living with one or more chronic conditions for which we, as yet, have no cure.

Patients need medical information, and doctors need patient information. But what kind of education do patient advocates need? Although most advocates do not undergo a formalized academic training process, this option is available. Currently, a few academic institutions in the United States offer graduate-level training in patient advocacy. In Chapter 18, case examples from two of these programs illustrate a major goal of advocacy education is patient empowerment. Among other reasons, advocates seek training so that they can help patients or communities make good healthcare decisions, teach them how to navigate organizations, assist them when they encounter obstacles, and change health systems overall that so they are more accessible, transparent, and equitable. As Chapter 18 illustrates, distinguishing between when it is appropriate to help patients take action on their own behalf versus performing tasks for them when they are too exhausted and demoralized to do so on their own requires judgment, discretion, and sympathy. As underscored by Lown and Kalet (Chapter 7) and by Zoppi, Sodomka, and Moretz (Chapter 12), an advocate needs to cultivate self-awareness, constantly assessing whether and what kind of advocacy is needed. The job of the patient advocate is not always to become the patient's voice; often, as appropriate, advocates' most far-reaching actions come when they coach patients in how to speak effectively for themselves and create environments where their voices can be heard.

Activated patients are finding ways to speak, not only in the context of their own unique experiences, but also in ways that inform medical research. In Chapter 17, Michaels and Collyar examine this trend. No longer limited to the role of research subjects, patients are now serving as advisors on the design and conduct of clinical trials and advocating for increased funding for medical research. These new roles require a certain level of sophistication, including an understanding of basic and clinical science as well as research protocols and institutional norms. Although the inclusion of lay persons on research review panels has not been achieved without controversy, some members of the scientific community have begun to recognize the importance of including the patient perspective when conducting clinical trials (see Chapter 17), and some funding agencies now require evidence of patient input into study design and data collection processes; however, the practice of including advocates in research decisions is not so well-established that were advocacy groups or coalitions to stop demanding their inclusion on review panels, many gains made in this area in the last 15 years would likely disappear.

Innovation and Social Change

As with any social movement, understanding at least part of the historical context that gives rise to the current situation, as Pearson et al. highlight in their preface to this book, can help advocates identify effective strategies, strategic alliances, and pitfalls. The legacy of patient advocacy is connected to social and consumer movements taking place in the United States from at least the 1850s to the present, and particularly within the last 50 years. As Tomes describes in Chapter 14, consumers have played a key role in achieving healthcare reform. Successful campaigns include more stringent food and drug safety regulations, procedures requiring informed consent and respect for patient privacy, and protection for people with mental and physical disabilities. Yet, Tomes also draws attention to an interesting conundrum: although in many ways healthcare consumers have become empowered through education and consciousness raising, the exponential increase in the depth and breadth of medical knowledge has also served to inhibit patient participation in decision making. Indeed, Tomes suggests an almost inverse relationship between patient autonomy and physician expertise, indicating that our ancestors from the 1800s may have been significantly more empowered when it came to healthcare (albeit living less long) than we are today.

On the other hand, some clinicians are seeking to decrease the divide between patients and providers. Chapter 19 focuses on Renneker and Stritter, two physicians who found it impossible to practice their kind of medicine within the confines of the current healthcare system. In response to his frustration with time constraints and other aspects of modern medicine, Dr. Renneker finally closed his medical practice and began to offer his services as a clinical advocate. Within this self-defined role, he was able to achieve his goal of providing "gold standard" care by serving as a medical consultant for his patients. His job description now includes conducting extensive research for and engaging in lengthy conversations with his clients (and their physicians); he helps them understand often impenetrable medical information, obtain second opinions, and negotiate frustrations associated with the healthcare nonsystem. Renneker focuses on patients who are struggling with complex medical issues across the diagnostic spectrum and who need more information and support than their providers can or do give them. After establishing his own successful practice, he trained Stritter to do the same. As clinical advocates, both have found the career satisfaction that was lacking for them in traditional medical practice. Whether their choice is a feasible option for other than a small select group of physicians, regardless of how preferable it may be for a large segment of the patient population, remains to be seen.

Lawyers also play a critical role as patient advocates. No doubt the first thing that comes to mind when the topic is legal advocacy is medical malpractice litigation. George Annas (2006) makes the point that citizens' options to pursue malpractice cases in court is a necessary legal protection and a right and, moreover, has underpinned important safety measures that benefit entire classes of patients. Yet, as Morrison and Truppin describe in Chapter 20, the law has much more to offer the healthcare advocacy movement than lawsuits. As they point out, litigation frequently leaves all parties involved with a less than ideal outcome. Thus, often what patients want when they experience a medical error is not a large financial settlement or a successful court case. They want a complete and honest explanation of what happened and an apology from the person who was responsible for providing their, or their loved one's, care. When healthcare organizations "circle the wagons," however, patients' frustration can lead them into the courtroom. This costly, time-consuming process often fails to meet the patient's needs even as it drives up healthcare costs, motivates doctors to practice defensive medicine, and creates stress for patients, families, and providers.

As it turns out, several other options besides litigation can help patients, physicians, and administrative entities arrive at more satisfying solutions for all involved. For example, lawyers can facilitate mediation, a process that allows both parties to work together toward a mutually acceptable, fully transparent solution. According to Morrison, mediation often leads to more efficient, fair, and satisfactory outcomes for all parties than litigation, creating a climate where apologies can be offered and accepted. Research suggests that "an apology with acknowledged responsibility helps injured people feel more sympathy and less anger, making them more willing to forgive the people who harmed them" (Robbennolt, 2003). More broadly, the outcome many patients want when they seek more information (and ultimately file a suit when their initial inquiries are met with stone-walling) is to prevent errors of a similar kind from happening to others. The idea that loved ones have suffered for no larger purpose is agonizing to many plaintiffs. Yet lawsuits can neither require an apology nor demand a change in care delivery. Although some progress has been made on this front, more advocacy work is definitely needed.

Although legal experts continue to debate what kind of apology should be made and at what point in the process, Atul Gawande (2005), in *The Malpractice Mess*, argues that current attempts at apology within medicine are far from satisfactory. Unfortunately, in response to the data on the salutary effects of apology, some members of the legal and healthcare communities have suggested providing patients with a carefully phrased acknowledgment of the patient's experience while not admitting any legal responsibility. Merely saying "I'm sorry," however, without an acceptance of responsibility, an expression of remorse, and an offer to repair the wrong or a plan to avoid a repetition of such incidents is likely to fall far short of patient needs and expectations. The full disclosure and straightforward, transparent discussion of medical errors are recommended not only by Morrison (Chapter 20) and Conway (Chapter 10) but also by the Institute of Medicine, which identifies disclosure and transparency as key factors in improving healthcare quality (Institute of Medicine, 2000).

Advocates Think Big

Patient advocacy often involves individual experiences that can, at times, lead to big changes. In Chapter 16, Davenport-Ennis chronicles this progression in her own life—from her personal battle with breast cancer to serving as an advocate when her friend was diagnosed with the same disease to the creation of an organization that makes these same counseling and support services available to consumers across the country. Moreover, she did not stop there. She recognized that the Patient Advocacy Foundation had the opportunity not only to mediate insurance disputes for individual patients but also to collect valuable data. In turn, PAF's sister organization, the National Patient Advocacy Foundation, also created by Davenport-Ennis, then used those data to inform a political agenda, lobby legislators, and help institute federal and state policy changes around insurance issues and prescription drug benefits. There is no better illustration than the PAF/NPAF story of how one patient's experience can continue to radiate outward, encompassing ever more people in its expanding sphere of influence.

Holder and Frank chronicle a similar process in Chapter 15 as they describe the history of a small grassroots organization, the National Citizens' Coalition for Nursing Home Reform (NCCNHR), that for many years fought for radical reform in the nursing home industry. Although there remains considerable room for improvement in the way we care for older adults, NCCNHR's story is one of several major victories for elderly patients. As with Davenport-Ennis, widespread changes have been instituted as a result of the efforts of ordinary people—including ombudsmen and citizen advocates. Reforms achieved by this movement include increased nurse staffing levels at nursing homes, the promulgation of restraint-free care, improved nutrition and hydration standards, individualized care plans for each resident, and the establishment of resident and family advisory councils. Although the continuing demographic shift taking place in our nation and the increasing demand for long-term care suggest much more needs to be accomplished in this arena, NCCNHR serves as an excellent case example of how kitchen table advocates—not just clinicians, lawyers and professionals—can achieve major health system reform.

METHODS OF ADVOCACY

As is clear from the array of advocacy approaches outlined in this book, a wide range of strategies can help advocates address problems in healthcare from every imaginable angle. Advocates provide education to and raise the consciousness of individual patients and families, the medical community, and society as a whole. Advocates offer counsel, guidance, and support for those trying to negotiate the healthcare system. Advocates share their own experiences with individuals and groups, use media outlets to sway public opinion, and ideally gain the attention of decision-making bodies. They form coalitions and rely on strategic alliances. Advocates collect evidence, conduct research, prepare reports, serve on committees, testify to Congress, and occasionally take to the streets in protest. All of these endeavors, undertaken to advance the well-being of patients or groups, to improve the health of communities, or to enhance the quality and equity of healthcare, are methods of advocacy.

Of these methods, collaboration with other like minded (and sometimes not so like minded) individuals and groups may yield the most fruitful results. Holder and Frank underscore this point when they discuss the gains NCCNHR achieved by joining forces with leaders in the not-for-profit nursing home sector to get major nursing home reform legislation passed (Chapter 15). In a system in which the insurance and pharmaceutical industries enjoy a disproportionate share of societal power, patient advocacy is an uphill battle, especially without teamwork. Representatives of the medical industrial complex (Chapter 14) have abundant funding, articulate and ambitious leadership, and a unifying agenda. Indeed, one of the primary reasons certain individuals and groups need advocacy is precisely because they lack the organization, financial resources, and access to influence that insurance or pharmaceutical companies or medical professionals possess. It is not a fair fight, yet nothing is more powerful in a democracy than public opinion.

On rare occasions, confrontations may be necessary, even inevitable. Advocacy that adopts a nonadversarial approach in its efforts to mobilize public opinion, however, can often gain more traction and have more staying power. Advocates can risk losing their credibility by relying too heavily on adversarial tactics. As Holder and Frank emphasize (Chapter 15), patient advocates who are committed to their cause in the long-term understand that cooperation, collaboration, and coalitions, even with those who may not seem like natural allies, go far in bringing about system change. Unless advocates are able to partner with key stakeholders, including those with financial and political influence, the "haves" will not be swayed, and the "have nots" will only slip further behind.

Possibilities for partnerships in patient advocacy abound. First and foremost, viewing patients (and their families) as partners in all advocacy efforts, making sure that the advocacy agenda is driven by patient concerns and priorities, is the first concern of the ethical advocate. This step ensures that advocates' agendas resonate with their constituencies, that they are actually addressing problems vital to the community, and that they are using methods the community supports. Second, advocacy organizations need to challenge themselves to cooperate or work out their differences with one another. As this book emphasizes, cooperation is challenging because different organizations have different agendas, missions, and strategies and are often competing for funds that come from the same very small pot. In these situations, advocates need to think hard about the ways to mesh their agendas.

Finally, the advocacy world, not unlike other political worlds, is about tradeoffs—tradeoffs between effectiveness and equity, between user preferences and feasibility, between "now" and "eventually." For those who have been hurt by medical errors or who have suffered from healthcare inequities, the task of working through compromises can be challenging. This approach may seem like a prescription for incrementalism, when a more radical "start over from the beginning" social movement is needed. It bears remembering, however, that the first responsibility of advocates is to leave a situation better than they found it and to avoid being so overwhelmed by the need to create a new system that we walk away from concrete, incremental solutions that can be implemented now or soon.

ETHICAL ISSUES IN PATIENT ADVOCACY

Within the context of the diverse partnerships and frustrating compromises, ethical dilemmas, and particularly conflicts of interest, abound. Many are addressed in this book, often implicitly. Our goal in creating this reader was not so much to provide answers to ethical dilemmas raised in the context of advocacy as to raise some of the right questions, questions that advocates currently wrestle with in the pursuit of achieving safe, accessible healthcare for patients and their families.

One fundamental question for advocates concerns loyalty. For whom, to whom, is the advocate responsible? In addition to the patient, what responsibility does the advocate have for addressing the often conflicting needs of the family, the healthcare provider, the hospital, and society? In this book, we talk not only about patient-centered care but relationship-centered and family-centered care, as well as about equity and access to care. What happens when these goals, or the priorities of different parties, collide in ways that Renneker and Stritter spotlight in Chapter 19? In some cases, a patient and a family member may disagree about the correct course of action. Family members may dispute one another or disagree with the physician in determining the appropriate course of action in a specific situation. In turn, physicians may disagree with each other or nurses with physicians. Sometimes what is best for the individual may not be best for the community and vice versa, or the most effective policy is not the most feasible one to implement, or the most equitable program is not the one preferred by influential stakeholders. In these circumstances, advocates need to be highly aware of the tradeoffs they are making, what is gained at what cost to whom. More broadly, as Meg Gaines put it during the Health Advocates Association meeting spotlighted in Textbox 21.2, "We need to be aiming for the goal not of bumping others out of the queue through our advocacy, but of making a bigger pie."

Textbox 21.2   The Future

After reading draft copies of the chapters in this book, students in our UNC-Chapel Hill patient advocacy class raised the following questions. These inquiries, by the next generation of advocates in training, suggest some of the questions this nascent field will face as patient advocacy research evolves into a full-fledged quality of care scientific endeavor. Many of the questions touch on the ethical core that defines what health and patient advocates do. For patient advocates wanting to make a difference in the way healthcare is delivered today, the 20 previous chapters have laid out precepts and pathways. Future patient advocacy researchers wanting to make a difference will need to put *their* efforts into asking researchable (i.e., measurable) questions, such as those our students have raised. We will need to solicit the perspective of many groups, ranging from people in poverty or with no health insurance to policy movers and shakers who vote on insurance plans or create strategic plans for improving the way the healthcare system delivers care. Why? Because what gets measured is what gets worked on. In other words, measurement and data are among the most central of tools we use to convince citizens and political and corporate leaders to adopt the progressive policies we are advocating for.

Student Questions

What would be the impact of allowing patients to see everything in their medical records? If a patient does not like the way a provider has described his or her behavior or condition, under what circumstances does he or she have the right to demand those statements be changed? Even if he or she is wrong? Who decides? Will providers write less or differently if patients can read their charts? If so, will this make a difference in outcomes?

To what extent do physicians practice defensive medicine? How fearful are doctors of diagnosing or giving patients information about their condition because of lawsuits? How can we change the healthcare system so that doctors can openly admit a mistake to a patient? If the healthcare system became more transparent, would patients still feel the need to seek answers in courtrooms? What is the possibility of creating responsive systems where patients could bring concerns? Would such systems, such as apologies, actually reduce the chance of lawsuits?

How do we evaluate provider performance so that patients know that they are receiving quality care? What hard evidence do we have that quality care is really patient-centered care? If we moved to a pay-for-performance system, what are the most important performance outcomes to measure? What is the best way, the most feasible way, to measure them? How will patients know that they are receiving quality care? If it doesn't "feel" patient centered,

(continued)

Textbox 21.2   The Future (continued)

can it still be quality care? Is being patient-centered a necessary component of quality care?

Is there an equally good way to increase empathy among providers who have not been "radicalized" by their own patient experience? Is it desirable, even necessary, to create empathy among providers to achieve more patient-centered care, or at least more respect for patient-centered care? Other then experiencing serious illness, or "the other side" of the healthcare system, what ways could we train physicians to become more aware of patients' experiences?

How do we overcome the stereotype that mentally ill patients are ill because of something they did while physically ill patients are ill because of something that happened to them? Even physical illness is often blamed on the patient (e.g., lifestyle behaviors). To what extent does such blaming interfere with, even suppress, empathy or patient-centered care? Are there any justifications for putting limits on insurance coverage of mental illness, or even "lifestyle-related illness?" Are such limits antithetical to quality care, or do they incentivize patients to change their behaviors?

Where should providers draw the line in a patient-centered care organization between caring for patients and caring for patients' families? If an emergency department is treating a patient whose family member needs emotional care, how much time, if any, should providers spend with family, rather than with a new, nontrauma, patient? Using a patient-centered approach, where should the line be drawn when resources are scarce? Is there a point in family-centered care where families can become too involved in their family members' illness and lose perspective on what is best for that sick family member? Is it the provider's job to know that point? If so, can we train providers to recognize the conditions under which this occurs?

It is not enough, but it is a first step to acknowledge that potentially competing interests exist at multiple levels of the socioecological framework. In the face of scarce resources, advocacy organizations may be inclined to form institutional alliances with hospitals, pharmaceutical companies, or academic institutions. Does doing so represent an inherent or potential conflict of interest or, as we have suggested in this chapter, a strategic opportunity for coalition building? Can advocacy groups resist being co-opted by the agenda of sponsors they partner with who are partially footing the bill? Should we pursue implementing patient-centered care throughout our health systems because it is inherently the morally correct road to take, even if we do not yet know whether we can make a business case for such practices? Can we use evidence-based outcomes to bolster our appeals to moral outrage, thereby creating sustainable health system change?

The reality is that, in the face of limited funding, advocacy groups may even be competing with one another. Some groups focus on a specific disease such as breast cancer, whereas others focus on meeting a specific need such as counseling patients about insurance issues. Several academic institutions may submit applications for the same grant when what society needs are diverse programs across a range of outcomes. If HIV/AIDs research gets funded, then something else might not. In a competitive environment, the most media-savvy, politically connected, and financially secure groups will almost inevitably be able to capture the attention of potential funders. Should funding mechanisms work this way, however? Although advocacy is fundamentally about giving voice to the voiceless, too often it is the demands of the loudest or best connected, and not the neediest, that prevail.

The 20 chapters in this text raise more specific ethical concerns. For example, advocates cannot address the needs of older persons and those who are dying without addressing the definition of a good life and a good death, the significance of quality of life versus length, the question of who makes decisions when the patient is unable to decide for him or herself. At the opposite end of the lifespan, the challenges faced by ill children and their parents present a similar conundrum. At what age is a child capable of making his own decisions? How can this ability be assessed? At the societal level, people of all ages are represented in the category of the uninsured. In fact, young adults are much more likely to lack health insurance than the older population. It is clear that we need a better safety net. Should we reform the current employer-based health insurance structure, expand public forms of assistance currently available, or discard the current nonsystem altogether in favor of a national health plan?

The relatively recent endorsement by the clinical research community of patient-reported outcomes as acceptable measures of health-related quality of life (National Cancer Institute, 2006) further emphasizes the importance of resolving these conflicts quickly so that patient advocacy researchers can get on with asking and answering hundreds of important-to-answer questions. We have adopted a powerful thesis, with suggestive evidence pointing us in radical directions. Yet education becomes propaganda if we fail to ground our claims with data and support our passion with evidence.

CONCLUSION

Although it may appear initially that increased funding would solve many of the healthcare problems in the United States, patient advocacy would be needed even if budgets doubled or tripled. The people most in need of advocacy—racial and ethnic minorities, inhabitants of rural areas or urban ghettos, the disabled, those with low literacy levels, people who exist on the margins of our society—need more than money to enjoy the same benefits those who have money take for granted. Until we address the social norms and societal values that create divisions between the haves and have nots, we will make little progress on a more patient-centered approach to healthcare delivery. Healthcare reform is not just about economics. It is also fundamentally concerned with ending racism, poverty, prejudice, and redistributing power. By giving a voice to the voiceless, by communicating hope to the hopeless, advocacy is about cultural change across the board.

The intent of this textbook is to give a face to the children, the parents, the older population, and the patients who represent those in need of advocacy. In addition to presenting research, evidence, science, and statistics, we also provide stories—stories of people whose lives have been transformed by illness and by advocacy, of kitchen table advocates who have helped achieve passage of revolutionary legislation. Patient-centered care begins with the patient, but patient advocacy extends to the needs of those who cannot truly be described as patients because they have no doctor. Patient advocacy is about more than providing information; it is about training people to communicate with one another, teaching doctors and administrators how to listen and patients how to speak. Over time, whispers become shouts and small gestures build pyramids to change. By telling today's stories, we stand a chance to change the future.

REFERENCES

Annas, G. J. (2006). The patient's right to safety: Improving the quality of care through litigation against hospitals. *New England Journal of Medicine, 354,* 2063–2066.

Berwick, D. M. (2002). *Escape fire: Lessons for the future of health care.* New York: The Commonwealth Fund.

Bishop, C. M., Earp, J. A., Eng, E., & Lynch, K. S. (2002). Implementing a natural helper lay health advisor program: Lessons learned from unplanned events. *Health Promotion Practice, 3,* 233–244.

Bodenheimer, T., Lorig, K., Holman, H., & Grumbach, K. (2002). Patient self-management of chronic disease in primary care. *Journal of the American Medical Association, 288,* 2469–2475.

Centers for Medicare and Medicaid Services. (2006). *CMS announces proposed changes to physician fee schedule methodology: Substantial increases for time spent with patients.* Retrieved November 1, 2006, from http://www.cms.hhs.gov/apps/media/press/release.asp?Counter=1887.

Clancy, C. (2003). Patient advocacy and patient safety. *Patient Advocacy Summit. Patients, Families and Health Care Providers: Partners in Decision Making, Advocates in Health Care.* Chapel Hill, NC.

Duggan, P. S., Geller, G., Cooper, L. A., & Beach, M. C. (2006). The moral nature of patient-centeredness: Is it "just the right thing to do"? *Patient Education and Counseling, 62,* 271–276.

Earp, J. A., Altpeter, M., Mayne, L., Viadro, C. I., & O'Malley, M. S. (1995). The North Carolina Breast Cancer Screening Program: Foundations and design of a model for reaching older, minority, rural women. *Breast Cancer Research and Treatment, 35,* 7–22.

Emmons, K., & Rollnick, S. (2001). Motivational interviewing in health care settings: Opportunities and limitations. *American Journal of Preventive Medicine, 20,* 68–74.

Gawande, A. (2005). The malpractice mess. *New Yorker, 81,* 62–71.

Grob, R., & Hurst, M. (2005). Workshop session 2.2.W5: Bull's eye: The patient's voice at front and center: Educating for advocacy at Sarah Lawrence College. *Where's the Patient's Voice in Health Professional Education? (An international conference sponsored by the University of British Columbia).* Vancouver, BC.

Institute for Healthcare Improvement. (2006). *100K lives campaign.* Retrieved November 1, 2006, from http://www.ihi.org/IHI/Programs/Campaign/Campaign.htm?TabId=3.

Institute of Medicine. (1999). In L. T. Kohn, J. M. Corrigan, & M. S. Donaldson (Eds.), *To err is human: Building a safer health system.* Washington, DC: National Academy Press.

Institute of Medicine. (2000). In L. T. Kohn, J. M. Corrigan, & M. S. Donaldson (Eds.), *To err is human: Building a safer health system.* Washington, DC: National Academy Press.

Institute of Medicine. (2001). *Crossing the quality chasm: A new health system for the 21st century.* Washington, DC: National Academy Press.

Institute of Medicine. (2003). In K. M. Gebbie, L. Rosenstock, & L. M. Hernandez (Eds.), *Who will keep the public healthy? Educating health professionals for the 21st century.* Washington, DC: National Academy Press.

Institute of Medicine. (2007). The promise of pay for performance. *Rewarding provider performance: Aligning incentives in Medicare (Pathways to quality health care series)* (pp. 25–45). Washington, DC: National Academy Press.

Institute of Medicine, Committee on Health Literacy. (2004). In L. Nielsen-Bohlman, A. M. Panzer, & D. A. Kindig (Eds.), *Health literacy: A prescription to end confusion.* Washington, DC: National Academies Press.

Joint Commission on Accreditation of Healthcare Organizations. (2006). *Root causes of sentinel events, 1995–2004, 2005.* Retrieved November 1, 2006, from http://www.jointcommission.org/NR/rdonlyres/FA465646-5F5F-4543-AC8F-E8AF6571E372/0/root_cause_se.jpg.

Kaiser Family Foundation. (2006). *Consumers' views of patient safety and quality information.* Retrieved November 1, 2006, from http://www.kff.org/kaiserpolls/pomr092706pkg.cfm.

Leape, L. L., & Berwick, D. M. (2005). Five years after *To err is human*: What have we learned? *Journal of the American Medical Association, 293,* 2384–2390.

Levin, A. A. (2005). Patient safety: Rejecting the status quo. *North Carolina Medical Journal, 66,* 91–95.

McClellan, M. (2006). *Champions of change: A national symposium on improving health care (J. Hockenberry, host): September 2006 symposium conducted prior to the release of the PBS broadcast Remaking American Medicine.* Washington, DC.

National Cancer Institute. (2006). *Improving patient-reported outcomes in clinical trials. (NCI Cancer Bulletin, 3, 9).* Retrieved November 14, 2006, from http://www.cancer.gov/ncicancerbulletin/NCI_Cancer_Bulletin_101006/page9.

Robbennolt, J. K. (2003). Apologies and legal settlement: An empirical examination. *Michigan Law Review, 102,* 460–489.

Smith C., Cowan C., Heffler S., Catlin A., & National Health Accounts Team. (2006). National health spending in 2004: Recent slowdown led by prescription drug spending. *Health Affairs, 25,* 186–196.

Index

A

AARP, 395
Abington Memorial Hospital, 555
Accreditation Council for Graduate Medical Education (ACGME), 173–174
Administrative hearings, 537
Advance care planning, 348
Advance directives, 335, 337–339, 348
Advisory Commission on Consumer Protection and Quality in the Health Care Industry, 425
Aetna Foundation, 344
Agency for Healthcare Research and Quality (AHRQ)
    National Healthcare Disparities Report, 122
    patient centeredness measurement and, 324
    patient quality improvement and safety and, 9, 538, 575–576
AIDS. *See* HIV/AIDS
AIDS Coalition to Unleash Power (ACT-UP), 451, 572
Alternative therapies, 303
American Academy of Pediatrics (AAP)
    family-centered care and, 64, 69, 76
    patient advocacy and, 5, 10–11
American Association of Health Plans, 431
American Association of Neurological Surgeons, 525
American Board of Hospice and Palliative Medicine, 349
American Board of Internal Medicine, 349
American College of Graduate Medical Education, 77, 349
American College of Physicians, 525
American Hospital Association (AHA), 272, 275, 376, 483
American Medical Association, 221, 226, 272, 368, 371, 484
American Nurses Association, 272
Americans with Disabilities Act, 131
The American Chamber of Horrors (Lamb), 370
Anesthesia Patient Safety Foundation (APSF), 266–267
Apology, 543–544, 592
Arbitration, 537
Arkansas Advocates for Nursing Home Residents (ANNHR), 406
Association of American Medical Colleges, 78

B

Ballentine, Marion, 389
Balm of Gilead program (Birmingham, Alabama), 131–132
Bates, David, 269

Behavioral change theory, 545
Belmont Report, 8
Berwick, Donald, 242, 269–270, 291–292, 580, 582
Biomedical approach, 192, 328
Biomedical provider-centered care, 315
Biopsychosocial communication approach, 186, 193
Blackwelder, Tracey, 71
Blakely, Harold, 98, 99
Block grant program, 47
Blue Cross, 32, 371
Blue Shield, 32, 371
Boston Medical Center, 549
Boston Women's Health Collective, 373–374
Boutique medicine, 524–527
Brain Talk Communities, 114
Breast cancer activism, 7–8, 452–454
Breast cancer patients/survivors, 7–8
Bugembe, Omega, 489
Bush, George, 274, 425

C

California Advocates for Nursing Home Reform (CANHR), 406
California Breast Cancer Research Program, 453
Campaign for Quality Care (National Citizen's Coalition for Nursing Home Reform), 402–403
Campaign for Quality Care (NCCNHR), 402
Cancer
    breast, 7–8, 452–454
    clinical advocate interventions related to, 513–515, 526
    diagnostic error, 513–514
    lung, 110–111
    nonprofit organizations funding research on, 457 (*See also* Research advocacy)
Cancer Drug Development Patient Consultant Program (Food and Drug Administration), 468
Care-by-Family Units program (University of Texas Medical Branch in Galveston), 67–70
Care partners, 302
Caring Connections, 344
Caring for Children and Families: Guidelines for Hospitals (Johnson, Jeppson, & Redburn), 75
Center for Medical Consumers, 266, 268
Center for Patient Partnerships (University of Wisconsin–Madison), 550

Center for Quality Improvement and Safety
(Agency for Health Care Research and
Quality), 575–576
Centers for Medicare & Medicaid Services
(CMS), 424, 586
Center to Advance Palliative Care, 344
Champions of Change, 587
Children
health insurance for, 40–46, 224
palliative, end-of-life, and bereavement care
for, 69
Children's Healthcare of Atlanta, 552, 556
Chronic illness
healthcare system reform for, 353
lifestyle change and, 587
management of, 227
patient activation and, 254
patient preferences related to, 341–342
Cincinnati Children's Hospital Medical Center,
71–75
Civil Rights Act of 1964, 124
Clancy, Carolyn, 571
Cleveland State University, 484
Clients, 13
Clinical advocacy
case examples of, 512–516
concierge medicine and, 524–527
example of different path to, 511–512
function of, 531
medical literature review, 524
obstacles and challenges to, 529–531
overview of, 508–509
physician as medical equalizer and, 509–511
physician vs. non-physician, 531
practice analysis of, 516–523
strategies toward, 527–529
Clinical research advocacy, end-of-life care,
344–347
Clinical Trial Initiative (National Breast Cancer
Coalition), 456
Clinton, Bill, 273, 376, 425, 432
Coaching, conflict, 550
Codes of Ethics, physician, 525
Codman, Emory, 266
Cohen, Jordan, 78
Cohen, Michael, 266
Collaboration, 436–437, 593–594
Collaborative law, 555–556
Collyar, Deborah, 453, 469
Committee on Quality of Health Care in
America, 8–10
Committee on the Costs of Medical Care, 370
Communication. See also Patient-centered
communication

of acknowledgment of responsibility and
apology, 543–544, 592
in family-centered care, 77–79
between hospital staff and administrators,
308–309
need for effective, 586
patient-physician, 163–166, 185–189,
191–195, 204–207, 320–323, 583
patient-provider, 18–19, 21, 196–199,
204–208, 287–289
physician-healthcare team, 169, 177
Communication strategies
for clients with limited health literacy, 229
for litigation reduction, 70–71
nonverbal, 196–198
for physicians, 314
psychosocial, 192–195, 204–207
to support advance care planning, 350
verbal, 198–199
Community health workers, 134–136
Complementary and alternative medicine
(CAM)
clinician views of, 530
patient communication regarding use of, 523
use of, 516
Concierge medicine, 524–527
Conflict coaching, 550
Congressionally Directed Medical Research
Programs (Department of Defense), 453–454,
458, 467
Connor, Maureen, 79
Consumer Advocates in Research and Related
Activities (CARRA) (National Cancer
Institute), 467
Consumer Assessment of Healthcare Providers
and Systems (CAHPS), 257
Consumer health assistance programs, 548
Consumerist approach, 193
Consumers
empowerment of, 374
explanation of, 13
healthcare demands of, 375, 377
Consumer satisfaction, 67–70
Conventional indemnity plans, 47
Conway, James B., 63, 70
Cooper, Jeff, 269
Co-Pay Relief Program (CPR) (Patient
Advocate Foundation), 429, 433–435
COPIC Insurance Company, 552
Corina, Ilene, 270, 274
Cost-sharing, 47
Cranmer, David, 465
Crossing the Quality Chasm: A New Health
System for the 21st Century (Institute of

Medicine), 5, 10–11, 64, 273, 289, 295, 320, 576
Cruzan, Nancy, 336–338
Cultural differences, healthcare access and, 127–130

D

Dana-Farber Cancer Institute (DFCI), 70, 269, 280–283
Data collection
  for family-centered care research, 83
  to influence state and federal policy, 430–431
  by nonprofit organizations, 427–428
  patient activation measurement and, 255–256
  program and service improvement through, 428–430
Davenport-Ennis, Nancy, 426, 427, 432, 438–440, 592
Decision making, shared, 199–201, 207–208
Department of Defense, 453–455, 458, 462, 467
Developmental Disabilities Assistance and Bill of Rights Act (1990), 64
Dialogue, 549–550
Diamond, Louise, 550
Dickie, Nancy, 269
Dingman, Jennifer, 270
Direct service, family-centered care and, 79–80
Disclosure programs, 551–553
Do not resuscitate order, 348
Drexel University College of Medicine, 555

E

East Tennessee State University, 322
Education. *See also* Health advocacy education; Medical education; Patient education; Training
  end-of-life, 347, 349, 351
  interest in advocacy, 22
  need for, 588–590
  safety, 278
  to support cultural competency, 353–354
Education Network to Advance Cancer Clinical Trials (ENACCT), 468
E-health. *See also* E-patients; Internet
  function of, 17–18, 114
  websites for, 53
Ehrenreich, Barbara, 374
ElderCare Rights Alliance, 399
End-of-life care
  for children, 69
  family-centered, 69
  future advocacy directions in, 350, 353–354
  healthcare delivery and, 341–342

  health professional education advocacy and, 347, 349, 351
  hospice and, 7, 342–343
  legal advocacy and, 335–341
  outcomes and risks of treatment and, 345–346
  overview of, 334–335
  palliative, 343–344
  patient advocacy in, 6–7
  physician communication approach for, 352
  resources for, 354–355
  SUPPORT study and surveys and, 346–347
  terminology related to, 348–349
End-of-life Nursing Education Consortium, 347
Englewood Hospital Library (Englewood, New Jersey), 98
English-language proficiency, 127–128
Entitlement program, 47
E-patients. *See also* Internet
  according to health status, 101–103
  activation levels of, 103–105
  description of, 100–101
  effects on clinician interactions, 106–107
  impact of and future for, 114–116
  online patient helpers for, 110–111
  service comments of, 105–106
  social network theory and, 107–110
  statistics regarding, 101
  support groups for, 110–114
E-Patient Scholars Working Group, 101, 110, 115–116
Escape Fire: Lessons for the Future of Health Care (Donald Berwick), 96, 291–292, 582
Ethical issues
  competing interests and, 597–598
  loyalty and, 595
  in patient advocacy, 170–171, 572–573
Evanston Northwestern Healthcare (Evanston, Il), 69–70
Evidence-based medicine, 380–381
Executive Order 13166, 127–128

F

Facilitative mediation, 553, 554
FAIR, 266
Families
  explanation of, 64–65
  focus on advocacy for, 68
  palliative, end-of-life, and bereavement care for, 69
  programs supporting involvement of, 301–302
Families as Faculty (University of Vermont College of Medicine), 69
Families in Resident/Student Teaching (FIRST), 78, 588

Family-centered care
  application of, 75
  benefits of, 65–66
  case study in, 71–75
  core principles of, 65
  direct service role in, 79–80
  explanation of, 63–65, 318–319
  function of, 582
  health outcomes and, 66–67
  medical education and training to provide,
    77–79
  medical error reduction from, 70–71
  parent-to-parent networking in, 76–77
  patient advocacy and, 62
  policies and practices for, 86
  research consistent with, 80–84
  satisfaction resulting from, 67–70
*Family-Centered Care and the Pediatrician's
  Role* (American Academy of Pediatrics), 64
Family Facility program (Children's Hospital of
  Philadelphia), 78–79
Fauci, Anthony, 451
Federal poverty guidelines (FPG), 47
Federal Trade Commission (FTC), 370–371
Federal Women's Health & Cancer Rights Act
  of 1998, 536
Federation of Families for Children's Mental
  Health, 83
Fetzer Foundation, 344
Flemming, Arthur, 306
Flesch-Kincaid Grade Level test, 232–234
Flexner Report, 483
Food and Drug Administration (FDA), 370–371,
  452, 468
Ford, Dan, 270
Frist, Bill, 438
Frydman, Gilles, 112, 114

G
Gaines, Meg, 595
Gawande, Atul, 487, 542, 592
Georgia State University Center for Law, Health
  & Society, 550
Global Access Project, 436–437
Goeltz, Roxanne, 270
Greene, Alan, 99, 108
Greenwall Foundation, 344
Griffin Hospital (Darby, Connecticut), 307–308
Grimmel, Cheryl, 426–427

H
Hafferty, Frederick, 323
Harm prevention
  methods for, 547

  need for, 544–546
Harvard Medical Practice Study, 540
Haskell, Helen, 274
Hatlie, Marty, 269
Health advocacy, 14, 62, 154
Health advocacy education
  case studies in, 494–502
  curriculum in, 490–492
  function of, 484–486
  future outlook for, 502–504
  historical background of, 482–484
  profile of students involved in, 488–489
  program structure for, 487–488
  thematic approach to, 492–493
Health Advocates Association (HAA), 576–580
Healthcare
  emphasis on technical and biological
    aspects of, 292–293
  goal of, 588–589
  patient involvement in, 14–16, 361–362
  relationship-centered approach to, 153–155
  terminology for, 47–49
  transparency in, 546–547
  types of, 315
"Health Care: Developing a Prevention,
  Education, and Research Agenda"
  (Annanberg Center for Health Services), 270
Healthcare access. *See also* Health insurance
  cultural differences and, 127–130
  English-language proficiency and, 127–128
  for individuals with disabilities, 125–126
  literacy and, 223–336
  poverty and, 126
  in rural communities, 125, 585
  for uninsured individuals, 49–50, 126, 423,
    584
Healthcare advocacy organizations
  access to decision makers by, 437–438
  boards of directors in, 431–433
  business models applied to, 433–435
  collaboration among, 436–437, 593–594
  data gathering and, 427–428
  effects of, 426–427
  examples of, 420–423
  function of, 419–420, 441
Healthcare costs
  family-centered care and, 66–67
  responses to, 375
  statistics related to, 422
Healthcare disparities
  cultural differences and, 127
  income and, 126
  for individuals with disabilities, 125–126
  lay health advisors to address, 135–145
  limited English proficiency and, 127–128

patient advocates and, 129–132, 144–145
race and, 124–125
in rural communities, 125, 585
strategies to address, 132–134
values, beliefs and practices and, 128–129
Health Care Ethics Consortium of Georgia, 550
Health Care for All, 535
Health Care News, 101
Healthcare providers
communication with, 18–19, 204–208, 287–289
end-of-life education for, 347, 349, 351
making transitions from one to another, 227–228
problems in finding, 224
understanding when to find, 225–226
Healthcare proxy, 348
Healthcare quality
inequities in, 122–124
movement for, 8–11
Healthcare system
helping patients navigate, 159–161, 176–177
historical background of, 30–33, 366–371
overview of, 422–423
reform for chronic disease care, 353
statistics regarding, 33–35
Health insurance. *See also* Healthcare access
access to, 223–224, 584–585
for children, 40–46
coverage denial and, 422
employer-sponsored, 35–37
examples of problems related to, 420–423
Medicaid, 38–41
medical billing disputes and, 430–431
Medicare, 42, 46, 49
nonprofit advocacy related to, 420–423
for palliative care, 353
preauthorizations and, 429
private, 37–38
safety net providers and, 50–52
State Children's Health Insurance Program (SCHIP), 41–42
statistics related to, 422
uninsured and, 49–50, 126, 423
Health Insurance Portability and Accountability Act (HIPPA), 424
Health insurance reform
background of, 423–424
federal initiatives in, 425–426
Health Insurance Portability and Accountability Act and, 424
Medicare prescription drug coverage and, 424–425
Health Law Advocates, 535
Health literacy, 218, 220–223. *See also* Literacy

Health maintenance organizations (HMOs), 36, 47
Health reimbursement accounts (HRAs), 37, 47
Health savings accounts (HSAs), 37, 48
Health status, e-patients and, 101–103
Hill Burton Act, 372
HIV/AIDS, 450–452, 572
Holder, Elma, 397–398
Hospice
explanation of, 7, 342–343, 348
policy reforms for, 350
Hospital Consumer Assessment of Healthcare Providers and Systems (HCAHPS), 307
Hospitals. *See also* Plantree hospital model
changing culture of, 296–299
design of, 300–301
historical background of, 31–32
palliative care programs in, 454–455
patient advocacy in, 20
patient safety initiatives in, 538
segregated, 124–125
standardization vs. personalization in, 293–295
use of mediation in, 555

I

Illich, Ivan, 362, 374
Illinois, children's health coverage in, 44–46
Illness. *See also* Chronic illness
literacy skills and management of, 226–228
theories related to, 449–450
IMPACT review form, 459, 474–477
Improving Access to Services for Persons with Limited English Proficiency (Executive Order 13166), 127–128
Indemnity coverage, 37
Individuals with disabilities
healthcare access for, 125–126
rights for, 373
Informed consent, 228
Inlander, Charles, 266
Institute for Family-Centered Care, 79, 80, 85–86, 274
Institute for Healthcare Improvement (IHI), 265–266, 274–277, 576
Institute for Safe Medication Practice, 266, 272
Institute of Medicine (IOM)
family-centered care and, 64
healthcare inequalities and, 127
health literacy and, 221
medical education and, 173
nursing home care and, 402, 403, 411
patient advocacy and, 4–5, 9
patient safety and, 265, 272–274, 278–279, 281
Summit on Crossing the Quality Chasm, 244
Insurance assistance programs, 548
Interest-based negotiation, 554

Internet. *See also* E-health; E-patients
    assisting patients with, 236
    drawbacks of, 115
    effect on clinical interactions, 106–107
    health information on, 17–18, 53, 99
    social network theory and, 107–110
    support groups on, 110–114
Interviews, motivational, 201–204, 587
Inui, Thomas, 323

J
John Deere Health Plans (Iowa), 430–431
Johns Hopkins Health System, 555
Joint Commission on the Accreditation of
    Healthcare Organizations (JACHO), 265,
    272–273, 344, 551, 586

K
Kaiser Permanente, 552
Kennedy, Edward, 376
Kenney, Linda, 274
King, Sorrel, 274, 544
Kolb, Ben, 270
Koop, Everett, C., 63
Kuhn, Maggie, 397, 398
Kuhn, Thomas, 97
Kushner, Rose, 452

L
Lay health advisors (LHAs)
    in clinic-based programs, 142–143
    explanation of, 134
    in medical facilities, 142
    in North Carolina Breast Cancer Screening
        Program, 133–134, 136–137, 140–141
    programs using, 141–142
    roles of, 140–141
Leape, Lucian, 269
Legal advocacy
    approaches to, 537, 591
    collaborative methods and, 549
    disclosure programs and, 551–553
    in end-of-life care, 335–341
    future outlook for, 556–557
    mediation and, 553–555
    medical-legal partnerships and, 548–549
    ombudsman programs and, 550–551
    transparency as component of, 546–547
Legal methods
    function of, 534–535, 556–557
    litigation as, 535, 537, 541–542, 545–546, 591
    overview of, 533–534
Legislation, healthcare, 536

Lehman, Betsy, 269, 270, 280
Levin, Art, 266
Lewin Group, 431, 436
Lindner, Kathy, 98
Literacy
    access to care and, 223–336
    assessment of adult, 217–220, 231
    explanation of, 217
    general information processing and, 228–230
    health, 218, 220–223
    illness management and, 226–228
    overview of, 215–216
Literacy strategies
    assessment as, 231
    distilling information as, 231–232
    document readability improvement as,
        232–235
    healthcare system change as, 236–237
    media use as, 233, 235–236
    problem recognition as, 230
Litigation
    communication skills to reduce use of,
        70–71
    explanation of, 535
    financial settlements resulting from,
        541–542
    negative aspects of, 545–546
    prolonging grieving process during, 542
Living will, 348
Long-term care
    barriers to reform of, 392–393
    current state of, 390–392
    organizational resistance to, 393–394
    overview of, 387–389
Long-term care advocacy
    background of, 394–395
    citizen advocacy in, 389, 396–402
    conclusions regarding, 412–413
    at local and state levels, 404–406
    Nader and, 395–396
    Nursing Home Reform Law and, 403–404
    ombudsman programs and, 405, 407–410
    reform effects of, 410–412
Long-Term Care Ombudsman, 551
Ludmerer, Kenneth, 174–175, 368
Lung Cancer Online, 111
Lung-Onc, 110

M
Malone, Deborah, 270
The Malpractice Mess (Gawande), 592
Mammography. *See also* North Carolina Breast
    Cancer Screening Program (NC-BCSP)
    disparities in use of, 130–131
Managed care, 514–515

Managed Care Ombudsman (Massachusetts), 551
Managed care organization (MCO), 48
Marine Hospital Service, 31
Martins, Becky, 270
Massachusetts Coalition for the Prevention of Medical Errors, 272
Massachusetts Hospital Association, 272
Maternal and Child Health Bureau, 63
McCain, John, 376
MDVIP, 526
Mediation, 553–555
Medicaid
    applying for, 224
    for children, 41–43
    dental coverage under, 535
    eligibility for, 39, 40, 585
    enrollment in, 40
    explanation of, 38–39, 48
    nursing home coverage by, 395, 397
    origins of, 32
    spending for, 40, 41
    in Washington State, 43–44
Medical bills, 229–230
Medical College of Georgia, 324–325, 327–329
Medical education. *See also* Education; Training
    biomedical model of, 315–318
    communication skills as aspect of, 314
    curriculum development in, 176–178
    drivers of change in, 179
    in family-centered care, 77–79
    future directions for, 174–176
    graduate, 173
    hidden curriculum in, 322–324
    Medical College of Georgia and, 324–325, 327–329
    patient advocacy and, 153, 588–589
    to support patient-centered care, 320–322, 324–325, 327–328
    undergraduate, 171–173
Medical equalizer, 509–511
Medical errors
    family-centered care and reduction in, 70–71
    issues related to, 8–9, 586
    national recognition of problems related to, 268–270, 587
Medical home
    characteristics of, 81
    explanation of, 79–80
Medical-legal partnerships, 548–549
Medical Nemesis (Illich), 362
Medicare
    applying for, 224
    explanation of, 42, 46, 48

hospice benefit under, 342
mediation use by, 555
nursing home coverage by, 395, 397
origins of, 32, 33
prescription drug coverage, 42, 46, 424–425
supplemental policies for, 46–47
Medicare Advantage (Medicare Part C), 42, 46, 48
Medicare Coverage Advisory Committee (Centers for Medicare & Medicaid Services), 424
Medicare Modernization Act (2003), 433
Medicare Prescription Drug Improvement and Modernization Act of 2003, 424–425
Medications
    data on access to, 428–429
    Medicare coverage for, 42, 46, 424–425
Methodist Hospital (San Antonio), 555
Micalizzi, Dale, 274
Michaels, Margo, 469
Millenson, Michael, 270
Minneapolis Children's Hospital, 552
Motivational interviews (MIs), 201–204, 587
Murphy, Edwin, 98–99
Mutuality, 188–189

N

Nader, Ralph, 395–397
Nance, John, 270
Narrative, 571–572, 587
National Adult Literacy Survey (1992), 217–218
National Assessment of Adult Literacy (NAAL) (2003), 217–220, 237
National Board of Medical Examiners, 321
National Breast Cancer Coalition (NBCC), 453, 456
National Cancer Institute (NCI), 426, 437, 454–455, 462–463, 467, 514
National Center for Medical Home Initiatives, 80
National Citizen's Coalition for Nursing Home Reform (NCCNHR)
    explanation of, 388
    origins of, 389–390
    platform of, 398–400
    role of, 401–402, 411–412, 593–594
National Community Health Advisor Study, 140
National Council of Senior Citizens, 395
National Council on the Aging, 395
National Gray Panther movement, 397
National Healthcare Disparities Report (Agency for Healthcare Research and Quality), 122
National Health Planning and Resource Development Act of 1974, 374
National Hospice and Palliative Care Organization, 344
National Institute of Health (NIH), 451–452, 454

National Library of Medicine, 221
National Naval Medical Center, 552
National Patient Advocate Foundation (NPAF)
    alliances formed by, 436–437
    establishment of, 426–427
    explanation of, 419–420, 432, 441, 592
    Policy Consortium, 435
    policy issues and, 430–433, 438
National Patient Safety Foundation (NPSF), 265, 271, 275
National Patient Safety Goals, 273
National Practitioner Data Bank, 540
National Quality Forum (NQF), 265, 271–272
National Welfare Rights Organization, 482
New Mexico Coalition for Youth and Families, 65
New York City Project for Mediating Malpractice Cases, 554
New York University School of Medicine, 162–163
Nightingale, Florence, 266
Nonprofit organizations. *See* Healthcare advocacy organizations; National Patient Advocate Foundation (NPAF); Patient Advocate Foundation (PAF)
North Carolina Breast Cancer Screening Program (NC-BCSP)
    compensation in, 138–139
    coordination and community involvement in, 139–140
    function of, 133–134, 585
    lay health advisor and staff recruitment and, 136–137
    lay health advisors in, 134–136, 140, 141
    training in, 137–138
North Carolina Medical Board, 525
Northern Westchester Hospital, 304
Nurses
    end-of-life education for, 347, 349, 351
    as patient advocates, 6
Nursing Home Reform Law (1987), 403–404, 413
Nursing Home Residents' Advocates, 399
Nursing homes. *See* Long-term care; Long-term care advocacy
Nursing Homes: A Citizen's Action Guide, 397–398

O

Old Age: The Last Segregation, 395–396
Older Americans Act amendments, 405
O'Leary, Dennis, 269
Ombudsman programs
    explanation of, 407
    function of, 548, 550–551
    long-term care, 405, 407–412
Omnibus Budget Reconciliation Act (1989), 64

100% Campaign, 224
100,000,000 Guinea Pigs (Kallet & Schlink), 370–371
One Voice Against Cancer, 426
Open Society Institute, 344
OPTION (Observing Patient Involvement) scale, 258
O'Regan, Hart, 270
Organizational change
    measurement of, 305–306
    ombudsman programs promoting, 409
    patient satisfaction and, 306–307
    staff-administration communication and, 308–309
    staff satisfaction and, 307–308
Organizational culture
    explanation of, 290–291
    patient care and, 291–295
Outcomes. *See* Patient outcomes

P

Palliative care
    for children, 69
    explanation of, 343–344
    insurance reforms for, 353
    for long-term care settings, 353
    patient advocacy in, 7
Parameter separation, 248
Parent-to-parent networking, 76–77
Parent to Parent of Vermont, 78
Parent to Parent USA, 76, 85
Parles, Karen, 110–111
Partnerships
    medical-legal, 548–549
    in patient advocacy, 594
Patel, Shilpa, 78
Patient activation
    explanation of, 242–243, 246
    function of, 243–244, 582–583
Patient activation measure (PAM)
    applications for, 242, 256–258
    development and testing of, 245–251
    importance of, 244–245
    research on, 258
    studies using, 255–256
    used to manage enrolled populations, 254–255
    used to tailor individual care plans, 251–254
Patient advocacy
    barriers to, 154
    for breast cancer patients, 7–8
    commitments, competencies, and curricular domains of, 156–157
    communication and, 586–588
    curriculum development for, 176–178

educational needs and, 588–590
for end of life and palliative care, 6–7
in end-of-life care, 333–335
ethical issues and, 170–171, 572–573, 595,
    597–598
family-centered care and, 62, 84–85
as field, 22, 570
healthcare disparities and, 129–132,
    144–145, 584–586
legal methods used in, 534–535
literacy problems and, 223–237 (*See also*
    Literacy)
mandates for change and, 173–174
medical education and training barriers to,
    171–173
methods for, 593–595
nursing and, 6
obstacles of, 365–366
overview of, 3–5, 569–570
patient case histories and, 158–161, 163,
    165, 167–169
patient-centered care and, 581–584
present state of, 378–382
professionalization of, 575–576, 579–581
reform achieved through, 592–593, 596
relationship-centered approach to, 153–155
resources for, 59
role of narrative in, 571–572, 587
safety and quality issues and, 8–11
social change and, 590–592
terminology for, 13–14
traditions in, 5–8
University of North Carolina survey on,
    25–26
Patient advocacy continuum
explanation of, 16–17
individual level of, 17–18
interpersonal level of, 18–19
by levels of influence, 23–24
organizational and community levels of,
    19–20
policy level for, 21–22
Patient advocacy goals
description of, 570–571
patient-centered care as, 11–12
patient involvement as, 14–16
safer systems as, 12, 14
Patient Advocate Foundation (PAF)
board of directors of, 432–433
business principles followed by, 433–435
data collection by, 427–430
establishment of, 426–427
explanation of, 419–420, 432
function of, 420–421, 427, 441, 592

Patient advocates
function of, 573–575
training for, 162–163
Patient and Family Advisory Councils
    (Cincinnati Children's Hospital), 79
Patient Assessment of Chronic Illness Care
    (PACIC), 258
Patient Bill of Rights, 425, 432, 482
Patient-centered care
case example of, 326
curriculum reform to support, 320–322
disclosure and, 552
explanation of, 11–12, 63, 315, 318–319
function of, 186–187, 581–584
historical perspective on, 319–320
issues in, 363–364
levels of influence for, 23
link between outcomes and, 190–195
motivational interviews in, 201–204
shared decision making in, 199–201
use of term, 13
Patient-centered communication. *See also*
    Communication
elements of, 189–190
examples of, 190
motivational interviews as aspect of, 201–204
nonverbal strategies for, 196–198
during office visits, 195
in office visits, 195
psychosocial, 192–195
verbal strategies for, 198–199
Patient Date Analysis Report (PDAR) (Patient
    Advocate Foundation), 428
Patient education
function of, 299–300
need for, 589–590
physician view of, 362
Patient injury
acknowledgment of responsibility and
    apology following, 543–544, 592
grieving process following, 542
harm prevention measures following, 544–546
information needs following, 542
litigation and, 535, 541–542, 545–546
patient needs following, 539–541
statistics regarding, 538
validation need following, 542
Patient Navigator Outreach and Chronic
    Disease Prevention Act (2005), 425–426
Patient outcomes
end-of-life care and, 345–346
family-centered care and, 66–67
link between patient-centered care and,
    190–192

measures of, 598
psychosocial communication and, 193–195
Patient-physician communication. *See also*
    Communication
    curriculum reform to support, 320–323
    function of, 187, 583
    health outcomes and, 191–192
    importance of, 185–186
    mutuality in, 188–189
    nature of effective, 163–166
    psychosocial, 192–195, 204–207
Patient-provider relationship
    communication in, 18–19, 21, 196–199,
        204–208, 287–289
    historical background of, 187–189
Patients
    commitment to understanding, 160, 176
    empowerment of, 374
    explanation of, 13
    imbalance of power between physicians and,
        291
    involvement in healthcare, 14–16, 361–366
    legal steps for injured, 540–541
    levels of influence for involvement of, 24
    measurement of satisfaction of, 306–307
    needs of injured, 539–541
    rights of, 367–368, 536
    supporting and empowering, 18–19
    validation, need of, 542
Patient safety
    advocacy for, 8–10, 277–278
    Dana-Farber Cancer Institute and, 280–283
    dialogue to address issues of, 549–550
    guidelines for, 275, 277, 286
    high-profile errors and, 268–270
    historical perspective on, 266, 268
    leadership in, 276–277
    legal issues related to, 538–539, 547–548
    levels of influence for, 24
    in long-term care facilities, 392–393
    medical-legal partnerships to benefit,
        548–549
    national measures to promote, 272–274
    organizational involvement in, 274–275
    overview of, 263–266
    patient involvement in, 278
    print resources on, 283–285
    public conferences on, 270–272
    terms and concepts related to, 278–281
    transparency as component of, 546–547
Patient Safety and Quality Improvement Act
    (2005), 274
Patient's Bill of Rights, 376–377
Patient Self-Determination Act, 338

Peer networking, 76–77
People's Medical Society, 266
Person-centered care, 13
Pew Internet and American Life Project, 101, 111
Physician-assisted suicide, 339–340, 348–349
Physician orders for life-sustaining treatment
    (POLST), 349
Physicians. *See also* Medical education; Patient-
    physician communication
    communication between healthcare team
        and, 169, 177
    communication between patients and, 163–166
    concierge medicine and, 524–527
    end-of-life communication approach for, 352
    imbalance of power between patients and, 291
    obstructionism by, 513
    as patient advocates, 153–157, 174–176
    professional codes of conduct for, 525
    survey results on, 508
Physicians Reimbursement Fund, 552
Picker Commonwealth Program for Patient-
    Centered Care, 63
Picker Institute, 11
Pierce, Jeep, 269
Plantree hospital model, 583–584
    business case for, 303, 305
    cultural audits and, 305
    explanation of, 290, 295–296
    family involvement programs and, 301–302
    hospital design and, 300–301
    Northern Westchester Hospital and, 304
    patient-centered policies and, 301
    patient education and involvement and,
        299–300
    patient satisfaction and, 306–307
    staff education and training and, 296–299
    staff satisfaction and, 307–308
    stress reduction and alternative therapies
        and, 303
Point-of-service plans, 37, 48
Poverty, 126
Preauthorizations, 429
Preferred provider organizations (PPOs), 36, 48
Prescription drug plans (PDPs), 42, 46, 48
President's Advisory Commission on Consumer
    Protection and Quality in the Health Care
    Industry, 271
Preventing Medication Errors (Institute of
    Medicine), 9
Principled negotiation, 554
Project DOCC (Delivery of Chronic Care), 78, 588
Project LEAD (National Breast Cancer
    Coalition), 461–462
Project on Death in America, 344

Project on Medical Liability (Pennsylvania), 552
Prospective payment systems, 48–49
Psychosocial communication
    barriers to, 204–205
    importance of, 192–193
    patient outcomes and, 193–195
    strategies for, 205–207
Public Health System, 31
PULSE, 272, 274
Punishment, 545

Q

Quality Improvement Organization (QIO), 555
Quality Interagency Coordination Task Force, 273
Quinlan, Karen Ann, 336–338

R

Race, 122–125
Rainbow Babies and Children's Hospital (Cleveland, Ohio), 67
Rasch modeling, 247–249
Ravitch, Ruth, 483
Readability level, 232–235
Relationship-centered advocacy, 153–155
Relationship-centered care, 315
Remaking American Medicine (Public Broadcasting System), 587
Renneker, Mark, 509–511, 513–514, 590
Research
    end-of-life, 345–347
    family-centered care, 80–84
    on shared decision making, 207–208
Research advocacy
    activities related to, 446–447
    benefits of, 447–448
    competencies for, 460–462
    funding supplements and, 457
    future outlook for, 466
    grant review process and, 454–455
    impact of, 455–457, 465
    for individuals with HIV/AIDS, 450–452
    overview of, 445–446
    representation and, 463–465
    resource list for, 467–468
    role of, 458–459
    selection process and, 463
    as social movement, 448–450
    for women with breast cancer, 452–454
Responsibility, 543–544
Retired Professional Action Group, 397
Robert Wood Johnson Foundation, 344
Roper, William, 571, 575

Rosenberg, Charles, 366
Rural communities, 125, 585

S

Safety. *See* Patient safety
Salamendra, Arlene, 266, 270
Sandmaier, Marian, 99, 100
Sarah Lawrence College, 484, 487–488, 490
Schiavo, Terri, 336, 338
Sebok, Anthony, 541
Second Annenberg Conference on Enhancing Patient Safety and Reducing Errors in Health Care (1998), 271
Self-awareness, 168–169, 177–178
Self-management, 583
Senate Special Committee on Aging, 395–396, 398
Seyda, Beth, 68
Shared decision making
    in patient-centered care, 199–201
    research on, 207–208
Sheridan, Susan, 274
SMOG formula, 233–235
Social change, 590–592
Social ecological perspective, 17–24
Social movements, 448–450
Social network theory, 107–110
Society for Healthcare Consumer Advocacy, 483
Soros Foundation, 344
Staff satisfaction, 307–308
Stanford School of Medicine, 484
State Children's Health Insurance Program (SCHIP), 41–43, 49, 585
Stress, function of reducing, 303
Stritter, Gwendolyn, 511–512, 515, 590
Study to Understand Prognoses and Preferences for Outcomes and Risks of Treatment (SUPPORT), 345–346
Support groups, e-patient, 110–114
Szasz, Thomas, 374

T

Texas Advocates for Nursing Home Residents (TANHR), 406
To Err Is Human: Building a Safer Health System (Institute of Medicine), 4–5, 8–9, 70, 272, 538, 576
Training, 77–79. *See also* Education; Medical education
Transactional law, 537
Transparency, 546–547

U

Unequal Treatment (Institute of Medicine), 127
Uninsured individuals
    explanation of, 49–50
    healthcare access for, 126, 423, 584
    safety net providers for, 50–52
The Uninsured: Voice of Despair (Patient
    Advocate Foundation), 438
United Hospital Fund, 344
United States Medical Licensing Examination
    (USMLE), 174
University of Michigan Health System, 552, 553
University of North Carolina (UNC), 25–26,
    484, 596
University of Rochester, 322
University of Vermont College of Medicine, 78
University of Wisconsin–Madison, 484,
    487–488, 490, 491, 550
Utilization review, 49

V

Values-clarification methods, 199–200
Veteran's Administration hospitals, 124, 344
Veteran's Administration (VA), 31, 33, 344
Veterans Affairs Medical Center (Lexington,
    Kentucky), 551
Visco, Fran, 454
Voyce, Charlene, 109, 113–114

W

War on Poverty, 31
Washington State, Medicaid in, 43–44
White, Laurens, 529
White, Ryan, 572
Work Centre for Dialogue (Vancouver), 550
World Health Organization (WHO), 220–221,
    274–275, 343